T0202672

Lecture Notes in Computer Science 13036

More information about this subseries at http://www.springer.com/series/7407

Tiziana Margaria · Bernhard Steffen (Eds.)

Leveraging Applications of Formal Methods, Verification and Validation

10th International Symposium
on Leveraging Applications of Formal Methods, ISoLA 2021
Rhodes, Greece, October 17–29, 2021
Proceedings

Editors
Tiziana Margaria
University of Limerick
Limerick, Ireland

Lero
Limerick, Ireland

Bernhard Steffen
TU Dortmund
Dortmund, Germany

ISSN 0302-9743 ISSN 1611-3349 (electronic)
Lecture Notes in Computer Science
ISBN 978-3-030-89158-9 ISBN 978-3-030-89159-6 (eBook)
https://doi.org/10.1007/978-3-030-89159-6

LNCS Sublibrary: SL1 – Theoretical Computer Science and General Issues

This Springer imprint is published by the registered company Springer Nature Switzerland AG
The registered company address is: Gewerbestrasse 11, 6330 Cham, Switzerland

Introduction

As Symposium and Program Chairs we would like to welcome you to the proceedings of ISoLA 2021, the 10th International Symposium on Leveraging Applications of Formal Methods, Verification and Validation which was planned to take place in Rhodes (Greece) during October 17–29, 2021, and endorsed by EASST, the European Association of Software Science and Technology.

This year's event was very special due to the very special circumstances. It comprised most of the contributions that were submitted to ISoLA 2020, only a few of which were presented last year in a remote fashion. ISoLA was planned to take place in October 2021 in a hybrid fashion, now comprising also the contributions contained in this volume. Only one track was postponed for yet another year, and we hoped very much to experience the other tracks in Rhodes.

As in the previous editions, ISoLA 2021 provided a forum for developers, users, and researchers to discuss issues related to the adoption and use of rigorous tools and methods for the specification, analysis, verification, certification, construction, testing, and maintenance of systems from the point of view of their different application domains. Thus, since 2004 the ISoLA series of events has served the purpose of bridging the gap between designers and developers of rigorous tools on one side and users in engineering and in other disciplines on the other side. It fosters and exploits synergetic relationships among scientists, engineers, software developers, decision makers, and other critical thinkers in companies and organizations. By providing a specific, dialogue-oriented venue for the discussion of common problems, requirements, algorithms, methodologies, and practices, ISoLA aims in particular at supporting researchers in their quest to improve the usefulness, reliability, flexibility, and efficiency of tools for building systems and users in their search for adequate solutions to their problems.

The program of ISoLA 2021 consisted of a collection of special tracks devoted to the following hot and emerging topics:

- Engineering of Digital Twins for Cyber-Physical Systems
  (Organizers: John Fitzgerald, Pieter Gorm Larsen, Tiziana Margaria, Jim Woodcock)
- Verification and Validation of Concurrent and Distributed Systems
  (Organizers: Cristina Seceleanu, Marieke Huisman)
- Modularity and (De-)composition in Verification
  (Organizers: Reiner Hähnle, Eduard Kamburjan, Dilian Gurov)
- Software Verification Tools
  (Organizers: Markus Schordan, Dirk Beyer, Irena Boyanova)
- X-by-Construction: Correctness meets Probability
  (Organizers: Maurice H. ter Beek, Loek Cleophas, Axel Legay, Ina Schaefer, Bruce W. Watson)
- Rigorous Engineering of Collective Adaptive Systems

(Organizers: Rocco De Nicola, Stefan Jähnichen, Martin Wirsing)
- Automating Software Re-engineering
(Organizers: Serge Demeyer, Reiner Hähnle, Heiko Mantel)
- 30 years of Statistical Model Checking!
(Organizers: Kim G. Larsen, Axel Legay)
- From Verification to Explanation
(Organizers: Holger Hermanns, Christel Baier)
- Formal methods for DIStributed COmputing in future RAILway systems (DisCo-Rail 2020)
(Organizers: Alessandro Fantechi, Stefania Gnesi, Anne Haxthausen)
- Programming: What is Next?
(Organizers: Klaus Havelund, Bernhard Steffen)

It also included two embedded events:

- Doctoral Symposium and Poster Session (A.-L. Lamprecht)
- Industrial Day (Falk Howar, Johannes Neubauer, Andreas Rausch)

Co-located with ISoLA 2021 was:

- STRESS 2021 – 5th International School on Tool-based Rigorous Engineering of Software Systems (J. Hatcliff, T. Margaria, Robby, B. Steffen)

Altogether ISoLA 2021 comprised contributions from the proceedings originally foreseen for ISoLA 2020 collected in four volumes, Part 1: Verification Principles, Part 2: Engineering Principles, Part 3: Applications, and Part 4: Tools and Trends, and the content of these proceedings which also cover contributions of the associated events.

We thank the track organizers, the members of the Program Committee and their referees for their effort in selecting the papers to be presented, the local Organization Chair, Petros Stratis, and the Easy Conferences team for their continuous precious support during the entire two-year period preceding the events, and Springer-Verlag for being, as usual, a very reliable partner for the proceedings production. Finally, we are grateful to Christos Therapontos for his continuous support for the Web site and the program, and to Markus Frohme and Julia Rehder for their help with the editorial system Equinocs.

Special thanks are due to the following organizations for their endorsement: EASST (European Association of Software Science and Technology) and Lero – The Irish Software Research Centre, and our own institutions—TU Dortmund and the University of Limerick.

We hope that you, as an ISoLA participant, had a wonderful experience at this edition, and that those of you reading the proceedings at a later date gain valuable new insights that hopefully contribute to your research and its uptake.

Tiziana Margaria
Bernhard Steffen

Organization

Symposium Chair

Margaria, Tiziana	University of Limerick and Lero, Ireland

Program Committee Chair

Steffen, Bernhard	TU Dortmund, Germany

Program Committee

Beyer, Dirk	LMU Munich, Germany
Bojanova, Irena	National Institute of Standards and Technology, USA
Fantechi, Alessandro	Università degli Studi di Firenze, Italy
Gnesi, Stefania	ISTI-CNR, Italy
Hatcliff, John	Kansas State University, USA
Havelund, Klaus	Jet Propulsion Laboratory, USA
Howar, Falk	TU Dortmund, Germany
Margaria, Tiziana	University of Limerick and Lero, Ireland
Robby	Kansas State University, USA
Schordan, Markus	Lawrence Livermore National Laboratories, USA
Steffen, Bernhard	TU Dortmund, Germany
Wirsing, Martin	LMU Munich, Germany

Contents

6th International School on Tool-Based Rigorous Engineering of Software Systems

Industrial Track

6th International School on Tool-Based Rigorous Engineering of Software Systems

STRESS

John Hatcliff[1], Tiziana Margaria[2], Robby[1], Bernhard Steffen[2]

[1] Kansas State University, USA
[2] University of Limerick and Lero, Ireland
[3] TU Dortmund University, Germany

Keywords: CI/CD · Collaborative development · DIME · DevOps · Requirement analysis · Service integration

Introduction

Welcome to STRESS 2021, the 6th International School on Tool-based Rigorous Engineering of Software Systems held in Alila, Rhodes (Greece) on October 2021,19–23th, in association with ISoLA 2021.

Following the tradition of its predecessors held 2006 in Dortmund, 2012 in Crete, 2014 and 2016 in Corfu, and 2018 in Limassol, also this year's School aims at providing interactive lectures, hands-on experience, and other innovative pedagogical material that provide young researchers with instructions in existing and emerging formal methods and software engineering techniques that are tool-supported and process-oriented, providing insights into how software is developed in the real world.

This year's program focuses on graphical modeling of CI/CD workflows [3], accompanied by lectures on collaborative development of data analytics process [4], and on the integration of external services in DIME [1], as well as a soft-skills lecture on WHY-based requirement analysis for a better understanding of the economical value of IT [2].

We thank the ISoLA organizers, the local Organization Chair, Petros Stratis, and the EasyConferences team for their continuous precious support during the week. Special thanks are also due to our home institutions for their endorsement.

References

1. Chaudhary, H.A.A., Margaria, T.: Integrating external services in DIME. In: Margaria, T., Steffen, B. (eds.) ISoLA 2021. LNCS, vol. 13036, pp. 41–54. Springer, Cham (2021)
2. Steffen, B., Steffen, B.: Asking why. In: Margaria, T., Steffen, B. (eds.) ISoLA 2021. LNCS, vol. 13036, pp. 55–67. Springer, Cham (2021)
3. Tegeler, T., Teumert, S., Schürmann, J., Bainczyk, A., Busch, D., Steffen, B.: An introduction to graphical modeling of CI/CD workflows with Rig. In: Margaria, T., Steffen, B. (eds.) ISoLA 2021. LNCS, vol. 13036, pp. 3–17. Springer, Cham (2021)
4. Zweihoff, P., Steffen, B.: Pyrus: An online modeling environment for No-code data-analytics service composition. In: Margaria, T., Steffen, B. (eds.) ISoLA 2021. LNCS, vol. 13036, pp. 18–40. Springer, Cham (2021)

An Introduction to Graphical Modeling of CI/CD Workflows with Rig

Tim Tegeler(✉), Sebastian Teumert, Jonas Schürmann, Alexander Bainczyk, Daniel Busch, and Bernhard Steffen(✉)

Chair for Programming Systems, TU Dortmund University, Dortmund, Germany
{tim.tegeler,sebastian.teumert,jonas.schurmann,alexander.bainczyk, daniel.busch,bernhard.steffen}@cs.tu-dortmund.de

Abstract. We present an introduction to the usage of Rig, our CINCO product for the graphical modeling of CI/CD workflows. While CI/CD has become a de facto standard in modern software engineering (e.g. DevOps) and the benefits of its practice are without a doubt, developers are still facing inconvenient solutions. We will briefly outline the basic concept of CI/CD and discuss the challenges involved in maintaining such workflows with current implementations before we explain and illustrate the advantages of our model-driven approach step by step along on the treatment of a typical web application.

Keywords: Continuous Integration and Deployment · DevOps · Domain-specific tools · Graphical modeling · Language-driven engineering · Purpose-Specific Language · Software engineering

1 Introduction

The growing popularity of agile software development and the rise of cloud infrastructure led to a rethinking of traditional software engineering: An accelerated rate of change requests, and the increasing complexity of system architectures demand a closer cooperation between Development and Operations. DevOps [2,4,9] is a popular response to this challenge which aims at bridging the gap, by involving experts from both sides and encouraging a continuous cross-functional cooperation. The enabling, and thus central element of DevOps is *Continuous Integration and Deployment* (CI/CD). CI/CD workflows [8,11,21] describe and automate the complete assembly process of even highly distributed applications and offer great value by improving the developer experience through quick feedback on their changes. Since tool support is still limited, the initial setup of CI/CD workflows is error-prone and the subsequent evolution of existing workflows remain tedious [23,24].

In this paper, we present our model-driven approach to the challenges of maintaining complex CI/CD workflows [23] and introduce graphical modeling of such workflows with Rig [24] along a running example of a typical web application. We will show that Rig uses a simplicity-driven [16] graphical *Purpose-Specific Language* (PSL) [22] that alleviates the need for developers to familiarize

T. Margaria and B. Steffen (Eds.): ISoLA 2021, LNCS 13036, pp. 3–17, 2021.
https://doi.org/10.1007/978-3-030-89159-6_1

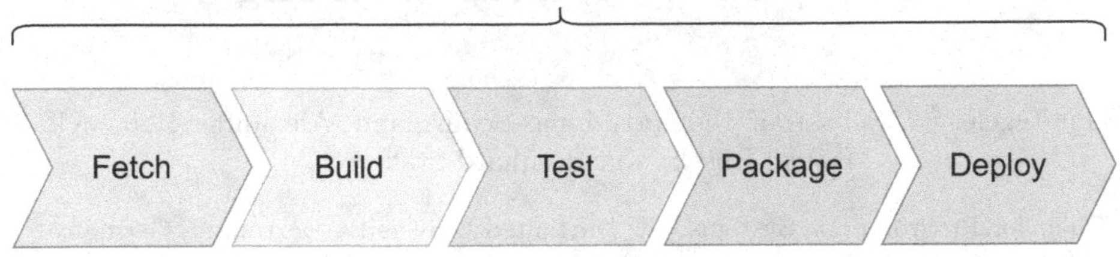

Fig. 1. Typical Jobs of a CI/CD Pipeline (cf. Listing 1.1).

themselves with the intricacies of current CI/CD implementations and the concrete structure of corresponding configuration files.

The paper is structured as follows. In Sect. 2 we briefly discuss CI/CD workflows and its basic concepts. Afterwards we introduce a typical web application in Sect. 3 and show in this context how CI/CD workflows can be 'programmed' manually. Section 5 presents Rig, before we demonstrate how it enables the graphically modeling of CI/CD workflows. In Sect. 7 we discuss prominent issues of current CI/CD implementations and highlight how our graphical modelling approach resolves them. We conclude in Sect. 8 by discussing related work and giving an outlook on the future development of Rig.

2 Continuous Integration and Deployment

Continuous Integration and Deployment is one of the most important building blocks of modern software engineering and a de facto standard in the context of DevOps. CI/CD is highly intertwined with *Version Control Systems* (VCSs), since the goal is to automatically assemble a specific version of the software – typically the latest commit on a branch. The continuous execution of so-called CI/CD pipelines (cf. Fig. 1), improves the development experience through automated feedback cycles, and the support of even complex assembly processes. Unfortunately, the term *pipeline* is often used ambiguously in the context of CI/CD. It is used to describe the overall concept of CI/CD, as well as concrete CI/CD configurations of a software project. For the sake of clarity, we distinguish between pipelines, workflows and configurations in the following way:

- *Pipeline:* Each execution is realized in a CI/CD pipeline (cf. Fig. 1) and must contain at least a single job. Jobs are the smallest logical entity from which more complex pipelines are composed. They are typically responsible to resolve tasks like building, testing or deploying an application. Jobs of a pipeline can depend on each other and use the outcome of previous jobs (e.g. compiled artifacts). The dependency between jobs of a pipeline forms a *directed acyclic graph* (DAG) indicating the possible orders of execution and

determining which jobs can be parallelized. The concrete pipeline, which is reflected by the contained jobs, depends on several constraints (e.g. branch).
- *Workflow:* From our point of view, a CI/CD workflow is the abstract, but comprehensive representation of all properties included to realize *Continuous Integration and Deployment.* It is the blueprint for all potential pipelines of a software project, from which a pipeline can be derived: When a new version of the software is pushed to the VCS, the workflow is evaluated upon constraints, and a concrete pipeline is executed. Workflows are typically serialized in configurations files, but we will show that they can be represented ideally by graphical models.
- *Configuration:* Workflows are serialized as low-level instructions that are read and interpreted by CI/CD engines. These instructions are stored as plain text files (e.g. `.gitlab-ci.yml`) in the corresponding repository. We call them configurations. Existing solutions (e.g. GitLab) make use of data serialization languages (e.g. YAML) for the required configuration files (cf. Listing 1.1). It is still the norm to write CI/CD configuration files manually, very often without IDE-based assistance like autocomplete or error analysis.

The jobs of a pipeline are executed on dedicated systems, often provided by software development platforms, like GitLab and GitHub. They integrate VCSs with CI/CD and maintain centralized and well-defined infrastructure to ensure predictable and reproducible builds. As mentioned above, common implementations are based on YAML (cf. Listing 1.1). While YAML is an adequate data serialization language aiming to be "human friendly" [6], the lacking visualization or validation of CI/CD configuration lets existing solutions fall short. Re-use of job definitions is often limited, with textual duplication being a commonly accepted solution. Applications built for multiple target platforms (e.g., Windows, Linux, MacOS) often require the duplication of these jobs with only slightly altered configurations, e.g., regarding infrastructure. Some platforms, e.g., GitLab, have adopted "job templates" to ease re-use of jobs, but practice shows that writing correct configurations remains an error-prone task [23,24] (cf. Sect. 7).

3 TodoMVC

TodoMVC [20] is a collection of numerous[1] implementations of the same web–based, purely client–side task management software written in different programming languages and frameworks by different developers. In order to make different implementations comparable, TodoMVC is based on a specification given in a textual, natural language format that dictates behavioral as well as visual characteristics that any TodoMVC implementation has to fulfill. For example, each implementation must have the user interface displayed in Fig. 2 and must allow users to create, read, update and delete tasks (e.g. *do the laundry*) as well as to filter tasks based on their state (i.e. finished or unfinished). This way,

[1] At the time of writing, the main repository contains 48 different implementations.

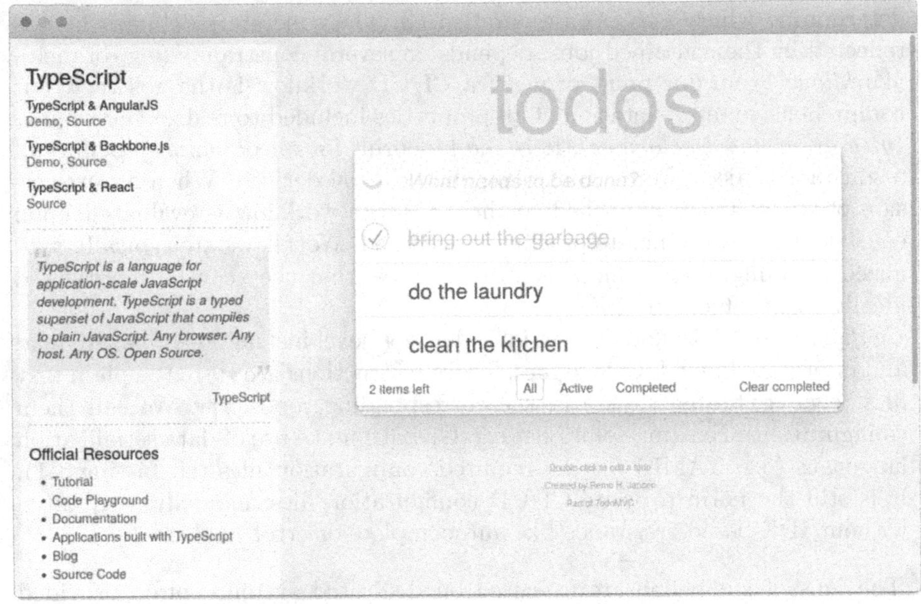

Fig. 2. Example Implementation from TodoMVC.

all implementations should look and functionally behave identically, which has also been verified in a previous case study [3]. As a result, developers can compare different frameworks easier and make themselves comfortable with frontend technologies such as client–side storage, routing, component–based development and state management to find a framework that suits the given use case.

By default, the repository already contains pre–compiled and pre–built versions for each implementation, so that all a developer has to do in order to run an implementation is to serve the static HTML, CSS and JavaScript files from a specific directory and access them from a browser. Although it is generally considered a bad practice to have generated or compiled code stored in VCSs, it suffices the purpose in this case: The entry hurdle to review the corresponding frameworks at runtime is lowered. Because of this design decision, delivering and testing all implementations in a local environment is straightforward. TodoMVC provides two global executable scripts for automated user interface testing and delivering all implementations via an integrated web server. The individual compile and build scripts are completely decoupled from that and are the responsibility of the corresponding implementations and even have to be triggered manually before each commit.

To conclude, in its current state, TodoMVC is designed to be built, tested, operated and used locally. There is no strict pipeline in place as e.g. displayed in Fig. 1 and some jobs, such as compile, package and deploy do not even exist. As a demonstration of the capabilities of our tool Rig, we will use a single TodoMVC implementation as our target application (in the following referred to as TodoMVC) to model and generate a GitLab–based CI/CD workflow. The workflow and the forked project can be found in the corresponding repository[2].

4 Programming a CI/CD Workflow

Before we demonstrate the capabilities of our model-driven approach to *Continuous Integration and Deployment* workflows, we present how such workflows are "programmed" traditionally. As a short recap, CI/CD workflows describe and automate how applications are built, tested and even deployed to production. Typically workflows are written as plain text in YAML and not visualized nor validated until they are executed by compatible software development platforms.

In order to feature an expressive example, we choose one of the more complex TodoMVC implementations that builds upon TypeScript and React[3]. As a consequence, our CI/CD workflow must not only support the fetching of dependencies (e.g. React and transitive dependencies) and the compiling of TypeScript to JavaScript, but also a dedicated packaging job to bundle a deployable artifact.

While several software development platforms exist, in this paper we will focus on GitLab. Therefore, the displayed configuration in Listing 1.1, is compatible with the CI/CD implementation of GitLab [1]. By default, GitLab expects this configuration to be serialized in a YAML file called `.gitlab-ci.yml`[4], stored in the root folder of the project's repository. The YAML specification supports three basic types of content: Scalar data types (e.g. strings, numbers and booleans), sequences for representing ordered lists, and mappings (i.e. hash or dictionary) for an unordered set of key/value pairs [6]. The first level of a `.gitlab-ci.yml` file is, always structured as a mapping. Except for some reserved keywords (e.g. `image`, cf. line 1), a key on the first level represents a name of the job (e.g. `fetch` , cf. line 3). In order to highlight the jobs of the CI/CD workflow, we colored the background of the corresponding lines with matching colors of Fig. 1. Please note, that the colors have no semantic meaning and serve presentation purposes only.

Since CI/CD aims at building a wide variety of applications, all with their own dependencies, providers commonly offer their users the ability to specify build environments using images of container engines (e.g. Docker[5]). The build environment of TodoMVC is Node.js[6] (for the sake of simplicity, often just called *node*). In line 1 we reference the container `image` of `node` in the version `16.7` and thus, declare the build environment globally for all following jobs. Part of the container image of node is the *Node Package Manager* (NPM), which provides a command line interface (called `npm`) for interaction. During our example, we heavily use `npm` for most of the jobs.

---

[2] https://gitlab.com/scce/stress2021/todomvc.
[3] https://reactjs.org.
[4] https://docs.gitlab.com/ee/ci/yaml/gitlab_ci_yaml.html.
[5] https://www.docker.com/.
[6] https://nodejs.org/.

```
1  image: node:16.7
2
3  fetch:
4      script:
5          - npm ci
6      artifacts:
7          paths:
8              - node_modules/
9          expire_in: 1 hour
10
11 build:
12     script:
13         - npm run build
14     artifacts:
15         paths:
16             - js
17     needs:
18         - fetch
19
20 test:
21     script:
22         - npm test
23     needs:
24         - fetch
25         - build
26
27 package:
28     script:
29         - npm run bundle
30     artifacts:
31         paths:
32             - out
33     needs:
34         - fetch
35         - build
36         - test
37
38 pages:
39     script:
40         - mv out/ public
41     artifacts:
42         paths:
43             - public
44     needs:
45         - package
```

Listing 1.1. Textual CI/CD Configuration of TodoMVC (cf. Fig. 1).

The main part of our configuration starts after the definition of the global build environment. Beginning with line 2, the actual jobs are configured. A job definition is also implemented as a mapping, but in contrast to the first level mapping of the CI/CD configuration, all keys are predetermined where each one serves a particular goal. The most important and also mandatory key of a job is **`script`** (cf. line 4). A script is usually a sequence of strings, each representing a shell command (cf. line 5). In order to define the dependencies of a job, the **`needs`** keyword (cf. line 17) can be used to reference other jobs by their names and form the aforementioned DAG. In the following, we will describe details of the jobs:

- **`fetch`** : At first, the pipeline fetches all necessary dependencies to build the application. In this example (using Node.js and NPM), this is done via the command `npm ci`. NPM uses a global package registry at `npmjs.org` and stores dependencies locally in a folder called `node_modules`. In order to pass these along to subsequent jobs (and thus avoiding the need to fetch them in every job), we define this folder as our artifact (cf. line 6).

- `build` : Building the application relies on the dependencies (stored in `node_modules`) being available, and thus references the `fetch` job as a needed dependency with the keyword `needs` in line 18. This enables the passing of the artifact from the required job. This jobs then compiles TodoMVC from TypeScript to JavaScript, by calling the build script with `npm run build`. The output of this process is stored in the `js/` folder, which is defined as the artifact of this job in order to enable passing it along to the next job.
- `test` : Running the tests of the TodoMVC application is done via `npm run test`. Since the job needs not only the assembled application, but also heavily depends on testing frameworks, it defines both a dependency on the `build` job and the `fetch` job to get both the built application, as well as the fetched modules (which are not passed transitively by default).
- `package` : This job bundles the application for deployment via `npm run bundle`. It uses the compiled outcome of `build` , but also depends on having the necessary modules available from `fetch` , and thus again defines both of these dependencies. Since only changes that pass the test suite should be deployed, the job also requires the `test` job, ensuring that it only runs when all tests were successful. It then recursively bundles all required dependencies and stores all relevant files in the folder `out/`. The files in the folder `out/`, are ready to be served locally or by a web server. They are defined as the artifact (or output) of this job.
- `pages` : This job facilitates deployment of the built application. It is not named "deploy", as one would expect for such a job (cf. Fig. 1), but "pages", since jobs named in this way have special treatment when using GitLab: Static websites can be hosted by GitLab via their own subdomain, `gitlab.io`, using a feature called "GitLab Pages"[7]. When naming a job "pages" as done here, users *must* also provide an artifact with a `public/` folder, which is subsequently deployed and served. Therefore, it moves the output from the previous job from `out/` to `public/` via the `mv` command. GitLab will then continue to deploy the static files. In our example, this means that the TodoMVC app is deployed and available under https://scce.gitlab.io/stress2021/todomvc/. This job depends only on the `package` job, since it does not use NPM, but solely works on the output from the previous job.

In this example, the jobs follow a linear order (`fetch` ↦ `build` ↦ `test` ↦ `package` ↦ `pages`). In more complex examples, jobs might also execute in parallel. An example would be building the frontend and backend of a web application separately, then packaging them together for deployment in a job that depends on both.

[7] https://docs.gitlab.com/ee/user/project/pages/.

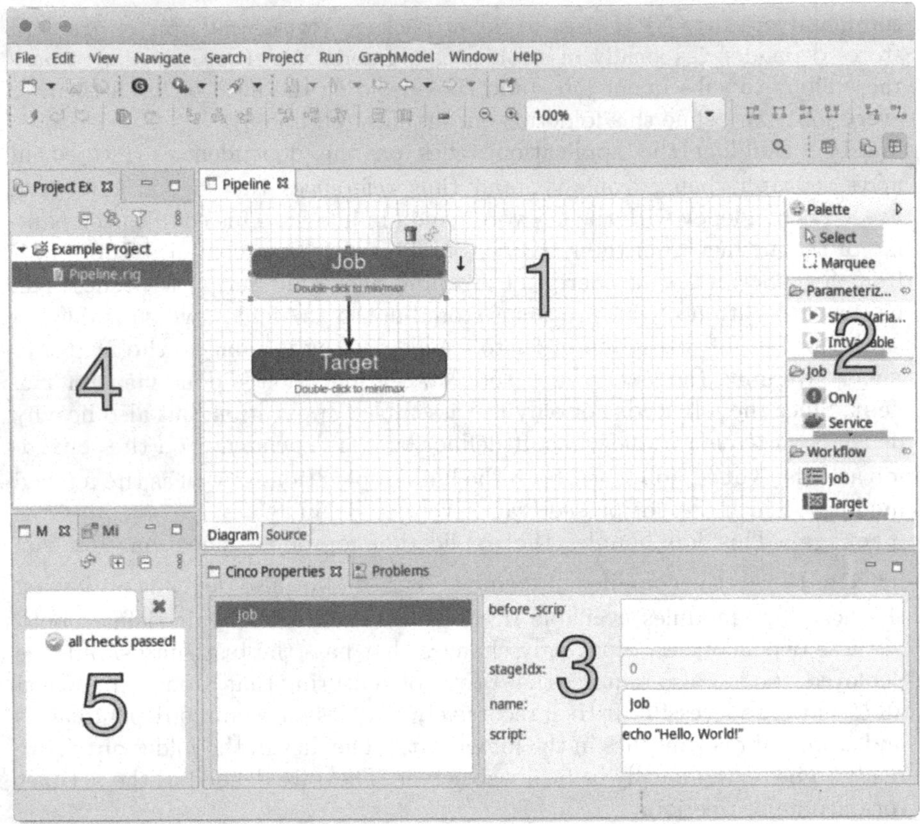

Fig. 3. CI/CD Modeling Environment of Rig.

5 Rig

Rig is an *Integrated Modeling Environment* (IME), that enables users to model CI/CD workflows for GitLab as its target platform. It has been created using CINCO and is therefore a CINCO product [18], which also means that it is based on the Eclipse Rich Client Platform [17]. Rig uses and expands a model-based approach introduced by Tegeler et al. in [23]. In their paper, the authors introduce a model utilizing *jobs*, *script arguments*, *build targets* and *parameters*. Targets are a newly introduced concept that offers freely configurable parameters used to parameterize jobs. These parameters are used to provide the values for script arguments, thus allowing customization of jobs for different build targets. This mechanism significantly eases re-use of job definitions and provides a powerful visual alternative to template-based approaches. The Rig PSL greatly expands on this concept by introducing *properties* and *variables* as well as additional configuration *nodes*. Since CI/CD workflows can be modeled as DAGs, dependencies between jobs can be described by edges in Rig's PSL, allowing the user to visually connect jobs in the correct order without the need to manually track and set the correct dependencies.

This section will give an overview of the IME Rig and will briefly describe how to use it. Through this, this section will also prepare readers to easily model their own CI/CD workflows in Rig.

Figure 3 shows the Rig IME with a small modeled example. The canvas of the graphical editor (see 1 in Fig. 3) contains two nodes "Job" and "Target". These nodes are used to express and visualize the desired CI/CD workflows. Nodes can be rearranged and edited as the user pleases. As can be seen in Fig. 3, nodes can also be deleted by clicking the bin symbol in the icon pad near the Job node, or be connected to other nodes through edges by drag-and-dropping, starting at the arrow symbol in the icon pad. Edges connect nodes with other nodes and are automatically created in a matching type upon releasing the mouse button of the drag-and-drop action. The most fitting edge type will be created, considering the underlying abstract syntax of the metamodel of the graph model.

New nodes can be created using the palette of the graphical editor (marked as 2 in Fig. 3). The palette contains all creatable nodes the graph model may contain. Simple drag-and-dropping of the desired nodes from the palette into the canvas area of the graphical editor will create the node in its concrete syntax style. Every model element may also possess more information than just their relationships between one another. This additional information may be stored as attributes of the respective model element. Attributes may be data of different types (text, number, enums).

To inspect and modify these attributes the "Cinco Properties" view is used (cf. 3 in Fig. 3). This view lists all non-hidden attributes of the model element currently select in the graphical editor of the IME (1 of Fig. 3). The properties may be edited directly in the property view, if not explicitly forbidden in the metamodel of the underlying graph model. Beside multiple model elements within the same graph model, it is of course possible to create multiple graph models (here: Rig models) as well. This is simply done by adding new graph model files to the project. A project explorer, that lists all files of the project, can be seen marked as 4 in Fig. 3.

Rig offers full code generation [14] from the created models. Its code generator is straight-forward and transforms the models of the graphical PSL into complete YAML files, by traversing the graph model backwards, starting from *Targets*. Simple transformation rules are executed in a fixed order: When processing a *Job*, the generator emits a *Job* by taking in account the parameterization by *Targets*. This way, each *Job* is emitted once for each *Target*. All incoming edges that point to *Properties* are evaluated and the proper configuration is emitted for each *Job*. *Properties* themselves can have incoming edges, either from *Variables* or *Target* parameters, so these are taken into account as well. When writing configurations manually, users must keep track of the dependencies between jobs and ensure they have set the correct dependencies on each job, potentially rewriting large parts of the file when re-ordering or renaming jobs. Rig can derive the correct dependencies trivially from the given model.

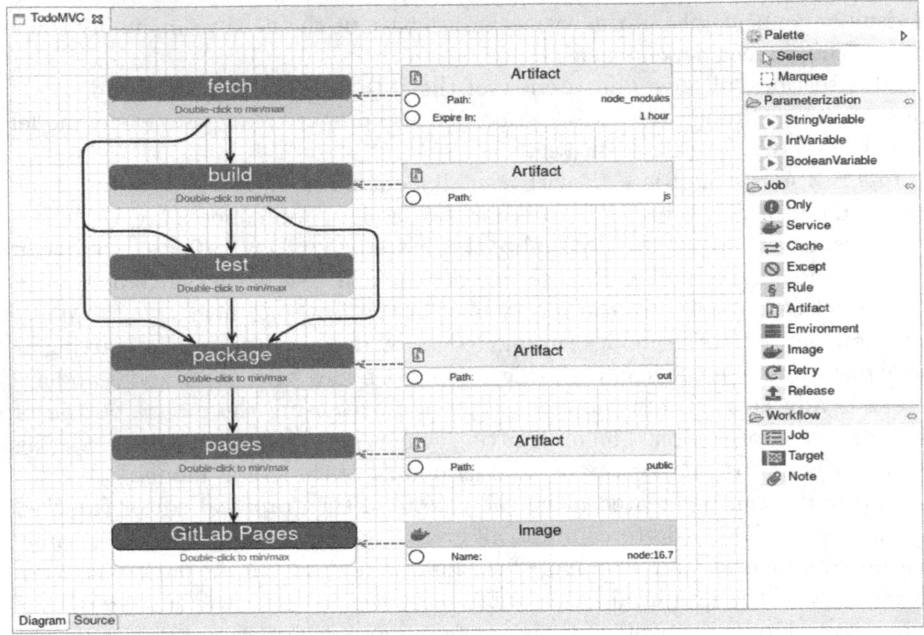

Fig. 4. Graphical CI/CD Configuration of TodoMVC (cf. Listing 1.1).

As an additional user-friendly feature, Rig also provides a "Model Validation" view (cf. 5 in Fig. 3), which offers validation and checks to ensure that only models with reasonable semantics are created. Rig not only uses many of the powerful checks inherent to models of CINCO products, like checking cardinalities of edges and other model elements, but also supports domain-specific validation. These custom checks detect cycles in the graph model, ensure that jobs have unique names, and prevent targets from parameterizing jobs that do not reach the target. Additionally, Rig includes grammars which offer auto-completion and suggestions for certain textual properties of the configurations, e.g. for the conditions in "Except", "Only" and "Rules" elements or for the pre-defined variables that our target platform GitLab offers. These grammars guide users towards writing correct expressions for these textual properties. We plan to replace those grammars with more generic and powerful models in the future (cf. Sect. 8).

6 Modeling a CI/CD Workflow in Rig

This section will provide a step-by-step guide to create the CI/CD pipeline depicted in Fig. 4. For a more in-depth look into the usage of Rig, please consult the official user manual at https://scce.gitlab.io/rig/.

Table 1. Overview of Script and Artifact Path Settings.

Job Name	Script	Artifact Path
fetch	`npm ci`	`node_modules`
build	`npm run build`	`js`
test	`npm test`	
package	`npm run bundle`	`out`
pages	`mv out/ public`	`public`

Creating a Target Node. Every CI/CD pipeline needs at least one target from which the parameterized jobs are later instantiated by the generator. To create a target node, first click on the corresponding button in the toolbox on the right, then click on the canvas to place the node. Select the target node and give it the name "GitLab Pages" in the properties panel on the bottom, as this is our deployment target.

Job Nodes. Next, we need nodes to define the jobs of the pipeline. Create five job nodes and give them the names "fetch", "build", "test", "package" and "pages". The last job must necessarily be named "pages" so that GitLab will deploy the final artifacts to GitLab Pages. Connect each job with their successor by holding the mouse down on the arrow symbol that appears on hover and releasing it on the following job. The last job, "pages", must be connected to the previously created target node, completing the basic pipeline structure. Now for each job the command line script has to be defined that is to be executed in the pipeline. In the properties panel, fill in the values of the *Script* column of Table 1 into the script property.

Specifying the Docker Image. Jobs are executed within a Docker container, so we have to specify what images should be used for each job. As we are only using npm in this example, one Docker image suffices as the global build environment for all jobs. Create an image node, select the name attribute and in the properties panel, enter "node:16.7" in the value field. Now connect the image node to the target node to simply apply it to all jobs.

Handling of Artifacts. Last, we define how artifacts produced by the jobs are captured and provided to following jobs as necessary. For each capture, create an artifact node and connect it to the job. Right-click on the artifact and choose "(+) Path", select the newly created entry and enter the path in the properties panel. We want to capture the artifacts paths for the jobs like listed in the *Artifact Path* column of Table 1.

At the end of the pipeline, GitLab will take the contents of the `public` directory produced by the "pages" job and deploy the files to GitLab pages, making the demo application publicly available. Additionally, we will let the artifact of the "fetch" job expire after an hour, because it is rather large and not needed afterwards. To do this, right-click on the artifact node, select "(+) Expire in" and set the value to "1 h" in the properties panel. Now, we need to add a few more connections between jobs to correctly pass on the artifacts to other jobs. Add the following edges between jobs:

- fetch → test
- fetch → package
- build → package

Now the pipeline is complete! Save the file and select "GraphModel" → "Generate Code" from the application menu. The generated `.gitlab-ci.yml` file should appear in the `src-gen` directory.

7 Discussion

Admittedly, our example of a CI/CD workflow written in YAML (cf. Listing 1.1) is not very daunting. Investing about 50 lines of code to achieve an automated assembly and deployment process into production sounds like a good deal, but well-functioning CI/CD configurations can be elusive. The effort of constructing a CI/CD workflow lies not in the resulting lines of code, it lies in understanding the elemental mechanics of CI/CD in the first place and dealing with the idiosyncrasies of its implementation. Creating (even just syntactical) correct configurations, often involves trial & error programming by uploading new versions of the configuration to the repository and waiting for the result [24]. A prominent example of not anticipated behaviour when dealing with YAML is the "Norway Problem" [13,19], where `NO`, two unescaped alphabetic characters, are parsed as boolean (cf. Listings 1.2 and 1.3).

```
countries:
  - GB
  - IE
  - FR
  - DE
  - NO
```

Listing 1.2. Sequence of Country Codes Written in YAML.

```
{"countries": [
    "GB",
    "IE",
    "FR",
    "DE",
    false ]}
```

Listing 1.3. Sequence of Country Codes Represented as Parsed JSON.

Most of these issues are rooted in the fact that YAML is a general-purpose configuration language that simply does not support the CI/CD domain very well. A strict YAML parser[8] would make the semantics of the configuration more predictable, and a full-blown textual *Domain-Specific Language* like Nix [10] would be able to integrate domain concepts and offer suitable abstractions. But we believe that narrowing the scope even further into a PSL and using a graphical modeling language with an accompanied IME gives even more benefits and offers the best support for maintaining CI/CD workflows. The generator of Rig

[8] https://github.com/crdoconnor/strictyaml.

properly quotes values in the YAML configuration files derived from our PSL, freeing the user from thinking about YAML semantics.

Aside from the fact that CI/CD workflows are typically represented textual, the discoverability of features is low [24]. From our experience, the *Time To Hello World* [15] is dramatically longer when compared to other programming or workflow languages. Beginners have to pursue extensive documentation to even start with basic workflows [24]. While platforms, like GitLab, offer a linting tool [12], users often can not leverage any substantial IDE-support [24]. Rig on the other side considers modeling assistance a prime objective, by following principles of "Correctness-by-Construction" [5] and the model validation approach of CINCO [7,25].

Since CI/CD pipelines are typically executed on provided and managed infrastructure, maintainers of CI/CD workflows are forced to keep up with changes in the specification of the CI/CD configuration. The graphical PSL of Rig uses a higher-level abstraction which can survive even more radical changes and allows seamless integrations of new features (e.g. stageless pipelines[9]). The full code generator approach lets maintainers overwrite existing CI/CD configurations without worrying about syntactic or semantic changes.

So called "*visual editors*" have been introduced as a solution to the difficulty of handling large CI/CD workflows, for example by SemaphoreCI[10], and – more recently – by GitLab[11] itself. These visual editors focus on deriving a *visualization* from the pipeline configuration, but only by showing jobs and their dependencies, and no other elements of the pipeline [24]. In case of SemaphoreCI, limited editing of the configuration can be done through the user interface. Neither solution visualizes the complete workflow model. Rig on the contrary introduces a graphical PSL as *single source of truth*, from which the CI/CD configuration is automatically generated.

8 Conclusion

In this paper, we have presented Rig, a visual authoring tool for CI/CD workflows, which follows our model–driven approach to *Continuous Integration and Deployment*. Rig enables us to visually model CI/CD workflows that, in contrast to YAML, benefit from a strict type–system that greatly reduces the potential of human–made errors when authoring corresponding files in an unchecked text file. Our full code generation approach then guarantees that the generated YAML configuration file is compatible with the target CI/CD provider, i.e. in our case GitLab. Not only that, but by leveraging graphical models, we also create a common basis for discussion that allows DevOps–teams to better reason about CI/CD workflows. For example, the graph–based approach allows us to easily comprehend how the different CI/CD jobs are interdependent and especially the order in which they are executed in.

---

[9] https://about.gitlab.com/blog/2021/08/24/stageless-pipelines/.
[10] https://semaphoreci.com/.
[11] https://about.gitlab.com/blog/2021/02/22/pipeline-editor-overview/.

To demonstrate the capabilities of Rig, we have modeled a CI/CD workflow targeted at GitLab for the TypeScript and React implementation of TodoMVC. The workflow not only includes the automated building and testing of the application within a pipeline, but it also deploys compiled artifacts to GitLab Pages, a service that provides hosting of static files, such as HTML, CSS and JavaScript. As a result of this, we have automated all steps we previously had to perform manually in order to build and publish TodoMVC to the web.

We believe that apart from improving Rig's potential to serve as a documentation and communication tool, future work should focus on lowering the barrier for adoption of CI/CD, especially for smaller projects. To achieve that, we are currently investigating how to make Rig available as a web application which would enable us to integrate supported CI/CD providers seamlessly. Rig currently only supports GitLab as the target platform, but following the generator approach of CINCO [18,26,27], different providers can be supported in the future. We have also identified potential generalizations of Rig to make this process easier [24] and to gradually develop a generic PSL for CI/CD modeling. We believe that these enhancements provide a good foundation for a better understanding of the potential of DevOps and, in the long term, for establishing an *industry standard* for CI/CD workflows.

References

1. GitLab CI/CD (2021). https://gitlab.com/gitlab-org/gitlab/-/blob/45150e2706 5257f0251484de55fc3d42d9dd5dbd/doc/ci/index.md. Accessed 31 Aug 2021
2. Allspaw, J., Hammond, P.: 10+ deploys per day: Dev and ops cooperation at Flickr. In: Velocity: Web Performance and Operations Conference, June 2009. https://www.youtube.com/watch?v=LdOe18KhtT4
3. Bainczyk, A., Schieweck, A., Steffen, B., Howar, F.: Model-based testing without models: the TodoMVC case study. In: Katoen, J.-P., Langerak, R., Rensink, A. (eds.) ModelEd, TestEd, TrustEd. LNCS, vol. 10500, pp. 125–144. Springer, Cham (2017). https://doi.org/10.1007/978-3-319-68270-9_7
4. Bass, L., Weber, I., Zhu, L.: DevOps: A Software Architect's Perspective. Addison-Wesley Professional, Boston (2015)
5. ter Beek, M.H., Cleophas, L., Schaefer, I., Watson, B.W.: X-by-construction. In: Margaria, T., Steffen, B. (eds.) ISoLA 2018. LNCS, vol. 11244, pp. 359–364. Springer, Cham (2018). https://doi.org/10.1007/978-3-030-03418-4_21
6. Ben-Kiki, O., Evans, C., döt Net, I.: YAML Ain't Markup Language (YAML™) Version 1.2 (2009). https://yaml.org/spec/1.2/spec.html. Accessed 22 June 2021
7. Boßelmann, S., et al.: DIME: a programming-less modeling environment for web applications. In: Margaria, T., Steffen, B. (eds.) ISoLA 2016. LNCS, vol. 9953, pp. 809–832. Springer, Cham (2016). https://doi.org/10.1007/978-3-319-47169-3_60
8. Chen, L.: Continuous delivery: overcoming adoption challenges. J. Syst. Softw. **128**, 72–86 (2017)
9. Debois, P., et al.: Devops: a software revolution in the making. J. Inf. Technol. Manag. **24**(8), 3–39 (2011)
10. Dolstra, E.: The Purely Functional Software Deployment Model. Ph.D. thesis, Utrecht University, Netherlands (2006). https://dspace.library.uu.nl/bitstream/handle/1874/7540/?sequence=7

11. Fowler, M.: Continuous Integration (2000). http://martinfowler.com/articles/continuousIntegration.html. Updated version from Mai 2006
12. GitLab Inc., contributors: Validate.gitlab-ci.yml syntax with the CI Lint tool. https://docs.gitlab.com/ee/ci/lint.html. Accessed 03 Sept 2021
13. Huntley, G.: No YAML. https://noyaml.com/. Accessed 3 Sept 2021
14. Kelly, S., Tolvanen, J.P.: Domain-Specific Modeling: Enabling Full Code Generation. Wiley-IEEE Computer Society Press, Hoboken (2008). https://doi.org/10.1002/9780470249260
15. Macvean, A., Church, L., Daughtry, J., Citro, C.: API usability at scale. In: PPIG, p. 26 (2016)
16. Margaria, T., Steffen, B.: Simplicity as a driver for agile innovation. Computer **43**(6), 90–92 (2010). https://doi.org/10.1109/MC.2010.177
17. McAffer, J., Lemieux, J.M., Aniszczyk, C.: Eclipse Rich Client Platform, 2nd edn. Addison-Wesley Professional, Boston (2010)
18. Naujokat, S., Lybecait, M., Kopetzki, D., Steffen, B.: CINCO: a simplicity-driven approach to full generation of domain-specific graphical modeling tools. Int. J. Softw. Tools Technol. Transfer **20**(3), 327–354 (2017). https://doi.org/10.1007/s10009-017-0453-6
19. O'Connor, C.: The Norway Problem - why StrictYAML refuses to do implicit typing and so should you. https://hitchdev.com/strictyaml/why/implicit-typing-removed/. Accessed 3 Sept 2021
20. Osmani, A., et al.: TodoMVC - Helping you select an MV* framework (2021). https://todomvc.com/. Accessed 31 Aug 2021
21. Shahin, M., Babar, M.A., Zhu, L.: Continuous integration, delivery and deployment: a systematic review on approaches, tools, challenges and practices. IEEE Access **5**, 3909–3943 (2017). https://doi.org/10.1109/ACCESS.2017.2685629
22. Steffen, B., Gossen, F., Naujokat, S., Margaria, T.: Language-driven engineering: from general-purpose to purpose-specific languages. In: Steffen, B., Woeginger, G. (eds.) Computing and Software Science. LNCS, vol. 10000, pp. 311–344. Springer, Cham (2019). https://doi.org/10.1007/978-3-319-91908-9_17
23. Tegeler, T., Gossen, F., Steffen, B.: A model-driven approach to continuous practices for modern cloud-based web applications. In: 2019 9th International Conference on Cloud Computing, Data Science Engineering (Confluence), pp. 1–6 (2019). https://doi.org/10.1109/CONFLUENCE.2019.8776962
24. Teumert, S.: Visual Authoring of CI/CD Pipeline Configurations. Bachelor's thesis, TU Dortmund University (2021). https://archive.org/details/visual-authoring-of-cicd-pipeline-configurations
25. Wirkner, D.: Merge-Strategien für Graphmodelle am Beispiel von jABC und Git. Diploma thesis, TU Dortmund (2015)
26. Zweihoff, P.: Cinco Products for the Web. Master thesis, TU Dortmund (2015)
27. Zweihoff, P., Naujokat, S., Steffen, B.: Pyro: generating domain-specific collaborative online modeling environments. In: Proceedings of the 22nd International Conference on Fundamental Approaches to Software Engineering (FASE 2019) (2019). https://doi.org/10.1007/978-3-030-16722-6_6

Pyrus: An Online Modeling Environment for No-Code Data-Analytics Service Composition

Philip Zweihoff(✉) and Bernhard Steffen(✉)

Chair for Programming Systems, TU Dortmund University, Dortmund, Germany
{philip.zweihoff,bernhard.steffen}@tu-dortmund.de

Abstract. We present Pyrus, a domain-specific online modeling environment for building graphical processes for data analysis, machine learning and artificial intelligence. Pyrus aims at bridging the gap between de facto (often Python-based) standards as established by the Jupyter platform, and the tradition to model data analysis workflows in a dataflow-driven fashion. Technically, Pyrus integrates established online IDEs like Jupyter and allows users to graphically combine available functional components to dataflow-oriented workflows in a collaborative fashion without writing a single line of code. Following a controlflow/dataflow conversion and compilation, the execution is then delegated to the underlying platforms. Both the inputs to a modeled workflow and the results of its execution can be specified and viewed without leaving Pyrus which supports a seamless cooperation between data science experts and programmers. The paper illustrates the fundamental concepts, the employed domain-specific language, and, in particular, the role of the integrated IDE's in an example-driven fashion which can be reproduced in the available online modeling environment.

Keywords: Graphical languages · Domain-specific languages · Data-analytics · Service composition

1 Introduction

In the domain of applied data science there are several challenges to overcome in order to develop a concrete service. First, data must be collected, cleaned, analyzed and then visualized to construct a so-called data-pipeline [37]. Each step has to be realized by multiple mechanisms and algorithms and usually requires extensive manual implementation. This means that the developer of a data analysis pipeline must have broad programming skills in addition to the domain-specific knowledge.

Of course, developers can draw on a large number of open source algorithms and functions, but integrating these poses an additional major challenge. This is because the composition of various functions combined from different sources requires overarching compatibility. However, since this is usually not the case, the individual functions must be subsequently analyzed and adapted, which represents an enormous effort.

T. Margaria and B. Steffen (Eds.): ISoLA 2021, LNCS 13036, pp. 18–40, 2021.
https://doi.org/10.1007/978-3-030-89159-6_2

In addition, there is a different mindset between domain experts of applied data science and programmers. Programmers think in imperative and controlflow-driven processes whereas data-pipelines are modeled conceptually dataflow-driven.

Projects like ETI [47], its successor jETI [26] and Bio-jETI [16,18,19] have already addressed this problem of remote service integration and composition by creating a global service repository. For each service, an interface for integration and usage could be stored to instrument them in the jETI tool. However, the modeling within ETI is done with controlflow based processes which contradicts the dataflow-driven modeling established in data analysis. The Taverna tool [33] addresses this issue by implementing the ETI approach of a centralized service repository in a dataflow-driven process environment. Nevertheless, it became apparent that it would require a great deal of additional effort to manage the central service repository and keep it synchronized with the respective services.

With the increasing use of web-based development and execution environments such as Jupyter [3], Gitpod [2] and Eclipse Che [1], it is now possible to simplify the concept of ETI and Taverna by bypassing the central service repository. For this reason we have developed the Pyrus tool which addresses three challenges:

- *Duality:* For optimal support, users should be able to work in their preferred domain. Accordingly, data analysis modelers and programmers should each use tailored environments. In this way, both can benefit simultaneously from each other in parallel.
- *Interoperability:* Established online development environments such as Jupyter have to be instrumented without detours in order to be able to compose and execute the functions and existing libraries implemented there.
- *Accessibility:* Users should be able to work from anywhere and platform independently without the need for installation or special system resources.

The web-based modeling environment *Pyrus*[1] presented here enables direct discovery and execution of the available services and functions within an online IDE without the detour via a central repository. By integrating an online development environment like Jupyter via API, Pyrus can automatically discover the functions available there and make them available to a user for composition within the process modeling environment. The created composition process of Pyrus can then be compiled and delegated to the connected runtime environment for execution via the same API. For modeling, Pyrus provides a graphical DSL for dataflow-driven processes with a linear type system, following the *Language-Driven Engineering* (LDE) [46] paradigm by aiming at bridging the semantic gap [35] for the user.

Pyrus itself was built using the CINCO Language Workbench [34], which is specialized to the development of graphical domain-specific languages (DSL) [11, 32]. By using Pyro [52], the Pyrus tool can be used as a web-based, collaborative

[1] Project: https://gitlab.com/scce/ml-process, Demo: https://ls5vs023.cs.tu-dortmund.de, (For reviewing only) Login:isola21 Password:isola21.

modeling environment where users can work together to create their processes. Both CINCO[2] and Pyro[3] are open-source and have already been used to develop several graphical DSLs for Eclipse and the web such as: Webstory[24], AADL [52] and DIME [7].

By integrating an online IDE into Pyrus, it is possible to instrument the algorithms, services and functions implemented there on an abstract level. In this paper, we illustrate the integration by the example of a Jupyter IDE[4] to show the advantages for the domain of data analysis. This gives domain experts from the applied data science environment the opportunity to concentrate on the composition and concrete parameterization of the individual functions without the hurdle of manual implementation. This clear separation between "how" and "what" is in line with the principles of Separation-of-Concern (SoC) [50], the One-Thing-Approach (OTA) [27] and Service-Orientation [29] by creating a user-specific intuitive environment. In turn, programmers are able to simultaneously tweak and change the implementation without the need for manual interface synchronization or mutual obstruction. In addition, Pyrus provides a dataflow-driven process language to support the user of the applied data-science domain as intuitively as possible.

In the further course of this paper, an overview is first given of how the Pyrus tool was conceptually developed and how the individual components within the system are interrelated. Subsequently, the metamodel for the dataflow-driven process DSL and the service interfaces declared with CINCO and EMF [49] are described. Based on the abstract syntax, the semantics of the process language is explained to show how the individual discovered functions and services are controlled. Next, the type system is described, which is used to check the correctness of the function composition. In Sect. 6, the usage of the Pyrus tool is demonstrated, showing the integration of Jupyter for the automatic discovery of the services, process modeling, compilation and delegation for execution. Sect. 7 provides a short corresponding tutorial for illustration. The related approaches are analyzed and compared in Sect. 8, followed by a conclusion and outlook for the next steps in Sect. 9.

2 Concept

Pyrus focuses on the composition of functions implemented and provided within external web-based IDEs. This clear separation makes it possible to decouple the function development from the orchestration. In addition, the graphical domain-specific modeling environment created in Pyrus supports the creation of dataflow processes without the need for programming skills. To ensure that the designed models are syntactically correct and executable, a linear type system is used that directly alerts the user to where incompatibilities exist. In this way, the user can

[2] https://gitlab.com/scce/cinco.

[3] https://gitlab.com/scce/pyro.

[4] Demo: https://ls5vs026.cs.tu-dortmund.de/. (For reviewing only) Login:isola21 Password:isola21.

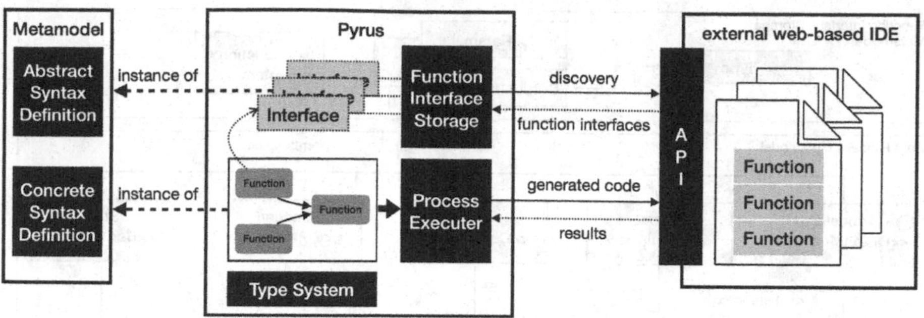

Fig. 1. Conceptual overview from the metamodel to the Pyrus tool and to the connection of an external IDE.

fully concentrate on the tasks in his domain and does not have to deal with the concrete details of the implementation.

The system architecture provides the Pyrus tool (see Fig. 1 in the middle) to be used for process modeling. The implementation and execution of the actual functions is performed within external web-based IDEs (see Fig. 1 on the right). IDEs such as Jupyter, Gitpod or Eclipse Che allow users to program directly in the browser. For this purpose, the corresponding source code is stored on an associated server and executed in an execution environment there. For communication between Pyrus and an external IDE, the respective API is controlled. On the one hand the available functions are discovered and analyzed with regard to the signature and on the other hand the composed functions are called. This describes likewise the prerequisites for the binding of an external IDE, which are fulfilled in the case of Juypter.

Pyrus uses the discovered functions to manage a user-specific Function Interface Storage (FIS). The FIS persists signatures by collecting information about the source, parameter types, return types and documentation. Based on the stored function interfaces in the FIS, users can graphically model dataflow-driven processes in Pyrus. The graphical representation of a functions visualizes the interface by corresponding input and output ports.

The graphical DSL used in Pyrus is based on a metamodel created with CINCO and EMF (see Fig. 1 on the left), which describes both the abstract and concrete syntax of the language. With the help of Pyro, the DSL is delivered within a collaborative, web-based modeling environment that allows direct access via browser.

In order to ensure within the modeling environment that the composition of external functions can be executed, a static linear type system [38] is used. The parameters determined within the function discovery are provided with the corresponding nominal monotypes, which are checked within the modeled hierarchical process using a type-inference algorithm.

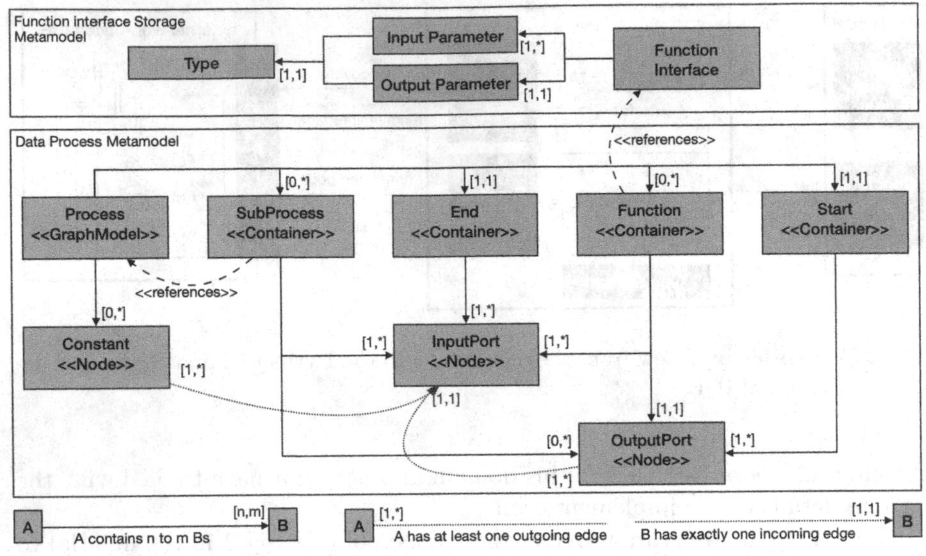

Fig. 2. Metamodel of the dataflow-driven process language of Pyrus.

The execution of a model created with Pyrus is handled by a model transformation and generation step in contrast to Remote Procedure Calls (RPC) [36] used by the majority of the existing tools (see Sect. 8). The code thus generated is then delegated as a complete program to the respective IDE for execution. Finally, the results of the execution are transmitted back to Pyrus to be displayed to the user directly in the modeling environment.

3 Metamodel

There exist many different description forms of the Unified-Modeling-Language (UML) [42] or the Eclipse-Modeling-Foundation (EMF) [49] to define a metamodel for graphical languages. However, these general-purpose meta-modeling languages are not specialized for the definition of graphical languages and accordingly require additional mostly implicit assumptions.

For this reason, CINCO was used to create the metmodel of the dataflow-driven graphical process language present in the Pyrus tool. CINCO is a Language Workbench for creating graphical domain-specific languages based on the meta-types: Graphmodel, Node, Container and Edge. Then, the definition of a graphical language is done by specializing the four meta-types and declaring composition possibilities.

Due to the focus on graph-based languages, only compositions in the form of embedding and connection constraints has to be defined in the metamodel. The constraints are described by cardinalities, which can express static semantics already in the metamodel. In addition, CINCO allows the use of the object-oriented meta-types known from UML and EMF like: Type, Attributes and Association. In addition to the structural metamodels, which represent the abstract syntax, CINCO also offers its own meta-modeling language for defining the concrete syntax. The so-called Meta-Styling-Language (MSL) offers different meta-types for the declaration of shapes, appearances and decorators, which is not described in this paper.

The dataflow-driven process language of Pyrus is based on a metamodel defining a graphmodel containing Function containers, Constant nodes and Dataflow edges. The goal of the language is to allow a user to compose and instrument external functions. The language is based on the following principles:

- A process composes external functions by describing data dependencies between them.
- The dataflow between the functions of a process is acyclic, so that they can be sorted topologically.
- A process can contain another process to form a hierarchically structure and enable reuse.

To do this, it must first be possible to represent the functions from the FIS in a Process. The user can then determine how the data can be transferred between the functions to enable pipelining. Besides the functions, constants should be defined which allow static data to flow into the process. In addition, it should be possible for the user to reuse created processes elsewhere in encapsulated form.

3.1 Function Interface Storage

For the implementation of the dataflow-driven process language and the function interface storage, two meta-models are created which are shown in Fig. 2. The meta-model of the function interface storage shows in which form the determined functions of an external IDE are represented in Pyrus. Each function is identified by a fully qualified name (FQN), which specifies how the actual function can be called. The FQN consist of the file path inside the external IDE as well as the name of the function. The signature of a function is determined by the input and output parameters. Each parameter is named and associated with a named type.

3.2 Process

The Process metamodel describes the abstract syntax of the dataflow-process DSL, which includes the enclosing Process graphmodel type. As a specialization of the graphmodel meta-type, it describes the root element of a graphical DSL in the context of CINCO. From the end user's point of view, the Process can be edited via canvas in which the other node types, edge types and container types described in the metamodel can be instantiated. Which node and container types can be created within the graphmodel is described by the solid edge representing the embedding constraints. The cardinalities at the end of the edge indicate the minimum and maximum number of instances of a specific type.

3.3 Function

To represent function interfaces recorded in the IFS, the Function container type is defined, which holds a reference to a Function Interface in the FIS. In the context of CINCO, the so-called prime references are defined as not nullable association, so that a Function can only exist in a Process as long as the referenced Function Interface exists. As shown in the metamodel (see Fig. 2), a Function container can contain the nodes InputPort and OutputPort. Both node types are used to map the input and output parameters of the referenced Function Interface. The dotted line defines that an edge can be drawn from an OutputPort to an InputPort, which describes the dataflow. The cardinality at the beginning of the dotted edge defines that at least one edge must be drawn from the OutputPort. In contrast, the cardinality at the InputPort node type limits the number of incoming edges to exactly one.

3.4 Constant

For the declaration of constant values, the metamodel defines the Constant node type, which may be contained arbitrarily often in a Process graphmodel. Just like the OutputPort node type, a Constant node can be connected to InputPort nodes via outgoing edges. The lower bound of the cardinality defines that a Constant node must have at least one outgoing edge for a valid structure.

3.5 SubProcess

The hierarchical composition of a Process graphmodel is achieved by using a representative container. The corresponding SubProcess container type can be instantiated any number of times in a Process and holds a reference to the underlying Process. Just like the Function container type, the SubProcess container type is defined to contain at least one InputPort node and an arbitrary number of OutputPort nodes. In this case, however, the parameters of a Function Interface are not represented, but rather the signature of the underlying Process. To define this signature, each Process contains a Start and an End container. The OutputPorts within a Start container define the data which can be passed into the Process and are represented as InputPort nodes inside the SubProcess container above. Analogously InputPort nodes within the End container are represented by OutputPort nodes inside the SubProcess container. Thus processes can be structured hierarchically, by the use of SubProcess containers as representatives within a superordinate process model.

4 Semantics

In the context of textual programming languages the semantics can be formalized for example by structural operational semantics (SOS) [39] along the syntax described in a BNF. In the area of graphical domain-specific languages, however,

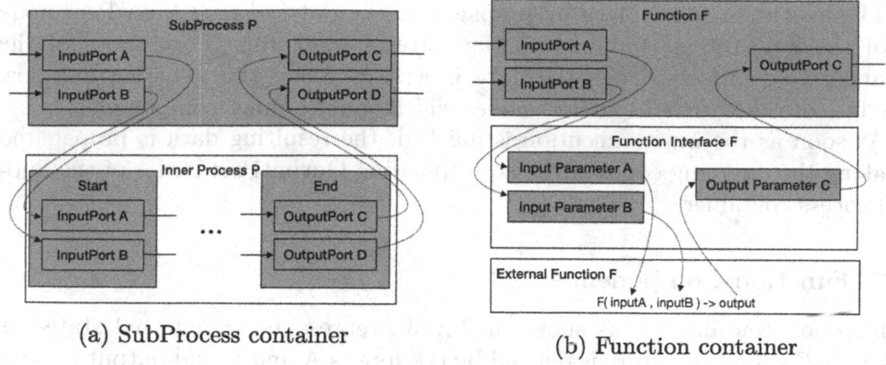

(a) SubProcess container

(b) Function container

Fig. 3. Schematic representation of the component's semantics in a Process model.

these established semantic descriptions can be complicated to use. With respect to the semantics of the dataflow-driven process language of Pyrus, the semantic is applied along the individual components defined in the metamodel by following the approach of Kopetzki [15]. For each component a fire-rule similar to Petri nets [40] can be specified, under the following restrictions:

- The dataflow inside a Process model is acyclic.
- No tokens are consumed.
- A component is enabled if every InputPort node is occupied with data.
- All enabled components are executed in an arbitrary order.
- After execution the resulting data is propagated over the outgoing edges of the OutputPort nodes, which can enable subsequent components.

Accordingly, the semantics for each component can be defined.

4.1 SubProcess Component

A SubProcess container represents the underlying Process model P as shown in Fig. 3a. The inputs A and B and resulting outputs C and D required for the subprocess are represented by corresponding InputPort and OutputPort nodes within the SubProcess container. For each InputPort of the SubProcess container there is an InputPort within the Start container of the underlying Process model. Similarly, the OuputPort nodes of the SubProcess container represent the OutputPort nodes of the End container. Semantically, the SubProcess container symbolizes the delegation to the underlying process, for which a fire rule can also be described:

- As soon as all InputPorts within the SubProcess container are occupied it is enabled.
- All enabled SubProcess containers are executed in an arbitrary order.

- The execution takes place by propagating the data of each InputPort node of the SubProcess container to the corresponding InputPort nodes of the underlying process. Then the data is written along the outgoing dataflow edges of the Start's InputPort nodes which enables inner components.
- As soon as the inner execution is finished, the resulting data is propagated along the outgoing edges of the corresponding OutputPort nodes of the SubProcess container.

4.2 Function Component

A Function container F as shown in Fig. 3b represents an external state-less function F whose signature is defined by the inputs A and B and output parameter C of the Function Interface F. Thus, the semantics of the external function is dependent on the actual implementation outside of Pyrus, since the function is only called during execution. The semantics of the Function container as a component of Pyrus can only specify when the external function is executed and what happens after execution. Thus, the semantics of a Function container can be described as follows:

- As soon as all InputPort nodes within the Function container are occupied, the Function is enabled.
- All Function containers that are enabled, are executed in a arbitrary order.
- An enabled Function container is executed by calling the external function.
- After the function has been executed, the data is propagated along all edges coming from the OutputPort of the Function container.

Although the execution of a hierarchical dataflow process is concurrent and non-deterministic, a deterministic behavior is achieved by the exclusive use of side-effect free external functions and the acyclic structure of a process. This means that it is irrelevant for the result of a process in which order the enabled components are executed, since there is no interference between them.

5 Type System

To ensure that the models created in Pyrus are valid, it is necessary to check whether the dataflow between the included functions is type-correct. For this reason, similar to textual programming languages, each language construct is assigned a type. It is then possible to check whether there are incompatibilities between the constructs associated with dataflow. For this reason, a type system [38] is realized within the modeling environment which is classified and explained in the following.

5.1 Classification

The type system present in Pyrus belongs to the class of strongly typed systems, since there are no possibilities of explicit or implicit type conversion. Type checking is done only at modeling time and not during execution, so it is a static type system. As the metamodel in Sect. 3 has already made clear, type definition takes place exclusively within the Function Interface Storage. During process modeling, the resulting typings of the ports are derived by this definition. Thus, Pyrus is based on an implicit static stong type system with inference.

5.2 Data Types

Pyrus is based on three different primitive data types: string, number, boolean, each of which can be declared and initialized via Constant nodes. Additionally there is the possibility to create an array of each primitive data type. With regard to the strong type system of Pyrus, no operations or transformation of the primitive data types are possible inside a process model. Additional type definitions cannot be modeled and come only from a nominative Type of the Function Interface Storage. The FIS manages the types of all input and return parameters of all determined external functions. Thereby the types are distinguished only by their name, whereby they represent nominal types.

5.3 Type Inference

Type correctness checking within Pyrus is done via type inference. Type inference is used in programming languages to avoid unnecessary additional typing where it can already be reconstructed from existing type definitions and rules. Pyrus realizes type inference related to the system described by Milner [9]. For the implementation of type inference, unification [41] is used to determine the corresponding most general type of a term with predicate logic.

With regard to the nominal types used by Pyrus, the type inference proceeds along the dataflow edges up to a port of a Function container. The ports of a Function container reflect the parameters of a Function Interface within the FIS and reference the corresponding nominative type. Thus the type of a port can be derived by the following unification algorithm:

- If the port is inside a Function container, its type can be determined by the referenced Function Interface and the corresponding Parameter.
- If the port is inside a SubProcess container, the dataflow is followed at the corresponding port of the inner Process model.
- The type inference is performed recursively until a Function container is reached. Since in each process at least one SubProcess or Function container is present, finally the appropriate port in a Function container is found and the type for inference is determined.

However, since the dataflow can split at an OutputPort, the type system must additionally ensure that all outgoing edges ultimately have the same type.

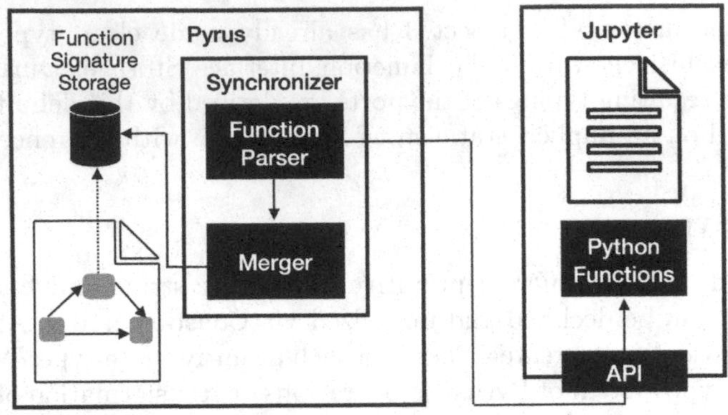

Fig. 4. Synchronization mechanism of Pyrus for function discovery in an external web-based IDE.

6 Usage

The goal of the Pyrus tool is to separate the domain of applied data analytics from the development in a loosely coupled fashion. The concept illustrated in Sect. 2 describes the cross-tool architecture established for this purpose, in which functions are implemented in Jupyter, graphically modeled in Pyrus and executed by delegating generated code.

In this chapter it will be discussed which mechanisms are used by Pyrus to discover the external functions on the one hand and to execute the created process model on the other hand. Furthermore, the modeling environment will be demonstrated with an example from cluster analysis on two dimensional data.

6.1 Function Discovery

In order to use the functions implemented in an external web-based IDE, they must first be discovered. Figure 4 shows the individual components and interactions involved in this process. For this it is necessary that the external IDE offers an appropriate API to access the source code. The Synchronization component implemented in Pyrus controls this API and discovers all existing files and the declared functions inside. At the moment Pyrus supports Python files to be analyzed in the discovery step. After the content of a file has been loaded, the source code is examined with regard to function declarations present in the global scope. Subsequently the Function Parser analyzes the documentation in front of each function. Only if the documentation contains a `Method` keyword followed by the function name and the parameter declaration starting with the `Inputs` and `Outputs` keywords, the function is considered for the use in Pyrus by adding it to the FIS.

This way the developer can decide in Jupyter which functions should be published. Besides the keyword, the function documentation must also contain

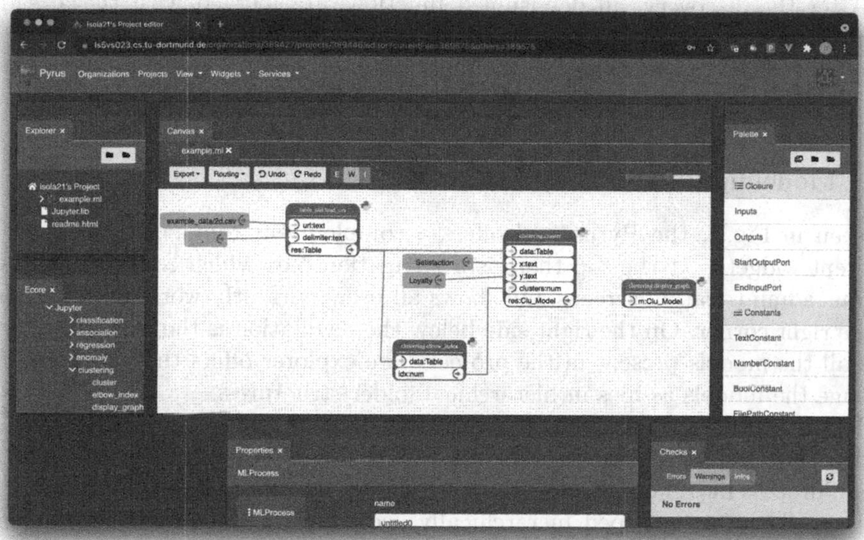

Fig. 5. Pyrus editor user interface screen shot.

information about the input parameters and the return. To enable correct instrumentation on the modeling side, the developer of a function must name the respective parameters and assign a nominative type. The naming of parameters is for user comprehension and to assist during modeling. The nominative type is used by Pyrus to realize the type inference and checking.

Listing 1.1 shows an example of the `cluster` Python function implemented inside Jupyter. In order for the function to be discovered and parsed by Pyrus' Synchronizer, a comment is added before the declaration as shown in lines 1 to 3. The function performs a cluster analysis on a given dataset `data` by first specifying two column names `x` and `y` and the number of clusters to find by `clusters`. The result `res` of the function includes the found clusters which can be further processed or visualized by subsequent functions. To ensure that the `cluster` function can be correctly combined with other functions, a nominative type is assigned to each input and the output parameter.

```
1 # Method: cluster
2 # Inputs: data:Table, x:text, y:text, clusters:num
3 # Output: res:Clu_Model
4 def cluster(data,x,y,clusters):
```

Listing 1.1. Example `cluster` analysis Python function which can be discovered by the synchronizer due to the documentation.

After the discovery, all determined functions are merged with the already existing ones from the function interface storage. Once the synchronization is complete, the Pyrus user can use the function interfaces to create dataflow Process models.

6.2 Modeling

As seen in Fig. 5, the Pyrus tool offers a complete environment consisting of different widgets. At the top there is a navigation bar, which contains links to various administration screens and shows all users currently working in parallel in the right corner. On the right side below the navigation is the explorer which lists all the models present in the project. The explorer offers the possibility to manage the models as files in hierarchical folder structures.

In the center is the modeling Canvas, which displays the currently selected model. The user can move and resize nodes and edges in the model by drag'n'drop. The function interfaces of the IFS are displayed right below the explorer. They are grouped hierarchically according to the files in which they were discovered. A function can be dragged from the widget onto the Canvas to create the corresponding Function container.

On the right side is the Palette widget, which lists all node types available in the language, such as various Constant nodes, Port nodes, Start containers and End containers. To create the elements, the entries of the Palette can be dragged directly onto the canvas. Pyrus also offers the possibility to display the elements of the Palette in their actual form.

Below the palette is the Check widget, which shows whether the currently visible model is valid. The error messages of the type system are listed, in case incompatible ports were connected. In addition, integrity checks are performed to ensure that the Function Interface referenced by a Function container is still present.

The model visible in Fig. 5 shows an example process for cluster analysis. First, several Constant nodes were created, which define the data source as a CSV file and a delimiter. Both constants are connected via dataflow edges to the `load_csv` function, which loads a CSV file. The output port of type `table` is in turn connected to the input of the `cluster` function. The `cluster` function implements the k-means method [22] which requires the numbers of clusters to be determined. This can be defined statically by Constant nodes, or it can be determined with the `elbow_index` function as shown here. The `elbow_index` function implements the heuristic elbow method [6] to determine the amount of present clusters in a given data set. Next, two more textual Constant nodes are created, which indicate the respective column names of the CSV on which the cluster analysis should be performed. Finally, the determined `Clu_Model` is displayed with the `display_graph` function.

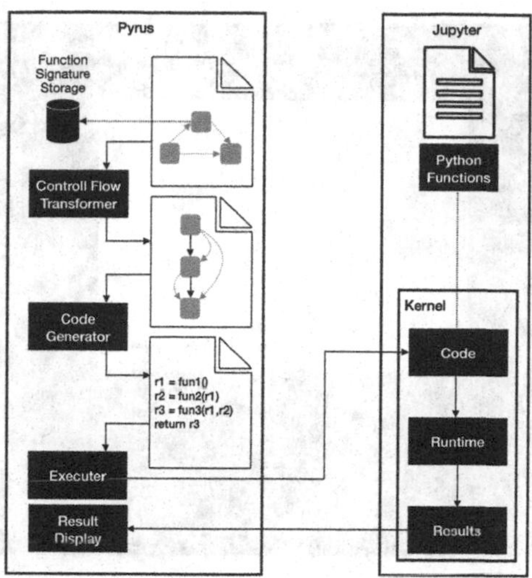

Fig. 6. Pyrus process model execution by transformation and code generation and subsequent delegation to the Jupyter IDE runtime.

6.3 Execution

After a user has created a valid model in Pyrus, it can be executed directly in the environment. The execution is done in several steps, which are demonstrated in Fig. 6.

A created dataflow-driven Process model must first be translated into a imperative controlflow graph because the external execution environment of Jupyter supports only imperative programming languages. For this purpose, a topological sorting is performed according to the semantics formulated in Sect. 4, which orders the Function and SubProcess containers contained in a model based on their distance from the start. Due to the concurrency of a dataflow-driven process, the creation of the execution order is not unique, but equivalent with respect to the result. Based on the determined order, a controlflow graph is created.

Subsequently, the controlflow graph can simply be translated into the target language with the help of a code generator. The code generator creates the respective calls of the external functions in the given order and sets the variables according to the ports and dataflow. In addition it reassembles the hierarchy of all involved process models.

The actual execution of the code generated from the model is realized by delegating it to the Jupyter online IDE by calling the API. Once the code is completely transferred, it is executed by the Jupyter runtime environment. Finally, the execution results are returned to Pyrus, to be displayed to the user (see Fig. 7). The results can be primitive data in the form of e.g. text as well as images, charts or tables, depending on how the external functions are implemented.

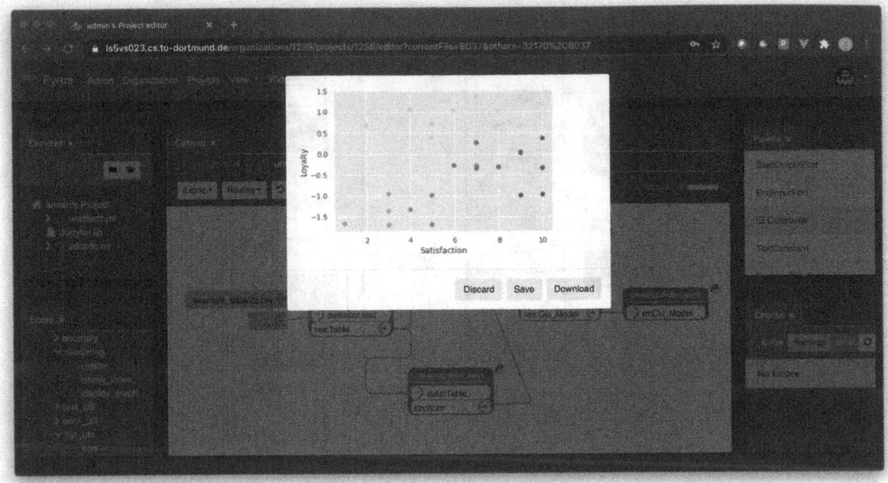

Fig. 7. Cluster analysis example result presentation in Pyrus.

7 Tutorial

In this section we describe a step-by-step guide on the use of Pyrus. We will demonstrate the creation and execution of the data-driven process for a k-means cluster analysis example as mentioned before in Sect. 6.2 and 6.3.

1. **Login** using the credentials: isola21/isola21
2. **Enter organization** by clicking on: `isola21`
3. **Enter the example project** by clicking on: `isola21's project`. A complete example model has already been created that can be executed directly. If you only want to run the model, you can click on the model `example.ml` (see Fig. 5) in the explorer on the top right and jump directly to step 9.
4. **Create a new empty model.** Right click on the project name in the explorer on the top left: isola21's Project and select new to open the creation dialog. Enter a name for the file and click on create button to open a new empty model.
5. **Add functions to the canvas.** All discovered functions are located in the Ecore widget in the bottom left. Expand the Jupyter entry and then the clustering entry. Drag and drop the `cluster`, `elbow_index` and `display_graph` entries to the canvas (see Fig. 8a). To load a CSV file, expand the `table_util` entry and drag and drop the `load_csv` entry to the canvas.
6. **Add data-flow between the functions.** Click on the `table` output port of the `load_csv` function and then click and hold the black circle to the right to draw an edge to the `table` input port of the `cluster` function container (see Fig. 8b). In the same way create connections:

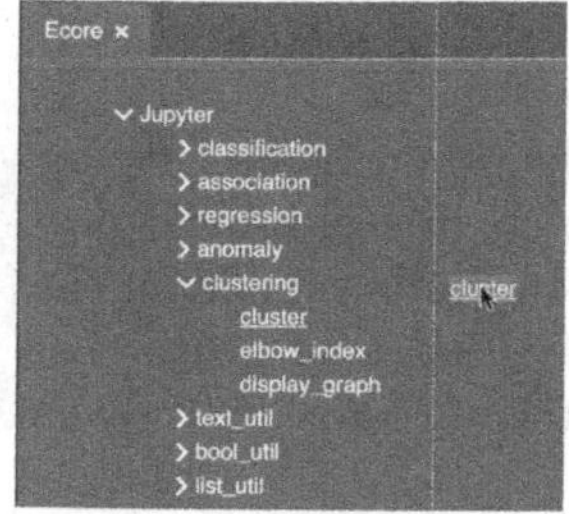

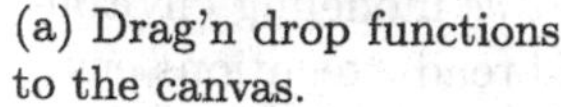
(a) Drag'n drop functions to the canvas.

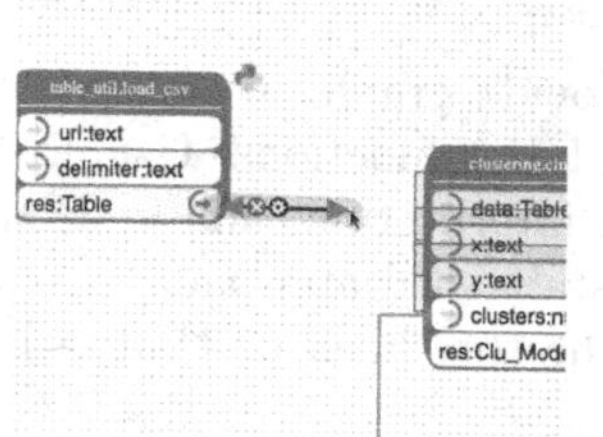

(b) Connect ports by data flow edges.

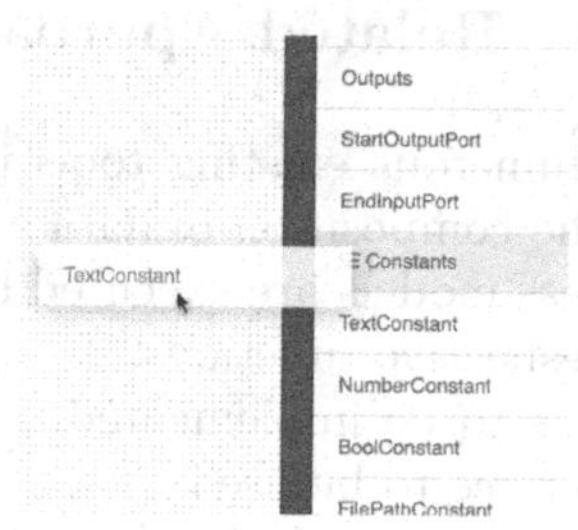

(c) Drag'n drop constants to the canvas.

Fig. 8. User interaction example screenshots.

   (a) from `load_csv` function's `res` output port to the `data` input port of the `elbow_index` function
   (b) from `clusterfunction`'s `res` output port to the `m` input port of the `display_graph` function
   (c) from `elbow_index` function's `idx` output port to the `clusters` input port of the `cluster` function
7. **Add constants to the canvas.** To create static inputs, darg an drop the corresponding entries from the palette widget on the top right to the canvas. Drag and drop the `TextConstant` entry four times from the palette to the canvas (see Fig. 8c). By clicking a `TextConstant` node on the canvas, the properties view at the bottom shows a text field to edit the value. Set the values and connect each `TextConstant` to an input port:
   (a) Set value to `example_data/2d.csv` and connect it to the `url` port of `load_csv`. This path refers to a file located in Jupyter.
   (b) Set value to , and connect it to the `delimiter` port of `load_csv`.
   (c) Set value to `Satisfaction` and connect it to the `x` port of `cluster`.
   (d) Set value to `Loyalty` and connect it to the `y` port of `cluster`.
8. **Check the model validity.** The validation view should show a green message: No Errors. If this is not the case, read the error messages and try to fix the model.
9. **Execute the model.** Right-click an empty spot on the canvas and click on *Execute on Jupyter*. The execution for the cluster analysis takes up to 15 s. The result is displayed in a popup (see Fig. 7) which can be download to the computer or save in the project.

Each function is located in a Jupyter workspace as part of our Jupyter Hub[5]. To explore the functions use the credentials isola21/isola21. The functions used for this example are located inside the library folder, which can be opened by the `File` menu and `Open...`. Inside the `library` folder the `clustering.py` file, used in the example above is located. The `clustering.py` file contains the implementation and signature description of the functions used in the example: `cluster`, `elbow_index` and `display_graph`.

[5] https://ls5vs026.cs.tu-dortmund.de/.

8 Related Approaches

Numerous existing tools provide graphical process modeling environments for the composition of data analytics functions. Usually the created graphical process models are executed by interpreting each node step-by-step and calling the respective functions. The established approaches require either that a function has to be implemented in the tool itself or that it has to be realized as a web service to be used.

None of the state-of-the-art tools provides a *collaborative* modeling environment and and is able to *delegate* the execution to best of bread executions environments, like Jupyter, via compilation. In contrast, Pyrus allows data analysts and domain experts to design data analysis models in tandem, each using their own browser, and then to delegate the execution to the execution environment of their choice, as illustrate in this paper for Jupyter.

Whereas the advantage of browser-based collaboration is obvious in particular these days, execution via delegation has also numerous advantages:

- it optimizes the data transfer,
- it supports data security, as the individual data may remain at the execution environments location, and only the aggregated results are communicated via the net, and
- using Pyrus interpreter, it is even possible to distribute the computation to dedicated execution environments for local computation and aggregate the results at the end. The execution environments may be different instantiations of Jupyper, but also entirely different execution environments like Gitpod, CodeAnywhere and Eclipse Che.

In the remainder of this section, we analyze and compare other open-source and commercial tools, focusing on the following characteristics:

- **Ext.** The extension possibilities and tool support to manually implemented functions to be used inside the modeling environment.
- **Execution.** The mechanism used to execute the model, which is performed by a stepwise *interpreter* or prior *compilation* to executable code.
- **Runtime.** The runtime environment executing the composed functions of a process model and how it is called: *remote* procedure calls, complete *delegation* to an external runtime or inside the *local* tool environment
- **Access.** The access possibilities of a tool: direct *online* access or *local* installation.
- **Collaboration.** Model sharing via *export* or collaborative *real-time* editing.
- **License.** Open-source (*OS*) or commercial (*Com.*).

We provide our discussion based on past publications describing the tools as well as the qualitative analysis presented in [13]. Table 1 summarizes our comparison regarding the characteristics of the data-analytics modeling tools. Each of the following subsections elaborates on one of the table's rows compared to Pyrus.

Table 1. Data-analysis modeling tool comparison.

Tool	Ext.	Execution (Runtime)	Access	Collaboration	License
Pyrus	Jupyer et al.	Compilation (delegation)	Online	Real-time	OS
MaramaEML	None	Interpreter (remote)	Local	Export	OS
ETI, Bio-jETI	None	Interpreter (remote)	Local	Export	OS
Taverna	None	Interpreter (remote)	Local	Export	OS
Kepler	Inline	Interpreter (remote)	Local	None	OS
SDLTool	None	Interpreter (remote)	Local	Export	OS
Azure ML Studio, Google Cloud ML, AWS ML	Inline	Interpreter (local)	Online	None	Com.
RapidMiner Studio	Inline	Interpreter (local)	Local	Export	Com.

8.1 MaramaEML

MaramaEML [21] is a desktop based modeling environment for the enterprise modeling language (EML) [20] which can be used to instrument data-analysis services via BPMN [51] processes. The modeled processes have to be generated to WS-BPEL [45] code which can be executed in a corresponding engine by instrumenting web services. To use a function in MaramaEML, it must be manually implemented and served over the web to be callable by the WS-BPEL engine. Users of Marama cannot collaborate in the tool directly and have to distribute serialized models by a version control system (VCS) [44].

8.2 ETI, Bio-jETI

ETI [47] is based on a controlflow-driven language in which the sequence of the individual services can be modeled. The services must be specified and stored in a central repository before they can be used in ETI. The latest version Bio-jETI [16] is a desktop application developed for the jABC platform [27,48].

8.3 Taverna

Taverna [33] utilize a centralized service repository which results in the same drawbacks as ETI. The modeling environment provides a dataflow-based service composition workflow language without ports. Taverna requires a local installation and setup which complicates the direct usability.

8.4 Kepler

Kepler [23] is a graphical modeling tool for combining R scripts and remote services to create scientific workflows. A workflow component can be implemented inline by a text editor to extend the available so-called actors. Since Kepler workflows can only be exported as archives, the collaboration is limited to file sharing. Kepler requires a local setup based on the Ptolemy framework [10] to create desktop applications for actor-oriented design.

8.5 SDLTool

The SDLTool [14] provides a visual language to define statistical surveys as a part of data analytics in a holistic modeling environment. The local desktop development environment allows users to publish designed process as web service so that they can be used by other applications. SDLTool cannot be used collaboratively by multiple users because the created model can only be exported to a repository. In addition, the analysis functions must be manually programmed and integrated within SDLTool.

8.6 Azure ML Studio, Google Cloud ML and AWS ML

There are many different commercial tools for creating data analysis processes based on serverless functions [5] such as Azure ML Studio, Google Cloud ML and AWS ML which have already been investigated by [12]. The integrated environments can be used via browser and operate on the corresponding platform infrastructure. Pre-defined components can be extended by Python and R scripts implemented inside the environment.

8.7 RapidMiner Studio

RapidMiner Studio [8] is a commercial local modeling tool to compose pre-build functions for data analytics and machine learning. Additional functions have to be manually imported as Python and R scripts to be used in a graphical process. RapidMiner Studio provide collaboration by exporting serialized models to a VCS.

9 Conclusion and Outlook

We introduced Pyrus as a new tool for bridging the semantic gap between the two worlds of imperative programming and dataflow-driven modeling in the domain of data analysis. The key to achieving this goal is the use of domain-specific process languages adapting to the established concepts for describing data-pipelines for machine learning and artificial intelligence. The possibility of directly integrating established online IDEs like Jupyter and delegating compiled process models for execution allows domain experts and programmers to work together and benefit from each other.

The concept of Pyrus is based on the principles of the One-Thing-Approach [27] and Continuous Model-Driven-Engineering [28] by enabling service-oriented instrumentation [31] of external functionalities in a central tool. Tools such Bio-jETI and Taverna showed the need to enable domain experts to independently use existing technologies without the technical expertise of a programmer.

The use of model-driven tools is particularly suitable for enabling a user to concentrate on the "what" and thus make design decisions independent of the "how" level of a concrete implementation. The advantage of this approach has already been shown in various studies by Lamprecht [17], Saay [43] and Margaria on the so-called eXtreme model-driven design (XMDD) [30]. It turned out that students of natural sciences without programming knowledge can get an intuitive access to process execution frameworks by using XMDD tools.

Pyrus has taken this approach and improved it with respect to current technologies. Unlike ETI and the Semantik-Web [25], Pyrus instruments external web-based IDEs directly, instead of a high-maintenance intermediate repository. In this way, functions can be discovered and used without detours.

The current architecture and technical implementation opens up the possibility for a variety of extensions on different levels. First, the previous validation, which is based on the static strong type system, can be extended by model checking methods. For this purpose, the external functions must be supplemented by further annotations in order to specify various properties to be checked. These annotations can be used to support the user during the modeling process by checking the semantic correctness. In a further step, the existing properties can be used to apply synthesis methods, as already done in the Bio-jETI tool. In this way, automatically missing process parts could be added to resolve existing type incompatibilities.

In addition to these enhancements on the usage level, we plan to increase the amount of usable programming languages to be integrated as functions in Pyrus. Jupyter offers a variety of languages which can be used through the integration of so-called kernels. In order to give users the freedom to choose which languages are used to create functionality, the function discovery and code generation of Pyrus can be extended. Functions of different languages can be called during the execution for example over remote-procedure-calls or with the help of interoperability frameworks like rpy2 [4]. In this way, functions of different programming languages can be combined in the modeling environment for specific purposes.

In order to be able to address different domains with Pyrus, it is necessary to integrate further web-based IDEs such as Gitpod, Eclipse Che, Codeanywhere or AWS Cloud9. For this purpose, a standardized interface and protocol should be established how online IDEs can communicate with each other.

We are convinced that the concept of Pyrus is promising. Due to the growing number of available web-based IDEs, it is possible to integrate more functionalities in a service-oriented way so that a user can handle complex problems on his own. Especially the fact that programmers and Pyrus users can work together in parallel without an intermediary enables a very agile way of working which has already been successfully demonstrated in several student projects.

References

1. Eclipse Che. https://www.eclipse.org/che
2. Gitpod. https://www.gitpod.io
3. Jupyter. https://jupyter.org
4. rpy2 - R in Python. https://rpy2.github.io/
5. Baldini, I., et al.: Serverless computing: current trends and open problems. In: Chaudhary, S., Somani, G., Buyya, R. (eds.) Research Advances in Cloud Computing, pp. 1–20. Springer, Singapore (2017). https://doi.org/10.1007/978-981-10-5026-8_1
6. Bholowalia, P., Kumar, A.: EBK-means: a clustering technique based on elbow method and k-means in WSN. Int. J. Comput. Appl. **105**(9) (2014)
7. Boßelmann, S., et al.: DIME: a programming-less modeling environment for web applications. In: Margaria, T., Steffen, B. (eds.) ISoLA 2016. LNCS, vol. 9953, pp. 809–832. Springer, Cham (2016). https://doi.org/10.1007/978-3-319-47169-3_60
8. Chisholm, A.: Exploring Data with Rapidminer. Packt Publishing Ltd, Birmingham (2013)
9. Damas, L., Milner, R.: Principal type-schemes for functional programs. In: Proceedings of the 9th ACM SIGPLAN-SIGACT Symposium on Principles of Programming Languages, pp. 207–212 (1982)
10. Eker, J., et al.: Taming heterogeneity-the ptolemy approach. Proc. IEEE **91**(1), 127–144 (2003)
11. Fowler, M., Parsons, R.: Domain-Specific Languages. Addison-Wesley/ACM Press (2011)
12. Khalajzadeh, H., Abdelrazek, M., Grundy, J., Hosking, J.G., He, Q.: Survey and analysis of current end-user data analytics tool support. IEEE Trans. Big Data (2019)
13. Khalajzadeh, H., Simmons, A.J., Abdelrazek, M., Grundy, J., Hosking, J.G., He, Q.: Visual languages for supporting big data analytics development. In: ENASE, pp. 15–26 (2020)
14. Kim, C.H., Grundy, J., Hosking, J.: A suite of visual languages for model-driven development of statistical surveys and services. J. Vis. Lang. Comput. **26**, 99–125 (2015)
15. Kopetzki, D.: Generation of domain-specific language-to-language transformation languages (2019)
16. Lamprecht, A.L.: User-Level Workflow Design. LNCS, vol. 8311. Springer, Heidelberg (2013). https://doi.org/10.1007/978-3-642-45389-2
17. Lamprecht, A.L., Margaria, T., Neubauer, J.: On the use of XMDD in software development education. In: 2015 IEEE 39th Annual Computer Software and Applications Conference, vol. 2, pp. 835–844. IEEE (2015)
18. Lamprecht, A.-L., Margaria, T., Steffen, B.: Seven variations of an alignment workflow - an illustration of agile process design and management in Bio-jETI. In: Măndoiu, I., Sunderraman, R., Zelikovsky, A. (eds.) ISBRA 2008. LNCS, vol. 4983, pp. 445–456. Springer, Heidelberg (2008). https://doi.org/10.1007/978-3-540-79450-9_42

19. Lamprecht, A.L., Margaria, T., Steffen, B.: Bio-jETI: a framework for semantics-based service composition. BMC Bioinformatics **10**(10), 1–19 (2009)
20. Li, L., Hosking, J., Grundy, J.: EML: a tree overlay-based visual language for business process modelling, pp. 131–137 (2007)
21. Li, L., Hosking, J., Grundy, J.: MaramaEML: an integrated multi-view business process modelling environment with tree-overlays, zoomable interfaces and code generation. In: 2008 23rd IEEE/ACM International Conference on Automated Software Engineering, pp. 477–478 (2008)
22. Lloyd, S.: Least squares quantization in PCM. IEEE Trans. Inf. Theory **28**(2), 129–137 (1982)
23. Ludäscher, B., et al.: Scientific workflow management and the Kepler system. Concurr. Comput. Pract. Exp. **18**(10), 1039–1065 (2006)
24. Lybecait, M., Kopetzki, D., Zweihoff, P., Fuhge, A., Naujokat, S., Steffen, B.: A tutorial introduction to graphical modeling and metamodeling with CINCO. In: Margaria, T., Steffen, B. (eds.) ISoLA 2018. LNCS, vol. 11244, pp. 519–538. Springer, Cham (2018). https://doi.org/10.1007/978-3-030-03418-4_31
25. Margaria, T., Kubczak, C., Steffen, B.: The XMDD approach to the semantic web services challenge. In: Blake, B., Cabral, L., König-Ries, B., Küster, U., Martin, D. (eds.) Semantic Web Services, pp. 233–248. Springer, Heidelberg (2012). https://doi.org/10.1007/978-3-642-28735-0_15
26. Margaria, T., Nagel, R., Steffen, B.: jETI: a tool for remote tool integration. In: Halbwachs, N., Zuck, L.D. (eds.) TACAS 2005. LNCS, vol. 3440, pp. 557–562. Springer, Heidelberg (2005). https://doi.org/10.1007/978-3-540-31980-1_38
27. Margaria, T., Steffen, B.: Business process modeling in the jABC: the one-thing approach. In: Handbook of Research on Business Process Modeling, pp. 1–26. IGI Global (2009)
28. Margaria, T., Steffen, B.: Continuous model-driven engineering. Computer **42**(10), 106–109 (2009)
29. Margaria, T., Steffen, B.: Service-orientation: conquering complexity with XMDD. In: Hinchey, M., Coyle, L. (eds.) Conquering Complexity, pp. 217–236. Springer, London (2012). https://doi.org/10.1007/978-1-4471-2297-5_10
30. Margaria, T., Steffen, B.: eXtreme model-driven development (XMDD) technologies as a hands-on approach to software development without coding. In: Encyclopedia of Education and Information Technologies, pp. 732–750 (2020)
31. Margaria, T., Steffen, B., Reitenspieß, M.: Service-oriented design: the roots. In: Benatallah, B., Casati, F., Traverso, P. (eds.) ICSOC 2005. LNCS, vol. 3826, pp. 450–464. Springer, Heidelberg (2005). https://doi.org/10.1007/11596141_34
32. Mernik, M., Heering, J., Sloane, A.M.: When and how to develop domain-specific languages. ACM Comput. Surv. **37**(4), 316–344 (2005)
33. Missier, P., et al.: Taverna, reloaded. In: Gertz, M., Ludäscher, B. (eds.) SSDBM 2010. LNCS, vol. 6187, pp. 471–481. Springer, Heidelberg (2010). https://doi.org/10.1007/978-3-642-13818-8_33
34. Naujokat, S., Lybecait, M., Kopetzki, D., Steffen, B.: Cinco: a simplicity-driven approach to full generation of domain-specific graphical modeling tools. Int. J. Softw. Tools Technol. Transfer **20**(3), 327–354 (2018)
35. Naur, P., Randell, B. (eds.): Software Engineering: Report of a Conference Sponsored by the NATO Science Committee, Garmisch, Germany, 7–11 October 1968. Scientific Affairs Division, NATO, Brussels 39 Belgium (1969)
36. Nelson, B.J.: Remote procedure call (1982)

37. O'Donovan, P., Leahy, K., Bruton, K., O'Sullivan, D.T.J.: An industrial big data pipeline for data-driven analytics maintenance applications in large-scale smart manufacturing facilities. J. Big Data **2**(1), 1–26 (2015). https://doi.org/10.1186/s40537-015-0034-z
38. Pierce, B.C., Benjamin, C.: Types and Programming Languages. MIT Press, Cambridge (2002)
39. Plotkin, G.D.: A structural approach to operational semantics. Aarhus university (1981)
40. Reisig, W.: Petri Nets: An Introduction, vol. 4. Springer, Heidelberg (2012). https://doi.org/10.1007/978-3-642-69968-9
41. Robinson, J.A.: A machine-oriented logic based on the resolution principle. J. ACM (JACM) **12**(1), 23–41 (1965)
42. Rumbaugh, J., Jacobson, I., Booch, G.: The unified modeling language. Reference manual (1999)
43. Saay, S., Margaria, T.: XMDD as key enabling technology for integration of large scale elearning based on NRENs. In: 2020 IEEE 20th International Conference on Advanced Learning Technologies (ICALT), pp. 45–46. IEEE (2020)
44. Spinellis, D.: Version control systems. IEEE Softw. **22**(5), 108–109 (2005)
45. Standard, O.: Web services business process execution language version 2.0 (2007)
46. Steffen, B., Gossen, F., Naujokat, S., Margaria, T.: Language-driven engineering: from general-purpose to purpose-specific languages. In: Steffen, B., Woeginger, G. (eds.) Computing and Software Science. LNCS, vol. 10000, pp. 311–344. Springer, Cham (2019). https://doi.org/10.1007/978-3-319-91908-9_17
47. Steffen, B., Margaria, T., Braun, V.: The electronic tool integration platform: concepts and design. Int. J. Softw. Tools Technol. Transfer **1**(1–2), 9–30 (1997)
48. Steffen, B., Margaria, T., Nagel, R., Jörges, S., Kubczak, C.: Model-driven development with the jABC. In: Bin, E., Ziv, A., Ur, S. (eds.) HVC 2006. LNCS, vol. 4383, pp. 92–108. Springer, Heidelberg (2007). https://doi.org/10.1007/978-3-540-70889-6_7
49. Steinberg, D., Budinsky, F., Merks, E., Paternostro, M.: EMF: Eclipse Modeling Framework. Pearson Education, London (2008)
50. Tarr, P., Ossher, H., Harrison, W., Sutton, S.M.: N degrees of separation: multi-dimensional separation of concerns. In: Proceedings of the 1999 International Conference on Software Engineering (IEEE Cat. No. 99CB37002), pp. 107–119. IEEE (1999)
51. White, S.A.: Introduction to BPMN. IBM Cooperation **2** (2004)
52. Zweihoff, P., Naujokat, S., Steffen, B.: Pyro: generating domain-specific collaborative online modeling environments. In: Hähnle, R., van der Aalst, W. (eds.) FASE 2019. LNCS, vol. 11424, pp. 101–115. Springer, Cham (2019). https://doi.org/10.1007/978-3-030-16722-6_6

Integrating External Services in DIME

Hafiz Ahmad Awais Chaudhary[1,2](✉) and Tiziana Margaria[1,2,3]

[1] CSIS, University of Limerick, Limerick, Ireland
ahmad.chaudhary@ul.ie

[2] Confirm - Centre for Smart Manufacturing, Limerick, Ireland

[3] Lero - The Science Foundation Ireland Research Centre for Software, Limerick, Ireland

Abstract. We show how to extend the (application) Domain Specific Languages supported by the DIME low-code development environment to integrate functionalities hosted on heterogeneous technologies and platforms. Developers can this way utilize within DIME entire platforms like e.g. R for data analytics, and collections of services, like e.g. any REST-based microservices. In this paper we describe the current architecture of the DIME-based Digital Thread platform we are building in a collection of interdisciplinary collaborative projects, discuss the role of various DSLs in the platform, and provide a step by step tutorial for the integration of external platforms and external services in DIME. The goal is to enable a wide range of DIME adopters to integrate their application specific external services in the DIME open source platform, bootstrapping a collaborative ecosystem where the low-code activity of integrating external capabilities facilitates an increasingly no-code application development on the basis of pre-integrated Application DSLs.

Keywords: Domain Specific Language (DSL) · Model Driven Development (MDD) · eXtreme Model Driven Development (XMDD) · Service Independent Building Blocks (SIBs) · Low code development environments · DIME

1 Introduction

We address the problem of integrating external services into the DIME integrated modelling environment. As shown in [14], we are building in Limerick a significant ecosystem of collaborations spanning various application domains, with the collective goal of contributing application domain specific collections of services to a DIME-centered low-code application development environment able to use all those services in the application design, in a possibly seamless way. In the terminology that is currently emerging in the advanced manufacturing context, this end-to-end integration of all what is needed to collaboratively deliver a complex, interoperable capability in a potentially cyberphysical cooperation is called the "Digital Thread".

Its definition is not yet settled, but to give an idea, according to the CEO of iBASEt, a company offering Digital Thread products and consultancy, *"the Digital Thread encompasses model data, product structure data, metadata, effectual*

T. Margaria and B. Steffen (Eds.): ISoLA 2021, LNCS 13036, pp. 41–54, 2021.
https://doi.org/10.1007/978-3-030-89159-6_3

data process definition data – including supporting equipment and tools" [6], and *"Product Lifecycle Management (PLM) provides "the what" (modeling, BOM management, process planning, process simulation, and engineering change management). Enterprise Resource Planning (ERP) provides "the when, where, and how much" (scheduling, financials, and inventory). To have a fully developed model-based enterprise—and a fully functioning Digital Thread—manufacturers also need "the how". That's what Product Lifecycle Execution (PLE) provides through process execution, process control, quality assurance, traceability, and deviation handling."*

In our view, the Digital Thread requires an end-to-end integration of the data and processes that guide and deliver such complex operations, and it is our goal to provide this integration and orchestration in a model driven and low-code, formal methods-supported fashion. In this paper, we address specifically the task of integrating external services provenient from various platforms and made available in various programming languages, into the DIME integrated modelling environment. DIME's extension and integration with external systems through the mechanism of native services DSLs extends the capabilities of the core platform to meet wider communication needs (e.g., in the cloud), and also to take advantage of existing sophisticated enterprise services (e.g. AWS).

Low-code programming both at the API and the platform level is considered to be a game changer for the economy of application development. Gartner Inc., for example, predicts [5] that the size of the low-code development tools market will increase by nearly 30% year on year from 2020 to 2021, reaching a $5.8 billion value in 2021. They state that so far, this is the fastest and probably the simplest and most economical method of developing applications.

In this paper, we briefly recall the DIME-based architecture of the Digital Thread platform in Sect. 2, including the central role of Low-code and DSLs in it. Section 3 presents the integration methodology in DIME with a quick tutorial, followed in Sect. 4 details the step by step integration of the R platform and of RESTful services. Finally, Sect. 5 contains our summary and a brief discussion of the perspectives.

2 The Digital Thread Platform in DIME

DIME [3] is a graphical Integrated Modelling Environments for low-code/no-code application development, used to develop research [9,16] as well as industrial applications. It is a general purpose MDD platform-level tool, suitable for agile development due to its rapid prototyping for web application development. It follows the One Thing Approach based on XMDD [18], in a lineage of development environments that traces back to the METAFrame'95 [25,26]. DIME supports both control flow and data flow modelling in its process diagrams. Control flow models admit a single start node but may have multiple end nodes, and nodes (called SIBs) representing single functionalities or sub-models are graphs, i.e. formal models. The SIBs are connected via directed edges depending on the business logic, with distinct edge types for dataflow and control-flow.

Software systems in general, and especially web apps in internet-centered ecosystems and digital threads in an Industry 4.0 context, are not isolated in nature: they demand interaction with various external systems, libraries and services. Frequent needs are (but not limited to)

- acquire sensors data from external systems,
- feed data to external dashboards for analytics and publishing,
- utilize the compute power of cloud systems,
- reuse sophisticated enterprise services.

We will use DSLs to virtualize the technological heterogeneity of the services, delivering a simple, coherent and efficient extension to this low-code modelling platform. The extension by integration adds to the tools the capability to communicate with sophisticated enterprise ecosystems, without sacrificing the flexible yet intuitive modelling style for the no-code users, who just use the DSLs that are available.

2.1 The Current Architecture

The current architecture of the Digital Thread platform is depicted in Fig. 1 (from [14]).

DIME's own **Language DSL** (in orange), designed in Cinco [21], encompasses for the moment in our application settings primarily the Data, Process and GUI models. This is the layer defining the expressive power of the DIME modelling language. Data, Process and GUI models are used to design the applications, thus the Digital Thread platform makes use of these facilities "as is". We do not extend nor modify this layer.

The concrete applications designed and implemented in DIME (in blue) use the modelling and orchestration language of the Language DSL, and as vocabulary a number of service collections provided in directly in the core DIME platform (the Common DSLs, e.g. concerning the supported GUI elements and their functionalities), but also a growing collection of Process DSLs that may be application specific or still generic.

All these are part of the **Application DSL** layer, that includes also quite a number of **Native DSLs** external to DIME (in green). These DSLs collect the atomic SIBs that expose to the application design layer the encapsulated code provenient from a rich and growing collection of external service providers. For example, in [8] and [7] we have integrated a number of EdgeX Foundry services [1] that support a variety of IoT devices and relative communication protocols. The same has happened for AWS and other services in [4].

The DSLs may concern specific application domains, but the parameter that determines the specific kind of integration is the technology on which they run. To give and example, one can use data analytics in R to analyze cancer-related data, census data, proactive maintenance data in the manufacturing domain, or risk and insurance related data in financial analytics. As long as they use the same R functions, the integration in DIME is exactly the same and needs to be

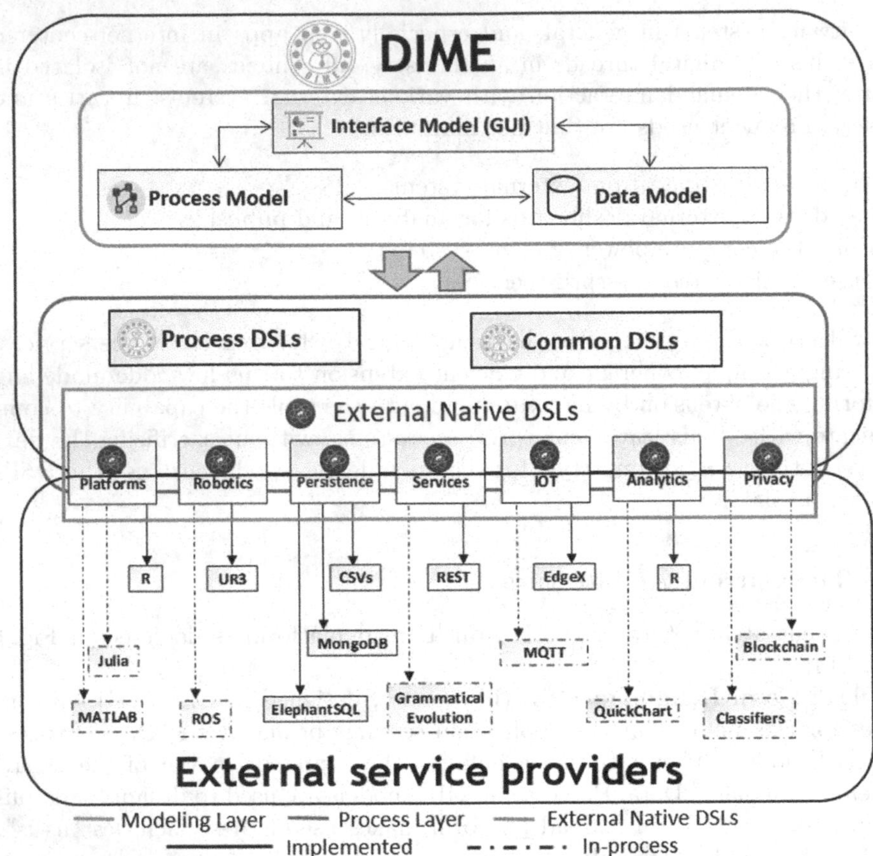

Fig. 1. Architecture Overview of DIME and Custom DSLs

done just once. The same applies for example to Julia and Matlab: we will address the integration of a DSL for each of them in the context of a biomechanical simulation collaborative project, but the corresponding DSLs will be reusable "as-is" for any other application that requires the same functionality.

In that sense, it is realistic to talk of the Digital Thread platform under construction as a large, heterogeneous, collaborative ecosystem where reusal is promoted well beyond the walled garden of a specific application domain. This is still a novelty to many, who are used to think in terms of their discipline and specialty, and see this possibility of direct reuse as an unexpected benefit, given that they are used to re-code rather than reuse.

In this respect, our value proposition sits clearly at the upper, application development layer, where we see the interoperability challenge truly reside.

We also see ourselves as systematic users of such pre-existing platforms, who are for us indeed welcome providers of Native DSLs. In this context, a number of integrations in DIME relevant to the advanced manufacturing domain have already been addressed.

2.2 Low Code and DSLs

Low code development platforms enable their users to design and develop applications with minimal coding knowledge [27], with the support of drag-and-drop visual interfaces that operate on representations of code as encapsulated code wrappers. The main aim [24] of these platforms is to produce flexible, cost effective and rapid applications in a model driven way. Ideally, they are adaptive to enhancements and less complex is terms of maintenance. Model-driven development (MDD) is an approach to develop such systems using models and model refinement from the conceptual modelling phase to the automated model-to-code transformation of these models to executable code [19]. The main challenges with traditional software development approaches are the complexity in development at large scale, the maintenance over time, and the adaptation to dynamic requirements and upgrades [27]. Doing this on source code is costly, and it systematically excludes the application domain experts. who are the main knowledge and responsibility carriers. At the same time, the cost of quality documentation and training of new human resources for code-based development are other concerns in companies and organizations that depend on code.

Domain Specific Languages (DSLs) conveniently encapsulate most complexities of the underlying application domain. Encapsulation of code and abstraction to semantically faithful representations in models empowers domain experts to take advantage of these platforms. They can develop products in an efficient manner and also meet the growing demands of application development without having deep expertise in software development. Based on a study [2] from 451 researches, the maintenance effort with low code platforms proved to be 50–90% more efficient as compared to changes with classical coding languages.

3 Integration in DIME: A Quick Tutorial

The extension mechanisms of DIME concern two distinct levels: adding Services and adding Platforms.

- **Service integration** follows the *Native library* philosophy of DIME and can be carried out by following the steps described in Sect. 3.2 and Sect. 3.3. We illustrate this step by step on the basis of a REST integration, which is applicable also to the general microservice architectures.
- In **Platform integration** there is the additional challenge of the preparation of the platform in such a way that it addresses the needs of the underlying application. We will show this in the case of the R platform in Sect. 3.1.

In either case, the goal is to create adequate wrappers around the code one wishes to call or execute, an adequate call mechanism, and an appropriate signature representation of each of these SIBs within the DIME SIB Native library.

When the new SIB is utilised in an application, it is expected to communicate with the respective external service, technology, platform or infrastructure for the purposes of connection creation, system call, or movement of data. It is thus important that the runtime infrastructure is compatible, optimised and scalable in order to handle the required collection of data sets, instructions and generated results, e.g., strings, tables and graphs.

We describe now the three key steps of the DIME extension mechanism for the integration of external services or platforms, concerning the runtime infrastructure, the SIB declaration and the SIB implementation.

3.1 Runtime Infrastructure

Normally, the individual services are already optimised and deployed in some cloud service with a public or private access. The preparation of the platform is however still a challenge. Being DIME a web based application, the network latency can be reduced if the platform or technological infrastructure is deployed on the same network. The following steps are required to prepare a runtime docker container for the infrastructure.

1. Prepare and deploy a docker container for the desired technology or platform.
2. Get the network and connectivity details of the deployed container to be fed into DIME extended SIBs at runtime (or compile time, if the endpoint is constant).
3. Make sure to close all the connections after the successful communication with the client SIB in order to avoid dangling open connections.

Once this is done, we can define the new DSL in DIME via the SIB declaration mechanism. As an External native DSL is a collection of SIBs, we describe now how to add a SIB.

3.2 SIB Declaration

To develop a new (atomic) SIB in DIME, the SIB declaration is the first step: the declaration defines the SIB signature, with the data and control flow dependencies of the new SIB. The SIB declaration process is the same in both the Service and the Platform integration. To define a new atomic SIB,

1. Firstly, in the DIME-models section of the project explorer, we add a new empty file with extension ".sib"
2. This new file contains the signature of the new SIB. It starts with the keyword "sib", followed by the new SIB name, a colon and the path to the attached Java function. This is the function be invoked when the SIB will be used in the process modelling.
3. The subsequent lines contain the input parameters accompanied with the variable names and data types

```
sib sib_name : Java_file_path#function_name
    input_1: integer
    input_2: text
    -> control_branch_1
       output_1: text
    -> control_branch_2
```

Fig. 2. Sample SIB declaration signatures

4. Finally, considering the set of possible execution outcomes, a list of outgoing control branches is defined, one for each execution outcome. Each control branch starts with the symbol "—>", followed by the branch name and the output variable name and data type.

A sample SIB declaration signature is shown in Fig. 2.

When the DSL contains many SIBs, this declaration has to be done individually for each SIB.

3.3 SIB Implementation

Following the OTA philosophy, the two key considerations for SIB implementation are autonomy and modularity. The implementation of any SIB declared in Sect. 3.2 follows the following steps.

1. A Java file must be created (if not already available) under the "native-library" section of the "dependency" section in the project explorer, on the same path defined in the SIB declaration process.
2. In this file, write the implementation of all the Java functions against the respective signature declaration in the ".sib" file, i.e.,. matching the function name, return types and input data types.
3. Dependency management is an essential part of any project in order to interact correctly with any external service or platform. The services and platforms of interest normally expose some interface for interactions and system calls, frequently in form of APIs or drivers. The dependency management must be done both in the . POM file and in the header of the Java file of the project, to respectively download and import the drivers.
4. Finally, the Java implementation of the SIB could vary on the basis of the business logic of the application. This logic usually has three sections:
   - **Connection Establishment:** Normally, the first interaction with any external entity is the connection establishment. This happens by calling a constructor with the appropriate parameters, e.g., server name, IP, credentials.
   - **Function Call:** Once the connection is established, the subsequent logic may carry out with a sequence of system calls to send some parameters, data, code and instructions to the external entity, for it to act upon.

- **Result Parsing:** After the completion of the function/system calls, the result is returned in a raw format and must be parsed for the underlying platform to understand and use it appropriately according to control and data flow.

While this seems at first sight a lot, it is a simple and quite general mechanism. In the case of service integration, the runtime platform phase may not be needed, simplifying the task.

In the following section we exemplify the described procedure step by step for a platform and a service integration.

4 Case Studies: The R Platform and REST Services

We selected as examples the integration of the R platform and REST services, as they are good illustrations of the two main cases of native DSL integration.

4.1 R Integration as Platform Integration

R is a specialised language for statistical computing, optimised for data processing and analytics. We show now, how to integrate the R platform with DIME as a Native DSL and utilize its capabilities as drag-able SIBs.

Runtime Infrastructure: R is a different platform from Java, thus it requires a separate, independent execution infrastructure. First of all, a separate container must be deployed on docker to run a R infrastructure stack. Once the container is up and running, then we need to collect the connection details (container name, IP, and credentials) for the DIME app to be able to properly communicate. For this we use the docker command `build`, `run` and `network inspect`.

1. To build a new R infrastructure, open CLI, create a new directory and run the command:
   `docker build -t rserve Rserve/ --no-cache`
2. Once the image is built, deploy the image on the docker container using the command:
   `docker run --name EnvR -p 6311:6311 --rm rserve:latest`
3. Once the docker is deployed, then type the following command to get the IP and other network details of the image:
   `docker network inspect bridge` .

SIB Declaration: The SIB signatures for R (the function `plot_R_histogram` in this case) as shown in Fig. 3, consists of SIB keyword followed by its name and its I/O parameters. This signatures also contains the path of the Java function to be invoked whenever this SIB will be used in an application.

```
sib plot_R_histogram : info.App#plot_R_histogram
    file_name: text
    col_name: text
    title: text
    x_label: text
    y_label: text
    color: text
    -> success
        result: file
    -> noresult
    -> failure
```

Fig. 3. Sample SIB declaration signatures

1. Create a new DSL file under “dime-models” with the extension .sib, where multiple SIBs can be defined within the same domain.
2. Copy the same signatures from Fig. 3 to create your new SIB file.
3. Refresh your SIB explorer. The newly developed SIB must be visible in the SIB explorer as a draggable item.

SIB Implementation: For the SIB implementation we will do the following:

1. Create a Java file under the “native-library” section of “dependency” and write the Java function with the same name and parameters order as mentioned in the SIB signatures.
2. For the dependency management, copy the “REngine.Rserve” reference under the dependency tag in the POM file and import the Rserve libraries (RConnection, RFileInputStream, RFileOutputStream and RserveException) in your Java file.
3. To establish a connection with the R infrastructure, copy the R container IP and port number in the RConnection constructor. Once the connection is established, it will return a R_pointer, and at this point the R platform is ready to accept any command from this Java based DIME SIBs.
4. Move the dataset / CSV as BufferedInputStream from the DIME application to the R container using the established connection pointer, e.g., R_pointer.
5. Once the data is moved to the R server, the R commands can be sent from the DIME application to the R server as a suite of subsequent instructions to be executed on the R server on the already transported dataset. e.g. read data file, generate histogram with given parameters and name of output file handler. The R commands must be passed in double quotes as a parameter, inside the parseAndEval function referenced by the connection pointer. e.g. R_pointer.parseAndEval (“read.csv(‘a.csv’)”)
6. After the successful execution of subsequent R instructions, the generated result (in this case a histogram) is transported back as BufferedOutputStream, parsed into the DIME readable image and passed as a resulting data flow of the SIB using the getDomainFileController handler.

```
package app.demo
sib rest_read_str_list : file_path#Java_fn
    url : text
    input_var : text
    input : text
    output : text
    -> success
        output: [text]
    -> noresult
    -> failure
```

Fig. 4. SIBs explorer with the new Native SIBs

Following the same approach, the SIB declaration and SIB implementation process can be replicated to extend the R-DSL with any R capability.

4.2 RESTful Extension as Service Integration

RESTful services provide a great flexibility for communication with external systems through exposed APIs. The increasingly popular microservice architectures [23] are typically exposed as REST services. They play an important role at the enterprise level. The microservice paradigm helps design software services as suites of independently deployable components with the purpose of modularity, reusability and autonomy [23]. Different versions of these services may coexist in a system as a set of loosely coupled collaborative components and must be independently replaceable without impacting the operations of heterogeneous systems. We see now in detail how to integrate REST services along the template introduced.

Runtime Infrastructure: Services are normally provided by third parties and are already deployed on private or public servers. So they do not require any infrastructural preparation, unless we are developing and deploying our own REST services. We consider here a pre-built PHP based REST service that is already deployed on a public server and accessible via its URL.

SIB Declaration: The SIB declaration is shown in Fig. 4. We proceed as follows:

1. Create a new DSL file under "dime-models", with the extension .sib. Here, multiple SIBs can be defined within the same domain.
2. To create a new SIB, write the keyword `sib` followed by the SIB name, : (colon) and the path to the corresponding Java function.
   In subsequent lines, write the names of the input variables with their data types (in our case it is the URL of an external server), the input variable name and data type, and the output variable name where to retrieve the

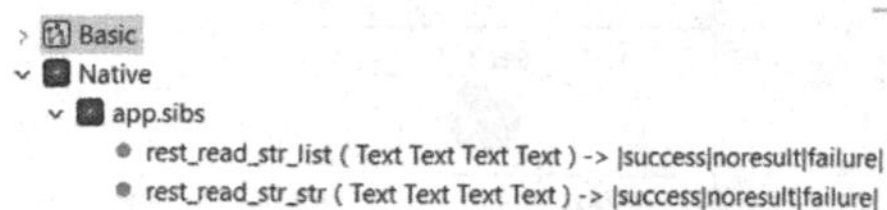

Fig. 5. SIBs explorer with the new Native SIBs

server response.
Finally, define the list of outgoing control branches based on the distinct outcomes, starting with symbol --->. In our case the three branches are "success", "noresult" and "failure".

3. Refresh your SIB explorer. The newly developed SIB must now be visible in the SIB explorer as a draggable item, as shown in Fig. 5.

SIB Implementation: For the SIB implementation we will do the following

1. Create a Java file under the "native-library" section of "dependency" and write a Java function with the same name and parameters order as mentioned in the SIB signatures.
2. For the dependency management, copy the "org.json" reference under the dependency tag in the POM file and import the HttpURLConnection and JSONObject libraries in your Java file.
3. To establish a connection with the REST service, copy the public URL and input parameters of the REST service and invoke the HttpURLConnection constructor followed by the getResponseCode() function.
4. On the successful response status, i.e. code 200, the service returns a JSON object that is further parsed into a Java readable string using the already imported JSONObject library functions, i.e. getString(JSON response).

Figure 6 shows the visual representation of the newly developed SIB as it appears when it is used in a process model. The required four inputs are being fed to this block using data flow (dotted) arrows. On success, the result will be conveyed as a string (or list of strings) to the successive SIB.

5 Conclusion and Discussion

In our Digital Thread efforts we are currently targeting primarily the application domain of advanced manufacturing including manufacturing analytics, and the data analytics field. In this context, data, processing and communications are expected to concern a large variety of devices, data sources, data storage technologies, communication protocols, analytics or AI technologies and tools, visualization tools, and more. This is where the ability to swiftly integrate external native DSLs plays a key role.

We presented therefore a generic extension mechanism for the integration of external services and platforms to DIME, an offline low-code IME, illustrating

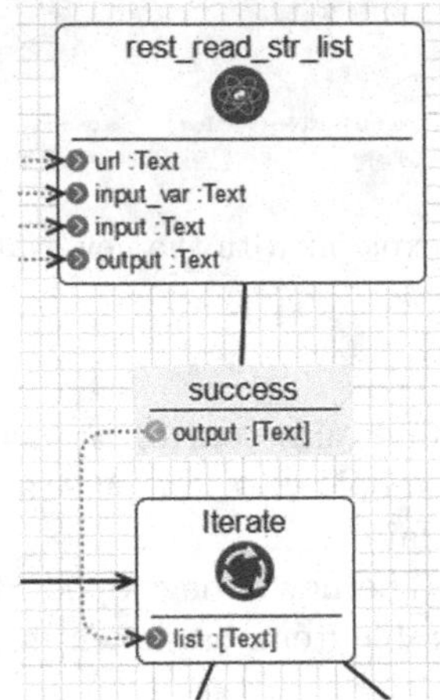

Fig. 6. The REST Read SIB in use: Visual representation in a model

in detail the technique on the basis of the R platform for data analytics and a REST service.

We used DIME's native library mechanism, with signature declaration, linked Java backend code, and where the code is merged with the logic layer at compile time. In previous work [4] we already showed how to address also the integration in Pyrus, an online no-code graphical data analytics tool based on Pyro [28] and linked with Jupyter Hub for functions discovery and code execution also discussed in detail in [29].

The Pyrus integration is simpler as it is tightly connected with Jupyter Hub. For example, to display new python functions as components in Pyrus, custom signatures are added to the python files defined in Jupyter Hub, and the data flow pipeline of the service is modelled in the Pyrus frontend.

In comparison with prior integration techniques, e.g. in jABC [11,15], ETI [13], jETI [12] and jABC/DyWA [22], this is a much simpler mechanism, and it follows much more tightly the One Thing Approach philosophy of integration [17].

As shown in Fig. 1, the span of External native DSLs we are currently building is quite impressive. It will cover proactive maintenance and building automation applications in the collaborations in Confirm, devoted to Smart Manufacturing, an open source biomechanical prosthetic socket design and optimization platform based on Gibbon [20] in Lero, analytics for the Digital Humanities [10], and various healthcare applications in the context of the Limerick Cancer Research Centre. In this sense we are hopeful to indeed bootstrap the effect of reuse of many DLSs and also processes across several application domains. This way, we also wish to showcase the power of model driven low code application development on real life examples from research and industrial applications.

Acknowledgment. This work was supported by the Science Foundation Ireland grants 16/RC/3918 (Confirm, the Smart Manufacturing Research Centre) and 13/RC/2094_2 (Lero, the Science Foundation Ireland Research Centre for Software).

References

1. Edgex foundry: The edgex foundry platform. https://www.edgexfoundry.org/. Accessed July 2021
2. Research: Intelligent process automation and the emergence of digital automation platforms. https://www.redhat.com/cms/managed-files/mi-451-research-intelligent-process-automation-analyst-paper-f11434-201802.pdf. Accessed February 2021
3. Boßelmann, S., et al.: DIME: a programming-less modeling environment for web applications. In: Margaria, T., Steffen, B. (eds.) ISoLA 2016. LNCS, vol. 9953, pp. 809–832. Springer, Cham (2016). https://doi.org/10.1007/978-3-319-47169-3_60
4. Chaudhary, H.A.A., Margaria, T.: Integration of micro-services as components in modeling environments for low code development. Proc. ISP RAS **33**(4) (2021)
5. Gartner: Gartner forecasts worldwide low-code development technologies market to grow 23% in 2021. https://www.gartner.com/en/newsroom/press-releases/2021-02-15-gartner-forecasts-worldwide-low-code-development-technologies-market-to-grow-23-percent-in-2021. Accessed February 2021
6. iBASEt: The digital thread explained. https://www.ibaset.com/the-digital-thread-explained/. Accessed July 2021
7. John, J., Ghosal, A., Margaria, T., Pesch, D.: DSLS and middleware platforms in a model driven development approach for secure predictive maintenance systems in smart factories. In: Margaria, T., Steffen, B. (eds.) ISoLA 2021, LNCS, vol. 13036, pp. 146–161, Springer, Heidelberg (2021)
8. John, J., Ghosal, A., Margaria, T., Pesch, D.: Dsls for model driven development of secure interoperable automation systems. In: 2021 Forum for Specification and Design Languages (FDL). IEEE (2021, September (in print))
9. Jorges, S., Kubczak, C., Pageau, F., Margaria, T.: Model driven design of reliable robot control programs using the jabc. In: Proceedings EASe'07, vol. 07, pp. 137–148 (2007). https://doi.org/10.1109/EASE.2007.17
10. Khan, R., Schieweck, A., Breathnach, C., Margaria, T.: Historical civil registration record transcription using an extreme model driven approach. Proc. ISP RAS **33**(3) (2021)
11. Kubczak, C., Margaria, T., Steffen, B., Nagel, R.: Service-oriented Mediation with jABC/jETI (2008)
12. Lamprecht, A.L., Margaria, T., Steffen, B.: Bio-jETI: a framework for semantics-based service composition. BMC Bioinform. **10**(Suppl 10), S8 (2009). https://doi.org/10.1186/1471-2105-10-S10-S8
13. Margaria, T.: Web services-based tool-integration in the ETI platform. Softw. Syst. Model. **4**(2), 141–156 (2005). https://doi.org/10.1007/s10270-004-0072-z
14. Margaria, T., Chaudhary, H.A.A., Guevara, I., Ryan, S., Schieweck, A.: The interoperability challenge: building a model-driven digital thread platform for CPS. In: Margaria, T., Steffen, B. (eds.) ISoLA 2021, LNCS, vol. 13036, pp. 393–413. Springer, Heidelberg (2021)

15. Margaria, T., Nagel, R., Steffen, B.: Remote integration and coordination of verification tools in JETI. In: Proceedings of the 12th IEEE International Conference on the Engineering of Computer-Based Systems, pp. 431–436. IEEE Computer Society, Los Alamitos, CA, USA (2005). https://doi.org/10.1109/ECBS.2005.59
16. Margaria, T., Schieweck, A.: The digital thread in Industry 4.0. In: Ahrendt, W., Tapia Tarifa, S.L. (eds.) IFM 2019. LNCS, vol. 11918, pp. 3–24. Springer, Cham (2019). https://doi.org/10.1007/978-3-030-34968-4_1
17. Margaria, T., Steffen, B.: Business process modeling in the jabc: the one-thing approach. In: Handbook of Research on Business Process Modeling, pp. 1–26. IGI Global (2009)
18. Margaria, T., Steffen, B.: Extreme model-driven development (xmdd) technologies as a hands-on approach to software development without coding. In: Encyclopedia of Education and Information Technologies, pp. 732–750 (2020)
19. Mellor, S.J., Clark, T., Futagami, T.: Model-driven development: guest editors' introduction. IEEE Softw. **20**(5), 14–18 (2003). issn 0740–7459
20. Moerman, K.M.: Gibbon: the geometry and image-based bioengineering add-on. J. Open Source Softw. **3**(22), 506 (2018)
21. Naujokat, S., Lybecait, M., Kopetzki, D., Steffen, B.: CINCO: a simplicity-driven approach to full generation of domain-specific graphical modeling tools. Int. J. Softw. Tools Technol. Transfer **20**(3), 327–354 (2017). https://doi.org/10.1007/s10009-017-0453-6
22. Neubauer, J., Frohme, M., Steffen, B., Margaria, T.: Prototype-driven development of web applications with DyWA. In: Margaria, T., Steffen, B. (eds.) ISoLA 2014. LNCS, vol. 8802, pp. 56–72. Springer, Heidelberg (2014). https://doi.org/10.1007/978-3-662-45234-9_5
23. Newman, S.: Building microservices: designing fine-grained systems. O'Reilly Media, Inc. (2015)
24. Sanchis, R., García-Perales, Ó., Fraile, F., Poler, R.: Low-code as enabler of digital transformation in manufacturing industry. Appl. Sci. **10**(1), 12 (2020)
25. Steffen, B., Margaria, T., Claßen, A., Braun, V.: The METAFrame'95 environment. In: Alur, R., Henzinger, T.A. (eds.) CAV 1996. LNCS, vol. 1102, pp. 450–453. Springer, Heidelberg (1996). https://doi.org/10.1007/3-540-61474-5_100
26. Steffen, B., Margaria, T., Claßen, A., et al.: Heterogeneous analysis and verification for distributed systems. In: Software-Concepts and Tools, pp. 13–25 (1996)
27. Waszkowski, R.: Low-code platform for automating business processes in manufacturing. IFAC-PapersOnLine **52**(10), 376–381 (2019)
28. Zweihoff, P., Naujokat, S., Steffen, B.: Pyro: generating domain-specific collaborative online modeling environments. In: Hähnle, R., van der Aalst, W. (eds.) FASE 2019. LNCS, vol. 11424, pp. 101–115. Springer, Cham (2019). https://doi.org/10.1007/978-3-030-16722-6_6
29. Zweihoff, P., Steffen, B.: Pyrus: an online modeling environment for no-code data-analytics service composition. In: Margaria, T., Steffen, B. (eds.) ISoLA 2021, LNCS, vol. 13036, pp. 18–40. Springer, Heidelberg (2021)

Asking Why

Barbara Steffen(✉) and Bernhard Steffen(✉)

TU Dortmund University, Dortmund, Germany
barbara.steffen@tu-dortmund.de, steffen@cs.tu-dortmund.de

Abstract. In this paper, we illustrate the impact of simple Why questions as a means to reveal global aspects that may easily be forgotten during traditional requirement analysis. For illustration we use the introduction of the General Data Protection Regulations (GDPR), a prime example to observe that adequate solutions may require to think out of the box, beyond just stepwise trying to fulfill individual requirements. Our Why analysis revealed the traditional, scattered data handling as the essential bottleneck, which we believe can be overcome by a cloud-based knowledge management across departments and applications.

Keywords: Why analysis · Alignment · Wicked world · VUCA · Knowledge/Data management · GDPR · IT infrastructure · Requirement analysis · DevOps

1 Introduction

A Gartner report from 2020 (p. 3) found that today's "business environment (is) marked by significant change, competition, uncertainty—and opportunity" [1]. This underlines that we live in a wicked world challenged by the VUCA characteristics in which learnings from the past do not ensure correct predictions for the future [2–4]. VUCA stands for vulnerability, uncertainty, complexity and ambiguity [5]. Organizations face constant changes and developments of their industries due to e.g., new trends, regulations and technologies and are forced to adapt to ensure their survival in the long-term. These constant changes increase the *vulnerability* and unpredictability of an industry's further developments leading to great *uncertainty* and thus challenges for an organization's management. Each strategic decision needs to be carefully designed and analyzed as potential scenario for the future which requires interdisciplinary collaboration and alignment. The interdisciplinary collaboration and its imposed stakeholder diversity enhance the *complexity* and *ambiguity* of decisions which are often interpreted differently due to stakeholder-specific expertise, interests and opinions [6].

The more factors and aspects are considered the less it becomes obvious what to emphasize and what the right/logical thing to do is. The challenge is to consider sufficient aspects/facts/trends while simultaneously preventing to run into the '*cannot see the forest for the trees*' dilemma. To support the strategy development and guide the brainstorming sessions business experts have defined many frameworks, methods and schemata like canvases. In particular, canvases are useful as they allow one to successively focus on

T. Margaria and B. Steffen (Eds.): ISoLA 2021, LNCS 13036, pp. 55–67, 2021.
https://doi.org/10.1007/978-3-030-89159-6_4

specific issues without losing the global overview during the planning phase (see the Business Model and Platform Alignment Canvases [7, 8]).

On the other hand, the planning-based approach often leads organizations to prematurely decide on implementation steps which is contra-productive in the VUCA world. Here change-driven approaches are advantageous which are based on continuous creativity, collaboration and validation to enable interdisciplinary innovation and learning in an evolutionary fashion in the sense of *'survival of the fittest/most adapted to today's environment'* [9, 10]. Change-driven approaches continuously modify their initial plan based on new learnings – or VUCA developments - over time according to a global vision - a *why* (do we do this)?. They then define the global goal - *what* (do we want to achieve)? The combination of vision and goal constitute the pillars to define a milestone-based roadmap.

Change-driven approaches are characterized by only committing to what is necessary at each point in time to provide sufficient leeway to adapt measures and milestones based on new learnings. This enables an open-minded and solution-driven continuous as-is and should-be comparison approach that reacts to identified deviations in an agile fashion.

In order to demonstrate the difference between the plan and change-driven approaches of either committing to plans or to visions this paper analyzes how organizations typically reacted to the introduction of the General Data Protection Regulation (GDPR) in May of 2018. It turns out that organizations try to avoid invasive changes and accept obviously unsatisfactory solutions despite the fact that GDPR already led to individual fines of up to €746 million in 2021 [11]. We will argue that this is mainly due to the organizations being caught in their traditional IT infrastructure and mindset which is inadequate to live up to typical GDPR requests like erasing all personal data of a certain person. This leads us to the main research question addressed in this paper:

Can implementing the GDPR regulations be considered an IT problem, and if so, what has to be done?

We will illustrate the power of (continuously) asking *Why* in a change-driven approach. In fact, many important Why's only arise during implementation and may lead to significant reconsiderations.

The next section therefore reviews the state of the art of many organizations, while Sect. 3 concerns the GDPR regulations, typical implementation (Sect. 3.1), a Why-based analysis of the corresponding design decision (Sect. 3.2), and a solution proposal. Subsequently, Sect. 4 provides a generalized discussion of the issues, and Sect. 5 our conclusion.

2 State of the Art

In this Section we introduce the constant external changes imposed on organizations. Then we dive into the state of the art of organization's internal knowledge management practices.

2.1 Today's Challenges of Organizations

"Across many industries, a rising tide of volatility, uncertainty, and business complexity is roiling markets and changing the nature of competition" [12, p. 7]. To survive, organizations need to rethink their strategies, business models and dynamic capabilities referring to their agility with regard to how fast and how well they can adapt to change [13]. Despite these pressures most organizations tend to address this change traditionally in the sense of "Why shall we change? We have always done it (successfully) this way". External pressures like Industry 4.0 either get ignored or addressed in an incremental almost "alibi" fashion via digitizing processes and documents or adding cloud services. These steps are considered Industry 4.0 measures and allow organizations to preserve what they currently excel at. Unfortunately, this approach misses to leverage the Industry 4.0 potential [14].

It also ignores the threat around the corner that established organizations and even market leaders are just one competitor's revolutionizing innovation away from significantly be threatened and potentially even forced out of the market [15]. Christensen calls this calm before the storm the innovator's dilemma [16, 17]. It underlines that once today's established organizations were the innovators, but as soon as they became successful, they lost their innovation potential and became "traditional" organizations. This approach is successful as long as no competitor outperforms the others. However, with every innovation it can be too late for established organizations bound by their legacy, as it can take them years to catch up.

One often ignored factor is that disruptive innovations with revolutionizing potential start targeting only very dedicated niche segments outperforming current offers at one particular functionality and/or service but underperform at most others have the potential to catch up with and even leave the established competition behind [18]. These disruptive innovations often are mistakenly overlooked as e.g., Kodak's ignorance of the digital camera opportunity [19], and so are the disruptive innovation-"makers". These organizations are often unknown potential industry entrants and thus not taken seriously. However, Porter made an important observation when he stated that each industry is driven by five forces: direct competition, customers, suppliers, substitutes and potential entrants [20]. New potentials and technological trends like Industry 4.0 and digitization open e.g., manufacturing industries to novel IT and software innovations. One has to understand the strategic potential of software and software-driven business models like digital platforms. They e.g., deprive established organizations of the direct contact with their customers and are therefore a major unstoppable threat. Great examples are Amazon for retail and Booking.com for hotels. Especially, IT and software create opportunities which significantly reduce the entry barriers for substitute providers and potential market entrants. And this is not all – they cannot just enter but overtake the market.

2.2 Today's Internal Knowledge Management Challenges

Already in the early 2000s estimated the IDC an annual loss of about $31.5 billion due to ineffective knowledge management for the US Fortune 500 organizations alone [21]. This indicates the competitive advantage of teams being able to access the relevant expert knowledge [6, 22]. The unsatisfactory state-of-the-art of knowledge management (KM) is due to four categories of knowledge management barriers: organizational, technology, individual and semantic [6].

Organizational barriers cover e.g., the missing integration of KM strategies into an organization's overall vision and strategy, competitive culture and missing adoption of KM systems. Technology barriers comprise the lack of a global and connected IT infrastructure, limited access to knowledge sources, mismatches between needs and solution and missing user-friendly tool-support. The individual barriers address employee's lack of trust, hesitance to share knowledge and lack of time and resources to do so. The final semantic barriers are unique in that they even act as barriers to 'shared understanding' even if no other barriers are in place and people would like to and know how to share knowledge. They refer to all the reasons why even perfect communication and knowledge exchange still leads to misunderstandings due to the stakeholders' different backgrounds, expertise, experiences, languages, and education.

In this paper we focus especially on the technology barriers and their impact on an organization's knowledge and data management as well as on collaborative work. Today, technology plays a major support role when using, sharing, saving and retrieving data to support an organization's internal processes and tasks and has the potential to increase quality while reducing required resources and time. Achieving this on a global, aligned, personalized, effective and efficient level is one of organizations' great challenges [23–25].

The following overview depicts today's state-of-the-art tool-landscape in many organizations. The list covers findings from Hessenkämper & Steffen in 2014, Steffen (2016) and Steffen et al. (2016) [6, 26, 27]:

- Localized and organization if not employee-wide distributed data storage,
- Incompatible tools with separate data handling (e.g., ERP, CRM and CMS systems),
- Missing integration and process support,
- Excessive use of inadequate communication media like E-mails, chats and calls and
- Incoherent document and data handling via tools like, e.g., PowerPoint, Word and Excel.

This situation hinders if not excludes an adequate alignment of

- Interdisciplinary work and communication
- Gathered data and knowledge, and
- Organizational processes across tools and platforms

In the data-driven world of today, this increasingly impairs the usability of the overall technical infrastructure and essentially affects the entire business of an organization: the missing alignment has to be compensated by the employees which slows down productivity.

Thus, the potential for the improvement of knowledge management, internal process support and business modeling is high. For now, everyone just tries to make the best of it and gets the projects/products finished on time. This short-term pressures and focus are quite successful in the here and now, but in the long-term organizations need to make a major leap to compete with potential entrants which are not held back by these legacy structures.

3 Case Study GDPR

In this Section we will discuss today's approach towards solving external changes along the example of the General Data Protection Regulation (GDPR) introduction. The typical corresponding state-of-the-art sketched in Sect. 3.1 will be challenged by Why questions in Sect. 3.2 which is followed by a proposal for a more fundamental solution in Sect. 3.3.

3.1 Typical GDPR Solutions in Practice

GDPR aims to protect a person's personal data which covers all information addressing an identified or identifiable real and living person directly via their name, date of birth and address, or indirectly via e.g., telephone number, social security number and IP address or cookies [28]. Although the introduction, deadline and implications of the GDPR guidelines were clear for years many organizations just engaged in a final sprint in April and May of 2018 to meet the deadline. The remaining short time frame typically led to rather non-invasive bureaucratic add-on solution approaches.

According to GDPR, it is the organization's task to protect all personal data of employees, customers, suppliers and collaboration partners. Organizations are obliged to define a data protection officer who is responsible for ensuring that the organization obeys to the rules, educates the management and employees and defines internal data protection guidelines, processes and responsibilities.

Here, organizations must ensure that personal data processing is [28]:

- lawful, fair and transparent in relation to the data subject
- only collected for specified, explicit and legitimate purposes
- minimized to the adequate, relevant and limited time and purpose
- accurate and, where necessary, kept up to date and erased without delay
- limited to the necessary purposes for which the personal data are processed
- appropriately securing the personal data ensuring integrity and confidentiality.

Given the description of today's state-ot-the-art of IT landscapes in Sect. 2.2., it becomes obvious why the GDPR integration is a major challenge for most organizations:

1) How can organizations identify where personal data got used and saved? Given the legacy of the last centuries organizations built a siloed IT landscape in which many employees work on and safe documents locally. So, the data owners are not centralized but rather decentralized as every employee potentially saves documents containing personal data.
2) How to ensure that only people/employees with access rights have access to the personal data? This is difficult to achieve as normally complete documents like PowerPoint presentations and complex Excel tables get distributed via E-mail or

central storage spaces. In the past no one had to personalize these views and ensure that personal data gets protected. Thus, personal data is highly distributed and exists in all versions of the corresponding documentation.

3) How to ensure that personal data can be deleted on demand? As data is saved locally all employees who potentially processed the personal data in questions need to search all their (corresponding) documents for the personal data and delete it following the detailed instructions of the data protection officer.

Given the isolated and incompatible tool landscape and the distributed data handling on notebooks and phones organizations do not have much choice but to delegate the GDPR handling to the employees. They are the ones having access to and storing the data (locally) and thus must be the ones deleting it.

To delegate and inform the employees/data owners about the GDPR challenge the management/data protection officer tend to design PowerPoint presentations instructing the employees about their personal GDPR responsibilities. These presentations are distributed per E-mail to all employees (and hopefully read and not perceived as spam). From here onwards the employees must obey to the general guidelines and find and delete all personal data when requested.

This is how the *solution* will look like in practice:

1) The organization receives a request from e.g., a customer's employee to delete all of his/her personal data.
2) This request gets forwarded to the data protection officer.
3) The data protection officer must check which IT systems and employees might have had access to this particular personal data and have stored them in their 'shadow IT'.
4) Then the data protection officer contacts the IT administrators and relevant employees e.g., via E-mail with the request to delete this specific personal information in all documents (e.g., including all versions of a specific document). This requires that all triggered employees must search the globally and locally shared documents and E-mails for this personal information and delete it manually.

Unfortunately, this process cannot ensure that all relevant personal data is found and deleted. Thus, organizations typically plead for their best effort and deal with missing deletion when they are detected. Looking at recent fines, it is more than questionable whether current best effort will be considered sufficient in the future. However, whatever will happen in the future, the result of this traditional approach is:

Almost any device and any document of any employee
has to be searched for personal data.

This is unrealistic and has no chance for completeness: some to be erased personal data will inevitably remain undetected. The next section therefore questions this state-of-the-art in a Why fashion.

3.2 *Why*-Based Quality Analysis

In this section we question the result of Sect. 3.1 *"Almost any device and any document of any employee has to be searched for personal data"* by repeatedly asking *Why* questions.

Root-Why: It must be possible to identify and erase *all* personal data of individual persons *everywhere* on request.

We will concentrate here on the problem of identifying all locations where such information is stored. Our solution proposal (Sect. 4) also deals with the adequate erasing of information.

The importance of this *Why* can be confirmed by just one more *Why* question:

Why: GDPR demands to satisfy such requests.

Thus, we can consider the Root-Why as given. But does this really justify that *"Almost any device and any document of any employee has to be searched for personal data"*?

In the traditional setting this is again confirmed via a chain of *Why* questions:

Why: The personal data cannot be found otherwise.

> *Why*: Data are transferred as PDFs, text files, PowerPoint presentations and Excel documents via broadcast E-mails to the team members and/or other targeted groups. These are often processed *locally* for the simplified use/ editing.
>
> > *Why*: The different used systems have their own *local* data management (Outlook, Excel, Atlassian, ERP, etc.) and the involved users need to be able to access this data.
> >
> > > *Why*: Due to today's traditional *localized* IT infrastructure setup (cf. Sect. 2.2).

A better solution must therefore break this chain of argumentation. But how can this be achieved? Investigating the explaining *Why* chain one characteristic appears to be common to all levels: *locality*! In the next subsection we will sketch how a centralized solution may overcome all the mentioned problems in an elegant and efficient way.

3.3 *Why*-Based Solution Proposal

In this section we sketch how a centralized solution naturally solving all the aforementioned problems can look like. In fact, we argue that this solution has major positive side-effects also on other, apparently unrelated issues which will then also get better addressed and dealt with.

As revealed by the *Why* analysis in Sect. 3.2, *centralization* addressing today's issue of locality is the key towards overcoming the discussed problems. But what does this mean precisely? In essence it means that every source of data has a *single source of truth*, i.e., a single location where it is stored, and that all locally kept data automatically adjust to this single source[1]. Illustrative examples for this principle are cloud-based solutions like Dropbox, Google Docs, and similar solutions to collaborative work [29–31].

In addition, the treatment of GDPR requires an adequately modularized and relation-based data management in a fashion that connections between data are explicitly modelled in ontological relations see Fig. 1. E.g., a person's record (i.e., information that just concerns this very person) is related to all relevant other data sources, e.g., via an address relation to the contact information or a health relation to the health records, etc. With such a data organization, erasing the data corresponding to a person just means to erase the relational connections to the record.

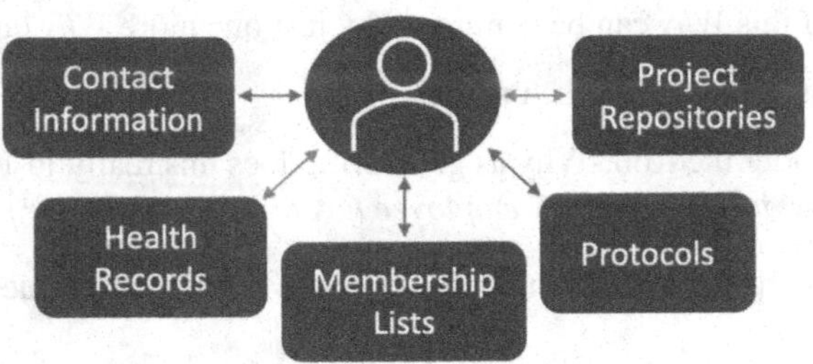

Fig. 1. Relational modeling of personal data

The benefit of this relational data organization seems marginal in the mentioned examples, as one could alternatively simply put all this information into the corresponding person record. This is, however, no longer true for data sources that concern many persons like membership lists, protocols and project repositories.

Please note that the described centralization approach provides many more benefits. Being able to dis-associate a person from some (data) resources is vital, e.g., when a person leaves an organization. Based on our observations many organizations would give a lot for a data management that is guaranteed to be consistent, let alone for a knowledge management which allows one to seamlessly address all data (of course in a secure, role-based fashion) in an aggregated form as illustrated in Fig. 2. This vision is quite straightforwardly realized on an adequately centralized data organization. And there are many more benefits, in particular concerning the inter-departmental exchange.

Admittedly, achieving such a data organization and management requires major reconstruction, is very expensive, and may take quite some time. Think of the impact such a change (digital transformation, cf. Fig. 3) would have on prominent ERP, SCM, HR, and supply chain solutions which essentially all base on a local data management (typically, every application requests the control over the data!).

Thus, a movement towards centralization imposes a major threat to many of today's IT solution providers which will fight for keeping as many data as possible, as it is the data that makes organizations dependent on these providers. The adaptation to the centralization approach, despite its numerous advantages, will therefore hardly be realized

[1] This does, of course, not exclude replications of data for technical purposes like e.g., backups.

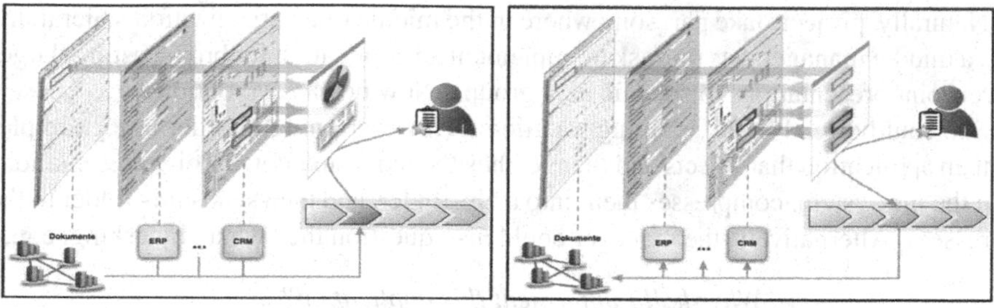

Fig. 2. Central data storage with personalized view and processing

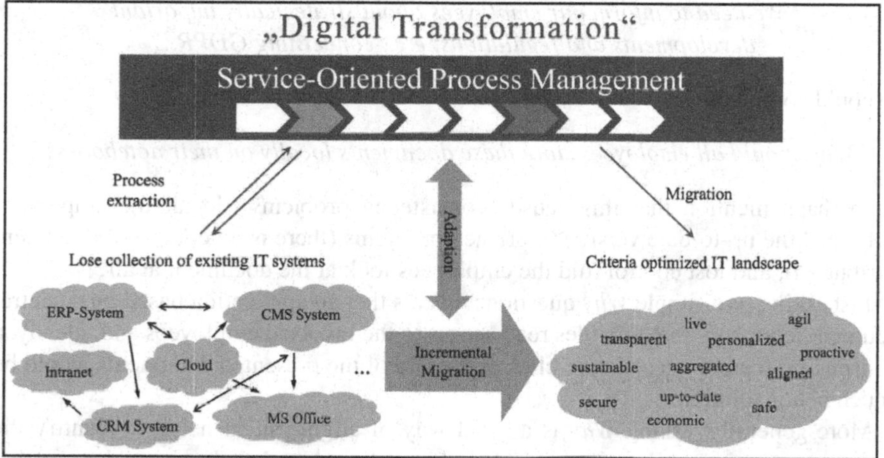

Fig. 3. Digital transformation from decentralized solutions to a global solution

in the near future for larger organizations. On the other hand, it is a great opportunity for smaller organizations which, this way, will gain quite a significant competitive advantage.

4 *Why*-Based Alignment

In this Section we reflect on the paper's observations from a more general perspective. To evaluate the decisions made in a top-down fashion from the requirements to the implementation we questioned them in a 'bottom-up' fashion (cf. Fig. 4). Looking at the proposed solution for an implementation we have asked ourselves, now in a bottom-up fashion, whether and why this proposal is (in)adequate, and whether there are alternatives and at which price. We have observed that the state-of-the-art IT-infrastructure of a typical organization is in the way to obtain natural and efficient solutions to the GDPR problem which can be solved much more elegantly and efficiently when changing from the today very localized data management to a centralized data or even better knowledge management.

Naturally, projects take part somewhere in the middle of an organization's hierarchy. E.g., a middle manager gets the task to implement an application for broadcasting (large) PowerPoint presentations to specific user groups. Now he has two options:

She could directly start applying traditional *How*-reasoning in order to e.g., implement an application that selects and then fetches the requested PowerPoint presentations from the file system, compresses them into a zip-folder, and then sends this folder to the addressees. Alternatively, the manager could also question the "what" by asking, e.g.,

"Why shall I implement this application?".

And on the response

"We need to inform our employees about strategically important developments and regulations, e.g., concerning GDPR."

she could continue with

"Why should all employees store these documents locally on their notebooks?"

and perhaps mention that this causes consistency problems (do all the employees really read the up-to-date version?), privacy problems (there is no control of document distribution), and lost control (did the employees look at the document at all?).

Just asking two simple *Why* questions reveals that an application based on a central document repository that provides read access to the involved employees and, ideally, a confirmation feature via a simply click at the end of the presented documents would be a much better solution.

More generally, asking *Why* is a good way of alignment: it helps to identify the relevant context, to get the affected stakeholders aboard, and to develop solutions that are accepted because they were commonly designed and fit the addressed need.

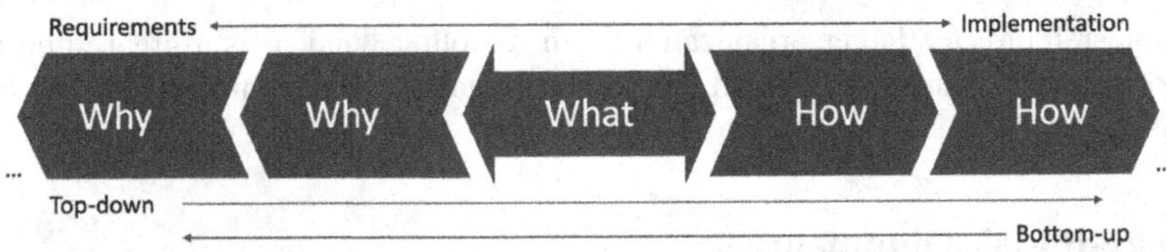

Fig. 4. Bottom-up analysis of top-down decision-making

This down and up reminds of the V-Model in software engineering, where the top-down requirement phase from desired concepts to implementation is complemented by a bottom-up integration and validation phase that provides the envisioned running systems. In fact, our *Why* approach has structurally a lot in common with the V-Model-based, plan-driven thinking, even though it does not aim at the realization of systems, but at a better (more global) understanding of the corresponding decision process and its frame conditions. Like for good system design, achieving a better global understanding typically requires feedback cycles, a fact, that led to numerous refinements of the originally hierarchical V-Model-based approaches. The One-Thing Approach (OTA) can be regarded as such a refinement: It is conceptually hierarchical, but allows to re-enter the process at any time, however at dedicated task-specific positions only, and in a way that avoids cyclic dependency propagation in order to guarantee global consistency [32]. Handling feedback cycles in the OTA fashion is also a good means for a goal oriented, consistent *Why* handling.

It often turns out that high hurdles at the implementation level can often be overcome by stepping back and altering the frame conditions. The GDPR example with its proposed change from local to global knowledge management is an extreme case: both the measure (re-structuring of the data management) and the impact are extremely high. Popular other examples can be observed in DevOps scenarios. In fact, the advantages gained by DevOps can be regarded as being the result of a *Why*-based analysis: Having an operations expert aboard allows one to adjust the early design in a way such that the step towards operations has no unnecessary hurdles [33]. Or, more concretely, the operations expert can ask the *Why* question whenever she observes a pattern that may cause problems in the later lifecycle. In fact, the GDPR example of a data elimination request also requires a treatment which strongly profits from a tight cooperation between development and operations.

In this light, the *Why* approach is nothing but a means to globalize the decision space in order to find better solutions. This globalization can be extremely powerful, in particular in cases, where the envisioned solutions are part of a bigger picture. Today's practice focusses far too much on local optima rather than considering what needs to be achieved globally. Asking *Why* is a good practice in these cases to overcome the so-called 'silo mentality' of individual cases by connecting and aligning them globally.

5 Conclusion

In this paper we sketched the current economic situation which is under pressure due to the increasing IT influence. Organizations need to change, to either achieve a leading edge or to prohibit that other organizations overtake their market leadership. We have also argued that established organizations have problems to take this challenge up, and that they typically hardly touch the opportunities offered by today's IT systems. Even radical contextual changes like, e.g., the ones imposed by the GDPR regulations, do not seem enough to act as a wake-up call. Rather, they are answered with traditional means that, in the long-term, are economically disastrous, imposing a lot of manual work and, as in the GDPR case, may lead to high penalties.

We have discussed the reasons for this status quo which seems, in particular, to be the result of a too local and short-term thinking: Even the necessity of global searches for personal data across an entire organization for satisfying certain GDRP regulations do not seem to suffice to question the status quo.

We have illustrated how simple *Why* questions may lead to simple answers. In case of GDPR, the local and distributed data management can be regarded as a root problem prohibiting efficient solutions: a centralized knowledge/data management with an adequately modeled data space, e.g., relational, in terms of ontologies, would essentially trivialize the system-wide search for all personal data.

Admittedly, this insight alone is not a solution, and applying it to large organizations is a major challenge. Thus, we envision that insights like this will be taken up first by smaller organizations which may then grow due to their competitive advantage.

That solutions to presumably very difficult problems may become commodity is, in fact, not too rare. A prominent example is enterprise-wide communication: Being able to offer a global communication system to an organization was still a vision in the eighties but is now almost for free due to the Internet. Today, clouds ease the centralization of knowledge. We are therefore convinced that the described changes will happen, and that early adopters will be the winners of this development.

Progress is often achieved because somebody asked a *Why* question. In our eyes this happens far too seldom. At least whenever something seems unreasonable one should automatically ask "*Why* can this be?". This (critical) reflection is the way to progress and innovation. Unfortunately, the many regulations we are confronted with are rarely well explained, a fact that makes us lazy, and surely, we cannot question everything. We should, however, question the seemingly unreasonable in our area of expertise.

References

1. Gartner: Top Insights for the C-Suite 2018–2019. Gartner. 1–90 (2019).
2. Bennett, N., Lemoine, G.J.: What a difference a word makes: understanding threats to performance in a VUCA world. Bus. Horiz. **57**, 311–317 (2014)
3. Hogarth, R.M., Lejarraga, T., Soyer, E.: The two settings of kind and wicked learning environments. Curr. Dir. Psychol. Sci. **24**, 379–385 (2015)
4. Epstein, D.: Range: Why generalists triumph in a specialized world. Penguin, New York (2021)
5. James, L., Bennett, N.: What VUCA really. Harv. Bus. Rev. **92**, 2014 (2014)
6. Steffen, B.: Inter-& Intradepartmental knowledge management barriers when offering single unit solutions (2016)
7. Osterwalder, A., Pigneur, Y.: Business model generation. Wiley, Hoboken (2010)
8. Steffen, B., Möller, F., Nowak, L.: Transformer(s) of the Logistics Industry - Enabling Logistics Companies to excel with Digital Platforms. In: Proceedings of the 55th Hawaii International Conference on System Sciences (2022, to appear)
9. Darwin, Charles annotated by Bynum, W.: On the Origin of Species. Penguin Group, London (2009)
10. Steffen, B., Howar, F., Tegeler, T., Steffen, B.: Agile business engineering: from transformation towards continuous innovation. In: Margaria, T., Steffen, B. (eds.) ISoLA 2021. LNCS, vol. 13036, pp. 77–94. Springer, Cham (2021)
11. Tessian: 20 Biggest GDPR Fines of 2019, 2020, and 2021 (So Far). https://www.tessian.com/blog/biggest-gdpr-fines-2020/. Accessed 5 Sept 2021
12. Doheny, M., Nagali, V., Weig, F.: Agile operations for volatile times. McKinsey Q. **3**, 126–131 (2012)
13. O'Reilly, C.A., Tushman, M.L.: Ambidexterity as a dynamic capability: resolving the innovator's dilemma. Res. Organ. Behav. **28**, 185–206 (2008)
14. Steffen, B., Boßelmann, S.: GOLD: global organization alignment and decision - towards the hierarchical integration of heterogeneous business models. In: Margaria, T., Steffen, B. (eds.) ISoLA 2018. LNCS, vol. 11247, pp. 504–527. Springer, Cham (2018). https://doi.org/10.1007/978-3-030-03427-6_37

15. Bechtold, J., Kern, A., Lauenstein, C., Bernhofer, L.: Industry 4.0 – the capgemini consulting view - sharpening the picture beyond the hype (2014)
16. Christensen, C.: The Innovator's Dilemma. Harvard Business School Press, Boston (1997)
17. Christensen, C.M.: The innovator's dilemma: when new technologies cause great firms to fail. Harvard Business Review Press, Boston (2013)
18. Christensen, C., Raynor, M.E., McDonald, R.: Disruptive Innovation. Harvard Business Review (2013)
19. Lucas, H.C., Jr., Goh, J.M.: Disruptive technology: how Kodak missed the digital photography revolution. J. Strateg. Inf. Syst. **18**, 46–55 (2009)
20. Porter, M.E.: Competitive advantage: Creating and Sustaining Superior Performance. The Free Press, New York (1985)
21. Babcock, P.: Shedding Light on Knowledge Management (2004). https://www.shrm.org/hr-today/news/hr-magazine/pages/0504covstory.aspx
22. Riege, A.: Three-dozen knowledge-sharing barriers managers must consider. J. Knowl. Manag. (2005)
23. Argote, L., Ingram, P.: Knowledge transfer: a basis for competitive advantage in firms. Organ. Behav. Hum. Decis. Process. **82**, 150–169 (2000)
24. Chang, C.L., Lin, T.-C.: The role of organizational culture in the knowledge management process. J. Knowl. Manag. (2015)
25. Ragab, M.A.F., Arisha, A.: Knowledge management and measurement: a critical review. J. Knowl. Manag. (2013)
26. Hessenkämper, A., Steffen, B.: Towards standardization of custom projects via project profile matching. In: Fernandes, João. M., Machado, Ricardo J., Wnuk, Krzysztof (eds.) ICSOB 2015. LNBIP, vol. 210, pp. 186–191. Springer, Cham (2015). https://doi.org/10.1007/978-3-319-19593-3_17
27. Steffen, B., Boßelmann, S., Hessenkämper, A.: Effective and efficient customization through lean trans-departmental configuration. In: Margaria, Tiziana, Steffen, Bernhard (eds.) ISoLA 2016. LNCS, vol. 9953, pp. 757–773. Springer, Cham (2016). https://doi.org/10.1007/978-3-319-47169-3_57
28. Regulation (EU) 2016/679 of the European Parliament and of the Council. https://eur-lex.europa.eu/legal-content/EN/TXT/?qid=1528874672298&uri=CELEX%3A02016R0679-20160504. Accessed 5 Sept 2021
29. Gitpod: Gitpod. https://www.gitpod.io/. Accessed 5 Sept 2021
30. Eclipse Che - The Kubernetes-Native IDE for Developer Teams. https://www.eclipse.org/che/. Accessed 5 Sept 2021
31. Zweihoff, P., Tegeler, T., Schürmann, J., Bainczyk, A., Steffen, B.: Aligned, purpose-driven cooperation: the future way of system development. In: Margaria, T., Steffen, B. (eds.) ISoLA 2021. LNCS, vol. 13036, pp. 426–449. Springer, Cham (2021)
32. Margaria, T., Steffen, B.: Business process modelling in the jABC: the one-thing-approach. In: Cardoso, J., van der Aalst, W. (eds.) Handbook of Research on Business Process Modeling. IGI Global (2009)
33. Tegeler, T., Teumert, S., Schürmann, J., Bainczyk, A., Busch, D., Steffen, B.: An introduction to graphical modeling of CI/CD workflows with rig. In: Margaria, T., Steffen, B. (eds.) ISoLA 2021. LNCS, vol. 13036, pp. 3–17. Springer, Cham (2021)

Industrial Track

Formal Methods for a Digital Industry
Industrial Day at ISoLA 2021

Falk Howar[1(✉)], Hardi Hungar[2], and Andreas Rausch[3]

[1] Dortmund University of Technology and Fraunhofer ISST, Dortmund, Germany
falk.howar@tu-dortmund.de
[2] German Aerospace Center, Braunschweig, Germany
hardi.hungar@dlr.de
[3] Clausthal University of Technology, Clausthal-Zellerfeld, Germany
andreas.rausch@tu-clausthal.de

Abstract. The industrial track at ISoLA 2021 provided a platform for presenting industrial perspectives on digitalization and for discussing trends and challenges in the ongoing digital transformation from the perspective of where and how formal methods can contribute to addressing the related technical and societal challenges. The track continued two special tracks at ISoLA conferences focused on the application of learning techniques in software engineering and software products [4], and industrial applications of formal methods in the context of Industry 4.0 [3,7]. Topics of interest included but were not limited to Industry 4.0, industrial applications of formal methods and testing, as well as applications of machine learning in industrial contexts.

1 Introduction

In 2011, The Wall Street Journal published Marc Andreessen's essay "Why Software Is Eating the World" in which the author predicted the imminent digital transformation of the world's economies and societies [2]. In the nearly ten years that have passed since publication, the scope and impact of that transformation has only become bigger. Without any doubt, the infrastructure of the twenty-first century is defined by software: software is the basis for almost every aspect of our daily live and work: communication, banking, trade, production, transportation - to name only a few. This has led to a situation in which for many industrial and manufacturing companies with no particular background in software, software crept into processes and products - first slowly then with an ever increasing pace and scope, culminating in the mantra that "every company needs to become a software company". From a technological perspective, the current situation is defined by a number of transformative technological innovations:

Ubiquitous Compute and Connectivity. IoT Devices and 5G technology will make it possible to put computing power and sensory equipment everywhere and connect decentralized computing power in huge distributed, heterogeneous architectures, spanning IoT devices, edge-resources, and cloud platforms. The main novel capabilities of such cyber-physical systems are (a) the

T. Margaria and B. Steffen (Eds.): ISoLA 2021, LNCS 13036, pp. 71–76, 2021.
https://doi.org/10.1007/978-3-030-89159-6_5

distributed observation, analysis, and processing of data, and (b) decentralized control of the physical world.

Data Becomes a Primary Resource. The systems described above will be used as a basis for establishing digital twins of physical devices (machines in production, harvesting equipment, supply-chains, etc.). Digital twins will act as proxies (observing and controlling physical machines) and enable the digitalization and automation of most processes and new services and features that are based on data, e.g., predictive maintenance, an autonomous harvest, or a fully synchronized supply-chain.

Machine Learning as the Basis of Applications. Applications like the aforementioned ones require the analysis of data, the discovery of patterns, and autonomous reactions to observed situations. Such features are typically realized with the help of machine learning technology, i.e., data is used to train a system instead of programming the system. The scope and complexity of learned applications is projected to increase dramatically over the next couple of years (cf., e.g., German AI strategy [13,14]).

Virtualization. Digital twins will not only act as proxies for physical devices (think shadows in the used analogy) but will become valuable assets in their own right. Processes and methods can be developed in virtual reality based on virtual twins (more precisely based on models obtained through the systems that enable digital twins): Calibration of processes, configuration of assembly lines, optimization of harvesting strategy can be computed in simulations, minimizing resources and ramp-up times, and maximizing yield in the physical world.

These trends will have an impact on virtually every enterprise. Potential cost-reductions and new services and products are expected to disrupt entire industries. This expectation has produced mantras like "Uber yourself before you get Kodaked", alluding to Uber's transformation of the taxi business and to Kodak's going out of business after not pursuing digital photography as one of the early companies in that market. The challenge faced by companies is to not miss key technological opportunities while being forced to take decisions and make investments without a full understanding of the exact impact. Additionally, the discussed technological innovations are associated with new challenges and specific risks, some examples of which are:

Safety and Security. Big heterogeneous, distributed, and networked systems have many attack vectors: A plethora of libraries, frameworks, and basic systems lead to a vast space of possible configurations and combinations of software stacks on individual devices. Moreover, being connected to the Internet makes these systems easy to attack. Systems that control machines in the vicinity of humans are safety-critical—the new quality of safety-related risks in these systems originates in their openness and in the new relation of safety and security.

(Data) Eco-Systems. The full potential for value-creation of data-centric applications oftentimes cannot be realized in classical value-chains but requires eco-systems [9]. The most obvious example of such a new business model may be so-called app stores that open platforms of a vendor (classically mobile phones) to app vendors, adding value for customers through third party apps. These new business models require a degree of openness and collaboration that is not easily organized between companies that are otherwise competitors. Moreover, it is often unclear a priori which business models will be profitable in the end. For the "pure" software companies and VC culture of Silicon Valley it is easy to simply try and adapt. For a manufacturing company with long-lived physical products and processes such an agility can probably not be achieved as easily.

Machine Learning as an Engineering Discipline. In traditional software development, a set of practices known as DevOps have made it possible to ship software to production in minutes and to keep it running reliably. But there is a fundamental difference between machine learning and traditional software development: Machine learning is not just coding, it is coding plus data. Data engineering does provide important tools and concepts that are indispensable for succeeding in applying machine learning in production. Practices from DevOps and data engineering need to be integrated into an engineering discipline for ML-based software.

Quality Assurance for Machine Learning. Quality assurance of distributed applications that rely on Machine Learning as a design principle is an open challenge—scientifically and engineering-wise. A classical safety argumentation (or case) starts with a high-quality requirements specification, which should ideally be correct and complete. This specification is later used as main input for testing and verification. For the development of an AI-based system, a huge data collection is used to partially replace a formal requirements specification. This data collection is incomplete, biased, and may even contain a small percentage of incorrect data samples. In a sense, AI-based systems are "machine-programmed" using training data selected by engineers. Safety assurance then has to be based on guarantees on the quality of training data and on rigorous testing of relevant application scenarios. Such methods are being researched today but are still far from being standardized or available in certification processes.

These challenges have a tremendous impact on the engineering of software systems. The security-related essential requirement of frequent system updates, e.g., does affect architectural decisions and development processes, requiring iterative improvements during the whole software life cycle, including during operation. At the same time, the amount of data that can be obtained during operation at a massive scale by far exceeds what can be processed or stored cost-efficiently, making a purely agile development approach or blunt re-training of learned models (which are frequently hailed as silver bullets today) infeasible. System architectures as well as business models must be carefully planned and evaluated before making major investments.

Complexity and uncertainty lead to a situation in which companies wait for others to make the first move or start following hyped trends and buzz words (agile, data-lakes, or social intranet, to name only a few) instead of making informed decisions. What is required, is a software engineering discipline that allows companies to move deliberately towards their digital transformation in the face of uncertainty about future eco-systems, business models, software- and system-architectures, and applications. The aforementioned mantra to "Uber yourself before you get Kodaked" is not to be taken literally in this respect: it ironically uses Uber, a company without a sustainable business model that is alleged to exploit employees and is banned in many European countries, as a symbol of a successful transformation of an industry. Instead, the case of Uber can rather be seen as an indication of the need for a holistic approach to software engineering and digital transformation: an approach that does not simply aim at disruption but also includes a societal perspective, aims for sustainable business models, and supports sound financial and technical planning.

Formal methods can be one crucial enabler for building and scaling the software infrastructure sketched above: constructive techniques will enable systems that are correct by construction, formal verification can deliver guarantees on existing systems. Domain-specific languages may enable the seamless application of formal methods at multiple levels of abstraction. Eventually, formalization can hopefully enable (automated) alignment and integration of systems and automation of processes and quality control. Formal methods are, however, far from being able to do that today and will have to be made into enablers through the development of tools, by finding beneficial applications, and by leveraging domain knowledge. The industrial track aims at bringing together practitioners and researchers to name challenges, to look for potential contributions, to outline approaches, to name useful tools and methods, and to sketch solutions.

2 Contributions

The track featured seven contributions with accompanying papers. Contributions focused on software-enabled knowledge management and business engineering, use cases of simulation in the context of developing autonomous systems, modeling languages for industrial automation, and machine learning techniques for the assisting the assessment of data quality.

2.1 Software-Enabled Business Engineering

The paper *"Agile Business Engineering: From Transformation Towards Continuous Innovation"* by Barbara Steffen, Falk Howar, Tim Tegeler, and Bernhard Steffen [11] presents the results of a qualitative study of analogies and differences in business engineering and software engineering, starting from the observation that a high degree of automation through purpose-specific tools and other "DevOps" techniques usually has a positive impact on outcomes in innovative software projects. The authors investigate whether a meaningful analogy can be drawn to challenges in business engineering during a digital transformation.

The paper *"Towards Living Canvases"* by Barbara Steffen, Stephen Ryan, Frederik Möller, Alex Rotgang, and Tiziana Margaria [12] (in this volume) presents a proposal for improving the quality of information that is gathered in the early stages of projects (e.g., elicitation of requirements from stakeholders) by providing tools that semantically integrate information pertaining to different aspects of a system or business. The authors report on a small initial study in which multiple canvases (usually used in pen-and-paper mode) were implemented and successfully integrated.

2.2 Simulation-Based Testing of Software for Autonomous Systems

The paper *"Use Cases for Simulation in the Development of Automated Driving Systems"* by Hardi Hungar [5] (in this volume) explores potential benefits, limitations, and open challenges in the application of simulation (i.e., an inherently incomplete and inaccurate technique) during the development and validation of autonomous systems.

The contribution *"Simulation-based Elicitation of Accuracy Requirements for the Environmental Perception of Autonomous Vehicles"* by Robin Philipp, Hedan Qian, Lukas Hartjen, Fabian Schuldt, and Falk Howar [10] (in this volume) presents one concrete use case for simulation in the development of autonomous vehicles: the elicitation of formal accuracy requirements for the integration of different components (perception and planning) of an autonomous driving function.

2.3 Domain-Specific Languages for the Industry 4.0

The paper *"DSLs and middleware platforms in a model driven development approach for secure predictive maintenance systems in smart factories"* by Jobish John, Amrita Ghosal, Tiziana Margaria, and Dirk Pesch [6] (in this volume) presents a result from a case study in industrial automation in which a language workbench has been used to design a tailored domain-specific language for modeling secure predictive maintenance systems in the context of smart factories.

The contribution *"From Requirements to Executable Rules: An Ensemble of Domain-Specific languages for Programming Cyber-Physical Systems in Warehouse Logistics"* by Malte Mauritz and Moritz Roidl [8] (in this volume) presents a similar application of domain-specific languages to the one above: domain modeling and domain specific languages are used to specify and automate the behavior of a cyber-physical warehouse system that collaborates with human operators.

2.4 Applications of Machine Learning in Software Engineering

Finally, the contribution *"Mining Data Quality Rules for Data Migrations: A Case Study on Material Master Data"* by Marcel Altendeitering [1] (in this volume) reports on an industrial application of machine learning techniques for learning rules that can be used to assess the quality of data in the context of data migration.

References

1. Altendeitering, M.: Mining data quality rules for data migrations: a case study on material master data. In: Margaria, T., Steffen, B. (eds.) ISoLA 2021. LNCS, vol. 13036, pp. 178–191. Springer, Cham (2021)
2. Marc, A.: Why software is eating the world. In: The Wall Street Journal (2011/08/20) (2011)
3. Hessenämper, A., Howar, F., Rausch, A.: Digital transformation trends: Industry 4.0, automation, and AI - industrial track at ISoLA 2018. In: Leveraging Applications of Formal Methods, Verification and Validation. Industrial Practice - 8th International Symposium, ISoLA 2018, Limassol, Cyprus, November 5–9, 2018, Proceedings, Part IV, pp. 469–471 (2018)
4. Howar, F., Meinke, K., Rausch, A.: Learning systems: machine-learning in software products and learning-based analysis of software systems. In: Margaria, T., Steffen, B. (eds.) ISoLA 2016. LNCS, vol. 9953, pp. 651–654. Springer, Cham (2016). https://doi.org/10.1007/978-3-319-47169-3_50
5. Hardi, H.: Use cases for simulation in the development of automated driving systems. In: Margaria, T., Steffen, B. (eds.) ISoLA 2021. LNCS, vol. 13036, pp. 117–128. Springer, Cham (2021)
6. Jobish, J., Amrita, G., Tiziana, M., Dirk, P.: Dsls and middleware platforms in a model driven development approach for secure predictive maintenance systems in smart factories. In: Margaria, T., Steffen, B. (eds.) ISoLA 2021. LNCS, vol. 13036, pp. 146–161. Springer, Cham (2021)
7. Margaria, T., Steffen, B. (eds.): Leveraging Applications of Formal Methods, Verification and Validation: Discussion, Dissemination, Applications, ISoLA 2016. LNCS, vol. 9953. Springer, Cham (2016). https://doi.org/10.1007/978-3-319-47169-3
8. Malte, M., Moritz, R.: From requirements to executable rules: an ensemble of domain-specific languages for programming cyber-physical systems in warehouse logistics. In: Margaria, T., Steffen, B. (eds.) ISoLA 2021. LNCS, vol. 13036, pp. 162–177. Springer, Cham (2021)
9. Boris, O., et al.: Data Ecosystems: Conceptual Foundations, Constituents and Recommendations for Action (2019). http://publica.fraunhofer.de/documents/N-572093.html. Accessed September 2021
10. Robin, P., Hedan, Q., Lukas, H., Fabian, S., Falk, H.: Simulation-based elicitation of accuracy requirements for the environmental perception of autonomous vehicles. In: Margaria, T., Steffen, B. (eds.) ISoLA 2021. LNCS, vol. 13036, pp. 129–145. Springer, Cham (2021)
11. Barbara, S., Falk, H., Tim, T., Bernhard, S.: Agile business engineering: from transformation towards continuous innovation. In: Margaria, T., Steffen, B. (eds.) ISoLA 2021. LNCS, vol. 13036, pp. 77–94. Springer, Cham (2021)
12. Barbara, S., Stephen, R., Frederik, M., Alex, R., Tiziana, M.: Towards living canvases. In: Margaria, T., Steffen, B. (eds.) ISoLA 2021. LNCS, vol. 13036, pp. 95–116. Springer, Cham (2021)
13. The German Federal Government. Strategie Künstliche Intelligenz der Bundesregierung (2018). https://www.bmwi.de/Redaktion/DE/Publikationen/Technologie/strategie-kuenstliche-intelligenz-der-bundesregierung.html. Accessed September 2021
14. The German Federal Government. Strategie Künstliche Intelligenz der Bundesregierung - Fortschreibung (2020). https://www.bmwi.de/Redaktion/DE/Publikationen/Technologie/strategie-kuenstliche-intelligenz-fortschreibung-2020.html. Accessed September 2021

Agile Business Engineering: From Transformation Towards Continuous Innovation

Barbara Steffen(✉), Falk Howar, Tim Tegeler, and Bernhard Steffen

TU Dortmund University, Dortmund, Germany
{barbara.steffen,falk.howar,tim.tegeler}@tu-dortmund.de,
steffen@cs.tu-dortmund.de

Abstract. We discuss how to overcome the often fatal impact of violating integral quality constraints: seemingly successful (software) development projects turn into failures because of a mismatch with the business context. We investigate the similarities and differences between the today popular DevOps scenarios for aligning development and operations and the more general alignment problem concerning software and business engineering based on 33 structured expert interviews. It appears that both scenarios are driven by creativity in a continuous collaboration process relying on continuous goal validation. On the other hand, differences appear when considering Thorngate's trade-off between accuracy, generality and simplicity: the different level of accuracy is the main hurdle for transferring the automation-driven DevOps technology. The paper closes with the hypothesis that this hurdle may be overcome by increasing the accuracy within the business context using domain-specific languages, a hypothesis supported by the interviews that now needs further confirmation via case studies.

Keywords: Agile business engineering · Software engineering · Integral quality constraint · DevOps · Domain-specific languages

1 Introduction

Today, organizations are under continuous pressure of their industry's evolution to survive the natural selection in a world of everchanging customer preferences, new technologies and competitors' developments and offers [21]. This selection is won by the organizations most responsive to or even driving the change. The Red Queen effect underlines the challenge: "[...] it takes all the running you can do, to keep in the same place" (p.2 [10]) [4]. Thus, organizations have to continuously track the external developments to initiate the according iteration and transformation measures internally.

Daepp et al. found that independent from the industry an organization's half-life is only roughly a decade based on a sample of 25.000 publicly traded organizations in North America [12]. In Christensen's opinion the worst enemy of industry leaders are the disruptive innovations/technologies they do not take seriously

T. Margaria and B. Steffen (Eds.): ISoLA 2021, LNCS 13036, pp. 77–94, 2021.
https://doi.org/10.1007/978-3-030-89159-6_6

enough due to an initial underperformance of their offers, but that still have the power to drive them obsolete [11]. This trend amplified with the fourth revolution including Industry 4.0 and digitalization shortens the innovation and change cycles dramatically with the effect that traditionally successful big bang[1] transformations are increasingly replaced by continuous change/transformation [1].

There are two strategies to tackle this continuous request for change. First, organizations can develop dynamic capabilities to ensure the organization's survival in the long run [26,33]: The more dynamic an organization is, the better it can adopt new technologies and thus adapt to new trends. Second, organizations may decide to go beyond this 'reactive' approach and to attack by driving the industry's change via designing radical innovations continuously challenging their own offers or via applying the blue ocean strategy of creating entirely new markets/customer segments [25].

Thus, the holy grail of surviving is becoming an ambidextrous organization and to simultaneously exploit current technologies and offers via further incremental innovations while, at the same time, exploring new paths via radical innovations and disruptive technologies [33]. In fact, Ries postulates that any (established) organization should have an entrepreneurship department in order to ensure that exploration receives the needed attention [34].

Invasive changes and innovations require cross-departmental collaboration to ensure the solution's fit. Due to different backgrounds, experiences, and set performance targets these collaborations face diverging agendas and semantic gaps complicating the smooth and aligned understanding and collaboration [8,28].

A great example of the status-quo and business engineering's shortcomings is Bosch's lawnmower Indigo Connect for roughly € 1200. Bosch is known for its high quality products. Thus, it was not surprising that the lawnmower's advertisement stated easy, live and remote controllability via smartphone. However, Keese summarized his experience as spending 3,5 days on his knees to install the boundary wires in his garden and a fight with an app that was never up to date [23].

How can it happen that the product's marketing promises diverge so much from the customer experience? Concerning the app performance, the answer is easy: Engineering developed, tested and pitched a lawnmower with two (identical) chips, one for driving autonomously and one for tracing and sending the position. The marketing campaign was based on this experience and promised an 'active and live control via app'. Controlling, on the other hand, considered the two chips as too expensive which led to the final product only having one chip. Together with the decision for a reduced data line (again a cost factor) this caused a totally unacceptable app performance, in particular, for a high-end product of a market leader [23].

The problem was the silo structure of today's market leaders with completely different competencies, objectives and metrics [19,36]. This silo structure supports local (department-centric) optimizations that are all too often in conflict with organization's global interest [23].

---

[1] https://airbrake.io/blog/sdlc/big-bang-model (last access 15th June 2021).

Mismatches like this are even greater in the business engineering (BE) and software engineering (SE) context where the integral quality constraints (that the product must adhere to the existing (IT) infrastructure, process and products) are much less tangible [38]. It is therefore a major challenge to motivate all involved stakeholders to support the changes/solutions, and to align and adapt the different objectives, requirements, and preferences [36]. This requires continuous communication and cooperation between the different stakeholders in order to establish a common understanding and vision by doing to reach the status of a scalable agile organization [19,27].

As stated in a Fraunhofer report (2021) [2], organizations need to understand software as enabler of business engineering and not just as internal business process support or add-on functionality of hardware devices.

The research presented in this paper is motivated by two observations:

- The integration problems due to misalignment between the information systems (IS) development methods and the business development context that may cause failure of seemingly successful SE projects [13].
- The success story of DevOps for aligning SE development (Dev) methods and outputs with the requirements of operations (Ops) [3,5]

These observations lead to two research questions:

1. What are the essential similarities and differences between the BE/SE and the Dev/Ops scenarios?
2. Is it possible to transfer some of the DevOps techniques to the BE/SE scenario?

The paper's structure is as follows: After the introduction, Sect. 2 outlines the foundations, parallels and differences of BE and SE. Section 3 details the methodology. Section 4 summarizes the interview study results. In Sect. 5 we derive the implications and answer the research questions before reflecting on the results in Sect. 6. This paper finalizes in Sect. 7 with a conclusion, limitations and outlook.

2 State of the Art

We briefly compare concepts, terminology, and methods of the BE and SE disciplines by summarizing the state of the art in both fields as found in the literature. We then make some initial observations on parallels, key differences, and potentials for alignment in Sect. 2.3. The observations provide a basic conceptual framework for the empirical study.

2.1 Business Engineering

In this paper we use Österle's definition of Business Engineering from 1995 [41]. It focuses on adapting and transforming the business in accordance to internal and external developments and is divided into optimization and development driven changes. These transformations are ideally implemented in a structured top-down fashion focusing on three specifications: strategy, organization and IT system [40,42]: From the business strategy encompassing the organization's strategy and the derived goals to the organization's business processes and finally to the definition of the corresponding IT system support and implementation. This rather engineering (also referred to as plan-driven) process is suggested to handle the transformation's complexity and interdisciplinary collaboration and alignment to ensure that all relevant aspects are considered in the right order.

However, since the continuous introduction of technology innovations businesses face the pressure to constantly observe and react to the industry's dynamics leading to rather invasive and radical innovations and adaptations of current internal processes and/or business models [1,6]. In these challenging settings of high uncertainty regarding the project's business execution and business development method this plan-driven approach does not suffice. Thus, organizations need to embrace change-driven project execution.

Many organizations already try to leverage agile methods like design thinking, scrum, SAFe etc. to reduce the uncertainty and adapt implementation measures and processes based on new learnings [9,27]. This focus on collaboration and regular meetings addresses and reduces the semantic gap (e.g. misunderstandings due to different backgrounds and experiences) and supports alignment and buy-in along the process. In practice this leads to better and holistic outputs but is a very time-consuming process to derive at acceptable compromises.

Nevertheless, Dahlberg & Lagstedt observed that even successful (Information Systems (IS)) projects that benefited from the necessary competencies and a well-defined plan may never be successfully integrated and used in the business environment [13]. From the business perspective the reason for this failure boils down to a violation of the integral quality constraint [38]: great and well functioning products and/or solutions do not fit the needs of the actual business development context in which they shall be integrated. Unfortunately, this mismatch often just becomes visible after the product is finalized and ready to be integrated.

The risk for failure increases with the scope of change and the underlying uncertainty: In engineering it is still comparatively simple to detail the machine specifications and to ensure its fit into the production line. It becomes more complicated with increasing degrees of freedom.

Software projects are known for their high degrees of freedom (see Sect. 2.2) as are invasive business changes: Both often depend on many parameters that are typically hardly constrained by something like physical laws. E.g. new business models and internal processes typically depend on cross-departmental collaboration and alignment and therefore on individuals with their specific character and their willingness to cooperate [35]. In such complex scenarios it is virtually impossible to sufficiently predict the solution's and the business context integration's requirements upfront. Rather a flexible approach is required that allows to react to arising challenges. To summarize, today's businesses face major uncertainties and thus need to embrace an internal continuous improvement approach.

This requires ongoing learning by doing in interdisciplinary teams via developing creative ideas and innovations which are continuously tested and validated.

2.2 Agile Software Engineering

In the 1990 s, Agile Software Engineering (ASE) arose as a response to two decades of failing waterfall-oriented software development projects, which had aimed at controlling risks via detailed contract specifications [7, 30]. The observation that software projects are very hard to specify upfront because customers are typically unable to express their wishes in sufficient detail for experts to decide on adequate implementations was central to the paradigm shift. This problem, also known as the semantic gap, led to the **Agile Software Engineering manifesto** [17] that postulated the following four key insights:

1. Individuals and interactions over processes and tools
2. Working software over comprehensive documentation
3. Customer collaboration over contract negotiation
4. Responding to change over following a plan

The manifesto considers software system development[2] as a mutual learning process in which customers and developers converge towards a mutual understanding. Key to convergence is the incremental development style in which partial products serve as unambiguous means for common design decisions.

DevOps [3, 5] complements ASE in this line by (semi-) automatically supporting partial product construction, management, and validation. More concretely, experts of operations are involved to bridge the gap between the logical design (e.g. the program) and the product running on some complex physical infrastructure. This comprises:

1. **Construction:** Version-controlled development supporting roll back and merge.
2. **Management:** Continuous version-based documentation in 'one shared repository' style where essential dependencies and design decisions are maintained in a combined fashion.
3. **Cooperation:** Dedicated domain-specific languages (DSLs) supporting the Dev/Ops cooperation.
4. **Validation:** Automated test environments enabling continuous validation via so-called CI/CD (Continuous Integration/Continuous Deployment) Pipelines.

The combination of ASE and DevOps supports an incremental, collaborative development style which continuously maintains running partial products (extremely high-fidelity prototypes) that successively converge towards (successful) products which oftentimes differ quite drastically from the initially conceived product.

[2] Here meant to comprise SE and IS.

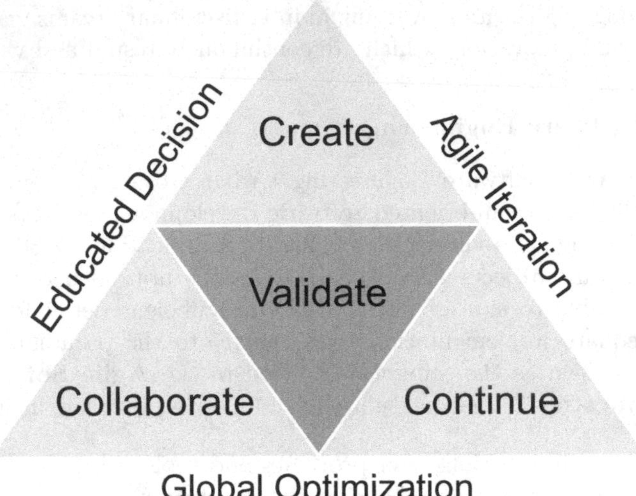

Fig. 1. BE and SE Parallels

The early integration of the operations team does not only lead to better infrastructure for scaling up operations and performance but it allows all stakeholders to experience and test the intended product during its development in its foreseen environment [18].

2.3 Parallels, Differences, and Potentials

As detailed in the previous two sections, BE and SE have a similar problem domain. Both disciplines face the challenges of (a) continuously dealing with change which requires (b) creative solutions that, to be successful, can only be found in (c) interdisciplinary collaboration. Moreover, in particular, due to the semantic gaps there is a strong need to continuously (d) validate the state of the creative collaboration process to detect misconceptions early. Figure 1 sketches the aspects of the problem domain and their interplay.

The labels on the outer sides of the triangle name requirements for solutions pertaining to the involved aspects: methods must enable global optimization through agile iteration, based on educated decisions. Key enabling techniques for the success of this approach concern the continuous validation of the reached achievements according to the strategic goals.

The main conceptual difference between BE and SE can elegantly be characterized by the well-known trade-off between accuracy, generality, and simplicity (see Fig. 2 [37]): by its nature, BE has to drastically simplify its complex highly heterogeneous scenarios, and, due to the high level of inherent uncertainty to aim for generality rather than accuracy. SE, in contrast, addresses software, i.e., descriptions precise enough to run on a computer. Programming languages are in other words generic, in order to allow programmers to potentially solve all

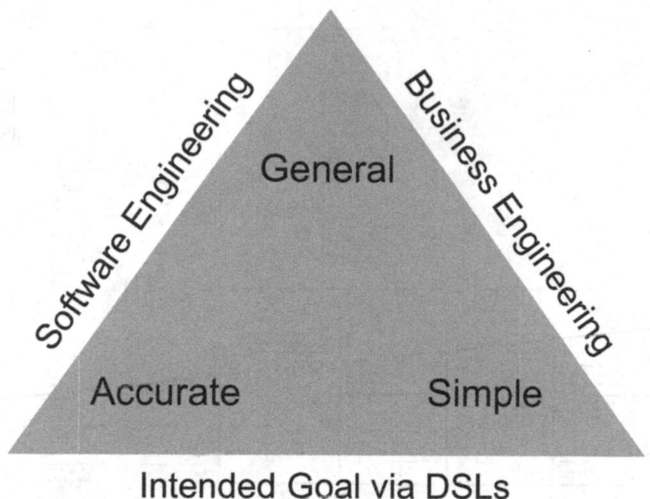

Fig. 2. Based on Thorngate's Trade-off

computable problems. Thus, SE only leaves room for trading between generality and simplicity.

The trade-off between simplicity and generality can be observed between general purpose programming languages and so-called domain-specific languages (DSLs, [16,22]) which are arguably one of the key enablers of DevOps [14].

Key characteristics of DSLs: Whereas programming languages are traditionally universal and consequently intricate, there is an increasing trend towards using (graphical) DSLs that aim at allowing application experts to cooperate in a no/low code style on specific problems. DSLs can be regarded as an ideal means to trade generality against simplicity in application-specific contexts. Together with corresponding Integrated Development Environments (IDEs, [24,29,31]) that typically provide sophisticated development support DSLs have the potential to become adequate alternatives to classical tool support whenever these are conceived to be too restrictive.

In the context of DevOps, this is witnessed by the success of DSLs that provide a dedicated support in particular for configuring IT infrastructure and to develop required CI/CD pipelines in an infrastructure as code style.

In the realm of business engineering, graphical DSLs that are designed on the basis of BE-oriented graphical notations (BPMN, CMMN, ER Diagrams, Organigrams, Canvases (BMC), etc.) may turn out to be good candidates for aligning the BE and ASE/Ops (Dev/Ops) cooperation and to transfer supporting technology for achieving (more) automation.

Our corresponding experience of combining the Business Model Canvas [32] with graphically modelled ontologies as sketched in Fig. 3 was very promising. It allowed us to (semi) automatically derive data structures for organizational structures without writing a single line of code.

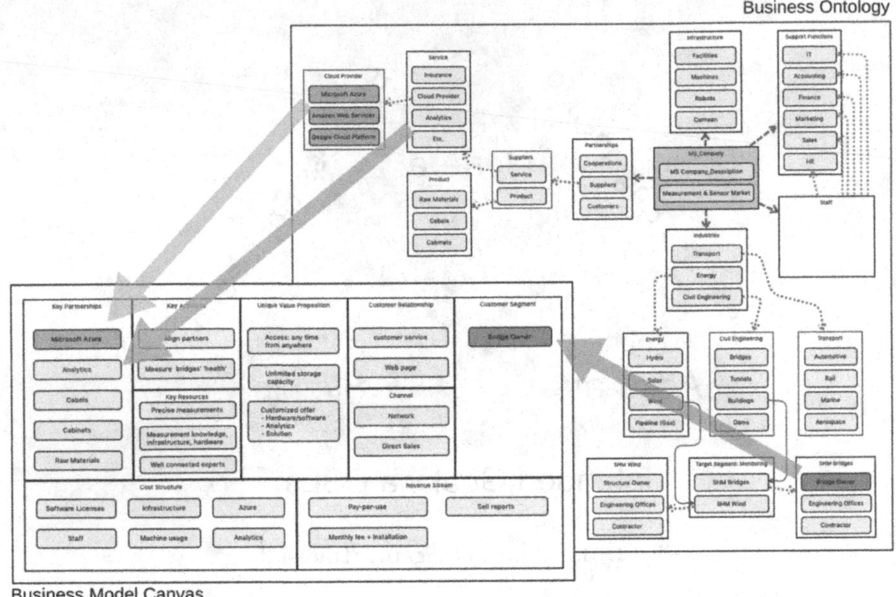

Fig. 3. Graphical DSL-based Enablement of Canvases

3 Method

In this section we define the paper's design method and interview study details. The design method is based on Hevner's three cycle view (see Fig. 4, [20]) which consists of the relevance, design and rigor cycles. In our case this led to a 10-step procedure as also sketched in Fig. 4:

- *Step 1 (Relevance):* The study of this paper was triggered by the observation of Dahlberg and Lagstedt (2021) [13] that the results of successful development projects may nevertheless lead to failure due to problems during the integration into the business context.
- *Step 2 (Design):* Based on this motivation and the corresponding research questions we designed this paper's method.
- *Step 3 & 4 (Rigor):* We reviewed the literature to define and compare BE and SE.
- *Step 5 (Design):* To further detail the parallels and differences between BE and SE we designed a structured interview guideline with closed and open questions.
- *Step 6 (Relevance):* To ensure the applicability of the structured interview guideline a pilot with four interviewees (two with IT and two with a business background) were conducted.
- *Step 7 (Design):* Based on the feedback gathered and issues identified via the pilot interviews we iterated the interview guideline accordingly.

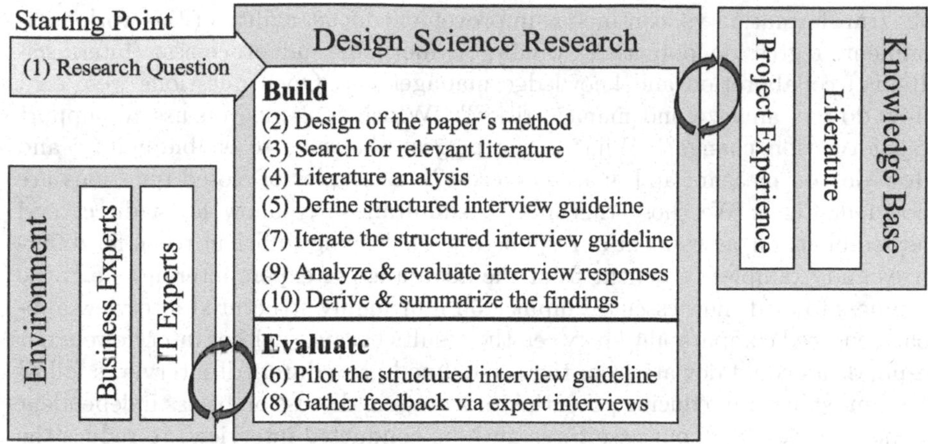

Fig. 4. Research Method Based on Hevner's Three Cycle View [20]

- *Step 8 (Relevance):* Then we gathered the business and IT expert feedback via 33 highly structured interviews.
- *Step 9 & 10 (Design):* Once all interviews were conducted, we analyzed and evaluated the responses to derive at the paper's final results and findings.

To ensure that the research questions can be answered based on actual experiences and assessments of the status quo and preferred outlooks we decided to conduct expert interviews. We interviewed a total of 33 interviewees:

- *7 business experts:* four senior consultants, two entrepreneurs, and one assistant to the board.
- *9 mixed business & IT experts:* four members of the board, one founder, three professors (who also led or worked in organizations), and one team leader with dedicated responsibility for digitalization. This group is especially important as they can compare the differences between BE and SE and their corresponding mind-set and tool-support firsthand.
- *10 IT experts:* four with dedicated DevOps experience and six with dedicated DSL experience four of which working as team leaders.
- *7 IT students:* all are almost finished with their masters, have experience with DSL application and participated in interdisciplinary IT projects.

Due to SARS-CoV-2 we executed the highly structured interviews via telephone and online (e.g. via Zoom). Each interview took roughly 45 to 60 minutes depending on the interviewees' level of detail. The interviews comprised a total of 57 questions and four additional questions regarding the general background. The 57 questions consisted of 25 quantitative (20x Likert-scale based response options from 1–5 and 5x multiple choice questions) and 32 qualitative (open questions) response options. The questions covered the interviewees' experiences and opinions on the following topics: confrontation with changes on the job, transformation vs. continuous improvement focus, agility of the work environment, regression potentials, validation methods and processes, (interdisciplinary) collaboration and knowledge management. Open questions were e.g., 'How do you analyze and manage risks?', 'Which tools do you use to support transformation/change?', What is the biggest challenge to enable agility' and 'How do you measure and analyze success?'. Examples of closed questions are shown in Fig. 5. We chose this mix to simultaneously allow for a direct and easy comparison/assessment of responses while leaving sufficient room for differences and examples to benefit from the advantage of expert interviews e.g. the openness towards new essential input [15]. Our highly structured interview approach ensured comparability between the results because neither interviewees nor respondents could deviate from the pre-defined procedure. All interviews follow the same structure reducing potential information/discussion biases independent of the interviewer. In our case three authors conducted interviews to reduce the interviewer bias: we matched the expertise and background of the respondents with the most similar interviewer to reduce potential semantic barriers and to increase the responses' objectivity [8,15,39].

4 Interview Results

In this section we sketch the results of the interview study. First, we will elaborate on the qualitative responses. Here, the main differences observed concern the understanding and status of the role of tools in BE and SE. Then we will briefly sketch and discuss the eight most relevant outcomes of the quantitative questions (Q1 to Q8) for our conclusion (see Fig. 5).

Via category-coding the named IT tools (used in the interviewees' work contexts) according to their purpose (communication/knowledge, operation, management, success metrics, requirements/validation, modelling, configuration management, and test/quality assurance), we observed that IT professionals frequently named tools (e.g. GitLab, GitHub, and CI/CD pipelines) automating tasks like operations, tests, and configuration management. In comparison, business experts, with two exceptions that also named tools to measure success metrics (e.g. Power BI and OKR Software), only mentioned tool support for communication/knowledge (e.g. MS Teams, Slack, Zoom, MS Office, Wikis, and SharePoint), information systems (e.g. SAP) and requirements/validation (e.g. survey tools and (software) prototypes).

More concretely, technical support for requirements elicitation (including prototypes) is present in both groups, indicating that both groups value early validation and use prototypes for improving the shared understanding. Business experts named significantly more tools for communication as IT professionals, but most answers qualified rather as conceptual frameworks than as tools in the sense of SE.

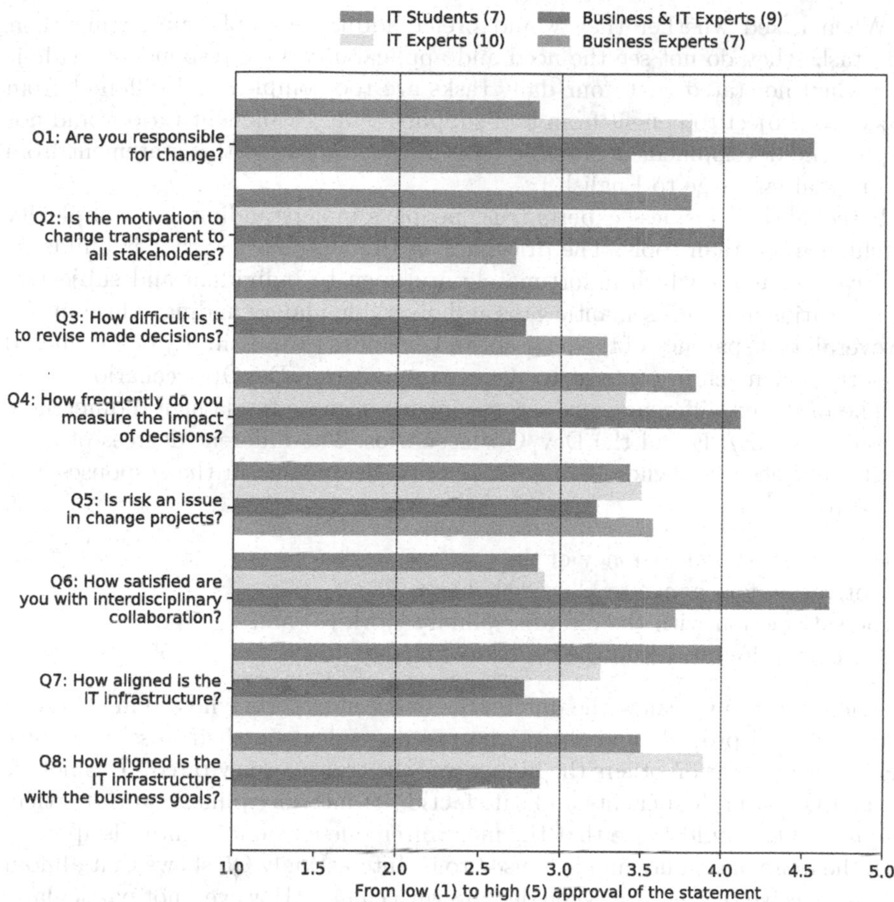

Fig. 5. The Results of the Exemplary Questions (Q1 to Q8)

For the group of professionals that qualify as both, the results were mixed, in some cases closer to the group of IT professionals (e.g. with regard to configuration management) and in some cases closer to the group of business experts (e.g. communication/knowledge). The higher the respective organization's IT core competency the more tools are used for (automated) support.

Interestingly business experts mentioned mostly decision and alignment support in the form of processes, methods and frameworks which currently do not benefit from direct tool support e.g. discussions in meetings, calls and workshops for SWOT, canvas and stakeholder analysis. Here one can see that today business experts handle the business transformation's complexity via meetings and shared documentation.

When asked whether they would prefer additional tools supporting their daily tasks they do not see the need and applicability. One respondent made it clear when he stated that "our daily tasks are too complex and different from project to project to benefit from tool-support. The cost-benefit ratio would not support the development of suitable tools". (We translated this statement from the original language to English.)

It seems that business experts trust people's understanding and complexity matching more than tools. The drawback of this approach is that it builds on intuitive semantics which unfortunately are open to individual and subjective interpretation and thus semantic gaps and diverging understanding. This impairs the overall transparency of the projects and excludes the possibility of automated support, very much in contrast to the accuracy-driven DevOps scenario.

The observed differences are a consequence of more fundamental differences between the BE/SE and the Dev/Ops scenarios: The different degrees of complexity and accuracy whose consequences are also visible in the responses (see Fig. 5) to

- the perceived transparency of the motivation for change to all stakeholders (2),
- the satisfaction with the interdisciplinary work (6) and
- the perception of risk in the context of change (5).

The replies to Q2 show the differences between experts who are in charge of their work and projects and those who are dependent on their boss' decisions. The less dependent on others the higher was the transparency rated. 'Business & IT experts' value the benefits and satisfaction of interdisciplinary work particularly high. One could argue that the more often one encounters interdisciplinary work the more one values and gets used to it. Interestingly Q5 shows that all four groups perceive risk as issue when dealing with change. However, not particularly high. The higher frequency of measuring the impact of decisions concerning both the SE and the Ops perspectives as seen in replies to Q4 indicates the impact of DevOps supporting higher degree of automation. As a consequence integral quality is continuously guaranteed in the DevOps scenario which prohibits bad surprises as reported in [13] where the results of a successful IS project never became operational because of a mismatch with the BE development contexts.

Put together with the other responses to the open questions the following picture arises:

- Automation support for configuration management, testing, operation, and continuous delivery (aka the DevOps support) is ubiquitous in SE but virtually absent in BE.
- Software engineers and business engineers have a different concept of what a tool is and likely also a different understanding of the degree of automation that can be achieved and the associated benefits.

- The agile mindset has already permeated all groups to some degree (as indicated by mentions of tools for requirements and early validation).
- Modeling tools (especially for business processes) have some success in BE.

These different perceptions of tools and their potential towards automation is essential for the proper understanding of the following answers to our two research questions.

5 Implications

In the following we will answer the paper's two research questions:

Research Question 1: What are the essential similarities and differences between the BE/SE and the Dev/Ops scenario?

There was a strong overall agreement in response to the qualitative and quantitative questions that both BE/SE and Dev/Ops face the challenge to continuously deal with and manage change. Here, interdisciplinary collaboration is particularly relevant to develop creative solutions like invasive and/or radical innovations. Moreover, as already mentioned in Sect. 2.3 and now confirmed by the interviews there is a strong need to continuously validate the progress of the creative (collaboration) process and the decisions' impact to detect misconceptions and misalignments early and allow for early and effective countermeasures.

On the other hand, the interviewees' responses revealed clear differences between the two scenarios when it comes to the required systematic support of the continuous and creative collaboration process. Particularly striking is the difference when it comes to the role of tools and validation:

1. Whereas in BE/SE there are hardly tools that support more than standard administrative tasks, DevOps is supported by a wealth of tools that (semi) automate most of the CI/CD pipelines comprising documentation, versioning and roll back.
2. Whereas in BE/SE processes typically follow some assumed best practices but are typically not tool supported or automated in any way, DevOps aims at automating the entire build process.
3. Whereas in BE/SE the gap between the SE/IS development methods and BE development context is considered too large to be bridged via standards and tools, DevOps explicitly addresses this gap with corresponding common DSLs in order to support automation.
4. Whereas the tool landscape of BE/SE is typically neither aligned itself (see Q7) nor towards the company goals (see Q8), DevOps is characterized by aligned tool chains.

Research Question 2: Is it possible to transfer some of the DevOps techniques to the BE/SE scenario?

The answers to the qualitative questions revealed that SE experts, in particular those with some experience with (graphical) DSLs, were quite optimistic concerning the transferability of the methods. The main reason mentioned was that DSL-based frameworks are much more flexible than 'classical' tools and may therefore proof to be able to bridge the larger gap. In fact, DSLs are also explicitly mentioned as the essential reason for DevOps to overcome the semantic gap between SE and Ops [14].

In fact, one of the nine 'business & IT' experts was a team leader of a larger software house where agility principles and tools known from software development and DevOps start to also enter the business level. In this company, organizing even customer presentations and company events like an agile software development project showed automation potential, easier goal adaptation, better prototyping and therefore, in particular, better cross stakeholder communication. These benefits even reached the board level and entered an explicit company-wide agile manifesto.

Certainly, this success story very much depends on the fact that it takes place within a software company, and that the application of software (development) tools is considered standard there. The feedback of the interviewees with experience in applying DSLs in customer projects suggests, however, that, using adequate DSLs, this success can be leveraged in a larger scope.

Our answer to the second research question can therefore be formulated as a hypothesis that cannot be confirmed by interviews but requires further systematic case studies and pilot projects:

Hypothesis for future research:
DSLs can be regarded as an enabler for tool-based automation in BE.

6 Reflections

Stepping back, it appears that compared with SE in particular DevOps the technological state of the BE scenario has certainly reasons in

- its much higher complexity in particular
  concerning the interdisciplinary scope
- its much higher level of variety and uncertainty

which both lead to the mindset that standardization, tools, and automation imply unacceptable restrictions that strongly impair the potential of BE. This explains the poor BE tool landscape and the appreciated value of informal best practice patterns (e.g. continuous improvement cycles and canvases). In particular the observed lack of automation hinders agility, as e.g., prototyping (in the sense of minimum viable products) or validations, e.g., via simulations, are extremely expensive and therefore hardly performed (at least in comparison to SE where, e.g., daily automated builds are kind of standard).

Our **Hypothesis for Future Research** indicates a way that may allow to overcome this situation: DSLs for interdisciplinary communication may provide a level of precision that allows for automation via dedicated generators for providing stakeholder-specific views, executable prototypes, or KPI analyzes. This may, in particular, also help to control the risk. Figure 5 is interesting in this respect: The 'business & IT expert' group which also considered a BE-oriented notion of risk sees fewer problems than the business expert group.

Please note that, in particular, the numbers of the other two groups are misleading in this respect as they were thinking, e.g., of security risks introduced by e.g. third party components (which the 'business & IT expert' group was also aware of), a phenomenon that was not considered by the interviewed business experts.

Reducing the (perceived) risk of a change is of vital importance for an agile organization and increasing the transparency of the impact of changes is a good way to guarantee the acceptance by all stakeholders. Thus, every means supporting validation is crucial.

7 Conclusion, Limitations, and Outlook

This paper **contributes** to the co-development potentials of BE and SE. It analyzed the similarities and differences between the BE/SE and DevOps contexts to derive an assessment on the applicability of the DevOps approaches, tools and mind-sets to BE/SE. We have identified that both contexts face continuous change which requires interdisciplinary collaboration as creativeness and innovation mostly originates from the intersection of several disciplines and especially requires them for their successful implementation. Moreover, as uncertainty increases with the number of stakeholders and the depth of change, frequent validation is crucial to enable educated decision-making and to achieve organization-wide acceptance.

To further detail our understanding we conducted an interview study with 33 experts. We chose to address four categories of interviewees: IT students with interdisciplinary experiences, IT experts, business experts and 'business & IT experts' with long experience in both fields of expertise enabling them to provide a rather objective view of the BE and SE contexts and their corresponding mind-sets.

Based on the highly structured interviews including quantitative and qualitative questions we have identified that these groups show major differences regarding current and wished for tool support.

The BE context faces more global challenges and greater interdisciplinarity than SE and in particular DevOps. This asks for rather manageable (as simple as possible) and generally/globally applicable solutions at the expense of accuracy. Today, these challenges are addressed via frequent meetings and presentations rather than concrete tool support.

SE and in particular DevOps on the other hand excel at accuracy to allow for (semi) automation and continuous tool support in addition to frequent meetings and awareness of diverging priorities. Here, DSLs allow for accurate and simple tools and solutions which fit in particular domain-specific contexts.

Based on these findings we derived at the following hypothesis for **future research**: DSLs can be regarded as an enabler for tool-based automation in

BE and, similar to DevOps, align cross community communication. Thus, the DSL-based approach would allow e.g. for tools/DSLs specifically designed for the cross-departmental cooperation required in a given project to achieve integral quality and alignment.

Due to the current exploration phase we focused on rather qualitative feedback on our questions at the expense of the generalizability of our findings. We propose to address this **limitation** via additional quantitative analyses to increase the reliability of our results. Further, in order to better meet the complexity of the BE context additional areas of expertise (e.g. finance and operations) should be addressed to account for their custom requirements and derive a more realistic picture of the overall complexity.

References

1. McKinsey Digital: Industry 4.0: How to navigate digitization of the manufacturing sector
2. Aichroth, P., et al.: Wertschöpfung durch software in deutschland: Aktueller zustand, perspektiven, handlungsempfehlungen
3. Allspaw, J., Hammond, P.: 10+ deploys per day: Dev and ops cooperation at flickr. In: Velocity: Web Performance and Operations Conference
4. Barnett, W.P., Hansen, M.T.: The red queen in organizational evolution (1996)
5. Bass, L., Weber, I., Zhu, L.: DevOps: A Software Architect's Perspective. Addison-Wesley Professional, Boston (2015)
6. Bechtold, J., Lauenstein, C., Kern, A., Bernhofer, L.: Industry 4.0 - the capgemini consulting view (2014)
7. Beck, K., et al.: The agile manifesto (2001)
8. Bloice, L., Burnett, S.: Barriers to knowledge sharing in third sector social care: a case study. J. Knowl. Manag. **20**, 125–145 (2016)
9. Brosseau, D., Ebrahim, S., Handscomb, C., Thaker, S.: The journey to an agile organization. McKinsey Insights 10
10. Carroll, L.: Through the Looking Glass. Project Gutenberg
11. Christensen, C.: The Innovator's Dilemma: When New Technologies Cause Great Firms to Fail. Harvard Business Essentials, Harvard Business School Press (1997). https://books.google.de/books?id=vWvixwEACAAJ
12. Daepp, M.I.G., Hamilton, M.J., West, G.B., Bettencourt, L.M.A.: The mortality of companies. J. Royal Soc. Interface **12**(106), 20150120 (2015)
13. Dahlberg, T., Lagstedt, A.: Fit to context matters-selecting and using information systems development methods to develop business in digitalization contexts (2021)
14. Debois, P., et al.: Devops: a software revolution in the making. J. Inf. Technol. Manag **24**, 3–39 (2011)
15. Fink, A.: How to Conduct Surveys: A Step-by-Step Guide. SAGE, Thousand Oaks (2015)
16. Fowler, M.: Domain-Specific Languages. Pearson Education, London (2010)
17. Fowler, M., Highsmith, J., et al.: The agile manifesto. Softw. Dev. **9**(8), 28–35 (2001)
18. Hemon, A., Lyonnet, B., Rowe, F., Fitzgerald, B.: From agile to devops: smart skills and collaborations. Inform. Syst. Front. **22**(4), 927–945 (2020)

19. Hessenkämper, A., Steffen, B.: Towards standardization of custom projects via project profile matching. In: Fernandes, J.M., Machado, R.J., Wnuk, K. (eds.) ICSOB 2015. LNBIP, vol. 210, pp. 186–191. Springer, Cham (2015). https://doi.org/10.1007/978-3-319-19593-3_17
20. Hevner, A.R.: A three cycle view of design science research. Scand. J. Inform. Syst. **19**(2), 4 (2007)
21. Hirst, D., Darwin, C., Ramm, N., Bynum, W.: On the Origin of Species. Penguin classics, Penguin Books Limited (2009). https://books.google.de/books?id=e3hwBxBTh24C
22. Hudak, P.: Domain-specific languages. Handb. Program. Lang. **3**(39–60), 21 (1997)
23. Keese, C.: Silicon Germany: Wie wir die digitale Transformation schaffen. Penguin Verlag, München
24. Kelly, S., Lyytinen, K., Rossi, M.: Metaedit+ a fully configurable multi-user and multi-tool case and came environment. In: International Conference on Advanced Information Systems Engineering, pp. 1–21
25. Kim, W., Mauborgne, R.: Blue Ocean Strategy. Harvard Business School Press, Brighton
26. King, A.A., Tucci, C.L.: Incumbent entry into new market niches: the role of experience and managerial choice in the creation of dynamic capabilities. Manag. Sci. **48**(2), 171–186 (2002)
27. Korpivaara, I., Tuunanen, T., Seppänen, V.: Performance measurement in scaled agile organizations. In: Proceedings of the 54th Hawaii International Conference on System Sciences, pp. 6912–6921 (2021)
28. Kukko, M.: Knowledge sharing barriers in organic growth: a case study from a software company. J. High Technol. Manag. Res. **24**, 18–29 (2013)
29. Ledeczi, A., et al.: The generic modeling environment, vanderbilt university. Institute For Software Integrated Systems
30. Martin, R.: Clean Code - a Handbook of Agile Software Craftsmanship. Prentice Hall, Hoboken
31. Naujokat, S., Lybecait, M., Kopetzki, D., Steffen, B.: Cinco: a simplicity-driven approach to full generation of domain-specific graphical modeling tools. Int. J. Softw. Tools Technol. Transf. **20**, 327–354 (2018)
32. Osterwalder, A., Pigneur, Y.: Business model generation: a handbook for visionaries, game changers, and challengers, vol. 1. John Wiley & Sons, Hoboken (2010)
33. O'Reilly, C.A., III., Tushman, M.L.: Ambidexterity as a dynamic capability: resolving the innovator's dilemma. Res. Organ. Behav. **28**, 185–206 (2008)
34. Ries, E.: The Startup Way: How Entrepreneurial Management Transforms Culture and Drives Growth. Portfolio Penguin (2017). https://books.google.de/books?id=er-iswEACAAJ
35. Steffen, B., Boßelmann, S.: GOLD: global organization alignment and decision - towards the hierarchical integration of heterogeneous business models. In: Margaria, T., Steffen, B. (eds.) ISoLA 2018. LNCS, vol. 11247, pp. 504–527. Springer, Cham (2018). https://doi.org/10.1007/978-3-030-03427-6_37
36. Steffen, B., Boßelmann, S., Hessenkämper, A.: Effective and efficient customization through lean trans-departmental configuration. In: Margaria, T., Steffen, B. (eds.) ISoLA 2016. LNCS, vol. 9953, pp. 757–773. Springer, Cham (2016). https://doi.org/10.1007/978-3-319-47169-3_57
37. Thorngate, W.: "in general" vs. "it depends": Some comments of the gergen-schlenker debate. Personal. Soc. Psychol. Bull. **2**(4), 404–410 (1976)

38. Weiber, R., Ferreira, K.: Transaktions- versus geschäftsbeziehungsmarketing. In: Backhaus, K., Voeth, M. (eds.) Handbuch Business-to-Business- Marketing, pp. 121–146. Springer Gabler, Wiesbaden
39. Wilson, M., Sapsford, R.: Asking questions. In: Sapsford, R., Jupp, V. (eds.) Data Collection and Analysis, pp. 93–123. SAGE, London
40. Winter, R., Müller, J., Gericke, A.: Der st. galler ansatz zum veränderungsmanagement. In: Organisationsentwicklung, pp. 40–47
41. Österle, H.: Business Engineering: Prozeß- und Systementwicklung. Springer-Verlag, Berlin Heidelberg, Berlin
42. Österle, H., Höning, F., Osl, P.: Methodenkern des business engineering - ein lehrbuch

Towards Living Canvases

Barbara Steffen[1(✉)], Frederik Möller[1,2], Alex Rotgang[3], Stephen Ryan[4,5], and Tiziana Margaria[4,5,6]

[1] TU Dortmund University, Dortmund, Germany
{barbara.steffen,frederik.moeller}@tu-dortmund.de
[2] Fraunhofer ISST, Dortmund, Germany
[3] Fraunhofer IML, Dortmund, Germany
alex.rotgang@iml.fraunhofer.de
[4] University of Limerick, Limerick, Ireland
{stephen.e.ryan,tiziana.margaria}@ul.ie
[5] Confirm - The Irish Smart Manufacturing Centre, Limerick, Ireland
[6] Lero - The Irish Software Research Centre, Limerick, Ireland

Abstract. We discuss how to better support practitioners in understanding, planning and executing their projects through visual guidance via e.g., canvases and diagram-based frameworks implemented as IT tools. Today, too many important aspects are overlooked during project development: opportunities to mitigate risks, innovation potentials and stakeholder alignment. We analyze whether a more holistic and integrated approach connecting different perspectives actually leads to new insights, relevant for a project's success. Based on our bespoke integrative analysis support, the case study indeed disclosed otherwise unaddressed important risks, that might lead to the project's failure if no mitigation strategies and new actions are introduced. This analysis stage is success critical, but often just gets done in a rudimentary fashion failing to reveal the most critical success factors, key actions and challenges. With missing benefits, it is obvious that it is often considered a waste of resources and left out altogether. To change this situation and standardize the analysis process in a customized way, we argue that adequate, advanced IT tool support is needed to better guide practitioners and integrate and aggregate the knowledge of the organization, teams and experts into a global organization-wide knowledge management infrastructure.

Keywords: Living canvas · Tool-enabled · Canvas tool · Project support · Global analysis · Knowledge management

1 Introduction

Since the Business Model Canvas (BMC) by Osterwalder was published in 2010 the canvas' role in brainstorming workshops received increasing attention [1]. In time, various authors proposed canvases (also called visual inquiry tools) for a wide array of application domains and applied them to business and research contexts [2, 3]. Each canvas supports a specific target segment/problem scope with a mapped-out overview of the most relevant aspects to consider and define. Canvases aim at supporting their users in

T. Margaria and B. Steffen (Eds.): ISoLA 2021, LNCS 13036, pp. 95–116, 2021.
https://doi.org/10.1007/978-3-030-89159-6_7

all kinds of decision-making e.g., from industry analysis (PESTEL [4]), status-quo analysis (e.g., SWOT [5]), competitor analysis (Porter's five forces [6, 7]), to Business Model design (BMC [1]). The unique selling proposition of using canvases is clear: the problem gets structured and tangible at one glance. This eases interdisciplinary communication, collaboration and alignment.

However, today's adoption of frameworks/canvases and their findings' integration into the e.g., project's implementation face three major shortcomings. First, the canvases guide the brainstorming sessions, but do not check, validate and integrate the findings into the organization's processes and tool landscape as they are generally just printed-out paper versions used with sticky notes or online versions on generic white-boards (e.g., miro [8]). In rare cases also rudimentary canvas-specific tools exist (e.g., Strategyzer [9]). Second, canvases are primarily used in single brainstorming sessions and do not get updated and challenged throughout the further design and implementation of the projects. Thus, the findings and insights are not "living" and thus cannot guide the project from definition to the final implementation [10]. Third, single framework/canvas analysis are not sufficient to get an overall understanding of the project, its opportunities, challenges and risks. Therefore, several suitable frameworks/canvases must be selected and connected to understand a project and its environment fully.

This paper aims to demonstrate the benefits of analyzing projects using several frameworks/canvases to integrate different perspectives and derive at a (more) global understanding of the project and its challenges. To do so, we defined a workshop study that consists of nine steps, including two self-developed canvases, a risk analysis complemented by externally proposed risks, and the interpretation of the findings from one project team's results to the overall project. We chose risk as add-on perspective as it is an often overlooked, but success critical factor. Further, we argue that this global, interconnected and living view can be best supported by an IT tool bringing the analysis, process and changes alive via e.g., DSL-driven canvas support.

Thus, this paper aims to answer the following **research questions**:

1. *What are the benefits of analyzing and guiding projects from multiple perspectives?*
2. *What are the key features a canvas tool needs to cover in order to be "alive" and support the challenges of traditional industries?*

The paper is structured as follows: Sect. 2 defines canvases, today's tool support and the risk standards. In Sect. 3, we briefly depict the paper's method. The case study introduction, workshop outline and workshop results are introduced in Sect. 4. Section 5 addresses the learnings and derives at requirements and implications for corresponding tool support. The paper finalizes in Sect. 6 with the conclusion.

2 State of the Art

In this section, we briefly introduce the benefits of canvases and today's application of canvases in practice and state the importance of analyzing risks and the hurdles along the way.

2.1 Today's Use and Application of Canvases

Canvases are collaborative 'frameworks' to design new solutions, foster innovation, and, in general, enable their users to work jointly even across disciplines [11–13]. Given the plethora of benefits, it is no surprise that canvases penetrate various application domains ranging from research processes [14] to developing novel services [15]. For example, Schoormann et al. (2021) propose a canvas for systematic literature reviews and expressively point to the benefit of shared ideation in structuring and communicating methodological rigor to reviewers [15]. Similarly, Elikan and Pigneur (2019, p. 571) point to the aspect of "(…) shared visualization of a problem (…)" [16]. One of the most well-known and acclaimed examples of a canvas is the BMC by Osterwalder and Pigneur [17, 18]. It is a two-dimensional canvas that enables its users to fill out nine fundamental building blocks which combined define a sound business model. Subsequently, one can identify a primary benefit: deconstructing a complex entity logically into understandable pieces, fostering lucid problem-solving. Additionally, a canvas is not restricted to be designed in isolation but instead spurs the potential for hierarchical problem-solving and establishing more-or-less fine or abstracted levels of analysis [12]. Chandra Kruse and Nickerson (2018) refer to the BMC as a 'mnemonic', acting as a memory aid reminding its user which building blocks should, mandatorily, be addressed in the business model design [19]. Canvases, generally, can differ greatly from one another. For example, Thoring et al. (2019) propose a morphology ranging from three up to fifteen building blocks [20]. Additionally, their purpose, i.e., what they are used for, is not bound to a specific purpose or domain.

Even though canvases have become popular, most users still need support in selecting the right canvases and understanding their correct application. This task becomes even more complex when identifying and selecting multiple canvases which together allow for a global understanding given their interlinkages and dependencies. Canvases aim to offer a standardized approach which needs to be applied in a customized fashion to the specific environment and requirements of the addressed problem scope. Most canvas designers offer printable templates, short descriptions, examples, videos and/or books to allow for an easy and fast adoption. E.g., the BMC can be downloaded free of charge. Nevertheless, a masterclass like *Testing Business* Ideas by Osterwalder himself costs about $1700 + VAT per person [21]. That shows that the successful transfer to a specific context requires more than a generic approach.

Traditionally, the BMC and canvases, in general, were bound to physical workshops, in which the users fill them out e.g., using post-its on canvas-posters [20]. For example, Elikan and Pigneur (2019) provide photographs of how they applied the Brand Identity Canvas with sticky notes [16]. Given that SARS-CoV-2 has forced the physical meeting to 'go digital', more and more workshops shifted to using online boards (e.g., *miro* [8]). Also, the BMC is a notable exception as it is integrated into an application provided by *Strategyzer*, yet, its design area revolves exclusively around business model components [9]. In addition, the *canvanizer* includes about 40 different canvas templates and allows for the development of private canvas templates [22]. However, a significant pitfall of these online boards and dedicated applications is the lack of transferability of results from one canvas to another. In addition, also the integration of the findings and plans into the actual processes and IT landscape of an organization is missing. For example, depicting a hierarchical order of canvases with integrated data management and data outflow to the ongoing processes is still an area left untapped in research. Steffen und Boßelmann (2018) outline an interdisciplinary approach intertwining different layers of abstraction using a hierarchy of modifiable canvases to align organizational business model design with other business areas and transcend typical 'silo-thinking' [23].

2.2 The Risk Standard as an Add-on Perspective

Risk has been studied in various corporate settings and functions e.g., decision-making in a managerial capacity [24]. The following definition of risk assessment was derived from the ISO 31000 standard: *how likely is an event to occur and what effect/impact does it have if/when it occurs* [25]. In addition, the theory of decision-making defines risk as the "reflection of variation in the distribution of possible outcomes, their likelihoods, and their subjective values" [24]. Today, analyzing and evaluating risk in organizations is somewhat tricky as no precise measures and processes exist. Here, organizations lack a single, easily understood and generally applicable risk definition, identification and evaluation process [26].

The first step in a more guided direction is the ISO 31000 standard [25]. It became the cornerstone of risk management within the corporate world. Its outlined standards support organizations in emphasizing and (better) understanding the fundamentals of risks by proposing and guiding the following steps: the identification, analysis, evaluation, treatment, communication and monitoring of risks. However, even this framework does not lead to objective measures of risks and factual outcomes.

That explains why the process is often considered time-consuming, costly and redundant as it does not lead to tangible and concrete outcomes. Thus, organizations tend to overlook or underrate risks incurring major consequences. This negligence ranges from missing to involve important expert opinions/feedback from layers of the organization to risk severity misinterpretations due to incorrect calculations. Hampton (2014, p.18), e.g., stated that "people can be too close to risk or just too busy to recognize impending critical problems" [27]. Alleviating such simple errors would prevent neglecting the risk perspective in the organization's overall strategic plans and instead allow for risk mitigations and radical reductions of risk-induced consequences. We argue that the risk perspective should be integrated into existing frameworks/canvases as add-on perspective to analyze and evaluate risks in a standardized and integrated fashion. In addition, a "living" approach could even integrate the ISO 31000 framework and thus the risk perspective into the project's analysis and planning phases to the final implementation in a continuous, agile and iterative fashion reacting to new insights.

3 Method

In this paper, we followed Hevner's three-cycle view [28]. It comprises the relevance, design and rigor cycles (see Fig. 1). The relevance cycle addresses the "real world" and triggers research questions and validates/falsifies e.g., hypotheses and artifacts. The paper's method and research are designed in the design cycle. The results must be

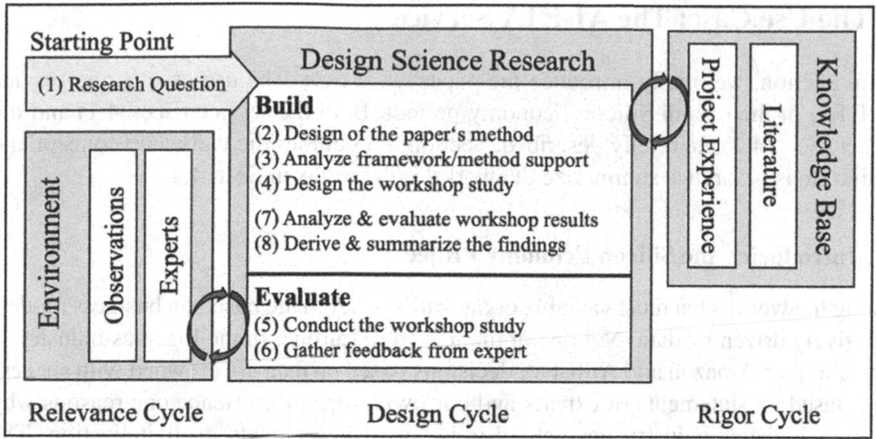

Fig. 1. The paper design is based on Hevner's three cycle view [28]

grounded in the existing knowledge base. Here, the rigor cycle ensures that literature and relevant experiences get analyzed and educate the paper's theory and conclusions.

In this paper the initial relevance cycle was triggered by our observations in past experiences that projects get addressed too one-sided. In practice relevant aspects stay unaddressed and thus often even mitigatable risks lead to (major) consequences which could have been avoided. We designed the paper and the case study based on observations of and conversations with experts as well as literature in the rigor cycle. The use case, the Silicon Economy project and particularly its AI-ETA service, was analyzed based on our workshop study design in the second relevance cycle. The study was intended to evaluate and test the multi-step analysis workshop design for its benefits.

The paper aims at analyzing the benefits of a multi-step analysis approach addressing a project from several perspectives. Thus, we designed a workshop study consisting of two canvases and the add-on perspective risk which are applied and detailed in nine sequential steps. In addition, based on the learnings and identified benefits and challenges we seek to identify functions and features a canvas tool support needs to cover to affordably guide and ease the multiple-step analysis in practice. As this tool does not exist yet we designed a "handmade" proof of concept (PoC), a pre-designed miro-board. It provides step to step guidance in the envisioned function of the canvas tool to test its benefits and derive feature and requirement requests.

We analyzed the case study and tested our multiple-step analysis in two workshops. We chose the workshop as a research methodology due to its benefits of studying cases in an authentic manner resulting in high reliability and validity output [29]. The workshop participants were the case study's – the AI-ETA service – product owner and three of the authors as each of us covered a different field of expertise which were necessary for the guidance, observation and interpretation of the workshops' multi-step approach. In addition, the workshop is the only format which allows to guide, support and observe the participants' understanding and progress.

4 The Use Case: The AI-ETA Service

In this section, we briefly introduce the paper's use case. The use case is one service (AI-ETA) of the overall Silicon Economy project. Both the service (Sect. 4.1) and the project (Sect. 4.2) are briefly described. Section 4.3 outlines the workshop concept and its nine steps before we summarize the workshop's results in Sect. 4.4.

4.1 Introducing the Silicon Economy Project

Among the world's ten most valuable organizations, seven are based on business models exclusively driven by data. Not one of them is from Europe. In the logistics industry in particular (see Amazon and Alibaba), decisions based on data are crowned with success [30]. Based on statements of experts and our own project experience one reasons why Europe's logistics industry lies behind is its small investments in digitalization. The successful data-driven organizations are based on a standardized data structure, high quantities, and great quality of data. In contrast to the American and Asian markets, the European market is characterized by many competitors, which currently prevents access to the quantity of data needed to build a data-driven business model realizing value [31–33].

To overcome these obstacles, the Silicon Economy project aims at establishing a platform, in cooperation with the logistics industry (leaders), to achieve:

- Standardization of data structures and APIs,
- Compatibility among different services/components in the logistics ecosystem,
- Easy access and modification of components and services,
- Tools and/or open-source components integrating e.g., public data sources and
- Services, e.g., the case study (AI-ETA), demonstrating the opportunities of adopting individual and combinations of the components as tools.

To address this challenge and achieve industry transformation, the German government-funded Silicon Economy project supports today's logistics organizations in developing their own digital platforms by offering logistics-specific open-source components. In addition, the project's approach of offering selectable and combinable components fits the modular design of digital platforms. Thus, it enables customized digital platforms compatible with the industry-standard [34].

That envisioned open-source-based platform requires a community and its management in addition to the developed components and case studies. On the one hand, it guarantees further development even after the completion of the project, and on the other hand, it also promotes the cooperation of different stakeholders. Since a multiplicity of different stakeholders/organizations comes together, also an orchestration is absolutely necessary to consolidate and neutrally evaluate the respective requirements and needs for its transfer into services [35].

To summarize, the project addresses three major challenges: First, the integration and use of public data sources, second, the standardization of data structures, and third the complementation of organization-specific data by the addition of public data sources. Overall, it is envisioned to create and offer a toolbox of individual components for logistics organizations to select, adapt to their needs and integrate in a problem-solving and value-creating way.

4.2 The AI-ETA Service

This section introduces the AI-based ETA (Artificial Intelligence based Estimated Time of Arrival) service, consisting of many Silicon Economy components. Based on the component canvas (see Fig. 2), we explain the necessity of this service and its contribution to the above-mentioned main goals of the Silicon Economy. The AI-ETA service aims at solving the currently inaccurate calculations of the ETA for different modes of transport. These inaccuracies have various causes like spontaneous events e.g., overtaking by rail, congestion on the road, vague estimates on the waterway. The results are inadequate resource planning at transshipment points and insufficient coordination between transport modes, preventing a significant improvement of the interconnection between the modes of transport. In addition, a shift from road to rail is necessary due to the climate targets of, e.g., a 65% CO2 reduction until 2030 and even a 100% reduction until 2045. Road transport emits many times more greenhouse gases than the other two transport modes [36].

The service aims at offering a fully automatic ETA of transport modes consisting of several modules and integrating many information sources. The users do not need to have access to the data sources themselves but can access the ones of interest. Based on connections to cloud platforms in the sense of a Silicon Economy the user can access and integrate the full service and/or individual modules. The natural transport mode-specific characteristics (e.g., the inland navigation dependence on the water level) are the basis for the service's developed algorithms achieving a fully automated ETA forecast and cross-modal networking. The main innovation lies in using and integrating public data sources, e.g., OpenStreetMap or mCloud, and in cross-modal considerations. In addition, a rule-based decision engine calculates the optimized route based on time, greenhouse gas emissions, or costs as preferred.

The Silicon Economy, in general, summarizes and implements existing standards component by component (e.g., geocoding), identifies processes and makes public data sources available (e.g., a weather service), and ensures the reusability of individual components by detailed documentation [37].

4.3 Workshop Execution

To analyze this paper's research question and identify the results of our approach, we designed a workshop to deliver the intervention and gather initial qualitative feedback. The current main goal is to identify whether our analysis steps help the workshop participants to refine their understanding of the AI-ETA service and of the overall Silicon Economy project. For example, can they derive new to-dos and propose best practices and/or improvement potentials for this service and new services? Based on these findings, we derive requirements for the ideal canvas support and translate them into specific requirements and solution proposals for an add-on IT tool support.

The workshop was carried out with one of two product owners of Silicon Economy's AI-ETA service. It addressed nine progressive steps, detailing our understanding of the

AI-ETA service and the Silicon Economy project as a whole. The workshop consisted of two meetings lasting an hour each. Both sessions took place via Zoom calls and were supported by the collaborative working platform miro. Here, the stepwise guidance led through tasks like filling out canvases, lists, and a matrix. The first meeting covered the definition of the AI-ETA service based on the component canvas and identification of the most important and risky entries (see Table 1, steps 1–2). The second meeting addressed steps 3–9 of the following workshop outline:

Table 1. Workshop outline - the nine steps

Step	Task description	Duration
	First Workshop	
1	Define the AI-ETA service with the Silicon Economy's Component Canvas.	45 min
2	Which entries are a) the most important for success? (mark them in turquoise) b) the riskiest? (mark them in red)	15 min
	Second Workshop	
3	What are the top risks of the AI-ETA service?	10 min
4	Please look at the following list of eight risks. a) Which of these are relevant in your opinion? b) Add the relevant risks to the list of top risks.	15 min
5	Select the top 10 risks.	10 min
6	Evaluate the risks based on the risk evaluation matrix, concerning each risks' likelihood of occurrence and its envisioned impact.	10 min
7	Which of the identified top ten risks for the AI-ETA service have implications/are relevant for the overall Silicon Economy project?	7 min
8	Please add and/or change the Silicon Economy description (on the Platform Alignment Canvas [38]) based on your current understanding and the now available risk analysis.	8 min
9	Please provide general feedback about the workshop (e.g., What did you like, what did you learn, identified benefits, what did you miss, next to-dos).	10 min

4.4 Workshop Results

This section outlines the results of the nine workshop steps. In the following, we briefly address each of the nine steps, including the service's risk analysis, present the insights gained from step to step, and discuss the evaluation of the identified risks.

In Step 1, the product owner defined the AI-ETA service based on the component canvas and filled out all 11 building blocks. Step 2 focused on the entries most important for success and most risky, leading to the identification of seven entries as most critical for success (sticky notes in turquoise), seven as the riskiest (sticky notes in red), and two which are both essential for success and risky (sticky notes in violet). In addition, this step focusing on importance/risk led to the complementation of the initial AI-ETA service description by six newly added entries. The participant added three entries due to their importance for the service's success and three further refining its riskiness. Figure 2 shows the filled-out component canvas as it looked after Step 2.

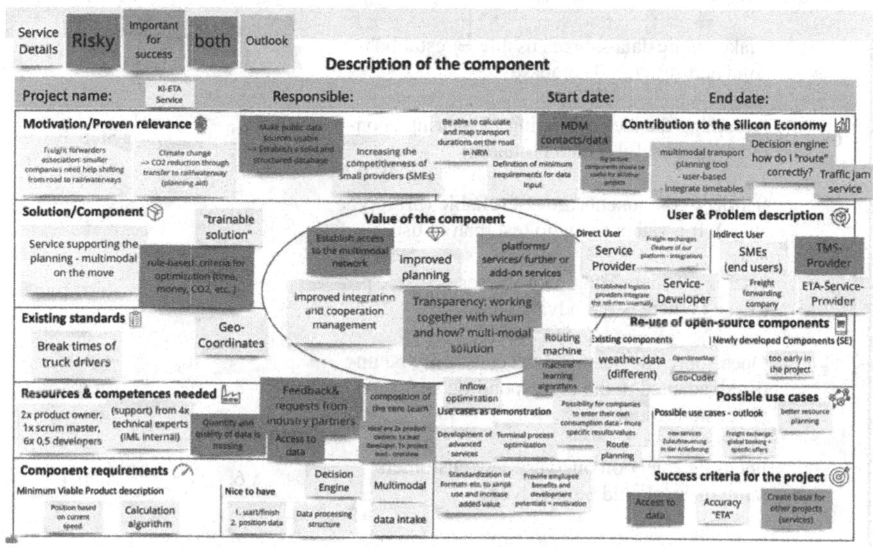

Fig. 2. Filled out Component Canvas after step 2

In Step 3, the product owner identified the service's top risks based on the prior identification of the risky entries. Eight pre-defined risks proposed by the workshop organizers were added to the pool of identified risks. In Step 4, the participant analyzed these eight new proposed risks. The participant identified one of these risks as already considered, two as not so relevant, and confirmed the relevance of the other five. This classification accounts for an 87,5% acceptance rate and a 62,5% relevance rate.

The fifth step asked to prioritize the top ten risks of the AI-ETA service, summarized in Table 2. Here, five risks came from the initial list of risks and five from our proposed risks pool in Step 4. Thus, 50% of the most critical risks for the service's success were identified only in Step 4.

Table 2. Identified top 10 risks of the AI-ETA service

Priority	Top Risks	Severity index	Identified in
1	Quantity and quality of (open) data is missing	25	Step 2
2	Receiving sufficient access to data	25	Step 2
3	Access to necessary core competences/expertise	16	Step 4
4	Innovation is not scalable	15	Step 4
5	Make public data sources usable → establish a solid and structured database	15	Step 1
6	Accepting the idea of sharing → sharing economy (only useful if data is shared)	12	Step 3
7	Services/components are not reliable (prototype stage). It is rather ready to test than to use.	10	Step 4
8	User is not interacting with the services/the prototype (Where is our advantage?)	10	Step 4
9	Open source device needs to constantly be updated/ adapted to the corresponding structures → customization	8	Step 3
10	Focusing solely on one/very few customers (aim: many should be involved)	6	Step 4

Step 6 asked the participant to rate each risk according to the ISO 31000 standard [25]. To quantify the risks correctly, it is crucial to evaluate the significance of each risk based on the likelihood of the risk to occur (y-axes) and the risk' envisioned impact on the service (x-axes). Combining both classifications into one matrix system was essential to correctly quantify these risks and weigh them for the AI-ETA service. The used matrix is depicted in Fig. 3: four risks were envisioned to have an extreme impact, one a significant impact, while the remaining five risks scored twice moderate impact and three times minor impact. Regarding the risks' likelihood of occurrence, four risks are almost certain to occur, three are likely, two are possible and one is unlikely.

In Step 7, the participant identified that seven of the top ten identified risks are also relevant for the Silicon Economy project because other services will also face similar challenges. These are all top risks except for risks 3, 5, and 9 in Table 2. The next step,

Step 8, showed the participant the Silicon Economy description based on the Platform Alignment Canvas [38] for the first time. He was asked to complement it based on his understanding as a product owner in the Silicon Economy context and the insights gathered from steps 1–7. He complemented the Silicon Economy description with six new entries (e.g., UVP: demonstrate the value of sharing, provider: service providers for "productification" and requirements: sufficient time and resources/feedback of 5–10 different stakeholders, etc.) shown in orange in Fig. 4.

	Negligible (1)		Minor (2)		Moderate (3)		Major (4)		Extreme (5)	
Almost Certain (5)	-	5	1	10	1	15	-	20	2	25
Likely (4)	-	4	1	8	1	12	1	16	-	20
Possible (3)	-	3	1	6	-	9	-	12	1	15
Unlikely (2)	-	2	-	4	-	6	-	8	1	10
Rare/ Remote (1)	-	1	-	2	-	3	-	4	-	5

Fig. 3. Risk evaluation Matrix including the top risks and their severity index (likelihood of the risk to occur (y-axes) and envisioned the impact of the risk (x-axes))

Step 9 asked the participant to provide overall feedback about the workshop, his learnings, and the next steps. He said that the workshop was organized straightforwardly and helpfully. Due to the Silicon Economy's and thus also each service's strict time constraints, the teams normally just dive into the service/component development and get started. In contrast, this workshop provided space to step back and reflect to identify the most relevant levers. The development of the AI-ETA service is already near its end, but nevertheless, the workshop supported the identification of new risks and success factors. In the participant's opinion, the workshop and its several analysis steps would be beneficial at the beginning and the end of the service/component development. In the beginning, it would help to deepen the team's understanding, increase transparency and alignment, and better prioritize the next steps. In the end, it would steer the reflection about the service development and its success. In general, it would be preferable to use the analysis method from the beginning as it allows for regular *should-be* comparisons, steering the modification along with the service's progress, if necessary.

Regarding the next to-dos concerning the AI-ETA service, he underlined the need to talk to (more) customers to ensure the service's usefulness, consider the scalability of the service, and how and what new services can re-use parts of existing services.

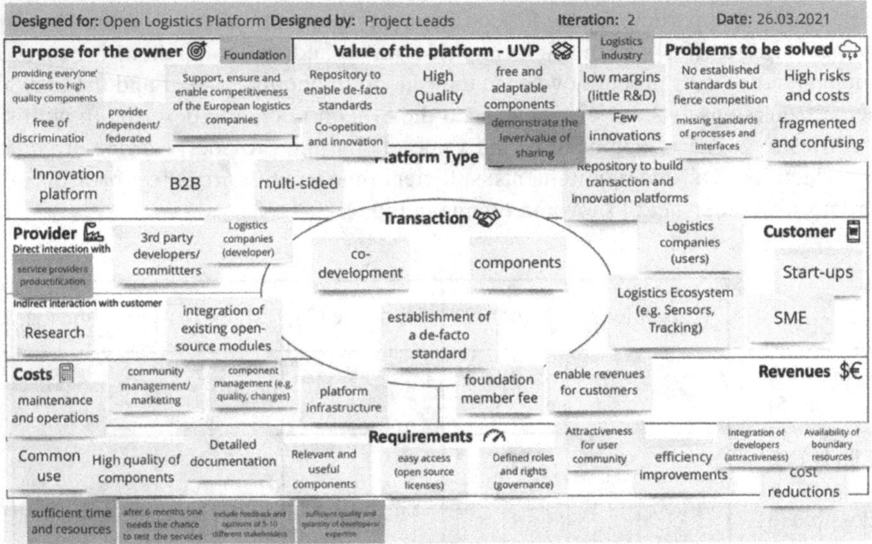

Fig. 4. Platform Alignment Canvas describing the Silicon Economy Project [38]

5 Lessons Learned and Implications

The conducted case study demonstrates that each of the nine workshop steps was useful: all added new insights or led to new findings on the local level, which could later be applied and adopted globally, as shown in Step 7. The participant perceived the workshop outline as supportive and solely focusing on essential topics. The steps were relevant in the global context of the Silicon Economy and especially for the success of the AI-ETA service.

It is important to state that these analyses are especially beneficial in the planning, execution and reflection phases. At the beginning, the analyses can support the product teams to better understand the challenges faced by the envisioned users and thus the problem at hand to design and develop the most suitable services/components. This approach animates the teams to seek user feedback and thus to ensure value for the users already in a first minimum viable product, i.e., it provides answers to questions like "What are the most relevant functionalities that must be finished in the six months period in order for the service to be useful and a success?". This clarity helps the team to prioritize and modify the implementation plan in an agile manner when needed. Further, the canvas and the approach allow the team to regularly check whether the set milestones were reached or can be reached, to monitor and reflect on the current progress, and at the end to reflect on the success of the overall project. This way, the teams can derive learnings that they can transfer to their next project/service development.

Especially the risk perspective was new to the product owner, showing that the Silicon Economy project currently does not emphasize the risk perspective as a success metric. In fact, several of the identified risks actually apply to the Silicon Economy project as a whole because many services deal with similar hurdles like, e.g., access to public data sources, sufficient validation via user feedback, service readiness, etc.

The workshop combined local analysis on the service level via a canvas and the complemented risk perspective. These learnings were further applied to the overall project level of the Silicon Economy, which is the global level of the entire platform. This transferability demonstrates the need to connect the different hierarchy levels, as the coherence of a top-down and a bottom-up development has strong implications for the overall project and its success.

In addition to the connectivity of the different layers, also the development phase would benefit from a continuous support, from goal setting to the final delivery of the service/components. Here, the planning and execution could be guided and complemented via add-on analyses of risks, opportunities etc. at the fitting moment along the implementation stages. Ideally, the developer teams would have their 'service-view' on the service's overall progress and a shared and up to date knowledge of the Silicon Economy project e.g., in the form of customized access to the relevant knowledge and developments. And those responsible for the Silicon Economy project should get access to the services' executive summary, their progress, and the as-is vs. to-be comparisons.

Further, the interdependent analyses and building blocks of e.g. the canvases should be connected and always make the users aware of changes and ask for corresponding updates. Also, suggestions of how to fill the analyses out correctly would be great, e.g. the analyses of the overall project could guide the definition and execution of each service to ensure that they are aligned and deliver the envisioned contribution.

5.1 Canvas Enhanced by Tool-Support

To answer the paper's research question, this section considers the requirements that need to be satisfied by visual tools to provide a "living" canvas support. Here, we focus especially on the three identified shortcomings of the current canvas use:

1. the missing *guidance and control* of the canvas' correct use,
2. the missing canvas /frameworks *selection support*, and
3. missing *interconnectivity* among building blocks, canvases and integration into the organization's running systems.

Addressing the *guidance and control* shortcoming, today canvases are still mostly used on paper, unguided whiteboard or in very locally supported dedicated apps. Thus, users face unsupported and unstructured graphs/constructs on a "piece of paper". Guiding questions on the canvas and examples in the documentation or tutorials help adopters to understand the canvases purpose and allow for a rough description of the problem scope to be analyzed by the team. However, the tricky part is to customize the standardized framework depicted as canvas in the correct manner. Taking the example of the widespread BMC, to properly use the BMC a project team must already have a good understanding of the organization, the product's goals, the customers already served, and the customers envisioned to be served in the future. Here, they must correctly distinguish between Business-to-Business, Business-to-Customer segments, and need to know a lot about the organization: key partners, key activities and resources, in order to properly understand and identify the organization's unfair advantages and unique selling propositions. Only if all this is known can they build upon them, rather than creating something in a siloed fashion, based on incomplete or incorrect assumptions rather than knowledge.

Here, we suggest that canvases connect via an ontology and are based on corresponding databases of what is known and what is happening in the organization and in its ecosystem. This further systematically ensures the re-use of knowledge and terminology within the canvas, and orientation on what the organization already excels at and does, rather than risking that each team works within their own limited horizon. This coherency of knowledge and terminology would allow for organization-wide transparency, orchestration, and analyses based on agreed-upon classifications.

We address the *selection support* shortcoming in the context of the solution to the guidance and control shortcoming. Based on the new level of transparency, a problem/challenge classification via a corresponding configuration allows to suggest which canvases are to be used to define and analyze the specific problem/challenge at hand in the best fitting way. Given that canvases are produced as an answer to needs that are general and relevant enough to justify dedicated tools, the match between problems and challenges of sufficient relevance and the canvas or canvas alternatives suitable to address them is known.

Here, we suggest that a configurator-like support pre-selects the suitable canvases and, depending on the level of integration with the relevant knowledge bases, it might already pre-fill them with already existing information/knowledge about the organization and insights generated by other in-house teams. This is achievable, for example, on the basis of rule-based support and integrations. Organizations would benefit from this support in the project execution, but also in general from the improved transparency and the internal learning effects resulting from the increasing amount of knowledge that is aggregated and brought into the right context.

Addressing the *interconnectivity* shortcoming, adequate tool support can also introduce or improve the connectivity among building blocks, canvases, and the integration into the organization's overall processes. Making these interlinkages transparent allows a better-informed decision making. Further, it allows to achieve a currently unrealistic learning curve because for the first-time actions and decisions can be better matched with their effects. This new track and tracing of processes, decisions and outputs would introduce a completely different way of working and make a more precise accountability feasible. This capability could increase the alignment, the output quality and create a path to success. Further, it allows to analyze the progress along the way: for example, in such a context unreached and unreachable milestones are already sufficient to push the teams to modify their plans and implementation strategy in an aligned and better-informed manner.

In addition to these three directions for improvements we further suggest that additional perspectives that are today often neglected (e.g., risk, sustainability, finance, HR, etc.) and relative frameworks should be analyzed and integrated to allow for 360-degree evaluations. As we have shown in the case study, adding the risk perspective led to new insights, massively impacting the further trajectory of the product's final development. Unfortunately, these aspects stay often unaddressed due to time constraints, lack of specific expertise, and limited guidance when planning and implementing projects and products in a holistic fashion. Thus, many opportunities for global rather than local optima are systematically missed which hinders the best prioritization based on the goals and resources at hand.

5.2 Required IT-Basis and Fundamental Aspects for a Technical Specification

For the new generation and new quality of canvases to become a reality, several technical aspects need to be considered and implemented in the IT-enabled canvases (also canvas-tool). These canvas tools should help the users to simplify (as much as possible) a complex situation, organize its key elements through building blocks, and then make use of guidance and support to ease first time adopters, but also to enforce alignment and a systematic approach when many groups use these canvas-tools within an organization or a collaborative ecosystem. In the context of the case study, the goal is to support the correct and competent adoption and use of the Component Canvas, a guided methodology to iteratively analyze, evaluate, complement and complete the specific perspective, a systematic way to enrich the overall analysis by adding perspectives (here the risk perspective) in a coherent, integrated and competent way (here, we followed the ISO 31000 standard process), and finally reflect at a higher, global level on the effects and insights that the specific tool-supported analysis has highlighted, in this case the Platform Alignment Canvas for the entire Silicon Economy project. More specifically, such an IT-tool or integrated tool landscape would need to provide the following nine requirements:

1. *A good demarcation between the different building blocks within a canvas: this can happen through good explanations, guiding questions and examples.*
   While most paper-based canvases print such questions in each building block, IT-supported canvases could customize this information for the industry segment, for the type of organization (e.g., SME, NGO and research project) and in other dimensions, greatly easing the accessibility to first time users. Given the reluctance many have, for example developers and product owners in IT projects, to adopt the so-called "business school tools", this IT-supported customization ability could be a big contributor to adoption by more IT-versed staff in a specific project situation.
   In terms of the technology, we have prior experience with such guidance and wizard implementation: in a large scale project concerning new business models in the personalized medicine [39], we realized a BMC tool embedding a wizard-based guidance [40], and validated it with the industry partners in the diagnostic and therapeutic industries. The first task of the wizard was to explain and characterize each BMC field in the specific context of that project, i.e., of the specific sector in pharmaceutics of these partners.
2. *Easy customization of the canvases through optional/additional building blocks.*
   While standard diagrams and canvases have the advantage of standardization, it is often the case that they oversimplify in their quest for generality, and that the specific use case would greatly benefit form the ability to add one to two building blocks that cover additional aspects essential to that use case. In an adequately IT tool-supported canvas, this would be easily possible. For example, using the Business Model Developer (BMD) tool or Global Organization aLignment and Decision (GOLD) tool [23, 40], it is possible to create custom canvases based on building blocks of a certain

type, and in particular it is possible to modify standard canvases (re)produced in the IT-tool to customize them to a specific and new canvas. The BMD and GOLD tools use the metamodeling and generation power of the CINCO framework [41] to define the syntax (look and feel) and the semantics of a (canvas), to define and generate fully functioning editors that are canvas tools.

3. *Display of answers from previous (important) building blocks to make sure that each element has at least one relation to another element.*
   This requires the canvas tool to have the ability to establish well-defined relationships between elements in different building blocks. In turn, this means that we treat building blocks like a semantic type, elements appearing in a building block assume that type, and the canvas tool (functioning as an intelligent editor) is then able to ensure that the same element is not appearing in different building blocks of different types (i.e., the diagram is well-typed), that the diagram is syntactically correct and complete (e.g., there are no empty building blocks). Additionally, relations or dependencies can be or must be established between elements of different building blocks. For example, Channels in the BMC must relate to one or more Customer Segments, and conversely each Customer Segment must have at least one Channel. Various analyses of plausibility can be implemented on an IT-supported canvas e.g., a BMC tool to make sure it is internally consistent in this sense, and none of them is currently available for any of the existing tools on the market. We have had previous experience here in the past [42–44]. The most valuable insight from these tools was the syntactic guidance provided to the users: while a wizard provides advice and helps filling up the canvas by sequentializing the fields in a logical order, this feature of the tool systematically prevented conceptual mistakes while the users were feeling free to edit at their pleasure. Here, the formal concepts of (semantic) type, type-based consistency, the use of formally defined relations of type compatibility, inclusion, and some basic logic reasoning find application.
4. *Ability to link elements, to simultaneously update/change other matching fields when changes are made.*
   This requirement builds upon the previous one, i.e., on the ability to establish and analyze relationships among elements in the canvas tool. The underlying technical capabilities rely on formal concepts of, e.g., equivalence, equality, compatibility, and on some simple inference in order to compute global consequences of local changes in a sort of chain propagation.
5. *Combination of different canvases or methods.*
   As we have seen, already this simple use case uses the Component Canvas and the Platform Alignment Canvas. In general, more than one canvas/framework is used and needed to cover different aspects, like PESTEL, SWOT or BMC. The current limitation of the tools is that they mostly support just one canvas/framework, so that using different diagrams means juggling with different tools that do not communicate. As already shown in GOLD, it is important to host and support the relevant diagrams and methods in one single environment, supporting a correct and controlled sharing of items, information and base knowledge. In this sense, it is useful to consider as a reference some of the capabilities of DIME [44], which is an advanced Integrated Modeling Environment for Web applications also realized as a CINCO-product. DIME shares one data model across many process models that all

refer to it, thus implementing the "write things once" rule is essential to guarantee coherence in complex IT systems. It also provides a GUI definition language for the Web application look and feel, interaction and navigation: this capability would be useful if one wishes to provide the tools as web applications, running in a browser, rather than as tools to be installed locally. Keeping in mind that canvases typically address non-IT experts, this can be a significant advantage for the simplicity of the uptake. DIME also includes a user access and security diagram that eases the management of role-based and in future also attribute-based access rights, which is a way to ensure a proper access control mechanism.

6. *Support in identifying the right tools and order, by asking questions and analyzing the current situation.*
   This can be useful also for orientation within the canvas, in case there are several possibilities, and different situations are better addressed by resorting to a different sequence of fields. For example, different team members may be responsible for different fields of, e.g., a BMC, so that it is not obvious where to start and who to involve next. A Wizard based approach to guidance, by video and interactive, stepwise support to filling out the canvas was already successful years ago in a large scale project concerning new business models in the personalized medicine [43], therefore we could build on that previous experience, that asked questions and helped analyze the current situation from different points of view.
7. *Support of prior knowledge/Corporate Dictionary* [45, 46].
   Here, various kinds of ontologies and taxonomies can help, both at the level of upper ontologies, defining the general concepts in a domain of interest, but also at the level of middle and lower ontologies, that become increasingly specialized and could even be organization specific. A proper tool support would need to be able to use linked external ontologies in some standard formats, and seamlessly maintain and extend the set of ontologies at the lower levels, for example by adding the concepts and items that appear in the canvas as well as the relations that emerge from the canvases and the analyses. A knowledge management/corporate dictionary level that is organized and maintained in this way would be an essential precondition for the global alignment and reuse of terminology, but also of information and knowledge, both in larger organizations like the global logistics organizations, and in ecosystems like the Silicon Economy.
8. *In terms of procedures to improve the corporate culture and processes, the tool should also be used as a vehicle to introduce the use of a canvas, if not yet known, to all the teams and the new hires.*
   For the generalized adoptability and ease of use, in particular the tool-internal embedded checks and guarantees are important: they can prevent erroneous use through syntax and semantic-aware editors and customizable wizards. From a technical point of view, wizards could be implemented by means of Web applications in DIME. The success of the BMC wizards in [42, 43] showed that the approach is congenial to adopters, as it provided immediate and often contextualized feedback that was easy to interpret, achieving a learning effect.
9. *In terms of corporate decision making and corporate culture, the subsequent elaboration of an action plan, to a) introduce the canvas through the tools in a systematic*

way in the corporate processes for business and product development, and b) the provision of adequate training, reward, and incentives for the individuals and teams that provide the best outcomes for the organization and the team through the use of the corporate knowledge internal alignment and of the tool-supported or tool-induced analyses.

This is a typical example of a digital transformation goal at the organization level.

In this constellation, we see the need of an interdisciplinary collaboration in order to respond to these requirements. From advanced software engineering and computer science come the technical components, like the intelligent Integrated Modelling Environments underlying the tools, and the embedded techniques. Here we see a role for analysis algorithms, e.g., for static analysis, dependency management, but also property checking, consistency monitoring, automatic generation of ontology-compliant entries and checkers. The business knowledge and the knowledge of the specific canvas tools is the general domain-specific expertise required from the "diagram experts". They are essential in the cooperation with the software experts in order to produce tools that are indeed correct in the canvas-specific knowledge and optimal in the contents of the guidance and support. User interaction and incremental improvement of the representational and informational aspects of the enriched canvas representation should be ideally led by user interaction and interaction design experts. This also applies to understanding the user feedback and user observation of how to prioritize and steer the successive improvement of the web applications, how to best design the integration between the different canvases, and how to organize the tutoring for different groups of adopters. The domain specific expertise in the various sectors would then ideally come from champions in the individual organizations, organization units, and teams, who are the knowledge carriers of the specific corporate culture and practice, in order to provide a transformation that is as conservative as possible and avoids to disrupt where it is not necessary.

6 Conclusion, Limitations and Outlook

This paper demonstrates the need for a different level of guidance for practitioners, deepening their understanding, supporting analyses and preparing for the challenges of the projects at hand. Today's approaches focus on single local aspects which the practitioners themselves need to select, connect and try to derive with educated decisions. As time equals money, and unguided brainstorming sessions do not lead to major benefits, practitioners tend to head-start into the execution of their projects without a prior careful 360-degree planning. This direct best effort approach ends too often in failed projects, cost explosions and results not fitting the prior envisioned goals.

To test whether a deeper and more holistic analysis, including several frameworks and canvases, leads to new insights and has the potential to guide projects and product development we have conducted a workshop study with a specific use case, the AI-ETA service of the Silicon Economy project. We focused on step by step refinements and the discovery and analysis of dependencies and interconnectivity of the different approaches, here the Component Canvas, Risk Analysis and the Project Alignment Canvas, and the resulting insights. This study accounts as a PoC for our guidance approach for e.g., project and product teams. The study followed a bespoke process that we prepared and worked with in miro. The workshop demonstrated that the holistic approach, combining the product description via a canvas, a risk analysis along the ISO 31000 standard, a corresponding risk evaluation and transfer from local insights to the global level, led to new insights that are currently unaddressed.

This study and our general observations in the contexts of other projects and product developments with industry partners demonstrated three major shortcomings of the current approaches. We then discussed how to address them in the context of advanced IT-supported canvas tools and derived several tool-support potentials and their corresponding technical and organizational requirements in the form of requirement specifications. Thus, our contribution focuses on merging the business and IT competencies to better guide and inform practitioners in their strategic and tactical tasks. The business support in the form of e.g., canvases and frameworks helped many practitioners for years. Nevertheless, the typically applied brainstorming session structure is too ad-hoc, and not sufficient to foster a culture of educated decision making, progress reports, as-is and to-be comparisons, with the integration of findings and learnings in the ongoing processes of an organization. Thus, the organizations' knowledge management potentials are currently not utilized. To adopt instead an agile and solution-driven mentality, today's business guidelines (available in form of many frameworks, like, e.g., SWOT, Porter's five forces and BMC, and checklists) need to be transferred into dedicated canvas tools, supported with the required interfaces to the organizations' existing tool landscapes and with tool-based guidance to learning and customized mastery of use.

The current research has two main *limitations*. First, its missing quantitative validation, e.g., more use cases, use cases from different industries etc., proving its general applicability. Instead we focused on a qualitative study to deepen our understanding and defer detailed requirements to be implemented into a first prototype. Second, we focused solely on the add-on perspective risk. Additional perspectives would have blown the workshop study out of proportion. Nevertheless, we are eager to analyze the benefits of add-on perspectives like, e.g., sustainability and finance.

Thus, we propose the following *outlook*. First, as a single detailed case study is not sufficient to derive a comprehensive list of specific requirements for a valuable tool support, we aim at additional case studies in the Silicon Economy context. Guided by the current experience and feedback, we will likely work next with the perishable goods import team and then extend the study to other industries for generalization, e.g., consulting, manufacturing, healthcare, start-up support etc. Second, the most relevant requirements need to be implemented in a first user friendly canvas tool. Here, a minimum viable product would be sufficient to test and validate the approach with users for educated iterations. That reference process and support will then form the basis for further developments regarding a broader applicability in other industries as well as broader support including the adoption and integration of additional frameworks, canvases and add-on perspectives like sustainability.

Acknowledgement. The project "Silicon Economy Logistics Ecosystem" is funded by the Federal Ministry of Transport and Digital Infrastructure.

This work was supported by the Science Foundation Ireland grants 16/RC/3918 (Confirm, the Smart Manufacturing Research Centre) and 13/RC/2094_2 (Lero, the Science Foundation Ireland Research Centre for Software).

References

1. Osterwalder, A., Pigneur, Y.: Business Model Generation. Wiley, Hoboken (2010)
2. Lecuna, A., Thoring, K., Mueller, R.: The idea arc: designing a visual canvas for fuzzy ideas. In: Proceedings of the 52nd Hawaii International Conference on System Sciences (2019)
3. Kronsbein, T., Müller, R.: Data thinking: a canvas for data-driven ideation workshops. In: Proceedings of the 52nd Hawaii International Conference on System Sciences (2019)
4. Jobber, D., Ellis-Chadwick, F.: Principles and Practie of Marketing. McGraw-Hill, Berkshire (2013)
5. Chen, W.-M., Kim, H., Yamaguchi, H.: Renewable energy in eastern Asia: renewable energy policy review and comparative SWOT analysis for promoting renewable energy in Japan, South Korea, and Taiwan. Energy Policy **74**, 319–329 (2014)
6. Porter, M.E.: The five competitive forces that shape strategy. Harv. Bus. Rev. **86**, 78 (2008)
7. Porter, M.E.: Competitive Advantage: Creating and Sustaining Superior Performance. The Free Press, New York (1985)
8. Miro. https://miro.com/. Accessed 05 Aug 2021
9. Strategyzer app. https://www.strategyzer.com/app. Accessed 02 Aug 2021
10. Steffen, B.: Living canvas. In: Proceedings, Part II, Leveraging Applications of Formal Methods, Verification and Validation. Specialized Techniques and Applications: 6th International Symposium, I SoLA 2014, Imperial, Corfu, Greece, 8–11 October 2014, pp. 634–635. Springer (2014)
11. Avdiji, H., Elikan, D.A., Missonier, S., Pigneur, Y.: Designing tools for collectively solving ill-structured problems. In: Proceedings of the 51st Hawaii International Conference on System Sciences (2018)
12. Avdiji, H., Elikan, D., Missonier, S., Pigneur, Y.: A design theory for visual inquiry tools. J. Assoc. Inf. Syst. **21**, 3 (2020)
13. Morana, S., et al.: Research prototype: the design canvas in MyDesignProcess. In: Proceedings of the 13th International Conference on Design Science Research in Information Systems and Technology (2018)
14. Schoormann, T., Behrens, D., Fellmann, M., Knackstedt, R.: On your mark, ready, search: a framework for structuring literature search strategies in information systems. In: Proceedings of the 16th International Conference on Wirtschaftsinformatik (2021)
15. Poeppelbuss, J., Lubarski, A.: Modularity Canvas-A framework for visualizing potentials of Service Modularity (2019)
16. Elikan, D.A., Pigneur, Y.: A visual inquiry tool for brand identity. In: Proceedings of the 52nd Hawaii International Conference on System Sciences (2019)
17. Osterwalder, A.: The Business Model Ontology: A Proposition in a Design Science Approach (2004)
18. Osterwalder, A., Pigneur, Y.: Business Model Generation: A Handbook for Visionaries, Game Changers, and Challengers. Wiley, Hoboken (2013)
19. Chandra Kruse, L., Nickerson, J.: Portraying design essence. In: Proceedings of the 51st Hawaii International Conference on System Sciences, pp. 4433–4442 (2018)
20. Thoring, K., Mueller, R., Badke-Schaub, P.: Exploring the design space of innovation canvases. In: Academy for Design Innovation Management Conference (ADIM) (2019)

21. Strategyzer training. https://www.strategyzer.com/training/virtual-masterclass-testing-business-ideas. Accessed 02 Aug 2021
22. Canvanizer. https://canvanizer.com. Accessed 02 Aug 2021
23. Steffen, B., Boßelmann, S.: GOLD: global organization alignment and decision - towards the hierarchical integration of heterogeneous business models. In: Margaria, T., Steffen, B. (eds.) ISoLA 2018. LNCS, vol. 11247, pp. 504–527. Springer, Cham (2018). https://doi.org/10.1007/978-3-030-03427-6_37
24. March, J.G., Shapira, Z.: Managerial perspectives on risk and risk taking. Manage. Sci. **33**, 1404–1418 (1987)
25. ISO: ISO 31000 Risk Management (n.d.). https://www.iso.org/iso-31000-risk-management.html. Accessed 05 July 2021
26. Shapira, Z.: Risk Taking: A Managerial Perspective. Russell Sage Foundation (1995)
27. Hampton, J.: Fundamentals of Enterprise Risk Management: How Top Companies Assess Risk, Manage Exposure, and Seize Opportunity. AMACOM (2014)
28. Hevner, A.R.: A three cycle view of design science research. Scand. J. Inf. Syst. © Scand. J. Inf. Syst. **19**, 87–92 (2007)
29. Ørngreen, R., Levinsen, K.: Workshops as a research methodology. Electron. J. E-learning. **15**, 70–81 (2017)
30. Suhr, F.: Apple ist das wertvollste Unternehmen der Welt. https://de.statista.com/infografik/25062/wertvollste-unternehmen-der-welt-nach-marktkapitalisierung/. Accessed 05 Aug 2021
31. Günther, W., Rezazade Mehrizi, M.H., Huysman, M., Feldberg, J.F.M.: Rushing for gold: tensions in creating and appropriating value from big data. In: International Conference on Information Systems 2017 (2017)
32. van Marwyk, K., Treppte, S.: Logistics Study on Digital Business Models (2016)
33. Bauer, I., Wortman, A.: Transport and logistics barometer: 2020 mid-year analysis of M&A deals, joint ventures and strategic alliances in the transport and logistics industry (2020)
34. Kenney, M., Zysman, J.: The rise of the platform economy. Issues Sci. Technol. **32**, 61 (2016)
35. Maruping, L.M., Matook, S.: The evolution of software development orchestration: current state and an agenda for future research (2020)
36. Ehring, G.: Die neuen Klimaziele für Deutschland (2021). https://www.deutschlandfunk.de/auf-dem-weg-zur-klimaneutralitaet-die-neuen-klimaziele-fuer.2897.de.html?dram:article_id=496894%3E
37. Gross, F., Landman, W.A., Balz, M., Sun, D.: Robust aim point strategy for dynamic solar tower plant operation. In: AIP Conference Proceedings, p. 30018 (2020)
38. Steffen, B., Möller, F., Nowak, L.: Transformer(s) of the logistics industry - enabling logistics companies to excel with digital platforms. In: Proceedings of the 55th Hawaii International Conference on System Sciences (2022, to appear)
39. Eppinger, E., Halecker, B., Hölzle, K., Kamprath, M. (eds.): Dienstleistungspotenziale und Geschäftsmodelle in der Personalisierten Medizin. Springer, Wiesbaden (2015). https://doi.org/10.1007/978-3-658-08403-5
40. Boßelmann, S., Margaria, T.: Domain-specific business modeling with the business model developer. In: Margaria, T., Steffen, B. (eds.) ISoLA 2014. LNCS, vol. 8803, pp. 545–560. Springer, Heidelberg (2014). https://doi.org/10.1007/978-3-662-45231-8_45
41. Naujokat, S., Lybecait, M., Kopetzki, D., Steffen, B.: CINCO: a simplicity-driven approach to full generation of domain-specific graphical modeling tools. Int. J. Softw. Tools Technol. Transfer **20**(3), 327–354 (2017). https://doi.org/10.1007/s10009-017-0453-6
42. Boßelmann, S., Margaria, T.: Guided business modeling and analysis for business professionals. In: Pfannstiel, M.A., Rasche, C. (eds.) Service Business Model Innovation in Healthcare and Hospital Management, pp. 195–211. Springer, Cham (2017). https://doi.org/10.1007/978-3-319-46412-1_11

43. Margaria-Steffen, T., Boßelmann, S., Wickert, A.: Der Business Model Developer – Entwicklung eines Tools zur Erstellung und Analyse von Geschäftsmodellen. In: Eppinger, E., Halecker, B., Hölzle, K., Kamprath, M. (eds.) Dienstleistungspotenziale und Geschäftsmodelle in der Personalisierten Medizin, pp. 95–115. Springer, Wiesbaden (2015). https://doi.org/10.1007/978-3-658-08403-5_4
44. Boßelmann, S., et al.: DIME: a programming-less modeling environment for web applications. In: Margaria, T., Steffen, B. (eds.) ISoLA 2016. LNCS, vol. 9953, pp. 809–832. Springer, Cham (2016). https://doi.org/10.1007/978-3-319-47169-3_60
45. Steffen, B., Boßelmann, S., Hessenkämper, A.: Effective and efficient customization through lean trans-departmental configuration. In: Margaria, T., Steffen, B. (eds.) ISoLA 2016. LNCS, vol. 9953, pp. 757–773. Springer, Cham (2016). https://doi.org/10.1007/978-3-319-47169-3_57
46. Hessenkämper, A., Steffen, B., Boßelmann, S.: Global communication infrastructure: towards standardization of customized projects via profile matching. In: Lamprecht, A.-L. (ed.) ISoLA 2012/2014. CCIS, vol. 683, pp. 83–96. Springer, Cham (2016). https://doi.org/10.1007/978-3-319-51641-7_5

Use Cases for Simulation in the Development of Automated Driving Systems

Hardi Hungar(✉)

Institute of Transportation Systems, German Aerospace Center, Lilienthalplatz 7, 38108 Brunswick, Germany
hardi.hungar@dlr.de

Abstract. Developing an automated driving system (ADS) is difficult, because a large, heterogeneous set of traffic situations has to be handled by the system. At present, data collection does not provide the means to capture them sufficiently comprehensive. And real-world testing is not feasible in the required amount. So virtual techniques, namely simulation, will play an important role in the development of an ADS, in particular in its verification and validation.

Because such a system is highly safety critical, the development will have to follow at least the process recommendations of the ISO 26262 (or similar directives). This permits to identify activities which can be supported by simulation within the overall development context.

This paper describes three such use cases for simulation in detail. Each use case is presented with its objective, the scope and level of the modeling, and tooling. Further, it is discussed what it takes or would take to realize the use case-what appears to be available and what might be lacking.

The paper thus contributes to an overview of the role virtual testing and exploration techniques might play in the development of ADS. It provides guidelines for practitioners who are faced with the task of selecting the methods to support a complex development process. And it hints at shortcomings of present-day tools, or necessary prerequisites to use those which are available.

Keywords: Simulation · Driving automation · Verification and validation · Safety critical system development

1 Introduction

1.1 Developing an Automated Driving System

The development of an automated driving system (ADS) is a very challenging task whenever the system is intended to operate on today's roads, and not in a very restricted, well controlled environment such as an industrial warehouse.

An example for the difficulties arising in traffic, taken from [1], is sketched in Fig. 1.

This research was partially funded by the German Federal Ministry for Economic Affairs and Energy, Grant No. 19A18017 B (SET Level 4to5), based on a decision by the Parliament of the Federal Republic of Germany. The responsibility for the content lies with the author.

T. Margaria and B. Steffen (Eds.): ISoLA 2021, LNCS 13036, pp. 117–128, 2021.
https://doi.org/10.1007/978-3-030-89159-6_8

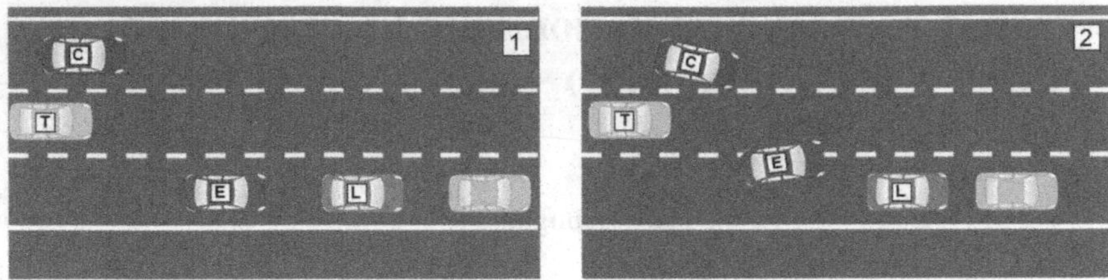

Fig. 1. Conflicting lane changes on a highway (Color figure online)

The scenario has started (not shown in the figure) in a stable situation where **E** (red, ego vehicle, automated) follows **L** (green, leading vehicle) at a constant velocity. **T** (yellow) on the middle lane is going at the same velocity, with a distance which would permit **E** to change safely to the middle lane. The vehicle **C** (blue, conflict vehicle) on the left lane is much faster, but in the beginning was far behind **T**.

The left part of the figure (Scene 1) shows the beginning of the critical part. **L** has decelerated, which might provoke **E** to overtake **L**, to keep its desired velocity. Since **C** was occluded by **T**, the automation might judge overtaking to be a safe maneuver. But once **E** starts its lane change (Scene 2), **C** completes its overtaking of **T** and changes to the middle lane, too.

This example illustrates one of the difficulties of situation assessment for automated vehicle control (and human control as well). And there are technical challenges, for instance reliable detection of road markings and other traffic participants even in the absence of occlusion, to name just one example.

So the ADS will be a complex technical system including a sophisticated control software and many components dealing with physical tasks. Since such a system shall not endanger human life, there are regulations for their development, and those require the safety to be proven convincingly. The most prominent standards to be adhered to are the ISO 26262 [1] and its extension ISO PAS 21448 [2].

These standards include mandatory requirements on the structure of the process, on artefacts to be produced, methods to be used, and verifications and validations to be performed. Figure 1 shows a simplified view of the well-known, standard conformant V process.

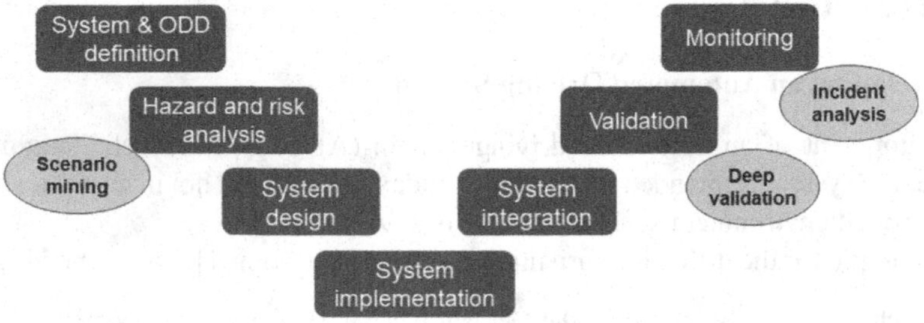

Fig. 2. Use cases for simulation in the life cycle of an ADS

Verification and validation provide the main factual evidence for the safety case. They are laborious activities, and in particular physical tests of subsystems in the laboratory or vehicles on the road are very expensive. It is hoped that using virtual techniques, i.e. simulation, will help to reduce this effort and render the construction of a safety case feasible.

The scenario from Fig. 1 might be the focus of a test in the validation phase. In that phase, the end result of the development is checked whether it meets the initial, user level requirements. A simulation of the scenario would reveal whether the control function correctly refrains from changing to the middle lane when it cannot be sure whether it will stay free long enough.

This might be one set of tests within a *deep validation* simulation campaign. Figure 2 indicates two further usages of simulation, *scenario mining* and *incident analysis.* These three types of potential usage of simulation will be presented in this paper. The project SET Level (Simulation based Engineering and testing of automated vehicles, [4]) considers these among other usages of simulation.

1.2 Simulation and Its Usage

Simulation has two advantages over real world tests: One need not be concerned about accidents, and one can perform a vast number of simulations for the cost of one real-world driving experiment. The downside is, of course, that simulation results are not really reliable, they have limited validity. For profitable use in the development, and in particular in safety arguments, simulation thus will have to be used with care, taking into account uncertainties of the virtual representation.

A use case for simulation is described by

0. Name: A name identifying the use case
1. Process phase: The phase in the (simplified) process from Fig. 2 where simulation is used in the described form
2. Objective: The objective of the use case is part of the output of the process phase where it is applied
3. Implementation: This describes the tools and formats which are to be employed in realizing the use case
4. Modeling scope and detail: Simulation may be performed on a broad range of levels of abstraction. The level is mainly defined by what is modeled to which degree of realism.
5. Validity requirements: A crucial question to be answered when intending to use simulation results is the validity of the outcome of the simulation.
6. Realizability: This item discusses tooling, whether tools are already available or what is missing.

1.3 Scope of the Paper

In this paper, we present three potential use cases for simulation. These range from very early in the system life cycle to the very last stage. These are just examples of how simulation might be used profitably (or might be desired to be profitably useful for). Future extension of this text will add more examples.

2 Simulation: Concepts and Tools

This section explains a few concepts from the field of simulation and its application, and it introduces some terminology used later in the description and discussion of the use cases.

Automated driving system (ADS): We are concerned with the use of simulation to explore properties of automated driving systems or components thereof.

Highly automated driving function (HAD-F): This function is the control component of an ADS. It interprets the traffic situation and takes decisions on the actions of the ADS.

Simulation: A *simulation* consists of the computation of a representation of some sequence of events. In our case, these will be traffic events. And either a complete ADS or components thereof will be part of the simulated objects.

Micro and nano simulation: A micro simulation [3] aims to reproduce the characteristics of the flow of traffic (throughput, congestions etc.). It uses rather abstract behavioral models of individual traffic participants, and it lets these models act in a virtual traffic network. The SUMO system [6] is one prominent example of such a system. For the analysis of the functionality of an ADS, more detail is needed. This is done in nano simulations, where effects like sensor performance come into play. There are several research and commercial nano simulation tools. Both micro and nano denote rather large classes of abstraction levels of simulation. Here, mostly nano simulation is considered.

System under test (SUT): In each use case of simulation, there will be a system which is the object of study, the SUT. In most cases, the simulation shall test this object.

Simulation tool: A *simulation tool* is a software system which performs the simulation. It uses *models* of elements of traffic (traffic participants, technical components of vehicles, etc.) to compute the effects of these elements on the sequence.

Simulation run: A single run of the simulation tool.

Scenario: A scenario (according to [6] is a description of sequences of events in traffic. "Sequence of events" is not limited to discrete sequences, but could also be some continuous development. Depending on the level of abstraction and the focus of attention, a scenario may include external conditions like weather or road conditions.

There are different forms of scenarios.

(Traffic) situation: A situation is a snapshot of a scenario. The result of a simulation run may be seen as a sequence of situations, namely the sequence of states of the simulated traffic elements at the points in time where those were computed by the tool.

Closed concrete scenario (CCS): Such a scenario fixes one sequence of events. It provides for some span of time the states of all traffic participants and other objects (e.g. traffic lights, weather). It may describe a sequence in real life in continuous time, or the result of a simulation run in discrete time. It is "fully defined" regarding a level of abstraction. Details not in the focus need not be included to make the scenario "fully defined". E.g., a traffic agent might be fully defined by just providing its trajectory for some application of simulation.

Open concrete scenario (OCS): In an open concrete scenario, the SUT is not restricted by the scenario description. The scenario is closed by providing the SUT (for instance, an automated vehicle, or a model of the highly automated driving function HAD-F). An OCS may be viewed as a function from SUTs to FCSs.

Logical scenario (LS): A logical scenario defines a set of scenarios in a parametrized form. I.e., certain values or conditions are parameters of the LS. Instantiating the LS by providing values for those parameters yields a concrete scenario. Thus, an LS defines a scenario space. It might be a set of fully defined concrete scenarios (FCLS), or a set of open ones (OLS). An OLS is used to define a task for simulation, where the simulation control may choose which concrete instances of the OLS will actually be simulated.

Evaluation function: One or more evaluation functions may be used to assess simulation runs or sets of simulation runs (sets may result from running a subset of the instances of an LS). In its simplest form, an evaluation function is a real valued function like time-to-collision.

3 Use Cases of Simulation

Here, we introduce and discuss the three use cases of simulation in the life cycle of an ADS indicated in Fig. 1. As said above, these are just three examples of where simulation might be used profitably.

3.1 Critical Scenario Mining

One important development activity is the collection of all system hazards. Often, hazards are classified as being external or internal. External ones origin from the environment of the system, internal ones from system faults or inadequacies. Though many hazards cannot be fully assigned to one of these categories, this distinction is helpful as a first hint in guiding the detection process. For an ADS, many hazards arise from the traffic situations encountered, and how they come to pass. These are mainly external hazards, and the search for them is addressed in this use case.

Use case summary

0. **Name**: Critical scenario mining
1. **Process phase**: Hazard and risk analysis
2. **Objective**: Detect scenario spaces potentially challenging the safety functionality of the ADS
3. **Implementation**: Combination of a microscopic traffic flow simulation and a detailed simulation, the latter detecting criticalities

4. **Modeling** scope and detail: synthetic road network, high level of traffic participant modeling
5. **Validity requirements**: low
6. **Realizability:** adaptation of available tools

Use case details

Process phase: The input to the phase include a description of the ADS and its ODD. This gives a handle to synthesize scenarios covering essential parts of the ODD, and to construct a rough model of the ADS behavior. These are important inputs to the simulation activities.

Objective: The objective is to generate sub-scenarios which may turn out critical for the system to be developed. These scenario (spaces) add to the hazard log which maintained during the development. They shall help to identify useful safety functionalities to be implemented. And they form a basis to construct test catalogues for later phases.

Implementation: This use case can be implemented in several forms. We describe one in some detail. In this instance, mining is performed by the combination of a micro and a nano simulation.

The first is a traffic flow simulation like the SUMO system. The flow simulation takes a road network and specifications of traffic densities, sources and sinks and such. It uses abstract models of traffic agents, whose behavior might be essentially determined by destination, desired velocity, lane and gap control. In that way, a broad spectrum of rather realistic scenarios (FCS) on a high level of abstraction can be generated.

This level of abstraction is too high, too high to permit a proper identification of relevant critical situations. For that, a nano simulation system like openPASS is combined with the micro simulation. It takes over the simulation in a limited part of the road network, e.g. a crossing. Each traffic participant entering the focus area is controlled by it until the participant leaves the area. Upon entering the area, a detailed agent model is initialized and then run. If a preliminary model of the ADS is available, it may be used for some selected participant.

An evaluation function is used to identify interesting runs. For instance those runs where an evaluation function indicating criticality exceeds a particular threshold. The output would then consist of a large set of FCS which might pose a safety challenge for an ADS.

Depending on further elaborations of the basic realization sketched above, one may generate output in a different, perhaps more useful format. For instance, one might generate an FCLS including variations of one particular concrete scenario.

Modeling scope and detail

The micro simulation models a large traffic network with little detail. Roads are modeled with approximated dimensions, their lane structure, and traffic regulations. Traffic participants are controlled by agents which produce stereotypical, largely regulation conformant behavior. Detailed physical modeling of e.g. braking curves is not necessary.

The nano simulation acts on a more concrete level of abstraction. This may still be rather high, if, for example, the focus of attention is the conformance to (basic) traffic regulations of the controlling HAD-F. In this case, detailed modeling of braking or sensor imperfection is not necessary. But one may also model common sources of hazards like occlusion to study other aspects of the automation.

Validity requirements
The requirements on validity in this use case are rather low. False positives, i.e. scenarios wrongly identified as critical, may induce unnecessary work in later phases but do not affect the validity of safety arguments. False negatives are more detrimental. Both micro and nano simulation may contribute to incompleteness of the output. The micro simulation may fail to produce relevant initial situations for the nano part, and the nano simulation may assess some scenarios erroneously. There does not seem to be much hope to make the method complete- One might even argue that there cannot be any complete automatic method in this early development phase. So the scenario mining by simulation will merely complement other approaches. And for providing *additional* information on potential hazards, the validity requirements are not too high.

Realizability: This use case can be realized with available tools. There are already some combinations of micro and nano simulation which do not need much additional machinery to be put to use.

3.2 Deep Validation

The safety case for an ADS will have to include an account of all verification and validation activities which have been performed during its development. *Verification* is performed to assure that one step of the development (e.g., hazard and risk analysis) has achieved its goals and its results are correct. Due to the multitude and intricateness of requirements on an ADS and the complexity of its implementation, verification will likely not provide enough confidence in the safety of the development result. *Validation* assesses whether the outcome meets the intentions, in our case whether the ADS is safe enough. It would be very helpful if some procedure could reliably measure how safe the result will behave. This is what *deep validation* tries to achieve.

As already indicated above, a logical scenario capturing the variants of the events sketched in Fig. 1 might be one of the LS examined in such an activity.

Use case summary

0. **Name**: Deep validation
1. **Process phase**: Validation
2. **Objective**: Asses the risk of the ADS when operating in its ODD
3. **Implementation**: Exploration of a comprehensive scenario catalogue with elaborate evaluation functions
4. **Modeling** scope and detail: full ADS with in various degrees up to highly realistic
5. **Validity** requirements: very high
6. **Realizability:** only partly realizable

Use case details

Process phase: Deep validation is intended for the final development phase of the ADS before the release.

Objective: The objective of deep validation is to provide a reliable estimate of the risk attributable to the ADS in its intended operation. Reliability means that the estimate comes with confidences and a convincing argumentation that these confidences can be relied on. The estimate and its reliability argumentation would then enter a safety case for the ADS. It would complement argumentations which show that the physical implementation of the ADS functionality meets its specifications, in particular, that the simulation models can be constructed to reproduce the specified behavior. If a realization of deep validation meets the objective, it might contribute substantially to fill the methodological gap in safety assessment procedures which motivated the work on the ISO/PAS 21448. Though this standard defines useful activities and goals, it cannot provide practitioners with a guideline to implement them.

Implementation: This use case needs a lot of ingredients for its realization.

1. *A scenario catalogue covering the ODD.* This would consist primarily of open logical scenarios (OLS) as the formal basis for exploring the ODD via simulation. These scenarios would also have to be equipped with occurrence distributions. These are similar in nature to continuous probability distributions, i.e. they define how frequent a subset of the OCS (the concrete test cases making up the space defined by the OLS) occurs. As with continuous probabilities, where any fixed outcome has probability zero, also any OCS has zero occurrence frequency. But a (small) range of OCSs (resulting from a range of parameter values) will have some occurrence frequency, measured in e.g. occurrences per driving hour.
2. *An evaluation function estimating accident severity*: If some test of the ADS in an OCS instantiating a logical scenario from the catalogue results in an accident, the severity of the accident in terms of likelihood of fatalities and injuries need to be assessed, For that, one needs a function providing good estimations.
3. *A faithful modeling of the ADS*: The ADS will have to be modeled rather well to produce reliable virtual representations of the real behavior.
4. *An exploration procedure detecting all potentially harmful OCS of a given logical scenario*: An OLS from the scenario catalogue defines a set of concrete test cases. In most cases, the set of these instances will be far too large to be simulated, even if we assume the parameter space to be discretized. Thus, to find all potential accidents in an OLS, some nontrivial exploration procedure will be necessary. One approach to construct such a procedure is sketched in [8]. This entails several more ingredients needed for the implementation of this use case.

Given ingredients such as described above, this use case can be implemented as follows. The risk to be computed is, essentially, the sum of the accident severity times accident probability over all scenarios of the catalogue. Each logical scenario is explored to find and assess accidents. Given the frequency information for the OLS, the risk can be computed in terms of expected fatalities, resp., injuries per driving hour. Summing over (disjunctive) scenarios gives the overall risk. Inaccuracies in defining the occurrence frequencies, assessing the outcome, and the simulation as a whole would have to be quantified to add the required reliability information.

Modeling scope and detail: Basis for the implementation of this use case are highly exact models of the physical reality-otherwise no reliable estimation of accident probability and severity cannot be computed. But a practical realization of the use case would employ also less detailed simulations to narrow the search space for the exploration by ruling out the vast majority of scenarios which are easily seem to be not critical. Iterating this over several layers of concretization will certainly be helpful to reduce the computation effort.

Validity requirements: The requirements for validity of a simulation are certainly very high. To be able to assess the severity of accidents in real traffic the simulation must be very precise. And typical challenges for automation like sensor inadequacies and malfunctions also call for very good virtual representations. If simulation results are not very reliable, the risk estimation figure will likely not be useful in a safety case, as its confidence interval will be too large.

Realizability: It is very challenging to realize this use cases. All four ingredients listed above will very often be missing for ADS where the ODD includes traffic on public roads. While it is conceivable to capture even complex urban traffic in a catalogue of logical scenarios, faithful frequency information will be hard to come by. A function assessing accident severity for road traffic seems even harder to get. Precise and faithful models of ADS components, a prerequisite for valid simulation results, are yet to be developed. And the same applies to exploration procedures providing the guarantees for accident detection.

So, this use case will likely be realized only for restricted applications of ADS, characterized by: a clearly definable ODD with well understood interaction patterns, few types of accidents, and automation components which can faithfully be modelled. Then, a deep validation by simulation might add strong evidence for the safety of the development result, and complement a thorough though per se not fully convincing verification performed before.

3.3 Incident Analysis

The development of an ADS reaches the most important milestone when the ADS is *released*, when it may be put in operation. The product life cycle does not end, though. After it has been released, the ADS is to be monitored how well it performs in practice. This is the monitoring phase. And any severe incident should be analyzed, to find out whether the design has some essential flaw, something which must or should be improved. In analyzing incidents, simulation may be used profitably.

Use case summary

0. **Name**: Incident analysis
1. **Process phase**: Monitoring
2. **Objective**: Discover the cause of road incidents involving the ADS
3. **Implementation**: replay incidents in simulation
4. **Modeling** scope and detail: full ADS
5. **Validity** requirements: high
6. **Realizability:** adaptations of available tools, some additional functionality needed

Use case details

Process Phase: Monitoring a safety critical system is a mandatory activity. It consists of observing the ADS in operation, recording (in some specified way) critical situations, and analyzing them.

Objective: The objective is, simply, to understand whether some observed unwanted situation is attributable to the automation. This entails a thorough assessment and evaluation of the situation and to understand its causes. In the end, this will be used to see whether the automation should be or must be improved in some way.

Implementation: The input to the simulation comes from the recording functionality installed in the automated vehicle, plus external information (weather, other devices observing the traffic, etc.). From that, a representation of the critical situation and the events leading to it is constructed. This is a fully concrete scenario (FCS), though it may not define all relevant behavior. It is complemented by additional information about internals of the automation like the list of detected objects during the scenario, or even raw sensor data.

Depending on the completeness of the available information and the detailed goals of the analysis, there are different instantiations of this use case.

If the recorded scenario is incomplete and the goal is to reconstruct plausible trajectories of all relevant participants, the FCS can be turned into a form where parameterized agents control the participants during unobserved points in time. Then, agent parameters are sought which plausibly complete the observations.

Given a complete (or a completed) FCS of the events, an important goal is to fill in information about the internal operation of the ADS. This is done by running the scenario with detailed models of the automation components. From that, malfunctions of the ADS can be deduced. These might be wrong results of sensor fusion, or a wrong situation assessment by the HAD-F.

Other lines of analysis, also simulation based, may address more complex questions. These might concern the likelihood of the observed critical situation, whether it is likely to recur, or whether it was a rare event. Another goal might be an assessment of the adequacy of the driving strategy. I.e., answering the question whether the situation could have been avoided if the ADS had acted more cautiously or proactively. For such analyses, it might help to consider variants of the observed FCS. The FCS would be turned into a logical or open logical scenario, and the scenario space would then be explored.

Modeling scope and detail: The most basic simulation consisting of a replay of a complete scenario requires to model the ADS or part of it in its inner workings. The focus of attention (sensor malfunction, situation assessment, …) will define which parts to model to which degree of precision.

The completion of missing trajectories will require usually only simple behavior models.

The estimation the frequency of situations might require somewhat realistic behavior models, incorporating frequency replication capabilities. For the involved ADS, a high level of modeling might be sufficient, provided that effects relevant to the scenario (e.g., occlusion) are taken care of. More or less the same is true for assessment of driving strategies: The strategy itself must be included in the form of a realistic model of the HAD-F, the rest may be abstracted out as long as the relevant effect are retained.

Validity Requirements: The validity requirements are moderate for these use cases. Most of the analyses detailed above will focus on the externally visible behavior, with the exception of inner workings of the ADS when analyzing internal error sources.

Realizability: The different instantiations of incident analysis rely mostly on core functionalities of (nano) simulation tools. These have to be extended by specific functionality. Some have already been implemented, like some trajectory completion procedures. Some cases seem challenging, like matching detailed data of sensor readings adequately in simulation, but overall useful solutions do not seem to be too difficult to come by.

4 Summary

The previous section includes a (short) description and discussion of three use cases for simulation in the development lifecycle of an ADS. Though there are many more, already these three examples show that simulation may play a very important role in the development of automated vehicles. That is, if the techniques and tools meet the sometimes rather high requirements. Validity of the simulation results is one main challenge. The virtual runs should match the events on the roads. And a necessary condition for that are, very often, models of physical components which correctly replicate the function of intricate devices influenced by a multitude of effects.

These and further topics are considered in many research and industrial activities. The ideas presented in this paper were inspired by the author's participation in three projects of the *PEGASUS family*. Besides the PEGASUS project [8] itself, which ended in 2019, these are SET Level [4], concerned with simulation tools and their applications, and VVM (Verification and Validation Methods, [9]), focusing on the proof of safety.

References

1. Hungar, H.: Scenario-based validation of automated driving systems. In: Margaria, T., Steffen, B. (eds.) ISoLA 2018. LNCS, vol. 11246, pp. 449–460. Springer, Cham (2018). https://doi.org/10.1007/978-3-030-03424-5_30

2. International Organization for Standardization: ISO 26262:2018 Road vehicles - Functional safety (2018)
3. International Organization for Standardization: ISO/PAS 21448:2019 Road vehicles - Safety of the intended functionality (2019)
4. SET Level Project. https://setlevel.de/en. Accessed 31 July 2021
5. Treiber, M., Kesting, A.: Traffic Flow Dynamics. Springer, Berlin Heidelberg (2013)
6. Lopez, P.A., et al.: Microscopic traffic simulation using SUMO. In: 21st IEEE Intelligent Transportation Systems Conference (ITSC) (2018)
7. Ulbrich, S., Menzel, T., Reschka, A., Schuldt, F., Maurer, M.: Defining and substantiating the terms scene, situation and scenario for automated driving. IEEE International Annual Conference on Intelligent Transportation Systems (ITSC) (2015)
8. Hungar, H.: A concept of scenario space exploration with criticality coverage guarantees. In: Margaria, T., Steffen, B. (eds.) ISoLA 2020. LNCS, vol. 12478, pp. 293–306. Springer, Cham (2020). https://doi.org/10.1007/978-3-030-61467-6_19
9. PEGASUS Project. https://www.pegasusprojekt.de/. Accessed 15 June 2020
10. VVM Project. https://www.vvm-projekt.de/en/. Accessed 31 July 2021

Simulation-Based Elicitation of Accuracy Requirements for the Environmental Perception of Autonomous Vehicles

Robin Philipp[1](✉), Hedan Qian[1], Lukas Hartjen[1], Fabian Schuldt[1], and Falk Howar[2]

[1] Volkswagen AG, Wolfsburg, Germany
robin.philipp@volkswagen.de
[2] Technische Universität Dortmund, Dortmund, Germany

Abstract. Novel methods for safety validation of autonomous vehicles are needed in order to enable a successful release of self-driving cars to the public. Decomposition of safety validation is one promising strategy for replacing blunt test mileage conducted by real world drives and can be applied in multiple dimensions: shifting to a scenario-based testing process, assuring safety of individual subsystems as well as combining different validation methods. In this paper, we facilitate such a decomposed safety validation strategy by simulation-based elicitation of accuracy requirements for the environmental perception for a given planning function in a defined urban scenario. Our contribution is threefold: a methodology based on exploring perceptual inaccuracy spaces and identifying safety envelopes, perceptual error models to construct such inaccuracy spaces, and an exemplary application that utilizes the proposed methodology in a simulation-based test process. In a case study, we elicit quantitative perception requirements for a prototypical planning function, which has been deployed for real test drives in the city of Hamburg, Germany. We consider requirements regarding tracking and the position of an oncoming vehicle in a concrete scenario. Finally, we conclude our methodology to be useful for a first elicitation of quantifiable and measurable requirements.

Keywords: Autonomous vehicles · Safety validation · Functional decomposition · Environmental perception · Error modeling

1 Introduction

Development of autonomous vehicles has hit a slump in the past two years. This slump (or trough of disillusionment in terms of the Gartner hype cycle) is caused by the so-called approval trap for autonomous vehicles: While the industry has mostly mastered the methods for designing and building autonomous vehicles, reliable mechanisms for ensuring the safety of such systems are still missing. It is generally accepted that the brute-force approach of driving enough mileage for documenting the relatively higher safety of autonomous vehicles (compared

T. Margaria and B. Steffen (Eds.): ISoLA 2021, LNCS 13036, pp. 129–145, 2021.
https://doi.org/10.1007/978-3-030-89159-6_9

to human drivers) is not feasible as it would require an estimated six billion kilometers for every new vehicle or even change in a vehicle's software [19, p. 458]. Since, as of today, no alternative strategies for the safety approval of autonomous vehicles exist, predictions for the availability of level 5 (fully autonomous) [1] vehicles have changed from early 2020s to mid 2030s.

Decomposition of safety validation into many sub-tasks with compositional sub-goals (akin to safety cases but for a vehicles intended functionality) is one promising strategy for replacing blunt mileage by combining validation tasks that together document the safety of an autonomous vehicle. Decomposition can be applied in several dimensions:

Scenarios. Autonomous driving can be decomposed into a sequence of different driving scenarios, varying widely in complexity. Driving on a straight, empty, well-marked section of a motorway in the middle of the day is relatively easy and has a low risk of endangering passengers or other traffic participants. Detection of lanes and following these is sufficient for driving safely. System failure can be mitigated by slowing down and moving over to the shoulder. Making an unprotected left turn across a crowded inner-city intersection at night in the presence of pedestrians and cyclists, on the other hand, is quite complex and has a comparatively high risk of endangering passengers and other traffic participants. It seems only natural that more effort is spent on validating the safety of an autonomous system in complex high-risk situations. Two notable efforts in this direction are the recent SOTIF (safety of the intended functionality) norm [13] that focuses on scenario-based safety validation for autonomous vehicles and the UN's draft specification for an automated lane keeping system [35], which lays out concrete scenarios in which the system has to drive safely.

Validation Methods. Another dimension of decomposition are the methods used for validation: instead of driving on the road, a hierarchy of validation approaches (ranging from simulation, to hardware-in-the-loop, to vehicle-in-the-loop, to augmented reality, to road tests) can be combined to reduce the number of actual miles on the road.

System Architecture. The software and system architecture of autonomous driving systems lends itself to an assume/guarantee-style decomposition of safety validation. Systems consist of three major components: *Sense*, *Plan*, and *Act* (cf. Section 2.1). The three components are based on different methods and principles and typically share lean, well-defined interfaces: *Sense* relies on trained components (e.g., deep neural networks for semantic segmentation and object tracking) and communicates a model of the environment to the *Plan* component. The *Plan* component works on this discrete representation of the environment and uses (non-deterministic) algorithms for generating an optimal future trajectory. The *Act* component is responsible for following this trajectory based on principles and techniques from the field of control theory. Assume/guarantee-style reasoning uses pairs of assumptions and guarantees on components for proving a property P on a system S of sequentially composed components $C_1, \ldots, C_n$ by proving guarantee G_i for component C_i under assumption A_i. Now, if additionally every guarantee G_i implies assumption A_{i+1} and G_n implies P, the sequence of proofs on the components establishes that the system S satisfies the property P under the assumption A_1.

Being based on different principles, different methods are required for verifying correctness and validating the safety of the *Sense*, *Plan*, and *Act* components. While (as of today) we cannot apply the above pattern in a rigid formal approach, we can still use the pattern in manually constructed and validated sequences of arguments. Validation methods for *Act* components already exist: Vehicles already ship with steer-by-wire and brake-by-wire functionality. Safety of these functions is ensured through functional safety approaches (fail operational modes, FMEA[1], FTA[2]). Correctness and performance of the *Plan* component can be validated through scenario-based testing (cf. SOTIF norm [13]). Validating the correctness of *Sense* components is a particular challenge since severity of perception errors is often not diagnosable without considering situational context and error compensation capabilities of the subsequent *Plan* component, which makes it difficult to specify general safety requirements. Correctness of trained models that are frequently included in *Sense* components is a topic of active research (cf. works on robustness, adversarial attacks, etc.).

Effective decomposition strategies of the validation task in all three of these dimensions (scenarios, simulation/reality, architecture) has to be the topic of future research and standardization efforts. A decomposed system architecture also yields the potential of independent development and updating processes for different components.

In this paper, we address one concrete challenge in this landscape: Identifying required accuracy guarantees for sense components (resp. required accuracy assumptions for plan components). As of today, it is not known if such properties can be established for autonomous vehicles or what their scope would be. The research question we address here, is whether there is a space of acceptable perceptual inaccuracy and whether it can be used for decomposing safety validation based on assume/guarantee-style arguments along the software architecture of the autonomous system in one driving scenario. We define a set of quality criteria (mostly systematic errors and allowed inaccuracy[3]) in the output of the *Sense* component for the scenario of an unprotected left turn in the presence of oncoming traffic and evaluate if guarantees on these aspects are useful as assumptions for the validation of the *Plan* component. Algorithmically, we use a sequence of closed-loop simulations of a given *Plan* component (developed as a prototype at Volkswagen Group and successfully deployed in the city of Hamburg, Germany in 2019[4]) in an urban scenario while iteratively degrading accuracy of the *Sense* component by injecting errors corresponding to defined quality criteria. By evaluating the performance of the driving task, we identify safe regions for quality aspects that can serve as assumptions on required quality of the *Sense*

[1] Failure Mode Effect Analysis.

[2] Fault Tree Analysis.

[3] In this work we follow the definition of *accuracy* given by ISO 5725-1 [12].

[4] Volkswagen AG, 04.2019 www.volkswagenag.com/en/news/stories/2019/04/laser-radar-ultrasound-autonomous-driving-in-hamburg.html.

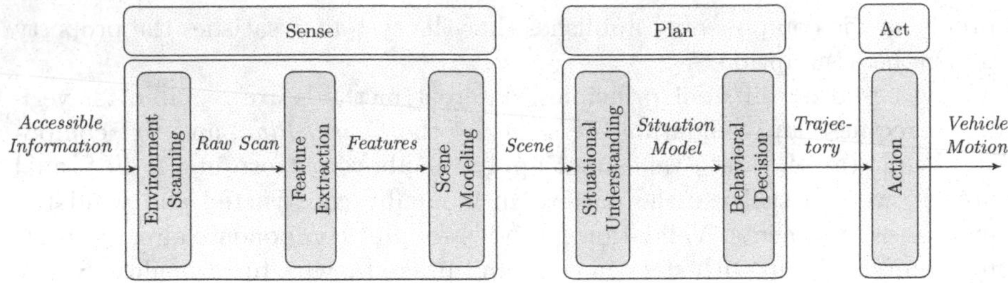

Fig. 1. Functional decomposition of autonomous vehicles [23]

component. Putting it blandly, we take a system metric (no collisions) and quantify its sensitivity towards errors at the interface between *Sense* and *Plan*. Our contribution is threefold:

1. We define concrete dimensions of inaccuracy regarding perceived traffic participants and enable their analysis by introducing exemplary error models.
2. We use simulation-based testing with error injection for the elicitation of accuracy requirements on the *Sense* component by testing a given *Plan* component in an autonomous driving software stack.
3. We show that such requirements and safe levels of inaccuracy can be identified for an urban driving scenario for the two types of investigated inaccuracies.

Outline. The remainder of the paper is structured as follows. Section 2 reiterates the decomposition of system architecture and decomposition into scenarios by discussing an exemplary urban scenario and its particular challenges. Section 3 presents our setup for simulation-based testing with injection of perceptual errors at a high level. Section 4 describes perceptual hazards and corresponding error models. These error models are utilized in Sect. 5 for eliciting quantitative requirements in the considered urban driving scenario. Finally, Sect. 6 discusses related work before Sect. 7 presents our conclusions and discusses future work.

2 Preliminaries

We will briefly detail the functional architecture that is commonly used in autonomous driving software stacks and the urban driving scenario addressed in this work.

2.1 Functional Decomposition

In order to investigate the interface between environmental perception and planning, we refer to the functional decomposition of autonomous vehicles proposed in past work [23]. The autonomous vehicle is decomposed into *Sense*, *Plan* and *Act* and then further refined into *Environment Scanning*, *Feature Extraction*,

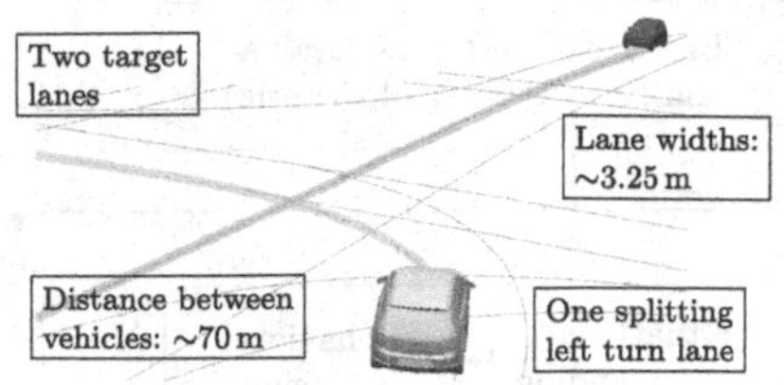

Fig. 2. Unprotected left turn scenario

Object Conceptualization		
Attribute	Unit	Description
x, y	[m]	Position
Ψ	[rad]	Yaw
v_x, v_y	$[m/s]$	Velocity
a_x, a_y	$[m/s^2]$	Acceleration
l, w	$[m]$	Length, Width
c		Classification

Fig. 3. Object attributes

Scene Modeling, *Situational Understanding*, *Behavioral Decision* and *Action* (see Fig. 1). *Plan* takes a conceptualization of the environment as input.

Since we are interested in requirements towards the *Sense* component based on the subsequent *Plan* component, we investigate what information is delivered to the *Plan* component by the *Sense* component. When composing a system and analyzing this interface towards requirements, there are in general two ways on how the system assembly can be approached: either for a given *Sense* component, deduce how robust the subsequent *Plan* component needs to be or for a given *Plan* component define how accurate the output from the *Sense* component needs to be. The focus of this contribution is the latter one. This can also be seen as a combination of assumptions and corresponding promises between these two components which is a common approach in the verification domain called assume-guarantee reasoning and also utilized in the field of contract-based system design [10,26].

The *Sense* component is decomposed into *Environment Scanning*, *Feature Extraction* and *Scene Modeling*. *Environment Scanning* is implemented as a combination of sensors and data processing and therefore consists of hardware-software systems. Environmental conditions or physical effects can cause disturbances while capturing the reality (e.g. glare of the sun) and influence the generated model of the environment (cf. environmental uncertainty [6]). An additional challenge is the association of extracted features when fusing data by multiple sensors in the *Feature Extraction* and *Scene Modeling* components.

The *Plan* component is decomposed to *Situational Understanding* and *Behavioral Decision* and can be regarded as an optimization problem with the goal of finding the trajectory with the least costs. This can be formulated as a mathematical problem and be approached with software. Especially in the aircraft domain, verification of *Plan* components as part of aircraft collision avoidance systems has been researched [14,16,32]. Recently, efforts have been made towards formal models for *Plan* components of autonomous vehicles [2,18,28].

2.2 Unprotected Left Turn Scenario

We investigate an exemplary scenario which is illustrated in Fig. 2. The simulated scenario comprises an unprotected left turn maneuver of the ego vehicle with one oncoming passenger car at a real intersection between *Jungiusstraße* and *Gorch-Fock-Wall* in the city of Hamburg, Germany. With the oncoming

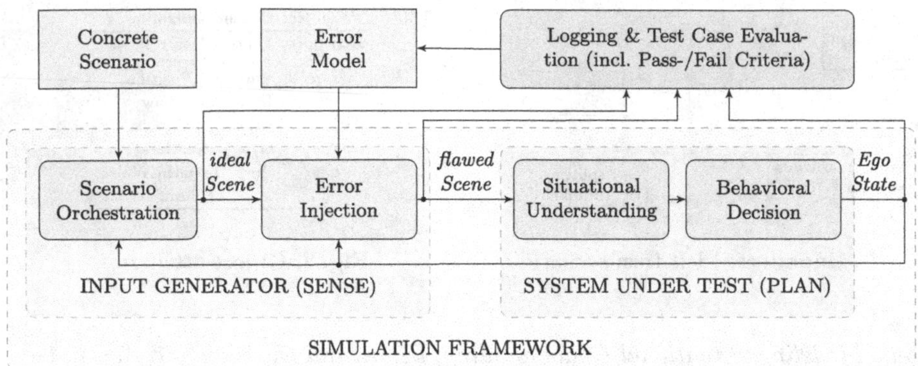

Fig. 4. Conceptual test design for the interface between *Sense* and *Plan*: Output of the *Sense* component is synthetically generated based on a concrete scenario and subsequently flawed to investigate the reaction of the *Plan* component

vehicle maintaining a velocity of $50\,\mathrm{km\,h^{-1}}$, the ego vehicle arrives right at the time when it needs to decide whether to turn in front of the oncoming vehicle or wait for it to pass. Making that decision requires a proper understanding of the scene and thereby an accurate perception. That encompasses an early and accurate detection of the oncoming vehicle. Position and velocity are both essential attributes for predicting the future trajectory and estimating the time of arrival. The object's width in combination with its position are crucial for estimating how far the ego vehicle can already pull into the intersection. The object conceptualization as part of the interface between *Sense* and *Plan* components of our system under test is specified in Fig. 3.

3 Simulation-Based Testing with Error Injection

The architecture of the used test setup is shown in Fig. 4: Components in the top row drive the exploration of variants of a scenario (varying errors and recording outcomes). Components in the lower row constitute the test harness (simulation framework and augmented *Sense* component) and the system under test (the *Plan* component).

Our intention is to investigate the response of the *Plan* component to errors in the perceived scene. Since the *Plan* component comprises multiple software modules and the input coming from the *Sense* component is generated and manipulated synthetically, we analyze the *Plan* component in a closed-loop simulation framework. The scene that is given to the *Plan* component is generated by simulating the *Sense* component and augmenting its output with errors. This comprises generating the scene based on a concrete scenario specification including traffic participant behavior and infrastructure elements as well as transforming the ideal scene into a flawed scene by injecting errors. To give an example, we could perturb the velocity of a distant oncoming vehicle to be perceived as being $40\,\mathrm{km\,h^{-1}}$ while the vehicle actually drives at a speed of $50\,\mathrm{km\,h^{-1}}$.

We quantify the behavior of the ego vehicle based on the ideal scene, the flawed scene the ego vehicle was aware of regarding its environment, and the states of the ego vehicle over time: By defining pass and fail criteria, the evaluation component can be used to assess whether a test case has passed or failed. Possible pass and fail criteria check for real collisions or unsafe distances. Due to the fact that we investigate iteratively worsening hazards, the results of the executed test cases will be taken into consideration by the error injection component for driving the variation of the scenario. When e.g. an inaccurate measurement regarding the oncoming vehicle's velocity with a deviation of $\Delta v = 10\,\mathrm{km\,h^{-1}}$ does not result in a failed test case, a greater inaccuracy is examined in the next simulation. The evaluation component logs the entire history of all simulations. This enables the use of an exit condition, e.g. when a threshold has been found or a defined parameter range has been explored in sufficient detail.

To utilize the proposed test setup and model iteratively worsening errors, a strategy for exploring of perceptual inaccuracy spaces is needed, especially when combining multiple types of inaccuracies. For this work we consider a multidimensional space of inaccuracies regarding a perceived object where each dimension describes a specific inaccuracy and therefore error (e.g. position, velocity, etc.) and use different approaches for sampling this space (grid-based and exploration around the origin) in different experiments.

4 Modeling Perceptual Inaccuracy and Errors

We identify multiple types of hazards and perceptual errors as a basis for error injection.

4.1 Perceptual Hazards

True Positive Inaccuracy. Surrounding traffic participants are often conceptualized as bounding box objects with attributes. These attributes can either be metric[5] variables (e.g. position, velocity) or categorical[6] variables (e.g. classification, light status). While the magnitude of an error regarding metric attributes can be calculated by looking at the difference between the true value and the measured value, measurements of categorical attributes can only either be true or false. Especially for the classification of other traffic participants, some misclassifications objectively seem worse, there is no way to assess the objective magnitude of the error without transforming the classification attribute to either an interval or ratio scale. That can e.g. be done by establishing similarity measures between two given classifications.

Field of View Delimiting. The field of view of an autonomous vehicle is made up out of the detection areas of the different sensors utilized. Traffic participants that are not within the range of the field of view can therefore not be perceived.

[5] Metric refers to a variable defined on either an interval or ratio scale.

[6] Categorical refers to a variable defined on either a nominal or ordinal scale.

Moreover, environmental conditions like sun glare, rainfall or occlusions by other traffic participants can temporarily limit the field of view. The field of view that is required by an autonomous vehicle moving in an operational design domain (ODD) is conditioned by the occurring infrastructure and surrounding traffic participant behavior. While highly automated driving on the highway especially necessitates perceiving objects in the far distance longitudinally, urban scenarios require a more uniform surround view due to cross traffic. Hence, eliciting the required field of view in a concrete ODD is not a trivial task. By systematically delimiting an ideal field of view, safety-critical areas can potentially be deduced. Delimiting the field of view can e.g. be implemented by defining a maximum range, specific opening angles or by individually defining sensor detection areas that are subsequently aggregated.

Object Track Instability. When perceiving traffic participants it is not only important to capture them accurately in a scene, but to also track them over the course of scenes. Ideally, as long as a traffic participant is in immediate range of the autonomous vehicle, the corresponding object track should not cease to exist. Although that can happen due to faults like extensive computation time for the association or occlusion by other traffic participants. Dealing with unstable object tracks is usually addressed by the *Situational Understanding* within the *Plan* component.

Object Track Decay/Multiple Track. Ideally, one traffic participant is conceptualized with one consistent track. However, when dealing with larger traffic participants such as busses, it can happen that their bounding box decays into multiple smaller ones. While these bounding boxes might still occupy around the same space as the previous larger one, this hazard results in more separate objects for the *Situational Understanding* to deal with. One traffic participant that is conceptualized by more than one object track is defined as *Multiple Track* by Brahmi et al. [3].

Multiple Object. In contrast to the hazard *Multiple Track*, it can also happen that multiple traffic participants are captured as one object track, e.g. when being close to each other. Such multiple object tracks are likely to decay into object tracks when they start moving resulting in the fact that these multiple object tracks are of special relevance to the *Situational Understanding* component. This hazard is defined as *Multiple Object* by Brahmi et al. [3].

4.2 Error Models

True Positive Inaccuracy: Systematic Object Position Shift. The position accuracy of the oncoming object in the investigated scenario is essential for the *Plan* component. The perceived longitudinal position is crucial for estimating the time until the oncoming vehicle arrives at the potential conflict zone. The perceived lateral position can directly influence how far the ego vehicle already pulls into the junction.

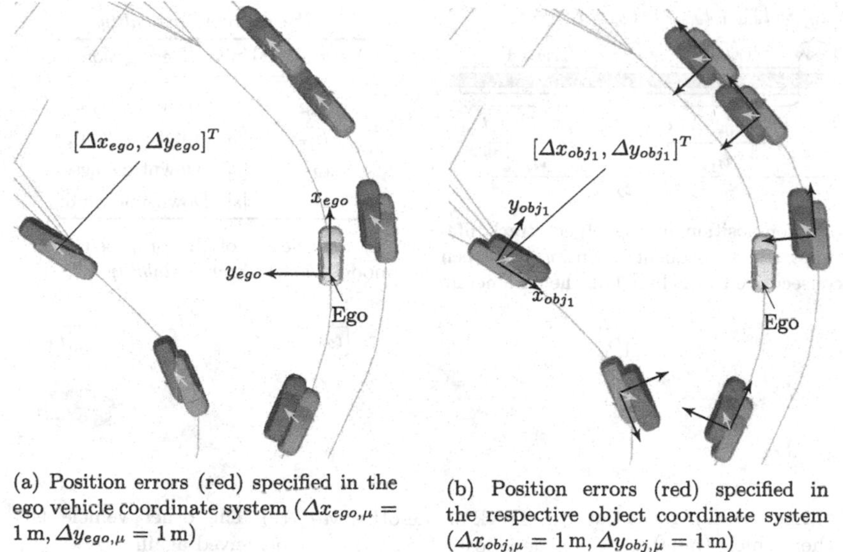

(a) Position errors (red) specified in the ego vehicle coordinate system ($\Delta x_{ego,\mu} = 1\,\text{m}, \Delta y_{ego,\mu} = 1\,\text{m}$)

(b) Position errors (red) specified in the respective object coordinate system ($\Delta x_{obj,\mu} = 1\,\text{m}, \Delta y_{obj,\mu} = 1\,\text{m}$)

Fig. 5. Error model *True Positive Inaccuracy: Object Position*

The object's position is a metric attribute defined in a Cartesian coordinate system consisting of two components. While an object's position is usually captured in an ego-centric coordinate system, it may also be of interest to not directly manipulate the ego-relative position components, but to define position shifts based on an object-centric coordinate system. The object-centric coordinate system resembles the ego-centric coordinate system rotated by the object's relative heading Ψ to the ego. In that way it is possible to separate an object's position shift distinctly into a longitudinal and lateral shift. Both coordinate systems and exemplary shifts in these are visualized in Fig. 5.

Our proposed error model for the object position covers both systematic errors μ and random errors σ and offers the possibility to define the deviation either in the ego-relative or object-relative coordinate system. Thus, the perceived position shift of the object $[\Delta x, \Delta y]^T$ can comprise a shift specified in the ego-coordinate system $[\Delta x_{ego}, \Delta y_{ego}]^T$ and a shift specified in the object-coordinate system $[\Delta x_{obj}, \Delta y_{obj}]^T$. It is defined as follows:

$$\begin{bmatrix}\Delta x\\ \Delta y\end{bmatrix} = \begin{bmatrix}\Delta x_{ego}\\ \Delta y_{ego}\end{bmatrix} + \begin{bmatrix}cos(\Psi) & -sin(\Psi)\\ sin(\Psi) & cos(\Psi)\end{bmatrix} \begin{bmatrix}\Delta x_{obj}\\ \Delta y_{obj}\end{bmatrix} \tag{1}$$

$$\begin{bmatrix}\Delta x_{ego}\\ \Delta y_{ego}\end{bmatrix} = \begin{bmatrix}\Delta x_{ego,\mu} + \Delta x_{ego,\sigma}\\ \Delta y_{ego,\mu} + \Delta y_{ego,\sigma}\end{bmatrix}, \qquad \begin{bmatrix}\Delta x_{obj}\\ \Delta y_{obj}\end{bmatrix} = \begin{bmatrix}\Delta x_{obj,\mu} + \Delta x_{obj,\sigma}\\ \Delta y_{obj,\mu} + \Delta y_{obj,\sigma}\end{bmatrix}. \tag{2}$$

Object Track Instability: Lifetime and Downtime. When dealing with object tracking in general, it is of interest how stable the object tracks generated by the perception have to be. Regarding a single object in one scene there either is an object track and thus the object is perceived or there is no object

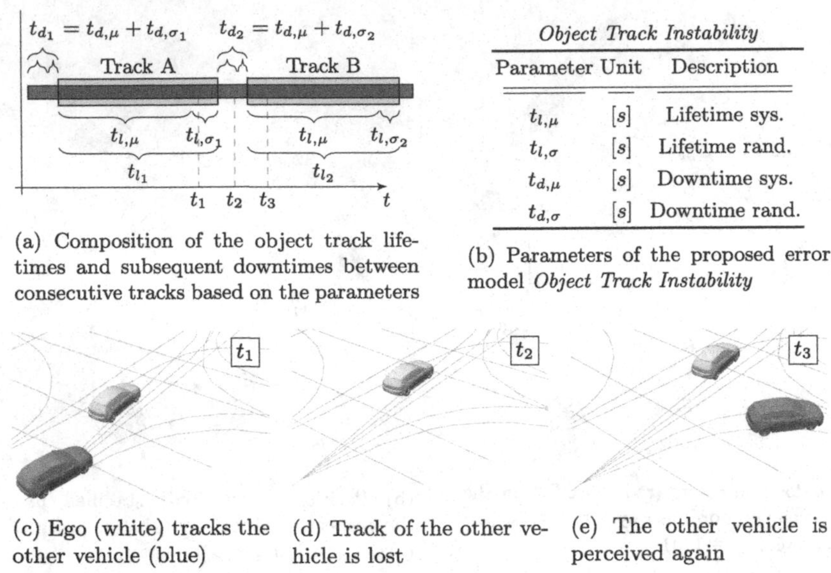

(a) Composition of the object track lifetimes and subsequent downtimes between consecutive tracks based on the parameters

Object Track Instability

Parameter	Unit	Description
$t_{l,\mu}$	$[s]$	Lifetime sys.
$t_{l,\sigma}$	$[s]$	Lifetime rand.
$t_{d,\mu}$	$[s]$	Downtime sys.
$t_{d,\sigma}$	$[s]$	Downtime rand.

(b) Parameters of the proposed error model *Object Track Instability*

(c) Ego (white) tracks the other vehicle (blue)

(d) Track of the other vehicle is lost

(e) The other vehicle is perceived again

Fig. 6. Error model *Object Track Instability: Lifetime and Downtime*

track and the object is therefore not perceived. Cumulating these over time and associating object tracks of two consecutive timestamps with one another allows the subsequent planning to consider past behavior of a perceived object. The two main aspects of object tracks we are therefore interested in is loss of an object track as well as the time gap until there is a new track for the same object.

The proposed error model (cf. Figure 6) varies both the lifetime of object tracks and the downtime between two consecutive object tracks for the same object. Additionally, a new object track also comes with a new ID. Therefore, it is not trivial for the system under test to associate the new object track with the old one and by that deduct the past behavior of the traffic participant. Both the lifetime and the downtime consist of a systematic component μ and a random component σ. While the systematic component is defined by a constant time, the random component is generated by a folded random distribution. Consequently, since the folded random distribution always produces a positive value, the systematic component also equals the minimum lifetime (or minimum downtime respectively). The subsequent equations for object track lifetimes t_l and downtimes t_d are therefore defined as follows:

$$t_l = t_{l,\mu} + t_{l,\sigma}, \qquad t_d = t_{d,\mu} + t_{d,\sigma}. \tag{3}$$

5 Evaluation

We have used the proposed test setup for analyzing accuracy requirements in two series of experiments based on the unprotected left turn scenario. This section presents results from these experiments before discussing generalizablity and threats to validity.

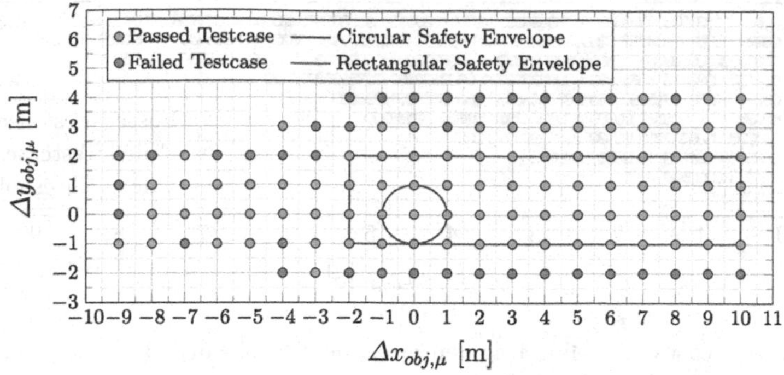

Fig. 7. Test cases and resulting safety envelopes regarding position inaccuracy

5.1 True Positive Inaccuracy: Systematic Object Position Shift

For an initial application of the proposed error model, we investigate the effect of a systematic object shift based on the object coordinate system. This means that the two parameters $\Delta x_{obj,\mu}$ and $\Delta y_{obj,\mu}$ are being utilized during the test process. We specify an initial step size of 1 m for both parameters and the range to be $[-10\,\text{m}, 10\,\text{m}] \times [-10\,\text{m}, 10\,\text{m}]$. Collisions of the ego vehicle with the ground truth object bounding box are considered for evaluating whether a test case is declared as either passed or failed. Also, one test case is repeated several times to cope with potentially occurring non-deterministic effects caused by the prototypical system under test or the experimental simulation framework. When only one of the test case repetitions is declared as failed, the whole test case is declared as failed. The results of the test process comprising a perceived systematic object position shift are visualized in Fig. 7.

There is a higher tolerance for an inaccurate longitudinal position while smaller errors regarding the lateral position component already propagate up to a failure earlier. This effect seems plausible since the lateral position of the oncoming vehicle is relevant to how far the ego vehicle can enter the intersection while it waits for the oncoming vehicle to pass (see Fig. 2). Even longitudinal position errors of higher severity do not necessarily result in a failure. The higher tolerance for longitudinal position errors can be explained by the cautious behavior of the ego vehicle. This behavior is observable by the time needed to accelerate again and finish the left turn maneuver after braking for the inaccurately perceived oncoming vehicle. Moreover, there is also a higher tolerance for a positive longitudinal shift than for a negative one. This does also seem plausible due to negative longitudinal shifts tricking the ego vehicle into overestimating the time gap between itself and the oncoming vehicle. These negative longitudinal shifts can therefore be the reason for the ego vehicle to decide for a quick left turn before the apparent arrival of the oncoming vehicle. Based on the resulting circular safety envelope, we state the following observation:

Requirement 1. *The tested Plan component requires a Sense component that reports an oncoming vehicle's position with less than 1 m inaccuracy in the simulated scenario of an unprotected left turn in an urban setting.*

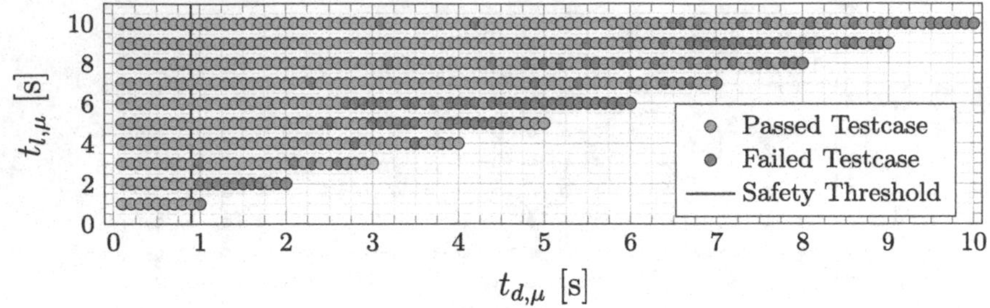

Fig. 8. Test cases regarding fragmentary object tracks utilizing $t_{l,\mu}$ and $t_{d,\mu}$

5.2 Object Track Instability: Lifetime and Downtime

The proposed error model can be utilized to investigate two aspects for a defined scenario. Firstly, whether the system under test (SUT) is sensitive to changing object IDs caused by insufficient tracking consistency. Secondly, when exactly a loss of track and the subsequent misdetection leads to a failure.

A first test process focuses on the former, considering a systematic lifetime of object tracks with no downtime in between ($t_{l,\mu} \in [1\,\text{s}, 10\,\text{s}]$ with a step size of $1\,\text{s}, t_d = 0\,\text{s}$). Each concrete test case is repeated several times.

However, none of the executed test case repetitions fail. This shows that even a frequently changing object ID ($t_{l,\mu} = 1\,\text{s}$) of the oncoming vehicle is not leading to a collision. Therefore, we consider a varying lifetime as well as a downtime between consecutive tracks in a subsequent test process.

For a first analysis of the SUTs response regarding a fragmentary object track, a test process with parameters $t_{d,\mu} \in [0\,\text{s}, 10\,\text{s}]$ (step size 0.1 s) and $t_{l,\mu} \in [1\,\text{s}, 10\,\text{s}]$ (step size 1 s) under the condition $t_{d,\mu} < t_{l,\mu}$ is conducted. This results in 550 concrete test cases (cf. Figure 8). While there is still no obvious influence coming from frequently changing object IDs, collisions occur first for downtimes of 1 s when track lifetimes are set to 1 s, 2 s and 3 s.

Not detecting the oncoming vehicle for 1 s means that the SUT is not perceiving it for nearly 14 m of its covered distance. Longer downtimes become acceptable with increased lifetimes. This seems plausible, since the object track lifetime $t_{l,\mu}$ serves as an indirect trigger for the track loss. Losing track of the oncoming vehicle is less critical, when it is either at a farther distance or has already crossed the intersection. This emphasizes, that timing of such errors in conjunction with the concrete scenario plays an important role regarding acceptable track instability. Based on the results, we state the following observation regarding object track instability in the investigated scenario:

Requirement 2. *The tested Plan component requires a Sense component to never miss an oncoming vehicle for more than 0.9 s during the simulated unprotected left turn maneuver in an urban setting.*

5.3 Discussion

Let us briefly discuss the obtained results, the generalizability of the approach and threats to vality of the presented test setup and results.

Obtained Assumptions/Guarantees. We conjecture that the investigated scenario is adequate for identifying meaningful requirements regarding inaccuracy of the lateral position since an unprotected left turn scenario can comprise a relatively small lateral distance between the ego-vehicle and the oncoming vehicle (even when executed perfectly safely). For the elicitation of meaningful requirements regarding the acceptable longitudinal position shift, another scenario might have been more suitable, e.g. following a fast leading vehicle while keeping a safe distance. As emphasized earlier, timing is an important factor regarding loss of an object track. The decisive concrete test cases for accepted time gaps between two object tracks comprised the situation that the SUT was not able to detect the oncoming vehicle right before it entered the crossing area. While this can already be seen as critical, it cannot be ruled out that there exists a shorter downtime in the scenario linked to another situation that would subsequently lead to a stricter requirement. For the automatic identification of critical situations including such errors, reward functions [20] or optimization [5] could be considered as strategies for further exploring the inaccuracy space.

Generalizability. Our initial application shows that the proposed technique can be utilized for identifying requirements on a *Sense* component for a concrete *Plan* component in a concrete driving scenario. By applying the technique to multiple scenarios and by investigating more perceptual hazards, it would certainly be possible to specify initial quantifiable and measurable quality criteria for a *Sense* component which are needed for safety validation—either per scenario or aggregated, e.g., for road types or for an urban setting vs. the motorway. A key question to address will then be the right level of aggregation, trading many, bespoke requirements in individual scenarios for fewer, more stringent requirements covering a range of different scenarios.

In a next step, the identified acceptable errors need to be analyzed together and not isolated from one another to identify potential dependencies. Together with more classes of perceptual errors and hazards, the space to explore grows quickly and it will not be possible to explore it exhaustively. Scalability will hinge on adding other techniques than simulation-based testing: e.g., a theory of combining the effects of errors or a feedback loop with software verification that can actually discharge guarantees and use assumptions in formal proofs. An exemplary verification of requirements for a flight-critical system is conducted by Brat et al. [4].

Validity. The obtained results pertain to one concrete *Sense* component and one concrete *Plan* component and as such can only be understood as a first step.

Concept Validity. As discussed above, many more steps will be required in order to arrive at an actual assume/guarantee-style safety argument for autonomous vehicles. The presented approach seems to suitable for providing sensible initial accuracy requirements.

Internal Validity. Safety validation relying on black-box methods has its limitations due to the fact that there can never be a proof of correctness and only statements about the performance based on expert-knowledge and statistics will be available. What this work has shown, however, is that sensible assumptions/guarantees seem to exist for which safe behavior can be achieved consistently in the presence of perceptual inaccuracies.

External Validity. While we did only analyze one concrete scenario, this scenario (as stated above) allows for relatively small distances between vehicles. To us this indicates that even in scenarios that require precision, requirements can be reliably identified with a quantifiable amount of inaccuracy.

6 Related Work

We first discuss the assessment of *Sense* components in the context of safe *Plan* components, then mention decomposed and structured testing approaches for cyber-physical systems, and lastly touch on the topic of requirement mining.

Sense Assessment for Safe Planning. Stellet et al. [31] point out existing safety validations approaches for automated driving systems which also include a decomposition strategy of combining statistically validated sensing and formally safe planning. They discuss the need to validate sensing towards situations being erroneously considered unsafe and erroneously considered safe, while also stressing that not every perception error must lead to a failure of the overall system. Stahl et al. [29,30] propose an online verification concept for a *Plan* component. Their concept requires that all objects in the scene have to be detected and perceived properly (without any further specification) in order to assure a safe trajectory. Klamann et al. [17] further emphasize the difficulty of defining pass-/fail criteria on component level. Schönemann et al. [27] propose a fault tree-based definition of general safety requirements for cooperative valet parking following the sense-plan-act paradigm. Among other safety requirements, they derive an allowed object position inaccuracy of 7.5 cm. Requirements for object position accuracy are also investigated and quantified in our work, using simulation tests instead of a mathematical derivation. Recently, efforts have been made towards novel metrics for *Sense* components that also consider situation-dependent error severity regarding the subsequent planning [22,36]. While an accurate perception is a prerequisite for safe planning and a safe overall system, general quality criteria which can be assessed to validate a *Sense* component are yet to be defined. In this work, we are not only defining but also quantifying exemplary requirements regarding acceptable inaccuracies of the *Sense* component for a given *Plan* component.

Decomposed and Structured Testing. The increasing complexity of cyber-physical systems as well as enormous parameter spaces for possible test inputs emphasize the need for novel testing methods. Systematic analysis of input stimuli and compositional falsification are recent approaches to meet the challenge of increasing complexity. Fremont et al. [9] perform structured testing to identify scenarios that lead to a failure of a neural network-based aircraft taxiing system by Boeing and subsequently retrain the system to achieve a better performance. Dreossi et al. [7] conduct a compositional falsification of a machine learning-based perception component and an advanced emergency brake system to identify potentially relevant misdetections. Tuncali et al. [33,34] present a framework for test case generation which they utilize to test both a machine learning-based perception component and a collision avoidance controller. They further emphasize the need to not only evaluate *Sense* components isolated but to consider closed-loop behavior of the whole system. While testing strategies of the listed contributions share similarities with our test design, we specifically focus on the performance of a *Plan* component under the influence of synthetically generated perception errors. The contribution that is the closest in spirit to our research is given by Piazzoni et al. [24,25]. While also utilizing simulation and handcrafted perception error models, they propose two test cases incorporating different *Sense* errors, i.e. non-detections, tracking loss and position inaccuracies of perceived objects. However, test case results are not aggregated to elicit acceptable errors. All the error types mentioned above are considered in this work and corresponding requirements are subsequently elicited.

Requirement Mining. As a last direction of research we want to mention requirement mining by falsification utilizing temporal logic. Both Hoxha et al. [11] and Jin et al. [15] explore properties of a given automatic transmission model that is expressed by a set of ordinary differential equations and subsequently elicit requirements regarding input signals. The requirement elicitation approach proposed in our work relies on structured testing rather than mathematical optimization, since the implementation of the *Plan* component under test is not known and therefore analyzed in a black-box manner.

7 Conclusion and Future Work

We have presented an approach for the elicitation of requirements based on closed-loop testing of a given *Plan* component. This comprises the concept of subsequently executing test cases while degrading the perception performance based on consecutive evaluation. For that, we also introduce a non-exhaustive set of perceptual hazards. Our results show that it is possible to elicit measurable and quantifiable initial requirements for the *Sense* component in one investigated scenario. These quality criteria are a first step towards assume/guarantee-style decomposition of system validation at the interface between *Sense* and *Plan*.

Future work should address modeling of further perceptual errors, also in a combined manner and including random errors. Moreover, various different scenarios should be utilized and investigated to further specify the assumption of *Plan* on *Sense*. A systematic way is required to identify categories of relevant traffic participants and areas which need to be perceived in urban traffic and thus should be considered by quality criteria for the *Sense* component. Further examination of suitable quality criteria for the interface between *Sense* and *Plan* components is needed to promote contract-based design. Closely related to that, correct-by-construction approaches [8,21] in the context of autonomous vehicles should also be further researched. Having an understanding of the behavior of *Sense* and *Plan* components in different scenarios and handling of faults and errors will be essential for finally establishing a safety argument.

References

1. SJ3016: Taxonomy and Definitions for Terms Related to Driving Automation Systems for On-Road Motor Vehicles (2018)
2. Bohrer, B., Tan, Y.K., Mitsch, S., Sogokon, A., Platzer, A.: A formal safety net for waypoint-following in ground robots. IEEE RA-L **4**(3), 2910–2917 (2019)
3. Brahmi, M., Siedersberger, K.H., Siegel, A., Maurer, M.: Reference systems for environmental perception: requirements, validation and metric-based evaluation. In: 6. Tagung Fahrerassistenzsysteme (2013)
4. Brat, G., Bushnell, D., Davies, M., Giannakopoulou, D., Howar, F., Kahsai, T.: Verifying the safety of a flight-critical system. In: FM: Formal Methods (2015)
5. Bussler, A., Hartjen, L., Philipp, R., Schuldt, F.: Application of evolutionary algorithms and criticality metrics for the verification and validation of automated driving systems at urban intersections. In: IEEE IV Symposium (2020)
6. Chechik, M., Salay, R., Viger, T., Kokaly, S., Rahimi, M.: Software assurance in an uncertain world. In: Fundamental Approaches to Software Engineering (2019)
7. Dreossi, T., Donzé, A., Seshia, S.A.: Compositional falsification of cyber-physical systems with machine learning components. J. Autom. Reason. **63**, 1031–1053 (2019)
8. Eiras, F., Lahijanian, M., Kwiatkowska, M.: Correct-by-construction advanced driver assistance systems based on a cognitive architecture. In: IEEE CAVS Symposium (2019)
9. Fremont, D.J., Chiu, J., Margineantu, D.D., Osipychev, D., Seshia, S.A.: Formal analysis and redesign of a neural network-based aircraft taxiing system with VerifAI. In: Computer Aided Verification (2020)
10. Guissouma, H., Leiner, S., Sax, E.: Towards design and verification of evolving cyber physical systems using contract-based methodology. In: IEEE ISSE (2019)
11. Hoxha, B., Dokhanchi, A., Fainekos, G.: Mining parametric temporal logic properties in model-based design for cyber-physical systems. In: STTT, vol. 20 (2017)
12. ISO 5725–1:1994: Accuracy (trueness and precision) of measurement methods and results - part 1: General principles and definitions. Standard (1994)
13. ISO/DIS 21448: Road vehicles - Safety of the intended functionality. Standard, International Organization for Standardization (ISO), Geneva, Switzerland (2021)
14. Jeannin, J.B., et al.: A formally verified hybrid system for the next-generation airborne collision avoidance system. In: TACAS (2015)
15. Jin, X., Donze, A., Deshmukh, J.V., Seshia, S.A.: Mining requirements from closed-loop control models. In: IEEE TCAD, vol. 34 (2015)
16. Julian, K.D., Kochenderfer, M.J.: Guaranteeing safety for neural network-based aircraft collision avoidance systems. In: IEEE DASC (2019)
17. Klamann, B., Lippert, M., Amersbach, C., Winner, H.: Defining pass-/fail-criteria for particular tests of automated driving functions. In: IEEE ITSC. IEEE, October 2019. https://doi.org/10.1109/ITSC.2019.8917483

18. Luckcuck, M., Farrell, M., Dennis, L.A., Dixon, C., Fisher, M.: Formal specification and verification of autonomous robotic systems. ACM CSUR **52**(5), 1–41 (2019)
19. Maurer, M., Gerdes, J.C., Lenz, B., Winner, H. (eds.): Autonomes Fahren (2015)
20. Moradi, M., Oakes, B.J., Saraoglu, M., Morozov, A., Janschek, K., Denil, J.: Exploring fault parameter space using reinforcement learning-based fault injection. In: IEEE/IFIP DSN-W (2020)
21. Nilsson, P., et al.: Correct-by-construction adaptive cruise control: two approaches. IEEE Trans. Control Syst. Technol. **24**(4), 1294–1307 (2016)
22. Philion, J., Kar, A., Fidler, S.: Learning to evaluate perception models using planner-centric metrics. In: Proceedings of the IEEE/CVF CVPR (2020)
23. Philipp, R., Schuldt, F., Howar, F.: Functional decomposition of automated driving systems for the classification and evaluation of perceptual threats. 13. Uni-DAS e.V. Workshop Fahrerassistenz und automatisiertes Fahren (2020)
24. Piazzoni, A., Cherian, J., Slavik, M., Dauwels, J.: Modeling perception errors towards robust decision making in autonomous vehicles. In: IJCAI (2020)
25. Piazzoni, A., Cherian, J., Slavik, M., Dauwels, J.: Modeling sensing and perception errors towards robust decision making in autonomous vehicles (2020). https://arxiv.org/abs/2001.11695
26. Sangiovanni-Vincentelli, A., Damm, W., Passerone, R.: Taming dr. frankenstein: contract-based design for cyber-physical systems. Eur. J. Control **18**(3), 217–238 (2012)
27. Schönemann, V., et al.: Fault tree-based derivation of safety requirements for automated driving on the example of cooperative valet parking. In: 26th International Conference on the Enhanced Safety of Vehicles (ESV) (2019)
28. Shalev-Shwartz, S., Shammah, S., Shashua, A.: On a formal model of safe and scalable self-driving cars (2017). https://arxiv.org/abs/1708.06374
29. Stahl, T., Diermeyer, F.: Online verification enabling approval of driving functions–implementation for a planner of an autonomous race vehicle. IEEE Open J. Intell. Transp. Syst. **2**, 97–110 (2021)
30. Stahl, T., Eicher, M., Betz, J., Diermeyer, F.: Online verification concept for autonomous vehicles – illustrative study for a trajectory planning module (2020)
31. Stellet, J.E., Woehrle, M., Brade, T., Poddey, A., Branz, W.: Validation of automated driving - a structured analysis and survey of approaches. In: 13. Uni-DAS e.V. Workshop Fahrerassistenz und automatisiertes Fahren (2020)
32. Tomlin, C., Mitchell, I., Bayen, A., Oishi, M.: Computational techniques for the verification of hybrid systems. Proc. IEEE **91**(7), 986–1001 (2003)
33. Tuncali, C.E., Fainekos, G., Ito, H., Kapinski, J.: Simulation-based adversarial test generation for autonomous vehicles with machine learning components. In: IEEE IV Symposium (2018)
34. Tuncali, C.E., Fainekos, G., Prokhorov, D., Ito, H., Kapinski, J.: Requirements-driven test generation for autonomous vehicles with machine learning components. IEEE Trans. Intell. Veh. **5**, 265–280 (2020)
35. UNECE: Proposal for a new UN Regulation on uniform provisions concerning the approval of vehicles with regards to Automated Lane Keeping System. Tech. rep. (2020). https://undocs.org/ECE/TRANS/WP.29/2020/81
36. Volk, G., Gamerdinger, J., von Bernuth, A., Bringmann, O.: A comprehensive safety metric to evaluate perception in autonomous systems. In: IEEE ITSC (2020)

DSLs and Middleware Platforms in a Model-Driven Development Approach for Secure Predictive Maintenance Systems in Smart Factories

Jobish John[1,3(✉)], Amrita Ghosal[1,4(✉)], Tiziana Margaria[1,2,4(✉)], and Dirk Pesch[1,3(✉)]

[1] CONFIRM, SFI Research Centre for Smart Manufacturing, Limerick, Ireland
[2] Lero, SFI Research Centre for Software, Limerick, Ireland
[3] School of CS and IT, University College Cork, Cork, Ireland
{j.john,d.pesch}@cs.ucc.ie
[4] CSIS, University of Limerick, Limerick, Ireland
{amrita.ghosal,tiziana.margaria}@ul.ie

Abstract. In many industries, traditional automation systems (operating technology) such as PLCs are being replaced with modern, networked ICT-based systems as part of a drive towards the Industrial Internet of Things (IIoT). The intention behind this is to use more cost-effective, open platforms that also integrate better with an organisation's information technology (IT) systems. In order to deal with heterogeneity in these systems, middleware platforms such as EdgeX Foundry, IoTivity, FI-WARE for Internet of Things (IoT) systems are under development that provide integration and try to overcome interoperability issues between devices of different standards. In this paper, we consider the EdgeX Foundry IIoT middleware platform as a transformation engine between field devices and enterprise applications. We also consider security as a critical element in this and discuss how to prevent or mitigate the possibility of several security risks. Here we address secure data access control by introducing a declarative policy layer implementable using Ciphertext-Policy Attribute-Based Encryption (CP-ABE). Finally, we tackle the interoperability challenge at the application layer by connecting EdgeX with DIME, a model-driven/low-code application development platform that provides methods and techniques for systematic integration based on layered Domain-Specific Languages (DSL). Here, EdgeX services are accessed through a Native DSL, and the application logic is designed in the DIME Language DSL, lifting middleware development/configuration to a DSL abstraction level. Through the use of DSLs, this approach covers the integration space domain by domain, technology by technology, and is thus highly generalizable and reusable. We validate our approach with an example IIoT use case in smart manufacturing.

An earlier version of this work was presented at the Irish Manufacturing Council's International Manufacturing Conference (IMC 37) 2021, Athlone, Ireland.

T. Margaria and B. Steffen (Eds.): ISoLA 2021, LNCS 13036, pp. 146–161, 2021.
https://doi.org/10.1007/978-3-030-89159-6_10

Keywords: Predictive maintenance · EdgeX-Foundry · Secured access · Domain-specific languages

1 Introduction

The Industrial Internet of Things (IIoT) enables the transformation of traditional manufacturing systems into highly flexible, scalable and smart interconnected automation systems widely known as Industry 4.0 [1,5,23]. Decentralized decision making through real-time monitoring, using a large number of networked devices form the basis of IIoT [21]. To realize future smart factories, many field devices operating with both wired and wireless communication technologies need to coexist and interoperate seamlessly, which is one of the significant challenges for IIoT adopters.

Extracting meaningful insights from the large volume of data generated by devices poses another significant challenge. It is usually done at two levels, at the on-premise network edge (widely referred to as edge computing) and at the cloud level (cloud computing) [3,21]. With advancements in edge computing, decisions can be taken at the local edge, especially in delay-sensitive situations. Remote monitoring, diagnosis and maintenance of complex equipment/ machines is one of such applications that is widely used in smart manufacturing. Maintenance of assets in a factory is carried out with three different approaches: i) Reactive maintenance (e.g., repair the system once it breaks down), ii) preventive maintenance (e.g., regular checks), and iii) predictive maintenance (e.g., IIoT smart sensing-based solution that predicts and schedules the machine maintenance at the right time) [7]. Predictive maintenance schemes provide the best utilization of assets by minimizing their downtimes.

In this paper we study a predictive maintenance system (PreMS) from a system integration point of view, encompassing heterogeneous system elements involved in an architecturally sound solution that provides reliable interoperability. These elements include IIoT components, middleware, specific application logic needed to build the PreMS solution, and also security aspects. In doing this, we leverage as far as is possible a platform approach instead of bespoke programming or even bespoke code-based integration. A well-designed IIoT platform at the network edge can act as a seamless service-based transformation engine between field devices and enterprise applications. To deal with the field device heterogeneity in a flexible, scalable and secured fashion, industry consortia have been developing several IoT middleware platforms such as EdgeX Foundry [10], IoTivity [22], FI-WARE [22]. To overcome interoperability issues between field devices of different standards we consider the EdgeX Foundry platform as our IIoT middleware of choice at the network edge.

For the solution design and implementation, we adopt the approach proposed in [15], which shows the use of a flexible, low-code platform for enhanced interoperability with characteristics well suited for our PreMS application. While [15] shows its use in a building automation setting, this flexible, low-code platform for enhanced interoperability serves our purposes for building an IIoT platform here too. Our contributions are

- an architectural approach to edge computing based integration and deployment of middleware based model driven software applications for IIoT including EdgeX and DIME, a graphical application development methodology backed by formal models [6]
- a role based, Ciphertext-Policy Attribute-Based Encryption (CP-ABE) security policy development approach for security, privacy and compliance policies compatible with DIME.

Our previous work [15] showed that such a combination can yield a uniform paradigm and platform for the design of both applications and their properties.

The remainder of the paper is structured as follows. Section 2 provides an overview of the EdgeX Foundry middleware and system integration platform. Section 3 presents the PReMS use case application including device provisioning, data and alert handling and reusable application development using Domain Specific Languages (DSLs). Section 4 presents the security policy approach and Sect. 5 concludes the paper.

2 EdgeX Foundry as IIoT Middleware Platform

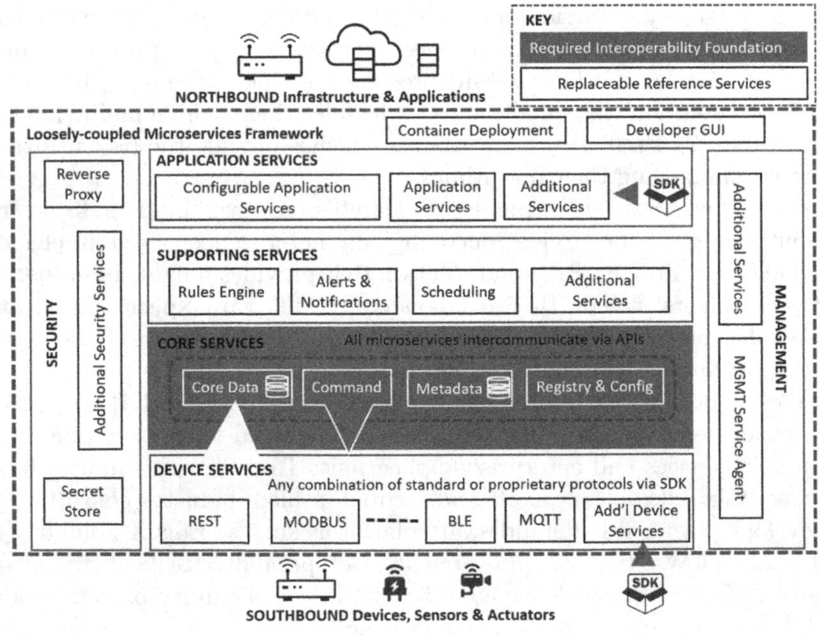

Fig. 1. EdgeX Foundry - platform architecture [10]

Although there are several IIoT middleware platforms available [22], we choose to use EdgeX Foundry at our network edge since it is an open-source, hardware agnostic, highly active, plug and play IIoT middleware platform aimed at edge computing. It is also supported by several industrial organisations, many of which are partners in our national research centre [8]. A commercial-grade version of EdgeX and associated IIoT device connectors (detailed in Sect. 3.1) is also available [14]. EdgeX Foundry [10] consists of six different layers (four service layers + two system layers) as shown in Fig. 1, implemented using loosely coupled microservices that are container deployable. Details about each layer are discussed in [15]. External devices, such as sensors and actuators of different protocols interact with the EdgeX platform using device connectors present in the device service layer. EdgeX includes security elements for protecting data while managing IoT entities. As an open-source platform, security features are developed with open interfaces and pluggable, replaceable modules. The secret store is implemented through the open source Vault [15], and communication with microservices is secured using TLS. A secure API gateway is the sole entry point for EdgeX REST traffic and safeguards unauthorized access to EdgeX's REST APIs.

Recent literature shows how to exploit **EdgeX Foundry** as a ready-made middleware platform. Xu et al. [25] propose a microservice security agent that provides secure authentication by integrating the edge computing platform with an API gateway. Han et al. [13] designed a monitoring system using EdgeX to deal with diverse communication protocols and insufficient cloud computing resources. Kim et al. [17] design an EdgeX-based general-purpose, lightweight edge gateway with low-end CPU and low-capacity memory. The gateway processes small load data to monitor control systems for smart homes, smart farms, and smart meters. Zhang et al. [26] describe a trusted platform to preserve data privacy of edge computing clients via an edge secured environment that integrates EdgeX and the Hyperledger Fabric blockchain network. Platform portability is enhanced by using EdgeX and extending it to incorporate the Hyperledger via a collection of well-defined security authentication microservices. Xu et al. [24] present an EdgeX-based edge computing environment that covers implementation and deployment at the edge. Devices are connected via CoAP and HTTP-based REST APIs on a Raspberry Pi, showing experimentally that CoAP is more stable and faster than HTTP.

In [15] we showed how to design and develop a low-code application for building automation that uses EdgeX's capabilities as an integration service. For the specific low-code support, we used a model-driven approach based on Domain Specific Languages at two levels:

1. *language DSLs* as a mechanism to design and implement the application design environment itself, i.e. the Integrated Modeling Environment DIME, and
2. *application domain DSLs* at application design time. The *Native DSL* mechanism in DIME is used as a means to integrate and expose both capabilities offered by end-devices and EdgeX middleware services to application designers. Additionally *Process DSLs* are used as a means to foster reuse of medium and large-grained business logic as reusable features across applications.

The native and process DSLs have been previously applied also to robotic scenarios [19], and [18] shows how to craft REST services and cloud services in the DIME environment. In [15] we also adopted the ADD-Lib [12] for policy definition. The policies designed with ADD-lib translate to efficient code that is integrated in DIME through its Native DSL mechanism.

Altogether, this shows flexibility, ease of extension, support of high-assurance software quality, agility, security, a service-oriented approach, and containerization, as well as proven compatibility with EdgeX. The contributions of this paper concern the portability of the architecture, methodology, and the reuse of many artefacts also in the Predictive Maintenance domain.

3 Industrial Automation Use Case: Predictive Maintenance

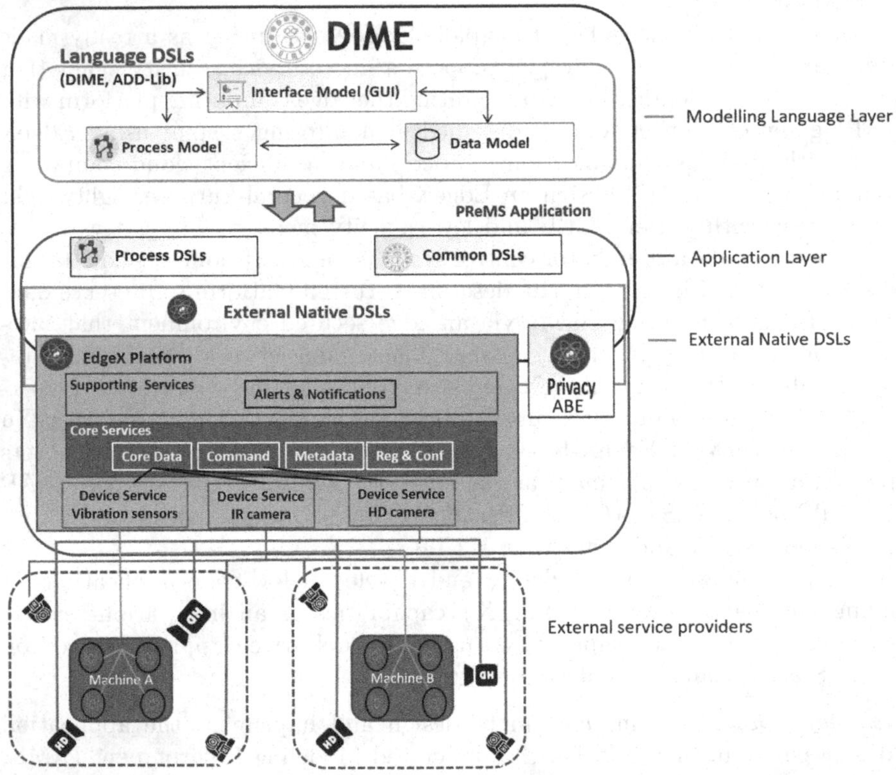

Fig. 2. EdgeX along with DSLs for an IIoT use case - predictive maintenance system (PreMS)

We illustrate the approach with a simple industrial automation use case concerning predictive maintenance, shown in Fig. 2. We consider a monitoring system to monitor machine health, whose purpose is to make decisions on machine maintenance, avoiding unscheduled downtime and preventing machine failure.

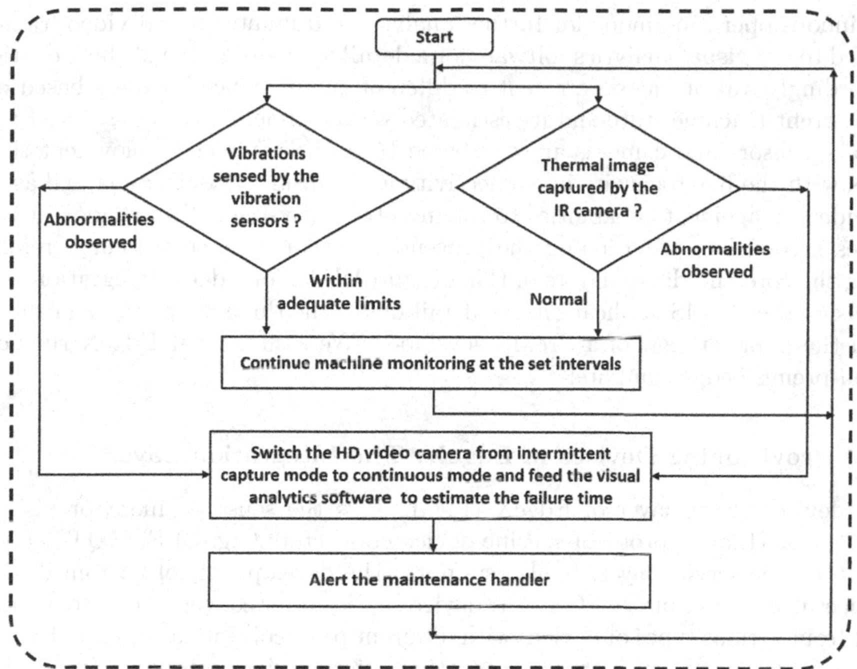

Fig. 3. Predictive maintenance system - an excerpt from the application logic

The monitoring system consists of *wireless vibration sensors* attached to the machine in key locations, an *infrared camera* and a *high definition video camera* that monitor the machine from a short distance and deliver image data for visual analytics to identify machine states. The sensors are wirelessly connected using Bluetooth technology, and the cameras are connected using Wi-Fi (infrared camera) and 5G (high definition camera) technologies. The *edge analytics* collecting and analysing data creates maintenance alerts to machine handlers indicating machine state and likely failure time. This allows the machine handlers to schedule planned downtime of particular machines avoiding machine failure and disrupting the manufacturing process. The general form of the platform architecture shown in Fig. 2 is detailed in [18]. Here we highlight the two layers of DSL and the specific PReMS instance of the External layers: Native DSLs and service providers.

Figure 3 details a high-level overview of the application logic of the Predictive Maintenance System (PreMS). The vibration sensors and the thermal imaging (infrared) cameras associated with each machine periodically report their data to the decision system. Under normal conditions, the HD cameras operate in an intermittent mode so that the industrial wireless network is not flooded with high volumes of unwanted data. Suppose any abnormalities are observed either in the machine vibrations or in the thermal conditions detected by the IR camera. In that case, PreMS switches the HD video camera from intermittent mode to continuous operating mode for further analysis and uninterrupted video frames are fed to the visual analytics software for a detailed investigation of the scenario. Accordingly, various alerts are sent to different maintenance handlers based on the current machine state and its estimated failure time.

The sensors and cameras are connected to an EdgeX edge deployment that deals with the heterogeneity in connectivity and sensing modalities as well as to provide management capabilities to the monitoring system. We now look at the stages involved in provisioning the preventative maintenance system (PreMS) using the core and device layers of EdgeX, and DIME for EdgeX integration and to design the PreMS application. We detail below the three main stages involved from the point of view of a PreMS developer. We assume that EdgeX runs on an on-premise edge computer.

3.1 Provisioning Devices in EdgeX: The Integration Layer

The device service layer of EdgeX (Fig. 1) aids the sensor/camera provisioning process through protocol-specific device connectors (e.g. BLE, MQTT, etc.) in the device service layer. It also supports the development of custom device services using an available SDK. The device service layer converts the data generated from various types of devices with different protocols into a common EdgeX data structure and sends the data to other microservices through REST calls. As shown in Fig. 2, our PreMS use case consists of three device services; one for each of the device protocol types (Vibration sensor-BLE interface, IR camera - WiFi interface, HD camera - 5G interface). A device service is only aware of the generic communication protocol, and the specific details about a particular device are uploaded to EdgeX through device profiles. The device specific details include the sensor data types, the sensing and actuation commands supported by the device (REST API calls) in addition to the generic information such as the manufacturer, model number, etc. The detailed process of registering an external device to EdgeX through its device profile for a building automation use case is detailed in [15]. In our case the procedure is the same: the *PreMS Native DSL* is an external Native DSL (see Fig. 2) for the devices encompasses a DSL per each IoT *device type*, and also here, the ability to use device profiles enables a very easy commissioning of multiple *device instances* of the same kind, e.g. the HD cameras for Machine A and Machine B in Fig. 2 as two instances of the HD camera device type.

As shown in Fig. 2, the Native DSLs expose to DIME collections of basic services across one or more application domains. They comprise "atomic" services which are implemented in code or as calls to external services, APIs and platforms. Once the devices are provisioned and connected to EdgeX, monitoring data can flow to EdgeX. Each device sends its data to the core-data service through its associated device services in the form of events/readings. The sensed data are stored in the database and made available on the common message bus (optional). The other microservices (e.g., Rules Engine) can operate on the data and derive local decisions based on various policies.

3.2 Data and Processes: The Application Layer

The PreMS application data model in DIME refers to the EdgeX entities, to the various device profiles, and includes the other entities relevant to the PreMS application, like users, locations of the machines and policies for later decision making. For every elementary or complex object in the data model, a set of services are automatically created in DIME (get and set services), so that the definition of an object and its attributes, as well as of an enumeration type, automatically produces a DSL for its management coherent with its structure and types without need of manual coding. This is particularly useful when we consider industrial users who are mostly not software developers.

At the application level, as shown in Fig. 2, DIME comprises of its own basic DSL, the *Common SIBs library*, with generic capabilities to handle files, decisions, comparisons, iterations, and more. It also provides a rich DSL for GUI element design. DIME addresses primarily Web applications, so GUI models using the design and functional elements provided in the GUI DSL are the way to define the look and feel of web pages, as well as their navigation structure.

Typically, applications have a hierarchical architecture, because processes can include other processes, therefore there are entire *Process DSLs* arising bottom-up from the design and sharing of processes for reuse in other processes. The process symbol is that of a graph because the processes (or workflows) are modelled as hierarchical graphs that define both control flow and data flow of the application. The Native DSLs on the contrary comprise of "atomic" services, hence the atom symbol on the icons. For example, the *UploadDevProfile, CreateDev* and *StartDev* services shown in Fig. 4 are atomic services belonging to the EdgeX native DSL in DIME, and the entire process in Fig. 4 implements the *SetupDevice* process, which is a process.

Figures 4 and 5 show how control flow and data flow are represented: the workflow logic is the control flow, denoted by solid arrows (e.g. from *Start* to *UploadDevProfile* in Fig. 4), and the data flow is denoted by dotted arrows, that connect directly the data elements (e.g., the output *devTypeID* produced by *UploadDevProfile* that is passed as input to *CreateDev* in Fig. 4), or refer in input or output to the Data context, as shown in Fig. 5 on the left, especially when complex data types are involved. Complex data types are typically created at once, but read or modified field by field in the process workflow. This is shown for the *device_type* record: its field *DeviceTypeID* is used (i.e., read) by three services but its *List_of_Services* field is used only by the *SendCommand* service.

3.3 Reuse Through DSLs

In the platform approach inherent to DIME and EdgeX, *reuse* of small and large components across applications in a domain and also across domains is an essential goal of the platforms, and a key benefit for the users. Referring again to the architecture in Fig. 2, the internal functionality offered by EdgeX is represented in DIME as a native palette to the application designers. The same applies to the EdgeX Core layer services, to the CP_ABE security service Native DSL for our

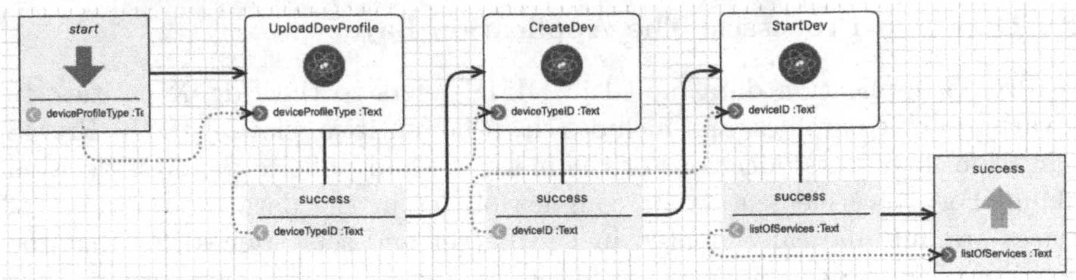

Fig. 4. EdgeXBAu processes: the SetupDevice process in DIME registers the device type and physical device to EdgeX

Attribute Based Encryption capabilities, as well as for other collections of services in the Common SIBs library, that include generic capabilities e.g. to handle files, decisions, comparisons, iterations, and more. In this sense, the "layers" in DIME differ from the layers in EdgeX.

From an EdgeX point of view, the granularity of services it provides in the four layers in Fig. 1 matters, and there is a clear hierarchy among the different service libraries at different levels. This is a service provider point of view, which refers to granularity and position in the internal service provision architecture.

For DIME, however, the point of view is that of the user, i.e. the consumer of services – whatever is external to the application layer is an external service, i.e. a "black box" seen as a *unit of functionality* ready to be used as a ready-made atomic entity. The important concept here is the unit – seen from DIME, any service provening from EdgeX is *atomic*, independently of their EdgeX-internal structure and complexity. This is a very powerful abstraction – not only EdgeX, but any external source of functionalities is treated the same way as is for example the UR3 robot command language in [19] or the Kinect and ROS related libraries in [11]. This virtualization and hiding mechanism is essential for a platform, in order to master heterogeneity and interoperability, so that DIME allows to mix and match services provening from different application domains, and service providers.

The important concepts are the *native DSLs* for the basic functionalities and the *process-level DSLs* for the hierarchical construction of applications within DIME. All the Common SIBs and the GUI DSL come with DIME, so they are written once but available to any application. DIME's EdgeX DSLs are also shareable across all the DIME applications that use EdgeX. The degree of generality and genericity in the specific domain is key to the degree of reusability. For example, our PreMS application "inherits" from the BAu application of [15] the collection of DIME Processes produced during the BAu application design that are specific to EdgeX, but not to BAu. Concretely, Figs. 4 and 5 show two such processes:

- Figure 4 shows the *SetupDevice process* in DIME, which registers the device type and physical device to EdgeX, originally called process *BAuSetupDevice* in [15], and

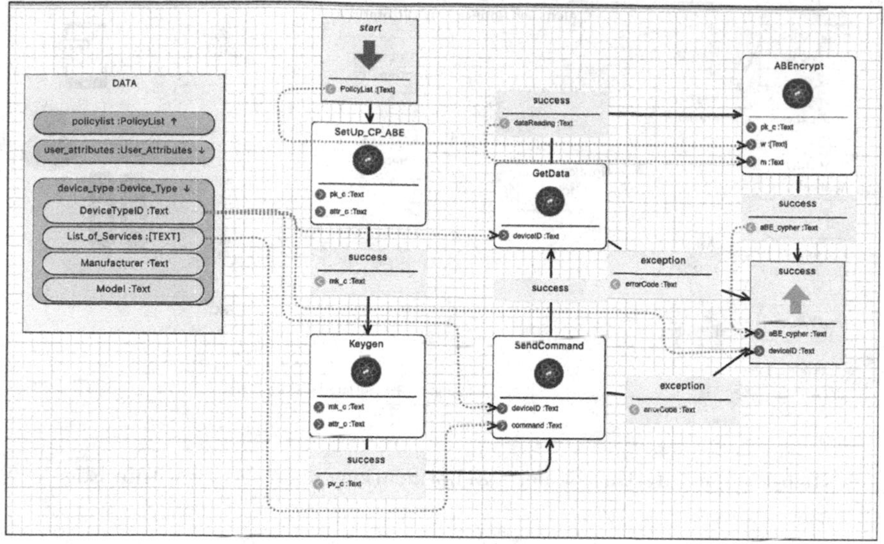

Fig. 5. EdgeX processes: simplified EdgeXOperations service

- Figure 5 shows the simplified EdgeXOperations service, which operates any specific application's system (originally the process BAuOperations in [15], or at any time allows users to decide to reconfigure, restart or stop the application and terminate.

Many other processes are application specific, thus do not carry over from a preexisting case study to the PreMS, and we have to design our own. Similarly, many native DSLs of the BAu application concern specific IoT devices (like PIR sensors, CO2 sensors etc.) not relevant to the PreMS application, so we have to design our own native DSL for the specific device types we use – vibration sensor, IR camera and HD video camera.

An MDD approach as supported by DIME through the models followed by code generation of the resulting application makes this reuse much easier and more intuitive than if we had to understand and reuse manually produced code.

3.4 Handling Alerts and Machine Failures

Here we detail the various stages involved in handling the alerts or machine failure scenarios. Once the PreMS detects any abnormal working conditions for any machine, alerts/notifications are sent to maintenance handlers for proper maintenance. Figure 6 shows the high-level internal architecture of the alerts and notification microservice provided by EdgeX as part of its *Alerts & Notification* library of the *Supporting Services* level (see Figs. 1 and 2). The *Notification Handler* receives the request to send out alerts or notifications from other microservices or applications (on-box/ off-box) through APIs of different application protocols (REST, AMQP, MQTT - shown on the left side of Fig. 6). In the

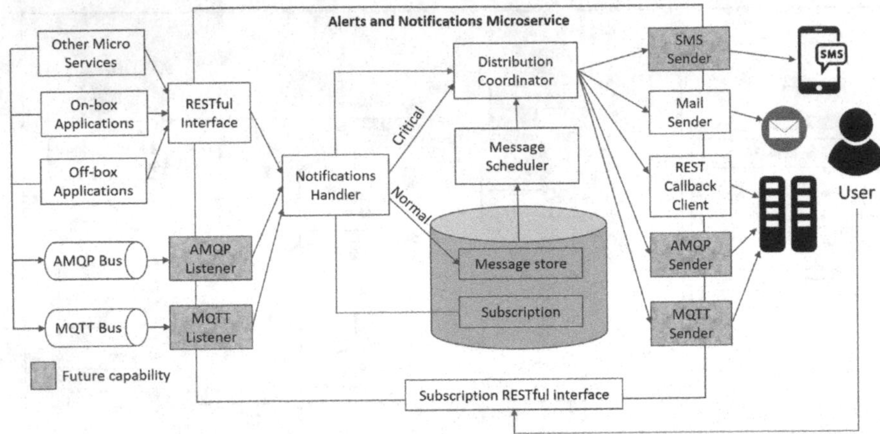

Fig. 6. High-level architecture of alerts & notifications microservice within EdgeX [9]

considered use case scenario, the alerts/notifications may be initiated either by the device service/ rules engine (when the vibration sensor readings fall outside the expected values), or by the thermal image inspection software (when any of the machine or its parts gets overheated), or by the visual analytics software. The *Notifications Handler* persists the received notification and hands it over to the *Distribution Coordinator*. The *Distribution Coordinator* queries the Subscription database to get the intended recipient details of the particular notification, including the communication channel information such as SMS, email, or API destination endpoint (REST, AMQP, MQTT). Accordingly, the Distribution Coordinator passes the alert/notification to the corresponding channel sender (shown on the right side of Fig. 6), which sends out the alert/notification to the subscribed recipients.

For us, at the application level in DIME, this is just yet another atomic service provening from EdgeX.

4 Secure Access Policy for PreMS

In the PreMS application, we use the EdgeX secret store security feature for storing sensitive data, while secure access of data is performed using the Ciphertext-Policy Attribute-Based Encryption (CP-ABE) [4]. For user authentication, we use the EdgeX API gateway security element. For the industrial automation application, we define a secure access policy mechanism as follows: we consider four attributes involved in our use case scenario, namely Maintenance Handler (MH), Mechanical (ME) department, Video Analysis (VA) department and Decision Management System (DMS), whose main functionalities are described as follows: (i) the MH of ME department is responsible for monitoring the health of the machine and have access to the data collected by the vibration sensor; (ii) the MH of VA department analyses the images captured by the infrared camera and the high definition video camera, and notifies the DMS Maintenance Handler if any deviation from normal behaviour is noticed; and (iii) the MH of the DMS takes the final call for the need of generating an alarm if any emergency situation occurs and notifying the same to the PreMS for further actions.

Table 1 shows the different types of devices used, the type of data they generate and the access policies. The access policies define which entities have access to specific data generated by the devices. As mentioned previously, we intend to allow fine-grained secure access control based on attributes, and for this we leverage public-key encryption, i.e., CP-ABE. In CP-ABE, the ciphertexts are identified with access policies and the private keys with attributes. Therefore, a message encrypted using CP-ABE produces a ciphertext which can be decrypted using a private key by a user who owns a set of attributes and satisfies the access policy. One of the key features of CP-ABE is that it enables the definition of top-level policies and is particularly suitable in settings, where it is necessary to limit the access of a particular information only to a subset of users within the same broadcast domain [2].

The CP-ABE scheme consists of the following four algorithms:

- SETUP(). The algorithm takes no input other than the implicit security parameters and returns the public key pk_c and master key mk_c.
- KEYGEN(mk_c, $Attr_c$). The key generation algorithm takes mk_c and the user attribute list $Attr_c$ as inputs and returns a private key pv_c.
- ABE$_{pk_c,w}(m)$. The encryption algorithm takes pk_c, an access policy w over the pool of attributes, and sensor reading m as inputs. It returns a ciphertext that can only be decrypted by a user that possesses a set of attributes $Attr_c$ such that $Attr_c$ satisfies w.
- ABD$_{pv_c}(c)$. The decryption algorithm takes pk_c, pv_c and the ciphertext c as inputs. It outputs the plaintext m if and only if the user $Attr_c$ satisfies w.

Table 1. Device type and access policy

Device type	Data type	Access policy
Wireless Vibration Sensor	[Integer/Float]	MH ∧ (ME ∨ DMS)
Infrared Camera	[H.264/ numeric array]	MH ∧ (VA ∨ DMS)
High Definition Video Camera	Float [H.264/ numeric array]	MH ∧ (VA ∨ DMS)

In order to implement this, we profit again from the work done in [15]: as the four algorithms are domain and application independent, we reuse the Native DSL for CP-ABE they produced, as well as the process in Fig. 5. What changes are the specific access policies for the PreMS from Table 1, which we will again define using the low code model driven development tool ADD-Lib [12] and the surrounding PreMS application logic.

5 Conclusions

We have shown how EdgeX simplifies integrating and managing a wealth of IoT devices and protocols that are central to applications in cyber physical manufacturing systems like predictive maintenance. The platform character of EdgeX and of modern low-code application design environments (LCADEs) is central to their ability to enable high reuse of existing resources, like microservices, components, and algorithms (e.g. CP-ABE), embedded through a Native DSL mechanism in DIME, our chosen LCADE. The DSL concept is central to the integration, the virtualization and the reuse. For example, the extension of existing middleware service platforms like EdgeX to include advanced security mechanisms like CP-ABE is made easy as CP-ABE is in DIME a native DSL plus a collection of domain and application independent processes. The DSLs also support application extension and evolution with minimum programming effort.

Because DIME adopts a generative approach to code, every time the models are modified or extended, the code is efficiently re-generated and redeployed, in a DevOps fashion. The consequence is that every version of the deployed code is "clean": it contains only what is needed (minimal), it contains no patches (it is most recent), and it is unspoiled by human intervention, which is known to inadvertently introduce bugs when fixing detected issues.

In terms of lessons learned, an integrated modeling environment like DIME is indeed superior to its predecessors, that addressed only the Native DSLs for integration and the processes. For example, in [16] the jABC tool, also a low-code and generative platform, while it supported a SIB palette for the commands available to steer a Lego robot, serving the same purpose as the Native DSLs, the data model was not supported in an integrated way, nor there was a possibility to define GUIs. We see the ability to work on all these design facets within the same environment as a clear asset. It eases adoption and better supports a multidisciplinary collaboration with experts of other domains.

From the point of view of modelling styles, in the CPS and engineering domain the prevalent approach is based on simulations or on hybrid models, e.g. for various kinds of digital twins that serve as virtual replicas of CPS. In the track dedicated to the engineering of Digital Twins for Cyber-Physical Systems in ISoLA 2020 [?], for example, providing a recent panorama of modelling approaches and applications in areas close to our own research, the considered models are predominantly quantitative, answering questions about uncertainty, precision and tolerance. Even when the applied model-based and formal techniques support some form of reasoning, this happens mostly in a statistical and AI or AI-like fashion. We concentrate here instead on a fully MDD approach to application design, which is still new to the CPS domain. Its relation with the Digital Twin concept is addressed in detail in [19], and the role of formal models for the low code, MDD application design as used here vs. a corresponding digital twin generated via active automata learning is discussed in [20].

The specific support of evolution is very attractive for our specific setting: our long term objective is to produce a collaborative design ecosystem and an open virtual testbed for intra-but also interorganizational advanced manufacturing, where we expect solutions to grow and evolve over time. We could envisage the EdgeX Distribution Coordinator shown in Fig. 6 to interface in the future with an advanced specialized alarm and notification escalation solution, like the Enterprise Alert product (Derdack, n.d.), and this extension should happen with minimum coding, minimum disruption to the underlying PreMS application, minimum effort, including testing, and minimum risk. We therefore value the simplicity, reuse, openness, and abstraction that these platforms jointly provide.

Acknowledgment. This project received funding from the European Union's Horizon 2020 research and innovation programme under the Marie Skłodowska-Curie Smart 4.0 Co-Fund, grant agreement No. 847577; and a research grant from Science Foundation Ireland (SFI) under Grant Number 16/RC/3918 (CONFIRM Centre)

References

1. Aceto, G., Persico, V., Pescapé, A.: A survey on information and communication technologies for industry 4.0: state-of-the-art, taxonomies, perspectives, and challenges. IEEE Commun. Surv. Tutor. **21**(4), 3467–3501 (2019). https://doi.org/10.1109/COMST.2019.2938259
2. Ambrosin, M., Busold, C., Conti, M., Sadeghi, A.-R., Schunter, M.: Updaticator: updating billions of devices by an efficient, scalable and secure software update distribution over untrusted cache-enabled networks. In: Kutyłowski, M., Vaidya, J. (eds.) ESORICS 2014. LNCS, vol. 8712, pp. 76–93. Springer, Cham (2014). https://doi.org/10.1007/978-3-319-11203-9_5
3. Antonini, M., Vecchio, M., Antonelli, F.: Fog computing architectures: a reference for practitioners. IEEE Internet Things Mag. **2**(3), 19–25 (2019). https://doi.org/10.1109/IOTM.0001.1900029
4. Bethencourt, J., Sahai, A., Waters, B.: Ciphertext-policy attribute-based encryption. In: Proceedings of IEEE S&P, pp. 321–334 (2007)
5. Bonavolontà, F., Tedesco, A., Moriello, R.S.L., Tufano, A.: Enabling wireless technologies for industry 4.0: state of the art. In: 2017 IEEE International Workshop on Measurement and Networking (M N), pp. 1–5 (2017). https://doi.org/10.1109/IWMN.2017.8078381
6. Boßelmann, S., et al.: DIME: a programming-less modeling environment for web applications. In: Margaria, T., Steffen, B. (eds.) ISoLA 2016. LNCS, vol. 9953, pp. 809–832. Springer, Cham (2016). https://doi.org/10.1007/978-3-319-47169-3_60
7. Christou, I.T., Kefalakis, N., Zalonis, A., Soldatos, J., Bröchler, R.: End-to-end industrial IoT platform for actionable predictive maintenance. IFAC-PapersOnLine **53**(3), 173–178 (2020)
8. Confirm: Confirm smart manufacturing - Science Foundation Ireland Research centre. https://confirm.ie/
9. EdgeX Foundry: "EdgeX Alerts and Notifications". https://docs.edgexfoundry.org/2.0/microservices/support/notifications/Ch-AlertsNotifications/
10. EdgeX Foundry: "Why EdgeX". https://www.edgexfoundry.org/why_edgex/why-edgex/
11. Farulla, G.A., Indaco, M., Legay, A., Margaria, T.: Model driven design of secure properties for vision-based applications: A case study. In: T.Margaria, M.G.Solo, A. (eds.) The 2016 International Conference on Security and Management (SAM 2016). Special Track "End-to-end Security and Cybersecurity: from the Hardware to Application", pp. 159–167. CREA Press (2016)

12. Gossen, F., Margaria, T., Murtovi, A., Naujokat, S., Steffen, B.: DSLs for decision services: a tutorial introduction to language-driven engineering. In: ISoLA 2018, Proceedings, Part I, pp. 546–564 (2018). https://doi.org/10.1007/978-3-030-03418-4_33
13. Han, K., Duan, Y., Jin, R., Ma, Z., Rong, H., Cai, X.: Open framework of gateway monitoring system for internet of things in edge computing. In: 2020 IEEE 39th International Performance Computing and Communications Conference (IPCCC), pp. 1–5. IEEE (2020)
14. IoTech: "IoTech The Edge Software Company". https://www.iotechsys.com/
15. John, J., Ghosal, A., Margaria, T., Pesch, D.: DSLs for model driven development of secure interoperable automation systems. In: Forum on Specification & Design Languages (Accepted for Publication) (2021), (in print)
16. Jörges, S., Kubczak, C., Pageau, F., Margaria, T.: Model driven design of reliable robot control programs using the jABC. In: Proceedings of 4th IEEE International Workshop on Engineering of Autonomic and Autonomous Systems (EASe 2007), pp. 137–148 (2007)
17. Kim, J., Kim, C., Son, B., Ryu, J., Kim, S.: A study on Time-series DBMS application for EdgeX-based lightweight edge gateway. In: 2020 International Conference on Information and Communication Technology Convergence (ICTC), pp. 1795–1798. IEEE (2020)
18. Margaria, T., Chaudhary, H.A.A., Guevara, I., Ryan, S., Schieweck, A.: The interoperability challenge: building a model-driven digital thread platform for CPS. In: Proceedings ISoLA 2021, International Symposium on Leveraging Applications of Formal Methods, Verification and Validation, Rhodes, October 2021. Lecture Notes in Computer Science, vol. 13036. Springer (2021)
19. Margaria, T., Schieweck, A.: The digital thread in Industry 4.0. In: Ahrendt, W., Tapia Tarifa, S.L. (eds.) IFM 2019. LNCS, vol. 11918, pp. 3–24. Springer, Cham (2019). https://doi.org/10.1007/978-3-030-34968-4_1
20. Margaria, T., Schieweck, A.: The digital thread in Industry 4.0. In: Olderog, Ernst-Rüudiger, S.B., Yi, W. (eds.) Model Checking, Synthesis and Learning. Lecture Notes in Computer Science, vol. 13030. Springer (2021)
21. Milić, S.D., Babić, B.M.: Toward the future-upgrading existing remote monitoring concepts to IIoT concepts. IEEE Internet Things J. **7**(12), 11693–11700 (2020). https://doi.org/10.1109/JIOT.2020.2999196
22. Paniagua, C., Delsing, J.: Industrial frameworks for Internet of Things: a survey. IEEE Syst. J. **15**(1), 1149–1159 (2021)
23. Wollschlaeger, M., Sauter, T., Jasperneite, J.: The future of industrial communication: automation networks in the era of the Internet of Things and Industry 4.0. IEEE Ind. Electron. Mag. **11**(1), 17–27 (2017). https://doi.org/10.1109/MIE.2017.2649104
24. Xu, R., Jin, W., Kim, D.H.: Knowledge-based edge computing framework based on CoAP and HTTP for enabling heterogeneous connectivity. Pers. Ubiq. Comput. 1–16 (2020)
25. Xu, R., Jin, W., Kim, D.: Microservice security agent based on API gateway in edge computing. Sensors **19**(22), 4905 (2019)
26. Zhang, J., et al.: A blockchain-based trusted edge platform in edge computing environment. Sensors **21**(6), 2126 (2021)

From Requirements to Executable Rules: An Ensemble of Domain-Specific Languages for Programming Cyber-Physical Systems in Warehouse Logistics

Malte Mauritz(✉) and Moritz Roidl

TU Dortmund University, 44227 Dortmund, Germany
{malte.mauritz,moritz.roidl}@tu-dortmund.de

Abstract. The fourth industrial revolution is driven by Software-enabled automation. To fully realize the potential of this digital transformation in a way that is beneficial to society, automation needs to become programmable by domain experts—the vision being a Software-assisted increase in productivity instead of replacing workers with Software. While domain experts, e.g., workers in production, typically have extensive experience with processes and workflows involving cyber-physical systems, e.g., production machines, they have little to no knowledge of programming and formal logic. In this paper, we present a framework for expressing executable rules in the context of a cyber-physical system at the conceptual level, akin to human reasoning, in almost natural sentences (e.g., *if a person is within 1 m of the machine then the light will turn red*). These requirements are automatically transformed by our framework into formal logic and can be executed and evaluated by a rule engine without additional input by domain experts. The framework is designed in a modular way that enables domain engineering, i.e., the development of new languages for individual application domains, with minimal effort. Only domain-specific entities and predicates (e.g., *is within*) need to be defined and implemented for a new domain. We demonstrate our framework in a logistics scenario on a shop floor that requires human-machine collaboration.

Keywords: Domain-specific languages · Logistics · Language programming · Language model transformation · Runtime monitoring

1 Introduction

Digitization by software automation is growing significantly in many organizations. In many companies with no particular background in Software (e.g.,

The Research has been executed within the centre of excellence Logistics and IT which is funded by the Ministry of Culture and Science of the State of North Rhine-Westphalia and the Fraunhofer Society for the Advancement of Applied Research.

T. Margaria and B. Steffen (Eds.): ISoLA 2021, LNCS 13036, pp. 162–177, 2021.
https://doi.org/10.1007/978-3-030-89159-6_11

in the industrial and manufacturing sector), Software crept into processes and products—first slowly but then with an ever-increasing pace and scope, culminating in the mantra that "every company needs to become a software company". This mantra comes with an inherently increasing demand for skilled software-engineers. Universities and colleges are unable to satisfy this demand adequately.

In many instances, Software is merely a means of automation, and we have to put the power of controlling automation into the hands of domain experts and the general public to bring digital transformation to its full potential in a way that is beneficial to society. Moreover, rules in automated systems need to be understandable at the conceptual level of human reasoning to be amenable, e.g., to ethical and legal considerations. Putting it bluntly, we need frameworks that enable "programming the real world", e.g., specifying the behavior of objects on a shop floor using observable events, conditions, and actions.

Classical systems engineering approaches fall short as in these approaches requirements on system behavior are decomposed to subsystems and refined to the level of signals, making the originally expressed intention hard to reconstruct (cf. [1,2] for examples). New or changed requirements need to be decomposed and translated from scratch, requiring expensive manual effort, involving domain experts and system developers.

We propose an alternative approach that uses domain-specific languages to bridge the gap between the conceptual level of human reasoning about the world and concrete signals and conditions in complex logistical systems enabling domain experts to write requirements like *"if a person carrying a box is within 1 m of the designated storage location then the light will turn green"*. Such requirements have a well-defined meaning in a system through domain-specific abstractions, computing the value of predicates like *"within 1 m of"* in a concrete cyber-physical system. System-wide relations and emergent behavior within cyber-physical systems can be evaluated in the form of natural predicates at runtime by preserving the meaning of requirements in domain-specific abstractions.

In this paper, we report on the results of an exploratory design effort, in which we have developed the generic architecture, languages, and abstractions of a framework that enables domain experts to program the behavior of cyber-physical systems (CPS) in the logistics domain. We present the development of a framework with domain-specific languages that allow to express executable rules about moving things in the real world at an abstract level, akin to human reasoning, e.g., *the light should turn green if a person carrying a box is within 1 m of the designated storage location.*

The resulting framework relies on three individual connected languages: (1) a language for the definition of requirements, (2) a language defining domain-specific objects, functions, and predicates as well as their interpretations in terms of concrete system signals and data, and (3) an extended first-order logic using arbitrary predicates for monitoring and controlling CPS at runtime.

We demonstrate our approach in a case study from the logistics domain: a scenario on a shop floor that requires human-machine collaboration.

Outline. The paper is organized as follows: Sect. 2 introduces logistics as our problem domain and related work. Section 3 presents our case study with our logistics research lab. Section 4 outlines our framework for the independent specification of domain and requirements. Section 5 describe the monitoring of the requirements at runtime and reports on results from our case study. Section 6 discusses the development of our framework and the results from our case study. Section 7 concludes the paper.

2 Related Work

Logistics is the science of moving things in the real world in a reasonable and efficient manner. Logistics applications permeate throughout the human inhabited world and exist in a plethora of different shapes and forms. Logistics systems scale from simple packaging stations to planetary-wide interdependent supply-chain networks. Although there are almost as many types of logistics systems as there are industries, they all share the same basic primitives of movement.

In order to sustain the pace of digital transformation, these logistics systems need to become programmable by domain experts. Moreover, rules in automated systems need to be understandable at the abstract level of human reasoning in order to be amenable to ethical and legal considerations.

Logistics automation is an engineering discipline with a disposition towards algorithms that use numeric methods for optimizing highly context-specific parameters. As such, it is a very different style of reasoning compared to what the shop floor workers are doing. Typical programming languages of field-level automated systems (i.e. Programmable Logic Controllers (PLCs)) are not usable by domain experts as they are rooted in control engineering. High-level requirements have to be related to the domain of these systems for execution in the real world and monitoring and controlling CPS at runtime. Entities, i.e., objects and predicates, which are used in high-level requirements have to be defined over the available signals and system data.

For this reason, *No Code* or *Low Code* platforms, e.g. DIME [3], Mendix[1], Creatio[2], Pega[3], among others, have become more and more popular in industry [4]. These platforms aim to facilitate the programming of mobile, Internet of Things (IoT), and are applications by non-technical employees based on domain-specific languages (DSL) [5] and models [6]. However, most solutions predominately target business process automation and user applications but are not suited for the programming of technical systems, e.g., robots.

In Academia, various languages and tools have been developed to address the definition of requirement and the automated processing. ASSERT [7] provides the constrained natural language SADL for formalizing domain ontologies and the requirements language SRL to express requirements as conditions over controlled system variables. FRET [8,9] provides the language FRETISH for

[1] https://www.mendix.com/.
[2] https://www.creatio.com.
[3] https://www.pega.com/.

specifying the requirements and transforming them into temporal logic formulas. However, these tools still utilize mathematical conditions over system variables in their requirements.

Academia has developed several controlled natural languages, e.g. Processable English (PENG) [10], Controlled English to Logic Translation (CELT) [11], Computer Processable Language (CPL) [12], which are close to natural languages but allow for knowledge representation and reasoning about the textual content. A good overview and classification of controlled languages are given in [13]. Attempto Controlled English (ACE) [14,15] provides a large subset of the English language to specify requirements which can be transformed unambiguously into a first-order logic [10]. However, ACE aims at knowledge representation and reasoning and does not provide a mechanism for the interpretation of text entities on system data for runtime monitoring and evaluation.

Other solutions for the requirements engineering in natural language aim at transforming natural language into machine-processable formats using fuzzy matching domain-based parsing techniques [16] or natural language processing (NLP) [17]. The problem with these tools is that their interpretation of the requirements within a real-world domain is undefined.

As the authors of [18], we see the importance for integrating multiple models wit specialized focus. We explicitly see the importance for the definition of domain entities and predicates over data of the CPS independent of the specification of requirements. We, therefore, have developed a framework which allows the specification of domain entities and predicates based on system data and their usage in requirements and first-order logic for the runtime monitoring and control.

The following Sect. 3 describe our use case. An overview of our framework with the engineering of the domain and the specification of monitorable requirements is given in Sect. 4.

3 Case Study: Warehouse Logistics

Our case study for the application of our framework has been implemented in a special purpose logistics research lab. This lab is designed as a highly flexible testbed environment for CPS and features a central experimentation area that is free of permanently installed equipment at ground-level. This central area is 22 m long and 15 m wide. It is surrounded by 40 infrared cameras that are part of a Motion Capturing System (MoCap). Additionally, eight laser projectors are installed on the ceiling that can project colored vector graphics on the floor. The graphic shapes can be changed with a very high frame rate and low latency.

Figure 1 shows the framework of the lab. Physical objects are tracked by the MoCap system via uniquely identifiable collections of retro-reflective markers. The generated data streams are sent to the simulation environment. The simulation environment mirrors the perceived objects into a virtual representation of the physical space. The simulation controls the laser projection system and displays virtual objects via a mapping to vector graphics directly in the experimentation area.

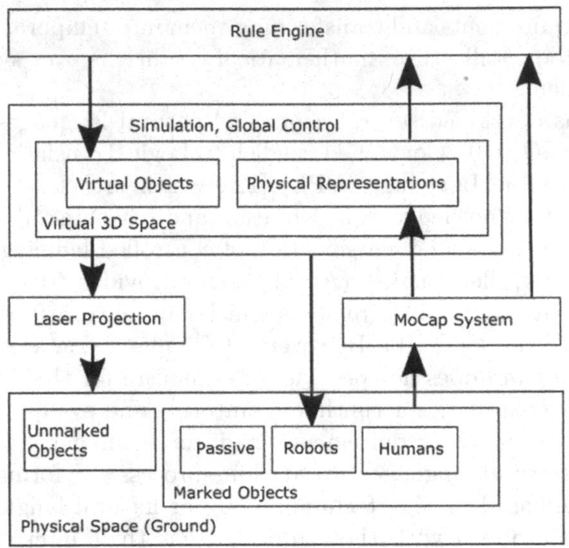

Fig. 1. Framework of the research lab

For the purpose of the application example, Message Queuing Telemetry Transport (MQTT) has been used as interface to allow the rule engine to generate virtual objects for laser projection to the floor. The incoming data stream of object positions could be either received by a subscription to the MoCap topic on the MQTT server or from the simulation environment. The latter option was used while developing the monitoring framework, as it allowed for faster testing of newly written code.

Our concrete scenario is the manual transports of assembly pieces between workstations, as it can be found in warehouses and plants. Assembly pieces are manually carried in a container between the workstations. The scenario consists of a worker carrying a container *KLT_2* for small assembly parts between two workstations *AS_1* and *AS_3* (cf. Figure 5). Positions of container and workstations are continuously tracked by a Motion Capturing System (MoCap) (cf. *position tracking* in Fig. 2). The tracking data is sent to a broker using the MQTT protocol [19] from where it is distributed to our rule engine.

The numerical data streams containing the objects' positions are transformed for the rule engine into abstract interpretations constituting logical constants, properties, and predicates (cf. *position abstraction* in Fig. 2). The abstract interpretations are used by the rule engine to reason about the relative positioning of container *KLT_2* and workstations *AS_1* and *AS_3*.

Based on the evaluation of formulas by the rule engine, actions within these formulas are executed to visualize relative positions of container *KLT_2* and workstations *AS_1* and *AS_3*. The rule engine emits the active actions within

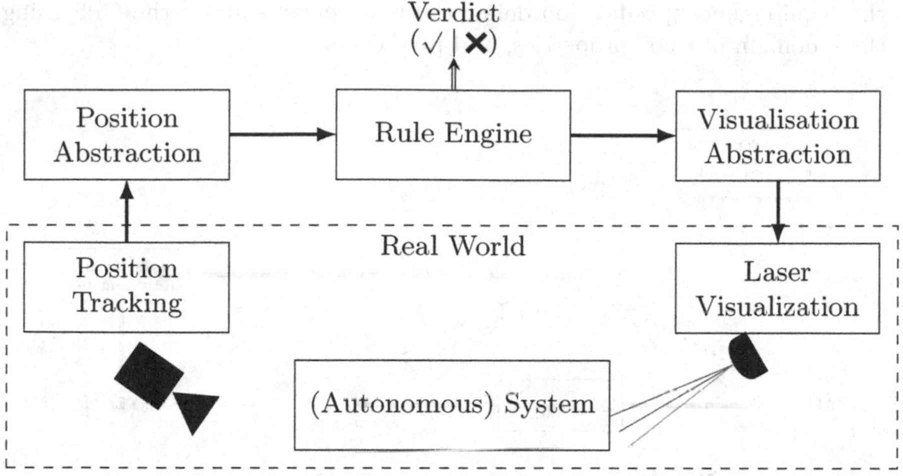

Fig. 2. Data flow at runtime

these formulas. These abstract actions are transformed into concrete visualization objects for the laser projectors of the testbed (cf. *visualization abstraction* in Fig. 2).

The following Sect. 4 gives an overview about our framework and presents the specification of domain and requirements in our case study.

4 Separation of Domain and Requirements

The behavior of logistics systems can become very complex, as these systems consist of many components with reactive behavior. The specification of emerging behavior in requirements solely based on internal signals and data can be difficult, if not impossible. Our vision is to bridge the gap between natural requirements and monitors or rules on the actual system through code generation and execution.

We want to enable domain experts to specify requirements for logistics systems akin to human reasoning, while directly monitoring and verifying these requirements at runtime. Domain experts do not need any knowledge about programming, language engineering, and formal methods. Otherwise, domain experts would be more concerned with technical or formal details, e.g., the syntax of first-order logic, than specifying the expected system behavior as requirements.

We hold domain experts away from the technical details of the domain and the logistics system by separating the requirements specification in into two main tasks - *domain engineering* and *requirements specification*:

1. The domain engineering defines the objects, properties, and predicates within the application domain and interprets these for the data of the CPS, and

2. the requirements specification define the requirements about the CPS using these domain objects, properties, and predicates.

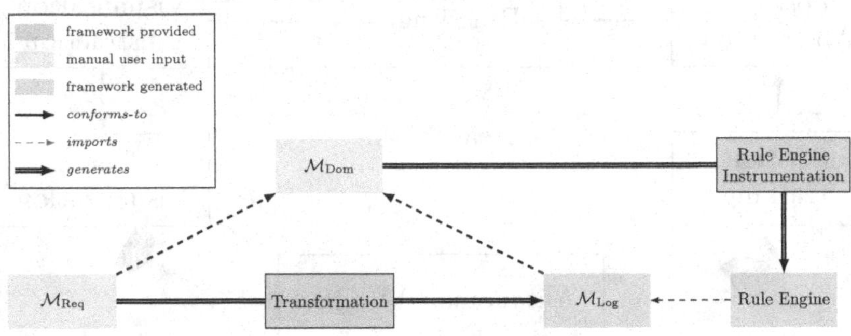

Fig. 3. Overview over the language framework

The separation in domain engineering and requirements specification (cf. Figure 4) is also represented by the models $\mathcal{M}$ in framework. Our framework incorporates three different domain-specific languages for specifying requirements akin to the reasoning of domain experts and executing these requirements at runtime to monitor and control these systems (cf. Figure 3):

1. Domain $\mathcal{M}_{\text{Dom}}$ describes the domain and its specific terminology which are used in the requirements $\mathcal{M}_{\text{Req}}$, the first-order logic $\mathcal{M}_{\text{Log}}$, and the rule engine.
2. Requirements $\mathcal{M}_{\text{Req}}$ enables specifying requirements akin to human reasoning.
3. Extended first-order logic $\mathcal{M}_{\text{Log}}$ provides the unambiguous syntax and semantics for monitoring and executing requirements at runtime.

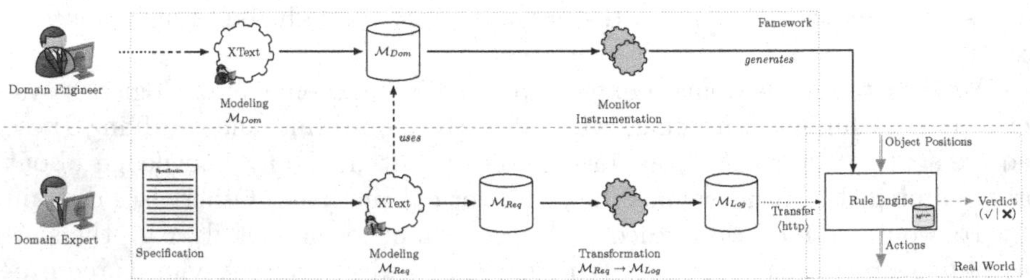

Fig. 4. Development workflow

As shown in Fig. 4, each task - domain engineering and requirements specification- requires a different skill sets. We, therefore, distinguish the roles *domain engineer* and *domain expert*:

- The *domain engineer* possesses sufficient knowledge about the application domain as well as programming and language engineering with domain-specific languages for comprehensively representing the application domain. From this domain specification, the rule engine is instrumented to interpret the entities and predicates in requirements for data from the monitored CPS.
- The *domain expert* has deep knowledge about the investigated CPS to exhaustively specify requirements about the system and its behavior akin to their natural reasoning. The natural requirements are automatically transformed into first-order logic for evaluation by the rule engine at runtime.

The domain engineering for warehouse logistics is described in Sect. 4.1, while the specification of requirements and their monitoring for the manual transport of goods in our logistics research lab are presented in Sect. 4.2.

4.1 Engineering the Warehouse Logistics Domain

The development in our use case commences with the definition of the domain $\mathcal{M}_{\text{Dom}}$ for Warehouse Logistics. The domain $\mathcal{M}_{\text{Dom}}$ is the central component in our solution and ensures that requirements $\mathcal{M}_{\text{Req}}$ and formulas $\mathcal{M}_{\text{Log}}$ reason about the identical application domain.

As shown in Fig. 3, respective interpretations within the domain $\mathcal{M}_{\text{Dom}}$ are imported into requirements $\mathcal{M}_{\text{Req}}$ and formulas $\mathcal{M}_{\text{Log}}$. The data interpretation of objects and predicates are used by the rule engine at runtime to evaluate domain objects and predicates for the current state of the CPS and process a verdict for requirements $\mathcal{M}_{\text{Req}}$ and in formulas $\mathcal{M}_{\text{Log}}$ at runtime e (cf. our case study in Sect. 5).

Domain $\mathcal{M}_{\text{Dom}}$ defines the domain's objects and predicates as they are used in our case study within our logistics research lab and associates these entities to the data in our logistics research lab. The domain $\mathcal{M}_{\text{Dom}}$ defines the item container *KLT_2*, workstations *AS_1* and *AS_3*, and predicates about the geometric relationship between objects, i.e., *besides*. An excerpt of the domain is shown in Listing 1.1.

Listing 1.1. Defintion of domain $\mathcal{M}_{\text{Dom}}$

```
def KLT_2 : Object {
  Requirement: KLT_2
  Logic: KLT_2
  Data: positionObjects[name==KLT_2]
}

def AS_1 : Object {
  Requirement: AS_1
  Logic: AS_1
  Data: positionObjects[name==AS_1]
}

def beside : Predicate {
```

```
  Requirement: beside dist:Float of
  Logic: beside(Con1:Constant,Con2:Constant,dist:Float)
  Data: ABS(positionObjects[name==Con2]->positon -
    positionObjects[name==Con1]) < dist
}
```

The objects *KTL_2* and *AS_1* both have the type *Object* and are identically expressed in the requirements $\mathcal{M}_{\text{Req}}$ and first-order logic $\mathcal{M}_{\text{Log}}$ (cf. keywords *Requirement* and *Logic* in Listing 1.1). The predicate *beside* is defined in $\mathcal{M}_{\text{Req}}$ by the word *within* and an arbitrary distance *dist* (cf. keyword *Requirement* in Listing 1.1). The objects which are compared by the predicate *beside* are determined by the sentence in which the predicate is used. For the first-order logic $\mathcal{M}_{\text{Log}}$, the predicate is defined with three parameters; the first two parameters take constants *Con1* and *Con2* as inputs while the third parameter takes a float value *dist* for the distance (cf. keyword *Logic* in Listing 1.1).

At runtime, predicate *beside* is interpreted and evaluated for the incoming streams of position data from the MoCap System. The data from the MoCap system is provided to the rule engine via the MQTT broker as JSON data [20, 21]. The interpretation of the system data is defined by the data function (cf. keyword *Data* in Listing 1.1); predicate *beside* will be evaluated as satisfied if the absolute amount of the distance between the position of object *Con1* and the position of constant *Con2* is below the given distance *dist*. Objects *Con1* and *Con2* are filtered in the list of objects *positionObjects* in the MQTT data based on their names and their common attribute *position* is assessed for the position values. These data interpretations are used in the abstraction of the numerical position data to abstract representations in first-order logic (cf. *position abstraction* in Fig. 2).

For our demonstration, we defined five additional predicates for evaluating the relative position of container and workstations. All six predicates are shown in Table 1.

In addition to the six predicates about the relative position of container and workstations, actions *draw rectangle* and *draw circle* are defined in the domain $\mathcal{M}_{\text{Dom}}$ (cf. Table 1). Action *draw circle* will result in a circle as laser visualization while action *draw rectangle* yields to the projection of a rectangle by the laser projectors. Both actions have parameters for `position`, `color`, `size`, `duration`, and `animation` of the projected `rectangle` resp. `circle`. Positions of the laser visualizations can be defined either as fixed positions in world coordinates or the visualizations can be attached to the positions of objects. Attachments to objects provide the advantages that the visualizations will change their positions according to the movement of these objects.

The following Sect. 4.2 describes how the requirements $\mathcal{M}_{\text{Req}}$ are defined for our logistics case study using the definitions in domain $\mathcal{M}_{\text{Dom}}$.

4.2 Specification of Requirements

Requirements $\mathcal{M}_{\text{Req}}$ are specified by domain experts using an almost natural but domain-specific language. Requirements $\mathcal{M}_{\text{Req}}$ have the basic clause

Table 1. Overview of predicates in the domain $\mathcal{M}_{\text{Dom}}$.

Predicate	Requirements	First-Order Logic
inside	[Obj] is inside [Box]	inside(Obj,Box)
rest on	[Obj] is on [Box]	reston(Obj,Box)
rest under	[Obj] is under [Box]	restunder(Obj,Box)
above	[Obj] is above [Box]	above(Obj,Box)
below	[Obj] is below [Box]	below(Obj,Box)
beside	[Obj] is within X m of [Box]	besides(Obj,Box,X)
draw circle	draw circle with position x in color y ... circle (position, color, ...)	
draw rectangle	draw rectangle with position x in color y ... rectangle (position, color, ...)	

$$\textbf{if } \langle \textit{conditions} \rangle \textbf{ then } \langle \textit{actions} \rangle$$

where ⟨*conditions*⟩ and ⟨*actions*⟩ can be conjunctions of multiple conditions resp. actions, e.g., *if a package is available in one of the loading areas, then an idling robot has to move to the leading area and pick up the package.* Requirements $\mathcal{M}_{\text{Req}}$ import the specific interpretations of domain-specific entities, i.e., item container *KLT_2*, workstations *AS_1* and *AS_3*, and predicates about the geometric relationship between objects, from domain $\mathcal{M}_{\text{Dom}}$ (cf. Section 4.1).

Listing 1.2. Initial definition of requirements.

```
1 Req Req1: If KTL_2 is within 4m of AS_1 and KTL_2 resides
      within 4m to AS_3 then show a rectangle with scale 6.0
      at position {1.0,0.0,0.0} with magenta color.
2 Req Req2: If KTL_2 is within 3m of AS_1 then print a
      rectangle over AS_1 in yellow color with scale 2.0.
3 Req Req3: If KTL_2 is within 3m of AS_3 then print a
      rectangle over AS_1 in yellow color with scale 2.0.
```

In our demonstration, we defined three requirements about the position of the container *KTL_2* in relation to the workstations *AS_1* and *AS_3* in the requirements $\mathcal{M}_{Req}$ using the definition of the domain $\mathcal{M}_{\text{Dom}}$. The requirements are shown in Listing 1.2. Requirement *Req1* will result in the drawing of a magenta rectangle with 6 m edges at the global position $\{1.0, 0.0, 0.0\}$ if the container *KLT_2* is within 4 m of both workstations *AS_1* and *AS_3*. The second requirement *Req2* will result in a yellow rectangle drawn around the workstation *AS_1* with edge of 2 m if the distance between container *KLT_2* and workstation *AS_1* is less than 3 m. Requirement *Req3* is identical to requirement *Req2* with workstation *AS_1* replaced by workstation *AS_3*.

The following Sect. 5 describe how the requirements $\mathcal{M}_{\text{Req}}$ are transformed into first-order formulas $\mathcal{M}_{\text{Log}}$ and monitor in our shop floor scenario in our logistics research lab.

5 Runtime Monitoring and System Control

Requirements $\mathcal{M}_{\text{Req}}$ are automatically transformed by our framework into formulas $\mathcal{M}_{\text{Log}}$ in first-order logic for monitoring and controlling the CPS at runtime. Our framework uses classic first-order logic extended by operators for equality $==$ and the implication $|>$ between conditions and actions.

Similar to the requirements $\mathcal{M}_{\text{Req}}$, the specific interpretations of entities in domain $\mathcal{M}_{\text{Dom}}$, i.e., item container *KLT_2*, workstations *AS_1* and *AS_3*, and predicates about the geometric relationship between objects, are imported into the formulas $\mathcal{M}_{\text{Log}}$. The semantics of formulas $\mathcal{M}_{\text{Log}}$ are given by the interpretation of these domain-specific entities for the data of CPS.

As shown in Listing 1.3, three formulas $\mathcal{M}_{\text{Log}}$ are generated in first-order logic from the three requirements in Listing 1.2. The requirement *Req1* in Listing 1.2 is transformed to formula *Req1* in Listing 1.3.

Listing 1.3. Formulas $\mathcal{M}_{\text{Log}}$ for the running example

```
Req1: beside(KLT_2,AS_1,4) AND beside (KLT_2,AS_3,4) |>
    rectangle (Req1_1, {-1.0,0.0,0.0},1,magenta,4,6,6,none)
    ;
Req2: beside(KLT_2,AS_1,3) |> rectangle (AS_1, 1,yellow
    ,4,2,2,none);
Req3: beside(KLT_2,AS_3,3) |> rectangle (AS_3,1,yellow
    ,4,2,2,none);
```

The container *KTL_2* and workstations *AS_1* and *AS_3* are equally used in requirements $\mathcal{M}_{\text{Req}}$ as well as formulas $\mathcal{M}_{\text{Log}}$. Therefore, representations of these objects in requirements $\mathcal{M}_{\text{Req}}$ are directly transformed into corresponding representations in formulas $\mathcal{M}_{\text{Log}}$ using the definitions in domain $\mathcal{M}_{\text{Dom}}$. The predicate *within* in $\mathcal{M}_{\text{Req}}$ maps to the predicate *beside* in formulas $\mathcal{M}_{\text{Log}}$. The container *KTL_2*, workstation *AS_1* resp. *AS_3*, and constraint *4 m* are assigned to the parameters *Con1*, *Con1*, and *dist* respectively. The preceding verbs *is* and *resides* for the predicate *within* in requirements $\mathcal{M}_{\text{Req}}$ are syntactic sugar and are not considered for the transformation of predicate *within* into the formulas $\mathcal{M}_{\text{Log}}$.

The action in the *action part* of requirements *Req1* in Listing 1.2 is transformed in the predicate *rectangle* in $\mathcal{M}_{\text{Log}}$ with its parameters derived from the additional constraints in the *action part*, e.g., *at position* $\{-1.0,0.0,0.0\}$ and *in magenta color*. Requirements *Req2* and *Req3* are transformed into formulas similar to the transformation of requirement *Req1*. The semantics of these three formulas in Listing 1.3 is consistent with the semantics of their original requirements in Listing 1.2.

Results from runtime evaluation of the three formulas in Listing 1.3 for the manual transport of container *KLT_2* between the two workstations *AS_1* and *AS_3* are shown in Fig. 5. The rule engine for this demonstration has been instrumented for evaluating the three formulas in Listing 1.3 at runtime using the definition of the domain in Listing 1.1.

(a) Visualization for container *KLT_2* at workstation *AS_3*.

(b) Visualization for container *KTL_2* at workstation *AS_1*.

Fig. 5. Demonstration of logistics scenario.

In Fig. 5a, the container *KLT_2* is at the workstation *AS_3*. The formulas *Req1* and *Req3* are satisfied in this situation while requirement *Req2* fails due to the large distance to workstation *AS_1*. As result, a large magenta rectangle and a small yellow rectangle around workstation *AS_3* are drawn according to the satisfied formulas *Req1* and *Req3* (cf. Listing 1.2).

After carrying the container *KLT_2* over to the workstation *AS_1*, the yellow rectangle around workstation *AS_3* disappears while a new yellow rectangle appears around workstation *AS_1*. This behavior is consistent with formulas *Req2* and *Req3* (cf. Listing 1.2) because the predicate *beside* in formula *Req3* is now invalid while it is now true for formula *Req2*. Formula *Req1* is satisfied in both situations. Therefore, the large magenta rectangle is drawn throughout the complete transition of container *KLT_2* from workstation *AS_3* to workstation *AS_1*.

Our lessons from the development and application of our framework are presented in the following section.

6 Discussion

The work presented in this paper is highly explorative. We have aimed for a first technical prove-of-concept.

While the current implementation of our framework is a prototype, we can draw some initial conclusions from its development, the conducted application.

Remark 1: *Separation of languages seems to support the distribution and reuse in system development.*

Our case study has provided first indications that the separation of domain engineering and requirements specification has a positive impact in the development of logistical CPS. Requirements $\mathcal{M}_{\text{Req}}$ and domain $\mathcal{M}_{\text{Dom}}$ seem to be reusable in another context independent of each other. Requirements can be used for CPS in other domains by just redefining the objects and predicates in requirements for the new domain. The development of new systems, may reuse an existing domain $\mathcal{M}_{\text{Dom}}$ in its new requirements $\mathcal{M}_{\text{Req}}$ of the new system. There is no need to adapt the objects and predicates in the domain $\mathcal{M}_{\text{Dom}}$ to the new system.

Requirements and domain seem to be easily developed independent of each other, providing organizations with the opportunity to efficiently employ domain engineers within the development of these systems. As critical resource due to their technical knowledge, domain engineers may concentrate on the definition of domain $\mathcal{M}_{\text{Dom}}$ while domain expert with limited technical knowledge can define the relevant requirements akin to their natural reasoning. This approach enables organization to introduce more non-technical domain experts to the development of these technical systems.

Remark 2: *Designing a domain-specific language for natural requirements, akin to human reasoning, is expensive.*

The specification of requirements has to feel as natural as possible for domain experts—akin to their usual reasoning of these logistical systems—in order for domain experts to adapt languages and tools into their work. Otherwise, domain expert are more occupied with the expression of requirements in a specific language grammar than comprehensively representing the systems in their requirements.

English and other natural language provide various clauses that allow for different sentence structures with identical semantic meaning in requirements. Replicating this grammatical flexibility in domain-specific languages is difficult and expensive. The majority of clauses from the natural base language have to be defined in the requirements language to suggest grammatical flexibility. Furthermore, all these clauses have to be mapped to expressions in the first-order logic for the evaluation at runtime. However, clauses often contain similar sentence structure which can cause problems for parser generators, i.e., ANTLR [22]. Clauses with similar sentence structure hinder the parser to associate corresponding parts of requirements deterministically to a single clause for building an abstract syntax tree. As a result, the grammar of the requirements language has to be carefully specified for these parser generators to work correctly. There exist some controlled natural languages, e.g., Attempto Controlled English (ACE) [14,15], Processable English (PENG) [10], and Computer Processable Language (CPL) [12] among others, which provide the grammatical flexibility of English, but these languages miss the mapping of objects and predicates to real system data.

Remark 3: *Temporal Constraints are an essential part of today's technical requirements in logistics.*

Within our case study, we have recognized that many technical requirements in logistics are time-dependent, but our requirements and logic are currently not able to express such temporal expressions. We neglected temporal constraint in our framework because we focused on the architectural combination of the three models, i.e., requirements, domain, and logic, to enable the specification of monitorable requirements at runtime. It is essential that we address temporal expression in our requirements and extend the logic by temporal operators as they are used in, e.g., metric first-order temporal logic [23], in future work.

Remark 4: *System data has to be provided in sufficient quantity and quality.* An important part for monitoring requirements at runtime is the data provided by the CPS. This system data defines the scope of domain and requirements, which can be evaluated by the rule engine at runtime. The CPS has to provide data in the appropriate form, quantity, and quality to sufficiently represent the real application domain in domain $\mathcal{M}_{\text{Dom}}$. Objects and predicates without any processable data function in domain $\mathcal{M}_{\text{Dom}}$ could be potentially used in requirements $\mathcal{M}_{\text{Req}}$ to form syntactic correct requirements, but these requirements cannot be interpreted by the rule engine at runtime. There exist two possibilities for evaluating an object or predicate for the data from the CPS, if (1) the provided data contains a corresponding data item or (2) the object and predicate can be calculated from the available data items. For example, the rule engine will evaluate the velocity of a robot, only if the provided data from the robot does include a data item about the robot's velocity or the remaining data items allow to calculate the velocity.

7 Conclusion

We have presented a framework for the development of domain-specific languages that express executable rules about CPS in logistics at the conceptual level, akin to the reasoning of domain experts. The framework defines three individual languages: (1) the domain language allows to specify the application domain with its entities, and predicates over these entities, (2) the requirements language provides the grammatical flexibility to define requirements akin to human reasoning, (3) the first-order logic provides clear syntax and semantics for monitoring and controlling CPS at runtime. We have demonstrated our framework in a logistics scenario with human-machine collaboration. The case study shows that the control and monitoring of CPS in logistics is viable and beneficial under the separation of requirements and domain specification. The separate definition of domain entities, i.e., objects, their proprieties, and predicates, over the system data is essential for specifying requirements akin to human reasoning. However, the development of our framework has also shown that the design of an almost natural language for the requirements specification is very costly and difficult.

One point to consider for the future is the consideration of existing and proven controlled natural languages, e.g. ACE or PENG, for the specification of requirements. Additional future improvements for our framework to consider: (1) temporal expressions in our requirements language and formal logic, (2) different languages than standard English, and (3) the integration of our framework in a requirements engineering workflow. We also envisage a potential of our work in other domain than logistics and want to harden the expressive power within our framework through application in more diverse domains.

References

1. Brat, G., Bushnell, D., Davies, M., Giannakopoulou, D., Howar, F., Kahsai, T.: Verifying the safety of a flight-critical system. In: Bjørner, N., de Boer, F. (eds.) FM 2015. LNCS, vol. 9109, pp. 308–324. Springer, Cham (2015). https://doi.org/10.1007/978-3-319-19249-9_20
2. Geist, J., Rozier, K.Y., Schumann, J.: Runtime observer pairs and bayesian network reasoners on-board FPGAs: flight-certifiable system health management for embedded systems. In: Bonakdarpour, B., Smolka, S.A. (eds.) RV 2014. LNCS, vol. 8734, pp. 215–230. Springer, Cham (2014). https://doi.org/10.1007/978-3-319-11164-3_18
3. Boßelmann, S., et al.: DIME: a programming-less modeling environment for web applications. In: Margaria, T., Steffen, B. (eds.) ISoLA 2016. LNCS, vol. 9953, pp. 809–832. Springer, Cham (2016). https://doi.org/10.1007/978-3-319-47169-3_60
4. Vincent, P., Iijima, K., Driver, M., Wong, J., Natis, Y.: Magic Quadrant for Eterprise Lw-Code Application Platform. Gartner report (2020)
5. Fowler, M.: Domain-Specific Languages. Pearson Education (2010)
6. Zweihoff, P., Steffen, B.: A generative approach for user-centered, collaborative, domain-specific modeling environments. arXiv preprint arXiv:2104.09948 (2021)
7. Crapo, A., Moitra, A., McMillan, C., Russell, D.: Requirements capture and analysis in ASSERT™. In: 2017 IEEE 25th International Requirements Engineering Conference (RE), pp. 283–291 (2017)
8. Mavridou, A., et al.: The ten lockheed martin cyber-physical challenges: formalized, analyzed, and explained. In: 2020 IEEE 28th International Requirements Engineering Conference (RE), pp. 300–310 (2020)
9. Giannakopoulou, D., Pressburger, T., Mavridou, A., Schumann, J.: Generation of formal requirements from structured natural language. In: Madhavji, N., Pasquale, L., Ferrari, A., Gnesi, S. (eds.) REFSQ 2020. LNCS, vol. 12045, pp. 19–35. Springer, Cham (2020). https://doi.org/10.1007/978-3-030-44429-7_2
10. Schwitter, R.: Controlled natural languages for knowledge representation. In: Coling Posters, vol. 2010, pp. 1113–1121 (2010)
11. Pease, A., Li, J.: Controlled English to logic translation. In: Poli, R., Healy, M., Kameas, A. (eds.) Theory and Applications of Ontology: Computer Applications. Springer, Dordrecht (2010). https://doi.org/10.1007/978-90-481-8847-5_11
12. Clark, P., Harrison, P., Jenkins, T., Thompson, J.A., Wojcik, R.H., et al.: Acquiring and using world knowledge using a restricted subset of English. In: Flairs conference, pp. 506–511 (2005)
13. Kuhn, T.: A survey and classification of controlled natural languages. Comput. Linguist. **40**(1), 121–170 (2014). https://www.aclweb.org/anthology/J14-1005
14. Fuchs, N.E., Kaljurand, K.: Attempto controlled English meets the challenges of knowledge representation, reasoning, interoperability and user interfaces (2006)
15. Fuchs, N.E., Kaljurand, K., Kuhn, T.: Attempto controlled English for knowledge representation. In: Baroglio, C., Bonatti, P.A., Małuszyński, J., Marchiori, M., Polleres, A., Schaffert, S. (eds.) Reasoning Web. LNCS, vol. 5224, pp. 104–124. Springer, Heidelberg (2008). https://doi.org/10.1007/978-3-540-85658-0_3
16. Ambriola, V., Gervasi, V.: Processing natural language requirements. In: Proceedings 12th IEEE International Conference Automated Software Engineering, pp. 36–45. IEEE (1997)

17. Ghosh, S., Elenius, D., Li, W., Lincoln, P., Shankar, N., Steiner, W.: ARSENAL: automatic requirements specification extraction from natural language. In: Rayadurgam, S., Tkachuk, O. (eds.) NFM 2016. LNCS, vol. 9690, pp. 41–46. Springer, Cham (2016). https://doi.org/10.1007/978-3-319-40648-0_4
18. Steffen, B., Gossen, F., Naujokat, S., Margaria, T.: Language-driven engineering: from general-purpose to purpose-specific languages. In: Steffen, B., Woeginger, G. (eds.) Computing and Software Science. LNCS, vol. 10000, pp. 311–344. Springer, Cham (2019). https://doi.org/10.1007/978-3-319-91908-9_17
19. Hunkeler, U., Truong, H.L., Stanford-Clark, A.: MQTT-S-A publish/subscribe protocol for wireless sensor networks. In: 2008 3rd International Conference on Communication Systems Software and Middleware and Workshops (COMSWARE 2008), pp. 791–798. IEEE (2008)
20. Pezoa, F., Reutter, J.L., Suarez, F., Ugarte, M., Vrgoč, D.: Foundations of json schema. In: Proceedings of the 25th International Conference on World Wide Web, ser. WWW 2016. Republic and Canton of Geneva, CHE: International World Wide Web Conferences Steering Committee, pp. 263–273 (2016). https://doi.org/10.1145/2872427.2883029
21. Internet Engineering Task Force (IETF): The javascript object notation (json) data interchange format (2014). https://tools.ietf.org/html/rfc7159
22. Parr, T.: The Definitive ANTLR 4 Reference, 2nd edn. Pragmatic Bookshelf (2013)
23. Koymans, R.: Specifying real-time properties with metric temporal logic. Real-Time Syst. **2**(4), 255–299 (1990)

Mining Data Quality Rules for Data Migrations: A Case Study on Material Master Data

Marcel Altendeitering(✉)

Fraunhofer ISST, Emil-Figge-Straße 91, 44227 Dortmund, Germany
marcel.altendeitering@isst.fraunhofer.de

Abstract. Master data sets are an important asset for organizations and their quality must be high to ensure organizational success. At the same time, data migrations are complex projects and they often result in impaired data sets of lower quality. In particular, data quality issues that involve multiple attributes are difficult to identify and can only be resolved with manual data quality checks. In this paper, we are investigating a real-world migration of material master data. Our goal is to ensure data quality by mining the target data set for data quality rules. In a data migration, incoming data sets must comply with these rules to be migrated. For generating data quality rules, we used a SVM for rules at a schema level and Association Rule Learning for rules at the instance level. We found that both methods produce valuable rules and are suitable for ensuring quality in data migrations. As an ensemble, the two methods are adequate to manage common real-world data characteristics such as sparsity or mixed values.

Keywords: Master data · Data quality · SVM · Association rule learning · Data migration

1 Introduction

Data migrations are understood as the process of permanently moving data from a source system to a target system in the right quality [17]. For instance, whenever a new software is introduced or the corporate structure changes (e.g. due to M&A) the need for a data migration arises. Despite the fact that companies are regularly confronted with data migrations their success rates are low. They are often underestimated in size and complexity and companies lack the necessary specialist skills. As a result, the quality of the target data set is impaired by introducing low quality data, which can jeopardize organizational success [16,17].

As data, and in particular master data, is a valuable asset for organizations, it is vital to ensure high quality data. For this, numerous methods and tools are available that can support practitioners in detecting errors in a single column [5]. These are often embedded in database management systems (DBMS) and automatically detect errors like missing values, duplicate entries or invalid categorical data. Detecting errors that involve multiple columns (e.g. functional

T. Margaria and B. Steffen (Eds.): ISoLA 2021, LNCS 13036, pp. 178–191, 2021.
https://doi.org/10.1007/978-3-030-89159-6_12

dependencies) is much more difficult and rarely included in established automated data quality tools [10]. A common approach for identifying multi-column data errors is the 'consulting approach', in which internal or external domain experts clean data sets using data quality rules and metrics [23]. Therefore, the domain experts manually analyze dependencies between values and attributes in the data set and create rules. The downside of this approach is that the need for experts makes the process time-consuming and expensive [9]. Moreover, the experts can miss rules, which are hidden in the data set but not made explicit using quality rules. A solely consulting based approach is therefore not suitable for large scale data migrations, in which many entries are changed at once. There is a need for an automated detection of multi-column data errors that can support data migrations and reduce the amount of data quality work.

In this paper, we propose an extended data migration process that uses data quality rule mining for automated quality checks in data migrations. With data quality rule mining we are uncovering relationships between attributes in relational data sets and are evaluating incoming data against the derived rules. This way, we are able to reduce the amount of data quality work and prevent complex data errors that would normally require expert support. In contrast to other solutions, our work focuses on multi-column errors and uses a combined approach to identify rules at the schema and the instance level. This way we are able to handle diverse data sets and can support the generality of our solution. We conducted and evaluated our study in a real-world migration of a material master data.

The remainder of this paper is structured as follows. In Sect. 2, we describe the experimental setting we investigated in our study. In Sect. 3, we propose the extended data migration process and show how we automatically derive data quality rules to support data migrations. Afterwards, we present the findings of our study in Sect. 4. Finally, in Sect. 5, we will discuss related work and draw a conclusion in Sect. 6.

2 Case Description

2.1 Setting

For our case study, we investigated the data migration process at a large German pharmaceutical company, which we call PharmCo in this study. PharmCo has several affiliated companies and production sites around the globe. The diversified and international nature of the company led to a complex IT and data infrastructure. In order to harmonize the data infrastructure, data migrations are required in regular intervals, causing a substantial financial and organizational effort.

In particular, we investigated the migration of material master data from external sources (e.g. a remote production site) to a central SAP system. The data sets in this system are of high importance for the company and inherit a great value for business operations. For example, incorrect tax information about a material could cause fines and interrupt the supply and delivery chains. Thus, it is important that the overall quality of this database is high and must not be deteriorated during data migrations.

2.2 Current Data Migration Process

Currently, data quality is maintained by an established data migration tool, which automatically enforces data models and secures data quality. However, the data migration system is not capable of detecting complex data quality issues involving multiple attributes, which causes the introduction of new errors to the data set during each migration. The correction of these errors costs PharmCo up to 10,000 Euros per data migration. Specifically, the current data migration process consists of three steps that are conducted in sequence (see Fig. 1).

- *Step 1*: Once the data migration starts the external data sets are imported into the data migration tool. The tool performs schema matching and error detection to harmonize the data sets and find simple data errors.
- *Step 2*: All data that passes the checks in the data migration tool is introduced to the target data set.
- *Step 3*: After the migration is completed there often remain errors in the target data set that were not detected by the data migration tool. Therefore, an experienced employee checks all entries manually to find and resolve potential issues. As this process is very expensive the expert focuses on error prone attributes, that had errors in previous migrations.

To address the limitations of the current approach PharmCo is looking for an automated solution that improves the error detection accuracy of the data migration tool and supports domain experts in resolving errors. During a workshop with two members of the data migration team we were able to derive the general requirements for such a solution. Most importantly, both participants from PharmCo mentioned that errors in a data migration mostly occur on the instance and the schema level. They therefore formulated the requirement that:

> *"The tool needs to generate rules for both, the instance and the schema level, so we can evaluate incoming data against these rules"*

They provided two examples, one for each category respectively. An instance rule is for example one, which specifies that when there is a certain value for the field 'Base Unit' there must also be certain values in the fields 'Material Group' and 'Volume'. A rule on the schema level should for example specify that once the attribute 'Gross weight' is filled with any value the attribute 'Net weight' also needs to be filled. They also specified that these are simple examples and potential rules can include several attributes, which makes the detection and formulation difficult. Another important aspect is the execution time of the tool. One participant mentioned:

> *"Data migrations are time-critical projects. It is therefore important for the algorithms to run in a limited amount of time and be highly scalable."*

Moreover, PharmCo stated that the quality rules the tool derives must be 'actionable'. This means the output should be easy to interpret semantically and enable an integration with existing tools using standardized interfaces.

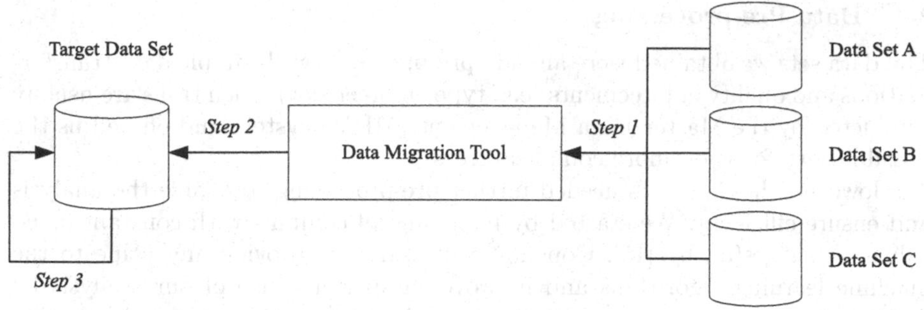

Fig. 1. Current approach for ensuring data quality in data migrations.

2.3 Data Set Description

For our study, PharmCo provided us with access to two real-world material data sets: trading goods and spare parts. The trading goods data set contains information about finished products that are ready to be sold on the market. Among others, this data set provides a description of the good, tax information, relations to other goods. The spare parts data set contains information about materials that are part of trading goods. This data set includes for instance the dimensions of the good, safety restrictions and weights.

There are several reasons why we selected to use material data sets and in particular these two kinds. (1) The material data sets do not contain any personal information and are not regulated by data privacy laws. It was therefore easier to gain access to these data sets as compared to supplier or customer data. (2) The data on trading goods and spare parts do not contain information about specific pharmaceuticals or ingredients, which could reveal company secrets. (3) The data definitions and data schemes vary between different parts of the company, which can lead to a large number of errors in data migrations. (4) The master data sets are important for business operations and can help to raise awareness about data quality.

Since we are working with real-world data sets, we are not able to present the actual data we used to protect intellectual property. However, we are able to describe the schema of the data in more detail. The trading goods data set has 173 attributes (46 constant, 84 categorical, 23 free text, 18 numerical, 2 date) and 15,904 entries. The spare parts data set also features 173 attributes (111 constant, 37 categorical, 7 free text, 12 numerical, 6 date) and has 92,869 entries. Overall, the trading goods data set has a sparsity of 10.5% and a size of 14.8 MB. The spare parts data set has a sparsity of 61.3%, which results in a size of 64.4 MB. The selected data sets originate from a real-world database and feature some typical challenges like high dimensionality, type mix, special characters and sparsity. It was therefore necessary to pre-process the data for analysis. Suitable methods for mining data quality rules must be able to incorporate these characteristics.

2.4 Data Pre-processing

The data sets we obtained were already pre-processed with simple data transformations and quality enforcements (e.g. type enforcement). Such tasks are usually conducted by the Master Data Management (MDM) system and offered us the possibility to focus on more complex errors.

However, the data sets needed further pre-processing to enable the analysis and ensure efficiency. We started by removing all columns with constant or no values as suggested by [15]. Constant values do not provide any value to the machine learning algorithms and improve the performance of our analysis by limiting the dimensionality of the data sets. As a result, we reduced the trading goods data set to 127 attributes and the spare parts data set to 62 attributes. We furthermore removed certain special characters like commas and semicolons from the free text values, which were hindering the import of the csv source files.

3 Proposed Solution

3.1 Extended Data Migration Process

With our study we want to support the currently manual process for ensuring data quality in data migrations with machine learning (ML) techniques. Therefore, we extended the manual process with a new capability that automatically derives data quality rules from a target data set and applies these to the data sets to be migrated. Following Chiang and Miller, data quality rules "define relationships among a restricted set of attribute values that are expected to be true under a given context" (p. 1166) [8]. Usually, these rules are developed manually by domain and business experts. However, obtaining a complete set of data quality rules is difficult as the process is time-consuming and costly. Additionally, there might be rules present in the data set that the experts are not aware of [8].

The proposed 'Data Quality Rule Mining' component tries to automatically identify such rules and apply them in a data migration. This way we want to reduce the amount of manual data quality checks by providing a hint on potential errors, which leads to reduced cost and better data quality. By extending the current data migration process with the proposed component, we get a new process consisting of four steps (see Fig. 2):

- *Step 1*: Using data mining and profiling techniques we derive suitable rules from a target data set on a schema and an instance level. Hereby, we assume that the given data set is correct. Optionally, a human-in-the-loop manually evaluates the derived rules to improve the accuracy of the result.
- *Step 2*: The derived data migration rules are implemented as executable rules in a data migration tool.
- *Step 3*: During a data migration the migration tool automatically checks if incoming data satisfies the rules. In case a check fails the issue is resolved manually or automatically by the tool.
- *Step 4*: Data that passes all checks is migrated to the target data set without further checks.

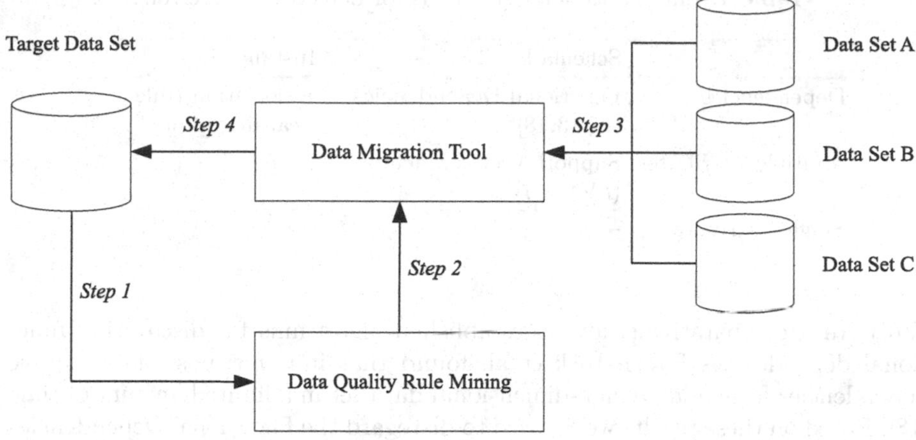

Fig. 2. The role of mining data quality rules in the data migration process.

3.2 Data Quality Rule Mining

Initial Selection. Since there is a large body of research available on mining and profiling relational data sets, we decided to return to the literature for selecting suitable methods for data quality rule generation. Several survey and overview papers in the domains of data mining and data profiling discuss potential approaches [1,2,8,10,12,19]. Following the requirement of PharmCo we can distinguish these methods between the schema and instance levels [19] and the dimensionality of a potential rule [2]. In terms of dimensionality, Abedjan et al. separate data profiling tasks in single-column, multi-column and dependency tasks [2]. In our case, we are only interested in multi-column and dependencies.

In each of these methodological categories there are numerous algorithms available. However, finding and selecting an algorithm that works on real-world data sets and satisfies our requirements remains difficult. The accuracy and usefulness of many methods is unclear when they are applied to a real-world data set. Most of them have either only been tested on synthetic data or on synthetically injected errors [1]. Another difficulty of real-world data sets is that they often contain multiple errors at the same time [19]. We therefore need to consider an ensemble of algorithms to derive suitable data quality rules, while maintaining a short execution time.

The literature review we conducted yielded in the selection of three methods for further investigation. Table 1 places these methods in their methodological categories and shows corresponding literature.

In a first step, we implemented algorithms for each of the four methods and used a small test data set to determine their usefulness for generating data quality rules. An analysis of the results showed promising results for the SVM and Association Rule Learning methods. The Functional Dependencies method suffered from large time and space requirements, which caused the algorithm to

Table 1. Initial selection of methods for detecting data errors.

	Schema-Level	Instance-Level
Dependencies	Functional Dependencies [11,13,18]	Association Rule Learning [3,6]
Multiple Attributes	Support Vector Machine (SVM) [7]	–
Single Attribute	–	–

abort. In a comparative study on established algorithms for discovering functional dependencies Papenbrock et al. found that it is not possible to derive dependencies from a large high-dimensional data set in a limited amount of time [18]. Based on these results we decided to disregard the Functional Dependencies approach and further investigate SVM and Association Rule Learning.

Support Vector Machine (SVM). The general idea of the SVM approach is to utilize the aspect that the material data sets at PharmCo are sparse. Given a tuple of a data set that contains some null and some concrete values we want to label if a value is expected for a certain attribute or not and determine a data quality rule on the schema level. Since a SVM works on numeric attributes, we transformed the given data set to a binary matrix consisting of 0 and 1 values. In this case, a 0 indicates that an attribute contains no value and a 1 indicates that some concrete instance is present. This way, we transferred the data set to a binary classification problem, which are well-suited for SVMs [21]. As SVMs are supervised learning models, a target attribute must be provided. This attribute can either be known as error prone or one of high-importance.

For the SVM analysis we start with a target data set and transform it to a binary matrix. We separate the data to a set of binary samples and a set of binary classes using the target attribute. With these two sets we train a linear SVM and obtain a trained binary classifier. During a migration incoming data is tested against this model. Therefore, we transform an entry of an incoming data set on-the-fly to a binary tuple. This tuple contains all attributes except for the target attribute. As classification result we will retrieve a 0 or 1, which indicates whether this field should be filled or not (see Fig. 3). In case a value is given but the model predicted a 0 or vice versa there is likely an error in the incoming tuple.

The main advantage of this approach is the fast training and classification time. On the contrary, this approach only works for sparse data sets and might therefore not always be useful. Furthermore, the SVM does not explicitly formulate the derived data quality rules, which makes it more difficult to interpret the results.

Association Rule Learning. Our goal with association rule learning is to discover relationships between multiple attributes on an instance level. This means that, in contrast to the SVM approach, we want to identify what values

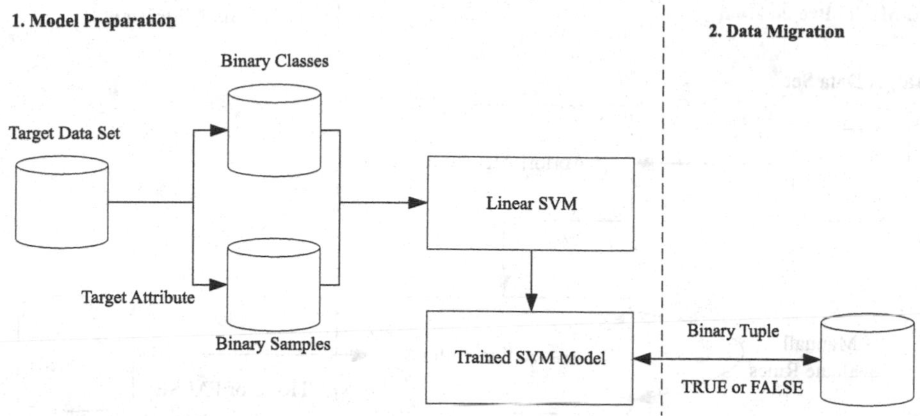

Fig. 3. Functional overview of the SVM method.

often appear together (i.e. frequent itemsets) and build data quality rules using these itemsets. Association rules are well suited for detecting multi-column data errors but are uncommon in professional data quality and migration tools, as these are focused on single column data errors [1,10]. Generally, association rules have the following format:

$$\{AttributeA|ValueA, AttributeB|ValueB \rightarrow AttributeC|ValueC\} \quad (1)$$

The most well-known algorithm for association rule learning is the Apriori algorithm by Agrawal et al. [3]. Although there are faster solutions available for discovering association rules (e.g. FP-Growth [6]) we decided to use the Apriori algorithm as it is well-established and there are several implementations in different programming languages available.

The Apriori algorithm is an unsupervised ML method that can handle different value types, but not null-values. We therefore filled the missing values in the data set with a fixed 'NA' value. The Apriori algorithm furthermore requires a *support* level, which determines how often a value pair needs to appear to be considered frequent and a *confidence* level, which defines how often a rule needs to be true. With these inputs the Apriori algorithm produces a set of association rules. During the data migration we can verify incoming data against the derived set of association rules. If a rule with a high confidence level is not met, we can reason that there is an error in the data set (see Fig. 4).

An advantage of association rule learning is that it is a multivariate method and is not limited to one kind of type. It also produces rules that are easy to understand and interpret for humans. A downside is the complexity of the algorithm and that it suffers from long execution times on data sets with many different or free-text values. Thus, it is vital to pre-process and filter the data from unnecessary attributes to limit the execution times.

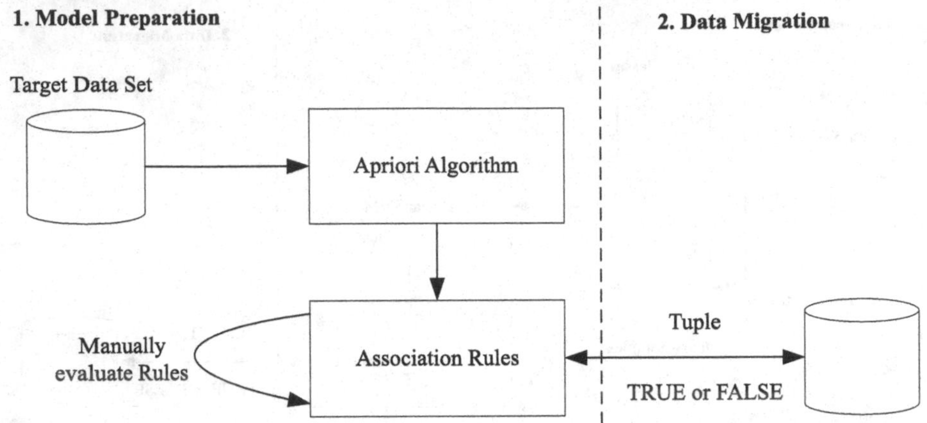

Fig. 4. Functional overview of the Association Rule Learning method.

4 Findings

For evaluating the soundness and suitability of our approach for data migrations we applied the methods to material data sets used in previous data migrations at PharmCo. We decided to use data sets from previous migrations as this offered us the possibility to compare our findings with the ground truth, in which all data quality issues were manually resolved. Specifically, we used a *training set* and a *test set* for the trading goods and spare parts data sets respectively. The *training sets* were old copies of the central SAP system and served as basis for training our ML models. The *test sets* were old copies from a material database of an external subsidiary of PharmCo. This data set simulated the incoming data during a migration. Moreover, we qualitatively evaluated our approach with data migration experts at PharmCo, who helped us to investigate the advantages and disadvantages of the proposed algorithms.

4.1 Support Vector Machine (SVM)

The SVM approach requires a certain target attribute to train a classifier. In discussions with the data migration team at PharmCo we selected three attributes (A: 'Product hierarchy', B: 'Transportation group', C: 'Purch Group') for the trading goods data set and five attributes (A: 'Product Hierarchy', B: 'Gross Weight', C: 'Material Type', D: 'Lot Size', E: 'Valuation class') for the spare parts data set as target attributes. We decided to train models for these attributes as according to PharmCo they have a tendency for missing values and needed manual review in previous migrations. We trained eight SVM models (S1 to S8) using the *training sets.* For each of these models we used the *test sets* to obtain a classification result and evaluated this against the ground truth to derive the fraction of false positive and false negative classifications. Following the definition of Abedjan et al., we set precision P as the fraction of cells that are correctly marked as errors and recall R as the fraction of actual errors discovered [1]. Table 2 summarizes our results.

Table 2. Evaluation of the SVM approach.

Data Set	*Trading Goods*			*Spare Parts*				
SVM Model	S1	S2	S3	S4	S5	S6	S7	S8
Attribute	A	B	C	A	B	C	D	E
P	0.99	1	0.99	0.99	0.98	0.96	0.99	0.98
R	0.94	0.93	0.96	0.96	0.94	0.9	0.97	0.93

The results show that the SVM approach is highly accurate in correctly detecting potential errors in an incoming data set. Using this approach we can significantly reduce the amount of manual data quality checks that would normally be required during a migration. The SVM approach is particularly useful for sparse attributes that have a tendency for missing values. However, our experiences are based on the two data sets provided by PharmCo. Further evaluations with other data sets should be part of future work to support the generality of the SVM approach for data migrations.

4.2 Association Rule Learning

For association rule learning we conducted several runs of the Apriori algorithm using the *training sets* with different parameter settings (see Table 3). Other than the attributes removed during the pre-processing step (see Sect. 2.4) we did not remove any attribute and conducted the analysis on the remaining 127 and 62 attributes for the trading goods and spare parts data sets respectively. For comparison and evaluation of the different settings we measured the number of rules produced, the execution time and the precision of the rules. We followed the approach of Chiang and Miller for calculating the precision value [8]. They define the precision P of association rule learning to be the fraction of the number of relevant rules over the total number of returned rules. To determine the amount of relevant rules we manually evaluated the derived rules with domain and data migration experts at PharmCo. In this process, we disregarded runs with no rules or with too many rules for manual review. We found the optimal configuration for the trading goods data set at $support >= 90\%$ and $confidence = 100\%$, which produced an output of 43 rules. For the spare parts data set we received an optimum of 14 rules with settings at $support >= 50\%$ and $confidence >= 80\%$.

During the manual review of the derived rules we found that some of the correct and relevant rules have a trivial meaning. For instance, we derived the following rule on dimensionality using the trading goods data set with 100% confidence and 100% support. It specifies that whenever two dimensions have a length of 0.0 the third must also be 0.0.

Table 3. Evaluation of association rule learning.

Data Set	*Trading Goods*				*Spare Parts*			
Settings % (sup. / conf.)	50/70	60/80	80/90	90/100	50/70	50/80	70/90	80/90
# of rules	2399	817	110	43	88	14	0	N/A
Exec. time (Sec.)	102	70	38	16	76	51	48	N/A
P	N/A	N/A	0.85	0.98	0.92	1	N/A	N/A

$$\{Height|0.0, Length|0.0 \rightarrow Volume|0.0\} \tag{2}$$

An example for a more complex rule we derived from the spare parts data set with a support level of 51.4% specifies that whenever a good is measured in kg and its trading is not restricted then its base unit is 'EA each'. This rule is true in 96.5% of the cases.

$$\{Weight|\text{KGM kg}, Cat|\text{Y001 Ambient no restrict} \rightarrow BaseUnit|\text{EA each}\} \tag{3}$$

Further to the manual review we evaluated the 43 and 14 rules we derived from the *training sets* against the *test sets* from a previous migration to find potential errors. This test showed that there are no violating tupels in the *test sets*. Nevertheless, this is still a useful result, as we have a validated proof that the data within the *test sets* is correct and do not need an additional manual review. This way we can reduce the amount of manual data quality work.

Overall, the results show that association rule learning is a suitable approach for detecting data errors in data migrations. However, it can be difficult to determine the optimal settings for support and confidence as the results need a manual review. Hereby, a user-friendly explanation of the algorithms and results can help to improve the usability of this approach [4].

4.3 Evaluation

After the case study we conducted a retrospective workshop with data migration experts at PharmCo. The workshop included the author of this paper and four experts from PharmCo. It lasted 90 min and provided valuable insights as the experts could draw on their personal experiences with data migrations. The workshop was structured by the two proposed methods and each one was discussed thoroughly regarding its usefulness and potential downsides.

Overall, we learned that our approach is well received and the prototypical application is still in use. However, a seamless integration into the existing system landscape at PharmCo is necessary for future use. Currently, the data migration team manually implements the rules derived from association rule learning into the existing data migration tool as executable rules. The SVM approach is used for certain attributes that the domain experts consider important. Therefore, the incoming data is tested against the binary classifier using a Python script, that was manually integrated into the data migration tool. PharmCo is planning to extend the current prototype and integrate it with the data migration tool as well as existing databases. This way, a fully integrated and automated tool for data quality rule learning emerges, which helps to simplify cumbersome data migration processes.

5 Related Work

The detection and cleaning of relational data sets (e.g., [1,19]) and the data quality challenges in data migrations (e.g., [16,20]) have both been widely discussed in the scientific literature. Yet, there is only a limited amount of prototypes available that combine both research directions and address data quality issues in data migrations.

For instance, with regard to quality rule learning Shrivastava et al. [22] presented a tool called DQLearn. The tool assists users in the development of data quality rules by providing a method for formalizing a data quality problem in a structured way. This way data quality rules become more explainable and easy to automate. In [4] the authors highlight the need for explainability and customization in automated data quality tools. They argue that the user needs to easily understand and interpret the results provided.

Drumm et al. proposed QuickMig, a system for semi-automatic creation and enforcement of schema mappings [9]. Their approach aims to reduce the complexity of data structures, which helps to lower the data migration efforts. Kaitoua et al. introduced a system called Muses [14]. Muses focuses on supporting data migrations between distributed polystores. Through efficient data reorganizations their system can improve the performance of data migrations by up to 30%. A data dependency graph is used for improving data migrations by Zou et al. [24]. The data dependency graph defines relationships between data components. Using pre-defined compliance criteria an algorithm checks whether a specific instance is migratable or not. This way data consistency and data quality are improved.

Unlike these systems, our approach features several distinct characteristics to support data migrations. (1) We are combining rule detection on a schema and an instance level to identify potential issues on both levels. Other solutions, like QuickMig, are focusing on the schema level [9]. (2) Our approach automatically discovers data quality rules in a limited amount of time. Solutions that utilize data profiling techniques (e.g. [1]) are of limited scalability and therefore not suitable for data migrations. (3) The methods we employ have been tested on real-world data sets. They are flexible to handle common data characteristics, such as sparsity or mixed values.

6 Conclusion

Although data migrations are part of a company's daily business, they are still considered error-prone, expensive and their success rates are low. In our study, we describe the lessons learned from impaired data sets due to data migrations and propose an extended data migration process that ensures data quality. Specifically, we combined a binary SVM classifier and association rule learning to mine data quality rules from a given data set. Incoming data must comply with these rules to be migrated without manual review. These automated checks lead to a reduced amount of manual data quality work and reduced cost. We evaluated both methods against a real-world data set. Our findings showed that both methods produce valuable results and are suitable for an application to data migrations.

With the proposed solution we are addressing the current limitations of data migrations at PharmCo. We created an automated solution that meets the requirements specified by the data migration and domain experts. Most importantly, our tool is capable of deriving data quality rules on the schema and instance level and can therefore prevent different kinds of data errors. Furthermore, the algorithms we used are scalable and have a limited execution time, which makes them suitable for time-critical data migration projects.

Despite the promising results, our study has several limitations. Most importantly, our findings are based on two material data sets. We are therefore planning to evaluate our solution in further data migration scenarios with different data sets and in different companies. This would also support the generality of our findings and help to formalize lessons learned that are generally applicable. It would also be useful to test our approach in a live data migration and investigate the impact our solution has on the performance and the overall migration process. Furthermore, our solution only works with structured data sets. In light of current trends, there is a need to investigate data quality rule generation for migrations of unstructured data sets.

References

1. Abedjan, Z., et al.: Detecting data errors: where are we and what needs to be done? Proc. VLDB Endowment **9**(12), 993–1004 (2016)
2. Abedjan, Z., Golab, L., Naumann, F.: Profiling relational data: a survey. VLDB J. **24**(4), 557–581 (2015)
3. Agrawal, R., Srikant, R., et al.: Fast algorithms for mining association rules. In: Proceedings 20th International Conference Very Large Data Bases, VLDB, vol. 1215, pp. 487–499 (1994)
4. Altendeitering, M., Fraunhofer, I., Guggenberger, T.: Designing data quality tools: findings from an action design research project at Boehringer Ingelheim, pp. 1–16 (2021)
5. Barateiro, J., Galhardas, H.: A survey of data quality tools. Datenbank-Spektrum **14**, 15–21 (2005)
6. Borgelt, C.: An implementation of the FP-growth algorithm. In: Proceedings of the 1st International Workshop on Open Source Data Mining: Frequent Pattern Mining Implementations, pp. 1–5 (2005)
7. Burges, C.J.: A tutorial on support vector machines for pattern recognition. Data Min. Knowl. Disc. **2**(2), 121–167 (1998)

8. Chiang, F., Miller, R.J.: Discovering data quality rules. Proc. VLDB Endowment **1**(1), 1166–1177 (2008)
9. Drumm, C., Schmitt, M., Do, H.H., Rahm, E.: QuickMig: automatic schema matching for data migration projects. In: Proceedings of the Sixteenth ACM Conference on Conference on Information and Knowledge Management, CIKM 2007, pp. 107–116. Association for Computing Machinery (2007)
10. Ehrlinger, L., Rusz, E., Wöß, W.: A survey of data quality measurement and monitoring tools. arXiv preprint arXiv:1907.08138 (2019)
11. Fan, W., Geerts, F., Li, J., Xiong, M.: Discovering conditional functional dependencies. IEEE Trans. Knowl. Data Eng. **23**(5), 683–698 (2010)
12. Hipp, J., Güntzer, U., Grimmer, U.: Data quality mining-making a virute of necessity. In: DMKD, p. 6 (2001)
13. Huhtala, Y., Kärkkäinen, J., Porkka, P., Toivonen, H.: TANE: an efficient algorithm for discovering functional and approximate dependencies. Comput. J. **42**(2), 100–111 (1999)
14. Kaitoua, A., Rabl, T., Katsifodimos, A., Markl, V.: Muses: distributed data migration system for polystores. In: 2019 IEEE 35th International Conference on Data Engineering (ICDE), pp. 1602–1605. IEEE (2019)
15. Kruse, S., et al.: Fast approximate discovery of inclusion dependencies. In: Datenbanksysteme für Business, Technologie und Web (BTW 2017) (2017)
16. Matthes, F., Schulz, C., Haller, K.: Testing quality assurance in data migration projects. In: 2011 27th IEEE International Conference on Software Maintenance (ICSM), pp. 438–447 (2011)
17. Morris, J.: Practical data migration. BCS, The Chartered Institute (2012)
18. Papenbrock, T., et al.: Functional dependency discovery: an experimental evaluation of seven algorithms. Proc. VLDB Endowment **8**(10), 1082–1093 (2015)
19. Rahm, E., Do, H.H.: Data cleaning: problems and current approaches. IEEE Data Eng. Bull. **23**(4), 3–13 (2000)
20. Sarmah, S.S.: Data migration. Sci. Technol. **8**(1), 1–10 (2018)
21. Shao, Y.H., Chen, W.J., Deng, N.Y.: Nonparallel hyperplane support vector machine for binary classification problems. Inf. Sci. **263**, 22–35 (2014)
22. Shrivastava, S., Patel, D., Zhou, N., Iyengar, A., Bhamidipaty, A.: DQLearn: a toolkit for structured data quality learning. In: 2020 IEEE International Conference on Big Data (Big Data), pp. 1644–1653. IEEE (2020)
23. Wang, P., He, Y.: Uni-detect: a unified approach to automated error detection in tables. In: Proceedings of the 2019 International Conference on Management of Data, pp. 811–828 (2019)
24. Zou, J., Liu, X., Sun, H., Zeng, J.: Live instance migration with data consistency in composite service evolution. In: 2010 6th World Congress on Services, pp. 653–656. IEEE (2010)

Programming: What is Next

Programming - What is Next?

Klaus Havelund[1(✉)] and Bernhard Steffen[2(✉)]

[1] Jet Propulsion Laboratory, California Institute of Technology, Pasadena, USA
klaus.havelund@jpl.nasa.gov
[2] TU Dortmund University, Dortmund, Germany
steffen@cs.tu-dortmund.de

Abstract. The paper provides an introduction to the track: "Programming - What is Next?", organized by the authors as part of ISoLA 2021: the 9th International Symposium On Leveraging Applications of Formal Methods, Verification and Validation. A total of 14 papers were presented in the track, with responses to the question: *what are the trends in current more recent programming languages, and what can be expected of future languages?*. The track covers such topics as general-purpose programming languages, domain-specific languages, formal methods and modeling languages, textual versus graphical languages, and application programming versus embedded programming.

Keywords: Programming · General-purpose languages · Domain-specific languages · Formal methods · Modeling · Textual languages · Graphical languages · Application programming · Embedded programming

1 Introduction

High-level main-stream programming languages (high-level wrt. to assembler languages and machine code) have evolved dramatically since the emergence of the Fortran language well over half a century ago, with hundreds of languages being developed since then. In the last couple of decades we have seen several languages appearing, most of which are oriented towards application programming, and a few of which are oriented towards systems and embedded close-to-the-metal programming. More experimental programming languages focusing e.g. on program correctness, supporting proof systems have appeared as well.

In addition, we see developments in the area of Domain-Specific Languages (DSLs), including visual as well as textual languages, easy to learn for experts in dedicated fields. Combined with approaches like generative and meta-programming this may lead to very different styles of system development. Related to these developments, we can also observe developments in modeling languages meant to support abstraction, verification, and productivity.

K. Havelund—The research performed by this author was carried out at Jet Propulsion Laboratory, California Institute of Technology, under a contract with the National Aeronautics and Space Administration.

T. Margaria and B. Steffen (Eds.): ISoLA 2021, LNCS 13036, pp. 195–201, 2021.
https://doi.org/10.1007/978-3-030-89159-6_13

This paper provides an introduction to the track: "Programming - What is Next?", organized by the authors as part of ISoLA 2021: the 9th International Symposium On Leveraging Applications of Formal Methods, Verification and Validation. 14 papers were presented in the track, with responses to the question: *what are the trends in current more recent programming languages, and what can be expected of future languages?*.

The papers presented cover various topics. There is a core of papers focusing on different ways of programming applications, and in particular embedded systems, using general purpose programming languages. Here classical programming languages such as C and C++ have been dominating for decades. However, these are low-level and unsafe, and better abstractions are needed. This includes formal specification and proof support. Related to this topic is the question how modeling and programming interacts, and it is emphasized that modeling and programming ought to be tightly integrated. Several papers discuss programming language concepts and constructs. New concepts are proposed, such as time as a core concept, an alternative to object-orientation, advanced type systems, and a suggestion to focus on non-linear dynamic systems. The alternative to general-purpose programming languages is domain-specific languages. Several papers advocate for their use, both textual and graphical. General-purpose as well as domain-specific languages are typically used/developed in IDEs. A browser-based approach is advocated in one paper.

The track can be seen as a followup of the tracks named *"A Unified View of Modeling and Programming"*, organized at ISoLA 2016 [2] and 2018 [3]. These tracks focused on the similarities and differences between programming languages and modeling languages. Whereas those tracks considered programming and modeling of equal interest, the "Programming - What is Next?" track is more focused on the programming activity.

2 Contributions

The papers presented in the track are introduced below. They are divided into subsections according to the track sessions, covering approaches to program development, programming language concepts, and domain-specific languages.

2.1 Program Development

Lethbridge [8] (*Low-code is often high-code, so we must design low-code platforms to enable proper software engineering*), argues that software written on low code platforms often accumulates large volumes of complex code, which can be worse to maintain than in traditional languages, because the low-code platforms tend not to properly support good engineering practices such as version control, separation of concerns, automated testing and literate programming. Based on his experience with low code platforms he claims that such technical debt can only be avoided by providing low-code platforms with just as deep a capability to support modern software engineering practices as traditional languages. As a side result sees a sign that traditional programming will maintain its value also in the (long) future.

Lee and Lohstroh [7] (*Time for all programs, not just real-time programs*), argue that the utility of time as a semantic property of software is not limited to the domain of real-time systems. This paper outlines four concurrent design patterns: alignment, precedence, simultaneity, and consistency, all of which are relevant to general-purpose software applications. It is shown that a semantics of logical time provides a natural framework for reasoning about concurrency, makes some difficult problems easy, and offers a quantified interpretation of the CAP theorem, enabling quantified evaluation of the trade-off between consistency and availability.

Havelund and Bocchino [6] (*Integrated modeling and development of component-based embedded software in Scala*), explore the use of Scala for modeling and programming of embedded systems represented as connected components. Four internal Scala DSLs are presented, inspired by an actual C++ framework, for programming space missions. The DSLs support programming of software components, hierarchical state machines, temporal logic monitors, and rule-based test generators. The effort required to develop these DSLs has been small compared to the similar C++ effort. It is argued that although Scala today is not suitable for this domain, several current efforts aim to develop Scala-like embedded languages, including the works [5,11] reported on in this volume.

Robby and Hatcliff [11] (*Slang: The Sireum programming language*), present the programming language Slang, syntactically is a subset of the Scala programming language, for programming high assurance safety/security-critical systems. The language supports specification and proof of properties, and omits features that make formal verification difficult. A subset, Slang Embedded, can be compiled to e.g. C. Slang can be used for prototyping on a JVM, and later re-deployed to an embedded platform for actual use. Slang is used as programming language in HAMR, see [5] in this volume, a High Assurance Model-based Rapid engineering framework for embedded systems. Developers here specify component-based system architectures using the AADL architecture description language.

Hatcliff, Belt, Robby, and Carpenter [5] (*HAMR: An AADL multi-platform code generation toolset*), present HAMR, a tool-kit for High-Assurance Model-based Rapid engineering for embedded cyber-physical systems. Architectures are modeled using AADL. HAMR is based on an abstract execution model that can be instantiated by back-end translations for different platforms. Elements of models can be programmed in the Slang programming language, translatable to C, also reported on in this volume [11]. The framework supports automated formal verification of models and code written in Slang. Since the infrastructure code and code generators are written in Slang, HAMR provides the convenience of a single verification framework to establish the correctness of code generation.

2.2 Program Language Concepts

Mosses [10] (*Fundamental constructs in programming languages*), presents a framework for defining the semantics of programming constructs at a high level of abstraction. A programming language construct is defined by translating it to fundamental constructs, referred to as funcons, in a compositional manner. The use of funcons is meant as a precise and complete alternative to informal explanations of languages found in reference manuals. Furthermore, specifying languages by translation to funcons appears to be significantly less effort than with other frameworks. Funcons abstract from details related to implementation efficiency, and are defined using a modular variant of structural operational semantics. A library of funcons has been developed, available online, along with tools for generating funcon interpreters from them.

Harel and Marron [4] (*Introducing dynamical systems and chaos early in computer science and software engineering education can help advance theory and practice of software development and computing*), argue that the concept of nonlinear dynamic systems, their theory, and the mathematical and computerized tools for dealing with them, should be taught early in the education of computer scientists. These systems are found in diverse fields, such as fluid dynamics, biological population analysis, and economic and financial operations. Such systems are complex and embody the notion of chaotic behavior. Focus on dynamic systems can lead to enrichment of e.g. programming languages, tools and methodologies in computer science.

Wadler [15] (*GATE: Gradual effect types*), highlights the value of advanced type systems, including effect types, and discusses how they can become mainstream. Traditional type systems are concerned with the types of data. Effect types are concerned with the effects that a program may invoke, such as input, output, raising an exception, reading or assigning to state, receiving or sending a message, and executing concurrently. It is argued that in order to make such advanced type systems main stream, a gradual approach is needed (the "gate" to types), where types can be gradually added, and which allow untyped languages to interoperate with strongly typed languages. The paper provides a survey of some of the work on these different advanced type systems.

Selić and Pierantonio [12] (*Fixing classification: a viewpoint-based approach*), argue that the classification scheme realized in traditional object-oriented computer languages is insufficient for modern software development, which is becoming increasingly more integrated with the highly dynamic physical world. The limitations of the traditional binary classification approach makes it difficult to model dynamic reclassification of objects, classification of objects from different perspectives, and representing in-between cases, where an entity may be categorized as belonging in more than one class. The paper outlines a new approach to classification based on viewpoints, overcoming these limitations. The proposed approach replaces the static multiple-inheritance hierarchy approach with multiple dynamic class hierarchies, including overlapping class membership.

2.3 Domain-Specific Languages

Stevens [13] (*The future of programming and modelling: a Vision*), argues that, despite impressive achievements, software development now suffers from a capacity crisis which cannot be alleviated by programming as currently conceived. Rather, it is necessary to democratise the development of software: stakeholders who are not software specialists must, somehow, be empowered to take more of the decisions about how the software they use shall behave. She proposes to describe this behaviour via a collection of models, each expressed in a (domain-specific) language appropriate to its intended users. Bi-directional transformations are then meant to serve for the corresponding global semantics. The paper also discussed required advances to guarantee the required progress.

Balasubramanian, Coglio, Dubey, and Karsai [1] (*Towards model-based intent-driven adaptive software*), argue that a model-based workflow for adaptive software may reduce the burden caused by system evolution like requirement changes and platform updates. In their vision, a modeling paradigm centered around the concepts of objectives, intents, and constraints, may uniformly comprise required functionalities as well as all managerial aspects. These concepts define, respectively, (1) what the system must do in terms of domain-specific abstractions, (2) the concretization choices made to refine a model into implementation, and (3) the system requirements not already expressed in terms of domain-specific abstractions.

Margaria, Chaudhary, Guevara, Ryan, and Schieweck [9] (*The interoperability challenge: building a model-driven digital thread platform for CPS*), argue that the traditional approach to achieve interoperability is inadequate and requires a model-driven platform approach supporting low-code application development on the basis of dedicated domain-specific languages. The paper illustrates the impact of such a platform by examples about robotics, Internet of Things, data analytics, and Web applications. In particular, it is shown how REST services can generically be extended, external data bases can be integrated, and new data analytics capabilities can be provided.

Voelter [14] (*Programming vs. that thing subject matter experts do*), argues that allowing subject matter experts to directly contribute their domain knowledge and expertise to software through DSLs and automation does not necessarily require them to become programmers. In his opinion, the requirement to provide precise information to unambiguously instruct a computer can be achieved more easily, of course requiring the basics of computational thinking. Völter believes that it is possible and economically important to provide accordingly 'CAD programs for knowledge workers'.

Zweihoff, Tegeler, Schürmann, Bainczyk, and Steffen [16] (Aligned, Purpose-driven cooperation: the future way of system development), argue that the future of software and systems development is collaborative, and will be supported globally in a cloud-based fashion. This way individual contributors do not need to worry about the infrastructural aspects which are all taken care of globally in the Web. This eases also the use of so-called purpose-specific languages that aim at directly involving application experts in the development process. The presentation of the vision is supported by details about the realization which, in particular, explain a simplicity-oriented way of language integration which can happen in a deep and shallow fashion.

3 Conclusion

The contributions of this track clearly indicate the expanse of what can be considered programming. It is therefore not surprising that the visions of where the evolution of programming will lead to, or should aim at, are very diverse. This diversity, however, does not imply that the visions are contradictory. Hopefully on the contrary. The embedded systems perspective, e.g., is envisaged to even deal with phenomena like chaos, application programming to successively comprise more computational paradigms and constructs to enable experts to elegantly solve dedicated tasks, and the future of user-level programming seems dominated by increasing ease and collaboration. Tools play a major role in all scenarios, which seem to have in common that programming and modelling will increasingly converge.

References

1. Balasubramanian, D., Coglio, A., Dubey, A., Karsai, G.: Towards model-based intent-driven adaptive software. In: Margaria, T., Steffen, B. (eds.) ISoLA 2021, LNCS 13036, pp. 378–392. Springer, Heidelberg (2021)
2. Broy, M., Havelund, K., Kumar, R., Steffen, B.: Towards a unified view of modeling and programming (track summary). In: Margaria, T., Steffen, B. (eds.) ISoLA 2016. LNCS, vol. 9953, pp. 3–10. Springer, Cham (2016). https://doi.org/10.1007/978-3-319-47169-3_1
3. Broy, M., Havelund, K., Kumar, R., Steffen, B.: Towards a unified view of modeling and programming (ISoLA 2018 Track Introduction). In: Margaria, T., Steffen, B. (eds.) ISoLA 2018. LNCS, vol. 11244, pp. 3–21. Springer, Cham (2018). https://doi.org/10.1007/978-3-030-03418-4_1
4. Harel, D., Marron, A.: Introducing dynamical systems and chaos early in computer science and software engineering education can help advance theory and practice of software development and computing. In: Margaria, T., Steffen, B. (eds.) ISoLA 2021, LNCS 13036, pp. 322–334. Springer, Heidelberg (2021)
5. Hatcliff, J., Belt, J., Robby, Carpenter, T.: HAMR: An AADL multi-platform code generation toolset. In: Margaria, T., Steffen, B. (eds.) ISoLA 2021, LNCS 13036, pp. 274–295. Springer, Heidelberg (2021)
6. Havelund, K., Bocchino, R.: Integrated modeling and development of component-based embedded software in Scala. In: Margaria, T., Steffen, B. (eds.) ISoLA 2021, LNCS 13036, pp. 233–252. Springer, Heidelberg (2021)
7. Lee, E.A., Lohstroh, M.: Time for all programs, not just real-time programs. In: Margaria, T., Steffen, B. (eds.) ISoLA 2021, LNCS 13036, pp. 213–232. Springer, Heidelberg (2021)
8. Lethbridge, T.C.: Low-code is often high-code, so we must design low-code platforms to enable proper software engineering. In: Margaria, T., Steffen, B. (eds.) ISoLA 2021, LNCS 13036, pp. 202–212. Springer, Heidelberg (2021)
9. Margaria, T., Chaudhary, H.A.A., Guevara, I., Ryan, S., Schieweck, A.: The interoperability challenge: Building a model-driven digital thread platform for CPS. In: Margaria, T., Steffen, B. (eds.) ISoLA 2021, LNCS 13036, pp. 393–413. Springer, Heidelberg (2021)

10. Mosses, P.D.: Fundamental constructs in programming languages. In: Margaria, T., Steffen, B. (eds.) ISoLA 2021, LNCS 13036, pp. 296–321. Springer, Heidelberg (2021)
11. Robby, Hatcliff, J.: Slang: The Sireum programming language. In: Margaria, T., Steffen, B. (eds.) ISoLA 2021, LNCS 13036, pp. 253–273. Springer, Heidelberg (2021)
12. Selić, B., Pierantonio, A.: Fixing classification: a viewpoint-based approach. In: Margaria, T., Steffen, B. (eds.) ISoLA 2021, LNCS 13036, pp. 346–356. Springer, Heidelberg (2021)
13. Stevens, P.: The future of programming and modelling: a vision. In: Margaria, T., Steffen, B. (eds.) ISoLA 2021, LNCS 13036, pp. 357–377. Springer, Heidelberg (2021)
14. Voelter, M.: Programming vs. that thing subject matter experts do. In: Margaria, T., Steffen, B. (eds.) ISoLA 2021, LNCS 13036, pp. 414–425. Springer, Heidelberg (2021)
15. Wadler, P.: GATE: Gradual effect types. In: Margaria, T., Steffen, B. (eds.) ISoLA 2021, LNCS 13036, pp. 335–345. Springer, Heidelberg (2021)
16. Zweihoff, P., Tegeler, T., Schürmann, J., Bainczyk, A., Steffen, B.: Aligned, purpose-driven cooperation: the future way of system development. In: Margaria, T., Steffen, B. (eds.) ISoLA 2021, LNCS 13036, pp. 426–449. Springer, Heidelberg (2021)

Low-Code Is Often High-Code, So We Must Design Low-Code Platforms to Enable Proper Software Engineering

Timothy C. Lethbridge(✉)

University of Ottawa, Ottawa, Canada
timothy.lethbridge@uottawa.ca

Abstract. The concept of low-code (and no-code) platforms has been around for decades, even before the term was used. The idea is that applications on these platforms can be built by people with less technical expertise than a professional programmer, yet can leverage powerful technology such as, for example, for databases, financial analysis, web development and machine learning. However, in practice, software written on such platforms often accumulates large volumes of complex code, which can be worse to maintain than in traditional languages because the low-code platforms tend not to properly support good engineering practices such as version control, separation of concerns, automated testing and literate programming. In this paper we discuss experiences with several low-code platforms and provide suggestions for directions forward towards an era where the benefits of low-code can be obtained without accumulation of technical debt. Our recommendations focus on ensuring low-code platforms enable scaling, understandability, documentability, testability, vendor-independence, and the overall user experience for developers those end-users who do some development.

Keywords: Low-code platforms · Modeling · Technical debt · End-user programming · Umple · Spreadsheets

1 Introduction

Low-code and no-code platforms are diverse in nature, but have some common features intended to allow people to build complex software mostly by configuring powerful underlying engines. Some applications built using low-code platforms have proved game-changing, or even life-saving, for example applications built rapidly to handle the Covid-19 pandemic [1].

Unfortunately, in practice it is common for people to write far more code and far more complex code than the low-code platform designers likely expected. The code can become exceptionally hard to understand and maintain, yet frequently needs to be modified, since low-code platforms are particularly prone to change for commercial reasons. What starts out as a good idea, building a powerful application with little code, turns into a mountain of technical debt. An example of this that many people can relate to is Excel, where individual formulas can sometimes span many lines, yet cannot even

T. Margaria and B. Steffen (Eds.): ISoLA 2021, LNCS 13036, pp. 202–212, 2021.
https://doi.org/10.1007/978-3-030-89159-6_14

be indented. A spreadsheet may be packed with many such formulas, and some of those may refer to macros or code in third-party plugins. None of this can easily be browsed, tested, documented, or reused.

It would seem reasonable to presume that low-code approaches are a key to the future of programming. But in this paper, we make the case that the designers of such platforms must always assume users will in fact write large amounts of code in their platforms, so they need to design the platforms to be high-code-ready – in other words ready for proper software engineering to be applied.

In the next section we will discuss low-code platforms and some of the challenges they present in practice. Then we illustrate some of the issues through case studies based on our experience. Finally, we will propose a set of principles that low-code platform developers should embrace.

2 No-Code and Low-Code as a Long-Standing and Growing Trend

No-code platforms provide a spectrum of core functionality for various classes of applications that can be tailored, typically through graphical or form-based user interfaces, to provide business-specific end-user experiences. Through the graphical interfaces, users select, arrange, configure and connect elements from built-in libraries of elements as well as from third-party plugins.

Examples of no code platforms include Shopify [2], which is at the core of a wide array of e-commerce web sites. WordPress [3], similarly, is at the core of a vast array of web sites. Spreadsheets, such as Microsoft Excel and similar products also fall into this category. Even software developers working with traditional programming languages use no-code platforms: Jenkins for example is one of several open-source platforms that can be configured for a wide range of automation tasks: It is most typically used for continuous integration (building and testing versions of software), but can do much more. A competing commercial no-code system is Circle-CI.

Low-code platforms share similarities with no-code platforms but with low-code there is expectation that a certain amount of code will be written, where code in this context implies small custom conditional expressions or algorithms. The idea is that such code operates on highly abstract and powerful features present in the system core, as well as on an ecosystem of plugins. Tools such as Appian, Oracle Application Express and Wavemaker are widely used to allow businesses to create information-systems on top of databases. The Eclipse platform used by developers, with its plugin capability can be seen as a low-code platform, as can some other IDEs.

Today many low-code and no-code platforms are cloud-native, meaning that the software runs as web applications. However, we include programmable downloadable apps in the low-code umbrella.

For simplicity, in the following we will refer to both no-code and low-code platforms as low-code even though there are some differences with regard to capabilities, scale and applicability. The difference between low-code and no-code is often merely in how it is used, and may be a matter of perception: For example, Excel clearly transitions from no-code to low-code when macros are used, but one might also say that the use of conditions in formulas means that Excel should not be considered no-code.

The low-code concept is far from new. Apple's original Hypercard was designed as a low code platform, and many interesting applications were built in it (e.g. [4]). The World Wide Web itself started as a low-code way to create static hypertext information systems, also pre-dating the invention of the low-code terminology. It is instructive to note how the Web has clearly become a high-code platform both on the front end and back end.

To further illustrate the long history, we can note that spreadsheets have been with us for over 40 years. The 1980's also saw the marketing of so-called fourth-generation languages (4GLs) [5, 6, 7]. These included languages such as Natural and Sperry's Mapper, which sold themselves as having many of the same benefits we attribute today to low-code platforms. Mapper, for example envisioned enabling business executives to generate their own analytic reports from mainframe databases.

The rise of model-driven engineering (MDE) and UML in the 1990's allows us to consider the low-code concept from another perspective: If one can describe an application's data in a class model and its behavior in state machine diagrams one can theoretically avoid a lot of textual coding. Reducing coding and enabling systems to be described in part by non-programmers has thus been part of the vision of many proponents of MDE.

Even many scripting languages can be seen as being motivated by the low-code vision. From the 1970's to today, every competent Unix/Linux programmer has written short scripts to automate operating system tasks and make their workflow easier; Apple Macintosh end-users similarly also have been able to use AppleScript and Automator.

Fast-forwarding to today, we see the confluence of low-code with ascendent technologies such as machine learning. Whereas it used to take a lot of coding to build machine learning into an application, tools like Google Auto-ML [8] provide a low-code experience. Low-code for quantum computing seems an inevitable next step – perhaps an essential step given the seeming complexity of describing quantum algorithms directly.

The benefits of low-code are clear: It allows for rapid deployment of powerful computerized functionality, tailorable by well-educated end-users, and certainly without the need for a developer to have deep knowledge of the underlying platform or of computer science. For basic use they merely require an understanding of a 'model' embodied by the platform (e.g. the tables in a database, or the layout of a spreadsheet), and some sense of how to extend and configure the system using mostly-declarative constructs.

However, in *actual practice from a software engineering perspective*, low-code applications deployed in industry turn out to be not really that different from traditional ones programmed in traditional 'high-code' languages like C++ or Java. The following subsections outline some of the reality.

2.1 Large Volumes and Complexity Make Low-Code a False Promise

The code volume found in deployed applications on low-code platforms is all-too often not 'low'. We have encountered app-control 'scripts' of thousands of lines, spreadsheets with many thousands of complex formulas, and programs in supposedly low-code business applications containing hundreds of thousands of lines. Clearly, code can accumulate to volumes that are just as high as in traditional languages. Such applications might be written entirely in the platform's built-in native domain-specific language (DSL), or else rely on programmed plugins or wrappers written in some other language.

Low-code applications can hence accumulate high complexity, bugs and other forms technical debt just as badly or even worse than traditional applications. However, the languages created for low-code platforms commonly lack features that would assist in their understanding and maintenance, such as the ability to organize them into files and modules, or even to add detailed comments attached to individual code elements.

2.2 Low Code Applications Often Lack Features Needed for Maintainability and Understandability

Low code applications are also often lacking documentation, both in terms of what developers write, and what documentation can feasibly be embedded with the code even if an attempt is made.

In traditional applications it was once thought that documentation should be found in external design documents, but over the last couple of decades that has been replaced by an ethos of literate programming (e.g. well-written names for data and functions, with carefully laid-out code), coupled with extensive code comments, in-repository files aligned with the code (e.g. Readme.md files) and auto-generated documentation enabled in part using code annotations (e.g. Javadoc). Opportunities to do this sort of documentation tend to be lacking in low-code platforms as some of the case studies below will testify.

Low-code applications are also often challenged with regard to separation of concerns and reusability. Although plugins are a dominant feature, the ability to make one's own code, written in a low-code language, modular or to re-use such code (without making a plugin) in multiple applications is often absent.

2.3 Turnover, Deprecation and Vendor-Dependence Further Challenge Low-Code

Whereas the code in many traditional platforms can be modified for years, with older code still runnable, there is a tendency (although not universal) for low-code applications to be vulnerable to rapid obsolescence.

The platforms on which low-code applications are built tend to be rapidly developed with new major versions requiring the low-code applications to be modified (i.e. maintained) to keep running. This is in part because most such platforms are commercial, and companies want to produce 'improved' or 'all-new' offerings. Historically, many low-code commercial platforms have just ceased to be developed. Many 4GLs of the 1980's are examples.

Extensive modification or replacement of low-code applications is hence needed at levels more frequent than would be the case for traditionally-programmed applications.

This would not be so much of a problem if the code were really 'low' in volume, and there was documentation and little technical debt. But the reality is that these assumptions tend to be false, resulting in premature death of large applications. Even open-source low-code platforms are subject to this problem, especially when the plugins on which low-code often depends are not maintained by other open-source developers. We have noted that this is the case with tools such as Jenkins.

3 Short Case Studies

In the following subsections we briefly give some case studies highlighting challenges with low-code platforms. Each of these summarizes the author's own experiences working in research, the public sector, the private sector, and the volunteer sector.

3.1 Excel and Other Spreadsheets

Spreadsheets like Excel are clearly low-code platforms and often no-code. At a base level, they are usable by almost any educated person; they have a layered-2D (table with sheets) model, an easily understandable instant-calculation semantics and a rich library of functions with a variety of plugins also available. Modern spreadsheets have migrated to the cloud, like other low-code platforms.

But spreadsheets can grow fantastically in complexity [9, 10]. Excess complexity can arise through five different types of scaling: the number of formulas, complex arrangement and interconnections of those formulas, massively complex formulas (many lines of text with no way to lay it out and comment it), macros (in Visual Basic for the case of Excel) and plugins.

Spreadsheets tend to be very fragile (proneness to bugs if modified incorrectly), and difficult to understand, with subtle differences in formulas not easy to notice, even if the spreadsheet makes some attempt to warn users. There is difficulty separating concerns: separate sheets or files can be used for this, but traditional languages are much more flexible in this regard, allowing almost-limitless flexibility in arranging files. It is almost impossible in spreadsheets to do proper detailed documentation (e.g. of complex formulae, patterns of cells, and so on); this is only possible in macros which have a traditional programming-language structure. Reuse of formulas in different spreadsheets is also not generally practical, so they tend to be cloned with the consequent problem of bug propagation.

Division of work among multiple developers is extremely challenging in a spreadsheet. Developers of code in languages like C++, Java and Python now are used to using configuration management and version control tools like Git, collaborating on code and using pull requests with code reviews and automated testing to reach agreement on what should become the next version. Although cloud-based spreadsheets do indeed allow multiple people to edit the code at once, and have 'change tracking' capability, this is far from the power available in traditional code.

Talented software developers can still create poor-quality spreadsheets, partly because Excel has core limitations regarding what is possible as described above, and partly because spreadsheets (as all software) tend to grow organically and inexorably, surprising even their own developers.

As an example of over-exuberance with low-code, the author witnessed a situation where a company put out a CFP for development of an application that might be expected to take over a person-year to develop. A talented Excel expert instead proposed that the requested requirements could all be satisfied in a few days of Excel spreadsheet development. The expert offered a company a completed product, developed in Excel from scratch within two days without even participating in the competitive bidding process. The application did more than the customer expected, so was welcomed almost as a miracle. But it was 'too clever'; it was only readily maintainable by its single developer. It had to be replaced within two years by a more traditionally-developed system.

3.2 WordPress

Vast numbers of websites rely on WordPress. Some are professionally maintained but very many are in the hands of people with zero training in software development, perhaps people maintaining a site for a local sports club.

Yet as new ideas for specialized information presentation, or uses of plugins are added, and as additional volunteers work on the site (often serially, as new people are elected each year), such sites often descend into the worst kind of software mess. The author has witnessed computer professionals stepping in to help such end users, and, finding the 'low code' incomprehensible, they have 'hacked' at it, making it worse.

Regular updates to WordPress or its numerous plugins, forces further hacking: The ugliness of the technical debt becomes ever more visible. The solution is often to 'start again'. But starting again on a different low-code platform just perpetuates the situation, since the new version will descend into the same sort of mess.

3.3 Jenkins

Jenkins, as a self-hosted automation and CI technology can be used with relatively little or no code, although technical expertise is needed for installation and maintenance. The real lesson, however, is the challenge of the plugins. These plugins mostly add additional configuration fields to various GUI panels in the classic no-code fashion. Many plugins have been created, yet many have ceased being maintained by their open-source developers. Many are marked as 'for adoption' yet are not adopted. They thus represent technical debt for people who incorporated them in their automation workflows.

3.4 Modeling Languages with Code Generation

As a final case study, we would like to mention the notion of modeling technologies often related to UML that allow code generation and integration of code using 'action languages'. An example is Papyrus. The reality is that although such technologies can save a lot of coding, our experience is that they can only reduce code volume by about half.

The action-language code then has to be managed in some way, and tends to be subject to the same weaknesses as we noted for Excel and WordPress. In some tools the action language code is embedded in XML files that also are used to convey the model (class model, state model, etc.), so can only be edited in the modeling tool. When this action code becomes extensive it suffers from low understandability, low testability, difficulty with collaborative development and so on.

The author's team have been working to overcome these limitations through the development of Umple [11, 12, 13]. Umple is a compiler, developed in itself, that translates a textual representation of models to both final systems and diagrams; it also allows editing of the diagrams in order to update the textual representation. Umple can be used in many environments including in the UmpleOnline website [14], where users can also experiment with a library of examples.

Our experience is that to build large systems with model-driven development, one has to deploy all the best software engineering practices that have been developed over the last half century for use with traditional code. Umple models are thus organized in the same sorts of files as used for traditional programming languages; they can be operated on using collaboration, version-control, and documentation-generation tools. Umple allows seamless blending of model representations with code in multiple traditional programming languages, and the instantly-generated documentation can consist of UML diagrams and Javadoc-style pages. Most Umple users do indeed use it in a low-code manner, but a few very large applications have been created without the limitations imposed by other low-code platforms.

4 Directions Forward

It seems likely that low-code platforms will continue to proliferate and will be the dominant way many types of software are developed in coming decades. But as discussed above, the amount and complexity of code in such systems will often not in fact be 'low', and may be exceedingly high.

The following are a few principles that, if adopted, we believe would help software to achieve the 'best of both worlds.' In other words, to allow applications to be developed with modest amounts of code on top of powerful platforms, while at the same time enabling the scaling of such code as needed, by enabling good software engineering practices.

4.1 Enable Low Code, but Plan for Lots of Code

Firstly, as a community, we should drop the pretense that low-code applications will remain low-code. There is nothing wrong with enabling powerful capability from very little code, but we need to understand that people *will* write high-code applications on low-code platforms.

4.2 Enable Documentability in Low-Code Platforms

Low-code platforms need to be designed to be documentable and written in a literate fashion. It should be possible to see live diagrams of the code as it is edited, or to edit the diagrams themselves to modify the underlying code. This is something we have achieved with Umple.

For example, in spreadsheet, it should possible to see formulas rendered as easy-to-understand textual entities with proper indentation and syntax highlighting. It should also be possible to write comments within the formulas.

Although spreadsheets have 'auditing' tools to do things like showing which cells depend on which others, much greater effort needs to go in to helping make complex code in spreadsheets and other low-code platforms understandable.

4.3 Improve Separation-of-Concerns, Re-use, and Collaboration Capabilities

Traditional languages have a variety of ways of separating concerns, such as using functions, multiple files organized in a hierarchy, mixins, traits and aspects. One can reuse one's own code in multiple contexts. In Umple we have arranged for all these features to be available in the action code added to models.

It would be nice if there were more effective ways of reusing formulas in spreadsheets. Macros go part way, but force the developer to delve into a totally different programing paradigm.

Separation of concerns and reuse go hand-in-hand with collaboration: As the volume of 'low code' gets high, multiple developers need to divide up development, and follow all the best practices of agile development.

4.4 Enable Automated Testing in Low-Code Platforms

One of the great revolutions in software over the last 20 years has been the now ubiquitous practice of automated testing (both unit testing and system testing). This prevents regression as all tests must pass when changes are made. Test-driven development takes that one step further, requiring tests to be delivered with each change. Pull-request testing allows testing of proposed changes against the current released version to ensure there is compatibility.

Automated testing has some distance to develop in the low-code context, yet it is desperately needed. There has been a small amount of research in this direction regarding Excel [15], but it is not part of the core platform yet needs to be. Testing in the context of model-driven development is also in its infancy [16].

4.5 Foster Multi-vendor Open Standards for Low-Code Languages

Although there are many traditional programming languages, and some form the basis for low-code platforms, there is still a lack of open-standard ways of creating code for related classes of low-code platforms. For example, Visual Basic macros and plugins written for Excel won't work in other spreadsheets; plugins for Jenkins won't work in Circle CI and code written for one of the database low-code platforms is not portable to others. This needs to change.

The solution we have chosen for Umple is to allow one or more of several traditional programming languages (Java, C++, Php, Ruby) to be used for the action code (i.e. the low-code). There will be some API calls this code needs to make to Umple-generated code, but using Umple's separation of concerns mechanism, these can be isolated, thus rendering most of the action code fully portable.

4.6 Emphasize Developer Experience at All Scales

There is a lot of emphasis on user experience (UX) in software engineering today. Developer experience [17] is a key subtopic. Low-code tools would benefit from strong focus on this, particularly when the code becomes large and complex. Most low-code tools seem to only pay attention to the experience of developers that create small amounts of code.

5 Some Other Perspectives

Low-code platforms with a very low barrier to entry are also widely called end-user development (EUD) platforms. There is considerable discussion in the literature of various aspects of these platforms that relate to the points we make in this paper.

Sahay et al. [18] provide a taxonomy of both terminology and features of such platforms. Central to their analysis are interoperability, extensibility, learning curve and scalability.

Paternò [19] points out that EUD platforms not only need to avoid intimidating beginners, but also need a to be able to scale to allow experts to use the tools more expansively, as we have indicated is indeed the reality. He also emphasizes the need for tools to support collaborative and social development.

Repenning and Ioannidou [20] emphasize ensuring that tools allow people to have a sense of flow (get neither bored nor anxious), and make syntactic errors hard or impossible. Similar to what we are suggesting, they highlight that such tools should support incremental development, testing and multiple views. They also suggest creating scaffolding examples that users can adapt, and building community-supported tools.

6 Conclusions

We should stop worrying about the end of the need for programmers as we know them. History shows that no matter whether a platform asserts it is low-code or even no-code, businesses will find requirements that expand the scale and sophistication of programs developed using the platform. Hence there will be a steady need for skilled developers.

History shows that code written in low-code platforms often becomes complex, and is hard to understand, document and reuse. This results in increasing technical debt and the need for replacement of systems, exacerbated by rapid obsolescence of the underlying low-code platforms.

As a result of this, we need to ensure low-code platforms have just as deep a capability to support modern software engineering practices as traditional languages. In particular they need to enable literate coding, self-documentation, separation of concerns, collaboration, and automated testing. Vendors of similar applications should find ways to work together to allow exchange of code among such applications. Finally, the user interfaces of all low-code and modeling tools should be subjected to focused work to improve their developer experience.

What is next in programming? New high-code languages with sophisticated textual syntax will continue to arrive on the scene, as has been happening for decades. However, in our view these will be applied more and more in tight synchrony with low-code technology such as editing of model diagrams, and blending domain specific languages (DSLs) with the high-code languages. This will enable greater abstraction and return on programmer investment. However, to ensure that the return on investment occurs, companies will need to recognize the need to apply key software engineering techniques such as test-driven development.

References

1. Woo, M.: The rise of no/low code software development-no experience needed? Eng. (Beijing China) **6**(9), 960–961 (2020). https://doi.org/10.1016/j.eng.2020.07.007
2. Dushnitsky, G., Stroube, B.K.: Low-code entrepreneurship: Shopify and the alternative path to growth. J. Bus. Ventur. Insights **16**, e00251 (2021). https://doi.org/10.1016/j.jbvi.2021.e00251
3. Stern, H., Damstra, D., Williams, B.: Professional WordPress: Design and Development. Wiley, Indianapolis (2010)
4. Estep, K.W., Hasle, A., Omli, L., MacIntyre, F.: Linneaus: interactive taxonomy using the Macintosh computer and HyperCard. Bioscience **39**(9), 635–639 (1989)
5. Aaram J.: Fourth generation languages. In: Rolstadäs, A. (eds.) Computer-Aided Production Management. IFIP State-of-the-Art Reports. Springer, Heidelberg (1988). https://doi.org/10.1007/978-3-642-73318-5_14
6. Nagy, C., Vidács, L., Ferenc, R., Gyimóthy, T., Kocsis, F., Kovács, I.: Complexity measures in 4GL environment. In: Murgante, B., Gervasi, O., Iglesias, A., Taniar, D., Apduhan, B.O. (eds.) ICCSA 2011. LNCS, vol. 6786, pp. 293–309. Springer, Heidelberg (2011). https://doi.org/10.1007/978-3-642-21934-4_25
7. Coulmann, L.: General requirements for a program visualization tool to be used in engineering of 4GL-programs. In: IEEE Symposium on Visual Languages, pp. 37–41 (1993). https://doi.org/10.1109/VL.1993.269576
8. Xin, D., Wu, E.Y., Lee, D.J.L., Salehi, N., Parameswaran, A.: Whither AutoML? understanding the role of automation in machine learning workflows. In: 2021 CHI Conference on Human Factors in Computing Systems, pp. 1–16, May 2021
9. Boai, G., Heath, A.: When simple becomes complicated: why excel should lose its place at the top table. Global Reg. Health Technol. Assess. (2017). https://doi.org/10.5301/grhta.5000247
10. Badame, S., Dig, D.: Refactoring meets spreadsheet formulas. In: 2012 28th IEEE International Conference on Software Maintenance (ICSM), pp. 399–409 (2012). https://doi.org/10.1109/ICSM.2012.6405299
11. Lethbridge, T.C., Forward, A., Badreddin, O., et al.: Umple: model-driven development for open source and education. Sci. Comput. Program. (2021). https://doi.org/10.1016/j.scico.2021.102665
12. University of Ottawa: Umple website. https://www.umple.org. Accessed Aug 2021
13. University of Ottawa: Latest Umple Release. http://releases.umple.org. https://doi.org/10.5281/zenodo.4677562
14. University of Ottawa: UmpleOnline. https://try.umple.org. Accessed Aug 2021
15. Khorram, F., Mottu, J.M., Sunyé, G.: Challenges & opportunities in low-code testing. MODELS 2020, pp. 70:1–70:10 (2020). https://doi.org/10.1145/3417990.3420204
16. Almagthawi, S.: Model-driven testing in Umple, Ph.D. thesis, University of Ottawa 2020. https://doi.org/10.20381/ruor-24577
17. Fagerholm, F., Münch, J.: Developer experience: concept and definition. In: 2012 International Conference on Software and System Process (ICSSP), pp. 73–77 (2012). https://doi.org/10.1109/ICSSP.2012.6225984
18. Sahay, A., Indamutsa, A., Di Ruscio, D., Pierantonio, A.: Supporting the understanding and comparison of low-code development platforms. In: 46th Euromicro Conference on Software Engineering and Advanced Applications (SEAA), pp. 171–178 (2020). https://doi.org/10.1109/SEAA51224.2020.00036

19. Paternò, F.: End user development: survey of an emerging field for empowering people. Int. Sch. Res. Not. Softw. Eng. (2013). https://doi.org/10.1155/2013/532659
20. Repenning, A., Ioannidou, A.: What makes end-user development tick? 13 design guidelines. In: Lieberman, H., Paternò, F., Wulf, V. (eds.) End User Development. Human-Computer Interaction Series, vol. 9, pp. 51–85. Springer, Dordrecht (2006). https://doi.org/10.1007/1-4020-5386-X_4

Time for All Programs, Not Just Real-Time Programs

Edward A. Lee(✉) and Marten Lohstroh

UC Berkeley, Berkeley, CA, USA
{eal,marten}@berkeley.edu

Abstract. We argue that the utility of time as a semantic property of software is not limited to the domain of real-time systems. This paper outlines four concurrent design patterns: alignment, precedence, simultaneity, and consistency, all of which are relevant to general-purpose software applications. We show that a semantics of logical time provides a natural framework for reasoning about concurrency, makes some difficult problems easy, and offers a quantified interpretation of the CAP theorem, enabling quantified evaluation of the tradeoff between consistency and availability.

Keywords: Time · Concurrency · Distributed systems · Design patterns

1 Motivation

The purpose of this paper is to address the question of the ISoLA 2021 track, "Programming: What is Next?" In short, we will argue for making **time** a first-class part of programs, not just for real-time programs, but for all programs.

Today, nearly all software runs on multicore machines and interacts with other software over networks. Programs, therefore, consist of concurrently executing components that are required to react in a timely manner to stimuli from the network. Unfortunately, building distributed programs with predictable, understandable, and resilient behavior is notoriously difficult. The ideal, sometimes represented by the acronym ACID (atomicity, consistency, isolation, and durability) proves too expensive and restrictive. A great deal of innovation over the last two decades has clarified the richness of possible models for distributed software [5], but the price is that every programmer writing software that interacts over networks has to become an expert in the surprisingly subtle ACID concepts, plus availability and resilience.

Fortunately, threads, semaphores, and locks, once the only widely available mechanisms available to programmers for dealing with concurrency, have been relegated to the basement, where highly trained experts use them to build concurrency-aware data structures and programming frameworks that enable programmers to reason about concurrency at a much higher level. For example, event loops with mutually atomic callback functions are the mainstay

T. Margaria and B. Steffen (Eds.): ISoLA 2021, LNCS 13036, pp. 213–232, 2021.
https://doi.org/10.1007/978-3-030-89159-6_15

of JavaScript and Node.js, and underlie much of today's client and server-side web software. Another paradigm for managing concurrency is the actor model [15], which is based on asynchronous message passing. Popular frameworks like Akka [1] and Ray [29] are based on actors. Publish-and-subscribe systems [13] also relay messages between concurrent processes, but rather than messages being sent directly, the dissemination of messages is organized around "topics" that can be published and/or subscribed to. This style of communication is prevalent in IoT and robotics middleware MQTT [16] and ROS [32].

Concurrency, as a concept, is entangled with the concept of time. It is odd, therefore, that few of these frameworks make any mention of time. When they do, the primary mechanism that they provide to influence timing or the order in which events occur is priority. A programmer can, for example, assert that one type of message or one computation has higher priority than others. By tweaking these priorities, programmers can improve responsiveness of programs, but priorities cannot reliably be used to ensure correctness properties. For example, priorities alone cannot guarantee that some action A always occurs before some other action B, particularly when the program is able to make use of a multiplicity of hardware resources such as cores and servers.

We begin by outlining four design patterns in distributed systems that we call **alignment**, **precedence**, **simultaneity**, and **consistency**. All of these patterns have many possible implementations that do not require any temporal semantics at all, but in each case, we will give a solution that uses temporal semantics. Our solutions will use a rather new programming framework called LINGUA FRANCA (LF) [25] that supports concurrent and distributed programming using time-stamped messages. We will then analyze these examples and hopefully convince the reader that their many subtleties are easier to reason about with temporal semantics than without it.

2 Alignment

The first pattern considers concurrent tasks that are invoked periodically and the invocations are expected to be **aligned** in a predictable way. By "alignment" we mean a form of synchronization that ensures that even though the task invocations are concurrent, any observer will see their occurrences locked together in some specified way. The simplest example, perhaps, is that if an observer sees that one task has been invoked N times, then that observer also sees that another task has been invoked N times. In a slightly more elaborate example, if one task is invoked with period T and another with period $2T$, then an observer will always see that the first task has been invoked $2N$ times if the second has been invoked N times. These periods need not be literally "real time" in the sense of time as measured by a wall clock. Practical examples include detecting failures by monitoring "heartbeat" messages or using timeouts when invoking remote services. Alignment may also require deterministic ordering of the tasks in the cycles at which both are invoked; this may be important, for example, if the tasks share state. Such predictable and repeatable alignments make programs less ambiguous and easier to test.

```
var x = 0;
function increment() {
  x = x + 1;
}
function decrement() {
  x = x - 2;
}
function observe() {
  console.log(x);
}
setInterval(increment, 100);
setInterval(decrement, 200);
setInterval(observe, 400);
```

Listing 1. JavaScript example illustrating weak temporal semantics.

Consider a simple JavaScript example from Jerad and Lee [19] that uses callback functions, shown in Listing 1. This uses the built-in JavaScript function `setInterval`(F, T), which schedules a callback function F to be invoked after T milliseconds and then periodically every T milliseconds. The actual time of the function invocations cannot be *exactly* every T milliseconds, since that would require a perfect timekeeper, which does not exist, and it would require that the JavaScript engine be idle at the requisite time. This imprecision is unavoidable, but it is no excuse for giving up on the *alignment* of these callbacks.

This program defines a variable `x` that is shared state. The program sets up periodic callbacks to increment `x` by one every 100 msec, decrement `x` by two every 200 msec, and observe the value of `x` every 400 msec. The programmer may expect that the observed value of `x` is always zero (or, at least, *near* zero), but this is not what occurs. Running this program in Node.js (version v12.8.1), we inexplicably see numbers starting with 2 and then decreasing monotonically without bound. The `decrement` function gets invoked significantly more frequently than half the rate of invocations of `increment`.

A simple, deterministic association between these callback functions is not hard to implement, as Jerad and Lee did, by providing their own variant of the `setInterval` and `setTimeout` functions that maintains an event queue and uses a single event loop that calls the built-in `setTimeout` function to advance time by the next expected increment [19]. But such logic is difficult to get right and quite separate from any application logic. And there are many subtleties. For example, for the intuitive idea of alignment of the scheduled callbacks to make sense for a program like that in the listing, we need a less intuitive idea that time does not elapse between the calls to `setInterval`. This requires a *logical* notion of time distinct from the physical notion. Time needs to become a *semantic* property of the program.

A comparable program in Lingua Franca is shown in Listing 2. This program deterministically prints "x = 0" repeatedly. Since the LF programs in subsequent patterns will become more intricate, we will use this example to explain some features of the language for readers who are unfamiliar with LF.

```
1 target C;
2 main reactor {
3     state x:int(0);
4     timer t1(100 msec, 100 msec);
5     timer t2(200 msec, 200 msec);
6     timer t4(400 msec, 400 msec);
7     reaction(t1) {=
8         self->x += 1;
9     =}
10    reaction(t2) {=
11        self->x -= 2;
12    =}
13    reaction(t4) {=
14        printf("x = %d\n", self->x);
15    =}
16 }
```

Listing 2. LINGUA FRANCA program comparable to Listing 1.

The first line specifies the target language, which in this case is C, but we could have chosen C++, Python, or TypeScript. The LF code generator takes this program as input and generates a standalone C program that realizes its semantics. In subsequent examples, we will omit the target line; all examples in this paper use the C target. There is only one **reactor** in this program (below we will see that reactors are concurrent objects that send messages to each other). This reactor has one state variable, `x`, defined on Line 3, that is accessible in all its reactions via a (code generated) struct called `self`. There are three timers, each with an offset and a period. There are then three **reactions** to the timers. The first two increment and decrement the state, respectively, and the last one prints the state.

The delimiters `{= ... =}` surround code written in the specified target language, and the mechanism for accessing inputs and state variables and for setting outputs is different in each target language (in C, via local variables associated with ports, the `self` struct, and the `SET` macro). That code is invoked in reaction to the specified triggers, which in this case are the timers. If a list of triggers is given, then any one of them can cause the reaction to be invoked. In LF, invocations of reactions belonging to the same reactor are mutually exclusive (because they share state), but reactions in distinct reactors may be invoked in parallel, modulo dependencies between them, as we will see. Moreover, if more than one reaction of a reactor is triggered at any logical time, then the reactions will be invoked in the order they are declared. Consequently, the reaction to `t4` is always invoked after the reactions to `t1` and `t2`, and hence its report of the state variable value always reflects what those reactions have done to the state at any logical time.

In LINGUA FRANCA, the time referenced by the timers is a **logical time**.[1] This can be aligned with physical time on a best-effort basis, or the program can be run as fast as possible with no reference to physical time. Either way,

[1] LINGUA FRANCA actually uses a richer model of time called "superdense time," but this is irrelevant to the present discussion, so we simplify to just refer to timestamps.

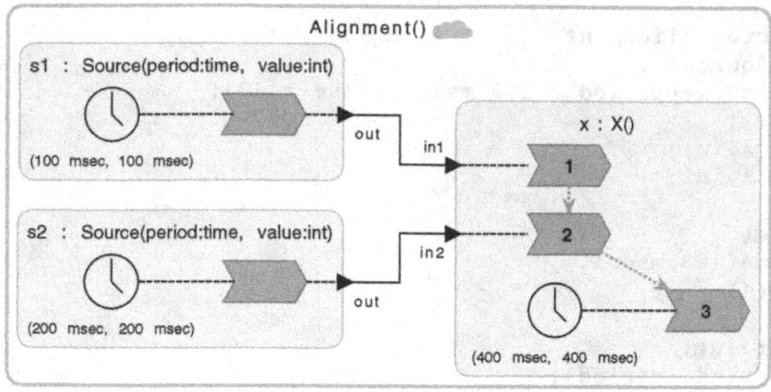

Fig. 1. Diagram of the LINGUA FRANCA example in Listing 3.

the runtime engine maintains alignment of the timers. Moreover, logical time does not elapse during the execution of a reaction. Hence, reactions are logically instantaneous.

Neither the JavaScript program of Listing 1 nor the LF program of Listing 2 has network interactions. In Listing 3, a version of the LF program is given that is **federated**.[2] The LF code generator generates a standalone C program for each top-level reactor and synthesizes the coordination between them to preserve the semantics. The result is a set of three programs (plus a fourth coordinator program) interacting over the network that exhibits exactly the same behavior as the unfederated version, even when the timers driving the updates to the state variable are realized on remote machines.

As LF programs get more complex, the diagram synthesized by the LF Eclipse-based integrated development environment (IDE) becomes useful for more quickly understanding the program.[3] The diagram for the program in Listing 3 is shown in Fig. 1. For a detailed explanation of this program and the diagram, see Sidebar 1.

In a federated execution, even one where communication between federates is over the open internet, the runtime infrastructure enforces the ordering constraints between reaction invocations defined by the program, and hence this program deterministically reports `x = 0` repeatedly. This is in stark contrast to the inexplicable behavior of the JavaScript program.

3 Precedence

Because the alignment pattern considered above makes explicit mention of time with periodic tasks, the reader may misconstrue our argument to apply only to

[2] The federated infrastructure of LINGUA FRANCA is currently rather preliminary, being built by Soroush Bateni and the two of us, but it is sufficiently developed for the examples described in this paper.

[3] The diagram synthesis infrastructure was created by Alexander Schulz-Rosengarten of the University of Kiel using the graphical layout tools from the KIELER Lightweight Diagrams framework [33] (see https://rtsys.informatik.uni-kiel.de/kieler).

```
federated reactor Alignment {
    s1 = new Source();
    s2 = new Source(period = 200 msec, value = -2);
    x = new X();
    s1.out -> x.in1;
    s2.out -> x.in2;
}
reactor Source(
    period:time(100 msec),
    value:int(1)
) {
    output out:int;
    timer t(period, period);
    reaction(t) -> out {=
        SET(out, self->value);
    =}
}
reactor X {
    input in1:int;
    input in2:int;
    state x:int(0);
    timer observe(400 msec, 400 msec);
    reaction(in1) {=
       self->x += in1->value;
    =}
    reaction(in2) {=
       self->x += in2->value;
    =}
    reaction(observe) {=
        printf("x = %d\n", self->x);
    =}
}
```

Listing 3. Distributed version of the program in Listing 2.

real-time systems. But here, time is being used to specify expected alignment, not real-time behavior. To further disavow the real-time interpretation, let's consider an example that has less to do with physical time. Specifically, we will consider a situation where one program invokes a service provided by a remote program, but this service may possibly be mediated by a third program (such as, for example, a third-party authenticator, a computation offloaded onto GPUs, an online image classification service, etc.). The challenge is that the results of the mediator must be available to the service provider before it can provide the service, and the results of the mediator need to be aligned with the service request. Hence, the mediator takes precedence over the service provider.

Figure 2 and Listing 4 provide a Lingua Franca program illustrating this precedence pattern. To keep the program to one page, the example is oversimplified, but the program is sufficient to illustrate this pattern. In this example, a Source reactor, when it chooses to request the service, sends a request message to the service provider and an authentication string to the Mediator. The request message is a random integer, but in more interesting applications, it could be a substantial payload like an image, and hence it may be desirable for the transport of the request to the Provider to proceed in parallel with the authentication of the Mediator. The Mediator checks the authentication string, and if it matches, forwards an authorization to the Provider. When the Provider receives logically simultaneous authorization and a service request, it provides the service.

In Listing 4, the `Source` reactor randomly sends either a valid authentication string ("good one") or an invalid one ("bad one") to the `Mediator`, and simultaneously sends a random number representing a service request to the `Provider`. The `Mediator` checks the authentication string, and if it valid, sends a boolean `true` to the `Provider`. The `Provider` provides the service only if receives a boolean `true` from the `Mediator` that is aligned with the service request.

The main point of this example is that the Provider has to match the service request with the results of the Mediator. There are many ways to do this without resorting to the timestamped semantics of LINGUA FRANCA, but we hope that the reader will appreciate simplicity that this solution provides. The application logic does not get polluted with the coordination logic. In LINGUA FRANCA, the program semantics ensures that, at each logical time, if a reaction of the Mediator is triggered, then that reaction will complete and its results will propagate to the Provider before any reaction of the Provider that depends on the Mediator is invoked. Hence, the *infrastructure* rather than the application logic handles the precedence relationship. The program is explained in detail in Sidebar 2.

One interesting observation is that in LINGUA FRANCA, the *absence* of a message conveys information. The job of the infrastructure is to ensure that every reactor sees inputs in timestamp order and that inputs with identical timestamps are simultaneously available. Hence, if the infrastructure is working

Sidebar 1: LINGUA FRANCA Alignment Program Explained

This sidebar provides a detailed explanation of the program in Listing 3 and its diagram in Fig. 1. LINGUA FRANCA keywords are shown in bold. Lines 1 through 7 define the main application program, which in this case contains three reactor instances that are interconnected. The **federated** keyword signals to the code generator that each of the three reactor instances should be instantiated in a separate program, which can be run on a distinct host, and that the code generator should generate the code needed for these separate programs to communicate. Had we used the **main** keyword instead of **federated**, only one program would be generated, and the concurrency of the application would be realized using threads rather than separate processes.

Lines 8 through 17 define a **reactor** class named `Source`. This class is instantiated twice, on Lines 2 and 3. These two instances are shown on the left in the diagram of Fig. 1 with connections to an instance of the class `X`, shown on the right. The connections are established on Lines 5 and 6. These are connections between distinct federates.

The `Source` reactor class has two parameters with default values defined on Lines 9 and 10. The default parameters are overridden by the second instance defined on Line 3. The parameters define the offset and period of the timer named `t` defined on Line 13 and the value sent in the output message on Line 15.

In the diagram of Fig. 1, reactions are shown as dark gray chevrons and timers with a clock symbol. The precedence relations between the three reactions of `X` are shown with arrows and numbers.

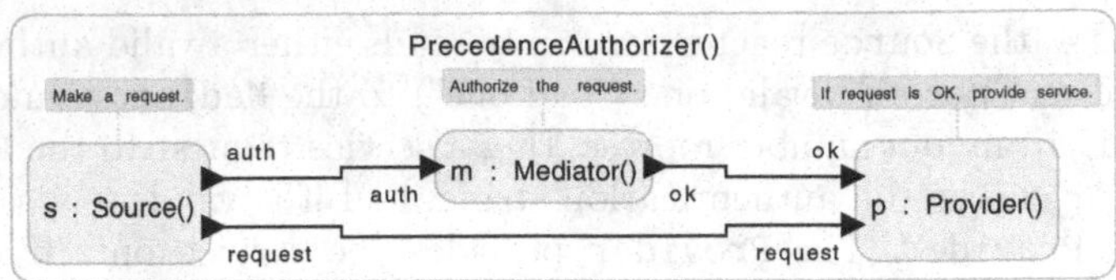

Fig. 2. Diagram of the LINGUA FRANCA example illustrating the precedence pattern.

```
federated reactor PrecedenceAuthorizer {
    s = new Source();
    m = new Mediator();
    p = new Provider();
    s.auth -> m.auth;
    s.request -> p.request;
    m.ok -> p.ok;
}
reactor Source {
    output auth:string;
    output request:int;
    timer t(0, 100 msec);
    reaction(t) -> auth, request {=
        static char* keys[] = {"good one", "bad one"};
        int r = rand() % 2;
        SET(auth, keys[r]);
        SET(request, rand());
    =}
}
reactor Mediator {
    input auth:string;
    output ok:bool;
    reaction(auth) -> ok {=
        static char* correct_key = "good one";
        if (strcmp(correct_key, auth->value)) {
            printf("AUTHORIZED\n");
            SET(ok, true);
        } else {
            printf("DENIED\n");
        }
    =}
}
reactor Provider {
    input ok:bool;
    input request:int;
    reaction(ok, request) {=
        if (ok->is_present && request->is_present
            && ok->value == true
        ) {
            printf("PROVIDE SERVICE\n");
        } else if (request->is_present) {
            printf("DENY SERVICE\n");
        }
    =}
}
```

Listing 4. Source of the LINGUA FRANCA example illustrating the precedence pattern.

correctly, then absence of a message at a logical time means that no such message is forthcoming. For example, if the Source reactor fails to send an authorization string to the Mediator, then the Provider will not receive an OK message. That message will be unambiguously absent at the logical time of the service request that it receives.

There are many applications that have similar structure. For example, the Mediator may be a bank, which authenticates the Source and testifies to the service Provider that funds are available without revealing any details about the requestor (identify, bank balance, etc.). The Mediator could be a vision subsystem that checks whether a service can be safely provided, as illustrated by the aircraft door controller example in Lohstroh, et al. [26], where the difficulties of realizing this pattern using actors are discussed. Menard, et al. [28] give an automotive application that has this pattern and illustrate the difficulties of correctly realizing the pattern using Adaptive AUTOSAR.

4 Simultaneity

A classic challenge program in concurrent programming is called the "cigarette smoker's problem" was introduced by Suhas Patil in 1971 [31] and is discussed

Sidebar 2: Lingua Franca Precedence Program Explained

This sidebar explains the program listed in Listing 4 and depicted in Fig. 2. Lines 2 through 4 create one instance of each reactor class. Lines 5 through 7 connect their ports. On Lines 14 to 17, the Source periodically produces requests and a randomly chosen correct or incorrect authentication key. In a real application, the Source might wrap a web server, for example, and produce requests and authentication keys when remote users request a service.[a]

On Lines 24 through 30, the Mediator checks that the provided authentication key matches the correct key, and, if so, issues an OK message. Since the execution of a reaction is logically instantaneous, that output has the same logical timestamp as the input. Consequently, when that OK message arrives at the Provider, it will be logically simultaneous with the request sent directly from the Source.

On Lines 37 through 43, the Provider checks that it has simultaneous inputs and that they match and, if so, provides the service. Otherwise, it denies the service.

[a] In Lingua Franca, an asynchronous interaction with the environment, such as a web server, is realized not with a timer, but rather with a **physical action**, which can be scheduled from outside the Lingua Franca program. Upon being scheduled, the physical action will be assigned a logical timestamp based on the current physical time at the machine where it is scheduled. The resulting timestamped event gets injected into the LF program where it can trigger reactions.

in Downey's *Little Book of Semaphores* [11].[4] Patil's original formulation goes like this:

> Three smokers are sitting at a table. One of them has tobacco, another has cigarette papers, and the third one has matches—each one has a different ingredient required to make and smoke a cigarette but he may not give any ingredient to another. On the table in front of them, two of the same three ingredients will be placed, and the smoker who has the necessary third ingredient should pick up the ingredients from the table, make the cigarette and smoke it. Since a new pair of ingredients will not be placed on the table until this action is completed, the other smokers who cannot make and smoke a cigarette with the ingredients on the table must not interfere with the fellow who can.

A naive solution realizes each smoker as follows (in pseudo code, shown for the smoker that holds tobacco):

```
while(true) {
    acquire_paper();
    acquire_matches();
    smoke();
    release();
}
```

The two "acquire" functions block until the specified resource is available and then acquire exclusive access to that resource. This realization, however, very likely deadlocks because after this smoker acquires paper, another smoker may acquire the matches (or the supplier process supplies tobacco instead of matches). At that point, no further progress is possible and all smokers freeze.

Patil imposed some constraints, that "the process which supplies the ingredients cannot be changed," and that "no conditional statements can be used." Patil argued that under these constraints, the problem cannot be solved using Dijkstra's semaphores [10].

In 1975, Parnas showed that Patil had imposed some additional unstated constraints on the use of semaphores and gave a solution that uses vector semaphores, but still avoids conditional statements [30]. Downey argued that the constraint to avoid conditional statements is rather artificial, but with the less artificial constraint that the supplier not be modified (it could, after all, represent an operating system), then the problem is interesting and the solutions can get quite convoluted [11]. Searching the web for solutions to this problem yields a few other attempts to solve it, including one that argues that the problem demonstrates the requirement for tests that enrich semaphores such as POSIX operations such as `sem_try_wait()` or `pthread_mutex_trylock()`.[5]

[4] The name of this problem illustrates how cultural norms have changed. In 1971, there was little cultural stigma around smoking cigarettes, and it was relatively common for smokers to roll their own.

[5] See for example OpenCSF: https://w3.cs.jmu.edu/kirkpams/OpenCSF/Books/csf/html/CigSmokers.html, although, unfortunately, the solution given there still exhibits the possibility of a form of deadlock, where one thread repeatedly, unfairly acquires a semaphore in a busy wait.

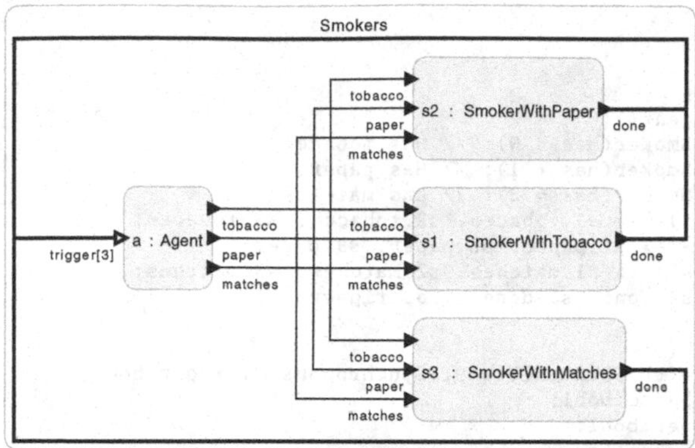

Fig. 3. Diagram of the LINGUA FRANCA example illustrating the **simultaneity** pattern.

A more commonly accepted solution, one implemented for example in the Savina actor benchmark suite [17], defines a centralized coordinator that first determines what the supplier has supplied, then decides which smoker should be given permission to take the supplies and dispatches a message to that smoker.

Addressing this problem in LINGUA FRANCA leads to radically different solutions that are not based on semaphores and locks at all. Hence, this does not really provide a solution to the problem Patil posed, but rather changes the problem into one that becomes trivially easy. A diagram is shown in Fig. 3 and the key portions of the code in Listing 5. Here, a Smoker class has a parameter named "`has`" (Line 35) that specifies which of the resources each smoker has. The instances of this class on Lines 3 and 5 give values to this parameter. The reaction starting on Line 46 is hopefully self-explanatory, showing how each smoker can independently decide whether to smoke without creating the possibility of deadlock. The key observation is that the reaction can test for the simultaneous presence of two distinct inputs, something that is not possible with basic semaphores. In fact, even programming errors will not manifest as a deadlock here. For example, if we erroneously instantiate two smokers with the same "`has`" parameter value, instead of deadlock, we will see two smokers smoking simultaneously. This program uses some features of the LINGUA FRANCA language that we have not yet explained. Those are explained in Sidebar 3.

Our LINGUA FRANCA program, of course, is not a solution to Patil's original problem, which was about how to use semaphores. It changes the problem, and semaphores are no longer needed. Instead, it uses the concurrency mechanisms of LINGUA FRANCA, where concurrent processes exchange time-stamped messages. With this solution, the problem becomes much less interesting. Unless your goal is to give programmers brain-teasing puzzles, this is a good thing!

```
main reactor {
    a = new Agent();
    s1 = new Smoker(has = 0); // Has tobacco.
    s2 = new Smoker(has = 1); // Has paper.
    s3 = new Smoker(has = 2); // Has matches.
    (a.tobacco)+ -> s1.tobacco, s2.tobacco, s3.tobacco;
    (a.paper)+ -> s1.paper, s2.paper, s3.paper;
    (a.matches)+ -> s1.matches, s2.matches, s3.matches;
    s1.done, s2.done, s3.done -> a.trigger;
}
reactor Agent {
    input\cite{ch15Benveniste:91:Synchronous} trigger:bool;
    output tobacco:bool;
    output paper:bool;
    output matches:bool;
    reaction(startup, trigger) -> tobacco, paper, matches {=
        int choice = rand() % 3;
        if (choice == 0) {
            SET(tobacco, true);
            SET(paper, true);
            printf("Agent putting tobacco and paper on the table.\n");
        } else if (choice == 1) {
            SET(tobacco, true);
            SET(paper, true);
            printf("Agent putting tobacco and matches on the table.\n");
        } else {
            SET(tobacco, true);
            SET(paper, true);
            printf("Agent putting paper and matches on the table.\n");
        }
    =}
}
reactor Smoker(
    smoke_time:time(1 sec),
    has:int(0)  // 0 for tobacco, 1 for paper, 2 for matches
) {
    input tobacco:bool;
    input paper:bool;
    input matches:bool;
    output done:bool;
    logical action smoke;
    reaction(smoke) -> done {=
        printf("Smoker is done smoking.\n");
        SET(done, true);
    =}
    reaction(tobacco, paper, matches) -> smoke {=
        if (self->has == 0 && paper->is_present && matches->is_present) {
            printf("Smoker with tobacco starts smoking.\n");
            schedule(smoke, self->smoke_time);
        } else if (self->has == 1
                && tobacco->is_present && matches->is_present) {
            printf("Smoker with paper starts smoking.\n");
            schedule(smoke, self->smoke_time);
        } else if (self->has == 2
                && tobacco->is_present && paper->is_present) {
            printf("Smoker with matches starts smoking.\n");
            schedule(smoke, self->smoke_time);
        }
    =}
}
```

Listing 5. LINGUA FRANCA program illustrating the **simultaneity** pattern.

5 Consistency

In the year 2000, Eric Brewer (of Berkeley and Google) gave a keynote talk [4] at the Symposium on Principles of Distributed Computing (PODC) in which he introduced the "CAP Theorem," which states that you can have only two of the following three properties in a distributed system:

- **Consistency**: Distributed components agree on the value of shared state.
- **Availability**: Ability to respond to user requests.
- tolerance to network **Partitions**: The ability to keep operating when communication fails.

This keynote is credited by many in the distributed computing community with opening up the field, enabling innovative approaches that offer differing tradeoffs between these properties. In 2012, Brewer wrote a retrospective [5] in which he observes that the "P" property is not really one you can trade off against the others. He clarified the design problem as one of how to trade off consistency against availability when network partitions occur. Moreover, he pointed out that network partitions are not a binary property; all networks have latency, and a complete communication failure is just the limiting case when the latency goes to infinity.

The tradeoff between consistency and availability arises in any distributed system where components are expected to agree on some aspect of the state of the system. Although this statement seems simple, it's actually quite subtle. When should they agree? What do we mean by agreement? These questions come into crisp focus when using a temporal semantics. We will argue that the tradeoffs are easier to reason about in this context.

Consider the reactor defined in Listing 6, Lines 19 to 36, which is inspired by Lamport's distributed database example [23]. This reactor is, perhaps, the smallest possible database. It contains one integer state variable named "`record`" and provides inputs that can add a value to that record. It also provides an input

Sidebar 3: Lingua Franca Simultaneity Program Explained

This sidebar explains some features of Lingua Franca that are used in Listing 5. Specifically, Lines 6 through 9 show a compact notation for certain connection patterns. The notation "`( portname )+`" means to use the specified port as many times as necessary to satisfy the right hand side of the connection. In this example, each such line establishes three connections. On the final line, 9, the right side of the connection references a **multiport**, a port that can accept a multiplicity of connections, defined on Line 12. The LF code generator checks that such connections are balanced. Messages that arrive on a multiport are handled in deterministic order, and each channel can be unambiguously absent while other channels have messages. The diagram in Fig. 3 can help the reader to understand these connections.

```
federated reactor Consistency {
    a = new Platform(update_amount = 100);
    b = new Platform(update_amount = -20);
    b.publish -> a.update;
    a.publish -> b.update;
}
reactor Platform(
    update_amount:int(0)
) {
    input update:int;
    output publish:int;
    c = new Client(update_amount = update_amount);
    r = new Replica();
    c.query -> r.query;
    (c.update)+ -> r.local_update, publish;
    r.current -> c.reply;
    update -> r.remote_update;
}
reactor Replica {
    input local_update:int;
    input remote_update:int;
    input query:bool;
    output current:int;
    state record:int(0);
    reaction(local_update, remote_update) {=
        if (local_update->is_present) {
            self->record += local_update->value;
        }
        if (remote_update->is_present) {
            self->record += remote_update->value;
        }
    =}
    reaction(query) -> current {=
        SET(current, self->record);
    =}
}
reactor Client(
    update_amount:int(0)
) {
    timer query_trigger(0, 150 msec);
    timer update_trigger(0, 100 msec);
    input reply:int;
    output query:bool;
    output update:int;
    reaction(query_trigger) -> query {=
        SET(query, true);
    =}
    reaction(update_trigger) -> update {=
        SET(update, self->update_amount);
    =}
    reaction(reply) {=
        printf("Balance is: %d.\n", reply->value);
    =}
}
```

Listing 6. Lingua Franca program illustrating the **consistency** pattern.

to ask for the current value of the record. Because inputs are timestamped, and because reactions are invoked in order when inputs are simultaneously present, the response to a **query** input will always reflect update inputs with timestamps equal to or less than that of the query input.

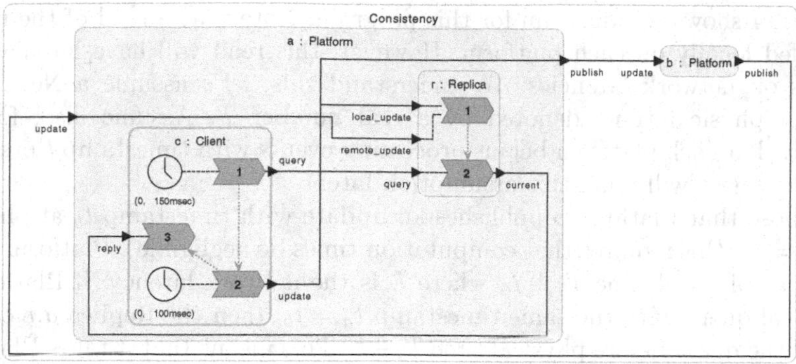

Fig. 4. Diagram of the LINGUA FRANCA example illustrating the **consistency** pattern.

Listing 6 shows an LF program that creates two instances of the Platform reactor (Lines 2 and 3), each of which contains one instance of the Replica reactor. The program ensures that the replicas remain strongly consistent. That is, given queries with the same timestamp, both replicas will always report the same value. This program also has a Client reactor that simulates users of the replicas by periodically generating updates and queries. In a real application, these updates and queries could be generated in response to network inputs, for example via a web server, rather than periodically, driven by timers.

The program is a bit more hierarchical than previous examples, where two instances of Platform are created, each with a Client and a Replica. Each Platform runs in a separate program (because the top-level reactor is federated) and can be run on different machines. Thus, the LINGUA FRANCA semantics ensures strong consistency across the replicas even when they are distributed.

Each Replica has three inputs, local_update, remote_update, and query. At any given logical time, if either local_update or remote_update (or both) are present, then the first reaction (Line 25) will be invoked and update the reactor's state using those inputs. If a query input is present, then the second reaction (Line 33) will be invoked. In LINGUA FRANCA semantics, if the query input is simultaneous with either local_update or remote_update, the first reaction is assured of being invoked before the second, and hence the response to the query will always reflect all updates, local or remote, with timestamps equal to or less than that of the query.

Here, the Replica reactors have a property that makes it easy to deal with simultaneous updates, which is that the update to the state is associative and commutative. Hence, one Client can add 100 to the state at the same (logical) time that the other Client subtracts 20 from the state, and both Clients will see a net change in the state of 80. Not all applications will have this associativity and commutativity, in which case the application logic needs to include mechanisms for resolving conflicts. For example, Clients could be assigned fixed priorities. Because of logical time, such conflicts are easy to detect and handle.

Figure 4 shows the diagram for this program. Note that a read of the record is handled locally on each platform. However, this read will have latency that depends on network latencies. To understand this, let's assume a Newtonian model of physical time, denoted by a real number T. Assume also, for the moment, that each platform begins processing events with timestamp t precisely when $t = T$ (we will relax this assumption later).

Suppose that Platform b publishes an update with timestamp t_b at physical time $T_b = t_b$ (this requires that computation times be negligible). Platform a will see this at physical time $T_b + L$, where L is the network latency. If Platform a has a local query with the same timestamp $t_a = t_b$, then the Replica $a.r$ cannot respond the query before physical time $T_b + L$. This means that it takes Platform a at least time L to respond to a query and to be ready for the next query.

The dependency on network latency implies that achieving perfect consistency, which this program does, comes at a quantifiable cost in availability. After receiving a query, the system cannot accept another query until time L has elapsed.

We can now relax some of these assumptions and draw a more general conclusion. Suppose that there is an offset O_a and O_b for a platform to begin processing events. That is, platform a will begin processing events with timestamp t_a at physical time $T = t_a + O_a$, and similarly for b. Suppose that a issues a query with timestamp t_a at physical time $T_a = t_a + O_a$, and b issues an update with the same timestamp $t_b = t_a$ at physical time $T_b = t_b + O_b$. Platform a will see the update at $T_b + L = t_b + O_b + L = t_a + O_b + L$. It cannot respond to the local query before physical time reaches

$$T = \max(t_a + O_b + L, t_a + O_a) = t_a + \max(O_b + L, O_a).$$

Since platform a starts processing events with timestamp t_a at $t_a + O_a$, then the time it takes to complete processing all events with timestamp t_a, which may include updates originating remotely, is

$$\Delta_a = (t_a + \max(O_b + L, O_a)) - (t_a + O_a) = \max(L + O_b - O_a, 0).$$

Correspondingly, the time it takes b to complete processing events at a timestamp is

$$\Delta_b = \max(L + O_a - O_b, 0).$$

Let us call these times the **unavailability**. We can adjust O_a or O_b to reduce the unavailability on one platform only at the expense of increasing it on the other! The fairest design is one where $O_a = O_b$, in which case the unavailability on both platforms is L, the network latency.

The best we can do, therefore, when maintaining perfect consistency, is limit queries to no more than one for each time period equal to L. This is a reduction in availability as a function of network latency, and therefore gives a quantitative interpretation to the CAP theorem. If the network fails altogether, L goes to infinity, and there is no availability.

We can now explore what happens if we relax consistency. In a timestamped language like LINGUA FRANCA, this is easy to do in a controlled way by manipulating timestamps. LINGUA FRANCA includes an **after** keyword that can be associated connections. We can, for example, replace Lines 4 and 5 in Listing 6 with

```
b.publish -> a.update after 10 msec;
a.publish -> b.update after 10 msec;
```

This means that the timestamp at the receiving end will be 10 msec larger than at the sending end. With this change, Δ_a and Δ_b both reduce by up to 10 msec, possibly making both of them zero, which will maximize availability.

There is a price in consistency, however. This means that on each platform, the results of a query reflect only remote updates that are timestamped at least 10 msec in the past. We can call this quantity the **inconsistency** C_{ab} and C_{ba}, and we now have

$$\Delta_a = \max(L + O_b - O_a - C_{ba}, 0)$$
$$\Delta_b = \max(L + O_a - O_b - C_{ab}, 0).$$

With perfect clock synchronization, the optimal values are $C_{ab} = C_{ba} = L$, which reduces the unavailability to zero at the cost of an inconsistency of L, the network latency. Any tradeoff in between perfect consistency and perfect availability can be chosen, with the caveat that L is likely not a constant and diverges to infinity upon network partitioning.

6 Related Work

In many ways, the ideas presented here are quite old, appearing in various forms in the work of Lamport, Chandy, and Lynch, for example, in the 1970s and 1980s. These ideas are worth a resurrection because of widespread prevalence of distributed computing today and because of the availability of much better programming frameworks and languages. LF and its runtime implementations leverage these classic results and wrap them in a programming model that abstracts away many of the complex details that are typically involved in realizing concurrent and distributed software.

LINGUA FRANCA is certainly not the first framework to give us concurrent components that exchange timestamped messages. Hardware description languages like VHDL and Verilog have always had this feature, as have simulation frameworks for discrete-event systems [7,36]. There is a long history of work on building parallel and distributed implementations of such frameworks [8,18], including the High Level Architecture (HLA) [21]. Some of these (like HLA) use centralized controllers that coordinate the advancement of time, while some, like Chandy and Misra [8] use decentralized control.

LINGUA FRANCA is also not the first framework to offer deterministic concurrency. The synchronous languages [3], such as Lustre, SIGNAL, and Esterel share key semantic features with LINGUA FRANCA, albeit not its timestamping.

In 1984, Lamport proposed a decentralized control strategy that links physical time with logical timestamps and leverages clock synchronizing to create an efficient decentralized coordination mechanism [23]. This technique was elevated to a programming framework with explicit timestamps in PTIDES [37] and then independently reinvented in Google Spanner [9]. These two latter efforts demonstrate that a timestamped framework is not just for simulation, but rather can be used efficiently at scale in large distributed systems. Moreover, they underscore the value of clock synchronization [12].

Timestamps have also appeared in a variety of forms, most famously in Lamport clocks [22] and vector clocks [24]. The relationship between these techniques and other uses of timestamps is subtle and fascinating.

This history of programming languages is punctuated with languages that include some notion of time, such as Modula [34,35], PEARL [27], Ada [6], Occam [14], Real-Time Euclid [20], and Erlang [2]. The notions of time introduced in these languages were more focused on exposing the mechanisms of a real-time operating system (RTOS) than on controlling concurrency. LF differs from these in many ways, not the least of which is that it is not a full-fledged programming language, but rather it is a polyglot coordination language. "Polyglot" means that program logic is written in a preexisting target language (C, C++, Python, JavaScript, etc.), and the coordination language simply orchestrates the execution of code in that language. In a federated Lingua Franca program, it is even possible to combine multiple languages in one application, although, as of this writing, that feature is not fully developed.

7 Conclusions

In light of the enormous increase in the prevalence of concurrent and distributed software, we need to continue to explore mechanisms beyond semaphores, locks, and threads. If these mechanisms include a notion of time with strong semantic properties, reasoning about concurrent programs becomes easier. Simple tasks, like aligning repeated computations, become simple again. Ensuring that precedences are respected become the responsibility of the infrastructure rather than of the application logic. Programming puzzles, like preventing deadlock in resource management problems, become trivial exercises. And exploring the tradeoff between availability and consistency becomes a quantifiable and systematic engineering task rather than ad hoc trial and error. Hence, taking time seriously is part of the answer to the question of what is next in programming.

Acknowledgments. The authors would like to acknowledge and thank the following people for their contributions to the design and implementation of Lingua Franca: Soroush Bateni, Shaokai Lin, Christian Menard, Alexander Schulz-Rosengarten, and Matt Weber. The work in this paper was supported in part by the National Science Foundation (NSF) award #CNS-1836601 (Reconciling Safety with the Internet) and the iCyPhy (Industrial Cyber-Physical Systems) research center, supported by Denso, Siemens, and Toyota.

References

1. Allen, J.: Effective Akka: Patterns and Best Practices. O'Reilly Media Inc., Newton (2013)
2. Armstrong, J., Virding, R., Wikström, C., Williams, M.: Concurrent Programming in Erlang, 2nd edn. Prentice Hall, Hoboken (1996)
3. Benveniste, A., Berry, G.: The synchronous approach to reactive and real-time systems. Proc. IEEE **79**(9), 1270–1282 (1991)
4. Brewer, E.: Towards robust distributed system. In: Symposium on Principles of Distributed Computing (PODC) (2000). Keynote Talk
5. Brewer, E.: CAP twelve years later: how the "rules" have changed. Computer **45**(2), 23 29 (2012). https://doi.org/10.1109/MC.2012.37
6. Burns, A., Wellings, A.: Real-Time Systems and Programming Languages: Ada 95, Real-Time Java and Real-Time POSIX, 3rd edn. Addison-Wesley, Boston (2001)
7. Cassandras, C.G.: Discrete Event Systems, Modeling and Performance Analysis. Irwin, Toronto (1993)
8. Chandy, K.M., Misra, J.: Parallel Program Design: A Foundation. Addison Wesley, Boston (1988)
9. Corbett, J.C., et al.: Spanner: Google's globally-distributed database. In: OSDI (2012). https://doi.org/10.1145/2491245
10. Dijkstra, E.W.: Cooperating sequential processes. In: The Origin of Concurrent Programming, pp. 65–138. Springer, New York (1968). https://doi.org/10.1007/978-1-4757-3472-0_2
11. Downey, A.B.: The Little Book of Semaphores, 2nd edn., vol. Version 2.2.1. Green Tea Press, Pennsylvania (2016). https://greenteapress.com/semaphores/LittleBookOfSemaphores.pdf
12. Eidson, J., Lee, E.A., Matic, S., Seshia, S.A., Zou, J.: Distributed real-time software for cyber-physical systems. In: Proceedings of the IEEE (Special Issue on CPS), vol. 100, no. 1, pp. 45–59 (2012). https://doi.org/10.1109/JPROC.2011.2161237
13. Eugster, P.T., Felber, P.A., Gerraoui, R., Kermarrec, A.M.: The many faces of publish/subscribe. ACM Comput. Surv. **35**(2), 114–131 (2003). https://doi.org/10.1145/857076.857078
14. Galletly, J.: Occam-2, 2nd edn. University College London Press, London (1996)
15. Hewitt, C., Bishop, P.B., Steiger, R.: A universal modular ACTOR formalism for artificial intelligence. In: Proceedings of the 3rd International Joint Conference on Artificial Intelligence, Standford, CA, USA, 20–23 August 1973, pp. 235–245 (1973)
16. Hunkeler, U., Truong, H.L., Stanford-Clark, A.: MQTT-S-A publish/subscribe protocol for wireless sensor networks. In: 3rd International Conference on Communication Systems Software and Middleware and Workshops (COMSWARE 2008), pp. 791–798. IEEE (2008)
17. Imam, S., Sarkar, V.: Savina - an actor benchmark suite enabling empirical evaluation of actor libraries. In: Workshop on Programming Based on Actors, Agents, and Decentralized Control (AGERE) (2014). https://doi.org/10.1145/2687357.2687368
18. Jefferson, D.: Virtual time. ACM Trans. Program. Lang. Syst. **7**(3), 404–425 (1985)
19. Jerad, C., Lee, E.A.: Deterministic timing for the industrial internet of things. In: IEEE International Conference on Industrial Internet (ICII), 21–23 October 2018. IEEE (2018)
20. Klingerman, E., Stoyenko, A.: Real-time Euclid: a language for reliable real-time systems. IEEE Trans. Softw. Eng. **12**(9), 941–949 (1986)

21. Kuhl, F., Weatherly, R., Dahmann, J.: Creating Computer Simulation Systems: An Introduction to the High Level Architecture. Prentice Hall PTR, Hoboken (1999)
22. Lamport, L.: Time, clocks, and the ordering of events in a distributed system. Commun. ACM **21**(7), 558–565 (1978). https://doi.org/10.1145/359545.359563
23. Lamport, L.: Using time instead of timeout for fault-tolerant distributed systems. ACM Trans. Program. Lang. Syst. **6**(2), 254–280 (1984)
24. Liskov, B.H., Ladin, R.: Highly available distributed services and fault-tolerant distributed garbage collection. In: Symposium on Principles of Distributed Computing (PODC), pp. 29–39. ACM, November 1986. https://doi.org/10.1145/10590.10593
25. Lohstroh, M., Menard, C., Bateni, S., Lee, E.A.: Toward a Lingua Franca for deterministic concurrent systems. ACM Trans. Embed. Comput. Syst. (TECS) **20**(4), 1–27 (2021). https://doi.org/10.1145/3448128. Article 36
26. Lohstroh, M., Menard, C., Schulz-Rosengarten, A., Weber, M., Castrillon, J., Lee, E.A.: A language for deterministic coordination across multiple timelines. In: Forum for Specification and Design Languages (FDL), 15–17 September 2020. IEEE (2020). https://doi.org/10.1109/FDL50818.2020.9232939
27. Martin, T.: Real-time programing language PEARL - concept and characteristics. In: Computer Software and Applications Conference (COMPSAC), pp. 301–306 (1978)
28. Menard, C., Goens, A., Lohstroh, M., Castrillon, J.: Determinism in adaptive AUTOSAR. In: Proceedings of the 2020 Design, Automation and Test in Europe Conference (DATE), March 2020. https://doi.org/10.23919/DATE48585.2020.9116430
29. Moritz, P., et al.: Ray: a distributed framework for emerging AI applications. CoRR arXiv:1712.05889 (2017)
30. Parnas, D.L.: On a solution to the cigarette smokers' problem (without conditional statements). Commun. ACM **18**(3), 181–183 (1975). https://doi.org/10.1145/360680.360709
31. Patil, S.S.: Limitations and capabilities of Dijkstra's semaphore primitives for coordination among processes. Report, Computation Structures Group, Project MAC. MIT, February 1971
32. Quigley, M., et al.: ROS: an open-source robot operating system. In: ICRA Workshop on Open Source Software, Kobe, Japan, vol. 3, p. 5 (2009)
33. Schneider, C., Spönemann, M., von Hanxleden, R.: Just model! - Putting automatic synthesis of node-link-diagrams into practice. In: Proceedings of the IEEE Symposium on Visual Languages and Human-Centric Computing (VL/HCC 2013), San Jose, CA, USA, pp. 75–82 (2013)
34. Wirth, N.: Toward a discipline of real-time programming. Commun. ACM **20**(8), 577–583 (1977)
35. Wirth, N.: Report on the programming language Modula-2. In: Programming in Modula-2, pp. 139–165. Springer, Heidelberg (1983). https://doi.org/10.1007/978-3-642-96757-3_33
36. Zeigler, B.P., Praehofer, H., Kim, T.G.: Theory of Modeling and Simulation, 2nd edn. Academic Press, Cambridge (2000)
37. Zhao, Y., Lee, E.A., Liu, J.: A programming model for time-synchronized distributed real-time systems. In: Real-Time and Embedded Technology and Applications Symposium (RTAS), pp. 259–268. IEEE (2007). https://doi.org/10.1109/RTAS.2007.5

Integrated Modeling and Development of Component-Based Embedded Software in Scala

Klaus Havelund(✉) and Robert Bocchino(✉)

Jet Propulsion Laboratory, California Institute of Technology, Pasadena, USA
{klaus.havelund,robert.l.bocchino}@jpl.nasa.gov

Abstract. Developing embedded software requires good frameworks, models, and programming languages. The languages typically used for embedded programming (e.g., C and C++) tend to be decoupled from the models and tend to favor efficiency and low-level expressivity over safety, high-level expressivity, and ease of use. In this work, we explore the use of Scala for integrated modeling and development of embedded systems represented as sets of interconnected components. Although Scala today is not suitable for this domain, several current efforts aim to develop Scala-like embedded languages, so it is conceivable that in the future, such a language will exist. We present four internal Scala DSLs, each of which supports an aspect of embedded software development, inspired by an actual C++ framework for programming space missions. The DSLs support programming of software components, hierarchical state machines, temporal logic monitors, and rule-based test generators. The effort required to develop these DSLs has been small compared to the similar C++ effort.

1 Introduction

Embedded software development. Developing software for embedded systems (for example, robotic vehicles) poses at least three specific challenges. First, without appropriate frameworks, embedded systems programming is difficult. All embedded systems have certain similar behaviors, such as commanding, telemetry, and inter-task communication. It is both tedious and wasteful to encode these behaviors by hand in a general-purpose language for each new application. Domain-specific frameworks such as F Prime (F') [4] and cFS [5] can alleviate this problem. The framework can provide the behavior that is common to many applications, and the developers can focus on the behavior that is specific to their application.

Second, even with a good framework, there is a semantic gap between the domains of design and implementation. For example, developers may express a

The research was carried out at Jet Propulsion Laboratory, California Institute of Technology, under a contract with the National Aeronautics and Space Administration.

T. Margaria and B. Steffen (Eds.): ISoLA 2021, LNCS 13036, pp. 233–252, 2021.
https://doi.org/10.1007/978-3-030-89159-6_16

design in terms of components and their connections, whereas the implementation may be in terms of C++ classes and functions. To bridge this gap, one can express the design in a modeling language and automatically generate code in a general-purpose language for further elaboration by the developers. F Prime uses a domain-specific modeling language named FPP (F Prime Prime, or F") for this purpose [10]. It is also possible to use a general-purpose modeling language such as SysML [36] or AADL [8]. This approach works, but it causes the model to be disconnected from the implementation, because the two are expressed in different languages, and the model does not generate a complete implementation. In particular, some hand-modification of generated code is usually required, and this makes it hard to update the model.

Third, embedded systems usually have tight timing and resource requirements compared to general applications. Therefore embedded developers are restricted in the programming languages they can use. The language must be compiled to efficient machine code, must provide low-level access to machine details, and must provide deterministic timing and scheduling. The traditional players in this space are C, C++, and Ada. More recent entries include D and Rust.

C, while groundbreaking in its day, has not advanced much since the 1980s; by the standards of modern languages, it is woefully primitive. C++ and Ada are better: they provide abstractions such as user-defined class types, and they are advancing with the times. However, these languages are incremental, sometimes awkward evolutions of decades-old designs. Further, C++, like C, has many devious behaviors that can trick even experienced and careful programmers into writing incorrect code. D improves upon C++ in many respects (e.g., cleaned-up syntax, improved type safety), but its design is strongly influenced by C++.

By contrast, Scala [30] is more recently designed from first principles. It has a clean syntax and semantics and is generally easier for programmers to understand and use than traditional embedded languages. Further, Scala's strong static type system rules out many basic errors that can lurk in even well-tested C and C++ programs. Rust is interesting because it adopts modern language design principles while being both efficient and safe. However, it relies on static analysis called "borrow checking" that is notoriously difficult to understand and use.

Overall, while both C++ and Scala can be used for both low- and high-level programming, C++ is more expressive for low-level programming (for example, it provides explicit control over the placement of objects in memory, whereas Scala does not), while Scala is more expressive for high-level programming (for example, Scala has ML-like functions and closures; in C++ functions and closures are separate concepts, and closures are syntactically awkward). Rust is somewhere in the middle.

Our work. We are exploring the use of Scala for modeling and developing embedded systems. Scala is a natural choice for modeling because it is has good high-level expressivity and good support for internal domain-specific languages (DSLs). Scala as it exists today is not suitable for embedded programming: it runs on the Java Virtual Machine, it is garbage collected, and it cannot express low-level machine interaction. However, several efforts are developing Scala-like embedded languages; we describe some of them below. Although it will take further research and implementation effort, we believe that it is possible to develop such a language. Arguably Swift [35] is already such a language, although its current focus is on iOS app development.

In this work, we imagine that Scala can be used for embedded software, and we explore what we could do if this were true. In particular, we imagine that we can use the same language (Scala) for both modeling and development. To do this, we leverage Scala's strong support for *internal DSLs*. Internal means that the domain-specific language is expressed using only features provided by the host language. By contrast, an *external DSL* has a separate implementation from the host language, with a standalone tool or tools for parsing, analysis, and code generation. Internal DSLs have the advantage that the programmer works with only one language and can use all the tools, such as integrated development environments (IDEs), available for that language. The DSLs are directly executable without the use of external tools.

We have implemented four internal DSLs in Scala 2.13.0. Two of them are inspired by the F′ (F Prime) C++ framework [4], developed at NASA's Jet Propulsion Laboratory (JPL) for programming flight systems as collections of interacting components. F′ has e.g. been used for programming the Mars Helicopter [22]. The four DSLs support programming respectively: components and their port connections; behavior as Hierarchical State Machines (HSMs) in the individual components; runtime monitors; and rule-based test generators. The HSM DSL was previously introduced in [15,16], and the monitor DSL was introduced in [13,14]. This work integrates these with the component DSL and the testing DSL in a combined framework.

Threats to validity. The main threat to validity is the considerable gap between Scala and efficient flight software. There are, however, two interesting different attempts in progress to address this problem. Scala Native [31] is a version of Scala, which supports writing low-level programs that compile to machine code. Sireum Kekinian [33] supports programming in the Slang programming language, a subset of Scala 2.13 but with a different memory model. Slang runs on the JVM, natively via Graal, and can be translated to C. It is furthermore supported with contract and proof languages designed for formal verification and analyses. A secondary threat to validity is the unruly nature of internal DSLs. Although internal DSLs are easy to develop and very expressive, they do have drawbacks. Whereas external DSLs have a hard boundary, offering a limited number of options, internal DSLs have a soft boundary, and allow perhaps too many options. Furthermore, whereas external DSLs can be easily analyzed, internal DSLs are harder to analyze and visualize, requiring analysis of the entire host language.[1] Finally, internal DSLs do generally not have as succinct syntax as external DSLs.

[1] This comment concerns *shallow* DSLs as the ones we present in this paper, where the host language constructs are part of the DSL. This is in contrast to *deep* internal DSLs, where a data type is defined, the objects of which are programs in the DSL, and which are analyzable.

Paper outline. Sections 2, 3, 4 and 5 present the four DSLs for creating respectively components and their connections, hierarchical state machines, runtime monitors, and rule-based test generators. Section 6 outlines related work. Section 7 concludes the paper.

2 Components

The first Scala DSL we shall illustrate allows one to model an embedded software system as a collection of interacting components. The DSL specifically reflects the F′ framework [4] developed at JPL. F′ is a component-based flight software framework. Components can be active or passive. Each active component runs an internal thread. A component communicates with other components through ports. Communication over ports can be asynchronous (via a message placed on a queue) or synchronous (via a direct function call). A component-based system is constructed by defining the components, and subsequently defining a topology: linking them together, connecting each output port of a component with an input port of another component.

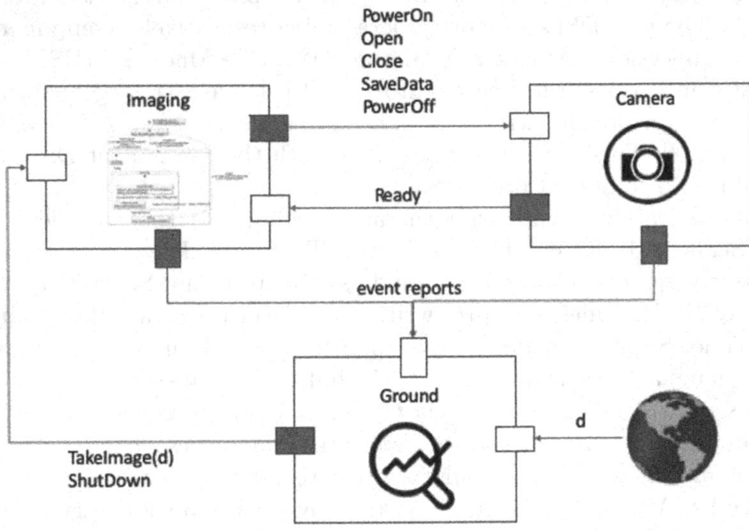

Fig. 1. The F′ Imaging, Camera, and Ground components.

We shall illustrate this DSL (and the other three DSLs) with a single example, shown in Fig. 1. The example is an elaboration of the example previously presented in [15], and concerns an imaging application on board a spacecraft, consisting of three components, Imaging, Camera, and Ground. The Imaging component is given commands from the ground to orchestrate the taking of an image by opening the shutter, controlled by the Camera component, for a certain duration. The Imaging and Camera components send event reports to the ground.

Each event report reports an event that occurred on board, such as taking an image. The Imaging component is programmed as a hierarchical state machine (see Sect. 3), and the Ground component contains a temporal logic monitor (see Sect. 4).

Importing DSLs. To start with, we import the four DSLs into our Scala program where we will build this system, see Fig. 2.

```
import fprime._
import hsm._
import daut._
import rules._
```

Fig. 2. Importing the four DSLs.

Defining Message Types. Then we define the types of messages that are sent between components. First commands, which are case classes/objects subclassing the pre-defined Command trait (a trait is an interface to one or more concrete classes), see Fig. 3. A command either causes an image to be taken, or shuts down the imaging system.

```
trait Command { ... }
case class TakeImage(d: Int) extends Command
case object ShutDown extends Command
```

Fig. 3. Commands.

In this simple system, all ground commands go to the Imaging component, and they all directly extend a single trait Command. In a more realistic system, commands to several components would be routed through a command dispatch component, and there might be separate command traits for separate components or subsystems.

We then define messages going between the Imaging and the Camera component, see Fig. 4. The Imaging component can instruct the Camera component to power on or off, to open or close the shutter, and to save the image. The Camera component can report back that it has followed the various instructions and is ready for a new instruction. For simplicity, we have made the camera's power interface part of the Camera component. In a more realistic system, there could be a separate power component. Also, in a realistic system the ground may command the camera directly.

```
trait CameraControl
case object PowerOn extends CameraControl
case object PowerOff extends CameraControl
case object Open extends CameraControl
case object Close extends CameraControl
case object SaveData extends CameraControl

trait CameraStatus
case object Ready extends CameraStatus
```

Fig. 4. Messages going between Imaging and Camera.

```
trait Event extends Observation
case class EvrTakeImage(d: Int) extends Event
case object EvrPowerOn extends Event
case object EvrPowerOff extends Event
case object EvrOpen extends Event
case object EvrClose extends Event
case object EvrImageSaved extends Event
case object EvrImageAborted extends Event
```

Fig. 5. Event reports to ground.

Finally we declare the kind of observation messages sent to the ground to report what is happening on board the spacecraft, see Fig. 5. These *event reports* (Evr) report on the take-image commands sent from the Ground component to the Imaging component, the instructions being sent from the Imaging component to the Camera component, and whether the image is being saved or aborted in the Camera component.

The Imaging Component. The Imaging component is shown in Fig. 6. It is defined as a class sub-classing the Component class, and defines two input ports, one for receiving commands from the ground, and one for receiving messages from the camera, and two output ports, one for sending messages to the camera and one for sending observation events to the ground.

```
class Imaging extends Component {
  val i_cmd = new CommandInput
  val i_cam = new Input[CameraStatus]
  val o_cam = new Output[CameraControl]
  val o_obs = new ObsOutput

  object Machine extends HSM[Any] {...}

  object MissedEvents {...}

  override def when: PartialFunction[Any, Unit] = {
    case input ⇒
      if (!Machine(input)) MissedEvents.add(input)
  }
}
```

Fig. 6. The Imaging component.

A component can, as we have seen, have multiple input ports. They are all connected to the same single *message input queue*. That is, when a message arrives at an input port, it is stored in this message queue. Our component contains a state machine Machine, and an auxiliary data structure MissedEvents, both to be described in Sect. 3.

A component must define the partial function when, which the Component class calls to process a message received on the queue. In this case, it applies the state machine, and if the state machine is not interested in the message (Machine(input) returns false), the event is stored in MissedEvents, to be processed later. Because when is a partial function, one can test whether it is defined for a certain message msg with the Boolean expression when.isDefinedAt(msg), a feature used to process messages.

The argument type is Any because the type of messages going into the message queue is the union of the messages coming into the input ports. We could statically constrain the type to be the union of the input types. However, writing out the union (say as a collection of Scala case classes) by hand would be inconvenient, since we have already provided this type information on the ports. This issue points to a limitation of using an internal DSL in this case. With an external DSL, we could use the types of the messages to infer and generate the case classes. More work is needed to find the sweet spot between internal and external DSLs meant to augment programmer productivity, in contrast to DSLs targeting non-programmers.

The Camera Component. The Camera component is a stub, and is not fully shown in Fig. 7. It receives messages from the Imaging component, sends messages back to the Imaging component, and otherwise just sends observation messages to the Ground component, and does not perform any real functions beyond that.

```
class Camera extends Component {
  val i_img = new Input[CameraControl]
  val o_img = new Output[CameraStatus]
  val o_obs = new ObsOutput
  ...
}
```

Fig. 7. The Camera component.

The Ground Component. The Ground component issues commands to the Imaging component, and takes as input observations from the Imaging and Camera components, see Fig. 8. In addition it takes inputs in the form of integers (i_int) supplied by the ground, where an integer *d* indicates that a command TakeImage(d) is to be sent to the Imaging component (take an image with the shutter being opened for *d* milliseconds).

The Ground component contains a monitor SaveOrAbort, formulated as a temporal logic property, and explained in Sect. 4. Each observation o of type Observation is submitted to the monitor with the call SaveOrAbort.verify(o).

```
class Ground extends Component {
  val i_int = new Input[Int]
  val i_obs = new ObsInput
  val o_cmd = new CommandOutput

  object SaveOrAbort extends Monitor[Observation] {...}

  override def when: PartialFunction[Any, Unit] = {
    case d: Int ⇒ o_cmd.invoke(TakeImage(d))
    case o: Observation ⇒ SaveOrAbort.verify(o)
  }
}
```

Fig. 8. The Ground component.

```
object Main {
  def main(args: Array[String]): Unit = {
    val imaging = new Imaging
    val camera = new Camera
    val ground = new Ground

    imaging.o_cam.connect(camera.i_img)
    imaging.o_obs.connect(ground.i_obs)
    camera.o_img.connect(imaging.i_cam)
    camera.o_obs.connect(ground.i_obs)
    ground.o_cmd.connect(imaging.i_cmd)

    ground.i_int.invoke(1000)
    ground.i_int.invoke(2000)
    ground.i_int.invoke(3000)
  }
}
```

Fig. 9. The main program.

Connecting the Components. The main program makes instances of the components and connects them, see Fig. 9. As an example, the statement imaging.o_cam.connect(camera.i_img) connects the output port o_cam of the imaging component with the input port i_img of the camera component. The main program then asks the ground component to take three images with exposure durations of respectively 1000, 2000, and 3000 ms.

3 Hierarchical State Machines

In this section we present the Scala DSL for writing the Hierarchical State Machine (HSM) that controls the Imaging component. An HSM supports programming with states, superstates, entry and exit actions of states, and transitions between states. The concept corresponds to Harel's state charts [12]. The DSL and this particular HSM has previously been described in [15].

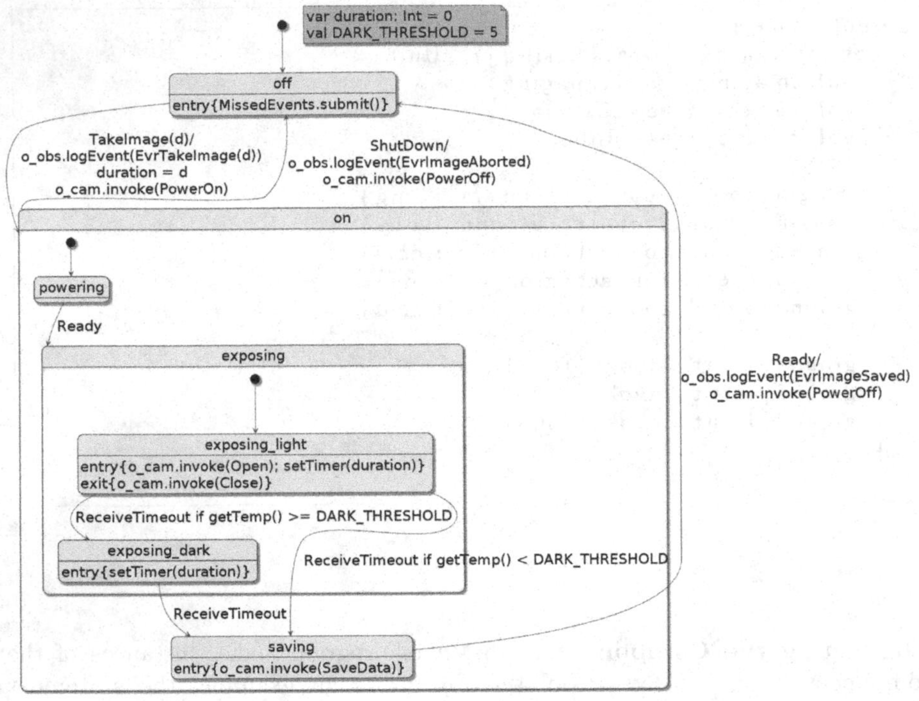

Fig. 10. The Imaging HSM visualized.

The Imaging HSM (referred to as Machine in the Imaging component) is shown graphically in Fig. 10. It can be automatically generated from the textual state machine in the corresponding Scala DSL, part of which is shown in Fig. 11, using PlantUML [25] and ScalaMeta [32]. The HSM can receive a TakeImage(d) command from ground, where d denotes the exposure duration. It responds to this request by sending a message to the camera to power on, and waiting until the camera is ready. It then asks the camera to open the shutter for the specified exposure duration, using a timer service which generates a timeout event after a specified period. Following this, it optionally takes a so-called dark exposure with the shutter closed (but only if the ambient temperature is above a specified threshold). A dark exposure allows determination of the noise from camera electronics, so that this can be subtracted from the acquired image. Finally, it saves the image data, and powers off the camera.

```
object Machine extends HSM[Any] {
  var duration: Int = 0
  val DARK_THRESHOLD = ...
  def getTemp(): Int = ...

  initial(off)
  ...
  object on extends state() {
    when {
      case ShutDown ⇒ off exec {
        o_obs.logEvent(EvrImageAborted)
        o_cam.invoke(PowerOff)
      }
    }
  }

  object powering extends state(on, true) {
    when { case Ready ⇒ exposing }
  }

  object exposing extends state(on)

  object exposing_light extends state(exposing, true) {
    entry { o_cam.invoke(Open); setTimer(duration) }
    exit {o_cam.invoke(Close) }
    when {
      case ReceiveTimeout ⇒ {
        if (getTemp() ≥ DARK_THRESHOLD) exposing_dark
        else saving
      }
    }
  }
  ...
}
```

Fig. 11. The Imaging HSM.

Following standard HSM notation, see Fig. 10, the filled-out black circles indicate the initial substate that is entered whenever a parent state is entered. Thus, for instance, a transition to the on state ends with the HSM being in the powering state. Associated with each state are also two optional code fragments, called the entry and exit actions. The entry action is executed whenever the HSM enters the state, whereas the exit action is executed whenever the HSM leaves the state. Finally, the labeled arrows between states show the transitions that are caused in response to events received by the HSM. A label has the form:

$\langle event \rangle$ **if** $\langle condition \rangle / \langle action \rangle$

which denotes that the transition is triggered when the HSM receives the specified ⟨*event*⟩ and the (optional) ⟨*condition*⟩ is true. In response, the HSM transitions to the target state, and executes the specified (optional) ⟨*action*⟩. As an example, suppose the HSM is in state exposing_light, and it receives the event ShutDown (for which a transition is defined from the parent on state). This would cause the HSM to perform the following actions (in order):

1. the exit actions for the states exposing_light, exposing (no action), and on (no action), in that order.
2. the action associated with the transition.
3. the entry action for the state off.

The entry action for the off state is MissedEvents.submit(). This re-submits an event that has been stored in the MissedEvents queue, which the HSM was not able to process in the past when in some state not prepared to process that event. Such "currently unwanted" events are stored for later re-submission. This is an artificial example, showing how one can deal with the fact, that an F′ component only has one input queue to which all input ports of the component connect. The MissedEvents data structure is defined in Fig. 12, where the submit function simply re-submits the next missed event to the component's input queue.

4 Monitors

In this section we briefly present the Daut (Data automata) DSL [7,13] for programming data parameterized temporal runtime monitors. The DSL supports writing event monitors that have either a temporal logic flavor, or a state machine flavor. We specifically program the Ground component to monitor observation events coming down from the Imaging and Camera components. The Ground component, Fig. 8, contains an instantiation of the SaveOrAbort monitor, the full definition of which is shown in Fig. 13.

The property states that whenever (always) an EvrTakeImage command is observed, then it is an error to observe another EvrTakeImage before either an EvrImageSaved or EvrImageAborted is observed. This reflects the property that taking an image should end with the image being saved or aborted before another image is processed.

The DSL for writing monitors is very expressive and convenient. An earlier version (TraceContract [1]) was used throughout NASA's Lunar LADEE mission [2] for checking command sequences against flight rules expressed as monitors, before being sent to the spacecraft.

```
object MissedEvents {
  private var missedEvents : List[Any] = Nil

  def add(event : Any): Unit = {
    missedEvents ++= List(event)
  }

  def submit(): Unit = {
    missedEvents match {
      case Nil ⇒
      case event :: rest ⇒
        missedEvents = rest
        selfTrigger(event)
    }
  }
}
```

Fig. 12. Data structure for storing missed events.

```
object SaveOrAbort extends Monitor[Observation] {
  always {
    case EvrTakeImage(_) ⇒ hot {
      case EvrTakeImage(_) ⇒ error("not␣saved␣or␣aborted")
      case EvrImageSaved | EvrImageAborted ⇒ ok
    }
  }
}
}
```

Fig. 13. The SaveOrAbort monitor.

5 Rule-Based Tests

In developing applications with the F′ flight software framework [4], we have found that it is useful to define tests in terms of *rules*. A rule R consists of a *pre-condition* and an *action*. The pre-condition is a Boolean function on the state of the system, expressing whether R is *enabled* in that state, in which case it can *fire* by executing the action. The action commands the system to do something and checks for the expected behavior. Armed with a set of rules, we can write *scenarios* that use the rules to generate tests, e.g. by randomly selecting enabled rules and firing them. By writing rules and scenarios, one can quickly construct tests that exercise much more behavior than would be practical by manually writing each test. In this section we present such a rule DSL.

Testing the Imaging Component. We show how to use the rule DSL to test the Imaging state machine, Figs. 10 and 11, explained in Sect. 3. We use the standard approach to unit testing F′ components. We construct a system consisting of two components:

1. The Imaging component that we want to test.
2. The Test component. This component simulates the rest of the system. It contains a rule-based object that sends input to the Imaging component and checks the resulting output.

Note that although the approach here is used for testing one component, it can be used for testing a collection of components as well.

The Test Component. The Test component, see Fig. 14, has an input port for each output port of the Imaging component: i_obs for observations, and i_cam for messages the Imaging component normally sends to the Camera component. In addition, the Test component has an i_tck input port. This is used to drive the Test component from the main program: one move at a time in this particular case, to control the speed of rule firing. Correspondingly, the Test component has an output port for each input port of the Imaging component: o_cmd for commands normally coming from ground, and o_cam for messages normally coming from the Camera component.

The when method in the Test component directs incoming "tick" messages (of type Unit) from the main program to the rule engine (TestRules), causing it to fire a single randomly chosen enabled rule. Observation events, on the other hand, are forwarded to the monitor (SaveOrAbort). All other messages are ignored. The SaveOrAbort monitor, Fig. 13, is the same that we previously used in the Ground component in Sect. 4, this time monitoring observation events emitted from the Imaging component only. It monitors that every EvrTakeImage is terminated by a EvrImageSaved or EvrImageAborted before the next EvrTakeImage is observed.

The rule-based tester, TestRules, is defined in Fig. 15. It contains three rules, each sending a message to one of the input ports of the Imaging component, taking an image, shutting down the imaging component, or a ready signal (symbolizing that the camera component is ready), with an upper limit on how many messages of each kind can be sent. The execution strategy chosen is 'Pick', which means: whenever the fire () method is called, pick **one** enabled rule randomly and execute it. The Test component is driven by the main program with tick messages: one tick - one rule fired. This way the main program has control over how fast the rule program executes its rules.

```
class Test extends Component {
  val i_tck = new Input[Unit]
  val i_obs = new ObsInput
  val i_cam = new Input[CameraControl]
  val o_cmd = new CommandOutput
  val o_cam = new Output[CameraStatus]

  object SaveOrAbort extends Monitor[Observation] {...}

  object TestRules extends Rules {...}

  override def when: PartialFunction[Any, Unit] = {
    case _: Unit ⇒ TestRules.fire()
    case o: Observation ⇒ SaveOrAbort.verify(o)
    case _ ⇒
  }
}
```

Fig. 14. The test component.

The rules DSL offers a sub-DSL for writing rule execution *strategy algorithms*, of type Alg, using the functions shown in Fig. 16. Random executes repeatedly a randomly chosen enabled rule, forever, or until no rule applies. A bounded version is provided as well. All executes the rules in sequence. An error is recorded if the pre-condition of a rule fails. Enabled executes enabled rules in sequence. If a pre-condition of a rule is not satisfied, the rule is just skipped. Until executes the rules in sequence, until a rule is reached where the pre-condition is false. First executes the first rule, from left, where the pre-condition evaluates to true. Pick executes a randomly chosen enabled rule once. Seq executes the sequence of algorithms. If executes one of two algorithms depending on a condition. While executes an algorithm as long as some condition is satisfied. Bounded executes the algorithm a bounded number of times.

The Main Test Program. The MainTest program in Fig. 17 instantiates the Imaging and the Test components, connects their ports, and then repeatedly 1000 times, with 100 ms in between, sends a tick message to the Test component, causing a rule to be fired for each tick (the repeat function is provided by the rule DSL).

```
object TestRules extends Rules {
  val MAX_IMAGES: Int = 1000
  val MAX_SHUTDOWNS: Int = 1000
  val MAX_READY: Int = 1000

  var imageCount: Int = 0
  var shutdownCount: Int = 0
  var readyCount: Int = 0

  rule("TakeImage") (imageCount < MAX_IMAGES) → {
    o_cmd.invoke((TakeImage(imageCount)))
    imageCount += 1
  }

  rule("ShutDown") (shutdownCount < MAX_SHUTDOWNS) → {
    o_cmd.invoke(ShutDown)
    shutdownCount += 1
  }

  rule("Ready") (readyCount < MAX_READY) → {
    o_cam.invoke(Ready)
    readyCount += 1
  }

  strategy(Pick())
}
```

Fig. 15. The TestRules component.

Detecting a Problem in the Imaging Component. Executing the above unit test does not reveal any violations of the SaveOrAbort monitor. However, setting the debugging flag to true yields output, part of which is shown in Fig. 18, illustrating two firings of the rule Ready. It demonstrates a problem with the handling of *missed events*: events which arrive in the Imaging component, but which it is not able to handle in the state it is currently in. These are put in the MissedEvents queue (the contents of which is shown as: `stored: [ ... ]`). When the imaging HSM gets back to the off state, it looks for the next event in the missed-queue. If such a one exists it takes it out and re-submits it to itself. The event, however, may not match what is expected even in the off state neither, which is only TakeImage events, and hence it is put back in the missed-queue. The result is that the missed-queue grows and grows with Ready and ShutDown events. This can be seen above in that the queue grows from `[Ready]` to `[Ready,Ready]`.

```
def Random(rules: Rule*): Alg
def Random(max: Int, rules: Rule*): Alg
def All(rules: Rule*): Alg
def Enabled(rules: Rule*): Alg
def Until(rules: Rule*): Alg
def First(rules: Rule*): Alg
def Pick(rules: Rule*): Alg
def Seq(algs: Alg*): Alg
def If(cond: => Boolean, th: Alg, el: Alg): Alg
def While(cond: => Boolean, alg: Alg): Alg
def Bounded(max: Int, alg: Alg): Alg
```

Fig. 16. Functions returning different test strategies.

```
object MainTest {
  def main(args: Array[String]): Unit = {
    val imaging = new Imaging
    val test = new Test

    test.o_cmd.connect(imaging.i_cmd)
    test.o_cam.connect(imaging.i_cam)
    imaging.o_cam.connect(test.i_cam)
    imaging.o_obs.connect(test.i_obs)

    repeat(1000) {
      Thread.sleep(100)
      println("=" * 80)
      test.i_tck.invoke(())
    }
  }
}
```

Fig. 17. The MainTest program.

From a functional correctness point of view, the program works since the ShutDown and Ready events probably should be ignored in the off state anyway. The problem, however, is that the queue of missed events keeps growing. This problem fundamentally is related to our failed attempt to deal with the fact that a component only has one input queue. It requires the programmer to pay careful attention to how to deal with messages arriving that are not expected in the state the component is currently in. The problem is in particular visible in components programmed as state machines. The F′ C++ team is currently considering how to deal with this problem. Note that this kind of problem also exists in the single input queue actor model [19], but not in the CSP [20] and CCS [24] channel-based models with multiple input queues (channels) that can be selected from.

```
...
===============================================================
[fpr] ? Test : ()                // Test receives a tick
[rul] executing rule Ready       // Rule Ready executes
[fpr] ! Test -[Ready]-> Imaging // Test sends Ready to Imaging
[fpr] ? Imaging : Ready          // Imaging receives Ready
Ready stored: [Ready]            // Ready unexpected and stored
===============================================================
[fpr] ? Test : ()                // Test receives a tick
[rul] executing rule Ready       // Rule Ready executes
[fpr] ! Test -[Ready]-> Imaging // Test sends Ready to Imaging
[fpr] ? Imaging : Ready          // Imaging receives Ready
Ready stored: [Ready,Ready]      // Ready unexpected and stored
===============================================================
...
```

Fig. 18. Debug output from running rule-based test.

6 Related Work

Among existing programming languages, there are a few potential alternatives to C and C++ in the embedded domain. Spark Ada [34] and Real-Time Java [27] have existed for some time. More recent languages include Rust [28], Swift [35], Go [11], and D [6]. Spark Ada is interesting due to the support for formal verification. Other languages are emerging supported by formal verification. We have previously mentioned the Scala Native effort [31], and the Slang [33] programming language, based on Scala's syntax, but with a different semantics suited for embedded programming, and supported by formal verification. The PVS theorem prover [26] has been augmented with a translator from PVS to C [9], permitting writing very high-level and verifiable (executable) specifications in PVS using PVS's highly expressive type system, and obtain C's execution speed. With respect to the modeling aspect, the BIP framework [3] supports component-based modeling with components containing C code, and specifically state machines. Interaction between components can be controlled with temporal constraints. The Quantum Framework [29] supports programming with hierarchical state machines in C and C++, and is used at JPL as target of a translation from statecharts drawn with MagicDraw [21]. Finally, an ongoing effort to design and implement a programming language explicitly supporting hierarchical state machines and monitors is described in [23]. That effort has been directly inspired by the work presented in this paper.

7 Conclusion

We developed four internal DSLs in Scala for modeling and developing embedded systems. The DSLs are inspired by the component-based C++ framework F′ developed at JPL for programming robotic vehicles. The work is part of a broader effort to explore alternatives to C and C++ for programming embedded systems. As part of this effort, we developed three non-trivial multi-threaded applications in both Rust [28] and Scala: an AI plan execution engine for the Deep Space 1 (DS-1) spacecraft, described and verified in [17]; a file transfer protocol, described and verified in [18]; and the F′ component framework, described in [4]. Rust's type checker includes the *borrow checker*, which verifies that memory operations are safe. This borrow checker is challenging to deal with. We are currently exploring features required for programming embedded systems in Scala as an alternative.

References

1. Barringer, H., Havelund, K.: TraceContract: a Scala DSL for trace analysis. In: Butler, M., Schulte, W. (eds.) FM 2011. LNCS, vol. 6664, pp. 57–72. Springer, Heidelberg (2011). https://doi.org/10.1007/978-3-642-21437-0_7
2. Barringer, H., Havelund, K., Kurklu, E., Morris, R.: Checking flight rules with TraceContract: application of a Scala DSL for trace analysis. In: Scala Days 2011. Stanford University, California (2011)
3. BIP. http://www-verimag.imag.fr/Rigorous-Design-of-Component-Based.html
4. Bocchino, R., Canham, T., Watney, G., Reder, L., Levison, J.: F Prime: an open-source framework for small-scale flight software systems. In: 32nd Annual AIAA/USU Conference on Small Satellites. Utah State University (2018)
5. cFS. https://cfs.gsfc.nasa.gov
6. D. https://dlang.org
7. Daut on github. https://github.com/havelund/daut
8. Feller, P., Gluch, D.: Model-Based Engineering with AADL: An Introduction to the SAE Architecture Analysis and Design Language. Addison-Wesley, Boston (2012)
9. Férey, G., Shankar, N.: Code generation using a formal model of reference counting. In: Rayadurgam, S., Tkachuk, O. (eds.) NFM 2016. LNCS, vol. 9690, pp. 150–165. Springer, Cham (2016). https://doi.org/10.1007/978-3-319-40648-0_12
10. FPP. https://github.com/fprime-community/fpp
11. Go. https://golang.org
12. Harel, D.: Statecharts: a visual formalism for complex systems. Sci. Comput. Program. **8**(3), 231–274 (1987)
13. Havelund, K.: Data automata in Scala. In: 2014 Theoretical Aspects of Software Engineering Conference, TASE 2014, Changsha, China, 1–3 September 2014, pp. 1–9. IEEE Computer Society (2014)
14. Havelund, K.: Monitoring with data automata. In: Margaria, T., Steffen, B. (eds.) ISoLA 2014. LNCS, vol. 8803, pp. 254–273. Springer, Heidelberg (2014). https://doi.org/10.1007/978-3-662-45231-8_18
15. Havelund, K., Joshi, R.: Modeling and monitoring of hierarchical state machines in Scala. In: Romanovsky, A., Troubitsyna, E.A. (eds.) SERENE 2017. LNCS, vol. 10479, pp. 21–36. Springer, Cham (2017). https://doi.org/10.1007/978-3-319-65948-0_2
16. Havelund, K., Joshi, R.: Modeling rover communication using hierarchical state machines with Scala. In: Tonetta, S., Schoitsch, E., Bitsch, F. (eds.) SAFECOMP 2017. LNCS, vol. 10489, pp. 447–461. Springer, Cham (2017). https://doi.org/10.1007/978-3-319-66284-8_38

17. Havelund, K., Lowry, M.R., Penix, J.: Formal analysis of a space-craft controller using SPIN. IEEE Trans. Softw. Eng. **27**(8), 749–765 (2001)
18. Havelund, K., Shankar, N.: Experiments in theorem proving and model checking for protocol verification. In: Gaudel, M.-C., Woodcock, J. (eds.) FME 1996. LNCS, vol. 1051, pp. 662–681. Springer, Heidelberg (1996). https://doi.org/10.1007/3-540-60973-3_113
19. Hewitt, C., Bishop, P., Steiger, R.: A universal modular actor formalism for artificial intelligence. In: Proceedings of the 3rd International Joint Conference on Artificial Intelligence, IJCAI 1973, San Francisco, CA, USA, pp. 235–245. Morgan Kaufmann Publishers Inc. (1973)
20. Hoare, C.A.R.: Communicating Sequential Processes. Prentice-Hall, Hoboken (1985)
21. MagicDraw. https://www.nomagic.com/products/magicdraw
22. Mars Helicopter. https://mars.nasa.gov/technology/helicopter
23. McClelland, B., Tellier, D., Millman, M., Go, K.B., Balayan, A., Munje, M.J., Dewey, K., Ho, N., Havelund, K., Ingham, M.: Towards a systems programming language designed for hierarchical state machines. In: 8th IEEE International Conference on Space Mission Challenges for Information Technology, (SMC-IT 2021). IEEE (2021, To appear)
24. Milner, R. (ed.): A Calculus of Communicating Systems. LNCS, vol. 92. Springer, Heidelberg (1980). https://doi.org/10.1007/3-540-10235-3
25. PlantUML. http://plantuml.com
26. PVS. http://pvs.csl.sri.com
27. Real-Time Java. https://en.wikipedia.org/wiki/Real_time_Java
28. Rust. https://www.rust-lang.org
29. Samek, M.: Practical UML Statecharts in C/C^{++}: Event-Driven Programming for Embedded Systems, 2nd edn. Newnes, Burlington (2009)
30. Scala. http://www.scala-lang.org
31. Scala Native. https://scala-native.readthedocs.io/en/v0.3.9-docs
32. ScalaMeta. https://scalameta.org
33. Sireum Kekinian. https://github.com/sireum/kekinian
34. Spark Ada 2014. http://www.spark-2014.org
35. Swift. https://developer.apple.com/swift
36. Systems Modeling Language (SysML). http://www.omg.org/spec/SysML/1.3

Slang: The Sireum Programming Language

Robby([✉]) and John Hatcliff([✉])

Kansas State University, Manhattan, KS 66506, USA
{robby,hatcliff}@ksu.edu

Abstract. This paper presents design goals, development approaches, and applications for Slang – a subset of the Scala programming language designed for engineering high assurance safety/security-critical systems. Rationale is given for specializing Scala for Slang so as to retain Scala's synergistic blend of imperative, functional, and object-oriented features while omitting and tailoring features that make formal verification and other analyses difficult. Strategies for enhancing the usability of Slang are discussed including integration with the broader Scala/JVM ecosystem, compilers, and development environments. A number of accompanying Slang tools are described including Slang scripting, meta-programming support, and translators to Javascript and native code that enable support for a wide range of deployment platforms. To support deployment on constrained embedded platforms, the Slang Embedded subset and an accompanying C translator generate efficient implementations that avoid garbage-collection and other aspects that hinder deployment and safety/security assurances. We conclude with a discussion of how our experiences with Slang may provide suggestions for the future of programming and programming language design for engineering critical systems.

1 Introduction

Fueled by accelerating hardware capabilities and algorithmic improvements, formal methods have made significant advances in recent decades and have increasingly gained adoption in industry. For example, there are now powerful SMT2 solvers (*e.g.*, [6,26]) that can scale to realistic problems in large-scale industrial use (*e.g.*, [3]). Groundbreaking and technically challenging work to formally prove correctness of complex hardware and software such as microprocessors (*e.g.*, [35]), OS kernels (*e.g.*, [22]), and compilers (*e.g.*, [25]), among others, have demonstrated the effectiveness of interactive theorem proving.

In our research, we have applied formal method techniques such as software model checking (*e.g.*, [13,16,30]), data/information flow analyses (*e.g.*, [2,32–34]), symbolic execution (*e.g.*, [7,17]), interactive and automated theorem proving (*e.g.*, [8,37]), and abstract interpretation (*e.g.*, [19,37]), as well as formal specification languages (*e.g.*, [2,14,31]), on extremally diverse kinds of systems

Work supported in part by the US Defense Advanced Research Projects Agency, US Air Force Research Lab, US Army, and US Department of Homeland Security.

T. Margaria and B. Steffen (Eds.): ISoLA 2021, LNCS 13036, pp. 253–273, 2021.
https://doi.org/10.1007/978-3-030-89159-6_17

such as real-time component-based embedded systems, concurrent Java, sequential SPARK/Ada, and mobile Android applications. Many of these recent tools were implemented in earlier generations of our Sireum platform, which is an outgrowth effort of the Bogor [30] model checking framework (which itself is an outgrowth of the Bandera software model checker project [13]). Sireum embraces the Bandera philosophy that usability in formal method tools is a crucial factor for gaining adoption and reducing application efforts. Moreover, it follows the Bogor philosophy of providing general basic building blocks and frameworks that can be customized for specific domains in order to better capitalize on the specific domain-inherent properties for reducing analysis costs.

In our teaching, in recent years, we were tasked to teach manual and automatic program verification for undergraduate sophomores, under the guise of an introductory course on logical foundations of programming that we inherited from David A. Schmidt – a highly-respected researcher and educator in programming languages and formal methods [4]. One might imagine that teaching manual/automatic formal verification to sophomores is a tall order, but Schmidt figured out how to package it effectively. As a teaching aid, he developed a semi-automatic program verifier (which includes its own arithmetic semi-decision procedure) for a "baby" Python language with contract and proof languages that produces an HTML-based verification report.

While it achieved its goals, we desired to have a more modern and automatic tool (while still supporting semi-manual proving as an option) that leverages SMT2 solvers and equipped with a seamless IDE integration that: (a) checks sequent proofs and verifies programs in the background as students type, and (b) asynchronously highlight issues directly in the IDE. This gave rise to the development of the Sireum Logika program verifier and proof checker [39], whose input language is a "baby" Scala script (with contract and proof languages expressed inside a custom Scala string interpolator). Since its initial deployment in the beginning of 2016, Logika has been used to teach around two hundred students each year at K-State. In addition, in the past couple of years, our colleagues at Aarhus University have adopted Logika for teaching logic courses.

Motivated and encouraged by these research and teaching experiences (and inspired by all the great work by others), we desired to consolidate all our efforts. Hence, in the beginning of 2017, we initiated the development of the next generation Sireum platform equipped with its own programming language with supporting specification and proof languages. These inter-connected languages and formal method tools aim to achieve higher levels of safety and security assurances by selectively designing the language features to significantly reduce formal analysis costs, as well as the cost to apply the analyses by making them more usable (*i.e.*, usable enough for teaching undergraduate sophomores).

In this paper, we present the Slang programming language – one result of the multi-year effort described above. Section 2 presents our design guidelines/decisions, which motivated the language features described in Sect. 3. Section 4 discusses Slang's implementation, and Sect. 5 describes how Slang have been applied to several domains as parts of our broader validation efforts. Section 6 relates Slang to other work, and Sect. 7 concludes with some future work.

2 Design

This section describes some of our design guidelines and decisions for Slang.

Usable safety/security first: We aim to provide a language that is amenable to formal verification and analysis. While one route is to emphasize powerful specification logics and verification using manually-oriented proof assistants to handle language complexity (*e.g.*, [10]), we instead choose to carefully engineer the language features and semantics to ease verification. Our (agile) approach is to start "small" and "grow" the language as desired while ensuring that new features do not introduce disproportionate analysis complexity. While we prioritize "verifiability" and "analyzability", we are also mindful of performance and memory footprint. We recognize that language usability is very important, since the ability to achieve safety/security is not worth much if the language is very hard to wield, detrimental to productivity, and impedes explanation of best principles of system engineering, coding, and logic-based program reasoning.

Gradual effort/reward assurance workflow: While we *design* the language for high assurance, we do not always *require* high assurance. Developers should be able to program in the language without being burdened about ensuring, *e.g.*, functional correctness. In these situations, automatic formal methods may be used "behind the scenes": (a) to help developers *understand the behavior of a program* (rather than for verification), and (b) to support other quality assurance techniques (*e.g.*, simulation and testing). As higher assurance levels are required, developers can incrementally employ various formal method techniques/tools.

Rich, high-level language features: As computing technology advances significantly, modern programming languages increasingly include a rich collection of high-level language features to increase productivity. Object-oriented programming language features (*e.g.*, classes and interfaces, dynamic dispatch, *etc.*) are useful for organizing large codebases while providing extensibility. Imperative programming language features are convenient and familiar to most developers. Functional programming language features provide simpler programming mental models (*e.g.*, side-effect free computations, *etc.*) and highly abstract features (*e.g.*, pattern matching, *etc.*). We would like to adopt a mix of these features.

Multi-platform support, from small to large: We want the language to support development of a variety of systems, from small embedded systems (*e.g.*, running inside a micro-controller with 192 kb memory) to large applications running on powerful workstations or servers. In addition, we want at least one platform that supports very easy deployment, prototyping, debugging, and simulation (*e.g.*, JVM). This is beneficial for classroom teaching as well as for introducing new researchers to the language and associated formal method tools. Moreover, industrial development can often benefit from: (a) capabilities to rapidly prototype systems on an easy-to-use platform, and (b) facilities that help re-deploy prototyped systems to hardened product platforms.

Integration with existing/legacy systems, libraries, and other languages: While we want our language to be used as often as possible, we need it to be able to integrate with existing systems and libraries and to provide interoperability with other languages. This allows gradual language adoption or a mixed system development involving different languages, as well as being able to reap benefits from existing efforts. In safety-critical systems, there will inevitably be low-level system code and device drivers that cannot be coded efficiently in a language that emphasizes verifiability and clean abstractions. So there needs to be some way to cleanly interface with such code.

Small-scale development/maintenance: As academics with limited resources and a high turn-over of team members (*i.e.*, students), one pragmatic criterion is that the language infrastructure and tooling should be able to be developed by a very small team (in fact, by a single person so far). This necessitates us to leverage thriving ecosystems instead of building a new one from the ground up.

Based on the above, we decided to realize Slang by leveraging the Scala programming language. Scala offers a good mix of object-oriented, imperative, and functional programming language features. It is built on top of the popular, multi-platform Java Virtual Machine (JVM) ecosystem, which brought about rich tooling support such as dependency management and compilation to native using GraalVM. Scala tooling also offers other compilation targets such as Javascript using Scala.js (and native code using Scala Native).

Despite its many strengths, Scala is a complex language, and thus difficult to highly assure for safety/security. However, its flexible language features (*e.g.*, powerful type inference, macros, *etc.*), open-source/development, and pluggable compiler pipeline architecture allow one to effectively customize the language. This is actually the primary reason why we settled on Scala as no other language tooling offered a similar customization level. Other weaknesses are Scala's slow compilation speed and IDE support issues (not as polished as Java's). All things considered, we deemed Scala's benefits far outweigh its downsides.

Hence, we *specialized* Scala for Slang. We adopted Scala's syntax (*i.e.*, Slang's syntax is a proper subset of Scala's), narrowed down its language features significantly (but still included many powerful features), and tailored its semantics via program transformations implemented in a compiler plugin and Scala macros (thus, enabling Scala/JVM tools to be used for Slang).

3 Features

In this section, we illustrate how Slang design goals are achieved using selected language features. Due to space constraints, we cannot illustrate all of the language features in detail. The Slang website [40] provides a repository of examples and an extensive language reference manual.

Reasoning about object references and heap-allocated data is one of the great challenges of program verification. Many research efforts have tackled this challenge by leaving the language largely unconstrained but then adopting separation logics (*e.g.*, [10]) or advanced type systems (*e.g.*, [12]) to support reasoning. Other efforts such as SPARK/Ada constrain the language to avoid introducing aliasing and other problems, which allows the specifications and logic to be simpler. We take the latter approach and constrain the language while attempting to preserve many features of Scala's type system and its synergistic fusion of imperative, functional, and object-oriented programming language features.

Distinct mutable and immutable objects: Slang distinguishes between mutable and immutable object structures *statically*. That is, object type mutability is declared as part of type declarations. Immutability is strict in Slang, *i.e.*, immutable objects cannot refer to mutable ones, and violations of this rule are detected by type checking. Mutable objects, however, can refer to immutable ones. The main benefit of using immutable structures is that they simplify reasoning because aliasing becomes a non-issue. On the other hand, mutable objects are often more convenient to transform via destructive updates for many developers.

Sole access path: One of the main difficulties in program reasoning is analyzing mutable object structure in the presence of aliasing. Slang reduces this reasoning complexity by adhering to the following runtime invariant property:

> *At any given program point, a mutable object is observationally reachable only by (at most) one access path.*

One (intended) consequence is that cyclic object structures are disallowed.[1] In general, immutable structures can form directed acyclic graphs while strictly mutable ones can only (at most) form trees.

Adherence to the invariant is facilitated by restricting aliasing on mutable objects. The typical language features that introduce aliasing are assignment (including pattern matching variable binding, for-each loop, *etc.*) and parameter passing. In Slang, assigning a mutable object to a variable (possibly) creates a deep mutable structure copy before updating the variable (if the object has previously been assigned to a variable).

This design choice trades off code performance and better memory utilization for ease of reasoning. In many cases, the decrease in performance/utilization is not detrimental to the coded application. When needed, the code can be rewritten and optimized (justified by empirical data such as profiling and memory analyses – not simply due to the pursuit of premature optimizations). Using an ownership type system is an alternate approach to tame aliasing [12] (*e.g.*, Rust). However, there is increased specification effort in using ownership types, and in languages that adopt them as the *default case*, developers must take on the increased specification burden even when the associated payoffs are small.

We prefer a gradual effort/reward approach in which developers can initially code without such burdens as the default, and only put in additional effort when the situation warrants. This enables developers to focus on code correctness (e.g., established using Slang's contract checking), and then code optimizations can be introduced when needed (and the contract checking framework can be used to

[1] This does not preclude graph algorithms from being written in Slang; in fact, the Slang runtime library provides a graph library (used in [33]), including cycle detection (graphs are realized using indexed node pools with pairs of indices as edges).

prove that the optimized code still satisfies its contract or equivalent to the less optimized version). The implicit copying of mutable structures does sometimes introduce unanticipated behaviors for developers new to Slang due to loss of anticipated data structure sharing. However, tools can be developed to highlight code regions where copying occurs. More approaches can be added to Slang in the future to further facilitate performance improvement/memory usage reduction, but they should not always be required if additional specifications are needed.

This leaves us with aliasing via parameter passing, which Slang allows with restrictions. Specifically, a method invocation sufficiently maintains the sole access path invariant when the mutable object structures being passed (and accessed "global", instance, or closure-captured variables) are disjoint/separate, and this can be established by ensuring that no two abstract access paths to mutable objects involved in the method invocation are a prefix of one to another. By abstract, we meant an access path p of the form: (1) variable reference x, (2) field access $p.x$, or (3) sequence indexing $p(\top)$, where the index value is abstracted away as $\top$. For example, consider a method invocation p_0.*m*(p_1,...,p_n) where each $p_{i\in\{0,...,n\}}$ is an abstract access path to a mutable structure, and where *m* accesses enclosing variables of mutable type represented as abstract paths $p_{n+1},...,p_{n+m}$ (which can be inferred [32]). The method invocation maintains the sole access path invariant if: $\neg\exists\ i,j \in \{0,...,n+m\}.\ i \neq j \wedge \mathit{prefix}(p_i,p_j)$. A more precise condition can be used if one is willing to prove all index values of same abstract path prefixes are all distinct at the invocation program point.

One useful Slang programming pattern to reduce implicit copying involves exploiting Slang's restricted aliasing by parameter passing. Instead of returning mutable objects as method results, which may trigger copying when returned objects are assigned to variables, mutable objects can be passed down the call chain to store computed results via destructive updates. This approach, which we nicknamed as the Slang "hand-me-down" maneuver, works very well even for programming small embedded systems (*i.e.*, to avoid dynamic memory allocation efficiently), but at the cost of what one might consider as "inelegant" code.

In short, Slang's approach to aliasing focuses the reasoning/verification concerns to statically-defined classes of objects (*i.e.*, mutable) at a single well-defined and easily-identifiable program construct (*i.e.*, method invocation), which is also the main location of concern in compositional program verification and formal analyses. Hence, addressing aliasing can go hand-in-hand with other compositional assurance approaches such as for ensuring absence of runtime errors (*e.g.*, buffer overflows), functional correctness, and secure information flow.

Type system: Slang does not have a notion of a "top" type like `Object` in Java or `Any` in Scala for more meaningful sub-typing relationships in program reasoning. Moreover, Slang does away with the problematic `null` value in favor of optional types.[2] There is no implicit type coercion in Slang as such coercion may

[2] Memory footprint optimizations in the Scala compiler plugin for Slang include flattening `None` into `null` and `Some` to its contained value internally for object fields, but optional values are used for field accesses.

be unintended and non-trivially affect program reasoning. Object identity is non-observable (one can always add a distinguishing field value when needed), and object equality tests are structural equivalences by default (*i.e.*, equality tests can be customized). Generics are supported, though currently unconstrained. In the future, type constraints over generics such as "sub-type of T" might be added, but as mentioned previously, we wanted to start "small".

Slang (immutable) built-in types are: `B` (boolean), `Z` (arbitrary-precision integer), `C` (character), `String`, `R` (arbitrary-precision decimal number), `F32` (32-bit floating-point number), `F64` (64-bit floating-point number), and `ST` (a template engine implemented using a custom Scala string interpolator).

Developers can introduce two kinds of custom integer types: (1) range integer types, and (2) bit-vector integer types. Range integer types can optionally specify min/max values (*i.e.*, they can be arbitrary-precision). Operations on range integers are checked that they stay within the specified min/max values. Range integer types do not provide bit-wise operations, which are offered by bit-vector integers. However, operations on bit-vector integers are not range checked, and they are backed and operated (in the generated code) using either 8-bit, 16-bit, 32-bit, and 64-bit values, using the smallest that fits. The reason why Slang distinguishes range and bit-vector integer types is because automated analyses on the latter are often significantly more expensive. That is, developers should use range integer types over bit-vector if bit-wise operations are not needed. Below are some examples of range and bit-vector integer type declarations.

```
@range(min = 0) class N                  // natural number (arbitrary-precision)
@range(min = 1, max = 10) class OneToTen // 1 .. 10 range int
@bits(signed = T, width = 8) class S8    // 8-bit signed bit-vector int
@bits(min = 0, max = 3) class U2         // 0 .. 3 unsigned bit-vector int
```

The Slang compiler plugin automatically generates supporting operations on such types (*e.g.*, addition, subtraction, *etc.*) as the (Scala value) class methods.

Slang built-in sequence (array) types are immutable `IS[`I`, `T`]` and mutable `MS[`I`, `T`]`, which are parameterized by index type I and element type T. The index type I has to be either `Z`, a range integer type, or a bit-vector integer type. A sequence's size is fixed after creation, and accesses on sequences are checked against the sequence index range. Append, prepend, and remove operations on `IS` and `MS` are provided, and they always create a new sequence. Tuple types `(`T_1`, ..., `T_N`)` are supported and their mutability is determined based on the contained element types. For (higher-order) closures, function types `(`T_1`, ..., `T_N`) => `U are also supported and classified based on their "purity" (discussed below). (When using (higher-order) closures in mixed paradigm languages like Slang, high assurance applications should use pure closures at present, if at all, as contract languages/analyses on "impure" closures are still subjects of our ongoing research.)

Slang interfaces (traits) and classes are distinguished by their mutability (and "sealing") as illustrated by the following example.

```
@sig trait I { ... }                  // immutable interface
@datatype trait ID { ... }            // immutable sealed interface
@datatype class D(...) { ... }        // immutable final class
@msig trait M { ... }                 // mutable interface
@record trait MR { ... }              // mutable sealed interface
@record class R(...) { ... }          // mutable final class
```

Traits can only define/declare methods (with/without implementations), but fields are disallowed. Traits can extend other traits, and classes can implement traits. Implementations of sealed traits have to be defined in the same file.

To keep it simple, classes are always final, hence, there is no class inheritance in Slang, only trait implementations. Inherited methods can be overriden. Method definitions that are inherited by a trait or a class T with the same name (and similar signatures) originating from different traits have to be overriden in T, so developers are explicitly made aware of a potential reasoning issue.

Classes can only have one constructor, and constructor parameters are fields. Fields can have read access (`val`, which is also the default) or read/write access (`var`), and both can refer to mutable and immutable objects. A `@datatype` class, however, can only have `val`s as fields, while a `@record` class can also have `var`s. All fields and methods have to be explicitly typed, which simplifies type inference and eases parallel type checking (after type outlining). All traits and classes regardless of mutability can have methods with side-effects (impure).

Slang `object` O `{ ... }` definitions are singletons like in Scala, except that they cannot implement traits and cannot be assigned to a variable or passed around. Therefore, they simply serve to group "global" fields and methods, and consequently, they are allowed to refer to mutable structure or define `var`s.

Method purity: Slang classifies methods based on the kinds of side-effects that they might make: (a) impure, (b) `@pure`, (c) `@memoize`, and (d) `@strictpure`. Impure methods are allowed to (destructively) update objects without restrictions. Methods (and functions) annotated with `@pure` cannot update existing objects but they can create and update the newly created objects as part of their computation. They can also define local `val`s and `var`s, use loops, and recurse. They cannot access any enclosing `val` which holds a mutable object or any enclosing `var` during their execution. `@memoize` is `@pure` with (non-observable) automatic caching. Hence, `@memoize` (and `@pure`) are observationally pure [28]. `@strictpure` methods have further restrictions; they cannot update any object, and they cannot define local `var`s (only `val`s) or use loops, but can recurse.

Pure methods simplify reasoning and are useful for specification purposes. We distinguished `@strictpure` methods since they can be directly translated to logical representations, and therefore they do not require explicit functional behavior contract specifications for compositional verification purposes. Thus, they can be treated directly as specifications (after checking for runtime errors).

Control structures: Slang supports Scala's if-conditional and while-loop, as well as for-loop and for-yield-comprehension, including forms with multiple iterators and conditions. Slang fully embraces Scala's pattern matching constructs with only minor constraints (related to loss of information due to erasure). Exceptions and exception handling are not supported as they complicate reasoning.

To simplify formal analyses (and improve readability), Slang restricts other Scala syntactic forms. For example, a code block that evaluates to a value expressed by e – {...;e}, is not part of Slang's expression language. Slang categorizes a special syntactic form ae that is only allowed as an assignment's right-hand side or as a function closure definition body (liberally) defined as:

ae ::= e | {...;ae} | **if** (e) ae **else** ae | **return** e | e **match** { $case$+ }

where each *case* pattern matching body evaluates to a value (`return` is disallowed in closure definitions). Note that an if-conditional without a code block (similar to Java's ternary `?:` operator) is part of Slang's expression language.

Extensions: As described above, many Scala features are excluded, partly because we wanted to simplify reasoning and partly because we wanted to start "small" in the language design. One additional noteworthy exclusion is concurrency features. This is in part due to the fact that in our current industrial research projects, we support concurrency using automatically generated real-time tasking structures derived from AADL [21] architecture models using our HAMR framework [18] described in Sect. 5. In the AADL computational model, component implementations (e.g., as written in Slang or C) are strictly sequential, implementing functions that transform values on component input ports to values on component output ports. Task scheduling, communication, and resolving contention on component ports is handled by the underlying run-time middleware. This organization of computation and tasks enables contract-based reasoning at the architectural level. Alternatively, there is a promising concurrency approach currently being incubated in Project Loom [38] – Java Fibers, which are lightweight and efficient threads powered by continuations implemented in the JVM, which seems worth waiting for. Regardless, Slang provides extension methods (akin to Bogor extensions [30]) to extend its capabilities by leveraging existing libraries as well as providing interoperability with other languages. Below is an example extension that provides a (pure) parallel map operation, which is heavily used in the Slang compilation toolchain described in Sect. 4.

```
@ext object ISZOpsUtil {
  @pure def parMap[V, U](s: IS[Z, V], f: V => U @pure): IS[Z, U] = $
}
```

For JVM, Scala.js Javascript, and GraalVM native compilation targets, the Slang compiler plugin rewrites `$` as method invocation `ISZOpsUtil_Ext.parMap(s, f)`, whose implementation is written in Scala using its parallel collection library for the JVM and native targets, and using a sequential map operation for the Javascript target. The `@ext` annotation can optionally accept a string of the target `object` name that provides the method implementation as an alternative of using the extension object identifier with the `_Ext` suffix convention. In general, the implementation can be written in any language of the hosting platform, and from this implementation one can call any library available on the platform.

One issue with extensions is that for Slang analysis/verification to be sound, an extension implementation has to adhere to Slang's sole access path invariant and obey any stated contract for the extension. However, conformance to these requirements cannot generally be established from within Slang or by using Slang tools. Thus, other assurance approaches have to be used, or conformance has to be considered as an undischarged assumption.

Language subsets: We recognize that not all Slang features are desirable for a certain application domain. For example, when targeting high assurance embedded systems, closures and recursive types are undesirable due to the dynamic memory management requirement for realizing such features. Thus, it is often handy to be able to create subsets of Slang for particular domains. These subsets can be enforced by a static analysis over fully resolved Slang abstract syntax trees. We have created a subset of Slang called *Slang Embedded* that is targeted for translation to efficient embedded C (see Sect. 4).

Specification and proof language support: As Slang is also an input language for the next generation Logika tool that we are currently developing, as well as for other formal analyses that we plan to develop, one of its design goals is to facilitate (possibly expanding) families of specification and proof languages.

As previously mentioned, we would like Slang's syntax to be a proper subset of Scala's syntax, because this allows existing Scala tooling (*e.g.*, IDEs) to work without much modification, thus lowering our tool development overhead. Drawing from an earlier work [29] that uses Java method invocations to represent contract forms, we also found that we could nicely simulate grammars using Scala's method invocation and special syntax features (internal DSLs). Below is an example behavioral contract of a method that `swaps` two sequence elements.

```
def swap[I, T](s: MS[I, T], i: I, j: I): Unit = {
  Contract(
    Reads(),           // read accesses (by default, parameters are included)
    Requires(s.isInBound(i), s.isInBound(j)),             // pre-conditions
    Modifies(s),                                          // frame-conditions
    Ensures(                                              // post-conditions
      s(i) == In(s)(j), s(j) == In(s)(i), s.size == In(s).size,
      All(s.indices)(k => (k != i & k != j) ->: (s(k) == In(s)(k)))))
  val t = s(i); s(i) = s(j); s(j) = t
}
```

`Contract`, `Reads`, `Requires`, `Modifies`, `Ensures`, `All`, and `In` are Scala methods:

```
object Contract {
  def apply(arg0: Reads, arg1: Requires, arg2: Modifies, arg3: Ensures): Unit =
    macro Macro.lUnit4
}
object All {
  def apply[I, T](seq: IS[I, T])(p: T => Boolean): B = { /* ... elided */ }
}
def Reads(accesses: Any*): Contract.Reads = ??? // throws NotImplementedError
def Requires(claims: B*): Contract.Requires = ???
def Modifies(accesses: Any*): Contract.Modifies = ???
def Ensures(claims: B*): Contract.Ensures = ???
def In[T](v: T): T = ??? // retrieve v's pre-state; usable only inside Ensures
```

`Contract` is realized using a Scala macro that effectively erases any invocation to it, thus it does not affect code runtime behaviors.[3] All other methods are

[3] A runtime contract checker (similar to [36]) can be developed in the future for testing purposes (or for contract enforcement with various mitigation options).

simply stubs with *types that enforce grammar rules*. Below is another example illustrating one of Slang theorem forms that proves a well-known syllogism using Slang's proof language, which also exploits Scala's syntactic flexibility:

```
@pure def s[U](human: U => B@pure, mortal: U => B@pure, Socrates: U): Unit = {
  Contract(Requires(All{(x: U) => human(x) ->: mortal(x)}, human(Socrates)),
           Ensures (mortal(Socrates)))
  Deduce(1 #> All{(x: U) => human(x) ->: mortal(x)}          by Premise,
         2 #> human(Socrates)                                by Premise,
         3 #> (human(Socrates) ->: mortal(Socrates))         by AllElim[U](1),
         4 #> mortal(Socrates)                               by ImplyElim(3, 2))
}
```

`Deduce`, like `Contract`, is erased in compilation. It serves to enumerate proof steps. Each step: (a) requires an explicit claim (for proof readability and auditability); (b) is uniquely numbered/identified in that particular proof context; and (c) has to be justified `by` using some proof tactics implemented as Logika plugins (*e.g.*, `Premise`) or applying lemmas/theorems (*e.g.*, `AllElim`, `ImplyElim`). (Details of these mechanisms will be provided in forthcoming documentation for the Logika next generation tool.)

`Contract`, `Deduce`, and other specification and proof language constructs described above are specially recognized by the Slang parser (described in the next section) and they are treated as first-class Slang constructs in Slang abstract syntax tree representations and downstream Slang compiler phases and toolchains. Hence, Slang has to be updated to support additional specification and proof constructs as more formal method tools for Slang are introduced or enhanced.

One disadvantage of this approach is that the specification and proof languages that can be introduced in Slang are limited by Scala's expressive power. However, we have found existing Scala tool support works well. For example, IntelliJ's Scala support for code folding, refactoring (*e.g.*, variable renaming), hyperlinking, type checking, *etc.*, works for Slang's specification and proof languages. This enables modern software engineering tool capabilities to be applied to the *specification and proof engineering* process.

4 Implementation

Slang compilation was first implemented using the Scala compiler extended with a custom compiler plugin and supporting macros. This provided compilation to JVM, Javascript, and native executables almost for free. With this approach, we prototyped Slang features rapidly (including IntelliJ integration using a custom plugin described later in this section). Because the Slang runtime library is written in Slang itself (aside from built-in types), this pipeline also continuously tested and validated Slang language features. After the prototype relatively stabilized (which took around half a year), we began a more ambitious validation by implementing the Slang front-end mostly using Slang itself and followed this by implementing, in Slang, a C back-end appropriate for embedded systems. This section describes the resulting compiler pipeline and Slang IntelliJ integration, as well as a supporting command-line build tool we recently developed.

The implementation guideline that we follow in our platform engineering effort is to think “BIG”. That is, we want to take advantage of the availability of powerful machines with multi/many-cores and high memory capacity to gain reduction in the most precious resource of it all, *i.e.*, time.

Front-end: Since Slang is based on Scala's rich and featureful syntax, building the parser itself was an early challenge. We ended up using the Scala parser from the open-source `Scalameta` library to produce parse trees, which are translated to Slang-based abstract syntax trees (ASTs). This is the only front-end part that is not written in Slang.[4] Another issue is how to (speedily) distinguish Slang vs. Scala programs during parsing. We resolved this by adopting the convention that Slang files should have `#Sireum` in its first line (in a comment).

Given this approach, the details of the front-end can be summarized as follows (assuming program well-formed-ness for presentation simplicity). The front-end accepts an input list of source paths which are mined for `.scala` files with `#Sireum` in its first line; found files are then read into memory. Each file's content is then (optionally `parMap`) parsed to produce Slang ASTs that are then processed to create file symbol tables. The file symbol tables are reduced into an overall symbol table, and programs are then type outlined. Type outlining processes type, field, method signatures (which, as we previously mentioned, have to be explicitly typed), and contracts, without processing field initializations and method bodies. This produces a transformed symbol table, ASTs, and a type hierarchy. Finally, each trait, class, and `object` AST is (`parMap`) type checked/inferred and reduced to produce yet another transformed symbol table and set of ASTs (type hierarchy is unaffected). All Slang symbol table, AST, and type hierarchy objects are implemented as immutable structures to enable safe (parallel) transformations. However, error, warning, and informational message reporting is done using a mutable `Reporter` that accumulates (immutable) messages as it is passed through the compilation routines using the “hand-me-down” maneuver (recall that `@pure` can create and mutate new objects).

Embedded C Back-end: We now summarize issues specific to the *Slang Embedded* subset of Slang and its translation to C. Since we target high assurance embedded systems, we decided that the generated C code should not dynamically allocate memory (a common restriction in safety-critical systems). This avoids runtime garbage collection, which helps ensure predictable behaviors.[5] Therefore, when using the Slang Embedded subset, all memory allocations must be either globally-allocated statically or stack-allocated. One consequence is that all sequences have to be bounded (the bounds are user-configurable). In addition, language features that require dynamic allocation such as recursive types (*e.g.*, linked-lists, *etc.*) and closures are prohibited. Recursion is allowed, but it is best if tail recursion is used (otherwise, call chain depths should be estimated/bounded). In summary, the features available in the Slang Embedded subset

[4] Aside from extensions in the Slang runtime library for file access (and spawning processes, OS detection, *etc.*), which are available on JVM and native targets.

[5] We initially planned to offer C compilation with garbage collection, but GraalVM or Scala Native can be used instead. We may reconsider such approach in the future.

align with what one would typically use when programming embedded software. Best practices include using statically-allocated bounded object pools if needed.

We want the generated C code to be compilable by the popular `gcc` and `clang` compilers. We also would like to leverage the great work on the CompCert verified C compiler [25], which provides strong guarantees that produced binary code faithfully reflect the semantics of its sources (this enables a possible certified translation from Slang to CompCert C sometime in the future). Thus, we ensure that the generated C code conforms to the C99 definition, which is supported by all three compilers above. We treat any warning from the C compilers as a bug in the Slang-to-C translation. In addition, we want the generated C code structure to match the structure of the corresponding Slang code to help enable traceability and to ease debugging/maintenance of the translator. Moreover, we want the generated C code to maintain Slang-level debugging stack information. For example, whenever there is an assertion error, one should get a similar stack trace to what is provided by the JVM, including Slang source filename and line number information. Finally, we would like to be able to edit, test, debug, and integrate the generated C code, so the translator should generate supporting files for use in an IDE. We decided to support CLion – IntelliJ's sister commercial product that accepts CMake configurations as project definitions.

To facilitate the above, the generated C code makes heavy use of C macros to ensure that generated code is similar in structure and appearance to the source. The macros also help maintain Slang-level source information (which can be optionally turned off). For example, the following two Slang methods:

```
def foo(): Unit = { println("foo") };     def bar(): Unit = { foo() }
```

are translated as follows (edited for brevity; macro expansions in comments):

```
typedef struct StackFrame *StackFrame;
struct StackFrame { StackFrame caller; /* ... */; int line; };

Unit foo(STACK_FRAME_ONLY) {                 // ...(StackFrame caller)
  DeclNewStackFrame(caller, /* ... */,       // struct StackFrame sf[1] = ...
                    "foo", 0);               //          .name = "foo", .line = 0 } };
  #ifndef SIREUM_NO_PRINT
  sfUpdateLoc(1);                            // sf->line = 1;
  { String_cprint(string("foo"), T);
    cprintln(T);
    cflush(T); }
  #endif
}

Unit bar(STACK_FRAME_ONLY) {                 // ...(StackFrame caller)
  DeclNewStackFrame(caller, /* ... */,       // struct StackFrame sf[1] = ...;
                    "bar", 0);               //          .name = "bar", .line = 0 } };
  sfUpdateLoc(1);                            // sf->line = 1;
  { foo(SF_LAST); }                          // foo(sf);
}
```

As illustrated above, each function stack-allocates `StackFrame` to store source information, which also maintains a pointer to the caller's stack frame. Source location information is updated for each corresponding Slang statement using `sfUpdateLoc`. Thus, at any given C program point, the Slang call stack information is available for, *e.g.*, printing to console (or when debugging in CLion). The `StackFrame` stack allocation strategy is the same that is used to stack allocate

Slang objects. Each Slang statement may be translated into several C statements as can be observed for the translation of `println` in `foo`. The C statements are grouped inside curly braces for structuring purposes, but more importantly, the grouping serves as a hint to the C compiler that the memory associated with stack-allocated objects inside the curlies can be safely reused after the statement has finished executing, thus reducing memory footprint. Console printing is guarded by a macro, allowing it to be disabled. This is handy when running the code in a small micro controller without a console; that is, the program can have console logging code for debugging purposes, but this functionality can be turned off when deployed to a system without a console.

There are some translation design choices related to namespaces, generics, type hierarchy, and dynamic dispatch. For namespaces, with the exception of Slang built-in types, we use underscore-encoded fully qualified names as C identifiers. This may yield long identifiers, but the approach is predictable and systematic. The translation specializes generics to the specific type instantiations used in the source program. For example, different code blocks will be generated for `Option[Z]` and `Option[IS[Z, Z]]`. This potentially generates a lot of code, incurring memory overhead. We reduce the problem by only translating methods reachable from a given set of entry points. The type hierarchy is realized by translating each trait as a C `union` of its direct subtypes and each class as a C `struct`; the `unions` and `structs` store an enumeration representing the object runtime type. Dynamic dispatch is handled by generating bridge code for each unique virtual invocation method target that switches on the runtime type stored in the translated `union`/`struct` and calls the corresponding implementation.

Given a set of program entry points, the C back-end first computes a whole-program Slang method call-graph. The type specializer uses the call-graph information to instantiate generic types and methods and specialize them. Finally, `ST` template-based translation processes each type, global field, and method and groups the output code based on the fully qualified name of types and `objects` to which the fields and methods belong. The results are then written to the disk.

The translation executes quickly, so we did not parallelize it. Moreover, unlike the front-end which we developed in a more "functional programming style" where new objects are created as part of the staged transformations, we purposely programmed the C template-based translation in a "more imperative style" that destructively updates template collections to add instantiated templates. We used Slang imperative features to see if there are inherent performance bottlenecks and/or memory consumption issues associated with these imperative features, and we did not experience any.

In our experience using Slang to code both the front-end and the C back-end, we found that mutating objects is convenient but best done locally with shallow mutable structures (which may hold deep immutable structures) to ease reasoning and code maintenance. We believe these are Slang *general* best practices:

"*Immutable globally and deeply. Mutable locally and shallowly.*"

IntelliJ integration and build tool: We strongly believe that IDE support is a crucial productivity enhancing tool that a language should be equipped with. IntelliJ is one of the best Scala IDEs available today. One nice feature is that IntelliJ's Scala type checking is both seamless and perceivably fast when running on modern hardware. IntelliJ's front-end runs in the background as one edits the code and asynchronously highlights issues as they are found. This speeds up development cycles considerably, thus mitigating Scala's slow compilation speed.

IntelliJ's Scala front-end is different than Scala standard compiler's. One issue is that it does not accept Scala compiler plugins and Scala macro support is limited. This means that it does not process Slang program transformations implemented in the Scala compiler plugin for Slang. For example, the `@range`/`@bits` classes do not have supporting operations from the perspective of IntelliJ's front-end as the operations are generated by the Slang compiler plugin.

Fortunately, Scala compiler plugins and macros are widely used in the Scala community, thus, IntelliJ offers injection extension points so compiler plugin developers can provide custom code transformations. Hence, we provide an IntelliJ plugin that implements the injection extension points to introduce Slang program transformations to IntelliJ's front-end. We also limit Slang macros to forms that works well with IntelliJ (*i.e.*, Scala "blackbox" macros). While it took some effort to integrate with IntelliJ, the gained productivity level is far more than enough to make up for it. IntelliJ's injection extension points are very stable so far, meaning that our Slang IntelliJ injection plugin has required little maintenance over time in spite of IntelliJ upgrades.

Another integration issue is configuring IntelliJ for Slang projects. In the past, we have used popular Scala build tools (*e.g.*, sbt and Mill), whose configurations can be imported by/exported to IntelliJ. However, they require some Scala finesse to use effectively. Thus, we developed a build tool for Slang, called Proyek (also written in Slang), whose module configurations are compositional and expressed via Slang `@datatype` class instances in Slang scripts (discussed in Sect. 5). Proyek can export its configuration to IntelliJ's, and it configures IntelliJ specifically for development using Slang. This enables IntelliJ's built-in build system to be used for compilation, testing, and debugging inside IntelliJ instead of running a separate third-party build tool for these tasks. In addition, Proyek provides command-line tasks for cross-compiling (module-incremental/parallel, including Scala and Java sources), testing, assembling, and publishing.

The above integration works well for using IntelliJ as an IDE for development using Slang. However, the approach by itself does not integrate Slang tools such as the Slang front-end (that checks for, e.g., Slang restrictions of Scala) and formal verification and analysis tools such as Logika. Thus, we recently developed another IntelliJ plugin as a client to a Sireum server that offers Slang tools as micro-services running locally (or, in the future, remotely). These integrations turn IntelliJ as an Integrated Verification Environment (IVE) for Slang – Sireum IVE (in the spirit of [11]), where formal method tools are parts of developers' toolbox for quality assurance that complement, for example, testing.

5 Applications

The previous section described how Slang was validated in part by using Slang to develop the Slang tooling itself. This section summarizes other significant applications that serve as further validation.

Sireum HAMR [18]**:** provides a multi-platform **H**igh **A**ssurance **M**odel-based **R**apid engineering framework for embedded systems. Developers specify component-based system architectures using the SAE standard AADL architecture description language. From an architecture specification, HAMR generates real-time tasking and communication infrastructure code. Developers complete the system by implementing the "business logic" for the components.

HAMR works by first generating a Slang-based intermediate representation of the AADL model (AIR) from the Eclipse-based AADL OSATE IDE which is then used as input for auto-generating the tasking and communication middleware in Slang Embedded. If developers use Slang Embedded to implement component business logic, the completed system can be run on the JVM for prototyping, simulation, and testing. The Slang Embedded system code can be translated to C (using the Slang Embedded C translator), which in turn can be compiled to a native application for macOS, Linux, or Windows. Additionally, a build can be created to run on the seL4 [22] verified micro-kernel to provide guaranteed spatial separation of tasks, which is useful for safety/security-critical systems. HAMR supports an alternate C-based workflow in which developers implement component business logic directly in C, while Slang is used by HAMR "behind the scenes" to generate the C tasking and communication middleware.

In summary, HAMR provides validation of Slang in a number of dimensions; it is used: (a) in meta-programming to describe the structure of models and templates for generating code, (b) to implement the AADL run-time libraries for tasking and communication, (c) to code component application logic for deployment on the JVM, and (d) as translation source for C or native-based applications deployed on multiple platforms.

Web applications: Rich web applications have surged in popularity in recent years; even some desktop applications (*e.g.*, Visual Studio Code) are now developed using web technologies. Using the Scala.js translator from Scala to Javascript, one can code aspects of web applications in Slang. We have found this convenient for building several Sireum tools. It is particularly effective for reporting and visualizing the results of Sireum analyses, because reports, highly interactive analysis visualizations, and even the analysis algorithms themselves can be presented/executed using existing web frameworks, and only a web browser is needed for viewing/executing. This has proved useful in our industrial interactions – engineers can view rich results of example analyses without having to install the full Sireum toolchain. For example, we used the strategy to provide AADL information flow analysis in the Sireum Awas tool [33]. Awas enables users to view and navigate the overall AADL system hierarchically, and to launch and interact with Awas information flow analyses that dynamically highlight how information flows throughout the system. While the Awas web application is mostly implemented in Scala (as part of the previous generation of Sireum), its core graph representation and algorithms are from the Slang runtime library, which are translated to Javascript via Scala.js.

Meta-programming: Slang has been used to implement several meta-programming tools that use Slang traits/classes as a data schema language. In one tool, Slang-based schemas are processed to generate Slang code to de/serialize the trait and class instances from/to JSON or MessagePack. In addition to AIR, this is used on fully resolved Slang AST, for example, as part of the Slang front-end regression suite that checks the property $AST = deserialize(serialize(AST))$ on the entire Slang front-end codebase itself. In a second tool, code is generated to perform pre/post-order visits/rewrites of the trait and class instances. This is used to implement the C back-end generic type specializer that transforms Slang AST objects into their specialized versions before translating them to C.

Scripting: Slang scripts leverage the Scala scripting facility, and they provide a lightweight way to utilize Slang code and associated formal methods tools. Scripts are ideal for teaching, *e.g.*, program reasoning, as mentioned in Sect. 1.

In addition to the conventional lightweight coding functionality provided by common scripting languages, Slang scripts can be used to capture contract specification and proof artifacts exclusively, even without executable code present in the script. This provides a convenient high-level specification/proof scripting language instead of having to interact directly with underlying SMT2 tools and theorem provers. For example, when verifying AADL interface contracts between two components in the HAMR framework above, verification conditions are expressed in a Slang script (which takes advantage of Slang high-level types and language features). The script can then be discharged by using Logika.

Scripting is also convenient when embedding domain specific languages (DSLs) in Slang. For example, we defined an embedded DSL for `bitcodec`, which takes a bit-precise "wire" message format specification in a script and generates Slang Embedded message encoder and decoder, for use in implementing communication between HAMR components when processing raw data bitstreams.

We also provide a Slang script variant, called Slash, that can be directly called from both POSIX `sh`-compatible and Windows `cmd` environments, which we heavily use as a means for universally shell scripting complex tasks. Proyek configurations are Slash scripts, which can optionally print module dependencies in GraphViz's dot for visualization purposes. We also use Slash scripts to ease Sireum installation and continuous integration testing on multiple platforms.

6 Related Work

Slang's design is inspired by our earlier work on SPARK in which we developed a symbolic execution-based framework for contract checking [2,7,20], information flow analyses [1,32], and a mechanized semantics in Coq [37]. In this work, we observed first-hand how language feature simplication significantly reduces formal analysis costs. We used the SPARK 2014 semantics concepts in [37] as the basis for Slang's approach to structure copying/updates, but also significantly extended the scope to address the modern features offered by Scala for small to large application development, with/without runtime garbage collection.

Slang differs from other work that adds custom contract specification notations to an existing language (*e.g.*, JML [23], Spec# [5], Frama-C [15], Stainless/Leon [9], VST [10]), in that Slang specializes/subsets the programming language (Scala) primarily to ease formal analyses. Thus, we have (so far) avoided becoming "bogged down" in complexities in both specification notations and verification algorithms due to having to treat complex language features that impede verification.

In contrast to other work on contract verification that develops an entirely new language specifically for verification purposes (*e.g.*, Dafny [24], Lean [27]), Slang leverages an existing multi-paradigm language with rich tooling support and integration of both Scala and Java ecosystems (*e.g.*, compilers, IDEs). This additional support and ecosystems have enabled us to use Slang to implement significant infrastructure (including Slang and many aspects of the Sireum tools that are bootstrapped and implemented in Slang) and industrial-strength tools such as the HAMR model-driven development framework [18]. This type of large-scale software development and tool engineering would be very difficult to achieve in a programming language that did not integrate with a larger development ecosystem.

7 Conclusion

In this paper, we presented the goals, development approach, and example applications of the Sireum programming language – Slang. With respect to the goals of this ISOLA Track "Programming: What is Next?", we believe our work with Slang explores several important issues related to the future of programming and programming language design described below.

- Increasing numbers of systems need high-assurance for safety and security. What are possible approaches that enable highly automated verification techniques for modern languages with rich features sets? For Slang, we argue that a language can be subsetted for particular domains (eliminating complex features unnecessary for that domain). Base languages that provide powerful syntactic frameworks, customizable compilers, and extensible tooling make it easier to develop usable development environments for such subsets. Scala is one of the few languages to provide these multiple customization dimensions. Thus, while language subsetting for safety-criticality and formal verification is not a new idea, we believe our work is providing additional insights into enabling technologies and specialized subset development approaches.
- Despite tremendous advances in formal methods, there is still a need for increased usability and better integration of specification and verification in developer workflows. Although Slang contracts and verification is not the

central subject of this paper, Slang illustrates what we believe are realistic and effective approaches for developer-friendly formal methods integration.
- Regarding development for embedded systems, we believe the approach we are taking with Slang (executable on the JVM for prototyping with rich Scala/-Java ecosystems, yet compilable to efficient embedded C code) is relatively unique and exposes possible directions for increasing flexibility and usability of embedded system languages that also utilize modern language features and type systems to avoid code vulnerability and flaws.

Slang is still in active development, though its focus has now shifted to specification and proof languages to support formal analyses. The Slang website [40] hosts a growing collection of language reference, example, and pedagogical resources.

References

1. Amtoft, T., et al.: A certificate infrastructure for machine-checked proofs of conditional information flow. In: Degano, P., Guttman, J.D. (eds.) POST 2012. LNCS, vol. 7215, pp. 369–389. Springer, Heidelberg (2012). https://doi.org/10.1007/978-3-642-28641-4_20
2. Amtoft, T., Hatcliff, J., Rodríguez, E., Robby, Hoag, J., Greve, D.A.: Specification and checking of software contracts for conditional information flow. In: Hardin, D.S. (ed.) Design and Verification of Microprocessor Systems for High-Assurance Applications, pp. 341–379. Springer, Cham (2010)
3. Backes, J., et al.: Semantic-based automated reasoning for AWS access policies using SMT. In: Formal Methods in Computer Aided Design (FMCAD), pp. 1–9 (2018)
4. Banerjee, A., Danvy, O., Doh, K., Hatcliff, J. (eds.): Semantics, Abstract Interpretation, and Reasoning about Programs: Essays Dedicated to David A. Schmidt [on occasion of his 60th birthday], EPTCS, vol. 129. OPA, September 2013
5. Barnett, M., Leino, K.R.M., Schulte, W.: The Spec# programming system: an overview. In: Barthe, G., Burdy, L., Huisman, M., Lanet, J.-L., Muntean, T. (eds.) CASSIS 2004. LNCS, vol. 3362, pp. 49–69. Springer, Heidelberg (2005). https://doi.org/10.1007/978-3-540-30569-9_3
6. Barrett, C., et al.: CVC4. In: Gopalakrishnan, G., Qadeer, S. (eds.) CAV 2011. LNCS, vol. 6806, pp. 171–177. Springer, Heidelberg (2011). https://doi.org/10.1007/978-3-642-22110-1_14
7. Belt, J., Hatcliff, J., Robby, Chalin, P., Hardin, D., Deng, X.: Bakar Kiasan: flexible contract checking for critical systems using symbolic execution. In: Bobaru, M., Havelund, K., Holzmann, G.J., Joshi, R. (eds.) NASA Formal Methods. NFM 2011. LNCS, vol. 6617, pp. 58–72. Springer, Heidelberg (2011). https://doi.org/10.1007/978-3-642-20398-5_6
8. Belt, J., Robby, Deng, X.: Sireum/Topi LDP: a lightweight semi-decision procedure for optimizing symbolic execution-based analyses. In: 7th joint European Software Engineering Conference and ACM SIGSOFT International Symposium on Foundations of Software Engineering (ESEC/FSE), pp. 355–364 (2009)
9. Blanc, R., Kuncak, V., Kneuss, E., Suter, P.: An overview of the Leon verification system: verification by translation to recursive functions. In: 4th Workshop on Scala, pp. 1:1–1:10 (2013)

10. Cao, Q., Beringer, L., Gruetter, S., Dodds, J., Appel, A.W.: VST-Floyd: a separation logic tool to verify correctness of C programs. J. Autom. Reason. **61**(1–4), 367–422 (2018)
11. Chalin, P., Robby, James, P.R., Lee, J., Karabotsos, G.: Towards an industrial grade IVE for Java and next generation research platform for JML. Int. J. Softw. Tools Technol. Transf. (STTT) **12**(6), 429–446 (2010)
12. Clarke, D., Östlund, J., Sergey, I., Wrigstad, T.: Ownership types: a survey. In: Clarke, D., Noble, J., Wrigstad, T. (eds.) Aliasing in Object-Oriented Programming. Types, Analysis and Verification. LNCS, vol. 7850, pp. 15–58. Springer, Heidelberg (2013). https://doi.org/10.1007/978-3-642-36946-9_3
13. Corbett, J.C., et al.: Bandera: extracting finite-state models from Java source code. In: 22nd International Conference on Software Engineering (ICSE), pp. 439–448 (2000)
14. Corbett, J.C., Dwyer, M.B., Hatcliff, J., Robby: Expressing checkable properties of dynamic systems: the Bandera Specification Language. Int. J. Softw. Tools Technol. Transf. (STTT) **4**(1), 34–56 (2002)
15. Cuoq, P., Kirchner, F., Kosmatov, N., Prevosto, V., Signoles, J., Yakobowski, B.: Frama-C - a software analysis perspective. In: Eleftherakis, G., Hinchey, M., Holcombe, M. (eds.) SEFM 2012. LNCS, vol. 7504, pp. 233–247. Springer, Heidelberg (2012). https://doi.org/10.1007/978-3-642-33826-7_16
16. Deng, X., Dwyer, M.B., Hatcliff, J., Jung, G., Robby, Singh, G.: Model-checking middleware-based event-driven real-time embedded software. In: de Boer, F.S., Bonsangue, M.M., Graf, S., de Roever, W.P. (eds.) 1st International Symposium Formal Methods for Components and Objects (FMCO). LNCS, vol. 2852, pp. 154–181. Springer, Heidelberg (2002)
17. Deng, X., Lee, J., Robby: Efficient and formal generalized symbolic execution. Autom. Softw. Eng. (ASE) **19**(3), 233–301 (2012)
18. Hatcliff, J., Belt, J., Robby, Carpenter, T.: HAMR: an AADL multi-platform code generation toolset. In: Margaria, T., Steffen, B. (eds.) ISoLA 2021. LNCS, vol. 13036, pp. 274–295. Springer, Cham (2021)
19. Hatcliff, J., Dwyer, M.B., Pasareanu, C.S., Robby: Foundations of the Bandera abstraction tools. In: Mogensen, T.E., Schmidt, D.A., Sudborough, I.H. (eds.) The Essence of Computation. LNCS, vol. 2566, pp. 172–203. Springer, Heidelberg (2002). https://doi.org/10.1007/3-540-36377-7_9
20. Hatcliff, J., Robby, Chalin, P., Belt, J.: Explicating symbolic execution (xSymExe): an evidence-based verification framework. In: 35th International Conference on Software Engineering (ICSE), pp. 222–231 (2013)
21. International, S.: SAE AS5506 Rev. C Architecture Analysis and Design Language (AADL). SAE International (2017)
22. Klein, G., et al.: seL4: formal verification of an OS kernel. In: 22nd ACM Symposium on Operating Systems Principles (SOSP), pp. 207–220 (2009)
23. Leavens, G.T., Baker, A.L., Ruby, C.: JML: a notation for detailed design. In: Kilov, H., Rumpe, B., Simmonds, I. (eds.) Behavioral Specifications of Businesses and Systems. The Springer International Series in Engineering and Computer Science, vol. 523. Springer, Boston (1999). https://doi.org/10.1007/978-1-4615-5229-1_12
24. Leino, K.R.M.: Dafny: an automatic program verifier for functional correctness. In: Clarke, E.M., Voronkov, A. (eds.) LPAR 2010. LNCS (LNAI), vol. 6355, pp. 348–370. Springer, Heidelberg (2010). https://doi.org/10.1007/978-3-642-17511-4_20

25. Leroy, X., Blazy, S., Kästner, D., Schommer, B., Pister, M., Ferdinand, C.: CompCert - a formally verified optimizing compiler. In: Embedded Real Time Software and Systems (ERTS) (2016)
26. de Moura, L., Bjørner, N.: Z3: an efficient SMT solver. In: Ramakrishnan, C.R., Rehof, J. (eds.) TACAS 2008. LNCS, vol. 4963, pp. 337–340. Springer, Heidelberg (2008). https://doi.org/10.1007/978-3-540-78800-3_24
27. de Moura, L., Kong, S., Avigad, J., van Doorn, F., von Raumer, J.: The lean theorem prover (system description). In: Felty, A.P., Middeldorp, A. (eds.) CADE 2015. LNCS (LNAI), vol. 9195, pp. 378–388. Springer, Cham (2015). https://doi.org/10.1007/978-3-319-21401-6_26
28. Naumann, D.A.: Observational purity and encapsulation. Theor. Comput. Sci. (TCS) **376**(3), 205–224 (2007)
29. Robby, Chalin, P.: Preliminary design of a unified JML representation and software infrastructure. In: 11th Formal Techniques for Java-like Programs (FTfJP), pp. 5:1–5:7 (2009)
30. Robby, Dwyer, M.B., Hatcliff, J.: Bogor: an extensible and highly-modular software model checking framework. In: 11th ACM SIGSOFT Symposium on Foundations of Software Engineering held Jointly with 9th European Software Engineering Conference (ESEC/FSE), pp. 267–276 (2003)
31. Rodríguez, E., Dwyer, M., Flanagan, C., Hatcliff, J., Leavens, G.T., Robby: Extending JML for modular specification and verification of multi-threaded programs. In: Black, A.P. (eds.) ECOOP 2005 - Object-Oriented Programming. ECOOP 2005. LNCS, vol. 3586, pp. 551–576. Springer, Heidelberg (2005). https://doi.org/10.1007/11531142_24
32. Thiagarajan, H., Hatcliff, J., Belt, J., Robby: Bakar Alir: supporting developers in construction of information flow contracts in SPARK. In: 12th Source Code Analysis and Manipulation (SCAM), pp. 132–137 (2012)
33. Thiagarajan, H., Hatcliff, J., Robby: Awas: AADL information flow and error propagation analysis framework. Innovations Syst. Softw. Eng. (ISSE) (2021). https://doi.org/10.1007/s11334-021-00410-w
34. Wei, F., Roy, S., Ou, X., Robby: Amandroid: a precise and general inter-component data flow analysis framework for security vetting of Android apps. ACM Trans. Priv. Secur. (TOPS) **21**(3), 14:1–14:32 (2018)
35. Wilding, M.M., Greve, D.A., Richards, R.J., Hardin, D.S.: Formal verification of partition management for the AAMP7G microprocessor. In: Hardin, D. (eds.) Design and Verification of Microprocessor Systems for High-Assurance Applications. Springer, Boston (2010). https://doi.org/10.1007/978-1-4419-1539-9_6
36. Yi, J., Robby, Deng, X., Roychoudhury, A.: Past expression: encapsulating prestates at post-conditions by means of AOP. In: Aspect-Oriented Software Development (AOSD), pp. 133–144 (2013)
37. Zhang, Z., Robby, Hatcliff, J., Moy, Y., Courtieu, P.: Focused certification of an industrial compilation and static verification toolchain. In: Cimatti, A., Sirjani, M. (eds.) Software Engineering and Formal Methods. SEFM 2017. LNCS, vol. 10469, pp. 17–34. Springer, Cham (2017). https://doi.org/10.1007/978-3-319-66197-1_2
38. Project Loom. https://openjdk.java.net/projects/loom
39. Sireum Logika: A program verifier and a natural deduction proof checker for propositional, predicate, and programming logics. http://logika.v3.sireum.org
40. Slang: The Sireum Programming Language. http://slang.sireum.org

HAMR: An AADL Multi-platform Code Generation Toolset

John Hatcliff[1(✉)], Jason Belt[1], Robby[1(✉)], and Todd Carpenter[2]

[1] Kansas State University, Manhattan, KS 66506, USA
{hatcliff,belt,robby}@ksu.edu

[2] Adventium Labs, Minneapolis, MN 55401, USA
Todd.Carpenter@adventiumlabs.com

Abstract. This paper describes the High-Assurance Model-based Rapid engineering for embedded systems (HAMR) tool-kit that generates high-assurance software from standards-based system architecture models for embedded cyber-physical systems. HAMR's computational model is based on standardized run-time services and communication models that together provide an abstract platform-independent realization which can be instantiated by back-end translations for different platforms. HAMR currently targets multiple platforms, including rapid prototyping targets such as Java Virtual Machines, Linux, as well as the formally verified seL4 space partitioned micro-kernel.

HAMR bridges the gap between architecture models and the system implementation by generating high assurance infrastructure components that satisfy the requirements specified in the model and preserving rigorous execution semantics. Based on the architecture model, including the components, their interfaces, run-time performance properties, and inter-component connections, the HAMR-generated code creates Application Programming Interfaces that provide developer-centric ease-of-use, as well as support automated verification.

HAMR currently interprets architecture models captured in the Architecture Analysis and Design Language (AADL). AADL is a rigorous standardized modeling language that has proven useful in the development of high assurance embedded systems. We describe using HAMR for building applications from safety and security-critical domains such as medical devices and avionics mission-systems.

1 Introduction

Advances in model-based engineering (MBE) have improved the development of Cyber-Physical Systems (CPS). A 2009 NASA study documented that nearly 80% of CPS's capability is implemented using software [15], and the trend is increasing. As system and software complexity increases, software integration risk has become a key limiting factor in the development of complex CPSs. A study by the SAVI initiative determined that while 70% of errors are introduced

Work supported in part by the US DARPA, US Air Force Research Lab, US Army, and the Software Engineering Institute.

T. Margaria and B. Steffen (Eds.): ISoLA 2021, LNCS 13036, pp. 274–295, 2021.
https://doi.org/10.1007/978-3-030-89159-6_18

at the design phase, most are not found and fixed until integration and test [2]. The study identified that fixing those errors late in the process costs orders of magnitude more than if they had been fixed earlier. This directly impacts system capability due to requirements being cut to keep on schedule or other systems not being built to address budget overruns. In their 2009 study, NASA recommended that the best way to address this is to focus on the system architecture at the design phase, both for new systems as well as system upgrades.

The SAE-standard Architecture, Analysis, and Design Language (AADL) [8] is an system architecture modeling and analysis approach that has obtained a fair amount of traction in the research and aerospace communities. For example, on the System Architecture Virtual Integration (SAVI) effort [3], aircraft manufacturers together with subcontractors used AADL to define a precise system architecture using an "integrate then build" design approach. Working with AADL models, important interactions are specified, interfaces are designed, and integration is verified before components are implemented in code. Once the integration strategy and mechanism are established, subcontractors provide implementations that comply with the architecture requirements. Prime contractors then integrate these components into a system. The integration effort, particularly schedule and risk uncertainty, is reduced due to the previous model-based planning and verification. Due in part to the NASA and SAVI studies, since 2012 the US Army has been investing in developing, maturing, and testing MBE and other engineering capabilities for the system development of the Future Vertical Lift (FVL), a top Army priority to modernize the vertical lift fleet.

One of the challenges inherent with modeling and analysis is maintaining consistency between the model-as-analyzed and the system-as-implemented. Any deviation can lead to inaccuracies in the predictions provided by the models, which can impact system performance against requirements. An example of this is if an implementation decision violates system partitioning requirements.

Another challenge is that many modeling approaches are design-time documentation exercises that are rapidly outdated as the system is implemented, deployed, and maintained throughout the life-cycle. If the models are merely documentation and not maintained and understood by developers, any system updates (e.g., bug fixes, new features) might violate the system-level concepts and requirements.

Yet another challenge is that some generic modeling approaches permit different interpretations of information contained in the models. One example of this is when modelers capture significant model information in comments. This makes it difficult to make system-level decisions based on the integration of components provided by different vendors.

To address these issues, we have developed a tightly integrated modeling and programming paradigm, called HAMR, to shift development to earlier in the design cycle, and thereby eliminate issues earlier, when they are less expensive to address. To accomplish this, HAMR encodes the system-level execution semantics, as specified in standardized models with clear and unambiguous specifications, into infrastructure code suitable for the given target platform. These execution semantics include component interfaces, threading semantics, inter-component communication semantics, standard system phases, scheduling, and application behavioral and non-functional performance properties.

Benefits of this approach include:

Extensible code-generation architecture capable of easily targeting new platforms: Complex industrial systems often include multiple platforms (e.g., in system-of-system architectures), and long-lived systems often need to be migrated to new architectures to support technology refresh.

Support for incremental development, from rapid prototyping to full deployment: Organizations can perform rapid prototyping and integration in spirals, moving in successive spirals (with different code generation back-ends) from simpler functional mockups of component behaviors and interface interactions to more realistic implementations on test bench boards, to final deployments on platform hardware.

Standard Development Environments. HAMR runs on widely-used platforms, leveraging development environments that are already familiar to students, graduate researchers, and entry-level industrial engineers. This helps reduce workforce training costs.

Direct support for formally-proven partitioning architectures: Industry teams are increasingly using micro-kernels, separation kernels, and virtualization architectures to isolate critical system components. Strong isolation provides a foundation for building safe and secure systems. It also enables incorporation of legacy components into a system (e.g., running legacy code on virtual machines within a partition of a micro-kernel). HAMR includes a back-end to directly target the seL4 micro-kernel whose implementation, including spatial partitioning, is formally proven correct using theorem-proving technology.

This paper describes HAMR, with specific contributions including:

- HAMR provides code generation for the SAE AS5506 Standard AADL. The code generated by HAMR conforms to the AADL standard's Run-Time Services, and further refines it towards a more precise semantics for safety-critical embedded systems.
- HAMR leverages Slang, a safety/security-critical subset of Scala. We define a Slang-based reference implementation of the above AADL Run-Time Services.
- Using the Slang AADL RTS, we define a Slang/Scala-based AADL code-generation, component development approach, and JVM run-time execution environment that can be used for JVM-based AADL system deployments or system simulations before further refinement to an embedded (e.g., C-based) deployment.
- We define a multi-platform translation architecture code AADL code generation by using the Slang AADL RTS reference implementation as an abstraction layer through which multiple back-ends can be supported.
- We implement C-based back-ends for the translation architecture targeting Linux OS and for the seL4 micro-kernel [13].
- We validate the translation framework using industrial-scale examples from multiple CPS domains including medical devices and military mission control systems.

The HAMR framework is being used by multiple industry partners in projects funded by the US Army, US Air Force Research Lab, US Defense Advanced Research Projects Agency (DARPA), and the US Department of Homeland Security (DHS). The HAMR implementation and examples described in this paper are available under an open-source license[1].

2 AADL

SAE International standard AS5506C [10] defines the AADL core language for expressing the structure of embedded, real-time systems via definitions of components, their interfaces, and their communication. In contrast to the general-purpose modeling diagrams in UML, AADL provides a precise, tool-independent, and standardized modeling vocabulary of common embedded software and hardware elements. Software components include data, subprogram, subprogram group, thread, thread group, and process. Hardware components include processor, virtual processor, memory, bus, virtual bus, and device. Devices are used to model sensors, actuators, or custom hardware. An AADL `system` component represents an assembly of interacting application software and execution platform components. Each component category has a different, well-defined standard interpretation when processed by AADL model analyses. Each category also has a distinct set of standardized properties associated with it that can be used to configure the specific component's semantics.

A *feature* specifies how a component interfaces with other components in the system. *ports* are features that can be classified as an *event port* (e.g., to model interrupt signals or other notification-oriented messages without payloads), a *data port* (e.g. modeling shared memory between components or distributed memory services where an update to a distributed memory cell is automatically propagated to other components that declare access to the cell), or an *event data port* (e.g., to model asynchronous messages with payloads, such as in publish-subscribe frameworks). Inputs to event and event data ports are buffered. The buffer sizes and overflow policies can be configured per port using standardizes AADL properties. Inputs to data ports are not buffered; newly arriving data overwrites the previous value.

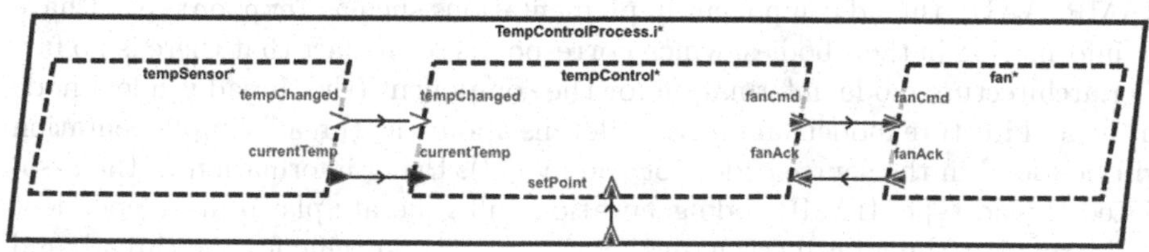

Fig. 1. Temperature control example (excerpts) – AADL graphical view

[1] Source code and supporting documentation available at https://github.com/santoslab/isola21-hamr-case-studies.

Figure 1 presents a portion of the AADL standard graphical view for a simple temperature controller that maintains a temperature according to a set point structure containing high and low bounds for the target temperature. The periodic `tempSensor` thread measures the current temperature and transmits the reading on its `currentTemp` *data port* (represented by a solid triangle icon). It also sends a notification on its `tempChanged` *event port* (represented by an arrow head) if it detects the temperature has changed since the last reading. When the sporadic (event-driven) `tempControl` thread receives a `tempChanged` event, it will read the value on its `currentTemp` *data port* and compare it the most recent set points. If the current temperature exceeds the high set point, it will send `FanCmd.On` `fan` thread via its `fanCmd` *event data port* (represented by a filled triangle within an arrow head) to cool the temperature. Similar logic will result in `FanCmd.Off` being sent if the current temperature is below the low set point. In either case, `fan` acknowledges whether it was able to fulfill the command by sending `FanAck.Ok` or `FanAck.Error` on its `fanAck` event data port.

AADL provides a textual view to accompany the graphical view. AADL editors such as the Eclipse-based Open Source AADL Tool Environment (OSATE) synchronize the two. The listing below illustrates the *component type* declaration for the `TempControl` thread for the example above. The textual view illustrates that data and event data ports can have types for the data transmitted on the ports. In addition, properties such as `Dispatch_Protocol` and `Period` configure the tasking semantics of the thread.

```
thread TempControl
features
 currentTemp: in data port TempSensor::Temperature.i;
 tempChanged: in event port;
 fanAck: in event data port CoolingFan::FanAck;
 setPoint: in event data port SetPoint.i;
 fanCmd: out event data port CoolingFan::FanCmd;
properties
 Dispatch_Protocol => Sporadic;
 Period => .5 sec;  -- the min sep between incoming msgs
end TempControl;

thread implementation TempControl.i
end TempControl.i;
```

The bottom of the listing declares an implementation named `TempControl.i` of the `TempControl` component type. Typically, when using HAMR, AADL thread component implementations such as `TempControl.i` have no information in their bodies, which corresponds to the fact that there is no further architecture model information for the component (the thread is a leaf node in the architecture model, and further details about the thread's implementation will be found in the source code, not the model). Using information in the associated thread type, HAMR code generation will generate platform-independent infrastructure, thread code skeletons, and port APIs specific for the thread, and a developer codes the thread's application logic in the target programming language. The generated thread-specific APIs serve two purposes: (1) the APIs limit the kinds of communications that the thread can make, thus help ensuring compliance with respect to the architecture, and (2) the APIs hide the implementation details of how the communications are realized by the underlying platform.

The listing below illustrates how architectural hierarchy is realized as an integration of subcomponents. The body of `TempControlProcess` type has no declared features because the component does not interact with its context in this simplified example. However, the body of the implementation has subcomponents (named component instances), and the subcomponents are "integrated" by declaring connections between subcomponent ports.

```
process TempControlProcess
  -- no features; no interaction with context
end TempControlProcess;

process implementation TempControlProcess.i
subcomponents
 tempSensor : thread TempSensor::TempSensor.i;
 fan : thread CoolingFan::Fan.i;
 tempControl: thread TempControl.i;
 operatorInterface: thread OperatorInterface.i;
connections
c1:port tempSensor.currentTemp -> tempControl.currentTemp;
c2:port tempSensor.tempChanged -> tempControl.tempChanged;
c3:port tempControl.fanCmd -> fan.fanCmd;
c4:port fan.fanAck -> tempControl.fanAck;
end TempControlProcess.i;
```

AADL editors check for type compatibility between connected ports. HAMR supports data types declared using AADL's standardized Data Model Annex [1]. For example, the data type declarations associated with the temperature data structure are illustrated below.

```
data Temperature
properties
 Data_Model::Data_Representation => Struct;
end Temperature;

data implementation Temperature.i
subcomponents
 degrees: data Base_Types::Float_32;
 unit: data TempUnit;

data TempUnit
properties
Data_Model::Data_Representation => Enum;
Data_Model::Enumerators=>("Fahrenheit","Celsius","Kelvin");
end TempUnit;
```

A standard property indicates that the `Temperature` type is defined as a struct and the struct fields and associated types are listed in the data implementation. The `degrees` field has a type drawn from AADL's standardized base type library. The `unit` field has an application-defined enumerated type.

AADL omits concepts associated with requirements capture and user interactions such as UML use cases, sequence diagrams, as well as class-oriented software units that are more appropriate when modeling general purpose object-oriented software. AADL is closer in spirit to SysML, although AADL elements are more precisely defined to enable analyzeability and tool interoperability. In industry applications of AADL, SysML may be used earlier in the development process to initially capture interactions between and the system and environment as well as rough architecture. AADL is then used to more precisely specify architecture and to support architecture analysis. Though having a workflow with multiple modeling languages is not ideal, the SysML + AADL approach utilizes the capabilities currently available to industry engineers that want to use AADL. In the broader vision of "programming: what's next?", AADL seems to be tracking the right course by more deeply integrating programming and modeling, but there is even more opportunity to integrate, in a single modeling framework, early design concepts that have both stronger semantics and traceability to eventually developed code-level artifacts.

AADL provides many standard properties, and allows definition of new properties. Examples of standard properties include thread properties (e.g., dispatch protocols such as periodic, aperiodic, sporadic, etc., and various properties regarding scheduling), communication properties (e.g., queuing policies on particular ports, communication latencies between components, rates on periodic communication, etc.), memory properties (e.g., sizes of queues and shared memory, latencies on memory access, etc.). User-specified property sets enable one to define labels for implementation choices available on underlying platforms (e.g., choice of middleware realization of communication channels, configuration of middleware policies, etc.).

The Eclipse-based OSATE tool provides an environment for editing AADL and has a plug-in mechanism that supports different AADL analysis tools. Controls for HAMR code generation are implemented as an OSATE plug-in.

3 Architecture

Since it is a code-generation framework, HAMR focuses on AADL software components – especially thread components and port-based communication between threads. The HAMR code-generation backend includes libraries for threading and communication infrastructure that help realize the semantics of AADL on the target platform.

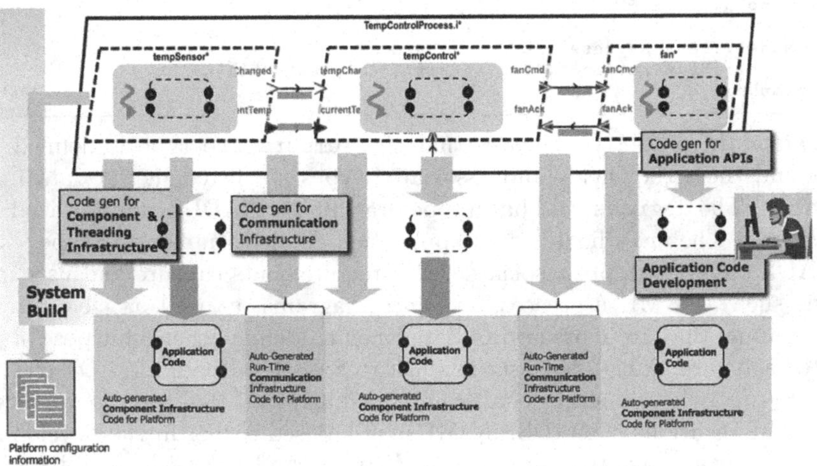

Fig. 2. HAMR code generation concepts

Figure 2 illustrates the main concepts of HAMR code generation. For each thread component, HAMR generates code that provides an execution context for a real-time task. This includes: (a) *infrastructure code* for linking application code to the platform's underlying scheduling framework, for implementing the storage associated with ports, and for realizing the buffering and notification semantics associated with event and event data ports, and (b) *developer-facing code* including thread code skeletons in which the developer will write application code, and *port APIs* that the application code uses to send and receive messages over ports. For each port connection, HAMR generates infrastructure code for the communication pathway between the source and target ports. On platforms such as seL4, pathways may utilize memory blocks shared between the components (seL4's *capability* mechanism can ensure that only the source/destination components can access the shared memory and that the information flow is one-way). On other platforms, middleware or underlying OS primitives are used. E.g., for Linux, HAMR uses System V interprocess communication primitives.

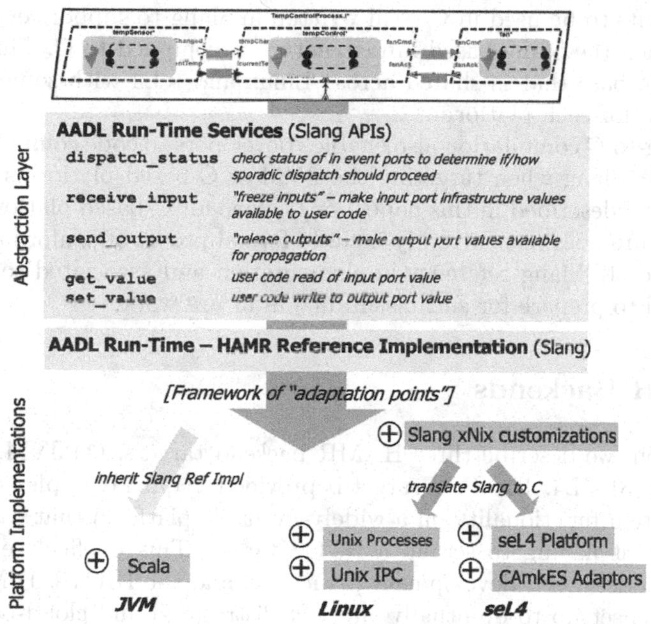

Fig. 3. Code generation factored through AADL RTS

Semantic consistency across platforms – that is, identical behavior of HAMR-generated code regardless of the target platform – is a fundamental HAMR goal. Semantic consistency is supported by carrying out the code-generation in stages. In particular, code is generated first for a platform-independent reference implementation of the AADL run-time services (RTS) (run-time libraries providing key aspects of threading and communication behavior) as illustrated in Fig. 3. These services are currently described informally in the AADL standard via textual descriptions of APIs for thread dispatching and port communication. HAMR specifies the APIs and platform-independent aspects of the AADL RTS functionality in Slang – a subset of Scala designed for high-assurance embedded system development. The HAMR-provided realization of these services is a "reference implementation" in the sense that (a) the highly-readable Slang APIs and service implementations can be directly traced to descriptions in the AADL standard and (b) the subsequent implementations on different platforms are derived from these Slang artifacts. For example, Slang can be compiled to Java Virtual Machine (JVM) bytecode and to efficient embedded C without incurring runtime garbage collection Slang's *extension facility* enables Slang programs to interface with full Scala and Java when compiling to the JVM and C when compiling to C.

Figure 3 illustrates that the HAMR translation architecture utilizes Slang to code platform-independent aspects of the AADL run-time and then uses Slang extensions in Scala and C to implement platform-dependent aspects. For example, for the JVM platform, a Slang AADL RTS Reference Implementation is used for most of infrastructure implementation with a few customizations (denoted by the circled "+") written in Scala. For the C-based (xNix) platforms, some of the Slang Reference Implementation is inherited but customizations define memory layouts to be used in C (still written in Slang to support eventual verification). Then the Slang-based infrastructure is compiled to C. This provides a sizable code base that is shared across Linux and seL4 with some further C customization for each platform.

The Slang-to-C compilation also enables developers to code component application logic in Slang when targeting the JVM or C-based platforms (including Linux and seL4 described in this paper) or C alone for C-based platforms. While this architecture does not currently include formal proofs of conformance of the generated code to Slang reference implementation and associated semantics, it is architected to prepare for such assurance in future work.

4 HAMR Backends

In this section, we describe three HAMR backend targets: (1) JVM, (2) Linux (native), and (3) seL4. The JVM target is provided to quickly implement component and system functionality on a widely-available platform that can be easily utilized without having to set up a RTOS target. This is effective for teaching AADL model-based development principles, and the HAMR JVM platform architecture is set up to eventually support distributed and cloud-based applications via industry-standard publish-subscribe frameworks like JMS, DDS, and MQTT. In two ongoing US DoD funded projects, a contract-based verification framework is being developed that supports integrated AADL and Slang-level contracts with automated SMT-based verification support. In a recently completed industrial project milestone, the JVM platform was used by industry engineers to quickly mock-up and test component functionality and simulate the overall system behavior, including being able to test specific component schedule orderings. If Slang is used to implement component behaviors, such implementations can also be compiled to C along with the Slang-based AADL RTS middleware that HAMR generates specific for the system. The overall system can then be run natively on Linux (as well as on macOS and Windows/Cygwin, with some environment setups). By leveraging Slang extension language facility, developers can opt to implement component behaviors partly/fully in C, for example, to leverage existing libraries, to access hardware, or to integrate legacy components. The seL4 verified micro-kernel backend supports on embedded system boards such as ODROID-C2/XU4. HAMR also generates deployments for seL4 on the QEMU simulation framework, which can be used for testing before deploying to actual hardware. As part of the DARPA CASE project, we provide a Vagrant file to automatically provision a VirtualBox Linux Virtual Machine (VM) with HAMR and its dependencies configured, including OSATE, compiler toolchains, and seL4; it is available at [18]. We continually update the Vagrant definition as we refine HAMR, as well as integrating new or enhanced seL4 features. HAMR has early support for additional targets such as FreeRTos, Minix3, and STM32, but these are less mature than the above.

Below we introduce the key concepts of code architecture using Slang, and then subsequent sections (relying on code examples in the appendix) illustrate the C-based coding.

4.1 Slang on JVM Platform

An AADL thread with sporadic dispatch mode is dispatched upon the arrival of messages on its input event or event data ports. To tailor the application code structure of a sporadic thread Compute Entry Point to the event-driven character, HAMR generates a message handler method skeleton for each input event and event data port. To program the application logic of the component, the developer completes the implementation of these method handlers.
For example, for the sporadic `TempControl` thread, HAMR generates the following Slang skeletons for entry points (excerpts).

```
@msig trait TempControl_i {
  // reference to APIs to support port communication
  def api : TempControl_i_Bridge.Api

  // == Skeleton for Initialize Entry Point ==
  def initialise(): Unit = {}

  // == Skeletons for Compute Entry Point ==
  // handler for the 'tempChanged' input event port
  def handletempChanged(): Unit = {
    // auto-generated default implementation simply logs
    //   messages
    api.logInfo("received tempChanged")
    api.logInfo("default tempChanged implementation")
  }

  // handler for the 'fanAck' input event data port
  def handlefanAck(value:TempControl.FanAck.Type):Unit={
     api.logInfo(s"received ${value}")
     api.logInfo("default fanAck implementation")
  }

  // handler for the 'setPoint' input event data port is
  // similar to above and omitted.

  // == Skeleton for Finalize Entry Point ==
  def finalise(): Unit = {}
}
```

To complete the Initialise Entry Point, the developer codes any initialization of component local variables that persist between activations of the thread, e.g., the variable caching the most recent set point structure is initialized. The initial values for all output data ports must also be set (not applicable in this case, because the component has no output data ports), and optionally, messages may be sent on output event and event data ports. The Finalise Entry Point is also coded to perform any clean up steps (omitted).

```
var setPoint: SetPoint_i = Defs.initialSetPoint

override def initialise(): Unit = {
  // The Initialize Entry Point must initialize all
  // component local state and all output data ports.

  // initialize component local state
  setPoint = Defs.initialSetPoint

  // initialize output data ports
  //  (no output data ports to initialize)
}
```

The primary application logic of the `TempControl` is coded by filling in the auto-generated skeletons for the message handler methods. The completed handler for `tempChange` port is given below. The code illustrates the use of auto-generated `api` methods to send and receive information on ports. These provide a uniform abstraction of the AADL communication semantics and allows HAMR to generate different implementations when deploying on different platforms.

```
override def handletempChanged(): Unit = {
  // get current temp from currentTemp data port
  // using auto-generated APIs for AADL RTS
  val temp = api.getcurrentTemp().get
  // convert current temp to Fahrenheit
  val tempInF = Util.toFahrenheit(temp)
  // convert stored setpoint values to Fahrenheit
  val setPointLowInF = Util.toFahrenheit(setPoint.low)
  val setPointHighInF = Util.toFahrenheit(setPoint.high)

  val cmdOpt: Option[FanCmd.Type] =
    if (tempInF.degrees > setPointHighInF.degrees)
      Some(FanCmd.On)
    else if (tempInF.degrees < setPointLowInF.degrees)
      Some(FanCmd.Off)
    // if current temp is between low and high set point
    // don't produce a command (None)
    else None[FanCmd.Type]()

  cmdOpt match {
    // if a command was produced, send it
    // using auto-generated API for AADL RTS
    case Some(cmd) =>
      api.sendfanCmd(cmd)
    case _ =>
      // temperature OK
  }
}
```

`TempSensor` is a periodic thread, and so instead of generating event handlers for the Compute Entry Point, HAMR generates a single `TimeTriggered` method.

```
object TempSensor_i_p_tempSensor {

def initialise(api:TempSensor_i_Initialization_Api):Unit={
    // initialize outgoing data port
    val temp = TempSensorNative.currentTempGet()
    api.setcurrentTemp(temp)
  }

def timeTriggered(api:TempSensor_i_Operational_Api):Unit={
    val temp = TempSensorNative.currentTempGet()
    api.setcurrentTemp(temp)
    api.sendtempChanged()
  }
}
// extension interface to step outside the Slang
// language subset
@ext object TempSensorNative {
  def currentTempGet(): Temperature_i = $
}
```

This example illustrates the use of the Slang *extension* mechanism that is used to interface to code outside of the Slang language subset. On the JVM platform, this typically involves interfacing to classes in full Scala or Java, e.g., to implement GUIs, simulation of sensors and actuators, or JNI interfaces to access GPIO facilities on a development board. In this example, a Slang extension interface is declared to pull a temperature value from the sensor. Multiple implementations of an extension interface may be set up to switch between, e.g., a simulated sensor and interfacing to an actual hardware sensor. The listing below illustrates a simple Scala-implemented sensor simulation that generates randomized values directed by the current state of extension simulation for the Fan hardware.

```
object TempSensorNative_Ext {
  var lastTemperature
        = Temperature_i(68f, TempUnit.Fahrenheit)
  var rand = new java.util.Random

  def currentTempGet(): Temperature_i = {
    lastTemperature = if (rand.nextBoolean()) {
      val delta =
        F32((rand.nextGaussian() * 3).abs.min(2).toFloat
          * (if (FanNative_Ext.isOn) -1 else 1))
      lastTemperature(degrees
          = lastTemperature.degrees + delta)
    } else lastTemperature
    return lastTemperature
  }
}
```

Corresponding to the gray areas of Fig. 2, HAMR generates code for each component infrastructure that links the developer-code application logic above to the threading/scheduling mechanisms of the underlying platform. The listing illustrates the pattern of an auto-generated Compute Entry Point for a sporadic thread, which processes messages on incoming event/event-data ports (using the AADL RTS (`Art`) `dispatchStatus` and `receiveInput`) and then calls corresponding developer-written message handlers. After handlers complete, the AADL RTS `sendOutput` is called to propagate data on output ports to connected consumers. During an execution, the `compute` method of each thread is called by an executive that follows a selected scheduling strategy.

This code illustrates some fundamental properties of the AADL computational model – namely, its input/work/output structure of task activations. First, similar to other real-time models designed for analyzeability (e.g., [5]), a task's interactions with its context are cleanly factored into inputs and outputs. At each task activation, inputs are "frozen" for the duration of the task's activity (which runs to complete within a WCET bound). The AADL RTS `receiveInput` freezes input by moving values from the communication infrastructure into the user thread's space (dequeuing event and event data port entries as necessary). During the task work, user code can read the frozen values using the `getXXX` APIs and can prepare outputs using `setXXX`. After the task's work is completed (e.g., event handler completes), the prepared outputs are released to the infrastucture using the `sendOutput` RTS.[2]

```
def compute(): Unit = {
    // get ids of ports that have pending messages.
    val EventTriggered(portIds)
             = Art.dispatchStatus(TempControl_i_BridgeId)
    // "freeze" data ports -- move data port values
    //          from infrastructure to application space
    Art.receiveInput(portIds, dataInPortIds)
    // --- invoking application code (event handlers) ---
    // for each arrived event, call corresponding handler
    for (portId <- portIds) {
      // if an event arrived on the 'fanAck' port
      if (portId == fanAck_Id){
        // get payload, call fanAck handler
        //  with the message payload as parameter
        val Some(BuildingControl.FanAck_Payload(value))
                = Art.getValue(fanAck_Id)
        component.handlefanAck(value)
      } else if(portId == setPoint_Id){
        val Some(BuildingControl.SetPoint_Payload(value))
                = Art.getValue(setPoint_Id)
        component.handlesetPoint(value)
      } else if(portId == tempChanged_Id) {
        // 'tempChanged' port is event (not event data)
        //     so there is no payload to pass to handler
        component.handletempChanged()
      }
    }
    // after all handlers run, propagate to consumers
    //   the values that they wrote to output ports
   Art.sendOutput(eventOutPortIds, dataOutPortIds)
 }
```

The overall system is run by launching a HAMR-generated JVM application of the system. Once launched, the application infrastructure initializes the AADL RTS middleware (e.g., allocate objects representing communication channels) calls the `initialize` entry point of each component. Then the executive infrastructure is called which repeatly invokes `compute` methods according to

[2] The `compute` code shown above deviates from the AADL standard description slightly in that the `for` loop processes one queued message on each incoming event port. An alternate implementation aligned with the standard is available that only processes a single event and then releases its output and yields.

the scheduling strategy. During a shut down phase, each component's `finalise` entry point is called.

HAMR auto-generates unit test harnesses for each component with helper methods for loading values into input ports, invoking the various entry points, and checking values on output ports. Also included is a run-time monitoring framework where, e.g., all send/receive actions on ports are logged on a Redis server which can be filtered in a variety of ways using a HAMR-generated framework that utilizes Akka and ReactiveX stream processing and filtering. This framework is used to generate multiple visualizations of the system execution (including dynamic generation of message sequence charts reflecting inter-component communication.

4.2 Linux

HAMR supports Linux natively by translating the Slang-based AADL RTS implementations to C. Slang has a memory model that enables memory to be statically allocated when translated to C, and it supports highly-controlled data type representations and other constructs that enable effective embedded code to be generated. The high-level infrastructure APIs, coordinating procedures of the Slang-based AADL RTS reference implementation, and Slang-based platform customizations for Linux constitute the infrastructure code that is translated to C. Using the Slang extension mechanism, only around 100 SLOC of C code are linked into the infrastructure to provide the lowest level aspects of the inter-component communication using Unix System V shared memory interprocess communication. Everything else is written in Slang, which lays the groundwork for future formal verification of the infrastructure code and makes it easy to establish traceability to the Slang-based AADL RTS reference model.

In the current organization of the generated infrastructure code, each thread component runs as a separate Linux process due to industrial project emphasis on separation. In the upcoming phases of projects, we will be investigating alternate approaches that allow multiple AADL threads to be grouped in the same AADL and Linux process. For implementing component application logic, two different workflows are supported: (1) a thread's behavior can be coded in Slang as in the previous section and compiled to C, or (2) C-level entry point APIs can be generated and coded/debugged in a C development environment.

4.3 seL4 Verified Microkernel

One of the goals of DARPA CASE program is help DoD industry teams harden systems to make them more resilient to cyber-attacks. The seL4 micro-kernel (formally verified using automated theorem-proving techniques) is a central part of the CASE approach. seL4 provides a *capability* mechanism that can be used to precisely configure which memory addresses, function interactions, and platform resources each thread can access. Similar to the concept of separation kernels long used to provide foundations for security [14], the precise formally-proven partitioning and information flow control that seL4 provides make it easier to include components of mixed criticality, to "sandbox" untrusted components, and to update portions of the system while ensuring that other parts can never be impacted by the changes. Building on the seL4 foundation, HAMR on CASE supports model-driven development for refactoring systems to achieve greater cyber-resiliency including automated wrapping of legacy components in virtual machines (VM) and automated insertion of high-assurance components such as message filters, network guards, and security health monitors.

In CASE, AADL is used to model system architecture which is automatically analyzed for cyber-resiliency properties and to capture architecture transformations that insert high-assurance components and VMs. HAMR translates an AADL architecture to produce configurations of the seL4 micro-kernel (especially the capability protection specifications), Specifically, HAMR translates AADL system architectures to seL4 architecture description language, called CAmkES [11], along with some C glue code to interface HAMR C AADL RTS with CAmkES. CAmkES is designed to make it easier to configure seL4 capabilities to align with component structures, and is rather agnostic to the particular computational model. The CAmkES framework has its own mechanism to generate low-level C kernel code as well as the seL4 "capDL" (Capability Distribution Language) file. These artifacts together with the kernel itself and CAmkES component code are used create a binary image which can be loaded onto an appropriate processor.

Leveraging the CAmkES code generation, HAMR generates CAmkES declarations to align with AADL, which, via the CAmkES code generation, configures seL4 so that AADL intercomponent information flow pathways are enforced by the microkernel. HAMR also generates additional code that adapts CAmkES threading and communication APIs to align with the AADL RTS and computational model. This includes generating infrastructure code that uses, e.g., seL4 protected shared memory to realize event buffering and dispatch logic of AADL RTS as implemented in the HAMR reference implementation. This is crucial for enabling AADL-level analysis and verification to be sound with respect to generated seL4 deployments. Leveraging the HAMR translation factored through the Slang reference model, the developer-facing C communication APIs and thread skeletons are identical to those generated for Linux (as described in the previous section). We are working with Data61 engineers to implement dedicated CAmkES connectors that realize the AADL semantics – thus, eliminating the need for a layer of adapter code used in the current code generation process.

HAMR also generates virtual machine configurations for CAmkES components that are used to host Linux VMs, e.g., for sandboxing legacy or less trusted code. This ensures that communication across VM boundaries also aligns with AADL communication semantics.

5 Applications

We have applied HAMR to several examples on multiple industrial research projects sponsored by US Department of Homeland Security (DHS), US Air

Force Research Labs, US Army, and US Defense Advanced Research Project Agency (DARPA). Below are two examples chosen for their scale, complexity, their coverage of different platforms, and the use of different programming language for code application logic.

5.1 PCA Pump – JVM Platform

The DHS-sponsored ISOSCELES project provides an open-source reference architecture for building medical devices [6]. The project supports device manufacturers and regulatory science by providing freely available resources that incorporate best-practices in MBE as well as architectures designed for safety and security. To validate the ISOSCELES reference architecture, the project utilized example medical device development artifacts from the Open PCA Pump Project (see [9] for an overview of the project and [19] for the project web-site that provides the open-source artifacts). PCA pumps are bedside devices used to infuse opioids into the IV line of a patient. Though the use of PCA pumps is wide-spread, they suffer from safety and security problems. In collaboration with engineers from the US Food and Drug Administration, the Open PCA Pump project developed a collection of realistic open-source development artifacts including an AADL model-based-development implementation of a pump.

The Open PCA Pump AADL model is one of the most complex publicly available AADL models. Just considering thread components and their interactions (excluding other component types not related to code generation), there are 12 thread components, 186 thread component ports, and 101 connections between thread ports. We used HAMR to develop a Slang-based JVM implementation of the pump software along with Slang, Scala, and Java-based simulations of several hardware elements of the pump, including the pump mechanism, fluid flow rate sensors, and operator interface. The resulting system has 14223 non-comment/space source lines of Slang/Scala code (NCSLOC) in the auto-generated infrastructure code and 1220 NCSLOC for the application logic.

5.2 UAV System – seL4 Platform

This example from the DARPA CASE program demonstrates HAMR's ability to support mission systems on a complex high-assurance partitioning platform. The CASE example is intended to demonstrate how CASE technology can harden legacy mission control software for unmanned air vehicles against cyber-attacks. AFRL's open-source UxAS framework, written in C++ using a publish/subscribe communication infrastructure, was used as the existing system to be hardened. A ground station communicates with a surveillance UAV. Before the UAV is launched, map information including operating regions and no-flys zones are loaded into the system. During the course of the mission, the UAV comes into contact with multiple ground stations who receive status information from the UAV and may send updated mission objectives. Mission objectives are processed by a flight planner module to produce collections of waypoints that are fed to the flight computer.

In the first step of the cyber-resilience hardening, the UxAS was broken into pieces to isolate different portions of the system to protect against intrusions and contain the effects of possible Trojan attacks. In this process, the communication stack on board the UAV was migrated into a Linux virtual machine in an seL4 partition. Similarly, the mission planner subsystem (which takes mission commands and map information and computes sets of waypoints for the flight controller) was also migrated to a Linux VM. Both of these are modeled as AADL processes (representing the spatially isolated functionality) bound to an AADL virtual process (representing a virtual machine). AADL properties on these components provide further configuration information. Next, various cyber-resiliency components auto-generated from high-level CASE formal specifications were inserted to filter messages coming from the untrusted legacy components and to monitor (and recover from) sequences of events from the legacy components that suggest that they have been compromised. These components, written in C or CakeML, each run on "bare metal" within their own seL4 partitions. The UxAS Waypoint Manager (which takes a collection of waypoints and feeds individual waypoints to the flight controller as the flight progresses) was considered to be trusted. Its existing C++ implementation was migrated to a bare metal seL4 partition with some hand-written C adapters at the boundaries to align the code with HAMR-generated C port APIs.

During the early phases of this effort, HAMR was first used by the industry team to build a JVM-based prototype of the system where component behaviors were first mocked up in Slang. Once interface design, data types, and other integration issues were solved, HAMR was used to generate a Linux prototype of the system which was refined to include more of the C-based implementations of the system components. Next HAMR was used to generate a fully functional seL4-based deployment (including VMs) for the QEMU simulation environment. Finally, HAMR was used to generate a deployment for seL4 running on an ODroid embedded platform. Thus, even though the initial CASE program goals did not seek to leverage the "multi-platform" nature of HAMR, the ability to quickly build Slang/Scala/Java JVM-based prototypes ended up being quite valuable. Industrial engineers are interested in continuing this approach in future phases of the program. Due to restrictions and proprietary information, we are unable to give precise metrics on the models and code base. The application code size is significantly greater than the other examples.

6 Related Work

The most closely related works to this paper are other AADL code generation frameworks.

Ocarina: Ocarina, led by Hugues [12], is the oldest AADL code generation project. Written in Ada and supported by a plug-in to OSATE, Ocarina provides backends for Ada and C code generation primarily using PolyORB-HI [16]. PolyORB-HI is a lightweight middleware designed for high-integrity systems. Ocarina generates real-time tasking and communication infrastructure for

C-based RT-POSIX threading, the Xenomai framework that provides real-time support on top of Linux, and the open source RTOS RTEMS. The PolyORB-HI Ada implementation is used with the GNAT compiler to support full Ada on native platforms (e.g., Linux, Windows) and the Ravenscar Ada subset profile to guarantee schedulability and safety properties. It also has a backend for POK, a partitioned operating system compliant with the ARINC653 standard, along with configuration file generation for ARINC653-compliant DeOS and VxWorks653 real-time operating systems (RTOS).

Ocarina has been used in several European defense industry projects over the last 12–15 years. Whereas the industry focus for Ocarina has primarily been for RTOSs, We have focused HAMR's on the seL4 microkernel for cyber-resiliency and information assurance. While Ocarina and HAMR both support multiple backends, Ocarina emphasizes targeting the common structure of the C and Ada PolyORB-HI implementations, while HAMR emphasizes factoring backends through language-independent standardized run-time services. AADL RTS is currently supported, but the system is modular so others can be supported.

Ocarina currently has a focus in integrating code generation for RTOS with integrated schedulability analysis. HAMR currently has an industrial research focus to move from the JVM-based framework for prototyping, visualization, and coding in a clean modern language subset (Slang) that can be compiled to C and from there to industry platform deployments. HAMR's current industrial research projects (e.g., DARPA CASE) are prioritizing the use of the machine verified seL4 micro-kernel. HAMR is being used in conjunction with Adventium Labs FASTAR AADL temporal analysis and schedule-generation tools.

RAMSES: The code generation approach of Refinement of AADL Models for Synthesis of Embedded Systems (RAMSES) [4] emphasizes successive automated AADL model refinement. The refinement steps are driven by developer-specified features for the target system, by capabilities and resources of the target platform, and by model-level analyses that assess system properties against requirements and platform capabilities. Such analyses include schedulability, timing properties, and resource analysis. By gradually exposing more implementation details in the model, those details can be considered in the analysis. The incremental transformations also form the basis of a correctness methodology in which the correctness of each transformation is considered. Once model transformations yield a sufficiently detailed implementation model, RAMSES generates C component infrastructure that when combined with developer-written component application C code can be deployed on Linux (with POSIX-compliant threading), nxtOSEK (open-source platform for LEGO Mindstorms), and POK. RAMSES has been used to develop systems for the avionics, railway, and robotics domains.

The differences in emphasis between HAMR's target application areas and RAMSES roughly correspond to the HAMR/Ocarina differences above. In addition, HAMR supports multiple languages and distinct platforms. RAMSES emphasizes model transformations as a basis for correctness arguments whereas Ocarina and HAMR emphasize factoring through abstract architecture layers. Like Ocarina, RAMSES focuses more on RTOS applications compared to

HAMR's current focus on micro-kernel-based information assurance and multi-platform support. Compared to HAMR, one challenge of the RAMSES approach is that the refinement steps produce multiple versions of AADL models. Multiple versions require additional work to maintain traceability and correspondence between the model-level contracts and information flow requirements and the source-code level contracts.

Trusted Build: HAMR can be seen as a successor to the Trusted Build (TB) concept prototype [7] developed in the DARPA High Assurance Cyber Military Systems (HACMS) Program by Collins Aerospace, University of Minnesota, and Data61. Like HAMR, TB generated component skeletons for seL4 from AADL using the Data61 CAmkES seL4 component modeling language. TB was the first AADL-to-seL4 translation framework. It was used in DARPA HACMS to construct several systems of roughly the same complexity as the UAV system described in Sect. 5.2.

HAMR provides significant functionality beyond TB. HAMR's port-based inter-component communication strategy now provides true one-way communication from the sender to the receiver on an AADL connection. With TB it was possible to have some back-flow of control and data information, which is undesirable from an information assurance perspective. The TB CAmkES patterns also had unnecessary complexity that require more complex information assurance arguments. In addition, the TB port-based communication structure introduced an extra thread for each connection, dramatically increasing the number of CAmkES components and associated support threads of the generated system, which vastly increases overhead. For example, if one considers deploying the small PCA Pump (Sect. 5.1) to seL4, the TB approach would generate 101 additional CAmkES components and threads compared to HAMR.

The TB generated structures also did not support standard AADL semantics for ports, so standard model-analysis results did not apply to the implementation. HAMR confirms to the standard, and handles additional AADL features including dispatching strategies (e.g., port urgency, explicit indication of ports that trigger dispatch) and port value freezing. HAMR also supports automated VM building, which reduces both manual labor and the potential for defects. HAMR also adds enhanced support for QEMU-based emulation and dramatically reduces the effort needed to create a working development environment by using a Vagrant set up framework.

7 Conclusion

HAMR is a new open-source multi-platform framework for model-driven development of cyber-physical systems using AADL. The framework has been vetted on a number of government/industry projects in both the medical device and mission control domains. HAMR complements existing AADL code generation tools like Ocarina and RAMSES by supporting additional industry-relevant platforms, and by providing an architecture designed for extensibility. The HAMR theme of supporting industry workflows through a progression of rapid prototyping to deployments on successively realistic platforms is also a new emphasis. HAMR significantly improves on the previous Trusted Build work and compared to other AADL code generation frameworks it provides a distinct area of emphasis: code generation for micro-kernels. Not only does this expand the opportunity to support rigorous CPS development, the experience with additional platforms and code generation architecture are providing inputs to the AADL standards committee for a re-design of the AADL run-time services and code generation annex in the upcoming major version of AADL (the organizations of the authors of this paper have a record of strong and extended participation in the AADL standards committee).

The HAMR approach is *not intrinsically tied to AADL*. Instead, it is linked to the paradigm of real-time tasking in communication in AADL – a paradigm based to real-time tasking models presented in classic textbooks on analyzeable real-time systems [5] and on communication approaches used in avionics buses like ARINC653. Thus, it is possible to replace the AADL front-end with other modeling frameworks that can be aligned with or instantiated to the computational paradigm of AADL. Our current Army SBIR Phase II research project is prototyping a SysML front-end for HAMR, based on the idea of defining a AADL-aligned profile for SysML. This can ease adoption of HAMR for companies that have significant investments in SysML tooling and find it challenging to integrate a different modeling language (AADL) and associated editors.

On a more foundational front, we are leveraging the layered design of HAMR to support the generation of evidence that generated code conforms to the AADL architecture. Aligning with the information assurance emphasis of some of our industrial and defense-related research projects, we are first tackling providing evidence of preservation of model-level information flow and spacial separation, e.g., as visualized in the Awas AADL information flow visualization tool [17]. We are also investigating framework for establishing stronger behavioral correspondence between lower-level generated code and the HAMR reference implementation abstraction layer in Slang.

Regarding the track theme *Programming: What's Next?*, HAMR emphasizes an approach where a modeling language (AADL) and a programming language (Slang, C, etc.) work hand-in-glove to provide the system implementation. The programming language is not used to code all of the system. Instead the model provides a high-level specification of inter-component communication and threading structure. Generative techniques are then used to generate a large amount of code. This is similar to other framework approaches like Spring that include high-level specifications of (a) building blocks (abstractions) from which code is derived for common services (b) integration of functionality specified with conventional source code.

What is different for HAMR is the is use of this type of framework for real-time and embedded systems, and in particular the use of building blocks that can be given a formal semantics. As a consequence, reasoning about the correctness of the system is done by reasoning about application source code together with the semantics of the integration abstractions. Given that the code generation is correct with respect to the semantics of the abstractions, the developer nor the verification tools need to be concerned with the details of the infrastructure code. Rather the can rely on the semantic properties of the abstractions.

Slang is not essential for the approach. One can also take this approach with C, for example. However, the use of Slang eases the verification of the application code. Moreover, since the infrastructure code and code generators are written in Slang, HAMR provides the convenience of a single verification framework to establishes the correctness of code generation for abstractions (done once) and the application code (done for each system).

From a bottom-up perspective, HAMR provides a significant contribution by layering application-oriented abstractions on top of the formally verified seL4 micro-kernel – thus providing the foundation for eventually scaling up the formally correctness proofs from the kernel to applications/systems programmed on top of the kernel.

In general, we believe that use of model/code frameworks based on formally-verified domain-specific abstractions with integrated semantics is important direction for engineering critical systems.

Acknowledgement. The authors wish to thank other DARPA CASE team members from Collins Aerospace, Adventium Labs, and Data61 for their work on applications of HAMR and their inputs on HAMR design.

References

1. SAE Architecture Analysis and Design Language (AADL) Annex Volume 2: Annex B: Data Modeling AnnexAnnex D: Behavior Model AnnexAnnex F: ARINC653 Annex
2. Aerospace Vehicle Systems Institute: motivation for advancing the system architecture virtual integration program (2020). https://savi.avsi.aero/about-savi/savi-motivation/
3. AVSI: System Architecture Virtual Integration (SAVI) Initiative (2012)
4. Borde, E., Rahmoun, S., Cadoret, F., Pautet, L., Singhoff, F., Dissaux, P.: Architecture models refinement for fine grain timing analysis of embedded systems. In: 2014 25nd IEEE International Symposium on Rapid System Prototyping, pp. 44–50 (2014)
5. Burns, A., Wellings, A.: Analysable Real-Time Systems: Programmed in Ada. CreateSpace (2016)
6. Carpenter, T., Hatcliff, J., Vasserman, E.Y.: A reference separation architecture for mixed-criticality medical and IOT devices. In: Proceedings of the ACM Workshop on the Internet of Safe Things (SafeThings). ACM, November 2017
7. Cofer, D., et al.: A formal approach to constructing secure air vehicle software. Computer **51**, 14–23 (2018). https://doi.org/10.1109/MC.2018.2876051
8. Feiler, P.H., Gluch, D.P.: Model-Based Engineering with AADL: An Introduction to the SAE Architecture Analysis & Design Language. Addison-Wesley, New York (2013)

9. Hatcliff, J., Larson, B., Carpenter, T., Jones, P., Zhang, Y., Jorgens, J.: The open PCA pump project: an exemplar open source medical device as a community resource. SIGBED Rev. **16**(2), 8–13 (2019)
10. International, S.: SAE AS5506 Rev. C Architecture Analysis and Design Language (AADL). SAE International (2017)
11. Kuz, I., Liu, Y., Gorton, I., Heiser, G.: CAmkES: a component model for secure microkernel-based embedded systems. J. Syst. Softw. **80**(5), 687–699 (2007)
12. Lasnier, G., Zalila, B., Pautet, L., Hugues, J.: OCARINA: an environment for AADL models analysis and automatic code generation for high integrity applications. In: Kordon, F., Kermarrec, Y. (eds.) Ada-Europe 2009. LNCS, vol. 5570, pp. 237–250. Springer, Heidelberg (2009). https://doi.org/10.1007/978-3-642-01924-1_17
13. NICTA, Dynamics, G.: sel4 microkernel (2015). sel4.systems
14. Rushby, J.: The design and verification of secure systems. In: 8th ACM Symposium on Operating Systems Principles, vol. 15(5), pp. 12–21 (1981)
15. West, A.: Nasa study on flight software complexity, March 2009. https://www.nasa.gov/pdf/418878main_FSWC_Final_Report.pdf
16. Zalila, B., Pautet, L., Hugues, J.: Towards automatic middleware generation. In: 11th IEEE International Symposium on Object-Oriented Real-Time Distributed Computing (ISORC 2008), pp. 221–228 (2008)
17. Sireum Awas website. https://awas.sireum.org
18. DARPA CASE Vagrant. https://github.com/loonwerks/CASE/tree/master/TA5/case-env
19. Open PCA Pump Project website (2018). http://openpcapump.santoslab.org

Fundamental Constructs in Programming Languages

Peter D. Mosses[1,2](✉)

[1] Delft University of Technology, Delft, The Netherlands
[2] Swansea University, Swansea, UK
p.d.mosses@swansea.ac.uk

Abstract. When a new programming language appears, the syntax and intended behaviour of its programs need to be specified. The behaviour of each language construct can be concisely specified by translating it to fundamental constructs (funcons), compositionally. In contrast to the informal explanations commonly found in reference manuals, such formal specifications of translations to funcons can be precise and complete. They are also easy to write and read, and to update when the language evolves.

The PLanCompS project has developed a large collection of funcons. Each funcon is defined independently, using a modular variant of structural operational semantics. The definitions are available online, along with tools for generating funcon interpreters from them.

This paper introduces and motivates funcons. It illustrates translation of language constructs to funcons, and funcon definition. It also relates funcons to the notation used in some previous language specification frameworks, including monadic semantics and action semantics.

Keywords: Funcons · Programming constructs · Formal specification

1 Introduction

Many constructs found in (high-level) programming languages combine several behavioural features. For example, call-by-value parameter passing in an imperative language involves order of evaluation, allocating storage and initialising its contents, local name binding, and lexical scoping. Such language constructs generally provide conciseness and clarity in programs, and may support efficient implementation techniques (e.g., stack-based storage); but their full behaviour can be quite difficult to understand, and tedious to specify directly.

Moreover, constructs in different languages may look the same but have very different behaviour (e.g., the notorious '`x=y`'), or look different but have exactly the same behaviour (e.g., '`while...do...`' and '`while(...){...}`'). Relatively minor differences between similar language constructs in different languages include order of evaluation in expressions, and the effect of arithmetic overflow. The evolution of programming languages has resulted in a huge diversity of language constructs and their variants. Some of the constructs are quite simple, but no programming *lingua franca* has emerged.

T. Margaria and B. Steffen (Eds.): ISoLA 2021, LNCS 13036, pp. 296–321, 2021.
https://doi.org/10.1007/978-3-030-89159-6_19

The PLANCOMPS project[1] has developed a large collection of *fundamental constructs* ('funcons') from which the behaviour of many high-level programming language constructs can be composed [26]. The behaviour of a complete programming language can be concisely specified by translating all its constructs, compositionally, to funcons. In contrast to the informal explanations commonly found in language reference manuals, formal specifications of translations to funcons can be precise and complete. They are also easy to write and read, and to update when the language evolves. This could make them especially useful during design and development of domain-specific languages.

Funcons are significantly simpler than typical language constructs, in general:

- Each funcon affects only a single behavioural feature, such as flow of control or data, name binding, storing, or interacting.
- Variants of funcon behaviour (e.g., evaluating their arguments in a different order) can be expressed by composite funcon terms.
- The funcons abstract from details related to implementation efficiency.

Funcon behaviour is defined using a modular variant [19,23] of small-step structural operational semantics [27], based on value-computation transition systems [7]. Any program behaviour that can be modelled by a labelled transition system can, in principle, also be specified by composing appropriately-defined funcons. Thus specification by translation to funcons does not, per se, restrict the features of specified languages. When the translation of a particular language construct is excessively complicated, however, its design may be questionable.

The definition of a funcon determines its *name*, its *signature*, and its *behaviour*. Each funcon name should have a *unique* definition, so that it always refers to the same signature and behaviour, regardless of where the reference occurs. To support reuse, funcon definitions need to be *fixed* and *permanent*: changing or removing funcons would undermine the validity of translations that use them. In particular, adding a new funcon to a collection must never require changes to the definitions already in it.

Version control is superfluous for funcons; translations of language constructs to funcons, in contrast, may need to change when the specified language evolves. For example, the illustrative language IMP includes a plain old while-loop with a Boolean-valued condition: '`while(`*BExp*`)` *Block*'. The following rule translates it to the funcon while-true, which has exactly the required behaviour:

Rule execute⟦ '`while`' '`(`' *BExp* '`)`' *Block* ⟧ =
while-true(eval-bool⟦ *BExp* ⟧, execute⟦ *Block* ⟧)

The behaviour of the funcon while-true is fixed. But suppose the IMP language evolves, and a *Block* can now execute a statement '`break;`', which is supposed to terminate just the *closest* enclosing while-loop. We can extend the translation with the following rule:

Rule execute⟦ '`break`' '`;`' ⟧ = abrupt(broken)

[1] https://plancomps.github.io.

The translation of '`while(true){break;}`' is while-true(true, abrupt(broken)). The funcon abrupt(V) terminates execution abruptly, signalling its argument value V as the reason for termination. However, the behaviour of while-true(true, X) is to terminate abruptly whenever X does – so this translation would lead to abrupt termination of *all* enclosing while-loops!

We cannot change the definition of while-true, so we are forced to change the translation rule. The following updated translation rule reflects the extension of the behaviour of while-loops with the intended handling of abrupt termination due to break-statements, and that they propagate abrupt termination for any other reason:

Rule execute⟦ '`while`' '`(`' *BExp* '`)`' *Block* ⟧ =
  handle-abrupt(
    while-true(eval-bool⟦ *BExp* ⟧, execute⟦ *Block* ⟧),
    if-true-else(is-equal(given, broken), null-value, abrupt(given)))

Computing null-value represents normal termination; given refers to the reason for the abrupt termination.

The specialised funcon handle-break can be used to specify the same behaviour more concisely:

Rule execute⟦ '`while`' '`(`' *BExp* '`)`' *Block* ⟧ =
  handle-break(while-true(eval-bool⟦ *BExp* ⟧, execute⟦ *Block* ⟧))

Wrapping execute⟦ *Block* ⟧ in handle-continue would also support abrupt termination of the current *iteration* due to executing a continue-statement.

Overview. The reader is assumed to be interested in programming languages, and familiar with their main concepts. The research on which this paper is based has been published elsewhere [4,7,8,19,21–23]. The main aims here are to motivate the general idea of funcons, and illustrate how they can be used to specify the behaviour of programming language constructs.

- Section 2 explains some general features of funcons.
- Section 3 considers how to manage large collections of funcons.
- Section 4 analyses various facets of funcon behaviour.
- Section 5 illustrates specification of translation of language constructs to funcons, and explains how to validate such translations.
- Section 6 illustrates how to define funcons independently.
- Section 7 relates funcons to the auxiliary operations defined in denotational semantics, to monads, and to the combinators used in action semantics.
- Section 8 concludes with plans for future development of funcons,
- Appendices A–G give an informal summary of the currently defined funcons.[2]

The rest of this paper is structured as responses to questions that readers might ask about funcons. The author welcomes further questions, as well as comments on the given responses.

[2] At the time of writing, the collection has not yet been released, and could change.

2 The Nature of Funcons

Let us start by explaining some general features of funcons.

- *What aspects of behaviour do funcons represent?*

Funcons abstract from details related to implementation efficiency, such as storage allocation algorithms and communication protocols. They express implementation independent behaviour that arises when programs are executed. They also express linguistic features on which that behaviour depends, such as scopes of bindings.

- *Can funcons be implemented efficiently?*

Funcons need to be executable, to support validation of language translations. Their current implementation uses HASKELL interpreters generated directly from their definitions [5]. The efficiency of evaluating funcon terms is adequate for running unit tests and typical test programs, but not applications. However, it should be possible to implement certain sets of funcons more efficiently, e.g., using virtual machines that support just the required features, or by optimised compilation of funcon terms to other languages.

- *How complicated are funcons?*

One might expect that funcons should be as simple as possible. In fact the aim is for funcons to be not too complicated, but not *too* simple – just right! In the physical sciences, molecules are characterised and understood primarily in terms of chemical bonds between their constituent atoms, and atoms are formed from protons, neutrons, and electrons; protons and neutrons are themselves composed from sub-atomic particles, such as quarks. To explain a molecule in terms of sub-atomic particles might be possible, but unhelpful. Language constructs are somewhat analogous to molecules, and funcons to atoms.

Introducing a funcon that corresponds directly to a complicated language construct would make the funcon analysis of that language construct trivial, but a direct definition of the funcon behaviour would necessarily be complicated. At the other extreme, taking pure function abstraction and application as the only funcons would make analysis and specification of language constructs as complicated as in (pre-monadic) denotational semantics.

Funcons aim to be unbiased towards any family of languages. Adding an intermediate layer of not-so-fundamental constructs that are closely related to some particular language constructs is thus undesirable. However, it is sometimes appropriate to define funcons that abbreviate particular compositions of other funcons. Section 1 mentioned handle-break, which handles abrupt termination caused only by abrupt(broken) in X; it abbreviates handle-abrupt(X, Y) where Y involves an explicit test whether a given signal is the value broken. Similarly, the funcon allocate-initialised-variable(T, V) abbreviates the sequential composition of allocate-variable(T) and initialise-variable($\_, V$).

– *Can funcons have alternative behaviours?*

No, never. The behaviour of common *language* constructs, such as assignment expressions, often varies significantly between different languages. For example, the order of evaluation of the two sides of an assignment expression is left to right in some languages, right to left in others, or may even be implementation-dependent; and the result may be the target variable or the assigned value. The *funcon* for assignment needs to have a behaviour from which all those variations can be obtained by composition with other funcons.

– *Are funcons independent?*

Funcons are often independent, but not always. For instance, the definition of the funcon while-true specifies the reduction of while-true(B, X) to a term involving the funcons if-true-else and sequential:

$$\textit{Funcon}\quad \mathsf{while\text{-}true}(B : \Rightarrow \mathsf{booleans}, X : \Rightarrow \mathsf{null\text{-}type}) : \Rightarrow \mathsf{null\text{-}type}$$
$$\rightsquigarrow \mathsf{if\text{-}true\text{-}else}(B, \mathsf{sequential}(X, \mathsf{while\text{-}true}(B, X)), \mathsf{null\text{-}value})$$

Duplication of B before starting to evaluate it is essential, in case it needs to be re-evaluated after the execution of X. We could introduce an auxiliary term constructor for that, but it is simpler to make use of if-true-else and sequential.

– *Do features of funcons interact?*

No. Feature interactions in software development tend to arise when requirement specifications are incomplete. An example of feature interaction in [2] involves a flood prevention system that turns off the water supply, and a sprinkler system that depends on that water; the requirements regarding flood prevention had better include checking the safety of turning the water off...

The complete requirement for each funcon is to provide just the behaviour specified in its definition, propagating all *unmentioned* effects of evaluating its arguments. The values of the arguments are required to be consistent with the types in the funcon signature, but *no* further requirements arise when combining funcons.

– *Can funcons be used as a programming language?*

Composing funcons is similar to the original idea of UNIX: plugging simple commands together to produce complex behaviour.[3] Not-so-fundamental constructs could be defined as abbreviations for frequently-needed funcon compositions; a coating of ‘syntactic sugar’ would be needed to avoid an unwelcome plethora of parentheses in larger funcon compositions.

The main drawback of programming directly with funcons would be the comparatively low efficiency of their current implementation, which uses interpreters written in HASKELL, generated directly from funcon definitions.

[3] Nowadays, a UNIX command often has a multitude of obscure options, documented in a manual ‘page’ that fills many screens.

– *Can funcons be higher-order?*

Funcons can represent higher-order functions as values, but funcons are not themselves higher-order: they do not take (non-constant) funcons as arguments. However, it is easy to define funcons for common idioms of higher-order programming (maps, filters, folds, etc.).

– *Do funcons have algebraic properties?*

Yes: many binary funcons are associative, with left and right units; some are also commutative. These properties hold for a notion of bisimulation for the value-computation transition systems [7] that provide the foundations for funcon definitions. This bisimulation is preserved when new funcons are added. Funcon terms are written as applicative expressions, and associativity allows binary funcons to be extended to longer sequences of arguments.

– *Can I use my favourite proof assistant to prove properties of funcons?*

Some years ago, the modular variant [19] of structural operational semantics used to define funcons was implemented in the Coq proof assistant, and modular proofs of some properties were carried out [14]. In a related line of work [33], a different method for modular proofs in Coq was developed.

Modular proofs depend only on the definitions of the funcons involved, and remain sound when funcon definitions are combined. In principle, they could be released together with the funcons.

3 Collections of Funcons

The current collection of funcons is called Funcons-beta. It includes several hundred funcons. Management of such a collection is non-trivial.

– *How can we classify funcons?*

Most high-level programming languages distinguish syntactically between commands (a.k.a. statements), declarations, and expressions. Commands may assign to variables; declarations bind names; and expressions compute values. However, such syntactic distinctions are not universal: for instance, expressions sometimes subsume commands, and sequences of commands may include declarations. Grammars for programming language syntax (abstract as well as concrete) often introduce many further syntactic distinctions. A universal set of syntactic sorts that encompasses all programming languages is not available.

For funcons, we have a single syntactic sort of *terms*, with *values* as a subsort. A funcon term is similar to an expression in an (impure) functional programming language: it computes values of a specific (possibly generic) type. A funcon term corresponding to a command computes a fixed null value, and a term corresponding to a declaration computes a value environment, mapping names to values.

We may also classify funcons according to their effects. The behaviour of many funcons involves *auxiliary entities*, representing various kinds of effects. For instance, funcons for name binding use an auxiliary environment entity to represent the current bindings; funcons for imperative variables use an auxiliary store entity to represent the currently assigned values of variables.

– *How do we refer to a particular funcon in a collection?*

A collection of funcons is like an *open* package: the names of all the funcons are visible externally (except those marked as auxiliary). Neither the classification of funcons nor the paths to their definitions affects references to funcon names.

The name of each funcon should clearly suggest its behaviour, to support casual reading of funcon terms and the potential use of funcons as a controlled vocabulary for informal discussion and comparison of programming languages. Type names are *plural* words (e.g., lists).[4] When a funcon corresponds directly to a familiar concept, a single well-chosen word can be adequate, but otherwise several words (joined by hyphens) may be needed. Moreover, different datatypes may have closely related operations, yet the names for the corresponding funcons have to be distinct, due to the absence of overloading: the name of the datatype can be added as a prefix of the name, e.g., integer-add.[5]

Suggestive names can be quite long, and abbreviations may be needed in some situations (e.g., classrooms, examinations, presentations). Abbreviations can be defined as explicit aliases for funcons; for instance, alloc-init is defined as an alias for allocate-initialised-variable.

– *Do funcons evolve?*

After a collection of funcons has been released, the behaviour of all the funcons in it needs to be *fixed* and *permanent*, since changes could affect or break their uses in language translations (which do not need to be public or registered). All uses of a particular funcon name thus refer to the same behaviour.

However, the collection itself *can* evolve: by extension with new funcons. This must not require changes to the definitions of the previous funcons. New funcons need to be carefully checked and tested before they are added, since their definitions cannot be revoked.

Names of funcons always refer implicitly to the current version of a collection. Evolving collections of funcons have no need for version *numbers*, since once a funcon has been defined, adding definitions for new funcons (or an alias for an already defined funcon) cannot invalidate existing references to names.

– *Will the* FUNCONS-BETA *collection of funcons ever be finalised?*

FUNCONS-BETA is a release *candidate*. After further polishing, review, and use in language specifications, the collection of funcons and their documentation are to be released for general use. However, it will always be possible to add new funcons to the collection, so as to support new concepts or provide alternative ways of expressing existing concepts.

[4] Singular forms of type names are used as value constructors.

[5] Currently, FUNCONS-BETA does not support namespaces in collections of funcons.

4 Facets of Funcons

When funcon terms are evaluated, their behaviour may have many *facets*: apart from computing values, funcon behaviour can involve name bindings, imperative variables, abrupt termination, interaction, etc. Facets that are not needed for a particular term can be ignored.

In this section, we introduce the main facets of the FUNCONS-BETA collection. Appendices A–G provide an informal summary of the funcons; their definitions are available online [26].

– *How are funcon terms evaluated?*

Evaluation of a funcon term may terminate *normally*, *abruptly*, or *never*. The evaluation takes a sequence of argument *terms*; on normal termination, it computes a sequence of *values* (where a sequence of length 1 is identified with its only element). The funcon signature specifies how many arguments it takes, the type of values to be computed by each argument, and the types of values that the funcon computes. Individual arguments may be required to be *pre-computed* values; the funcon definition specifies how its behaviour combines the computations of any remaining arguments.

– *Does each funcon take a fixed number of arguments?*

Not necessarily: a funcon signature can specify that an argument at some position is optional, or that it can be a sequence. Sequence arguments are often used to extend associative binary funcons to longer argument sequences. They are also used for funcons that correspond directly to conventional notation for (finite) lists and sets, e.g., $\mathsf{list}(V_1, \ldots, V_n)$ for $[V_1, \ldots, V_n]$.

– *How do funcons represent data?*

Data that programs process when executed is represented by funcon terms classified as values. Some funcons are value constructors: they are *inert*, and have no computational behaviour themselves. Values are themselves classified as *primitive values*, *composite values*, or (procedural) *abstractions*.

Conceptually, primitive values are atomic, and not regarded as constructed from other values. Booleans, unbounded integers, IEEE floats, UNICODE characters, and a null value are all classified as primitive. Some of them have constant constructors; the rest are computed by built-in funcons.

Composite values are constructed from finite sequences of argument values. Value constructors are injective: different argument value sequences give different composite values. The types of composite values include parametrised algebraic data types, with a generic representation. Various algebraic datatypes are predefined, and new ones can be introduced. Composite values include also built-in parametrised types of sets, maps, multi-sets, and graphs.

Abstractions are values formed by the value constructor $\mathsf{abstraction}(X)$ with an *unevaluated* argument X. Values are called *ground* when they are constructed entirely from primitive and composite values, without any abstraction values.

Appendix A summarises the funcons for types of data, and some funcons for data operations.

– *What kind of behaviour do funcons for data operations have?*

Data operations in programs are generally represented by funcons whose only behaviour is to compute values from *pre-evaluated* arguments. The arguments are evaluated in *any* order, possibly with interleaving (the order of argument evaluation is irrelevant when the evaluations have no effects). *Partial* data operations (e.g., integer division, or selecting the head of a list) compute the empty sequence when their arguments are not in their domain of definition.

Value *types* are themselves values, so funcons can take types as arguments and give them as results. Apart from supporting dependent types, this generality is needed to represent ordinary type constructors as funcons (e.g., lists(T), where T is the type of the list elements).

– *How do funcons express normal flow of control?*

A funcon intended purely for specifying normal control flow generally specifies the potential order of evaluation of its arguments, but does not otherwise contribute to behaviour. Such funcons include sequential or interleaved command execution and expression evaluation, deterministic and non-deterministic choice between computations, and command iteration.

Appendix B summarises the funcons for representing control flow.

– *How do funcons express flow of data?*

A computation may involve multiple uses of the same data (e.g., so as to assign it to a variable as well as provide it as a result). It may also involve repeating the same computation with different data. The computations of funcons for specifying such data flow involve an auxiliary entity given-value(V) that can be set to a computed value V; the funcon given gets the current value.

Appendix C summarises the funcons for representing data flow.

– *How do funcons specify scopes of bindings?*

An occurrence of a name in a program either *binds* the name, or *references* whatever is currently bound to the name. Binding occurrences are usually found in declarations, parameter specifications, and patterns; references to names are ubiquitous. Sequences of declarations have the effect of successively extending (or perhaps overriding) the current bindings with the bindings due to the individual declarations.

Funcons use conventional environments ρ (mapping names to values) to represent both the current bindings and bindings computed by declarations. The auxiliary entity environment(ρ) represents the current bindings; the current binding for an individual name I is inspected using the funcon bound-value(I). An environment representing computed bindings is an ordinary composite value, and can be inspected using data operations.

Some languages include various constructs for composing declarations, and these are represented directly by funcons that compute environments. However, the funcons corresponding to recursive declarations represent circularity by creating cut-points called links, which involves a separate auxiliary entity.

Appendix D summarises the funcons for representing name binding.

– *Do funcons have static scopes for bindings?*

The difference between static and dynamic scopes concerns procedural abstraction. A value that represents an abstraction is constructed from an *unevaluated* argument X by the funcon abstraction(X). The abstraction value can be subsequently enacted, which evaluates the argument X – potentially in a different context from that where the abstraction value was constructed.

Constructed abstraction values thus naturally have *dynamic* scopes for bindings. To obtain *static* scopes, the funcon closure(X) computes a closure value: an abstraction whose argument evaluation starts by ignoring the current bindings and (locally) re-declaring the abstraction-time bindings.

– *How do funcons distinguish between constant and mutable variables?*

In programming languages, imperative variables usually have names. It may be tempting to regard variable names as *bound* directly to values: bindings then need to be mutable, assignment to a variable name updates its binding, and constants correspond to single-assignment variables. However, such a simplistic analysis does not easily extend to features such as aliasing and call by reference.

A more satisfactory conceptual basis for imperative variables is to regard them as independent storage *locations*.[6] The declaration of a named variable involves allocation of storage (optionally with an initial value) together with binding the name of the variable to the storage location. Assignment to a named variable then affects what value is stored at the location, but leaves the bindings unchanged. Aliasing can now be understood simply as the simultaneous binding of different names to the same location.

The funcons for imperative variables involve an auxiliary mutable entity store(σ), mapping locations to their currently assigned values. The store supports allocation (and recycling) of locations for values of any type, and their initialisation, assignment, and inspection. It is completely independent of the auxiliary entity environment(ρ) used to represent the current name bindings.

In mathematical logic, a 'variable' corresponds to a name, and 'assignment' to binding. Imperative variables in programming languages are often called 'L-values', with 'R-values' being those that can be assigned to variables.[7] With funcons, all values can be assigned to variables – and variables are themselves values.

– *Can funcons represent structured variables with mixtures of constant and mutable fields?*

A simple variable consists of a location together with the type of values that it can store; assignment checks that the value to be assigned to the variable is in its type.[8] Simple variables may store primitive values (e.g., numbers) or composite

[6] Funcons have not yet been developed for 'relaxed' memory models or data marshalling.

[7] 'L' and 'R' refer to the left and right sides of typical assignment commands [32].

[8] Funcons for using un-typed locations as variables would be slightly simpler.

values (e.g., tuples), but assignment to a simple variable is always *monolithic*: the current value is replaced *entirely* by the new value.

Structured variables are composite values where some components are simple variables. These include hybrids having both mutable and immutable components. Assignment to a selected component variable corresponds to an in-place update; assignment of a composite value to an entire structured variable updates all the component simple variables with the matching values, and checks that the immutable components are the same.

Appendix E summarises the funcons for representing imperative variables.

– *How about abrupt termination?*

Various language constructs may cause abrupt termination when executed: throwing or raising an exception, returning the value of a function, breaking out of a loop, etc. Enclosing constructs can detect particular kinds of abrupt termination, and handle them appropriately. For example, a language construct may inspect an exception value, and conditionally handle it; a function application handles an abruptly returned value by giving it as the result; and a loop handles a break by terminating normally.

Funcons express abrupt termination and handlers *uniformly*. Evaluation of a funcon term may terminate normally, abruptly, or never. Abrupt termination leads to a stuck term, emitting an auxiliary entity abrupted(V) as a *signal* with a value V. The *closest* enclosing funcon that notices the emission of such a signal can inspect its value, and determine whether to handle it or not.

Appendix F summarises the funcons for abrupt termination.

– *Is it possible to define delimited control operators as funcons?*

Somewhat surprisingly, yes: see [26,30]. Control operators include continuation handling functions, such as '`call-cc`'.

– *Can non-terminating funcon evaluation have observable behaviour?*

Yes: through *interactive* input and output.

Program behaviour may depend on, and affect, data stored in files. Conceptually, files can be regarded as (complicated) structured variables: input from a file inspects the value stored at the current position, and advances the position; output to a file appends a value to it. Changes to a file system during program execution correspond to updating values stored in locations; they may subsequently be overwritten, so their *final* values can only be observed on program termination.

Interactive input and output, in contrast, *cannot* be regarded as effects on mutable storage. Acceptance of input data from a stream during program execution is irrevocable, as is output of data to a stream. Interaction may also involve inter-dependence between input and output. And a program that never terminates can have infinitely long streams of input and output.

Thus funcons for expressing interaction involve kinds of entities that differ fundamentally from those we previously introduced. The auxiliary entity standard-in(V^*) represents the (finite) sequence of values *input* at each step of a computation, where the empty sequence ( ) represents that no values are input. The value null-value indicates the end of the input. The auxiliary entity standard-out(V^*) represents the (finite) sequence of values *output* at a particular step, where the empty sequence ( ) represents the lack of output. Computations concatenate the input sequences of each step, and similarly for output – potentially resulting in infinite sequences for non-terminating computations.

Appendix G summarises the funcons for representing interaction. To support multiple streams, further entities and funcons would need to be added.

– *Do funcons currently support specification of any other language features?*

Tentative funcons for *multithreading* have been developed. They have not yet been rigorously unit-tested, nor used much in language definitions. These funcons are not included in FUNCONS-BETA, but in an unstable collection that extends FUNCONS-BETA [26].

The multithreading funcons involve multiple mutable auxiliary entities, representing the collection of threads, the set of active threads, the thread being executed, the values computed by terminated threads, and (abstract) scheduling information. Funcons that combine effects on multiple auxiliary entities are undesirable, and their definitions are somewhat verbose. It is currently unclear whether simpler funcons for multithreading can be developed.

Multithreading also involves *synchronisation*. The funcons for synchronising involve only the store entity. To inhibit preemption during synchronisation, multiple assignments need to be executed atomically, in a single transition.

Funcons for *distributed processes* have not yet been developed. They are expected to be based on asynchronous execution and message passing (cf. [17]).

Funcons for specifying *meta-programming* constructs have been defined [3]; they also enable a straightforward specification of call-by-need parameters.

5 Translation of Language Constructs to Funcons

In this section, we illustrate how a simple programming language construct can be specified by translation to funcons. Specifying such a translation for all constructs of a language defines the behaviour of programs, based on the behaviour of the funcons used in the translation. The PLANCOMPS project has developed some examples [26] and made them available for browsing on a website. We conclude this section with an overview of the examples, and indicate how they have been developed and tested.

– *How is call-by-value translated to funcons?*

The following fragments of a language specification illustrate how call-by-value parameter passing in an imperative programming language can be specified by translation to funcons. The fragments originate from a published specification [8] of the SIMPLE language; for brevity, however, we here restrict SIMPLE function applications and declarations to a single parameter.

The translation specification in Fig. 1 declares exp as a phrase sort, with the meta-variable *Exp* (possibly with subscripts and/or primes) ranging over phrases of that sort. The BNF-like production shows two language constructs of sort exp: an identifier of sort id (lexical tokens, here assumed to be specified elsewhere with meta-variable *Id*) and a function application written 'Exp_1(Exp_2)'.

Syntax Exp : exp ::= ⋯ | id | exp '(' exp ')' | ⋯

Semantics rval⟦ _ : exp ⟧ : ⇒ values

Rule rval⟦ Id ⟧ = assigned-value(bound-value(id⟦ Id ⟧))

Rule rval⟦ Exp_1 '(' Exp_2 ')' ⟧ = apply(rval⟦ Exp_1 ⟧, rval⟦ Exp_2 ⟧)

Fig. 1. Translation of identifiers and function applications in SIMPLE to funcons

The translation function rval⟦Exp⟧ maps phrases Exp of sort exp to funcon terms that compute elements of type values. Translation is compositional: the funcon term for a phrase combines the translations of its sub-phrases. The translation function id⟦Id⟧ maps lexical tokens Id of sort id to funcon values of type identifiers (its specification is omitted here).

In this illustrative language, the only values to which identifiers can be bound are simple imperative variables. When identifiers can be bound directly to other values (e.g., numbers) we would use current-value instead of assigned-value.

For call-by-value parameters in an imperative language, the argument value can be passed to the called function, which then has to allocate a variable to store the value. For call-by-reference, the argument would have to evaluate to a variable; for call-by-name, the evaluation of the argument would be deferred, which can be expressed by constructing a thunk abstraction value from it. When the mode of parameter-passing in function applications depends on the function, argument evaluation needs to be incorporated in the value that represents the function.

The translation specification for function declarations in Fig. 2 assumes a translation function exec⟦$Block$⟧ for phrases $Block$ of sort block. A block is a statement, which normally computes a null value; but here, as in many languages, a block can return an expression value by executing a return statement, which terminates the execution of the block abruptly.

The use of closure ensures static (lexical) bindings for references to names in the function body. For dynamic bindings, we would replace closure by abstraction. The construction of a function value from the closure is needed so that apply can be used to give the argument value to the body of the abstraction.

Syntax *Decl* : decl ::= ⋯ | '`function`' id '(' id ')' block

Semantics declare⟦ _ : decl ⟧ : ⇒ environments

Rule declare⟦ '`function`' Id_1 '(' Id_2 ')' *Block* ⟧ =
bind-value(id⟦ Id_1 ⟧,
allocate-initialised-variable(functions(values, values),
function(closure(
scope(
bind-value(id⟦ Id_2 ⟧,
allocate-initialised-variable(values, given)),
handle-return(exec⟦ *Block* ⟧)))))))

Fig. 2. Translation of function declarations in SIMPLE to funcons

The scope funcon adds the bindings computed by its first argument to the current bindings for the evaluation of its second argument. In this simplified illustration, functions have only one formal parameter, which is bound to a freshly allocated variable containing the given argument value; for multiple parameters, the given value would be a tuple of the same length, matched by a pattern tuple.

The handle-return funcon concisely handles abrupt termination of the function body arising from evaluation of the return funcon. It has no effect on normal termination, nor on abrupt termination for other reasons.

In languages where function identifiers can be bound directly to function closures, the first allocate-initialised-variable in the translation rule could be eliminated. However, the possibility of recursive function calls would then need to be expressed directly, using the recursive funcon.

The call-by-value example illustrates how directly the behaviour of a language construct can be specified by translation to funcons.

– *Which other language constructs have been translated to funcons?*

The PLANCOMPS project has developed the following language specifications based on FUNCONS-BETA, and made them available for browsing online [26].

- IMP: a very small imperative language, often used in text books on semantics. Its translation to funcons illustrates basic features of the framework.
- SIMPLE: a somewhat larger imperative language than IMP. Its translation to funcons [8] illustrates most features of the framework. It is comparable to the specification of SIMPLE in K [28], except that multithreading is omitted.
- MINIJAVA: a very simple subset of JAVA, used in [1]. Its specification illustrates translation to funcons for classes and objects.
- SL: the SIMPLELANGUAGE used for demonstration of GRAALVM [10]. Its translation to funcons illustrates how dynamic bindings can be specified.

- OCaml Light: a core sublanguage of OCaml. Its specification illustrates how translations to funcons scale up to a medium-sized language.

Further examples of language specifications involve funcons from an unstable collection that extends Funcons-beta [26]:

- Imp++: extends Imp with multithreading and various other features.
- Simple-Threads: adds the previously-omitted multithreading constructs.
- LangDev-2019: demonstrates extensibility of language specifications.

A funcon-based specification of C♯ is currently being developed.

- *How can we check translations of language constructs to funcons?*

Consider our translation of function declarations with call-by-value parameters. Potential mistakes include spelling errors in names (primarily funcons, but also syntax sorts, translation functions, and meta-variables) and misplaced parentheses. The syntax of the language construct in the translation rule might not be consistent with the specified grammar. A less obvious mistake is when the arguments of a funcon could compute values that are not in the types required by the funcon signature. We might also have used a funcon that does not have the intended behaviour (e.g., using abstraction instead of closure).

Clearly, tool support for checking is essential. A workbench for specifying translations of languages to funcons has been developed [21]. Tools for evaluating funcon terms [5] allow us to check whether they have the expected behaviour.

The workbench checks references to names, term formation, and the syntax in translation rules. It checks that funcons have the right number of arguments, but not yet that the arguments compute values of the required types; we currently rely on testing to check for that.

The workbench also supports parsing complete programs and translating them to funcon terms, using parsers and translators generated from the specified grammar and translation rules. It is based on the Spoofax language workbench [12], and implemented using the declarative domain-specific meta-languages SDF3, NaBL2, and Stratego. See [21] for further details. The tools for evaluating funcon terms [5] are implemented in Haskell, and can be called directly from the workbench.

6 Defining and Implementing Funcons

In this section, we illustrate how to define the behaviour of a funcon, once and for all, using a highly modular variant [19,23] of structural operational semantics [27]. Modularity of funcon definitions is crucial for extensibility of funcon collections.

Funcon $\mathsf{scope}(\_ : \mathsf{environments}, \_ : \Rightarrow T) : \Rightarrow T$

$$\textit{Rule}\quad \frac{\mathsf{environment}(\mathsf{map\text{-}override}(\rho_1, \rho_0)) \vdash X \longrightarrow X'}{\mathsf{environment}(\rho_0) \vdash \mathsf{scope}(\rho_1 : \mathsf{environments}, X) \longrightarrow \mathsf{scope}(\rho_1, X')}$$

Rule $\mathsf{scope}(\_ : \mathsf{environments}, V : T) \leadsto V$

Fig. 3. Definition of the funcon for expressing scopes of local declrations

– *How are funcons defined?*

The funcon signature in Fig. 3 specifies that scope takes two arguments. The first argument is required to be pre-evaluated to a value of type environments; the second argument should be unevaluated, as indicated by '$\Rightarrow T$'. Values computed by $\mathsf{scope}(\rho_1, X)$ are to have the same type (T) as the values computed by X.

The rules define how evaluation of $\mathsf{scope}(\rho_1, X)$ can proceed when the current bindings are represented by ρ_0. The premise of the first rule holds if X can make a transition to X' when ρ_1 overrides the current bindings ρ_0. Whether X' is a computed value or an intermediate term is irrelevant. When the premise holds, the conclusion is that $\mathsf{scope}(\rho_1, X)$ can make a transition to $\mathsf{scope}(\rho_1, X')$.

If X can terminate abruptly, or continue making transitions forever, then $\mathsf{scope}(\rho_1, X)$ can do the same. The last rule allows evaluation of $\mathsf{scope}(\rho_1, X)$ to terminate normally, computing the same value V as X. Transitions written with '$\leadsto$' correspond to term rewriting [7], and do not involve auxiliary entities.

– *How can funcon definitions remain fixed when new funcons are added?*

The use of the auxiliary entity $\mathsf{environment}(\rho_0)$ in the definition of scope restricts transitions to states that include it, but states might still include other auxiliary entities, such as $\mathsf{store}(\sigma)$ or $\mathsf{given\text{-}value}(V)$. If a transition $X \longrightarrow X'$ updates σ to σ', so does $\mathsf{scope}(\rho_1, X) \longrightarrow \mathsf{scope}(\rho_1, X')$; the transitions in the premise and conclusion use the same given value; and if $X \longrightarrow X'$ emits a signal on abrupt termination, so does the corresponding transition for $\mathsf{scope}(\rho_1, X)$.

Auxiliary entities are classified according to how they are *propagated*:

Contextual: A contextual entity remains *fixed* for successive steps in the computation of a term, but can be different for the computations of sub-terms.

Mutable: Sequential *changes* to a mutable entity are propagated between the computation of a term and the computations of its sub-terms.

Input: An input entity is a sequence of values *consumed* by evaluating a term, concatenating the sequences consumed by the computations of its sub-terms.

Output: An output entity is a sequence of values *produced* by evaluating a term, concatenating the sequences produced by the computations of its sub-terms.

Control: A control entity is a value that can optionally be *signalled* by a step. The corresponding step of an enclosing term may inspect the value, and signal the same value, signal a different value, or not signal.

The notation used for specifying auxiliary entities determines their classification. For instance, entities written before '$\vdash$' are classified as contextual.

- *Can static semantics for funcons be defined in the same way as dynamic semantics?*

The modular structural operational semantics rules for funcon term evaluation are in the *small-step* style, where each rule has *at most one* transition premise. A static semantics for funcons would naturally use *big-step* rules, with a premise for each sub-term. It is currently unclear whether the same classification of entities can be used for static and dynamic semantics; the static semantics of abstractions generally requires making latent effects explicit, in contrast to dynamic semantics.

- *How have funcons been implemented?*

The initial implementation of funcons was in PROLOG. Funcon definitions were translated to PROLOG clauses defining transitions,[9] based on the original implementation of MSOS in PROLOG.[10] Funcons have also been implemented in MAUDE.[11] The PROLOG implementation of MSOS was subsequently enhanced to support the rewriting relation used in value-computation transition systems [7]. The FUNCON TOOLS package [5] supports parsing funcon definitions and generating funcon interpreters in HASKELL, as described in [4].

- *Could funcons be used for language specification in other frameworks?*

The K-framework [28] has a high degree of modularity. For an experiment with using the K-framework to define funcons, see [24]. The distinction between pre-evaluated and unevaluated arguments in funcon signatures is represented by strictness annotations in K. However, rules in K are unconditional, so funcons such as scope cannot be defined straightforwardly. The specification of the structure of states is monolithic, and may need updating when adding new funcons.

REDEX [13] is a popular domain-specific metalanguage for operational semantics, embedded in the RACKET programming language. It is based on reduction rules and evaluation contexts. The reduction rules are highly modular, and grammars for language constructs and evaluation contexts can be specified incrementally. However, evaluation context grammars associated with control operators appear to be inherently global. It should be possible to define a particular collection of funcons in REDEX, but adding a new funcon could require updating the evaluation contexts for existing funcons.

7 Related Work

Many funcons are closely related to notation used in several previously developed language specification frameworks: denotational semantics, monads, abstract semantic algebras, and action semantics.

[9] https://pdmosses.github.io/prolog-msos-tool.
[10] https://pdmosses.github.io/msos-in-prolog.
[11] https://github.com/fcbr/mmt.

Denotational Semantics. The funcons for flowing, binding, and storing are directly based on Christopher Strachey's original conceptual analysis of imperative programming languages. Strachey initiated the development of denotational semantics at the IFIP Working Conference on *Formal Language Description Languages* in 1964 [31]. At the time, he was working on the design and implementation of the high-level CPL programming language, and aiming to specify its semantics formally. In the paper, he focuses on representing imperative features of programming languages as pure mathematical functions, avoiding the introduction of abstract machines. For assignment commands, he distinguishes between L-values and R-values of expressions, with locations in stores σ being a special case of L-values. He defines the operation C to get the current content of a location, and U to update the content. For flow of control, he uses composition of functions from stores to stores, and the fixed-point operation Y. In his widely-circulated 1967 lecture notes [32], he also introduces environments that map names to values, and represents procedures as closures.

Strachey's original operation C on stores is renamed *Contents* in [29], and U is renamed *Assign*. Many subsequent denotational specifications define a large number of such auxiliary operations (e.g., [16] defines about 80). However, the definitions are ad hoc, and they are based on the domains defined for the specified language. Even the way lambda-expressions are written, and the notation used for modifying environments and stores, vary between denotational specifications.

The VDM metalanguage for denotational semantics, developed from 1974 [11], introduced fixed notation for operations expressing basic mathematical and computational concepts. The notation for data flow, control flow, storing, and exception handling looks rather like a programming language, but it is intepreted as pure mathematical functions (the interpretation depends on whether exceptions are used).

Monads. The types of the mathematical functions used in denotational semantics can be quite complicated. In 1989, Eugenio Moggi suggested that each feature should be seen as a monad, where the elements represent computations of values in arbitrary domains [15]; moreover, the required domains could be defined modularly, by applying a series of monad constructors. Monads have a binary operation for composing a computation with a function that takes its computed value,[12] corresponding to the funcon give(X, Y), and a unary operation for giving a value as the result of a computation (not needed with funcons). Each monad constructor adds further structure to the domain of computations, together with associated operations. For example, the monad constructor for stores in a domain S makes computations of values in T take an argument in S and return both a value in T and a store in S. The associated operations are *lookup*(l), to return the value at location l in the argument store and the unchanged store, and *update*(l, v), to return a null value and a store where the value at l is v. The funcons assigned(Var) and assign(Var, V) correspond to (a typed variant of) the operations defined by the store monad constructor. Other

[12] See [20] for discussion of earlier uses of similar operations in denotational semantics.

funcons closely correspond to the operations associated with monad constructors for a wide range of notions of computation. Monad constructors also need to lift definitions of operations to the resulting domains, which is non-trivial. The notation for monad constructors and operations varies (also between functional programming languages and proof assistants that support monads).

Abstract Semantic Algebras and Action Semantics. In a series of papers in the 1980s, the present author proposed various sets of combinators, together with algebraic laws that they were supposed to obey, giving so-called *abstract semantic algebras*. The elements of abstract semantic algebras were intended to have a clear operational interpretation; they were referred to as 'actions' from 1985.

The action notation used in the action semantics framework [17,18] was developed in collaboration with David Watt [25]. It was defined [17, App. C] using a novel (but non-modular) variant of structural operational semantics, and use of action semantics was supported by tools implemented in the ASF+SDF Meta-Environment [6,9].

Action notation involves actions, data, and yielders. The performance of an action represents information processing behaviour. Yielders used in actions may access, but not change, the current information. The evaluation of a yielder always results in a data entity. Many funcons correspond closely to the combinators of action notation. The crucial difference is that action notation could not be extended with new features, due to the non-modularity of its operational definition. The development of modular structural operational semantics [19] was directly motivated by the aim of making the definition of action notation extensible, and avoiding reduction of the many facets of action behaviour to pure functions in monads [34].

8 Conclusion

The PLanCompS project has defined the behaviour of a substantial collection of funcons, and illustrated translation of functional and imperative language constructs to funcons [8,26]. It has also developed their theoretical foundations [7]. Specifying languages by translation to funcons appears to be significantly less effort than with other frameworks. Funcon definitions and translations have been validated by testing, using generated interpreters; web pages and PDFs are generated from the same source files, with hyperlinks from names to definitions to support browsing and navigation.

Much remains to be done. Current and future work includes: completion and release of the initial collection of funcons and further tool support; demonstration of scaling up to translation of a major language such as C♯; improvement of the definitions of funcons for multithreading; defining the static semantics of funcons; defining funcons for expressing static semantics of language constructs; proving algebraic laws for funcons; and investigating whether funcons can be used also for specifying the semantics of declarative and domain-specific programming languages. PLanCompS welcomes new participants who would like to contribute to the development of funcons!

Acknowledgements. Helpful comments on a previous version were provided by Thomas van Binsbergen, Cliff Jones, Neil Sculthorpe, members of the PL Group at Delft, and the anonymous reviewers. Thanks to the track organisers Klaus Havelund and Bernhard Steffen for extra space for the appendices.

The initial development of funcons was supported by an EPSRC grant to Swansea University for the PLANCOMPS project (EP/I032495/1). The author is now an emeritus at Swansea, and a visitor at Delft University of Technology.

A Data

A.1 Datatypes

Primitive values. Conceptually, primitive values are atomic, and not formed from other values. For large (or infinite) types of primitive values, however, it is infeasible to declare a separate constant for each value. So in practice, funcons used to construct primitive values usually take other values as arguments.

- booleans are the values true, false; funcons corresponding to the usual Boolean operations are defined.
- integers is the built-in type of unbounded integers, with funcons for the usual mathematical operations. Funcons corresponding to associative binary operations are extended to arbitrary numbers of arguments. Subtypes include naturals and bounded(M, N); compositions with casts to such subtypes correspond to partial operations representing computer arithmetic.
- floats is the built-in type of IEEE floating point numbers, with funcons for the required operations.
- characters is the built-in type of all UNICODE characters. Its subtypes include ascii-characters and iso-latin-1-characters. Its funcons incude the UTF-8, UTF-16, and UTF-32 encodings of characters as byte sequences.
- null-type has the single value null-value, alias null.

Composite values. Conceptually, composite values are constructed from finite sequences of argument values. The types of composite values include parametrised algebraic data types, with a generic representation. Various algebraic datatypes are defined, and new ones can be introduced. Composite values include also built-in parametrised types of sets, maps, multi-sets, and graphs.

Algebraic datatypes

- datatype-values are generic representations for all algebraic datatype values.
- tuples$(T_1, \cdots, T_n)$ are grouped sequences of values of the specified types.
- lists(T) are grouped sequences of values of type T, with the usual operations; strings are lists of characters.
- vectors(T) are grouped sequences of values of type T, accessed by index.
- trees(T) are finite, with values of type T at nodes and leaves.
- references(T) are values that refer to values of type T.

- pointers(T) are references to values of type T or pointer-null.
- records(T) are unordered aggregate values, indexed by identifiers.
- variants(T) are pairs of identifiers and values of type T.
- classes are collections of features, allowing multiple superclasses, used to classify objects.
- objects are classified collections of features.
- bit-vectors(N) has instantiations for bits and bytes.

Built-in datatypes

- sets(GT) are finite sets of ground values of type GT.
- maps($GT, T^?$) are finite maps from type GT to type $T^?$.
- multisets(GT) are finite multisets of ground values of type GT.
- directed-graphs(GT) have values of type GT as vertices.

See [26] for funcons that operate on the above types of values.

A.2 Abstractions

Generic Abstractions. These non-ground values are used for constructing thunks, functions, and patterns. An abstraction body of computation type $T \Rightarrow T'$ may refer to a given value of type T, and compute values of type T'.

- abstractions(CT) are procedural abstractions of computation type CT.
- abstraction(X) constructs an abstraction with dynamic bindings.
- closure(X) computes an abstraction with static bindings.
- enact(A) evaluates the body of the abstraction A.

Thunks. The abstraction body of a thunk does not reference a given value.

- thunks(T) are constructed from abstractions with bodies of type $( ) \Rightarrow T'$.
- thunk(A) constructs a thunk from the abstraction A.
- force(V) enacts the abstraction of the thunk V.

Functions. The abstraction body of a function may reference a given value.

- functions(T, T') are constructed from abstractions with bodies of type $T \Rightarrow T'$.
- function(abstraction(X)) constructs a function with dynamic bindings.
- function(closure(X)) computes a function with static bindings.
- apply(F, V) gives the value V to the body of the abstraction of function F.
- supply(F, V) determines the argument value of a function application, but returns a thunk that defers evaluating the body of the function.
- compose(F_2, F_1) returns the function that first applies F_1 then F_2.
- curry(F) takes a function F that takes a pair of arguments, and returns the corresponding 'curried' function.
- uncurry(F) takes a curried function F and returns a function that takes a pair of arguments.
- partial-apply(F, V) takes a function F that takes a pair of arguments, and determines the first argument, returning a function of the second argument.

Patterns. The abstractions of patterns match a given value.

- patterns are constructed from abstractions with bodies of computation type values ⇒ environments.
- pattern(A) constructs patterns from abstractions A.
- match(X, pattern(A)) enacts the abstraction A, giving it the value of X.

B Flow of Control

- left-to-right($\cdots$) evaluates its arguments sequentially, and concatenates the computed value sequences. Composing it with a funcon having pre-computed arguments prevents interleaving; e.g., integer-add(left-to-right(X, Y)) always executes X before Y.
  right-to-left($\cdots$) is analogous.
  interleave($\cdots$) evaluates its arguments in any order, possibly with interleaving, and concatenates the computed value sequences.
- sequential($X, \cdots$) executes the command X, then any remaining arguments, evaluating to the same value(s) as the last argument.
- effect($\cdots$) interleaves the evaluations of its arguments, discarding their computed values, and gives null-value.
- choice($Y, \cdots$) selects one of its arguments, then evaluates it.
- if-true-else(B, X, Y) evaluates B to a Boolean value, then evaluates either X or Y (which have to compute values of the same type).
- while-true(B, X) evaluates B to a Boolean value, then either executes X (which has to correspond to a command) and iterates, or terminates.

C Flow of Data

given evaluates to the current value of the auxiliary entity given-value.
- give(X, Y) evaluates X. It then executes Y with the value of X as the value of the auxiliary entity given-value.
- left-to-right-map(F, V^*) evaluates F for each value in the sequence V^* in the same order, computing the sequence of resulting values.
  interleave-map(F, V^*) allows interleaving of the evaluations.
- left-to-right-repeat(F, M, N) evaluates F for each integer from M up to N sequentially, computing the sequence of resulting values.
  interleave-repeat(F, M, N) allows interleaving of the evaluations.
- left-to-right-filter(P, V^*) evaluates P for each value in V^*, computing the sequence of argument values for which the value of P is true.
  interleave-filter(P, V^*) allows interleaving of the evaluations.
- fold-left(F, A, V^*) reduces a sequence V^* to a single value by folding it from the left, using A as the initial accumulator value.
  fold-right(F, A, V^*) is analogous.

For any list L, the funcon term list-elements(L) evaluates to the sequence V^* of elements in L, and list(V^*) reconstructs L. Composition with these funcons allows the above funcons on sequences to be used with lists; similarly for vectors, sets, multisets, and the datatype of maps.

D Name Binding

- bind-value(I, X) computes the singleton environment mapping I to the value computed by X.
- unbind(I) computes an environment that hides the binding of I.
- bound-value(I) computes the value to which I is currently bound (possibly recursively, via a link), if any, and otherwise fails.
- scope(D, X) first evaluates D to compute an environment ρ. It then extends the auxiliary environment entity with ρ for the execution of X.
- closed(X) prevents references to non-local bindings while evaluating X.
- accumulate(D_1, D_2) first evaluates D_1, to compute an environment ρ_1. It then extends the auxiliary environment entity by ρ_1 for the evaluation of D_2, to compute an environment ρ_2. The result is ρ_1 extended by ρ_2.
- collateral($D_1, \cdots$) evaluates its arguments to compute environments. It returns their union as result, failing if their domains are not pairwise disjoint.
- bind-recursively(I, X) makes bind-value(I, X) recursive. It first computes a singleton environment ρ mapping I to a fresh link L. It then extends the auxiliary environment entity by ρ for the execution of X, to compute a value V. Finally, it sets L to refer to V, and gives ρ as the computed result.
- recursive(SI, D) makes D recursive on the identifiers in the set SI. It first computes an environment ρ mapping all I in SI to fresh links. It then extends the auxiliary environment entity by ρ for the execution of D, to compute an environment ρ'. Finally, it sets the link for each I to refer to the value of I in ρ', and gives ρ' as the computed result.

E Imperative Variables

- variables is the type of all simple variables.
- allocate-variable(T) constructs a simple variable for storing values of type T in a location not in the current store.
- recycle-variables($Var, \cdots$) removes locations allocated to variables from the current store.
- initialise-variable(Var, V) assigns V as the initial value of Var.
- allocate-initialised-variable(T, V) is a composition of allocate-variable(T) and initialise-variable($\_, V$).
- assign(Var, V) stores V at the location of Var when the type contains V.
- assigned(Var) gives the value last assigned to Var.
- current-value(V) gives the same result as assigned(V) when V is a simple variable, otherwise V.
- un-assign(Var) makes Var uninitialised.
- structural-assign(V_1, V_2) assigns to all the simple variables in V_1 the corresponding values in V_2, provided that the structure and all non-variable values in V_1 match the structure and corresponding values of V_2.
- structural-assigned(V) computes V with all simple variables replaced by their assigned values. When V is a simple variable or a value with no component variables, structural-assigned(V) gives the same result as current-value(V).

F Abrupt Termination

- abrupt(V) terminates abruptly for reason V.
- handle-abrupt(X, Y) first executes X. If X terminates normally, Y is ignored. If X terminates abruptly for any reason, Y is executed, with the reason as the given value.
- finally(X, Y) first executes X. On normal or abrupt termination of X, it executes Y. If Y terminates normally, its computed value is ignored, and the funcon terminates in the same way as X; otherwise it terminates in the same way as Y.
- fail abruptly terminates for reason failed.
- else($X_1, X_2, \cdots$) executes the arguments in turn until either some X_i does *not* fail, or all arguments X_i have been executed. The last argument executed determines the result.
  else-choice($X_1, X_2, \cdots$) is similar, but executes the arguments sequentially in any order.
- check-true(X) terminates normally if the value computed by X is true, and fails if it is false.
- checked(X) fails when X computes the empty sequence of values ( ), representing that a value has not been computed. It otherwise computes the same as X.
- throw(V) abruptly terminates for reason thrown(V).
  handle-thrown(X, Y) handles abrupt termination of X for reason thrown(V) with Y.
  handle-recursively(X, Y) is similar to handle-thrown(X, Y), except that another copy of the handler attempts to handle any values thrown by Y.
- return(V) abruptly terminates for reason returned(V).
  handle-return(X) evaluates X. If X either terminates abruptly for reason returned(V), or terminates normally with value V, it terminates normally giving V.
- break abruptly terminates for reason broken.
  handle-break(X) terminates normally when X terminates abruptly for reason broken.
- continue abruptly terminates for reason continued.
  handle-continue(X) terminates normally when X terminates abruptly for reason continued.

Further funcons are provided for expressing delimited continuations [26, 30].

G Communication

- read inputs a single non-null value from the standard-in entity, and gives it as the result.
- print(V^*) outputs the sequence of values V^* to the standard-out entity.

References

1. Appel, A.W., Palsberg, J.: Modern Compiler Implementation in Java, 2nd edn. Cambridge University Press, Cambridge (2002)
2. Batory, D.S., Höfner, P., Kim, J.: Feature interactions, products, and composition. In: Denney, E., Schultz, U.P. (eds.) GPCE 2011, pp. 13–22. ACM (2011). https://doi.org/10.1145/2047862.2047867
3. van Binsbergen, L.T.: Funcons for HGMP: the fundamental constructs of homogeneous generative meta-programming (short paper). In: Wyk, E.V., Rompf, T. (eds.) GPCE 2018, pp. 168–174. ACM (2018). https://doi.org/10.1145/3278122.3278132
4. van Binsbergen, L.T., Mosses, P.D., Sculthorpe, N.: Executable component-based semantics. J. Log. Algebr. Meth. Program. **103**, 184–212 (2019). https://doi.org/10.1016/j.jlamp.2018.12.004
5. van Binsbergen, L.T., Sculthorpe, N.: Funcons-tools: a modular interpreter for executing funcons. https://hackage.haskell.org/package/funcons-tools. Software package. Accessed 08 Aug 2021
6. van den Brand, M., Iversen, J., Mosses, P.D.: An action environment. Sci. Comput. Program. **61**(3), 245–264 (2006). https://doi.org/10.1016/j.scico.2006.04.005
7. Churchill, M., Mosses, P.D.: Modular bisimulation theory for computations and values. In: Pfenning, F. (ed.) FoSSaCS 2013. LNCS, vol. 7794, pp. 97–112. Springer, Heidelberg (2013). https://doi.org/10.1007/978-3-642-37075-5_7
8. Churchill, M., Mosses, P.D., Sculthorpe, N., Torrini, P.: Reusable components of semantic specifications. In: Chiba, S., Tanter, É., Ernst, E., Hirschfeld, R. (eds.) Transactions on Aspect-Oriented Software Development XII. LNCS, vol. 8989, pp. 132–179. Springer, Heidelberg (2015). https://doi.org/10.1007/978-3-662-46734-3_4
9. van Deursen, A., Mosses, P.D.: ASD: the action semantic description tools. In: Wirsing, M., Nivat, M. (eds.) AMAST 1996. LNCS, vol. 1101, pp. 579–582. Springer, Heidelberg (1996). https://doi.org/10.1007/BFb0014346
10. GraalVM: Introduction to SimpleLanguage. https://www.graalvm.org/graalvm-as-a-platform/implement-language. Accessed 08 Aug 2021
11. Jones, C.B.: The transition from VDL to VDM. J. Univers. Comput. Sci. **7**(8), 631–640 (2001). https://doi.org/10.3217/jucs-007-08-0631
12. Kats, L.C.L., Visser, E.: The Spoofax language workbench: Rules for declarative specification of languages and IDEs. In: Cook, W.R., Clarke, S., Rinard, M.C. (eds.) OOPSLA 2010, pp. 444–463. ACM (2010). https://doi.org/10.1145/1869459.1869497
13. Klein, C., et al.: Run your research: on the effectiveness of lightweight mechanization. In: Field, J., Hicks, M. (eds.) POPL 2012, pp. 285–296. ACM (2012). https://doi.org/10.1145/2103656.2103691
14. Madlener, K., Smetsers, S., van Eekelen, M.C.J.D.: Formal component-based semantics. In: Reniers, M.A., Sobocinski, P. (eds.) SOS 2011. EPTCS, vol. 62, pp. 17–29 (2011). https://doi.org/10.4204/EPTCS.62.2
15. Moggi, E.: An abstract view of programming languages. Technical report, ECS-LFCS-90-113, Edinburgh Univ. (1989)
16. Mosses, P.D.: The mathematical semantics of Algol 60. Technical Monograph, PRG-12, Oxford Univ. Comp. Lab. (1974)
17. Mosses, P.D.: Action Semantics, Cambridge Tracts in TCS, vol. 26. Cambridge University Press, Cambridge (1992). https://doi.org/10.1017/CBO9780511569869

18. Mosses, P.D.: Theory and practice of action semantics. In: Penczek, W., Szałas, A. (eds.) MFCS 1996. LNCS, vol. 1113, pp. 37–61. Springer, Heidelberg (1996). https://doi.org/10.1007/3-540-61550-4_139
19. Mosses, P.D.: Modular structural operational semantics. J. Log. Algebr. Program. **60–61**, 195–228 (2004). https://doi.org/10.1016/j.jlap.2004.03.008
20. Mosses, P.D.: VDM semantics of programming languages: Combinators and monads. Formal Aspects Comput. **23**(2), 221–238 (2011). https://doi.org/10.1007/s00165-009-0145-4
21. Mosses, P.D.: A component-based formal language workbench. In: Monahan, R., Prevosto, V., Proença, J. (eds.) F-IDE@FM. EPTCS, vol. 310, pp. 29–34 (2019). https://doi.org/10.4204/EPTCS.310.4
22. Mosses, P.D.: Software meta-language engineering and CBS. J. Comput. Lang. **50**, 39–48 (2019). https://doi.org/10.1016/j.jvlc.2018.11.003
23. Mosses, P.D., New, M.J.: Implicit propagation in structural operational semantics. ENTCS **229**(4), 49–66 (2009). https://doi.org/10.1016/j.entcs.2009.07.073
24. Mosses, P.D., Vesely, F.: FunKons: component-based semantics in K. In: Escobar, S. (ed.) WRLA 2014. LNCS, vol. 8663, pp. 213–229. Springer, Cham (2014). https://doi.org/10.1007/978-3-319-12904-4_12
25. Mosses, P.D., Watt, D.A.: The use of action semantics. In: Wirsing, M. (ed.) Formal Description of Programming Concepts III, pp. 135–166. North-Holland (1987)
26. PLanCompS Project: CBS: A framework for component-based specification of programming languages. https://plancomps.github.io/CBS-beta. Accessed 08 Aug 2021
27. Plotkin, G.D.: A structural approach to operational semantics. J. Log. Algebr. Program. **60–61**, 17–139 (2004). https://doi.org/10.1016/j.jlap.2004.05.001
28. Rosu, G.: K: a semantic framework for programming languages and formal analysis tools. In: Pretschner, A., Peled, D., Hutzelmann, T. (eds.) Dependable Software Systems Engineering, pp. 186–206. IOS Press (2017). https://doi.org/10.3233/978-1-61499-810-5-186
29. Scott, D.S., Strachey, C.: Toward a mathematical semantics for computer languages. In: Fox, J. (ed.) Proceedings of the Symposium on Computers and Automata. Microwave Research Institute Symposia, vol. 21, pp. 19–46. Polytechnic Institute of Brooklyn (1971). Also Technical Monograph, PRG-6, Oxford University Computing Laboratory
30. Sculthorpe, N., Torrini, P., Mosses, P.D.: A modular structural operational semantics for delimited continuations. In: Danvy, O., de'Liguoro, U. (eds.) WoC 2016. EPTCS, vol. 212, pp. 63–80 (2015). https://doi.org/10.4204/EPTCS.212.5
31. Strachey, C.: Towards a formal semantics. In: Formal Language Description Languages for Computer Programming, pp. 198–216. North-Holland (1966)
32. Strachey, C.S.: Fundamental concepts in programming languages. High. Order Symb. Comput. **13**(1/2), 11–49 (2000). https://doi.org/10.1023/A:1010000313106. Lecture Notes, Int. Summer School in Comput. Prog., Copenhagen (1967)
33. Torrini, P., Schrijvers, T.: Reasoning about modular datatypes with Mendler induction. In: Matthes, R., Mio, M. (eds.) FICS 2015. EPTCS, vol. 191, pp. 143–157 (2015). https://doi.org/10.4204/EPTCS.191.13
34. Wansbrough, K., Hamer, J.: A modular monadic action semantics. In: Ramming, C. (ed.) DSL 1997. USENIX (1997). http://www.usenix.org/publications/library/proceedings/dsl97/wansbrough.html

Introducing Dynamical Systems and Chaos Early in Computer Science and Software Engineering Education Can Help Advance Theory and Practice of Software Development and Computing

David Harel(✉) and Assaf Marron

Weizmann Institute of Science, Rehovot, Israel
david.harel@weizmann.ac.il

Abstract. Dynamical systems, i.e., systems that progress along time according to fixed rules, exhibit many special phenomena like the emergence of interesting patterns, bifurcation of behavior, the appearance of chaos despite determinism and boundedness, and sensitive dependence on initial conditions. Such phenomena are encountered in diverse fields, such as fluid dynamics, biological population analysis and economic and financial operations. The study of dynamical systems, their properties, and the mathematical and computerized tools for dealing with them, are often designated as part of advanced curricula in physics or mathematics. Consequently, many computer science students, perhaps the majority thereof, graduate without ever being exposed to such concepts. We argue that with the pervasiveness of dynamical systems and manifestation of their properties in the real world, these concepts should be introduced early on; in undergraduate studies in computer science and related fields, and perhaps even in high school. Available introductory courses demonstrate that only a minimal foundation of knowledge in mathematics is needed for the basic understanding of the key ideas. Such an introduction would deepen one's understanding of the world and highlight important capabilities and limitations of mathematical and software tools for analysis, simulation, testing and verification of complex systems. In turn, this can lead to enhancement and enrichment of languages, tools and methodologies for dealing with dynamical systems, and of research in computer science and software engineering in general.

1 Motivation

The concept of emergent entities and emergent properties is central to the study of complex systems. Examples include a traffic jam, a spinning tornado, a swarm of bees, the organization and behavior of an ant colony, and the partition of the unfathomable number of organisms in nature into millions of distinct species. Depictions of an ant eater befriending an ant colony in Hofstadter's seminal book Gödel, Escher, Bach [14] are particularly illuminating of the distinction between

T. Margaria and B. Steffen (Eds.): ISoLA 2021, LNCS 13036, pp. 322–334, 2021.
https://doi.org/10.1007/978-3-030-89159-6_20

the emergent entity, i.e., the friendly colony, and its constituent components, namely the poor ants who may be served as food to maintain this friendship with the anteater.

In our own research on biological evolution and of biological modeling [4,5], we have encountered extensive interest by scientists in the emergence of new patterns and order either from seemingly disordered behavior or, more often, from well specified and seemingly constrained local behavior [15,22,28]. This, in turn, led us more deeply into the realm of dynamical systems and chaos, in which concepts like emergence, bifurcation, sensitivity to initial conditions, fractals, and never-exactly-repeated behavior (which are explained briefly in Sect. 2) are dealt with thoroughly using analytical and computational tools [8,11].

This, combined with our interest in computer science (CS) education and in making deep CS concepts accessible to the general public (see, e.g., [13]), made us realize that ideas and notions associated with dynamical systems, chaos and emergence are often absent from the curricula of basic CS and software and system engineering (SE). A brief check of curricula in leading universities confirms this observation. And while dynamical systems and chaos (DS&C) are usually introduced as part of the disciplines of physics or mathematics, they are often considered to be advanced optional material and are offered as part of an elective or on the graduate level.

In this paper, we argue that concepts in, or properties of, DS&C are relevant to CS and software and system engineering students and professionals, and indeed to people from other areas who are interested in science and the observation of nature, and in engineering and philosophy. Thus, we claim, these concepts should be introduced early on, in undergraduate studies and perhaps even in high school. The scope of such an introduction can range from a single overview lecture, through a unit in a broader course, to an entire introductory course.

Some courses, books, lectures and papers already address the aim of making dynamical systems accessible to individuals with only basic mathematical background. For example, Devaney's introductory book [6] is targeted at undergraduate students who have had only a one year calculus course, and does not require knowledge of differential equations. Feldman's book [8] and his highly accessible series of videos from the Santa Fe Institute and the College of the Atlantic under the Complexity Explorer series [7] can also serve as excellent starting points for students and teachers new to this domain; they do not even require calculus and the relevant aspects of derivatives and partial differential equations are taught as an integral part of the DS&C course. Further support for the claim that these seemingly advanced concepts can be understood by students with a more limited mathematical background is provided by the research on teaching dynamical system to high school students [10]. An invaluable, and even less technical introduction to the history and the beauty of the field is offered in Gleick's book [11].

The goals of such introductory information include: (i) broadening one's perspective of the world in action, in line with the maxim attributed to Albert Einstein *"look deep into nature, and then you will understand everything better"*; (ii) laying a foundation for individuals who will later actually work with common dynamical systems in academia and industry; (iii) alerting professionals to the existence of dynamical-system and chaotic traits and unpredictable behavior in systems that might not be considered as such at first; (iv) highlighting requirements and gaps in techniques for development, analysis, simulation, testing and verification of complex dynamical systems, thus offering leads into research on programming languages and abstractions, algorithms, and theory; and, (v) making available to students and scientists the theory and tools developed for dynamical systems that have been shown to be of value when working on problems that are considered to be at the core of computer science.

2 The Subject Matter: Key Phenomena in Dynamical Systems and Chaos

A dynamical system is defined as a mathematical system that progresses in time according to fixed rules. These rules can operate in discrete time via iterative recurrence relations, of the form $x_{n+1} = f(x_n)$, where x_n and x_{n+1} are the states of the system at time n and $n+1$, respectively, or continuously, expressed as differential equations like $\frac{\partial x}{\partial t} = f(x, y, z)$, $\frac{\partial y}{\partial t} = f(x, y, z)$, and $\frac{\partial z}{\partial t} = f(x, y, z)$, where $\langle x, y, z \rangle$ represents the state of the system (in this case, in a three dimensional space) and the derivatives are rates of change with respect to time of each component of the state. In both the discrete and continuous cases, the next state, or the next change in state, are a function of only the current state. All seemingly external events and conditions are incorporated as internal parameters of the model, and the only role of the passage of time has to do with the step size in calculating the next system state. The absolute wall-clock time, or the time that has elapsed since the beginning of a simulation or an observation, are not essential parts of the model.

In dynamical systems, the functions depicting changes in state are often nonlinear, that is, the changes in output are not directly proportional to the changes in input. This non-linearity makes the mathematical analysis more difficult, which may be one of the reasons for why the topic is not taught earlier on. However, as in the quote attributed to Stanislaw Ulam [1]: *"Using a term like nonlinear science is like referring to the bulk of zoology as the study of non-elephant animals."*, the pervasiveness of nonlinear systems mandates that scientists, students and engineers should be more familiar with them.

Specifically, the main phenomena we deem relevant to this paper's proposal are:

1. **Emergence:** General definitions of emergent entities and properties often relate to properties of a system, or a set of entities, that are not expressed by any one of the components of the system or elements of the set (see, e.g., [4] and references therein). In dynamical systems, one often observes unexpected patterns, arrangements, and self organization. Salt crystals, ocean waves, convection rolls in a slowly-heating liquid, flocks of flying birds, and living cells are examples of such emergent entities. More specifically, consider an autonomous vehicle (AV) out on the field, at some large distance from

a designated tree. The AV is programmed to always proceed in a direction that is close to being perpendicular to its line of sight to that tree, and to control the direction angle so as to keep the distance more or less constant. While these instructions are local, external observers would readily see that the vehicle's trajectory/orbit/phase-space forms a circle; also, local observers, like additional AV instrumentation with memory, or a human who is present in the AV, can also notice the circular nature of the trajectory.

2. **Bifurcation:** Some dynamical systems exhibit great qualitative differences in observed behavior when certain parameters are subjected to minute changes. For example, consider the famous logistic map function $x_{n+1} = x_n \cdot r \cdot (1 - x_n)$ (see, e.g., [6], and Fig. 1). It can be viewed as a population x, where $0 < x < 1$ (representing, say, the portion of the area of a Petri dish covered by bacteria) grows by a factor of r every time unit, and is restrained by a factor of $1-x$. The trajectory is computed by starting at some arbitrary initial value $0 < x_0 < 1$, and iteratively computing the map. For all values of r, with $r < 3$, each of the trajectories formed by the iterative operation of the map converges to a single value (with different fixed points for different values of r); for $3 < r <\sim 3.44$, each of the different maps eventually oscillates between two values; for $\sim 3.45 < r <\sim 3.54$ the maps long-term behavior is an oscillation with a period of 4, etc.; and, for $r = 4$ and other values, the function behavior is chaotic, visiting in an unpredictable order the entire $[0, 1]$ range.

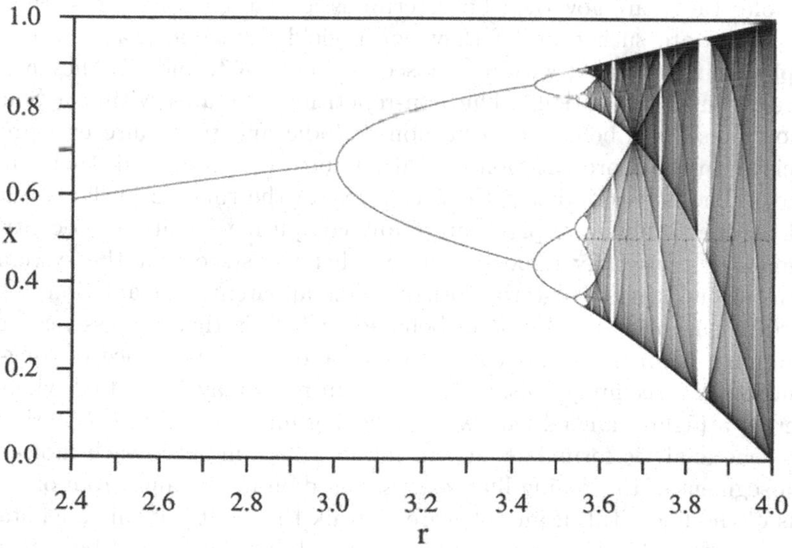

Fig. 1. The logistic map $x_{n+1} = x_n \cdot r \cdot (1 - x_n)$. The graph shows, for each value of r, the values that the map converges to after many iterations. For $r = 2.6$, this is a single value ~ 0.61; for $r = 3.2$, the map oscillates between two values, ~ 0.8 and ~ 0.51; for $r = 3.5$ the oscillation period is 4: ~ 0.50, ~ 0.87, ~ 0.38, ~ 0.83; and for $r = 4$, the map yields chaotic coverage of the entire range between 0 and 1. See the body of the text in the bifurcation paragraph for more details. Image source: Wikipedia; under fair-use licensing.

The transitions between these behaviors are sudden and occur in very narrow ranges of values of r. Similar sudden changes in behavior occur in other dynamical systems like the changes in patterns and periods in the behavior patterns of a dripping faucet in response to the incoming water flow, or the number of convection rolls in a heated container as a function of the rate of change in temperature.

3. **Sensitivity to initial conditions:** This phenomenon, highlighted by the discoveries of Lorenz (see Fig. 3), and which is often termed "the butterfly effect", means that certain functions, even very simple ones, can produce very different system trajectories when starting at arbitrarily close, yet distinct, states. These distinct states commonly reflect not a particular choice, or an uninvited deviation from some desired reality, but merely a measurement error due to instrument limitations, or constraints imposed by the finite representations of numbers in computing. The term butterfly effect alludes to the difficulty in predicting the long term path of a storm, when the formulas in the model are sensitive to minute details, such as, figuratively speaking, whether a far-away butterfly, which might have been included in the model, did or did not flap its wings at a certain point in time.
4. **Unpredictable chaotic behavior:** In the study of dynamical nonlinear systems, behavior is considered to manifest chaos, or be chaotic, when it is unpredictable, but not because it depends on randomness or pseudo randomness; the system's state changes, and its infinite trajectory through all its possible states, are governed by deterministic mathematical rules. However, these rules are such that (i) they never yield the same exact state twice, despite being bounded within a closed region of $\mathcal{R}^n$, and (ii) they are sensitive to initial conditions. The non-repetition of states within a bounded region causes the behavior to be non-periodic and to require ever-growing precision in the representation of real numbers (in order to distinguish near states). The non-periodicity, the sensitivity of the rules to initial conditions and the inevitable finite precision of any computing facility, then contribute to making it virtually impossible to predict the state that the system will be in beyond some near-term horizon. This apparent contradiction between determinism in intended system behavior, which is the very essence of programming, algorithms and computation, and the appearance of long-term behavior as a seemingly disordered random mess may be settled when considering a highly tangled thin wire or fishing line, as in Fig. 2. Clearly there is no one analytic formula that can tell us where in space each molecule or each segment of the fishing line resides, based on its distance from one of the ends of the line. Still, if an ant were to walk the length of this line, starting at one of its ends, the ant's near-term general direction would be reasonably well defined for any location on the line. It is also intuitive to think that if the fishing line can be infinitesimally thin, one can always insert (indeed, thread) an additional length of it into the tangle without disrupting or cutting through existing line segments. For a more formal example, we return to the logistic map mentioned earlier, and consider $r = 4$, where the behavior is chaotic. Given a fully specified initial value of x, if one wishes to compute

the map value after n iterations, one must first compute all preceding $n-1$ iterations to unbounded precision. One may then ask whether or not such a process can be considered to be a prediction.

Additional phenomena manifested by DS&C include the following: the formation of fractal structures, i.e., self-similar recursive structures and behaviors; the existence of strange attractors, i.e., the convergence of behavior towards a chaotic, sometimes fractal pattern (such as the three dimensional figure-eight continuous trajectory of Lorenz equations system shown in Fig. 3, or the fractal boomerang shape formed by the Hènon Map shown in Fig. 4, that is formed over time by points being drawn one at a time, in different locations); and, the existence of universal mathematical parameters, like Feigenbaum's constant(s), which appear in highly disparate systems, ranging from the logistic map and other quadratic maps, through a dripping faucet, to the formation of convection rolls. See, e.g., [9] for more details.

Fig. 2. A single filament fishing line. The "path" of the thread illustrates unpredictable, yet deterministic and bounded behavior, in which any particular $\langle x, y, z\rangle$ coordinate in space is visited at most once; the path is very sensitive to the precision of measurement and calculation; any misstep by someone following the path of the thread could cause a transition to a different segment of the thread resulting in a very different trajectory. For an infinitely thin thread, new paths can always be found without physically intersecting, i.e., sharing an absolute coordinate, with an already traversed location. Image source: Wikipedia; under fair-use licensing.

3 Linking DS&C Tenets to General Education and to CS and SE

In this section we offer several perspectives on how DS&C is tied to classical computer science and software development, and why learning DS&C early may be beneficial to scientists and engineers.

3.1 DS&C Phenomena are Real and Pervasive

Most generally, the phenomena discussed in the previous section are real, both in nature and in their abstract mathematical manifestations, and there is a general consensus about them being aesthetic in some sense. Hence there may not be a need for further justification for including them at some level in general education and in scientific and engineering curricula, and for having CS and SE be part of the disciplines offering languages, tools, methodologies and theoretical foundations for dealing with these phenomena.

$$\frac{\mathrm{d}x}{\mathrm{d}t} = \sigma(y - x)$$

$$\frac{\mathrm{d}y}{\mathrm{d}t} = x(\rho - z) - y$$

$$\frac{\mathrm{d}z}{\mathrm{d}t} = xy - \beta z$$

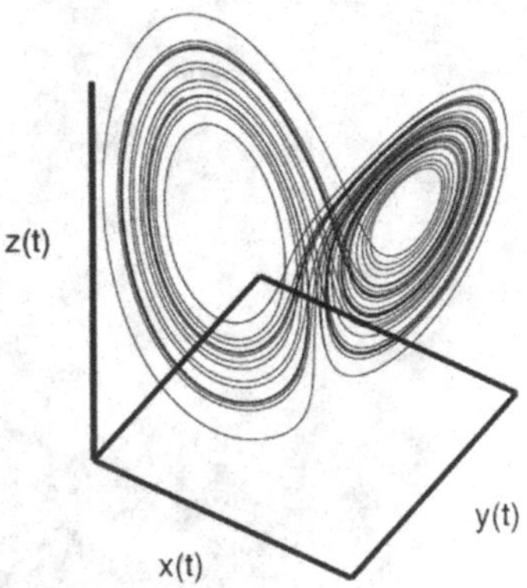

Fig. 3. Lorenz equations and trajectory. For any location of "the tip of the pen" drawing this graph in a three dimensional space, its speed along each of the axes, and thus its direction, is given by the respective partial derivative equations on the left. The result is the graph on the right. The equations are simple, and involve only elementary arithmetic operations over the current coordinates and some constants. Regardless of the starting point, the orbit is persistently attracted towards this well recognized, emergent, three dimensional "figure eight" shape. Still, given any current position of the traveling pen, it is impossible to predict far into the future in which lobe of the figure eight the pen will be at any particular time. Images sources: [7], under fair use licensing

3.2 CS and SE Already Deal with DS&C

At the other extreme of the links between DS&C and CS and SE is the fact that many sub-fields of CS and SE, as well as computer applications in other areas, already deal directly with dynamical systems. These include fluid/airflow dynamics, weather prediction, we transportation, robotics, manufacturing automation, economics and finance, storage/warehousing planning, disease control, livestock and agriculture management, and a variety of modeling and analysis applications in the study of biology, chemistry and physics. Therefore, it is only natural to expect CS and SE to be prepared to step in, attempting to address any technological, methodological or theoretical gaps or needs that may arise in such projects.

3.3 DS&C Issues May Emerge in *any* System

In between the two extremes listed in the preceding two subsections, we now list considerations related to DS&C concepts that affect requirements in the design of *any* system, whether perceived as a dynamic one or not. The bibliographic references given for each item serve to illustrate the issues via examples of in-depth treatment of well-scoped problems with relevant algorithms. Formulating succinct methodological principles that engineers and scientists should bear in mind, is yet to be done.

Pattern emergence. The emergence of unexpected patterns in images and other sensor input may cause incorrect classification or identification. This

$$\begin{cases} x_{n+1} = 1 - ax_n^2 + y_n \\ y_{n+1} = bx_n \end{cases} \qquad a = 1.4 \quad b = 0.3$$

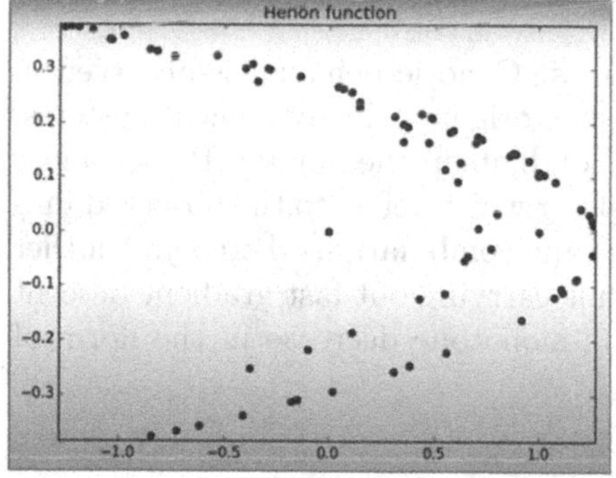

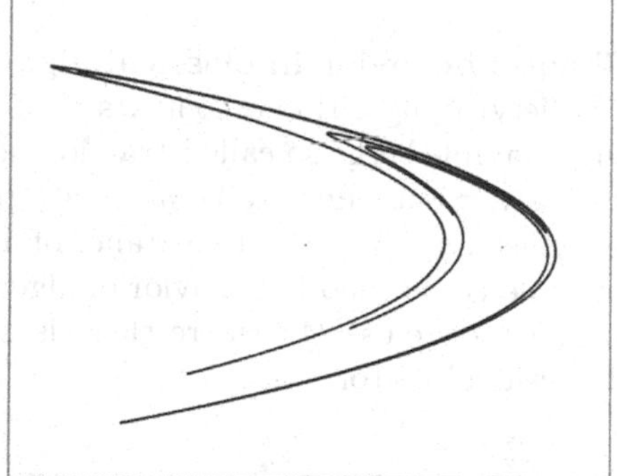

Fig. 4. Hènon Map. Starting at any point $\langle x, y\rangle$ in the two-dimensional plane, and computing the trajectory according to the equations at the top, and using the coefficients $a = 1.4, b = 0.3$, consecutive system states, i.e., coordinates of newly drawn points, may not be close to each other; after many steps, a boomerang-like shape emerges; the shape is fractal: when enlarging a sub-frame of the trajectory containing multiple lines (not shown here), one sees that each line is actually comprised of multiple thinner lines whose distances from each other are in proportions that are similar to the proportions of line distances in the original frame. Images sources: [9], under fair use licensing.

emphasizes the importance of redundancy in sensors of environment states and in the processing and analysis of their inputs (see, e.g., [2]) for causes of mistakes in image classification). Furthermore, such emergence of unexpected behavioral patterns may render a system more vulnerable to attacks that take advantage of the induced predictability, or cause excessive wear and tear in the system or in its environment (see, e.g., [18] for how repetition of a desired robot's path may form ruts in a field's soil).

Limitations in model-based prediction. Often, systems plan their behavior using on model-based algorithmic predictions. The development of such models and algorithms must accommodate the possibility of bifurcations in the behavior of the system and/or their environment throughout the allowable range of parameters (see, e.g., [12]). Furthermore, when an autonomous system explores new environments and new operational parameters, where it is not assured of the absence of bifurcations, it must be prepared for situations in which a very small change in parameters can cause dramatic and unexpected changes in behavior patterns.

Sensitivity to initial conditions. In computational/algorithmic models that affect operational decisions, the design must incorporate the level of sensitivity to initial conditions and to the finite precision in representing the current state, and set its prediction horizon accordingly. And, still, confident as the system may be in its predictions within the safe horizon, it must include mechanisms for appropriately reacting to unpredicted events and conditions, and, when possible, adapt its prediction process accordingly (see, e.g., [16,17]).

Chaotic behavior in classical algorithms. Chaotic behavior is observed in a variety of algorithmic contexts that do not originate in dynamical systems. One example is the so called "randomness" of digits in the number Pi (π) (more precisely, π is assumed to be *normal*, a property which refers to the observed uniform distribution of the appearance of digits and combinations thereof). Another example is the chaotic behavior of algorithms carrying out fast gradient descent in linear systems [24], where there is a non-monotone decrease in the norm of the residual vector.

3.4 CS and SE Research Can Help Close Gaps in Dealing with DS&C

There is a certain amount of published work on design principles for developing dynamical systems. For example [27] focuses on agent based models, [25] focuses on coding of society models, and [23] proposes principles for environmental and climate models. However, it appears that this sub-field is not as mature as software and system engineering for, say, traditional information processing systems, or control systems. Developing models of or controllers for dynamical systems can benefit from a variety of language idioms, and tools and methodologies, that are not readily available in existing languages and platforms for dealing with the various aspects of dynamical systems, such as the Modelica language (and tools implementing it), MATLAB and Simulink, NetLogo, AnyLogic, or Berkeley Madonna. To illustrate the need for language idioms and abstractions, we now list examples of challenges in monitoring a real or modeled dynamical traffic system. We focus on the detection, reaction to, and simulation of emergent entities (both expected and unexpected); languages for describing complex emergent behavior; dynamic incorporation of emergent entities as active programmable agents in a system, and more. Note that a human observer can readily handle the challenges in the examples below, yet programmed solutions require sophisticated procedural code:

- Detecting the existence of a traffic jam, and measuring its properties, such as its length. Note that the traffic jam entity exists despite its constituents being transient and dynamic, as vehicles leave its "head" and others join its "tail".
- Detecting a group of vehicles, like a truck convoy or a group of motorcyclists, and determining its relationship to other road users; for example, can others pass it safely?
- Detecting an unusual pattern in overall flow, as when a slow vehicle in a middle lane causes other vehicles to have to pass it on the right and left, with the difficulties and risks of changing lanes and merging.
- Detecting patterns in space and time; for example, whether the presence of certain kinds of vehicles, or of a certain kind of driver behavior is now more frequent/common than in the past.

While some such functions are carried out today using standard programming features, language idioms and development tools that address these directly could be of great value. And, not only can this be an important direction for computer scientists, we believe that studying DS&C can help attract undergraduate students to pursue graduate studies and research in this domain, further advancing the field.

3.5 Techniques Developed for DS&C Can Help Tackle Classical CS and SE Challenges

Approaches from dynamical system theory have been shown to be applicable in a variety of areas that are traditionally considered to be part of the computer science discipline. Example of such areas and one problem within each area are listed below. See the references for more details and examples.

- **Dynamical search** [19]. Consider the search for a minimum of a continuous function f in an interval where f is known to have only one such minimum; the search algorithm samples $f(x)$ at certain points within the current search interval e_n, and then narrows down the search interval $e_{n+1} = \psi(e_n)$ where ψ uses some algorithm-specific rules and the most recently found values of f.

This iterative computation of the intervals can be viewed as a dynamical system, and its behavior and convergence can then be analyzed using dynamical systems theory.
- **Algorithms for NP-hard problems** [21]. Consider the problem of partitioning a graph into equal size sets while minimizing the weights of cut edges; this problem arises in a range of settings, including gene networks, protein sequences, Internet routing algorithms and many more. To balance the cuts, the problem is often stated as minimizing the ratio between the inter-connection strength and the size of individual clusters. In this form, the problem is apparently intractable (NP-complete). An algorithm that uses dynamical system properties was developed for this task. It propagates waves in a graph in a completely decentralized setting, and has been shown to be orders of magnitude faster than existing approaches.
- **Machine Learning with Dynamical Systems** [3,20,26]. There is a growing body of work for introducing continuous dynamical system behavior and analysis into the theory of machine learning (ML) and neural nets. Elements of ML, like the propagation of information and computation within a neural net, the iterative training process that modifies the structure of a neural net based on prior results, and/or the behavior of the data itself in space (e.g., the processed image) are treated as continuous dynamical processes described using ordinary and partial differential equations.

4 Conclusion

Familiarity with the concepts and phenomena associated with nonlinear dynamical systems and chaos can enrich and enhance the work of scientists, engineers and educators in many fields. In particular, in the context of computer science and software & system engineering we expect that such broader and deeper awareness can trigger additional learning followed by valuable development and enhancement of languages, tools and methodologies. Based on already existing introductory material that does not require advanced knowledge of mathematics, we also believe that the first steps of such a shift in computer science education are in fact possible.

Acknowledgements. We thank Dror Fried for valuable comments throughout the development of this paper. Many thanks also to Irun Cohen, Smadar Szekely, Guy Frankel, and Meir Shani for constructive discussions and comments.

References

1. Campbell, D., Farmer, D., Crutchfield, J., Jen, E.: Experimental mathematics: the role of computation in nonlinear science. Commun. ACM **28**(4), 374–384 (1985)
2. Chakraborty, P., Adu-Gyamfi, Y.O., Poddar, S., Ahsani, V., Sharma, A., Sarkar, S.: Traffic congestion detection from camera images using deep convolution neural networks. Transp. Res. Rec. **2672**(45), 222–231 (2018)

3. Chen, R.T., Rubanova, Y., Bettencourt, J., Duvenaud, D.: Neural ordinary differential equations. arXiv preprint arXiv:1806.07366 (2018)
4. Cohen, I.R., Harel, D.: Explaining a complex living system: dynamics, multi-scaling and emergence. J. R. Soc. Interface **4**(13), 175–182 (2007)
5. Cohen, I.R., Marron, A.: The evolution of universal adaptations of life is driven by universal properties of matter: energy, entropy, and interaction. F1000Research **9** (2020)
6. Devaney, R.L.: A First Course in Chaotic Dynamical Systems: Theory and Experiment. Chapman and Hall/CRC Press, Boca Raton (2020)
7. Feldman, D.: Complexity Explorer Course on Dynamical Systems and Chaos. https://www.youtube.com/playlist?list=PLF0b3ThojznQwpDEClMZmIIssMsuPnQxZT. Accessed May 2021
8. Feldman, D.: Chaos and Dynamical Systems. Princeton University Press, Princeton (2019)
9. Feldman, D.P.: Chaos and Fractals: An Elementary Introduction. Oxford University Press, Oxford (2012)
10. Forjan, M., Grubelnik, V.: How well do students in secondary school understand temporal development of dynamical systems? Eur. J. Sci. Math. Educ. **3**(2), 185–204 (2015)
11. Gleick, J.: Chaos: The Amazing Science of the Unpredictable. Vintage Publishing, New York (1998)
12. Guan, X., Cheng, R., Ge, H.: Bifurcation control of optimal velocity model through anticipated effect and response time-delay feedback methods. Phys. A: Stat. Mech. Appl. **574**, 125972 (2021)
13. Harel, D., Feldman, Y.A.: Algorithmics: the Spirit of Computing. Pearson Education, London (2004)
14. Hofstadter, D.R.: Gödel, Escher, Bach: An Eternal Braid; 20th Anniversary Edition. Penguin Books (1999)
15. Kauffman, S.A.: Investigations. Oxford University Press, Oxford (2000)
16. Kewlani, G., Crawford, J., Iagnemma, K.: A polynomial chaos approach to the analysis of vehicle dynamics under uncertainty. Veh. Syst. Dyn. **50**(5), 749–774 (2012)
17. Marron, A., Limonad, L., Pollack, S., Harel, D.: Expecting the unexpected: developing autonomous-system design principles for reacting to unpredicted events and conditions. In: Proceedings of the IEEE/ACM 15th International Symposium on Software Engineering for Adaptive and Self-Managing Systems, pp. 167–173 (2020)
18. Ostafew, C.J., Schoellig, A.P., Barfoot, T.D., Collier, J.: Learning-based nonlinear model predictive control to improve vision-based mobile robot path tracking. J. Field Robot. **33**(1), 133–152 (2016)
19. Pronzato, L., Wynn, H.P., Zhigljavsky, A.A.: An introduction to dynamical search. In: Pardalos, P.M., Romeijn, H.E. (eds.) Handbook of Global Optimization, pp. 115–150. Springer, Boston (2002). https://doi.org/10.1007/978-1-4757-5362-2_4
20. Ruthotto, L., Haber, E.: Deep neural networks motivated by partial differential equations. J. Math Imaging Vis. **62**, 1–13 (2019)
21. Sahai, T.: Dynamical systems theory and algorithms for NP-hard problems. In: Junge, O., Schütze, O., Froyland, G., Ober-Blöbaum, S., Padberg-Gehle, K. (eds.) SON 2020. SSDC, vol. 304, pp. 183–206. Springer, Cham (2020). https://doi.org/10.1007/978-3-030-51264-4_8
22. Schrodinger, E.: What is Life? The Physical Aspect of the Living Cell. Cambridge University Press (1951)

23. Simm, W.A., et al.: SE in ES: opportunities for software engineering and cloud computing in environmental science. In: Proceedings of the 40th International Conference on Software Engineering: Software Engineering in Society, pp. 61–70 (2018)
24. van den Doel, K., Ascher, U.: The chaotic nature of faster gradient descent methods, pp. 1–27. The University of British Columbia, Canada (2011)
25. Vendome, C., Rao, D.M., Giabbanelli, P.J.: How do modelers code artificial societies? Investigating practices and quality of NetLogo codes from large repositories. In: 2020 Spring Simulation Conference (SpringSim), pp. 1–12. IEEE (2020)
26. Weinan, E.: A proposal on machine learning via dynamical systems. Commun. Math. Stat. **5**(1), 1–11 (2017)
27. Williams, R.A.: Lessons learned on development and application of agent-based models of complex dynamical systems. Simul. Model. Pract. Theory **83**, 201–212 (2018)
28. Wolf, Y.I., Katsnelson, M.I., Koonin, E.V.: Physical foundations of biological complexity. Proc. Natl. Acad. Sci. **115**(37), E8678–E8687 (2018)

GATE: Gradual Effect Types

Philip Wadler(✉)

University of Edinburgh, Edinburgh, UK
wadler@inf.ed.ac.uk
http://homepages.inf.ed.ac.uk/wadler/

Abstract. Two recent exciting trends in programming languages are gradual types and algebraic effect handlers. Several steps are required to bring algebraic effect handlers to wider use, one of the most important being the development of a suitable gradual type system.

1 Introduction

To type or not to type?

In the industrial world, dynamic languages are flavour of the month, with JavaScript, Python, and R on the rise. Meanwhile, in the academic world, exotic type systems are on the rise: dependent types in Agda, Coq, and Idris; session types in Links, Scribble, and Singularity OS; effect types in Eff, Frank, Koka, and Links. Even some interest among developers, with ownership types in Rust.

Bridging these is the rise in interest in gradually typed languages, which enable typed and untyped languages to interoperate. I had thought of these as assisting those poor schmucks that use dynamically-typed languages to migrate toward statically-typed languages with better maintenance properties. Whereas Facebook was once famous for "move fast and break things" now it is known for Hack and Flow, languages that supplement PHP and JavaScript, respectively, with types.

But now I realise that I am one of the poor schmucks. All of the legacy code out there, even in Haskell or OCaml, is in languages that don't support dependent types, session types, or effect types. If I want myself and others to use these in future, a way must be found for code with exotic types to interact with code without such types. Gradual types aren't just about typed vs untyped, they are also about more-precisely typed vs less-precisely typed. All our legacy code is less-precisely typed than some type system of interest. (The "poor schmuck" terminology is swiped from Wadler (2015).)

Traditionally, types describe *data* but not the huge range of *effects* that a program may invoke—such as input, output, raising an exception, reading or assigning to state, receiving or sending a message, executing concurrently, or the use of non-determinism or probability. One family of languages—the *functional* languages—address this problem by minimising the use of effects, but all such languages still support some form of effects. A line of research, going back to the *type and effect* system of Gifford and Lucassen in the late 1980s, aims to assign types to effects as well as values. A few languages, such as Java, permit type signatures that reflect a limited range of effects, such as raising exceptions.

T. Margaria and B. Steffen (Eds.): ISoLA 2021, LNCS 13036, pp. 335–345, 2021.
https://doi.org/10.1007/978-3-030-89159-6_21

Perhaps the most widespread combination of types and effects is the use of *monad* types to reflect effects, as in Haskell, and sometimes adopted in other languages such as F#, Rust, and Scala. One drawback to the monad approach is that there is no general way to combine two monads into a single monad supporting the effects of both. In the early 2000s, Plotkin and Power introduced a refinement of the monad approach known as *algebraic effects*, which does support combination of effects. This approach has attracted a great deal of interest and further development, including the introduction by Plotkin and Praetner of *effect handlers*. Several research languages, such as Eff, Frank, Koka, and Links, support the use of algebraic effects. A few languages, including Multicore O'Caml and WASM support specific algebraic effects, and we may see general algebraic effects make their way into mainstream languages in the future.

Several research questions must be answered before algebraic effects see widespread adoption.

How gradually type effects? That is, how to integrate legacy code that lacks typed effects with new code that supports typed effects? To date there is only a tiny amount of work in the area, and important aspects of effects, including algebraic effects and effect handlers, have yet to be addressed.

How to encapsulate effects? Typically, one effect (say, access to a database) may be built in terms of another effect (say, access to a file system). One would like to write types that mention only to the high-level effects while omitting the low-level effects in terms of which they are implemented. But most systems suffer from what has been dubbed *type pollution*, where invoking any effect requires also mentioning those in terms of which it is implemented. Proper support for encapsulation of effects is still poorly understood.

How to scope effects? Traditionally, variables in programming languages use static scope (a name matches the nearest declaration lexically) while exception handlers use dynamic scope (a name matches the nearest handler on the execution stack). By analogy with exception handlers, effect handlers use dynamic scope; but there is recent research suggesting this leads to problems, and that static scope may be more appropriate. But the current definitions of static scope are still complex. Can static binding of effect handlers be made as simple as static binding of variables?

How to subtype effects? A function that performs a smaller set of effects (say, only a read effect) may be returned where a function that performs a larger set of effects (say, both read and write effects) is expected. Various approaches to the issue exist, including both subtyping and row typing of effects. Promising new approaches to both subtyping (the work of Dolan) and row typing (the work of Morris and McKinna) have recently emerged, and await application to algebraic effects.

How to migrate effects to the mainstream? There is a large body of research on algebraic effects, and a number of implementations in research languages. However, work to date is often complex, and further attention is required to where idea can be simplified. Integration with the mainstream is easier to explore in the context of gradual types, which support running legacy code and new code in tandem. While the title of this paper derives from the key question of gradual types, the dyslexic acronym GATE refers to the combined effect of all of them: we need to open a gate through which effect types can enter the mainstream of programming languages.

2 Background

This section reviews some of the most interesting work in each of the related areas.

2.1 Gradual Types

Contracts. The enabling innovation for gradual types is the *contract*, introduced by Findler and Felleisen (2002). Contract monitor the flow of data between less-well-typed and more-well-typed regions of code, and checks that data entering the more-well-typed region satisfies the constraints imposed by the types. Many researchers built on this technique, including the dependent dynamic typing of Ou *et al.* (2004), the interlanguage migration of Tobin Hochstadt and Felleisen (2006), the hybrid typechecking of Flanagan (2006), and Siek and Taha (2006) who coincd the name *gradual typing.*

Blame. Wadler and Findler (2009) captured a common core of these ideas in the *blame calculus.* It uses casts to mediate between more-precisely-typed and less-precisely-typed code, where more-precisely-typed code depends on invariants that less-precisely-typed code may violate. Casts perform runtime tests to enforce the invariants, raising blame if they are violated. Each cast has a blame label; if the cast fails, the label indicates which side of which cast is at fault.

Blame is valuable to both theory and practice. For theory, blame enables one to state and prove blame safety, which guarantees that if a cast fails blame lies with the less-precisely-typed side. In practice, blame aids debugging; casts typically correspond to boundaries between modules, and the blame label indicates which of the two modules fails the relevant invariants. Wadler (2015) describes these issues at greater length.

As explained later, many systems for gradual typing fail to deal with blame. Which raises the question: why bother with blame safety? Surely it is obvious that type errors must lie with less-precisely-typed rather than more-precisely-typed code? It is important for the same reason as type safety: mathematical rigour helps us to avoid errors and corner cases in our designs.

Previous proofs of blame safety required sophisticated arguments based on program equivalence, as in Tobin Hochstadt and Felleisen (2006) and Matthews and Findler (2007). Blame calculus supports a simple proof, resembling the traditional progress and preservation formulation of Wright and Felleisen (1994).

Practice. Forms of gradual type systems in widespread use for industry include Dynamics in C#, Bierman *et al.* (2010), Microsoft's TypeScript, Bierman *et al.* (2014), Google's Dart, Ernst *et al.* (2017), Facebook's Hack, Verlaguet (2013), and Facebook's Flow, Chaudhuri *et al.* (2017), and from academia include Racket (formerly PLT Scheme), Tobin-Hochstadt and Felleisen (2006; 2008) and Reticulated Python Vitousek *et al.* (2017).

Gradual Guarantee. Siek *et al.* (2015b) introduced the Gradual Guarantee, which comes in two parts: the static guarantee asserts that typing is preserved as types become less precise, while the dynamic guarantee asserts that values are preserved as types become less precise. Increasing precision may make code fail to type check or yield blame more often, but will never make a program return a different answer. The Gradual Guarantee has become a valuable yardstick: a paper introducing a new gradual system will usually indicate whether or not it satisfies the static and dynamic guarantees.

Abstract Gradual Typing. Garcia *et al.* (2016) introduced Abstracting Gradual Typing (AGT), which connects gradual typing to the approach to abstract interpretation pioneered by Cousot and Cousot (1977). They propose a systematic method to gradualise any base language. A concretisation function takes a gradual type to a set of base types. One gradual type is more precise than another if the concretisation of the first is a subset of the concretisation of the second. The inverse function is abstraction, and concretion and abstraction form a Galois connection. This fundamental technique has proved productive, inspiring much further work, such as Bader *et al.* (2018) and Toro *et al.* (2018). AGT also includes a methodology for implementing gradual types based on runtime evidence, inspired by the threesomes of Siek and Wadler (2010). While the Galois connection is easy to understand and has proved influential, implementations based on evidence are more convoluted and might benefit from further improvement. In particular, it is not yet clear how evidence can support blame.

New Perspective. Another exciting development is the *new perspective* of Castagna *et al.* (2019), which shows how the transitive notion of *precision* of types can replace the non-transitive notion of *compatibility* used in most developments. They apply this perspective to union and intersection types, but it may well have other applications. Again, it is not yet clear how to support blame under this perspective.

Unifying Theories. Recently, several unifying theories of gradual types have begun to arise. Independently, two groups of researchers at Northeastern, Greenman and Felleisen (2018) and Chung *et al.* (2018) each give a single source language and then assign to it a number of different operational semantics, providing a framework to compare different approaches to gradual typing. In contrast, the *gradual type theory* of New *et al.* (2019) develops different theories of gradual types axiomatically, putting the properties one expects satisfied first, and deriving operational implementations from these.

Polymorphism and Parametricity. Parametric polymorphism, introduced by Milner (1978), is one of the most important features of functional languages. As observed by Reynolds (1983), parametric polymorphism imposes strong semantic conditions on terms, an idea popularised under the name "Theorems for free" by Wadler (1989). Remarkably, gradual typing can enforce these properties on untyped code that is cast to a polymorphic type, as discussed by Guha *et al.* (2007), Ahmed *et al.* (2011; 2017). There has been considerable discussion of whether semantic parametricity is compatible with the gradual guarantee, with Toro *et al.* (2019) arguing they are incompatible, while New *et al.* (2020) suggests they may be reconciled.

Dependent Types. Dependent types, as found in Agda, Coq, and Idris, attract much interest in the functional programming community, both for more precise types in programming and for validation. More widespread adoption of dependent types could be aided by gradual typing, for instance, to support migration from ordinary functional languages to dependently-typed ones. Eremondi *et al.* (2019) observe an important point, that since dependent types depend upon values, gradual typing may benefit from supporting not only less precise types but also less precise values. They apply AGT to design a new language with both, but don't support blame. Meanwhile, Zalewski *et al.* (2020) support blame, but not imprecise values. There remains much to do in this area.

Space-efficient Gradual Typing. Constant-space implementation of tail recursion is an important aspect of many functional languages. Naive implementations of gradual typing violate this property, and restoring it has been the subject of a line of work that includes Herman *et al.* (2007), Siek and Wadler (2010), Garcia (2013), and Siek *et al.* (2015a). The last provides a solution that is easy to understand, easy to implement, and accounts for blame. How to extend that solution beyond simple types, for instance, to polymorphism and dependent types, remains an open question.

2.2 Computational Effects

Effect Types. The seminal notion of tracking computational effects in the type system is due to Gifford and Lucassen (1986), and has been extended by many others, including Talpin and Juvelot (1994). Each effect type system is designed specifically to track particular effect, but they all have a similar design, and Marino and Millstein (2009) suggest a system that generalises many other such systems.

Monads. Moggi (1989; 1991) introduced monads as a semantic framework that describes many forms of effect. Wadler (1990; 1992) adopted monads for use in structuring functional programs, notably in Haskell. Various *ad hoc* methods of combining monads have been studied, starting with King and Wadler (1992) and Liang *et al.* (1995).

Wadler (1998), later jointly with Thiemann (2003), drew a connection between monads and effect types by indexing monads over a semi-lattice of possible effects. Combination of monads is also discussed by Filinski (1999). A closely related way of indexing monads over effects is *graded monads*, introduced by Katsumata (2014); a related notion of indexing was introduced by Orchared *et al.* (2014). Another form of indexing is *parameterised monads*, first described by Wadler (1994) and named and brought to wider attention by Atkey (2006; 2009). A generalisation of both forms of indexing is described by Orchard *et al.* (2020).

Algebraic Effects. A drawback of the monad formulation is that it does not support combining two arbitrary monads. This is rectified by *algebraic effects* as introduced by Plotkin and Power (2001a; 2001b; 2002; 2003). Logical reasoning over algebraic effects is discussed by Plotkin and Pretnar (2008), while optimisations based on algebraic effects are discussed by Kammar and Plotkin (2012).

Handlers. Next, Plotkin and Pretnar (2009) introduced *handlers*, which support custom definitions of algebraic effects. This was a key step forward and many researchers began to explore ramifications of this design, including the programming language *Eff* by Bauer and Pretnar (2015), *Koka* by Leijen (2017), and *Frank* by Convent, Lindley, McBride, and McLaughlin (2018; 2017), as well as the addition of row-based effect types to *Links* by Hillerström and Lindley (2016).

Effects without types. Almost exclusively, the focus of effects has been on static type systems. However, one can consider effects added to a *dynamically-typed* language such as Lisp or Javascript. One of the few explorations of this part of the design space is the programming language *Shonky* by McBride (2016).

Expressive power. Transformations between monads and delimited continuations is consider by Fillinski (1994), while transformations between both of those and effect handlers are considered by Forster *et al.* (2017). Compilation of effect handler to continuation passing style and considered by Hillerström *et al.* (2017).

Lexical binding. It used to be that many programming languages used *dynamic binding* for variables, where a name refers to the closest binding with the same name on the call stack. But since the advent of Scheme, most programming languages used *lexical binding* for variables, where a name refers to the binding that is lexically closest. Traditionally, exception handlers use dynamic binding, but Zhang *et al.* (2016) argue lexical binding, as specified by *tunnelling*, is more appropriate. By analogy, effect handlers again use dynamic binding, so Zhang and Myers (2019) adapt tunnelling to effect handlers. Similarly, Biernacki *et al.* (2020) also argue in favour of lexical rather than dynamic binding for effect handlers.

Gradual Typing and Effects. A gradual effect system has been proposed by Banados Schwerter *et al.* (2014; 2016), based on the generic effects of Marino and Millstein (2009). One particular effect type of importance is session types, with gradual session types considered by Igarashi *et al.* (2017).

2.3 Subtyping

To be useful in practice, a system of effect types must support some form of subtyping, or at least subeffecting. In particular, it must be possible to pass a function that performs fewer effects where a function that may perform more effects is expected. Pretty much all the effect type systems described above support some form of subtyping or subeffecting.

Unfortunately, combining subtyping with type inference tends to be problematic. Theoretically, there is no issue, as sound and complete inference systems for subtyping have been known since Mitchell (1984). But pragmatically, the types inferred by such systems may involve constraints that are unwieldy to write and read.

Recently, a new approach to subtypes that does not require constraints has been proposed by Dolan and Mycroft (2017), with further details in Dolan's dissertation (2017). The system appears to hit a "sweet spot" in that types and easy to write and read. A preliminary attempt to apply Dolan's system to algebraic effects has been made by Courant (2018).

Complementary advantages to subtyping are achieved by the row types of Wand (1989; 1991), where again the types are relatively easy to write and read. A recent generalisation of row typing due to Morris and McKinna (2019) seems particularly flexible and may be worth investigating.

Acknowledgements. Philip Wadler acknowledges support from UK EPSRC programme grant EP/K034413/1 *ABCD: A Basis for Concurrency and Distribution.*

References

Ahmed, A., Findler, R.B., Siek, J.G., Wadler, P.: Blame for all. In: Principles of Programming Languages (POPL) (2011)

Ahmed, A., Jamner, D., Siek, J.G., Wadler, P.: Theorems for free for free: parametricity, with and without types. Proc. ACM Program. Lang. (PACMPL) **1**(ICFP), 1–28 (2017)

Atkey, R.: Parameterised notions of computation. In: Mathematically Structured Functional Programming (MSFP). BCS (2006)

Atkey, R.: Parameterised notions of computation. J. Funct. Program. **19**(3–4), 335–376 (2009)

Bader, J., Aldrich, J., Tanter, É.: Gradual program verification. In: VMCAI 2018. LNCS, vol. 10747, pp. 25–46. Springer, Cham (2018). https://doi.org/10.1007/978-3-319-73721-8_2

Schwerter, F.B., Garcia, R., Tanter, É.: A theory of gradual effect systems. In: International Conference on Functional Programming (ICFP), pp. 283–295. ACM (2014)

Bauer, A., Pretnar, M.: Programming with algebraic effects and handlers. J. Logical Algebraic Methods Program. **84**(1), 108–123 (2015)

Bierman, G., Abadi, M., Torgersen, M.: Understanding typescript. In: Jones, R. (ed.) ECOOP 2014. LNCS, vol. 8586, pp. 257–281. Springer, Heidelberg (2014). https://doi.org/10.1007/978-3-662-44202-9_11

Bierman, G., Meijer, E., Torgersen, M.: Adding dynamic types to C♯. In: D'Hondt, T. (ed.) ECOOP 2010. LNCS, vol. 6183, pp. 76–100. Springer, Heidelberg (2010). https://doi.org/10.1007/978-3-642-14107-2_5

Biernacki, D., Piróg, M., Polesiuk, P., Sieczkowski, F.: Binders by day, labels by night: effect instances via lexically scoped handlers. Proc. ACM Program. Lang. (PACMPL) **4**(POPL), 48:1–48:29 (2020)

Castagna, G., Lanvin, V., Petrucciani, T., Siek, J.G.: Gradual typing: a new perspective. Proc. ACM Program. Lang. (PACMPL) **3**(POPL), 16:1–16:32 (2019)

Chaudhuri, A., Vekris, P., Goldman, S., Roch, M., Levi, G.: Fast and precise type checking for JavaScript. Proc. ACM Program. Lang. (PACMPL) **1**(OOPSLA), 48:1–48:30 (2017)

Siek, J., Taha, W.: Gradual typing for objects. In: Ernst, E. (ed.) ECOOP 2007. LNCS, vol. 4609, pp. 2–27. Springer, Heidelberg (2007). https://doi.org/10.1007/978-3-540-73589-2_2

Convent, L., Lindley, S., McBride, C., McLaughlin, C.: Encapsulating effects in Frank (2018)

Courant, N.: Safely typing algebraic effects (2018). http://gallium.inria.fr/blog/safely-typing-algebraic-effects/

Cousot, P., Cousot, R.: Abstract interpretation: a unified lattice model for static analysis of programs by construction or approximation of fixpoints. In: Principles of Programming Languages (POPL), pp. 238–252 (1977)

Dolan, S.: Algebraic Subtyping. BCS, The Chartered Institute for IT (2017)

Dolan, S., Mycroft, A.: Polymorphism, subtyping, and type inference in MLsub. In: POPL (2017)

Eremondi, J., Tanter, É., Garcia, R.: Approximate normalization for gradual dependent types. Proc. ACM Program. Lang. (PACMPL) **3**(ICFP) (2019)

Ernst, E., Møller, A., Schwarz, M., Strocco, F.: Message safety in dart. Sci. Comput. Program. **133**, 51–73 (2017)

Filinski, A.: Representing monads. In: Principles of Programming Languages (POPL), pp. 446–457. ACM (1994)

Filinski, A.: Representing layered monads. In: Principles of Programming Languages (POPL), pp. 175–188. ACM (1999)

Findler, R.B., Felleisen, M.: Contracts for higher-order functions. In: International Conference on Functional Programming (ICFP), pp. 48–59. ACM, October 2002

Flanagan, C.: Hybrid type checking. In: Principles of Programming Languages (POPL), pp. 245–256. ACM, January 2006

Forster, Y., Kammar, O., Lindley, S., Pretnar, M.: On the expressive power of user-defined effects: effect handlers, monadic reflection, delimited control. Proc. ACM Program. Lang. (PACMPL) **1**(ICFP), 13:1–13:29 (2017)

Garcia, R.: Calculating threesomes, with blame. In: International Conference on Functional Programming (ICFP) (2013)

Garcia, R., Clark, A.M., Tanter, É.: Abstracting gradual typing. In: Principles of Programming Languages (POPL), pp. 429–442. ACM (2016)

Gifford, D.K., Lucassen, J.M.: Integrating functional and imperative programming. In: LISP and Functional Programming, pp. 28–38. ACM (1986)

Greenman, B., Felleisen, M.: A spectrum of type soundness and performance. Proc. ACM Program. Lang. (PACMPL) **2**(ICFP), 71:1–71:32 (2018)

Guha, A., Matthews, J., Findler, R.B., Krishnamurthi, S.: Relationally-parametric polymorphic contracts. In: Dynamic Languages Symposium (DLS), pp. 29–40 (2007)

Herman, D., Tomb, A., Flanagan, C.: Space-efficient gradual typing. In: Trends in Functional Programming (TFP) (2007)

Hillerström, D., Lindley, S.: Liberating effects with rows and handlers. In: Proceedings of the 1st International Workshop on Type-Driven Development, pp. 15–27. ACM (2016)

Hillerström, D., Lindley, S., Atkey, R., Sivaramakrishnan, K.C.: Continuation passing style for effect handlers. In: Formal Structures for Computation and Deduction (FSCD), vol. 84. LIPIcs, pp. 18:1–19. Schloss Dagstuhl (2017)

Igarashi, A., Thiemann, P., Vasconcelos, V.T., Wadler, P.: Gradual session types. Proc. ACM Program. Lang. (PACMPL) **1**(ICFP), 38 (2017)

Kammar, O., Plotkin, G.D.: Algebraic foundations for effect-dependent optimisations. In: Principles of Programming Languages (POPL), pp. 349–360. ACM (2012)

Katsumata, S.-Y.: Parametric effect monads and semantics of effect systems. In: Principles of Programming Languages (POPL), pp. 633–646. ACM (2014)

King, D.J., Wadler, P.: Combining monads. In: Launchbury, J., Sansom, P. (eds.) Glasgow Workshop on Functional Programming, Workshops in Computing, pp. 134–143. Springer, London (1992). https://doi.org/10.1007/978-1-4471-3215-8_12

Leijen, D.: Type directed compilation of row-typed algebraic effects. In: Principles of Programming Languages (POPL), pp. 486–499. ACM, January 2017

Liang, S., Hudak, P., Jones, M.P.: Monad transformers and modular interpreters. In: Principles of Programming Languages (POPL), pp. 333–343. ACM (1995)

Lindley, S., McBride, C., McLaughlin, C.: Do be do be do. In: Principles of Programming Languages (POPL), pp. 500–514. ACM, January 2017

Marino, D., Millstein, T.: A generic type-and-effect system. In: Types in Language Design and Implementation (TLDI), pp. 39–50. ACM (2009)

Matthews, J., Findler, R.B.: Operational semantics for multi-language programs. In: Principles of Programming Languages (POPL), pp. 3–10 (2007)

McBride, C.: Shonky (2016). https://github.com/pigworker/shonky

Milner, R.: A theory of type polymorphism in programming. J. Comput. Syst. Sci. **17**(3), 348–375 (1978)

Mitchell, J.C.: Coercion and type inference. In: Principles of Programming Languages (POPL), pp. 175–185. ACM (1984)

Moggi, E.: Computational lambda-calculus and monads. In: Symposium on Logic in Computer Science (LICS), pp. 14–23. IEEE (1989)

Moggi, E.: Notions of computation and monads. Inf. Comput. **93**(1), 55–92 (1991)

Garrett Morris, J., McKinna, J.: Abstracting extensible data types: or, rows by any other name. Proc. ACM Program. Lang. (PACMPL) **3**(POPL), 12 (2019)

New, M.S., Licata, D.R., Ahmed, A.: Gradual type theory. Proc. ACM Program. Lang. (PACMPL) **3**(POPL), 15:1–15:31 (2019)

New, M.S., Jamner, D., Ahmed, A.: Graduality and parametricity: together again for the first time. Proc. ACM Program. Lang. (PACMPL) **4**(POPL), 1–32 (2020)

Orchard, D., Wadler, P., Eades III, H.: Unifying graded and parameterised monads. In: Mathematically Structured Functional Programming (MSFP), vol. 317. EPTCS, pp. 18–38 (2020)

Orchard, D.A., Petricek, T., Mycroft, A.: The semantic marriage of monads and effects. CoRR, abs/1401.5391 (2014). http://arxiv.org/abs/1401.5391

Ou, X., Tan, G., Mandelbaum, Y., Walker, D.: Dynamic typing with dependent types. In: Levy, J.-J., Mayr, E.W., Mitchell, J.C. (eds.) TCS 2004. IIFIP, vol. 155, pp. 437–450. Springer, Boston, MA (2004). https://doi.org/10.1007/1-4020-8141-3_34

Plotkin, G., Power, J.: Semantics for algebraic operations. Electron. Notes Theoret. Comput. Sci. (ENTCS) **45**, 332–345 (2001a)

Plotkin, G., Power, J.: Adequacy for algebraic effects. In: Honsell, F., Miculan, M. (eds.) FoSSaCS 2001. LNCS, vol. 2030, pp. 1–24. Springer, Heidelberg (2001). https://doi.org/10.1007/3-540-45315-6_1

Plotkin, G., Pretnar, M.: Handlers of algebraic effects. In: Castagna, G. (ed.) ESOP 2009. LNCS, vol. 5502, pp. 80–94. Springer, Heidelberg (2009). https://doi.org/10.1007/978-3-642-00590-9_7

Plotkin, G., Power, J.: Notions of computation determine monads. In: Nielsen, M., Engberg, U. (eds.) FoSSaCS 2002. LNCS, vol. 2303, pp. 342–356. Springer, Heidelberg (2002). https://doi.org/10.1007/3-540-45931-6_24

Plotkin, G.D., Power, J.: Algebraic operations and generic effects. Appl. Categ. Struct. **11**(1), 69–94 (2003)

Plotkin, G.D., Pretnar, M.: A logic for algebraic effects. In: Symposium on Logic in Computer Science (LICS), pp. 118–129. IEEE (2008)

Reynolds, J.C.: Types, abstraction and parametric polymorphism. In: IFIP congress, vol. 83 (1983)

Schwerter, F.B., Garcia, R., Tanter, É.: Gradual type-and-effect systems. J. Funct. Program. **26** (2016)

Siek, J., Thiemann, P., Wadler, P.: Blame and coercion: together again for the first time. In: Programming Language Design and Implementation (PLDI) (2015a)

Jeremy G. Siek and Walid Taha. Gradual typing for functional languages. In: Scheme and Functional Programming Workshop (Scheme), pp. 81–92, September 2006

Siek, J.G., Wadler, P.: Threesomes, with and without blame. In: Principles of Programming Languages (POPL) (2010)

Siek, J.G., Vitousek, M.M., Cimini, M., Boyland, J.T.: Refined criteria for gradual typing. In: Summit on Advances in Programming Languages (SNAPL), vol. 32. LIPIcs, pp. 274–293. Schloss Dagstuhl (2015b)

Talpin, J.-P., Jouvelot, P.: The type and effect discipline. Inf. Comput. **111**(2), 245–296 (1994)

Tobin-Hochstadt, S., Felleisen, M.: Interlanguage migration: from scripts to programs. In: Object-Oriented Programming: Systems, Languages, and Applications (OOPSLA), pp. 964–974. ACM (2006)

Tobin-Hochstadt, S., Felleisen, M.: The design and implementation of typed scheme. In: Principles of Programming Languages (POPL), pp. 395–406. ACM (2008)

Toro, M., Garcia, R., Tanter, É.: Type-driven gradual security with references. ACM Trans. Program. Lang. Syst. **40**(4), 1–55 2018

Toro, M., Labrada, E., Tanter, É.: Gradual parametricity, revisited. Proc. ACM Program. Lang. (PACMPL) **3**(POPL) (2019)

Verlaguet, J.: Facebook: analysing PHP statically. In: Workshop on Commercial Uses of Functional Programming (CUFP) (2013)

Vitousek, M.M., Swords, C., Siek, J.G.: Big types in little runtime: open-world soundness and collaborative blame for gradual type systems. In: Principles of Programming Languages (POPL), pp. 762–774. ACM (2017)

Wadler, P.: Theorems for free! In: Functional Programming Languages and Computer Architecture (FPCA) (1989)

Wadler, P.: Comprehending monads. In: LISP and Functional Programming, pp. 61–78. ACM (1990)

Wadler, P.: The essence of functional programming. In: Principles of Programming Languages (POPL), pp. 1–14. ACM (1992)

Wadler, P.: Monads and composable continuations. LISP Symb. Comput. **7**(1), 39–56 (1994)

Wadler, P.: The marriage of effects and monads. In: International Conference on Functional Programming (ICFP), pp. 63–74. ACM (1998)

Wadler, P.: A complement to blame. In: Summit on Advances in Programming Languages (SNAPL), vol. 32. LIPIcs, pp. 309–320. Schloss Dagstuhl (2015)

Wadler, P., Findler, R.B.: Well-typed programs can't be blamed. In: Castagna, G. (ed.) ESOP 2009. LNCS, vol. 5502, pp. 1–16. Springer, Heidelberg (2009). https://doi.org/10.1007/978-3-642-00590-9_1

Wadler, P., Thiemann, P.: The marriage of effects and monads. Trans. Comput. Logic (TOCL) **4**(1), 1–32 (2003)

Wand, M.: Type inference for record concatenation and multiple inheritance. In: Symposium on Logic in Computer Science (LICS), pp. 92–97. IEEE (1989)

Wand, M.: Type inference for record concatenation and multiple inheritance. Inf. Comput. **93**(1), 1–15 (1991)

Wright, A.K., Felleisen, M.: A syntactic approach to type soundness. Inf. Comput. **115**(1), 38–94 (1994)

Zalewski, J., Mckinna, J., Garrett Morris, J., Wadler, P.: λdb: blame tracking at higher fidelity. In: Workshop on Gradual Typing (2020)

Zhang, Y., Myers, A.C.: Abstraction-safe effect handlers via tunneling. Proc. ACM Program. Lang. (PACMPL) **3**(POPL), 5 (2019)

Zhang, Y., Salvaneschi, G., Beightol, Q., Liskov, B., Myers, A.C.: Accepting blame for safe tunneled exceptions. In: Programming Language Design and Implementation (PLDI), pp. 281–295. ACM (2016)

Fixing Classification: A Viewpoint-Based Approach

Bran Selić[1,2(✉)] and Alfonso Pierantonio[3]

[1] Malina Software Corp., Ottawa, Canada
selic@acm.org
[2] Monash University, Melbourne, Australia
[3] Università degli Studi dell'Aquila, L'Aquila, Italy
alfonso.pierantonio@univaq.it

Abstract. The concept of classification as realized in most traditional object-oriented computer languages has certain limitations that may inhibit its application to modeling more complex phenomena. This is likely to prove problematic as modern software becomes increasingly more integrated with the highly dynamic physical world. In this paper, we first provide a detailed description of these limitations, followed by an outline of a novel approach to classification designed to overcome them. The proposed approach replaces the static multiple-inheritance hierarchy approach found in many object-oriented languages with multiple dynamic class hierarchies each based on different classification criteria. Furthermore, to better deal with ambiguous classification schemes, it supports potentially overlapping class membership within any given scheme. Also included is a brief overview of how this approach could be realized in the design of advanced computer languages.

Keywords: Classification · Viewpoints · Computer languages

1 Introduction

As we build increasingly more sophisticated engineering systems, we seem to be approaching a level of complexity that may even be comparable to the complexity encountered in natural systems. It may be the case that classical engineering approaches, which are fundamentally based on the traditional divide-and-conquer strategy, may not be able to cope with this degree of complexity. The "crisp" modular nature of this approach, whereby individual functions tend to be isolated and encapsulated within dedicated modular units, is rarely reflected in natural systems. Although there certainly is modularity in nature, its module boundaries tend to be much more diffused, with a much greater degree of interlacing of functions.

For example, in medical science, the human body is deemed to have 11 distinct "body organ systems", representing groups of organs that jointly perform complex functions needed for survival and reproduction.[1] However, practically every organ in these systems

[1] https://www.verywellhealth.com/organ-system-1298691.

T. Margaria and B. Steffen (Eds.): ISoLA 2021, LNCS 13036, pp. 346–356, 2021.
https://doi.org/10.1007/978-3-030-89159-6_22

performs multiple functions, not all of which are necessarily associated with the body organ system to which they nominally belong. Thus, the liver, which secretes bile used in digestion, is classified as part of the *digestive system*, but it also filters blood which is considered to be the responsibility of the *cardiovascular system*. Similarly, bones, which are nominally part of the *skeletal system*, produce red and white blood cells, which is also part of the functionality of the cardiovascular system.

Clearly, the boundaries between these various organ "systems" are approximations at best. In fact, given such intermixing of functionalities, it is fair to ask whether these "systems" actually exist as concrete entities. A more accurate view, perhaps, is that the human body is simply one highly integrated complex system. The postulated separation into distinct systems is a simplified model of this complex reality, an artifact devised by humans to help our minds deal with what might otherwise be overwhelming complexity.

The mechanism behind this divide-and-conquer approach is *abstraction*. It is behind much of the success of modern engineering, including software engineering in particular since software is unique in its ability to implement abstract concepts. Highly effective programming paradigms such as Dijkstra's structured programming [4] and various component-based approaches [2] are some notable examples. Although abstraction in software usually comes at the cost of efficiency, this is more than compensated by gains in terms of conceptual simplicity (i.e., understandability and maintainability) and design reliability. But, as we gradually progress into attempting to construct what are popularly referred to as "smart" software-intensive systems,[2] the usually trustworthy divide-and-conquer method may have reached its limits. In fact, it may even prove counterproductive in these circumstances, adding to complexity by forcing a highly diverse and potentially confusing network that connects multiple different but inter-related functional modules. After all, as the human body exemplifies, nature has demonstrated that truly complex systems require a more sophisticated and more intricate approach to system design. It seems worthwhile, therefore, to study it and, possibly, use it as a guide to how to deal with the of extreme complexity that we are striving for these days.

With this in mind, we examine here the possibility of a more sophisticated approach to the problem of *classification*, one that is inspired by natural phenomena such as biological systems. The specific objective is to overcome some of the major limitations of the way that classification is defined in most modern object-oriented programming languages. Namely, that approach to classification is yet another example of an approximate representation of an inherently more complex natural phenomenon. The "body organ subsystems" example clearly demonstrates that reality can be far more complex than this particular classification scheme provides. Numerous other examples are easily found: from the peculiar nature of a duck-billed platypus (an egg-laying mammal[3]) to the confusing classification of the tomato plant (fruit or vegetable?[4]). The binary nature of

[2] https://smartanythingeverywhere.eu/.

[3] The first European scientists to examine the body of a platypus in 1799 declared it to be a fake, consisting of sewn-together parts of multiple different animals (https://en.wikipedia.org/wiki/Platypus).

[4] https://en.wikipedia.org/wiki/Tomato#Fruit_versus_vegetable.

classification in encountered in these traditional programming languages, where membership in a class is based solely on the binary presence or absence of specific structural and behavioral features, simply cannot reflect the true nature of such complex phenomena.

Furthermore, because of the way it is defined, the traditional approach makes it difficult to directly model the rather common natural phenomenon of *dynamic reclassification*, whereby an entity progresses through different existential modes, each of which is characterized by different characteristics. In the process, it may acquire new characteristics as well as shed or diminish existing ones. For example, a frog progresses from a tadpole with gills and a tail to a mature frog with legs, lungs, and no tail. Complicating classification further is the existence of transient intermediate forms in between those crisply-delineated phases, with dynamically changing combinations of features from both the initial and the final forms.

The section that follows provides a more detailed analysis of the limitations of traditional classification approaches and why they need to be overcome. Section 3 provides an outline of a different "viewpoint-based" model of classification. The possible realization of this model in computer programming or modeling languages is described briefly in Sect. 4. Although the traditional model of classification in programming languages has mostly remained unchallenged, some prior works have raised at least some of the issues discussed here and some have even proposed partial solutions. Those that are known to the authors of this paper are described in Sect. 5. The final section briefly summarizes the essential takeaways of this paper and also includes a short discussion of possible future research directions associated with this approach.

2 The Limitations of Traditional Models of Classification

The focus of this work is on enabling three principal modeling capabilities that are currently inhibited by current approaches to classification in object-oriented programming languages:

1. The ability to dynamically reclassify objects (and their capabilities) as they progress through their lifecycle,
2. The ability to classify objects from different perspectives, based on different categories of concerns,
3. The ability to accurately represent "in-between" cases, where an entity may be validly but ambiguously categorized as belonging in more than one class within a given classification scheme.

The reasons why these features are desirable and why they are not handled adequately by current programming languages are discussed individually below.

2.1 Dynamic Reclassification

One common property of most current models of classification found in popular programming languages such as Java, C#, or C++, is that an object can only be an instance of exactly one class throughout its lifetime. Unfortunately, since a class is defined by the set of structural and behavioral features that its members possess, this does not support modeling of important categories of *mutable objects* whose set of features changes over time.

Mutable entities occur naturally in many different contexts. One obvious example can be found in biological systems, such as the aforementioned frog example. Given that more and more of today's "smart" software interacts closely with the highly dynamic physical world, there is a clear need to be able to accurately model such phenomena in software. For instance, a "digital twin"[5] that represents some mutable physical object or process falls directly into this category. However, mutable entities can also occur in the virtual world of software. For example, a subsystem that is in the process of initializing or recovering from failures is likely to exhibit very different behavior and even different attributes in these circumstances when compared to its steady-state operational modes.

Traditional methods of dealing with this are either through multiple inheritance or via the State design pattern [6]. But, the problems of multiple inheritance are well known. The most notable is that it can lead to the well-known "diamond inheritance" problem,[6] whereby a given feature may be inherited from two or more different ancestors that ultimately share the same superclass. In addition, multiple inheritance may also lead to inheriting some redundant or even undesirable features from some of the ancestor classes. For example, in some system, the AmphibiousVehicle class may inherit from both an AquaticVehicle class and a SurfaceVehicle class. However, if the AquaticVehicle superclass includes a HomePort attribute, it would also appear in all instances of the merged AmphibiousVehicle class, where it may not be meaningful.

The State design pattern, on the other hand, requires defining an auxiliary branch of the class hierarchy for capturing the different operational modes of the original class. This also obscures the crucial fact that the various states captured by the pattern are an inherent property of the base class. It also requires the definition of an auxiliary variable for dynamically instantiating the appropriate instances of the operational classes as needed. In other words, the State pattern is merely a "manual" workaround in lieu of a missing first-class concept in the implementation language.

In summary, both approaches indirect and problematic solutions, for what should evidently be a first-class modeling capability.

2.2 Multiple Concurrent Classification Schemes

A second core limitation of strict and immutable inheritance is that it favors a single dominant classification scheme to the detriment of others. As a rule, modern object-oriented languages require that, at any given time, an object can only be an instance of a single class. This holds even with multiple inheritance since, in that case, a single class is still needed to merge the different ancestor branches, as in the case with the forementioned AmphibiousVehicle, which inherits from both its AcquaticVehicle and its SurfaceVehicle ancestors.

---

[5] https://en.wikipedia.org/wiki/Digital_twin.

[6] https://en.wikipedia.org/wiki/Multiple_inheritance.

But, even without dynamic reclassification, there is still a practical need to view a given object from different perspectives, depending on what is of principal interest at a given point in time. For example, as illustrated by the somewhat simplistic example in Fig. 1, we may choose to classify persons in a variety of different ways, such as based on their employment status, age, gender, etc. In general, each such classification scheme focuses only on a subset of available features, based on which ones are relevant to that scheme. In fact, in accord with the well-known principle of separation of concerns,[7] it may even be desirable to "hide" or abstract out features that do not belong to the classification that is currently of concern. (For example, the `jobFunction` attribute shown in Fig. 1 only makes sense in the context of a Person who is employed, and, therefore, its presence would only create "noise" in other viewpoints.)

While it may be that in some applications, one classification scheme may be deemed as more important than others, it seems inappropriate to always *force* a "dominant" one to which all other schemes must conform.

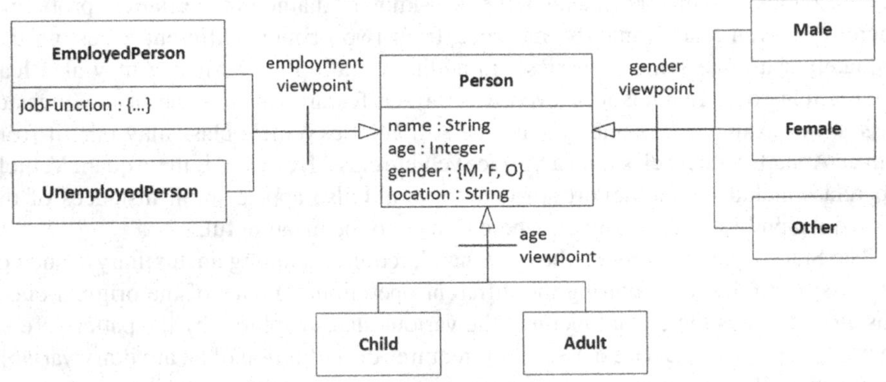

Fig. 1. A simple example of multiple different classification schemes for a given concept

In essence, classification is one more case of the divide-and-conquer approach. It works by dividing up a potentially large number of entities into smaller subsets. This reduces the dimensionality of the problem thereby making it more amenable to human reasoning. The resulting subsets comprise entities that are similar according to some chosen classification scheme (i.e., set of concerns), such as entities that share a common subset of possible features. The scheme used in this process and the concerns that it encompasses represent what is often called a *viewpoint*.[8] Since it is generally possible to define different partitioning schemes for practically a given population of entities, the possibility of a *viewpoint-based classification* approach naturally asserts itself. An outline of such an approach is provided in Sect. 3.

---

[7] This principle is, of course, yet another example of the divide-and-conquer strategy.

[8] For the purposes of this work, we use the definition of viewpoint as provided in the IEEE 42010 standard [7]. It defines a "view" as a description of a system "from the perspective of specific system concerns", and a "viewpoint" as the "conventions for the construction and interpretation…of views".

2.3 Transient and Overlapping Forms

This is a requirement that is needed to accurately represent cases where there is some ambiguity about how to classify some instances. Overlapping classifications occur when two or more classes within the same classification scheme do not have mutually exclusive membership constraints, allowing an instance to be a valid member of both classes. However, the strictly "binary" approach to classification supported in current object-oriented languages does not allow this. Designers are forced to choose exactly one class, thereby hiding this important characteristic.

Transient forms can occur when a feature of an object can either appear or disappear *gradually*. However, since traditional classification is based strictly on the presence of features it is inherently discrete, which means that it does not provide explicit support for cases of continuous feature dynamics. For instance, in its lifecycle, a frog will progress through a stage during which it is transitioning from a tadpole to a fully formed adult frog. In the course of that transformation, some of its features will gradually diminish (e.g., gills) and eventually disappear, while others (e.g., lungs) will appear and gradually increase until they reach full extent. Such transient phenomena are certainly common in the natural world and elsewhere and, consequently, it should be possible to model them accurately.

3 A Viewpoint-Based Model of Classification

The core of the argument posited in the preceding section is that classification is a subjective artifact that is "imposed" on a collection of entities for practical reasons (i.e., in support of human comprehension – but, as with all abstractions, at the cost of loss of accuracy). It is not an immanent property of the entities themselves. Because classification is based on selected viewpoints, it is possible in principle to define multiple different classifications strategies for the same set of entities, as illustrated by the Person example in Fig. 1.

However, the relationship between an object and its applied classifications is inverted in current popular programming languages. That is, instead of the class(es) of an object being a consequence of the set of its existing attributes and their values, the opposite holds: the attributes of an object are determined by its class, and new instances are created on the basis of a class specification. In other words, it is the abstraction that defines the object, rather than the other way around. Unfortunately, a class can only represent either (a) just one of many possible viewpoints or, (b) a forced and uncurated merge of multiple different viewpoints. Neither of these is satisfactory, because it cannot always provide an accurate representation of the modeled entity.[9] Classes that represent a single viewpoint suffer from the constraining "dominant viewpoint" problem noted above. The merged viewpoints approach, on the other hand, indiscriminately combines features from different possibly temporally exclusive viewpoints or modes.

The UML-based metamodel depicted in Fig. 2 captures our proposed viewpoint-based approach to classification. It is designed to overcome the limitations of traditional approaches described in the preceding section.

---

[9] Box and Draper in their work on empirical model building, state boldly that "essentially, all models are wrong, (but some are useful)" [1].

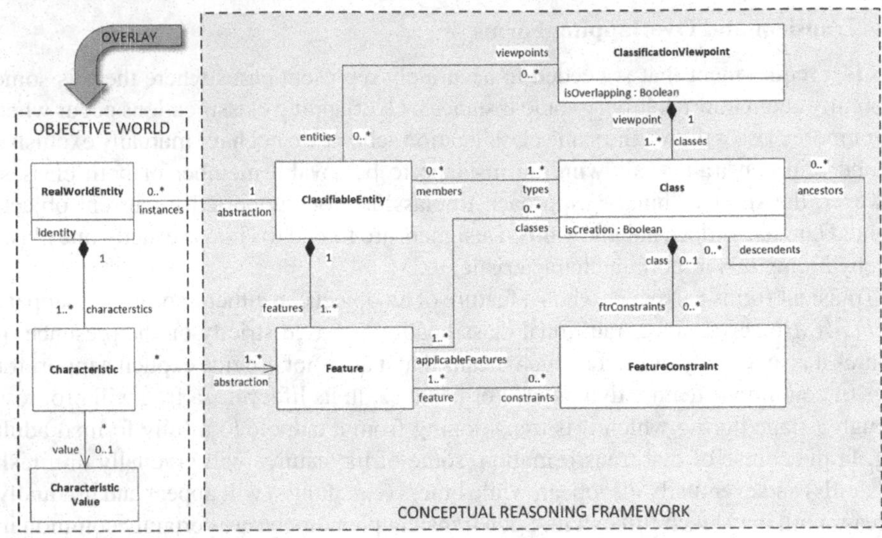

Fig. 2. The Objective World and the Conceptual Reasoning Framework

The dashed box on the left-hand side of the diagram represents elements of an "objective" world, that is, *an environment in which entities exist independently of any particular classification schemes that might be applied to them.* The concept `RealWorldEntity` represents an instance of some physical or conceptual entity or process. Each entity has a unique and permanent *identity*, which is constant and persists across its entire lifecycle. For instance, a tadpole has an identity that is preserved even as it is progressing into a fully-fledged frog. An entity possesses a number of Characteristics[10] that jointly fully define its structure and behavior. Characteristics can be dynamic: they can change their value, appear, or disappear over time. The value of a characteristic (`CharacteristicValue`) can be a complex element rather than something as simple as a data type. For instance, it could be the full lifecycle behavior of an animal.

The dashed box on the right-hand side of the diagram captures the essential concepts involved in classification. In other words, it represents the "subjective" world, that is, an artificial creation used to support one or more classification strategies that we can choose to apply (conceptually) to elements of the objective world. Thus, real-world entities are modeled by the abstraction, `ClassifiableEntity`. This is a conceptual stand-in for a set of corresponding real-world entities.[11] Each characteristic of a real-world entity is modeled by one or more Features, which are conceptual representations of corresponding real-world characteristics. Note that both `ClassfiableEntity` and its Features are independent of any particular classification imposed on them. Hence, there are no composition associations to any of the other elements of the conceptual framework. Ideally, they represent a fully time-collapsed model of the corresponding

[10] We intentionally chose a different name than "feature" for this real-world element to better distinguish it from its conceptual representation, which is called Feature in this framework.

[11] The concept of `ClassifiableEntity` can be viewed as a type in the traditional software interpretation of that term.

elements in the objective world. These could even be pure conceptual entities, with no concrete physical manifestation.

The remaining elements in the conceptual framework capture the core components of viewpoint-based classification. They specify the different ways in which classifiable entities can be categorized. The root concept here is `ClassificationViewpoint`, which is intended to group those real-world entities modeled by classifiable entities into one or more Classes defined by the viewpoint. As in traditional classification, each class is characterized by the subset of Features that all of its members share. However, for a feature to qualify for a given class, it also has to satisfy any associated `FeatureConstraints`. These constraints define the possible values of the associated features for the feature to be included in a class definition. For example, in an age-based classification of people, such as shown in Fig. 1, a given individual will be included as a member of the "Child" class as long as the value of its "age" feature is less than 18. Otherwise, it will be included in the "Adult" class.

When an object is created, it will possess a default set of features. These may be defined in one or more classes in different viewpoints. These "creation stage" classes are identified by their `isCreation` meta-attribute.

To support transient forms, classification viewpoints can be defined as "overlapping" (as specified via the `isOverlapping` meta-attribute). This means that it is possible for membership in the classes of a viewpoint to overlap. This can be achieved by means of overlapping feature constraints expressed using fuzzy logic, which allows for ambiguous set membership, or other similar means.

4 Computer Language Considerations

The viewpoint classification metamodel shown in Fig. 2 is generic, intended to be applicable to any domain. In this section, the focus switches to its interpretation in software. In particular, we examine computer language mechanisms that are needed to support it.

In this case, the Conceptual Reasoning Framework is actually realized in software, which means that the conceptual and objective worlds are unified. Therefore, the `RealWorldEntity` and the `ClassifiableEntity` concepts represent the same thing and are conflated into the concept of a *run-time object*. Similarly, the Characteristic and Feature concepts are also merged.

The first practical issue is to define how an object is created, given that it can be an instance of different classes based on different frameworks. In particular, which features and feature values will be assigned to a newborn object upon creation? The most direct and possibly most straightforward strategy is for the object to select the viewpoints that apply to it at creation time. As a result, all classes in the selected viewpoints with a positive value for its `isCreation` attribute will be scanned for their *applicable features*. If these features are structural attributes, they will be added to the object, along with their preset initial values. If they are behavioral features, they will be executed.

From this point on, there are several possibilities in the lifecycle of the created object. One option is for objects (i.e., the programmer) to choose (e.g., in response to inputs) which viewpoints they want to apply and when. In that case, the scenario is similar to the creation scenario. This may add new features to the object in case they were not already present. Objects can also "unapply" an applied viewpoint, which may either remove (or, more pragmatically, disable) features unless they are still present in one of the other applied viewpoints.

An alternative strategy would be for viewpoints to be applied or unapplied automatically, depending on changes in values of structural features or by the explicit software-controlled addition or removal of features. Which viewpoints are applied or unapplied in those situations is determined by evaluating the feature constraints of the affected features. If a feature constraint is no longer satisfied, the associated viewpoint will be unapplied with appropriate changes in the feature set. Conversely, if the change in value results in a feature constraint switching from unsatisfied to satisfied, the corresponding viewpoint in which it exists will be applied. Needless to say, this alternative may sometimes come with significant overhead since it involves evaluating all feature constraints associated with a changed feature every time its value changes. It may also lead to inconsistencies if the dynamically defined configuration of features does not correspond to any defined viewpoint.[12]

Additional utilities are likely to be needed, such as a primitive operation that checks whether a given set of viewpoints is applicable at the time when it is invoked. For example, in a traditional textual programming language form, it might look as follows:

```
if obj.applicable(ViewpointA, ViewpointB) then
    {… instructions that can access any features that
    are accessible in either ViewpointA or Viewpoint B …}
```

Although the mechanisms involved in this may not be simple, a clever implementation could significantly simplify matters. For instance, when an object is instantiated it could contain the merge of all the features belonging to all of its viewpoints (similar to multiple inheritance). But, only those features that are applicable at a given time (i.e., depending on applicable viewpoints and their feature constraints) would be enabled. The remaining ones would be disabled and, consequently, inaccessible, until they are enabled by a viewpoint change.

5 Prior Work

Problems with current forms of classification and inheritance were identified early. For example, in 1991, Michael Jackson published a critique that described some (but not all) of the limitations described in Sect. 3 [8]. In particular, he pointed out the consequences of the "dominant viewpoint" issue. In addition, he discusses the need for dynamic reclassification.

The latter capability is supported in some object-oriented languages. This was available in one of the first object-oriented languages, Smalltalk-80, which had a dedicated "become" method. This allowed an existing object to switch from being a member of

[12] This may not necessarily be an error, but it does imply that the classification schemes are incomplete, which may not have been the intent.

one class to a different one. However, this capability was not incorporated in any subsequent object-oriented languages that are in common use today (e.g., Java, C++, C#, Objective-C), most likely because it created difficulties for static type checking.[13]

Later, a dynamic reclassification capability was included in the experimental Fickle language [5]. But, this was primarily an experimental research language and was never picked up by a broader user base. An alternative to dynamic reclassification was later sought via the concept of typestates [3], which is, to an extent, a language-based realization of the State design pattern, with some additional useful features.

However, none of these prior efforts provided the ability to support simultaneous different classifications of an object, such as the viewpoint approach described here. Exceptionally, the Unified Modeling Language standard [9] includes the concept of a *generalization set*, which "provides a way to group Generalizations into orthogonal dimensions". This is, in effect, a mechanism intended to support viewpoint-based classification. Unfortunately, the standard also states that the mechanisms by which this type of capability is implemented are considered out of scope of the standard. This capability has not been picked up by any mainstream language, and is even explicitly excluded from the associated OMG standard that provides a formal semantics definition of UML [10].

6 Summary and Future Research Prospects

The core issue addressed in this paper is that current models of classification in common object-oriented programming languages are inadequate for the complex challenges that are facing modern software. The principal problem lies in the fact that they are insufficiently flexible to help us capture the complex and dynamic nature of the world that we are trying to manage with software, as is the case, for example, with digital twin models. In particular, they make it very difficult to model dynamic phenomena whose classification changes over time, as well as the ability to classify phenomena in multiple different but equally useful ways.

Classification is an abstraction conceived to help us approximate a complex reality with a simpler and more comprehensible representation. Like all abstractions, any given classification scheme is imperfect, suitable for some purposes but not necessarily for others that we might be of interest to us. In the proposed approach, the essential idea is to allow reasoning about the classification of objects to be chosen dynamically, based on (a) the state of an object and (b) what concerns us about the object at that point.

This paper is a call for new ways in how we model and use classification in software. The ideas described are quite preliminary, but they represent one possible and feasible solution. But, much more research is needed to understand its full ramifications and future possibilities. One obvious line of study is to determine the extent to which static verification can be used in these potentially dynamic circumstances. Prior work on static type checking of typesets suggests that it may be possible to an extent [3]. Another interesting area is the ability to explore classification viewpoint hierarchies,

[13] Smalltalk-80 was a dynamically typed language, so static type checking was impractical in any case.

whereby viewpoints can inherit from more abstract viewpoints, including the notion of a "powerset" viewpoint.

References

1. Box, G., Draper, A.: Empirical Model-Building and Response Surfaces. Wiley, Hoboken (1987)
2. Crnković, I., et al.: A classification framework for software component models. IEEE Trans. Softw. Eng. **37**(5), 592–615 (2011)
3. DeLine, R., Fähndrich, M.: Typestates for objects. In: Odersky, M. (ed.) ECOOP 2004. LNCS, vol. 3086, pp. 465–490. Springer, Heidelberg (2004). https://doi.org/10.1007/978-3-540-24851-4_21
4. Dijkstra, E.: Chapter I: Notes on structured programming. In: Dahl, O., et al. (eds.) Structured Programming, pp. 1–82. Cambridge, Academic Press (1972)
5. Drossopoulou, S., et al.: More dynamic object reclassification: Fickle. ACM Trans. Program. Lang. Syst. **24**(2), 153–191 (2002)
6. Gamma, E., Helm, R., Johnson, R., Vlissides, J.: Design Patterns: Elements of Reusable Object-Oriented Software. Addison-Wesley, Boston (1995)
7. ISO/IEC/IEEE: Systems and Software Engineering – Architecture Description, 1st edn. ISO/IEC/IEEE Standard 42010 (2011)
8. Jackson, M.: Object-orientation: classification considered harmful. In: Proceedings of NordData-91 (1991)
9. Object Management Group (OMG): OMG Unified Modeling Language (OMG UML) – version 2.5.1, OMG document number formal/2017-12-05 (2017). https://www.omg.org/spec/UML/
10. Object Management Group (OMG): Semantics of a Foundational Subset for Executable UML Models (fUML) – version 1.3 Beta, OMG document number ptc/2017-02-01 (2017). http://www.omg.org/spec/FUML/1.3

The Future of Programming and Modelling: A Vision

Perdita Stevens(✉)

Laboratory for Foundations of Computer Science School of Informatics, University of Edinburgh, Edinburgh, UK
Perdita.Stevens@ed.ac.uk
http://homepages.inf.ed.ac.uk/perdita

Abstract. What is the future of programming, and what does it have to do with modelling? In this paper we will first argue that, despite impressive achievements, software development now suffers from a *capacity crisis* which cannot be alleviated by programming as currently conceived. Rather, it is necessary to democratise the development of software: stakeholders who are not software specialists must, somehow, be empowered to take more of the decisions about how the software they use shall behave. We will suggest that a potential way to achieve this is that software should be delivered in the form of a collection of models, each expressed in a (domain-specific) language appropriate to its intended users, and all connected by bidirectional transformations. We emphasise the pragmatic need to accommodate a heterogeneous collection of formalisms so that solutions can incorporate pre-existing transformations, with automatic "fixing up" of their results as necessary. We discuss the advances that are needed to make this a reality, and some early progress in this direction.

Keywords: Programming · Modelling · Bidirectional transformation · Consistency maintenance

1 The Software Capacity Crisis

In the early days of the telephone, subscribers called one another, not by entering a number into their handset, but by lifting their receiver and talking to a telephone operator, who plugged the caller's wire into the callee's socket. Soon, it became clear that the number of telephone operators could not scale to match the growth in subscriber numbers. People began to point out, rhetorically, that in the not-too-distant future everyone in the demographic from which telephone operators were drawn would have to be employed in that way. For example, around 1886 the Chief Engineer of the British Post Office estimated that by the year 2000 every woman in Britain would have to be a telephone operator (reported in [48], p52). Fortunately for the author, such dreadful predictions did not come to pass. Instead, the automated telephone exchange was invented, enabling subscribers to control their own connections. In a certain sense, every

T. Margaria and B. Steffen (Eds.): ISoLA 2021, LNCS 13036, pp. 357–377, 2021.
https://doi.org/10.1007/978-3-030-89159-6_23

one of us is now a telephone operator: but we do not find the occupation too irksome.

Software development today is in a state analogous to that of telephony at the end of the 19th century. We struggle to find enough people – there are already hundreds of thousands of unfilled ICT positions in the European Union [11]. Looking further ahead, we expect the demand for software to continue to increase; one estimate [12] is that 1.6 *million* ICT professional jobs will need to be filled in the European Union between 2018 and 2030. Big data and the rise of AI make new frontiers of potential software visible, while they also intensify concern about the properties of the software, including correctness and privacy. Businesses desire to update their software ever faster. Despite their resulting popularity, agile and DevOps techniques such as continuous integration/continuous delivery (CI/CD) are far from a panacaea [31]. For example, even in a survey of businesses using agile development [47], just 4% of respondents – 71% of which were planning DevOps adoption within the next year – agreed that agile practices were enabling greater adaptability to market conditions! Capacity and hiring regularly appear at the top of lists of software companies' concerns (e.g. [46]).

What makes the software situation even worse than the telephony one is the sheer **difficulty of modern software development**. It pushes the limits of human cognition: in order to make productive use of the technology we have today, people typically have to devote their full-time efforts to learning, retaining, practising and updating their software-related skills. Universities are asked to turn out increasing numbers of students with an extraordinarily wide and fast-changing skill-set; the difficulty of doing so underlies apparent paradoxes such as that, in the UK, despite the unfilled positions, the unemployment rate for computer science graduates is above that of other STEM subjects [39]. While the fundamentals of our discipline do not change, the devil is in the detail – and there is a lot of detail, as anyone can attest who has had to develop (say) a web application with mainstream tools, after a few years of not doing so. Consequently not every person is able to succeed in modern software development, so even if, as a society, we were willing to devote the efforts of even more of us to software development, this would not solve the problem.

Impressive advances in software development have, however, been made since the "thirty year crisis" [40] of approximately 1960–1990. We now have better languages, tools, and frameworks; we have consensus on the importance of testing being integrated into development; we are beginning to understand how to combine the safety of a high-ceremony process with the responsiveness to change that agile methods can bring.

Each of these advances can be seen as (partially successful) attempts to employ **separation of concerns** in Dijkstra's terminology [8] to help manage **information overload**, which is the main root cause of the difficulty of software development, because the amount of information in even a medium-sized software project vastly exceeds what humans can easily hold in mind. For example, high level programming languages allow the programmer to remove focus from low level implementation details; the practice of unit testing enables someone investigating a bug to ignore certain parts of the code base with confidence; in a sprint, the developer focuses attention on a subset of the requirements and how to realise them.

Ideally decisions taken for the sake of one concern have no effect on any other; then different people may work with different concerns, independently. But usually this is not so (as indeed Dijkstra explained). Separating concerns is worthwhile because of the way it helps focus, but dependencies between them still have to be managed, usually manually and informally, relying on developers' knowledge. Unfortunately, we have (so far) not made advances, in this task of **reintegrating concerns**, that are comparable to those that we have made in managing each individual concern. Thus it turns out that the improvements in software engineering to date do not actually make it *easier* to develop software: they just enable the same software developers – tight-knit teams of people with a rare blend of up-to-the-minute technical, interpersonal and business skills – to achieve more, faster, than used to be possible.

In summary, the practice of software development has advanced enormously since the earliest days, so that we are now able to build large, complex software systems reliably. We have banished the original software crisis. However, current approaches to software development push the limits of human cognition. Acquiring and retaining the skills necessary to be effective in modern software development takes so much time and effort, even from the most talented people, that it is not possible to find enough skilled people to build all the software we would like built, given the way that software development is currently organised. Hence we have a software capacity crisis.

2 Modelling and Its Limitations

As we have seen, from the invention of the subroutine on, encapsulation, and, more generally, separation of concerns [8], have been understood to be important for managing the information overload that is characteristic of software development. This idea, together with the idea that, in particular, the concerns of different **stakeholders** should be separated, drove the rise of object orientation and the development of modelling.

In the 1990s many different modelling languages flourished, each typically promoted by a single guru and supported by a single tool. Eliding some political history: the Unified Modeling Language, UML [17], was developed in the late 1990s, with the aim of solving this Babel and permitting networking effects that would energise the tools market, permit easier transfer of people between projects, and generally increase the efficiency of software development by enabling decisions to be taken and recorded at higher levels of abstraction. The Object Management Group (OMG), many of whose members are tool development companies, standardised UML. (I wrote the first student textbook on it [49].) UML garnered a remarkable degree of buy-in and effectively wiped out most of the earlier modelling languages. It has since suffered a backlash, because

1. the need to get buy-in from all the key influencers (and to standardise using OMG's consensus-based process, which is itself designed to maximise buy-in) led to UML being huge and imprecise;
2. diagrams are slow to develop compared to code. It took the community a remarkably long time to appreciate the sense in which concrete syntax is superficial. We can have several concrete syntaxes for 'the same' language, e.g. graphical and textual presentations of the same information. For example, the metamodelling language Ecore has a textual syntax, Emfatic, in addition to the original diagrammatic syntax [14].[1]

Unsurprisingly, we have seen a succession of papers about how little UML is used (e.g. [35]), although in fact, developers' use of diagrams to help focus their design thinking is ubiquitous [26].

One way to analyse the problem is to say that UML has a cost-benefit ratio problem: point 1 above causes the benefit to be too low, and point 2 means that the cost is too high.

2.1 Increasing the Benefit that Derives from Modelling

Attempts to increase the benefit that is derived from the effort of developing models have led to **model-driven development** (MDD) and the related concepts of **language engineering** [23] and **low-code platforms** (estimated market size 27.23 billion US dollars by 2022 [29]). These can be seen as reactions to the backlash against UML: they make more use of tools, and hence, perforce, of languages as formal artefacts, in an attempt to increase the benefit derived from models and hence improve the cost-benefit ratio. A progenitor of this family of approaches was OMG's **model-driven architecture** [16]. This emphasised forward generation of platform-specific models from platform-independent models, and of code from platform-specific models: its underlying assumption was that important decisions about functionality could all be made at a high level of abstraction, so that human involvement in modifying code – programming – would be all but abolished. Modern, more flexible, successors of this approach include XMDD based on the "One Thing Approach" [27,28]. With an insistence on replacing, rather than integrating, the old-fashioned approach of humans editing code, they provide an conceptually efficient methodology for greenfield development, in which all modelling can take place under the same aegis and there can be a single point of control for generating code once the models are ready. If testing of the code reveals that early decisions, embodied in highly abstract models, must be revised, then the necessary changes are recorded in the models and the automatic process of synthesising code is re-run. When this is a practical way to proceed, it is undoubtedly the right thing to do: it avoids repeating information in more than one place, and recording it in inefficient ways, and uses automation to best advantage. Successful examples include the development of single-page web applications using DIME [4].

[1] Indeed, this is why, in this paper, we do not make a hard distinction between "model" (often assumed graphical) and "code" (always assumed textual).

A key difference between OMG's original MDA conception and these later approaches – with wider implications which we shall shortly come to – is that while MDA envisaged models would be expressed in general purpose languages like UML, later approaches make use of multiple **domain-specific (modelling) languages (DS(M)Ls)**, each made just expressive enough for the concern it targets and endowed with syntax suitable for its users. (Traditionally a program in a DSL is expressed in text, while a model in a DSML is expressed diagrammatically; but we have already observed that this distinction is superficial, and in the context of DS(M)Ls the deliberately limited expressivity makes it easier, than with general purpose languages, to provide both textual and graphical syntax for the same language, and hence makes it even more difficult and unproductive to draw a distinction between program and model. We shall not do so, and shall use the shorter term DSL from now on without intending to limit its scope to textual languages.) DSLs can benefit their users by providing uncluttered, straightforward means to access *all and only* the information required for a particular task; they can be provided with tooling which is efficiently usable; and they are amenable to programmatic manipulation for synthesis, model-checking, etc.

There is, of course, no such thing as a free lunch. The DSLs themselves and their tooling have to be developed and maintained and, even with the best of language engineering support, this carries a cost. The DSL's users have to learn them, and great care is needed to ensure that the initial effort of doing so really is repaid by greater efficiency coming from the suitability of the language for the task. Different users have different backgrounds and skills, hence they may need widely different languages and tools. A poorly designed DSL can give the worst of all worlds. Nevertheless, these problems and their solutions are becoming well-studied and mainstream (see e.g. [15]).

Overall, DSLs are an important step forwards towards better separation of concerns. However, concerns must still be related, so that eventually software can be produced that is correctly modelled by all the models in the various DSLs. In an ideal world, any decision is recorded in only one model, so that all the human-modified models are orthogonal, with no dependencies between them. Then models that combine information from several of them, including ultimately the delivered software system itself, can be generated, unidirectionally, from them. Most DSL engineering still works on this premise, whether the generation is done by **transformations** as usual in MDD, by global constraint solving, or by another kind of search. From now on we focus on model transformations as the mechanism by which models are related. The term refers to any program, however expressed, that has models among its inputs and/or outputs.

2.2 Bidirectionality

From the beginning, potential users of transformations recognised that the world would not generally be ideal in the sense just referred to: the interesting Object Management Group document [50], produced in the run-up to its call for proposals for model transformation languages, records that the ability to resolve *bidirectional dependencies* between models was important to potential users of such languages. Bidirectional dependencies, in which a change to either of two models may necessitate a change in the other, arise because information cannot, in fact, usually be partitioned between models. There is generally an overlap between the information that must be included in one model, and that which must be included in another, in order to allow the users of each to do their work. Thus it is not generally enough to accept arbitrary current states of all the models expressed in their DSLs, and synthesise code from them. It can, and does, happen that models get "out of sync": they record inconsistent information, and one or both must be modified before development can proceed. If only one of the models is user-facing, the other being generated from it, then of course there is no problem: we simply regenerate the generated model. However, if both models are under the control of human developers then these modifications have to be effected in a way which is acceptable to the humans. They may, for example, have to sit down together, identify the root causes of the inconsistencies between their models, and agree how to fix them. This can be an expensive, time-consuming and error-prone process, because it inherently requires the humans to understand information from outside their own model – precisely what DSL use was intended to avoid.

We use the term **bidirectional transformation** (abbreviated **bx**) for an *automatic* means of checking and restoring consistency[2] between two (or more) models, allowing for the possibility that a change in either might necessitate a change in the other. In an earlier paper [43] I listed the following three criteria as "the essence of bidirectionality":

1. There is separation of concerns into explicit parts such that
2. more than one part is "live", that is, liable to have decisions deliberately encoded in it in the future; and
3. the parts are not orthogonal. That is, a change in one part may necessitate a change in another.

Following the earlier observation about the superficiality of syntax, we call the parts "models", regardless of whether they are diagrams or text (including code), or recorded otherwise. ("Everything's a model".) Where bidirectional situations arise – and they do arise in any large cooperative software development – care must be taken to manage the relationship between the models. They sometimes need to be allowed to evolve separately – we say, to become "inconsistent" – for a while, especially when the owner of one model is making changes that may not prove to be durable [33]. At some points, though, it will be necessary to bring the models into consistency with one another. This can be done entirely manually, e.g. following discussion between the owners of the models. Restoring consistency automatically is the job of a bidirectional transformation.

[2] The now well-established use of the term "consistency" occasionally causes confusion. Consistency can be any desired relation between the models: models are consistent if the development they are part of is considered to be in a good state. The relationship between this and logical consistency is discussed in [43].

It is important to understand that, even though there may be many ways to restore consistency between two models, this does not imply that the bidirectional transformation must be non-deterministic, or must involve user interaction. It may do so, if desired: but the choice between different consistency restorations can be programmed in the bidirectional transformation. Indeed, this is the main job of the programmer of the transformation.

It has proved difficult to develop good languages and other technology to support bidirectional transformations, partly because the requirements for such a language cannot all be met simultaneously[3]. The various attempts have led to a **fragile tools problem**, in which solution approaches, each balancing the forces in different ways and making different compromises, are incompatible with one another and have idiosyncratic (and often incompletely documented) behaviour. Among other problems, we so far lack a principled way to allow **inter-operation of bidirectional transformations**. That is, it is difficult or impossible to manage a development that incorporates bidirectional transformations that have been developed in different ways at different times by different people and expressed in different languages.

Thus these model-based approaches have not (yet) solved the capacity problem. Whilst powerful walled-garden tools such as JetBrains MPS[4] can achieve amazing results in skilled hands, this leads to lock-in at personal and organisational level; it prevents the combination of advantages from different approaches, and makes network effects unavailable (although for commercial platform vendors, such lock-in gives a short-term advantage). And, despite the bullish projection of its market size, low-code platforms are reasonably seen as a "fad", the latest in a long sequence of candidate silver bullets, because "anybody coding really needs to understand what's going on behind it all" [36]: that is, today, the dependencies between concerns still have to be handled manually, which places a heavy burden on the developer.

3 A Vision for the Future

In summary, in order to address the software capacity crisis we need principled advances on several fronts.

1. Of course, we do need to continue to increase the productivity of today's best software specialists, that is, the speed at which teams of the most talented people – who can, for example, embrace techniques such as mechanised proof and functional programming with sophisticated type systems – produce dependable software. This is the aim of the vast majority of software engineering and programming language research today, but it is not the only important avenue to pursue.

[3] For example, it is extremely convenient if all one's bx have the property known as strong undoability, while not requiring auxiliary data beyond the models themselves, but insisting on this limits expressiveness too much.

[4] https://www.jetbrains.com/mps/.

2. We need to reorganise software development, so that the effort of the most skilled software specialists can be applied where it is most needed (e.g. writing the bidirectional transformations that support the integration of concerns) allowing technically easier tasks (e.g. updating a model of a single concern) to be done by developers with less experience. Taking this to the extreme:
3. We need to distribute more of the decision-making about software's behaviour to people who are not software specialists, but are stakeholders in the software, perhaps experts in some completely different domain.

Let us go into a little more detail about how such a reorganisation of software development might look.

In future, rather than delivering a software system with fixed behaviour, and standing ready to change it whenever the required behaviour changes, software specialists should deliver something more like a **cloud of potential software systems**:

- a collection of distinct **model spaces**, within which each stakeholder can safely and easily change their decisions about how the software should behave, using whatever tooling they find appropriate;
- within each model space, a starting model, which incorporates the specialists' current understanding of what the stakeholders want;
- a mechanism, involving a collection of bidirectional transformations, for bringing together the separate collections of decisions made by different stakeholders and melding them into *well-behaving* software that meets all of its requirements.

Here is a very simple example. Suppose that a system involves: a form-based user interface, controlled by a UI designer; a database, controlled by a database designer; and a report production engine, the format of the report being controlled by an accountant. Let us suppose that data that needs to appear in the report must be collected from the users and stored in the database: that is, the consistency condition between the three models, that must be maintained, includes this constraint. (It may, or may not, also say a lot more, such as that data should not be collected from the user *unless* it is needed in the report.) If the accountant modifies the report format to include some extra data, then the three models will be considered inconsistent. It might be that the bx, delivered with the model spaces, are capable of automatically restoring consistency, by adding a field to the UI in a default, programmed way, and by adding another column to the database schema (and creating any necessary migration scripts etc.). Of course, not every change that a stakeholder wishes to make to their model will break consistency with other stakeholders' models. For example, following the change just discussed, the UI designer might decide on a better way to collect the new data than the default one chosen by the bx, but this would be entirely within the UI designer's concern and would not affect consistency with the other models. We would still like to have a mechanism for checking that consistency holds.

More generally, the vision is that whenever it turns out that – because their requirements were misunderstood, or because they have changed – a stakeholder's needs are not served by the current software system, they can change their own model within the provided model space. They can then use the bx to update the whole software system accordingly, including automatically making any necessary modifications to other stakeholders' models. Only when something is needed that is outwith the delivered cloud of software systems do software specialists need to get involved again. Of course this will sometimes happen: a stakeholder may need something that is not expressible within the provided model space, or the provided bx may be unable to synthesise well-behaving software from all the current needs of the stakeholders. The more expressive the model spaces, and the more powerful the bx, the less often this will happen. As usual we may expect to see a trade-off between effort invested up front and effort likely to be required later; but we may hope there is potential to eliminate a lot of routine maintenance work and a vast amount of stakeholder frustration, by **making easy changes easy**. The reader who doubts whether this is possible at all should observe that we already have a degenerate case of it: we expect to have settings screens which enable us to modify the behaviour of software in certain small ways which have no effect on other stakeholders. What is proposed here is that we harness the power of bx to broaden the scope of changes that can be automatically effected: an open question is to what extent this can be done. Another, equally important, is "how do we get there from here?".

Summarising the argument so far: we have understood the importance of **separation of concerns** since Dijkstra gave us the phrase. We separate out a concern by capturing all, and only, the information relevant to that concern in one artefact – today we call this artefact a model. The language of this model functions as a high-level, abstract language for expressing the part of the solution relevant to the concern. This helps the developer by allowing them to focus attention on the most relevant information, and by giving them the ability to express their decisions concisely.

However, attempts to use such an approach to democratise the task of telling a computer what to do have had very limited success, despite attempts going back at least to the development of COBOL. Fundamentally this is because of inadequate separation of concerns, which in turn results from a lack of support for **putting concerns back together again**. It looked as though someone could write a COBOL program without understanding full details of what the computer would do as a result, but this was an illusion. If (as still generally happens today) the developer is permitted to *write* only a comparatively small model, but still has to *understand* how their model fits into the rest of the development, what will be generated from it, etc., we may have saved them typing, but we have not really relieved them of information overload; we have simply handed them yet another power tool with which to manage it. To get more benefit, it needs to be possible for a developer to understand in detail *just* the model of this one concern. By taking that seriously as an aim, we can get:

- benefits for software specialists, who are free to not spend brain space on knowing a lot of detail about how their model fits with the rest of the system; but even more
- the possibility of opening up the use of the model to people who are not software specialists.

One might think that it is natural to concentrate on the first of these benefits, taking software specialists as intended users, and only later expanding focus to include non-software-specialists. However, aiming at the second possibility has a crucial advantage for the technology developer. If the people using a model are software specialists anyway, and especially if they *already know* a low-abstraction way to solve the problem, then it may not be possible to overcome the startup cost of learning to work with high-abstraction modelling languages and separate bx. In the early stages at least, we are vulnerable to "I can code this directly, faster". Non-software-specialists are not vulnerable to this: they genuinely need the abstractions, because the rest of their cognitive attention is on things other than software. They therefore automatically get more benefit than software specialists do from using the new approach. This is the sense in which focusing on the harder aim is sensible: it may actually make us more likely to succeed.

4 Bidirectional Transformations

We have argued that it is desirable that different stakeholders should be able to work on different models, with the relationships between them maintained automatically, and we pointed out that this has long been recognised. However, even something as generic as UML-Java round-tripping has not been taken up as widely as one might expect, because in practice the accidental complexity [22] imposed by today's tools is too high; so maintaining consistency between models and code is perceived as an important barrier to the use of modelling [20,32,35], despite the long-standing availability of tools that target exactly this problem. If, rather than using general purpose modelling and programming languages like UML and Java, we want to use custom-designed DSLs, better adapted to the people using them, then we must also custom-design the means of maintaining the desired consistency relationships between the models. That is, we must have good ways to develop dependable bx. In this section we briefly consider the state of the art.

Consistency checking and restoration can be done by programs written in conventional – unidirectional – languages, and in practice, today's bidirectional situations are often handled that way. In the simplest formulation, we can write three distinct, but related, programs that each operate on two models m and n whose consistency is supposed to be maintained: one consistency-checker, which returns true iff m and n are consistent, and two consistency-restorers, one that returns an m' which is a version of m modified to be consistent with n, and dually one that returns a version n' of n, modified to be consistent with m. However, since the functionality for the consistency checking, and for the restoration in either direction, must then be written largely separately, it is tedious and error-prone. For example, the structure of the models tends to get encoded in all three programs, all of which must be updated if the structure changes. A bx language is a language in which one artefact can represent all of these tasks. A good example of what can be achieved today with bx languages is BiYacc [51]: this domain-specific language allows a single bx program to represent both a parser and a printer for the same grammar. Moreover, since BiYacc is based on a body of bx theory, it offers "reflective" printing with guaranteed round-trip properties, allowing it, for example, to avoid losing comments in program text which is parsed, optimised, and printed again.

The design space of general purpose, unidirectional programming languages has been extensively explored; although advances continue, much is understood about the options for structuring, typing and supporting such languages. Despite important advances in recent years, bx languages are nothing like so well understood. A handful of languages have been developed [3,7,19,37,38] and a few have had some success in applications [18,25]. However, they are very different from each other, difficult to learn and practically impossible to combine. Classification has been attempted [9] but is not yet mature. The Object Management Group developed a standard for a bidirectional language, QVT-R [34], but the standard has so many problems [5,41,42], including not only "accidental" problems but also "essential" problems with the structure of the language, that with hindsight this standardisation effort was premature.

The active Bx community, especially through its annual workshop and its collaborative events, brings together diverse constituencies – chiefly software engineering, programming languages, databases and graph transformations – and is making great progress in understanding the commonalities and differences between approaches to bx (e.g. [21]). It has also built up a useful catalogue of examples and benchmarks [1,6]. Nevertheless, the area is still desperately immature compared with that of unidirectional programming. We need experimentation with different languages to continue, but even more, we need investigation into the foundations of such languages, to improve our understanding of the design space of bx languages.

One axis on which approaches differ is which bx task should be uppermost in the bx programmer's mind. Let us explain in the special case of an asymmetric bx, where one of the models being reconciled is a **view** which is a strict abstraction of the other, its **source**. (The term **lens** is often used for such asymmetric bx, following seminal early work [13].) A programmer following a **bidirectionalization** approach [30] thinks principally of the get direction, from source to view, and in practice the same is true of the programmer in lens languages such as Boomerang [3]. There is a field explicitly called **put-back based programming** [19] in which the put direction, which takes an updated view and a source and updates the source, is primary. (One advantage of this approach is that the get function is then determined by the put behaviour, given mild well-behavedness assumptions.) Relation-based languages such as QVT-R, like constraint-based approaches [24], put the consistency relation itself first in the programmer's mind. Because this approach does not privilege one restoration direction, it is suitable for writing **symmetric** bx, where each model contains information that is not present in the other. These are ubiquitous in MDD: for example, source code typically omits the use-case information from a UML model, but includes detailed code which the UML model does not. In MDD understanding *what it means* for models to be consistent is both easier and more important than understanding *how* consistency can be restored after it has been lost. It is more likely to be specified correctly, and less susceptible to being generated automatically.

In summary, there is currently, for good reasons, a wide and growing range of bx languages and the field is still in its infancy. Unfortunately, it is not straightforward to compose transformations written in today's bx languages and this situation is not likely to improve any time soon. So, in order to "get there from here", we need to tackle this problem. As so often in software engineering, we may proceed by adding an extra level of indirection[5]. But first let us consider the broader implications of having more than two models in play.

5 Specifying Networks of Models: Megamodelling

As we have seen, there is a bewildering variety of approaches to the problem of maintaining consistency even between just two models. Until recently, most work on bidirectional transformations was focused on this binary case. This is unfortunate for our vision, since any non-trivial software system has more than two concerns! Elsewhere in MDD, however, more complex configurations of models were getting more attention. The term *megamodel* was coined by Jean Bézivin [2] in recognition of the fact that the collection of models and their relationships can itself be seen as a model (but that the term *metamodel* is already in use for something quite different!)

Concretely, consider Fig. 1 as a small but not trivial example of how models work together to separate concerns in software development. The diagram represents: a model `M` (say, a diagram showing the structure of the software to be built, together with a use-case diagram giving an overview of its requirements); a metamodel `MM` to which the model should conform; some `Code`; some `Tests`; and a `Safety` model. The model `M` and the `Code` are supposed to be related by a standard **round-tripping** relationship. For example, we might expect that the same classnames will appear in the structure diagram as in the code, while the detailed code has no equivalent in the model, and the use-case diagram has no equivalent in the code. There are several different possible relationships that might be desired between the `Code` and the `Tests`, for example a coverage criterion might or might not be included; the diagram represents that a `Safety` model, recording among other things whether the system is considered safety-critical, may have an influence on what relationship is desired.

In principle, the requirements for a way of restoring consistency between separated concerns do not imply presenting the concerns in the form of a megamodel

[5] See https://en.wikipedia.org/wiki/Fundamental_theorem_of_software_engineering.

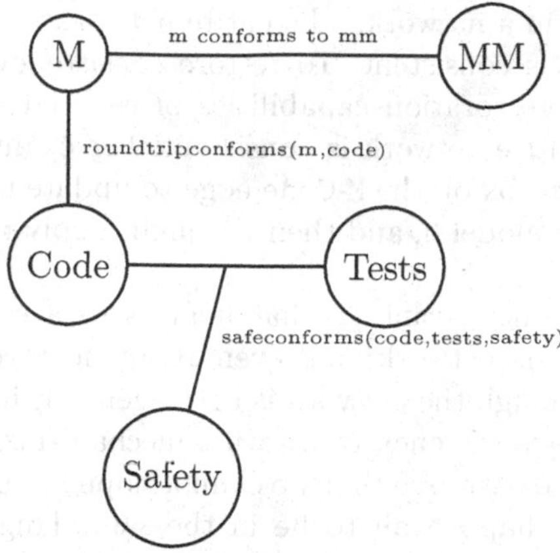

Fig. 1. A small megamodel: models connected by desired relationships (from [45]). Notation: lower-case `model` is instance of upper-case `Model`.

like this: we could in principle specify and restore a single, five-place consistency relation expressing precisely which collections of models $\mathtt{m} \in \mathtt{M}$, $\mathtt{code} \in \mathtt{Code}$ etc. are to be considered consistent. This is impractical, however, for many reasons. An important reason is that such a five-place consistency relation would be entirely bespoke, and would be prohibitively costly to specify. Since it most likely incorporates, conceptually, standard notions such as conformance between a model and its metamodel, and roundtrip consistency between a model and some source code, we would like to be able to reuse those bx, perhaps even buying them off the shelf. We expect, therefore, that some edges in a megamodel will represent such off-the-shelf standard bx, while others may represent bx written for a specific software system. Remember that, given the lack of a single best bx technology, these bx may well be written in different languages and executed by different bx engines. We should not assume *any* homogeneity or compatibility between their formalisms.

Particularly when considering what future, better bx languages should be like, one early question among many is: does it suffice to have languages in which to express consistency, and its restoration, between just two models – we say, languages to express binary bx – or do we need multiary transformations (multx for short), to express and restore consistency relations between more than two models? Fig. 1 illustrates a ternary bx between `Code`, `Safety` and `Tests`, although the other edges in this megamodel are all binary. This question is addressed in detail in [44]: here it suffices to say that in many situations it is reasonable to proceed by putting together binary bx in a network of models. Then each edge in the network represents a binary bx: a restorable consistency relation between two models.

Even if, as in Fig. 1, edges are not restricted to being binary, it is useful to express the consistency of a whole collection of models forming a megamodel by means of the edges in a network. The entire network is considered consistent when every edge in it is consistent. To restore consistency in the network, we apply the consistency restoration capabilities of each edge, in some sequence, until, hopefully, the entire network is consistent. For example, we might apply the `roundtripconforms` bx on the `M-Code` edge to update the `Code` with respect to some changes in the model `M`, and then we might apply the `safeconforms` bx to update the tests.

This approach has the advantage that it gives us a way to talk about the overall consistency of the network, and even about how we restore consistency in the network, even though the network is heterogeneous in both the expression of consistency and the consistency restoration mechanisms.

Unfortunately, it is easy to see that we cannot hope for an arbitrary collection of bx (even if they all happen all to be in the same language) to comprise a complete solution to the problem of maintaining consistency in the network. As explored in [44], several problems can arise. Most significant among them is that when a model $m \in M$ is connected by bx to several other models in the network, restoring consistency in the whole network requires that an $m' \in M$ be found which is consistent with *all* its neighbours. Even if each individual bx can restore consistency with *one* of m's neighbours, such an m' may not exist. Even if it does, reaching m' from m may not be possible using any sequence of applications of the consistency restoration procedures of the individual bx. And even if there is a simultaneous solution and it is achievable, we may not have confluence: that is, the eventual result achieved may depend on the order (and, in general, direction) in which bx are applied.

6 Restoring Consistency in Megamodels

The problem of how to reason about the restoration of consistency in a network of models can seem overwhelming. Even if we start with a collection of bidirectional transformations that are, in principle, adequate, how on Earth do we manage the process, avoiding confusion caused by the problems just discussed, viz., that solutions may not exist or may not be unique? There may be no practical alternative to doing some "fixing up" in order to make bx incident on the same model "play nicely together", e.g. preventing the second bx applied from undoing some necessary change made by the first; but requiring even a trivial amount of manual work to be done after applying the bx negates some of the value of using the bx. It is especially damaging to our vision of consistency restoration being done without reference to software specialists.

An example (from [45], referring again to Fig. 1) illustrates. Consider the bx incident on the `Code` (a particular instance will be referred to as `code` following our standard convention), and think about the problem of using these bx to change `code` so as to bring it into consistency with its neighbours. (For the sake of giving a simple example, we suppose that in this situation only `code` must be altered – we say, its neighbours are for the present *authoritative*, that is, must not be altered by the automated consistency restoration process.) For concreteness,

- Suppose the `roundtripconforms` edge requires that every class in `m`'s class diagram should have a corresponding (in some sense we need not go into) Java class in `code`. When the bx's consistency restoration is invoked in the direction of `code`, then if there is a class in `m` with no corresponding class in `code`, one will be generated. No comments will ever be inserted in the Java.
- Suppose the `safeconforms` edge requires (among other things) that every Java class in `code` corresponds to a test class in `tests`, *unless* the Java class is marked with a special comment (`// Not Yet To Be Tested` or similar). When this bx is invoked in the direction of `code`, any Java class that has neither that special comment nor a corresponding test class will be deleted. If there is a test class that lacks a corresponding Java class, then a Java class will be generated.

First, observe that the order in which these bx are applied matters (we say that they are not *non-interfering* [44]). One reason why this is so is that each of the two bx will generate a missing Java class if necessary. Consider the case that the "same" class exists in `m` and in `tests`, but there is currently no corresponding class in `code`. Then the first bx to be applied will generate Java code for the missing class, after which the second one will find the Java code already present and not need to generate it. However, it may be that one of the bx is better at generating useful Java code than the other. We would like human intelligence, not an automatic framework that proceeds in ignorance of the specific setting, to be making the choice of order of application of the bx, so that the better code generator is used.

More interestingly, consider a case where a class is present in `m`, but not in either `code` or `tests`. Here neither order of application of the available bx, without adjustment, will succeed in restoring both the consistency relations. For if `roundtripconforms` is applied first, it will create a Java class – but because it does not insert the special comment, application of `safeconforms` will then delete it again, breaking consistency according to `roundtripconforms`. On the other hand, if `safeconforms` is applied first, and then `roundtripconforms`, the result will be that a Java class is present in `code`, without the special comment, but is not present in `tests`, so the `safeconforms` consistency relation does not hold. However, some intelligent "fixing up" can easily solve this problem. What we want to do is:

1. apply the `roundtripconforms` consistency restoration first, possibly creating new classes in `code`, then
2. add the special comment to any such new classes, before
3. invoking the `safeconforms` consistency restoration.

In this way, a fully consistent state may be reached even though this would not be possible with any combination of the bx unaided. Of course, a human could carry out this procedure, manually invoking the bx and doing the "fixing up" as necessary. But in order to realise our vision of most software maintenance taking place without the involvement of software specialists, we need to automate the whole process.

Alongside tackling these semantic issues and ensuring that consistency can be restored in a sensible way, we also note that, in practice, model transformations can be computationally expensive and it will be important not to do unnecessary work. We will want to avoid applying model transformations in situations where we "should know" that they are not required.

It turns out we can make progress on all of these problems via the observation that the problem of restoring consistency in a network of models is closely related to the problem of *software build*, where both correctness (ensuring that software is built correctly from its sources, according to the build rules, incorporating the latest changes to every source) and optimality (ensuring that no unnecessary compilation etc. is done) have been the subject of extensive study. Work by Erdweg et al. on the *pluto* build system framework [10] is especially helpful: it gives us the means to handle the problem of wanting human intelligence to control the application of the bx and any necessary "fixing up", as follows.

For each model that might need to be modified in the process of restoring consistency overall, there is a **builder** which owns the responsibility of doing that modification. That is, this builder controls the invocation of any bx that will modify this model, and does any necessary "fixing up". The builder is a program: it might be a very simple one, which simply invokes one or more bx in a fixed order, or it might be arbitrarily intelligent. The effect is to allow the inter-operation of heterogeneous technologies; eliding some details, the builder's key post-condition is simply that, on successful completion, this model should, somehow, have been brought into consistency with its (relevant) neighbours. The builder provides the extra level of indirection advertised earlier.

Space forbids telling the full story of how the builders cooperate to restore consistency in the megamodel as a whole. To cut a long story short, it turns out that the *pluto* framework [10] can, with care, be adapted to our needs: provided that we write builders obeying some natural constraints, *pluto* can manage the invocation of the right builders in the right order, so that (if the build completes without error) consistency is restored in the relevant part of the whole network, without any unnecessary work having been done.

Key ingredients of the adaptation are:

- the decision to adopt a "pull" rather than a "push" model: rather than rolling changes in one model out through the network, a build request produces a version of a specified model, which has been brought into consistency with its dependencies (transitively, but without modifying any model on which the specified model does not depend);
- the use of an *orientation model* to capture project-level decisions about which models may be automatically modified (and which are authoritative, i.e. may not be modified right now) and in which direction bx should be applied (hence, which model takes priority, right now, in the case of conflicts).

For more details, see [45].

7 Further Work Needed to Realise This Vision

Programming. This vision has not, by any means, eliminated the need for programming. What it has done is to concentrate it. Someone has to program the bx, and the builders. There is something to be said for having the builders all in Java, or another general purpose language, but, as mentioned in Sect. 4, it is advantageous to write the individual bx in a specialist bx language. We have already remarked that the development of bx languages is in its infancy, and "bx programmer" is not yet a career. Perhaps it will be in future.

Modelling. Achieving separation of concerns which is effective enough to make it genuinely practical for non-software specialists to change the behaviour of software by using only their own model, without needing to understand the rest of the system into which their model fits, requires excellent support for both developers and users of DSLs. It remains to be seen how far the idea can be pushed, but it is a field which is already active [15].

Explainability, verification, validation. More challenging may be the need to achieve overall dependability of the framework into which the DSLs fit. When the consistency restoration process produces results that surprise someone, how can they tell whether there is a bug that should be reported? And, if the consistency restoration process fails – e.g. because different stakeholders have made decisions for which no simultaneous solution exists – what then? We will need *explainability* beyond anything achieved so far.

The correctness and optimality of any framework realising the vision suggested here is both crucial and subtle. Megamodelbuild [45], building on *pluto* [10], is supported by hand-written proofs, but, especially in order to explore more flexible variants, mechanisation is desirable. This is work in progress.

Enabling gradual adoption. Something which is both a challenge and an opportunity is the flexible range of possible ambition inherent in this approach. At the least ambitious end, we could have a set-up in which all we can do is *check* consistency: every builder checks consistency of its model with relevant neighbours and fails if any inconsistency is found. This might already be very useful, even if the actual restoration of consistency has to be done manually following meetings between stakeholders (and presumably, in this case, involving software specialists). For example, it would permit any stakeholder to make any change that does not break consistency. Over time, the builders, and the bx that they apply, could be replaced by more sophisticated versions that can more often succeed in restoring consistency automatically. We could even envisage a *learning* framework, in which the consistency restoration processes become automatically more powerful over time, as they incorporate knowledge of what humans do to restore consistency so that the next time a similar change is required it can be made automatically. There is intriguing crossover with artificial intelligence (principally good old-fashioned AI rather than machine learning, though that too might have its place).

8 Conclusions

In this paper I have argued that we need a radical change in how software is conceived, developed and delivered. Without it, we have little hope of solving the software development capacity crisis. I have suggested that a reorganisation of software decision-making that empowers stakeholders to take more of the decisions pertaining to their own concern has potential. To make this a reality we will still need all the old programming language skills, but they will be directed to where they are most needed: programming the consistency checking and restoration processes. If achieved, this vision might deliver more flexible software for us all; but many challenges need to be met to make it a reality.

Acknowledgements. I am grateful to NCSC/RIVeTSS project RFA20601-4214171 *Mechanising the Theory of Build Systems* for funding, and to Steffen Zschaler, Julian Bradfield, Robin Bradfield and all the participants of Dagstuhl no. 18491 on *Multidirectional Transformations and Synchronisations* [40] for helpful comments and discussion. I thank the anonymous reviewers for insightful comments, questions and pointers to relevant literature.

References

1. Anjorin, A., Diskin, Z., Jouault, F., Ko, H.-S., Leblebici, E., Westfechtel, B.: Benchmarx reloaded: a practical benchmark framework for bidirectional transformations. In: BX@ETAPS, vol. 1827. CEUR Workshop Proceedings, pp. 15–30 (2017). CEUR-WS.org
2. Bézivin, J., Jouault, F., Valduriez, P.: On the need for megamodels. In: Proceedings OOPLSA/GPCE Workshop: Best Practices for Model-Driven Software Development (2004)
3. Bohannon, A., Nathan Foster, J., Pierce, B.C., Pilkiewicz, A., Schmitt, A.: Boomerang: resourceful lenses for string data. In: PoPL (2008)
4. Boßelmann, S., et al.: DIME: a programming-less modeling environment for web applications. In: Margaria, T., Steffen, B. (eds.) ISoLA 2016, Part II. LNCS, vol. 9953, pp. 809–832. Springer, Cham (2016). https://doi.org/10.1007/978-3-319-47169-3_60
5. Bradfield, J., Stevens, P.: Enforcing QVT-R with mu-calculus and games. In: Cortellessa, V., Varró, D. (eds.) FASE 2013. LNCS, vol. 7793, pp. 282–296. Springer, Heidelberg (2013). https://doi.org/10.1007/978-3-642-37057-1_21
6. Cheney, J., McKinna, J., Stevens, P., Gibbons, J.: Towards a repository of BX examples. In: Selçuk Candan, K., Amer-Yahia, S., Schweikardt, N., Christophides, V., Leroy, V. (eds.) Proceedings of the Workshops of the EDBT/ICDT 2014 Joint Conference (EDBT/ICDT 2014), Athens, Greece, 28 March 2014, vol. 1133. CEUR Workshop Proceedings, pp. 87–91 (2014). CEUR-WS.org. http://bx-community.wikidot.com/examples:home
7. Cicchetti, A., Di Ruscio, D., Eramo, R., Pierantonio, A.: JTL: a bidirectional and change propagating transformation language. In: Malloy, B., Staab, S., van den Brand, M. (eds.) SLE 2010. LNCS, vol. 6563, pp. 183–202. Springer, Heidelberg (2011). https://doi.org/10.1007/978-3-642-19440-5_11

8. Dijkstra, E.W.: On the role of scientific thought. In: Selected writings on Computing: A Personal Perspective, pp. 60–66. Springer, New York (1982). https://doi.org/10.1007/978-1-4612-5695-3_12
9. Diskin, Z., Gholizadeh, H., Wider, A., Czarnecki, K.: A three-dimensional taxonomy for bidirectional model synchronization. J. Syst. Softw. **111**, 298–322 (2016)
10. Erdweg, S., Lichter, M., Weiel, M.: A sound and optimal incremental build system with dynamic dependencies. In: OOPSLA, pp. 89–106. ACM (2015)
11. Digital Economy European Commission and Skills (Unit F.4). Digital skills and jobs, November 2019. https://ec.europa.eu/digital-single-market/en/policies/digital-skills
12. Cedefop: European Centre for the Development of Vocational Training. ICT professionals: skills opportunities and challenges, November 2019. https://skillspanorama.cedefop.europa.eu/en/analytical_highlights/ict-professionals-skills-opportunities-and-challenges-2019-update
13. Nathan Foster, J., Greenwald, M.B., Moore, J.T., Pierce, B.C., Schmitt, A.: Combinators for bidirectional tree transformations: a linguistic approach to the view-update problem. ACM Trans. Program. Lang. Syst. **29**(3), 17 (2007)
14. Eclipse foundation. Emfatic: a textual syntax for EMF Ecore (meta-)models. https://www.eclipse.org/emfatic/
15. Fowler, M., Parsons, R.: Domain-Specific Languages. Addison-Wesley, Boston (2010)
16. Object Management Group: Model driven architecture (MDA) MDA guide Rev. 2.0 (2014)
17. Object Management Group: Unified modeling language v2.5.1. OMG document formal/17-12-05 (2017). https://www.omg.org/spec/UML/2.5.1
18. Hermann, F., et al.: Triple graph grammars in the large for translating satellite procedures. In: Di Ruscio, D., Varró, D. (eds.) ICMT 2014. LNCS, vol. 8568, pp. 122–137. Springer, Cham (2014). https://doi.org/10.1007/978-3-319-08789-4_9
19. Hu, Z., Ko, H.-S.: Principles and practice of bidirectional programming in BiGUL. In: Gibbons, J., Stevens, P. (eds.) Bidirectional Transformations. LNCS, vol. 9715, pp. 100–150. Springer, Cham (2018). https://doi.org/10.1007/978-3-319-79108-1_4
20. Hutchinson, J.E., Whittle, J., Rouncefield, M., Kristoffersen, S.: Empirical assessment of MDE in industry. In: ICSE, pp. 471–480. ACM (2011)
21. Johnson, M., Rosebrugh, R.D.: Symmetric delta lenses and spans of asymmetric delta lenses. J. Object Technol. **16**(1), 2:1–2:32 (2017)
22. Brooks Jr.,F.P.: No silver bullet - essence and accident in software engineering. In: Proceedings of the IFIP Tenth World Computing Conference, pp. 1069–1076 (1986)
23. Lämmel, R.: Software Languages. Springer, Cham (2018). https://doi.org/10.1007/978-3-319-90800-7
24. Lano, K.: Constraint-driven development. Inf. Softw. Technol. **50**(5), 406–423 (2008)
25. Lutterkort, D.: Augeas: a Linux configuration API, version 0.10.0, December 2011. http://augeas.net/
26. Mangano, N., LaToza, T.D., Petre, M., van der Hoek, A.: How software designers interact with sketches at the whiteboard. IEEE Trans. Software Eng. **41**(2), 135–156 (2015)
27. Margaria, T., Steffen, B.: Business process modeling in the jABC. In: Cardoso, J.S., van der Aalst W.M.P. (eds.) Handbook of Research on Business Process Modeling, pp. 1–26. IGI Global (2009)

28. Margaria, T., Steffen, B.: Service-orientation: conquering complexity with XMDD. In: Hinchey, M., Coyle, L. (eds.) Conquering Complexity, pp. 217–236. Springer, London (2012). https://doi.org/10.1007/978-1-4471-2297-5_10
29. marketsandmarkets.com: Low-code development platform market by component (solution and services (professional and managed)), deployment mode, organization size, vertical (telecom and it, BFSI, government), and region - global forecast to 2022, January 2018. https://www.marketsandmarkets.com/Market-Reports/low-code-development-platforms-market-103455110.html
30. Matsuda, K., Hu, Z., Nakano, K., Hamana, M., Takeichi, M.: Bidirectionalization transformation based on automatic derivation of view complement functions. In: ICFP, pp. 47–58 (2007)
31. Meyer, B.: Agile! The Good, the Hype and the Ugly. Springer, Cham (2014). https://doi.org/10.1007/978-3-319-05155-0
32. Mussbacher, G., et al.: The relevance of model-driven engineering thirty years from now. In: Dingel, J., Schulte, W., Ramos, I., Abrahão, S., Insfran, E. (eds.) MODELS 2014. LNCS, vol. 8767, pp. 183–200. Springer, Cham (2014). https://doi.org/10.1007/978-3-319-11653-2_12
33. Nuseibeh, B., Easterbrook, S.M., Russo, A.: Making inconsistency respectable in software development. J. Syst. Softw. **58**(2), 171–180 (2001)
34. OMG: MOF2.0 query/view/transformation (QVT) version 1.3. OMG document formal/2016-06-03 (2016). www.omg.org
35. Petre, M.: UML in practice. In: ICSE, pp. 722–731. IEEE Computer Society (2013)
36. Reselman, B.: Why the promise of low-code software platforms is deceiving, January 2018. https://devopsagenda.techtarget.com/opinion/Why-the-promise-of-low-code-software-platforms-is-deceiving
37. Schürr, A.: Specification of graph translators with triple graph grammars. In: Mayr, E.W., Schmidt, G., Tinhofer, G. (eds.) WG 1994. LNCS, vol. 903, pp. 151–163. Springer, Heidelberg (1995). https://doi.org/10.1007/3-540-59071-4_45
38. Schürr, A., Klar, F.: 15 years of triple graph grammars. In: Ehrig, H., Heckel, R., Rozenberg, G., Taentzer, G. (eds.) ICGT 2008. LNCS, vol. 5214, pp. 411–425. Springer, Heidelberg (2008). https://doi.org/10.1007/978-3-540-87405-8_28
39. Shadbolt, S.N.: Shadbolt review of computer sciences degree accreditation and graduate employability, April 2016. https://www.gov.uk/government/publications/computer-science-degree-accreditation-and-graduate-employability-shadbolt-review
40. Shapiro, S.: Research abstract. In: Aspray, W., Keil-Slawik, R., Parnas, D.L. (eds.) History of Software Engineering, pp. 45–46. Dagstuhl Seminar, August 1996
41. Stevens, P.: Bidirectional model transformations in QVT: semantic issues and open questions. J. Softw. Syst. Model. (SoSyM) **9**(1), 7–20 (2010)
42. Stevens, P.: A simple game-theoretic approach to checkonly QVT relations. J. Softw. Syst. Model. (SoSyM) **12**(1), 175–199 (2013). Published online, 16 March 2011
43. Stevens, P.: Is bidirectionality important? In: Pierantonio, A., Trujillo, S. (eds.) ECMFA 2018. LNCS, vol. 10890, pp. 1–11. Springer, Cham (2018). https://doi.org/10.1007/978-3-319-92997-2_1
44. Stevens, P.: Maintaining consistency in networks of models: bidirectional transformations in the large. Softw. Syst. Model. **19**(1), 39–65 (2019). In print January 2020. Online first, May 2019
45. Stevens, P.: Connecting software build with maintaining consistency between models: towards sound, optimal, and flexible building from megamodels. Softw. Syst. Model. (2020, in press). Online first, March 2020

46. Török, T.: Software development trends 2018: latest research and data, April 2018. https://codingsans.com/blog/software-development-trends-2018
47. VersionOne. 12th annual state of agile report. https://explore.versionone.com/state-of-agile/versionone-12th-annual-state-of-agile-report
48. Wessner, C.W. (ed.): New Vistas in Transatlantic Science and Technology Cooperation. National Academies Press (1999)
49. Stevens, P., Pooley, R.: Using UML: Software Engineering with objects and Components. Addison-Wesley Longman (1999). Current edition updated for UML2: first published 1998 (as Pooley and Stevens)
50. Witkop, S.: MDA users' requirements for QVT transformations. OMG document 05-02-04 (2005). www.omg.org
51. Zhu, Z., Zhang, Y., Ko, H.-S., Martins, P., Saraiva, J., Hu, Z.: Parsing and reflective printing, bidirectionally. In: van der Storm, T., Balland, E., Varró, D. (eds.) Proceedings of the 2016 ACM SIGPLAN International Conference on Software Language Engineering, Amsterdam, The Netherlands, 31 October–1 November 2016, pp. 2–14. ACM (2016). http://biyacc.yozora.moe/

Towards Model-Based Intent-Driven Adaptive Software

Daniel Balasubramanian[1], Alessandro Coglio[2], Abhishek Dubey[1], and Gabor Karsai[1](✉)

[1] Institute for Software-Integrated Systems,Vanderbilt University, Nashville, TN, USA
gabor.karsai@vanderbilt.edu
[2] Kestrel Institute, Palo Alto, CA, USA

Abstract. Model-based software engineering plays an increasing role in system development. The abstractions offered by models provide a basis for tasks such as analysis, synthesis, and automated reasoning. However, like traditional software engineering, model-based engineering must also deal with challenges that arise during system evolution, including requirement changes and platform updates. This paper describes our vision for a model-based workflow for adaptive software that reduces the burden caused by evolution. Our vision includes a modeling paradigm centered around the concepts of objectives, intents, and constraints, which define, respectively, (1) what the system must do in terms of domain-specific abstractions, (2) the concretization choices made to refine a model into implementation, and (3) the system requirements not expressed in terms of domain-specific abstractions. We also discuss a vision of integrated program synthesis via refinement in a theorem prover.

1 Introduction: Trends in Software Development

Software has become an essential part of all technological systems today [25], from the simplest household items to societal-scale systems. The proliferation of software-based solutions to complex problems introduced dramatic changes in the software development process as well. One change is that software is created more through composition and configuration [23]: developers build complex applications upon large and complex frameworks and from sophisticated libraries, or systems from existing (software) systems by making them interoperate. Another change is the need for continuous evolution and development: software systems are continuously being updated, due to market pressures, including new requirements, as well as due to the discovery of latent security flaws [28]. New releases of less complex 'apps' come out almost weekly, while even more complex software systems (for desktops) are updated monthly.

Such a radical change in the software development paradigm necessitates agile processes that quickly lead from changes in requirements to updated software. Arguably, today this is done mainly by sheer manpower, and there is very

T. Margaria and B. Steffen (Eds.): ISoLA 2021, LNCS 13036, pp. 378–392, 2021.
https://doi.org/10.1007/978-3-030-89159-6_24

little automation involved. We argue that the next step in model-based software engineering (MBSE) should focus on this problem. In this paper we present a vision for a next-generation approach to MBSE that aims at addressing this issue. The approach is based on tightly coupled models of salient aspects of software and its development, as well as the use of program synthesis methods for software evolution and adaptation.

2 Background: MBSE Today

Model-based software engineering (MBSE) is predicated on the assumption that models capture salient properties of software, on a higher level of abstraction than conventional code, and that this makes developers more productive, especially if models are directly compiled into code. In conventional MBSE, the main products of the software developer are: (1) the Application Model, i.e., a representation of the (typically) object-oriented design of an application; and (2) the software artifact, i.e. compilable and executable code [29]. If automatic code generation is used at all, the models are translated into code, but code is often produced (or modified) by significant manual effort. In observed industrial practice, models are often used for communication [15]: documentation, explaining the design, demonstrating (expected) behavior, etc., and, sometimes, for code generation, with a few notable exceptions, like Simulink/Stateflow [10], where the models *are* the code. Another example is DIME [4] where models are considered as the code, and, respectively, the single source of truth.

There are two major variants for the use of modeling languages in MBSE today: one is based on the general-purpose Unified Modeling Language (UML) standardized by the Object Management Group, and the other one is exemplified by Model-Integrated Computing (MIC) [33] (Fig. 1), which is based on narrow-scope Domain-Specific (Modeling) Languages (object-oriented design and thus UML being one of the potential domains). UML is the *de facto* standard for industrial MBSE and there are several tools available. While UML is well-defined (and it even includes an executable, object-oriented programming language), it suffers from the problem that it does not provide for domain-specific constructs: all conceptual constructs must be expressed in terms of UML, which, in this case, increasingly looks like a higher-level programming language. Note that UML support 'profiles' through user defined stereotyping [11], but they do not imply a concrete, diagrammatic or textual surface syntax. In MIC, domain-specific modeling languages (DSML) are used to express application domain concepts that are used to construct the software. Note that this approach subsumes UML-based MBSE. MIC developers define DSMLs, implement code generation and analysis tools for those languages, and then use domain-specific models to express the software to be built. The cost of building DSMLs for a domain (or a software product line) is amortized over all the software variants that could be built with such tooling. Our claim is that for large-scale development of complex software product lines, with high configurability requirements, this approach can make developers very productive and the code produced high-quality.

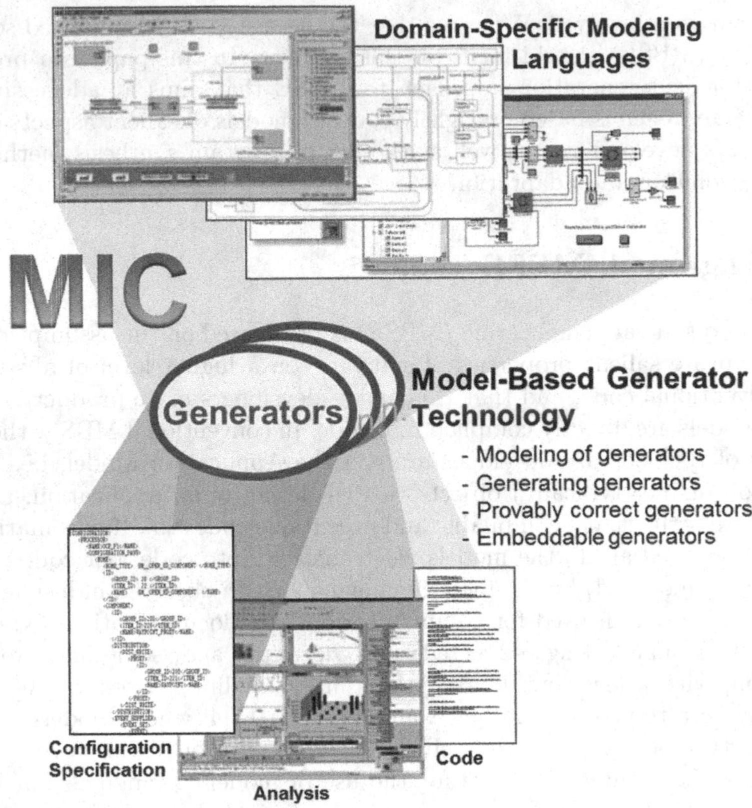

Fig. 1. Model-integrated computing.

In conventional MBSE there are additional models not always expressed in an explicit form: the model of the application domain (i.e., the abstract concepts of the 'world' in which the software operates), and the model of the 'target' (i.e., the implementation platform that could be the instruction set of a real or a virtual machine or a set of services provided by a software platform, framework, or operating system). The former may be directly "implemented" in the model of the application, and the latter is hidden in the "generation" step, which is implemented by a specialized code generator or by the manual effort of the developer. In this conventional scheme, when requirements change, the designer/developer is expected to translate those requirement changes into changes in the application model and/or in the code artifacts. If the code is changed, it is an extra effort to change the models. As a requirement change may impact many parts of the model and the code base, the size of the change in requirements can trigger an avalanche of changes in the models and the code. If automatic generation is used, the designer often has to figure out how the models should be updated so that the generated code will address the new requirement(s). If automatic generation is not used then the problem is even worse: both the model and the code base have to be updated, and then the correspondence between the two has to be restored. Clearly this is neither practical nor scalable.

3 MIDAS: A Vision for Modeling

The technical approach of our vision is summarized in Fig. 2 below. The lower part of the figure highlights where MBSE is today, while the overall diagram shows the concept for our proposed extension. We plan to realize the overall approach in a toolchain called MIDAS (Model-based Intent-Driven Adaptive Software): an integrated development environment (IDE) that integrates the models and supporting tools. For pragmatic reasons, MIDAS will leverage several research products—existing tools that are used in practice—and build upon this foundation. In the proposed new scheme we introduce a 'Model Design Language' (MDL): a higher-level design language that supersedes the existing MBSE approach in several ways, as listed below.

The goal of MDL is to represent as much knowledge as practically feasible about the software system, including its requirements, its environment, its target platform, as well as the process for synthesizing it (or its parts). This happens through a set of *models*, expressed either formally (in a precisely specified modeling language) or informally, in natural language. A key feature of this language is that such models are inter-linked, and such links (i.e., dependencies) are tracked and maintained by tools. Listed below are the various models in MDL.

Objectives, Intentions, and Constraints (OIC). These models represent, at a high level of abstraction, 'what' the system is expected to do (objectives), 'how' it is expected to do it (intentions), and under what 'restrictions' (constraints). These models may be relatively less formal with respect to the other models of the system, but they are to be linked to the other models, to provide traceability and an opportunity for analysis. Our goal is to express conventional system requirements as OICs.

Objective Model (OM). *Objectives* express what the system is expected to do. A software system always operates in a domain, exhibits an expected behavior, and interacts with various actors in an environment—hence the 'Objective Models' (OMs) shall be able to express these as high-level assertions. Note that OMs must be linked to Domain Models (DMs), discussed below. A system is anticipated to have several objectives, which may be related to each other. Hence, we envision a graph structure for objectives that makes the relationships explicit.

Intention Model (IM). *Intentions* represent decisions made by the developer based on input from the customer, about how the system should behave. An intention can be a refinement of one or more objectives into more concrete behaviors—a step towards a detailed specification; Sect. 4 below describes our formal approach to concretization through program synthesis. By 'concretization' we mean specific design and implementation choices that take the developer closer to an actual implementation.

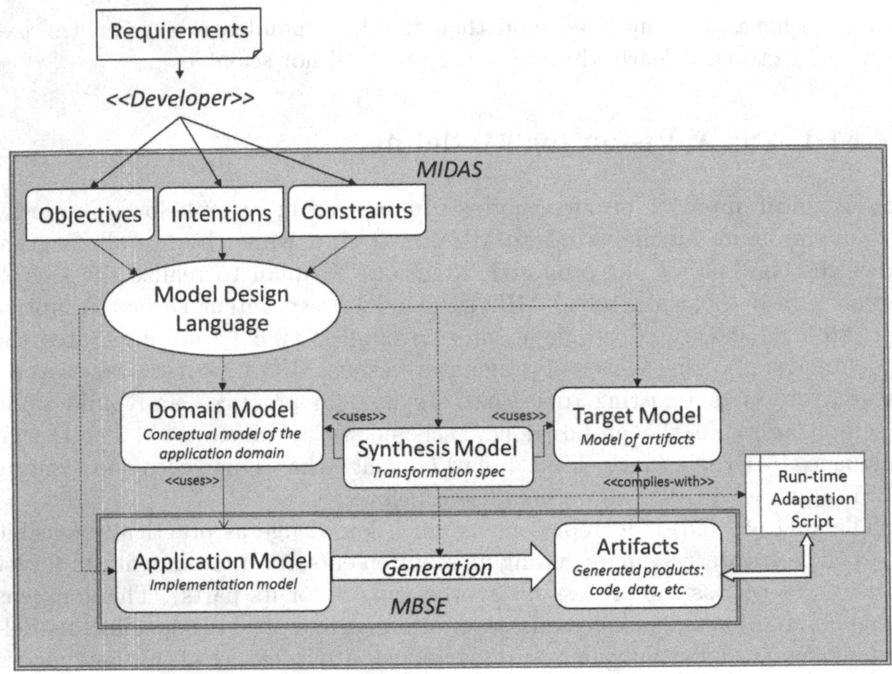

Fig. 2. High-level technical approach.

Again, 'Intention Models' (IMs) are linked to DMs. IMs can also be related to OMs—representing which objective(s) they are derived from. An IM is much more specific than an OM; it may, for instance, include high-level models of system behaviors, as finite state machines, etc. Intentions can also be organized into a graph structure, but the relationships (represented by graph edges) will likely have much more precisely defined semantics.

Constraint Model (CM). *Constraints* express restrictions on the system to be built that the implementation has to satisfy. 'Constraint Models' (CMs) can be informal (e.g. expected hardware capabilities) or formal (e.g. timing constraints); they are linked to OMs, IMs, and DMs. The constraints must be verifiable: either at design-time, or at run-time, the implementation has to satisfy all constraints. Similarly to objectives and intentions, constraints form a graph where the nodes are the actual constraints. The edges link the nodes to some system properties (if the constraint is formal) or to some intention (if the constraint is informal).

The representation of objectives, intentions, and constraints is a challenge. We envision that initially they are expressed informally, but possibly even then in some structured form (e.g., [8]), and later refined into a more formal representation. The key concept here is that these models are not standalone documents but are tightly linked to the other models.

Domain Model (DM). The DM makes the modeling of the *software application domain concepts* explicit. Such models describe the conceptual structure of the 'world' the software artifact is operating in. Domain models are represented in hierarchically organized concepts that are linked to each other via various relationships, and have attributes capturing salient properties. Specific domains often have domain-specific constraints (e.g. physical systems obey the laws of physics); if relevant, such constraints will be expressed in the DMs as well. Note that such constraints are different from the Constraint Models (CMs) described above. These models capture the designer's understanding of the domain, without any relationship to implementation. The DM is built by developers who understand the domain well.

As indicated above, OIC models are linked to DMs, as DMs provide the context in which OIC models are interpreted. The linkage provides for traceability: if an objective changes, a tool can immediately detect what intentions need to be revised, what constraints need to be checked, and how these are related to the domain concepts. In reverse, updates to the DM will enable tracking what OIC models are potentially affected. It is expected that building the OIC and domain models will take a significant effort (compared to straightforward coding). However, we argue that such modeling is worth the effort, as it helps and guides in understanding what the domain of the system is, what the system is expected to do, and under what restrictions. These models also have the added benefit of helping identify which pieces of the formal synthesis (described in Sect. 4) may need modification when requirements change. We plan to allow both formality and informality in the OIC models, to support accessibility for conventional developers. However, the developers will be required to organize the OIC models and link them to DMs: this is a critical, but easy-to-address requirement in our approach.

Application Model (AM). Application model (AM). The AM represents the actual *implementation* in the form of models, but it may also contain literal, concrete implementation artifacts, like code fragments that are directly included in the final engineering product artifacts.

We do *not* consider application modeling and application programming as two isolated activities, rather as two ends of a spectrum: models are high(er)-level programs that we should be able to mix with implementation code from the other end of the spectrum. We envision a programming style where implementation code can refer to model elements while models can contain implementation code[1]. To follow this principle, the AMs will allow the use and embedding of implementation code into the model, as opposed to allowing only models. We understand this carries a risk, as the (formal, potentially verifiable) models are intermixed with (potentially flawed) implementation code. While it is an important goal to move towards a completely formal development paradigm, the mixed approach is a pragmatic compromise that seems acceptable to current developers.

The AM extends the traditional application model by (a) relating AM elements to DM elements, and (b) linking AM elements to explicitly expressed

[1] This approach has been promoted by embedded and embeddable domain-specific languages [34], as practiced in the MPS toolsuite [35].

intentions and constraints. Note that not all DM elements are expected to have a corresponding AM, and vice versa, but all AM elements should be related to an intention. The AM is built by the application designers and developers.

The AM also has links to elements of the Target Model (TM), discussed below. The software developer may decide to explicitly link AM elements (models or code artifacts) to TM elements. Arguably, representing these dependencies is critical as changing the implementation platform (i.e. the 'targets') has far reaching consequences. As a minimum, the developer should be warned about the invalidation of some models or code. In a more advanced setting, such a change may trigger a re-synthesis of the target artifacts (as discussed below).

We *do* consider tests as integral part of the AM. Unit tests and integration tests are expected to be developed together with the system, and they will be linked to OIC models like everything else. We envision that such 'test models' will be used to verify that the system satisfies (formally modeled) requirements.

Target Model (TM). The TM makes the modeling of the 'target' or 'implementation' domain explicit. We envision that the 'target domain' is going to be a software 'platform' for which compilable source code (or other software artifacts, like Makefiles) should be generated. While the DMs represent the concepts of the problem domain, the TMs represent the concepts of the solution domain. As such, TMs are somewhat similarly organized to DMs: concepts, attributes, relationships, but they carry additional information, necessary for the automated synthesis. Hence, TM will include models that are associated with parametrized code (or data) templates that will be spelled out during the generation process. The TM is built by developers who understand the target domain (and its intricacies) well, but also have some experience with writing code templates and generation. Note that the TM may also include code templates for unit and system level tests.

Synthesis Model (SM). The SM is for the explicit representation of how AM elements are mapped into code and data artifacts (that are compliant with the TM elements). We envision that the SM will be built by skilled developers who are 'synthesis engineers', familiar with the synthesis technology. Our goal is to make the synthesis technology accessible to average developers, who may already be familiar with language tools like ANTLR [24], or template engines like Jinja2 [27].

We envision that some SMs are prefabricated and re-used across many applications (e.g. a synthesis tool that generates code from a finite state machine model). Note that the SM may involve generation of many different artifacts: production code, data, test code, etc. The SM is also used to generate changes to the running system: we envision that the requirement changes can be addressed by changing the configuration or properties of the deployed, active system. This will be facilitated by the 'Run-time Adaptation Script' shown on the right, which assumes a suitable adaptive software platform.

Formally, the SM defines the mapping from the AM to the TM. In other words, given an AM, SM specifies how it should be translated into 'artifacts' (code, configuration files, etc.) that are compliant with the abstract TM. The SM relies on the APT program synthesis technology, described in the next section.

Note that Fig. 2 should be viewed in the context of an incremental and iterative development process. In practice, objectives and constraints are stated often before a high-quality domain model is available, although a domain model is clearly necessary [3] as it provides the context in which to express objectives and constraints.

In summary, our approach relies on highly interlinked models of the objectives, intentions, constraints, domain, application, target platform, and synthesis process. The product of the development process is synthesized and/or instantiated executable code, plus other artifacts necessary for the further compilation and/or deployment of the system. We envision that the synthesis system and target models can be engineered to target a variety of languages.

4 Program Synthesis

As mentioned above, the synthesis model relies on automated program synthesis. The APT (Automated Program Transformations) toolkit [6,7,18], extended with new features, will provide this capability. We describe APT as it exists today, how it can address adaptation in MIDAS, and our planned extensions.

APT realizes the classic ideas of program transformation and stepwise program refinement in the state-of-the-art, industrial-strength theorem prover ACL2 [17]. Program development by transformation and stepwise refinement by now is a proven approach, but it has some limitations, which our envisioned work aims to bring a major step forward.

In our view, while completely automated synthesis of all the code for a system is not practical, the interactive, tool-assisted program transformation and stepwise refinement of critical software components is very feasible. Completely automated synthesis is possible if the ‘automation’ has all the skills of a human developer, but that implies that the human developer can explicate and formulate all the skills s/he has, which is doubtful. Fully exhaustive search of the solution space of algorithms and data structures is computationally infeasible, too. Hence, the pragmatic solution is to provide assistance to developers to enact the refinement and synthesis process, where the developer remains in ultimate control. For this to be feasible, we envision (and have partially implemented [14,31]) a library of generic program transformations.

In *stepwise refinement* [9,36], a program is derived from a specification via a sequence of intermediate specifications. Several refinement notions and formalisms and tools exist, e.g. [1,2,5,13,16,21,22,32]. A *derivation* is a sequence

$$s_0 \rightsquigarrow s_1 \rightsquigarrow \cdots \rightsquigarrow s_n \stackrel{C}{\mapsto} p, \tag{1}$$

where the specification s_0 captures requirements, $s_1, \ldots, s_n$ are intermediate specifications, p is the program that implements the specification, and $\rightsquigarrow$ represents a formal refinement relation; the last step typically involves a code generator C that translates the suitably refined executable specification s_n into a standard programming language like Java or C.

Each derivation step represents a concretization decision, e.g. the choice of a data structure or algorithm, or the application of a particular optimization. As different decisions may be taken at each stage, a derivation is one path in a tree whose branching nodes are specifications, whose branches are derivation steps, and whose leaf nodes are implementations, as shown in Fig. 3. All the leaves p, p', p'', etc. are implementations of the root specification s_0; they all satisfy the requirements captured by s_0, but they may use different algorithms, data structures, library functions, etc. In practice, the tree may be a graph, as different paths may lead to identical nodes, e.g. if two or more "orthogonal" transformations are applied in different orders.

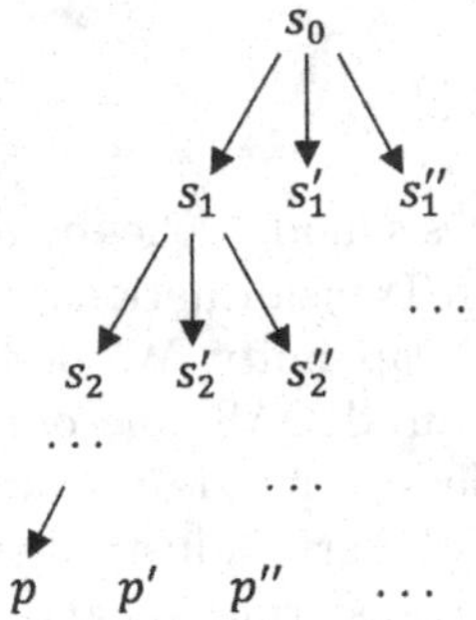

Fig. 3. A derivation tree.

In *refinement-based program synthesis*, derivation steps are carried out via *automated transformations* [6,7,18,19,30]. That is, given s_i, instead of writing down s_{i+1} and proving $s_i \rightsquigarrow s_{i+1}$ ('posit and prove'), an automated transformation $\mathcal{T}$ is applied to s_i to generate both s_{i+1} and a formal proof of the refinement assertion $s_i \rightsquigarrow s_{i+1}$ ('correct by construction').

Applying a transformation $\mathcal{T}$ may require proving suitable *applicability conditions*, from which a proof of the top-level refinement assertion $s_i \rightsquigarrow s_{i+1}$ is automatically constructed by $\mathcal{T}$. Proving applicability conditions is generally simpler than proving the top-level refinement assertion: transformations help reduce complex proof tasks to simpler proof tasks in a principled way.

In general a transformation $\mathcal{T}$ takes user-supplied parameters π that indicate where to apply the transformation and that provide, if needed, information to prove the applicability conditions. An example for a parameter could be a domain constraint that states the arguments of a specification to be transformed will be part of a domain (e.g. natural numbers), hence domain theories are applicable.

Using automated transformations for the derivation (1), for each $i \in \{1, ..., n\}$ we have $\mathcal{T}_i(\pi_i)(s_{i-1}) = \langle s_i, prf_i \rangle$, where prf_i is a proof of $s_{i-1} \rightsquigarrow s_i$. Thus the derivation can be represented as the sequence

$$[s_0; \mathcal{T}_1(\pi_1); \ldots; \mathcal{T}_n(\pi_n)]. \tag{2}$$

APT automatically produces (1) from (2): in particular, the program p is produced, along with an end-to-end proof. In the sequel, we generally use the term 'derivation' to refer to (2) rather than (1).

In regard to adaptability, consider the derivation path leading to the implementation p in Fig. 3. The implementation p is the "sum" of all the concretization decisions made along the path, starting from the root specification s_0. Besides the essential properties required by s_0, p satisfies other non-essential properties. The separation between essential and non-essential properties is not readily delineated in p itself, but can be discerned in the derivation path. The particular derivation path chosen is presumably adequate to, and informed by, the target platform and other constraints/requirements not explicitly captured by the specification s_0, such as performance requirements. A change in the platform or in these non-explicit requirements may necessitate a different set of concretization decisions, i.e. a different path in the tree, leading to a different implementation, say p'. So, in this framework, adaptation amounts to *re-derivation*. But the re-derivation need not be done from scratch: rather, it can be often constructed as a "delta" from the existing one, rendering the task easier.

When certain requirements change, the root specification s_0 changes, say, to a new specification $\hat{s_0}$. In this case, concretization decisions that start with the new specification lead to a new derivation tree with intermediate specifications $\hat{s_1}$, $\hat{s_1}'$, $\hat{s_2}$ etc., and with leaf implementations $\hat{p}$, $\hat{p}'$, etc.: picture a version of Fig. 3 where each node $\cdot$ becomes $\hat{\cdot}$. If the new specification $\hat{s_0}$ does not differ much from the old specification s_0, the two trees will likely not differ much from each other: this means that an existing derivation from the old specification s_0 can be often adapted to a new derivation from the new specification $\hat{s_0}$—again, adaptation amounts to re-derivation, which is generally easier than building a derivation from scratch. This is depicted in Fig. 4, which shows the general case in which s_0 changes to $\hat{s_0}$, but also applies to the case in which $\hat{s_0} = s_0$. These two cases are not fundamentally different, as platform requirements can be incorporated into specifications [5].

While program development via stepwise refinement, with or without automated transformations, has been successfully used in many domains, a significant amount of expertise is currently needed. Thus, we plan to extend APT as follows for MIDAS.

The Syntheto Front-End Language. Currently, the requirements and intermediate specifications s_0, s_1, s_1', $\hat{s_0}$, etc. are written in the ACL2 language, which may be unfamiliar to many developers. Therefore, we are developing a front-end specification language, called Syntheto, that is more familiar to developers. Syntheto uses a Java-like syntax, and has built-in strong typing. Syntheto syntax is translated to ACL2 syntax, and the Syntheto types are translated to ACL2 predicates. We are also developing a reverse translation from ACL2 to Syntheto, used for the code generated by the APT transformations.

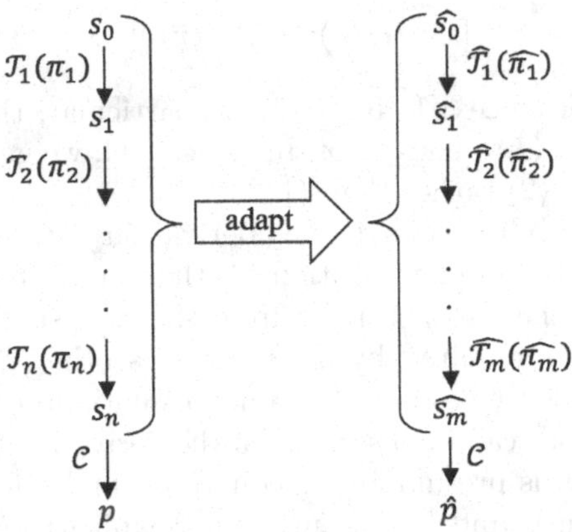

Fig. 4. Adaptation at the derivation level.

Higher-Level, More Automated Transformations. When constructing a derivation $[s_0; \mathcal{T}_1(\pi_1); \ldots; \mathcal{T}_n(\pi_n)]$, the developer must pick the individual transformations $\mathcal{T}_1$, $\mathcal{T}_2$, etc. to apply and their order, as well as (where needed) their parameters π_1, π_2, etc. We plan to reduce this effort by increasing automation at two levels. (i) At the level of an individual transformation $\mathcal{T}$, the choice of the parameters π could be partially or completely automated, sparing the user from supplying most or all of the information. Some initial experiments that we have carried out in this direction have been encouraging and give us confidence that we can significantly increase automation at this level. (ii) Besides automating the choice of π in a single transformation $\mathcal{T}(\pi)$, more automation can be also achieved in the construction of the sequence of transformations $\mathcal{T}_1(\pi_1); \ldots; \mathcal{T}_n(\pi_n)$, or at least sub-sequences of it. Our idea is to build a *derivation finder* that attempts to construct such a sequence, based on an examination of the specification.

Scaling to Complex Systems. A key question is whether the set of available transformations is or will be "complete", i.e. sufficient to build all foreseeable systems. It has been our experience that the more derivations are built, the fewer new APT transformations are needed. Furthermore, to address future cases in which new transformations (or extensions to existing transformations) are needed, we will investigate approaches to enable developers to not only use transformations, but also implement transformations. APT transformations are currently implemented in ACL2 as the programming language (not just as the language being transformed), and therefore require knowledge of ACL2. However, if we view APT transformations as a kind of application, then we should be able to use MIDAS, and APT itself under the hood, to synthesize new transformations. This could evolve into a domain-specific sub-tool of MIDAS for developing new transformations.

5 Comparison

We argue that current standards, notably UML, does not directly support the approach as envisioned. While UML includes a number of languages, it lacks the language categories of MDL. Also, some aspects (e.g. the Synthesis Model) are completely missing. Furthermore, we consider the linkage among models as first class concepts in the language, essential to the adaptation of the software to be produced. Arguably, such links are not necessarily expressed in concrete (diagrammatic or textual) syntax, but rather tool supported, hence their presentation is indirect.

The syntax and precise semantics of MDL is to be defined, but this clearly must be driven by the needs of adaptive software development. We argue that diagrammatic and textual expression formalisms should be both allowed—but probably not interchangeably. We argue that both diagrams and text are renderings of some underlying data structure (e.g. an abstract syntax tree for program text or an attributed typed graph for models), and ultimately what matters (i.e. edited, stored, managed) is this data structure. Whether the actual editing happens via a (syntax-driven) text editor or a diagram editors, is of less importance. What is important is how rapidly the constructs can be created and modified in a form that is easy to understand. One promising direction here is to use a textual representation for editing and an automatically generated diagram corresponding to the text [12].

The envisioned Application Model represents the final 'product': the implementation, but it may also include: (1) concrete models from which code can be immediately generated (e.g. state machine diagrams), (2) high-level specifications for behaviors from which code can be synthesized (using the synthesis approach described above), as well as (3) hand-written code. We recognize that not all code will be generated or synthesized from models, but rather handcrafted by skilled developers. Such code must be allowed and included in the development tools, and connected to the models (as all other artifacts in the IDE).

The main goal of MDL and its underlying tooling by the MIDAS IDE is to support evolution and adaptation. We envision that all, integrated models will be stored in a version-controlled, append-only graph database, in the style of [20]. The version control is over the state of the (very large) graph representing a particular state of the development process, with all, cross-linked artifacts stored as graphs included. Adaptation happens by making changes in various models (e.g., objectives, constraints, etc.). The support tool should determine which linked or derived models are (or should be) affected, and, in some cases, possibly automatically perform the adaptation. Naturally, this requires a high-performance graph database, however recent developments (e.g., [26]) indicate the feasibility of the approach.

A key problem with MBSE in general is that developers often consider model construction an extra burden over producing the working code. We argue that this needs to change by providing better tools to developers that can seamlessly integrate code-based and model-driven development. Using an integrated database for all artifacts: models, code, requirements, etc., as postulated in MIDAS could be a step in this direction.

6 Conclusion

We presented our vision for an advanced model-based software engineering framework that is responsive to requirement changes and the resulting evolution. Our vision includes a higher-level 'model-design language' with models for objectives, intents, and constraints. We also rely on explicit 'application design', 'target platform', and 'synthesis' models which are highly interlinked to provide traceability when parts of the system evolve and requirements change.

We also envision formal program synthesis via stepwise refinement as an integral part of this vision. The central idea is that when requirements change, the root specification is updated, and that many of the existing derivations can be re-used. In other words, an existing derivation (which concretizes a specification into an implementation) can be *adapted* to a new derivation using the updated specification (i.e., the updated requirements) resulting in synthesized code that conforms to the updated requirements. Ideally, changes made to the various models would generate a list of changes potentially needed in the formal specification and/or refinement steps.

We believe this combination of modeling and program synthesis provides an exciting and novel opportunity for model-based software engineering and evolution. We argue that software development will move from the current approach that is highly (source) code-oriented and that relies on version control of code modules towards a more artifact-oriented paradigm that is supported, possibly, by a version controlled graph database. By 'artifact' we mean all "documents": specifications, models, program synthesis transformation rules and their applications, source code, tests and test results, etc. that constitutes the body of the software system. These artifacts will be stored in a form that allows overall version control and, most importantly, linking across the artifacts. Developers will interact with these artifacts via a collaborative environment, where changes are tracked and propagated, assumptions verified, and synthesis steps re-enacted, as needed. Obviously, significant improvements in the development tools are needed, and possibly the entire interaction paradigm has to be re-designed. However, the increasing complexity and the need for the continuous and sustained evolution of our software systems will necessitate these changes.

Acknowledgement. The work was supported by the DARPA and Air Force Research Laboratory. Any opinions, findings, and conclusions or recommendations expressed in this material are those of the author(s) and do not necessarily reflect the views of DARPA or AFRL.

References

1. Abadi, M., Lamport, L.: The existence of refinement mappings. J. Theo. Comput. Sci. **82**(2), 253–284 (1991)

2. Abrial, J.R.: The B-Book: Assigning Programs to Meanings. Cambridge University Press (1996)
3. Bjørner, D.: Domain Engineering: Technology, Management, Research and Engineering. JAIST Press (2009)
4. Boßelmann, S., et al.: DIME: a programming-less modeling environment for web applications. In: Margaria, T., Steffen, B. (eds.) Leveraging Applications of Formal Methods, Verification and Validation: Discussion, Dissemination, Applications, pp. 809–832. Springer, Cham (2016)
5. Coglio, A.: Pop-refinement. Archive of Formal Proofs, July 2014. http://afp.sf.net/entries/Pop_Refinement.shtml, Formal proof development
6. Coglio, A., Kaufmann, M., Smith, E.: A versatile, sound tool for simplifying definitions. In: Proceedings 14th International Workshop on the ACL2 Theorem Prover and Its Applications (ACL2-2017), pp. 61–77 (2017). https://doi.org/10.4204/EPTCS.249.5
7. Coglio, A., Westfold, S.: Isomorphic data type transformations. In: Proceedings 16th International Workshop on the ACL2 Theorem Prover and Its Applications (ACL2-2020) (2020)
8. Crapo, A., Moitra, A., McMillan, C., Russell, D.: Requirements capture and analysis in assert(tm). In: 2017 IEEE 25th International Requirements Engineering Conference (RE), pp. 283–291 (2017). https://doi.org/10.1109/RE.2017.54
9. Dijkstra, E.W.: A constructive approach to the problem of program correctness. BIT **8**(3), 174–186 (1968)
10. Documentation, S.: Simulation and model-based design (2020). https://www.mathworks.com/products/simulink.html
11. Fuentes-Fernández, L., Vallecillo-Moreno, A.: An introduction to UML profiles. UML Model Eng. **2**(6–13), 72 (2004)
12. Heung, K.H.: A tool for generating UML diagram from source code (2013)
13. Hoare, C.A.R.: Proof of correctness of data representations. Acta Informatica **1**(4), 271–281 (1972)
14. Hunt, W.A., Jr., Kaufmann, M., Moore, J.S., Slobodova, A.: Industrial hardware and software verification with acl2. Philos. Trans. R. Soc. A Math. Phys. Eng. Sci. **375**(2104), 20150399 (2017)
15. Jolak, R., Ho-Quang, T., Chaudron, M.R., Schiffelers, R.R.: Model-based software engineering: a multiple-case study on challenges and development efforts. In: Proceedings of the 21th ACM/IEEE International Conference on Model Driven Engineering Languages and Systems, pp. 213–223. MODELS 2018. Association for Computing Machinery, New York (2018). https://doi.org/10.1145/3239372.3239404
16. Jones, C.: Systematic Software Development using VDM, 2nd edn. Prentice Hall (1990)
17. Kaufmann, M., Moore, J.S.: The ACL2 theorem prover. http://www.cs.utexas.edu/users/moore/acl2
18. Kestrel Institute: APT (Automated Program Transformations). http://www.kestrel.edu/home/projects/apt
19. Kestrel Institute: Specware. http://www.specware.org
20. Maróti, M., et al.: Next generation (meta) modeling: web-and cloud-based collaborative tool infrastructure (2014)
21. Milner, R.: An algebraic definition of simulation between programs. Tech. Rep. CS-205, Stanford University (1971)
22. Morgan, C.: Programming from Specifications, 2nd edn. Prentice Hall (1998)

23. Nierstrasz, O., Achermann, F.: Supporting compositional styles for software evolution. In: Proceedings International Symposium on Principles of Software Evolution, pp. 14–22 (2000). https://doi.org/10.1109/ISPSE.2000.913216
24. Parr, T.: The Definitive ANTLR 4 Reference. Pragmatic Bookshelf (2013)
25. Roberts, R.D.: Why software really will eat the world-and whether we should worry. Independent Rev. **20**(3), 365–368 (2016)
26. Rodriguez-Prieto, O., Mycroft, A., Ortin, F.: An efficient and scalable platform for java source code analysis using overlaid graph representations. IEEE Access **8**, 72239–72260 (2020). https://doi.org/10.1109/ACCESS.2020.2987631
27. Ronacher, A.: Jinja2 documentation. Welcome to Jinja2-Jinja2 Documentation (2.8-dev) (2008)
28. Sánchez-Gordón, M., Colomo-Palacios, R.: Characterizing DevOps culture: a systematic literature review. In: Stamelos, I., O'Connor, R.V., Rout, T., Dorling, A. (eds.) Software Process Improvement and Capability Determination, pp. 3–15. Springer, Cham (2018). https://doi.org/10.1007/978-3-030-00623-5_1
29. Selic, B.: Personal reflections on automation, programming culture, and model-based software engineering. Autom. Softw. Eng. **15**(3), 379–391 (2008)
30. Smith, D.R.: KIDS: a semi-automatic program development system. IEEE Trans. Softw. Eng. Spec. Issue Formal Method. **16**(9), 1024–1043 (1990)
31. Smith, E.: Software Synthesis with ACL2. https://www.cs.utexas.edu/users/moore/acl2/workshop-2015/slides/eric-smith-synthesis/eric-smith-software-synthesis.pdf
32. Spivey, J.M.: The Z Notation: A Reference Manual, 2nd edn. Prentice Hall (1992)
33. Sztipanovits, J., Karsai, G.: Model-integrated computing. Computer **30**(4), 110–111 (1997). https://doi.org/10.1109/2.585163
34. Voelter, M.: DSL Engineering: Designing, Implementing and Using Domain-specific Languages. CreateSpace Independent Publishing Platform (2013)
35. Voelter, M., Pech, V.: Language modularity with the MPS language workbench. In: 2012 34th International Conference on Software Engineering (ICSE), pp. 1449–1450. IEEE (2012)
36. Wirth, N.: Program development by stepwise refinement. Commun. ACM **14**(4), 221–227 (1971)

The Interoperability Challenge: Building a Model-Driven Digital Thread Platform for CPS

Tiziana Margaria[1,2,3(✉)], Hafiz Ahmad Awais Chaudhary[1,2], Ivan Guevara[1,2], Stephen Ryan[1,2], and Alexander Schieweck[1,2,3]

[1] CSIS, University of Limerick, Limerick, Ireland
tiziana.margaria@ul.ie
[2] Confirm - Centre for Smart Manufacturing, Limerick, Ireland
[3] Lero - The Science Foundation Ireland Research Centre for Software, Limerick, Ireland

Abstract. With the heterogeneity of the industry 4.0 world, and more generally of the Cyberphysical Systems realm, the quest towards a platform approach to solve the interoperability problem is front and centre to any system and system-of-systems project. Traditional approaches cover individual aspects, like data exchange formats and published interfaces. They may adhere to some standard, however they hardly cover the production of the integration layer, which is implemented as bespoke glue code that is hard to produce and even harder to maintain. Therefore, the traditional integration approach often leads to poor code quality, further increasing the time and cost and reducing the agility, and a high reliance on the individual development skills. We are instead tackling the interoperability challenge by building a model driven/low-code Digital Thread platform that 1) systematizes the integration methodology, 2) provides methods and techniques for the individual integrations based on a layered Domain Specific Languages (DSL) approach, 3) through the DSLs it covers the integration space domain by domain, technology by technology, and is thus highly generalizable and reusable, 4) showcases a first collection of examples from the domains of robotics, IoT, data analytics, AI/ML and web applications, 5) brings cohesiveness to the aforementioned heterogeneous platform, and 6) is easier to understand and maintain, even by not specialized programmers. We showcase the power, versatility and the potential of the Digital Thread platform on four interoperability case studies: the generic extension to REST services, to robotics through the UR family of robots, to the integration of various external databases (for data integration) and to the provision of data analytics capabilities in R.

Keywords: Interoperability · Digital Thread (DT) · Model Driven Development (MDD) · Low Code Development (LCD) · Software platforms.

T. Margaria and B. Steffen (Eds.): ISoLA 2021, LNCS 13036, pp. 393–413, 2021.
https://doi.org/10.1007/978-3-030-89159-6_25

1 Introduction

The manufacturing industry in the context of Industry 4.0 demands automated and optimized production lines and is moving towards connected and smarter supply chains processes [25,60]. Cyber Physical Systems (CPSs) are core building blocks of future factories [41] and researchers believe that, with the emergence of systematic industrial integrations of ICTs and external information systems, CPSs will contribute towards "smart anything everywhere" in particular also smart cities and smart factories [18]. This medium-to-large scale industrial integration implies interoperation of interconnected, heterogeneous virtual and physical entities and devices towards a shared goal [5]. Interoperation includes real time data from machines, production lines, IoT devices, networks, programmable logic controllers and external systems into a smarter, connected manufacturing systems [9].

In this context, the integration and interoperability among all these entities is a key challenge for the success of Industry 4.0. Due to architectural convergence, the holistic integration challenge can be organized in three levels [51]:

1. **Physical Integration**, handling the connectivity and communication among devices.
2. **Application Integration**, dealing with the coordination and cooperation among different software applications and data stores.
3. **Business Integration**, covering the collaboration between different functions, processes and stakeholders.

In this context, considering the "reprogrammable factory" vision brought forward within the CPS Hub of the Confirm research centre [32] and the high-level depiction in Fig. 1, we find a broad correspondence between the three layers above and the three layers implicit in the picture. The Digital Twin is there a "sosia" of any individual component, software or process, and the Digital Thread is a fitting analogy for the role played by any integration and interoperability layer delivering that ability to communicate and cooperate. Ideally, the digital thread should not be provided through a myriad of scripting quick fixes, nor through a vast patchwork of bespoke technologies, that may be adequate serve individual point-to-point interfacing needs, but become a nightmare to understand, test, validate, manage, and evolve.

In Fig. 1, the Digital Thread is the collection of blue lines (solid or dotted), that manage the communication and interoperation between the **Business layer** (at the top), the integration and communication middleware and their platforms (like e.g., EdgeX foundry) as well as the Digital Twins, both at the **Application layer** (in the middle), and the myriad devices, machines, sensors, dashboards, and more at the **Physical layer**, which may also include software for SDNs, SCADA, analytics, AI and ML, and more.

If properly provided and managed, these many heterogeneous vertical and horizontal integrations can enable CPSs to leverage the many advances in industrial systems, big data, AI/ML and cloud computing systems. This way, the

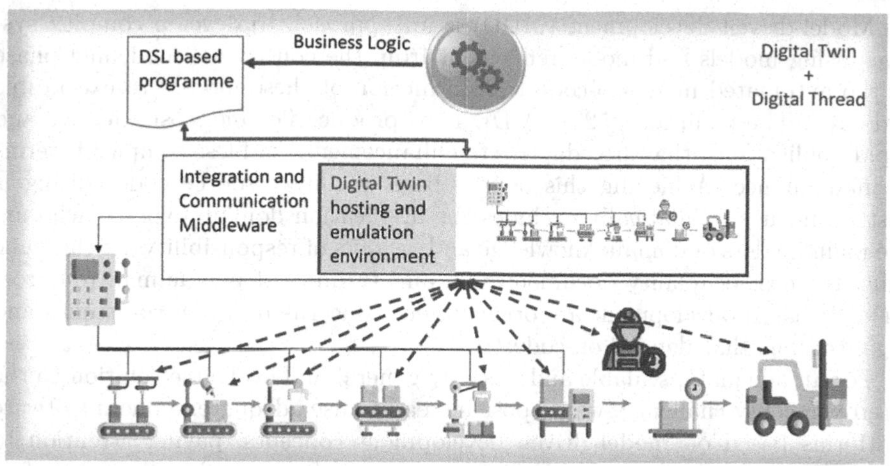

Fig. 1. Confirm HUB CPS – the Reprogrammable factory vision (source: Confirm HUB2)

seamless integration needs advocated by leading technology providers, vendors, and end-users [17] can be fulfilled.

The IEEE defines interoperability as "the ability of two or more systems or components to exchange information and to use the information that has been exchanged" [14]. The author highlighted this need and introduced best practices to develop smarter applications rather than fragmented applications [61]. Literature shows that five categories of interoperability can have quite different arrangements [49]:

1. Device interoperability
2. Network interoperability
3. Syntactical interoperability
4. Semantic interoperability
5. Platform interoperability

The effort of building interoperable systems is an outstanding challenge in the adoption of new technology. The integration layer is too frequently neglected and left for developers to solve as a side issue. This means that a number of experts are required over and over again to reprogram these complex systems in accordance with evolving needs and standards. This is a time-consuming and expensive task [45], and such systems are hard to produce and difficult to maintain. The author [23] also concluded that manual integrations between APIs reduces the agility, and that inaccuracies in the integration may also lead to financial losses and unexpected delays in production. CPSs are typically embedded into a more complex system via interfaces, so modularity (plug and play) and autonomy are important enablers to adapt the upgrades and reconfigurations effectively, in accordance with rapidly changing customer needs [24]. Trustworthy interoperability both at the vertical and horizontal level is critical for setting up Industry 4.0 operations [17].

Model-driven development (MDD) is an approach to develop complex systems using models and model refinement from the conceptual modelling phase to the automated model-to-code transformation of these models to executable code [38]. The main aim [52] of MDD is to produce flexible, cost effective and rapid applications, that are adaptive to enhancements and less complex is terms of maintenance. Achieving this on the basis of direct source code editing is costly, and it systematically excludes the application domain experts, who are the main holders of domain knowledge and carriers of responsibility. At the same time, the cost of quality documentation and training of new human resources for code-based development are other urgent concerns today in companies and organizations that depend on code.

For an adequate, scalable and possibly general and evolvable solution to the interoperability challenge, we propose instead to use adequate, modern software platforms based on model driven development concepts, paying attention to choose those that best support a) high assurance software and systems, b) a fast turnaround time through agility and a DevOps approach, and c) an inclusive understanding of the stakeholders, where few are professional coders. Therefore we adopt a low-code application development paradigm, combined with code generation and service orientation.

The paper is organized as follows: Sect. 2 introduces the digital thread concept and its relation with interoperability. Section 3 discusses the low-code environment platform we use to develop the digital thread platform itself. Section 4 describes the current status of the platform: latest integrations, ideas and enhancements that benefits the bootstrapping of components in the smart manufacturing domain. Section 5 addresses the specific questions posed by the Special track organizers. Finally, Sect. 6 concludes and sketches the planned future work.

2 Digital Thread in the Middle – Interoperability

Digital Twin and Digital Thread are two transformational technological elements in digitalization of the Industry 4.0 [47]. The Digital Twin covers individual aspects of physical assets, i.e., their virtual representation, their environments and the data integrations required for their seamless operations. Digital Twins and AI models are the two kinds of models that the manufacturing Industry has meanwhile accepted as useful. However, they are not the only ones. A Digital Thread connects the data and processes for smarter products, smarter production, and smarter integrated ecosystems. In the modern era, the Digital Thread provides a robust reference architecture to drive innovation, efficiency and traceability of any data, process and communication along the entire system (or system of systems') lifecycle. This is a new, much more structured and organized way to look at integration and interoperability. It is unfamiliar to the manufacturing world, and it is also still unfamiliar to many in some software engineering communities.

For this new paradigm to enter mainstream, systems and their models need to be connected through **an integrated platform** for automatic data and process transformation, analysis, generation and deployment that should be able to take systematic advantage of the formalized knowledge about the many immaterial and material entities involved. Referring to Fig. 1 again, data and operations from and to any of the heterogeneous elements (component, subsystem) in the picture, should be mediated (i.e., adapted, connected, transformed) through the Digital Thread platform, which becomes both the nervous and circulatory system of the overall system:

- The nerves, as whatever is sensed needs to be sent to the decision systems and the commands then relayed to the actuators.
- The circulatory system, as plenty of data is moved in order to "nourish" the information-hungry services that store, aggregate, understand, visualize what happens in the system, increasingly in real time or near-real time.

The choice of which concrete IT system to adopt for this central role is not an easy one, and it is not a choice that can be amended or reversed easily later on. The properties of the Digital Thread will depend very intimately on the characteristics and features of the IT platform on which it bases: whatever the IT platform does not support will be difficult to overlay a posteriori, and whatever is easy in that platform will likely be adopted and become mainstream for the community of users.

Bearing in mind all the desired characteristics, we chose DIME [8] as the IT platform of choice underlying the Digital Thread solution.

3 The Underlying Low-Code Development Environment

DIME is an Eclipse based graphical modeling environment developed with the Cinco SCCE Meta Tooling Suite [42] It is a low-code application development environment that follows the philosophy of OTA (One Thing Approach) [34] and the eXtreme Model Driven Development paradigm [36,37] to support the design, development, and deployment of (originally web) applications in an agile way. DIME empowers application domain experts that are not proficient coders/programmers to fully participate in the entire design, development and evolution process because it supports easy modelling, done by means of drag and drop of pre-existing components. For separation of concerns, DIME supports several model types that express distinct perspectives on the same comprehensive model. This "write once" rule is the essence of the coherence by construction principle central to the One Thing Approach. The DIME model types encompass:

- A **Data model**, which covers the persistence layer (both types and relations) of the application in a form similar to a UML class diagram.
- A collection of **Process models**, that define the business logic on the basis of internal and external libraries of basic functionalities provided by means of the

Native DSL mechanism. Each DSL exposes a collection of SIBs (for Service Independent Building blocks), that are reusable, instantiable and executable modeling components with either an associated code implementation or an associated hierarchical process model.
- A collection of **GUI models**, defining the elements (look and feel, actions and navigation) of the pages of the web application, and
- **Security and Access control models**, mainly handling the security and access permission aspects of the application.

This is different, for example, from the standard UML models [50]: UML and related tools support a variety of different model types (static, like UML class diagrams and DIME's Data model, and dynamic like UML's activity diagrams and DIME's process models) serving different purposes, but those models/model types are not connected among each other. Therefore, it is very easy in UML to breach consistency of the overall model collection, because changes do not propagate from one model to the other.

We value DIME's characteristics of open source, flexibility, ease of extension, support of high-assurance software quality, agility, service-oriented approach, and containerization. For the specific low-code support, its model-driven approach is based on DSLs at two levels:

1. **Language DSLs**, as a mechanism to design and implement the application design environment itself, i.e., the Integrated Modeling Environment (IME), and
2. **Application domain DSLs**, at application design time. We want to use **Native DSLs** as the means to integrate and expose collections of capabilities offered by end devices and other sources of functionalities to the application designers, and **Process DSLs** as the means to foster reuse of medium and large grained business logic across applications.

As different models cover different aspects of the target application, to ensure the intended behavior each model of the application is validated at compile time both at DSL and platform level for syntactic and semantic errors. After validation, these models act as input for subsequent model-to-code transformation phases. The key design principles of DIME are simplicity [39], agility [35] and quality assurance [59], hence, DIME is a promising "game changer" low code development environment (LCDE) for the realization of sophisticated web applications in tremendously shorter development cycles.

4 Digital Thread Platform: The Current Status

We target the application domain of advanced manufacturing including manufacturing analytics. Accordingly, we intend to support the conception, design and implementation of a set of applications, like for example robotics navigation and control, proactive maintenance, MES monitoring, but also analytics dashboards that analyse or summarise in real time or near-real time data provenient

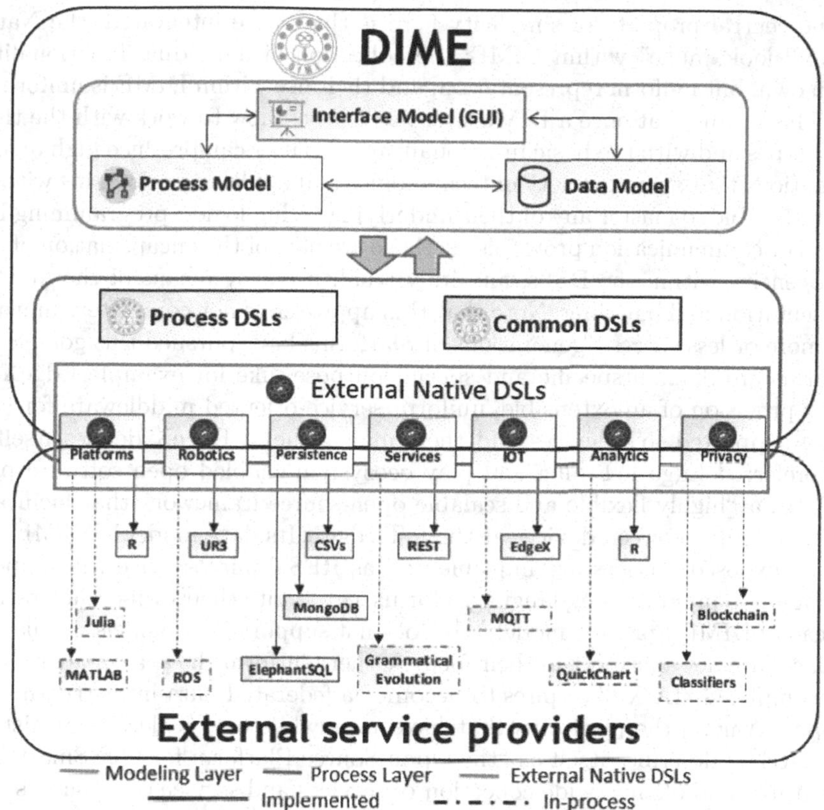

Fig. 2. Architecture Overview of DIME and Custom DSLs

from various systems and subsystems of a complex, possibly distributed production plant. In this context, data, processing and communications are expected to concern a large variety of devices, data sources, data storage technologies, communication protocols, analytics or AI technologies and tools, visualization tools, and more. This is where the integration of external native DSLs plays a key role. The current architecture of the Digital Thread platform is depicted in Fig. 2.

We see that DIME's **Language DSL**, used to design the applications, encompasses for the moment in the advanced manufacturing setting primarily the Data, Process and GUI models.

We also see that already a significant variety of external platforms (like EdgeX for IoT), technologies (like REST services, or R for analytics) and tools (like the UR family of robots) have been integrated. All these are part of the **Application DSL** layer mentioned in Sect. 3, including quite a number of **Native DSLs** external to DIME.

The central property of simplicity here is that, once integrated, the Native DSLs all look "alike" within DIME: the collection of individual functionalities has an own, but uniform representation, and their use within DIME is uniform as well. This means that once a DIME user has learned how to work with the three model types and with the basic functionalities, this user can produce high quality applications that span a variety of technologies and application domains without need to be able to master any of their underlying technologies, programming languages, or communication protocols, as these are part of the encapsulation of this heterogeneity within the DSLs, and its virtualization by means of the uniform representation and handling. Note that this approach is not completely unusual: with more or less success, generations of platforms have pursued this goal. Some platforms are domain specific and special purpose, like for example EdgeX [1] for the provision of an extensible, uniform service-oriented middleware for (any of the) supported IoT devices and their management. EdgeX defines itself as "the preferred Edge IoT plug and play ecosystem-enabled open software platform" [1], a "highly flexible and scalable open-source framework that facilitates interoperability between devices at the IoT edge". Its data model is YAML profiles, its exposed services are implemented as REST microservices, it supports the C and Go programming languages for users to write their own orchestrations (instead of DIME's process models). It does not support GUI models as this user interfaces are not an aspect in their focus. Other platforms have a broader scope. For example, GAIA-X [3] aspires to become "a federated data infrastructure for Europe". Among the platforms that have meanwhile over a decade of history, FI-WARE [2] describes itself as "the Open-Source Platform for Our Smart Digital Future" and offers a wide collection of services and service components that can be reused by application developers.

They all require programming ability, none of them offers a low-code approach, they all provide collections of reusable components, and do not envisage support for the orchestration on top. Their view is the bottom-up approach of component provision, that an expert will then somehow orchestrate.

In this respect, our value proposition sits clearly at the upper, application development layer, where we see the interoperability challenge truly reside.

We also see ourselves as systematic users of such pre-existing platforms, who are for us indeed welcome providers of Native DSLs. In this context, a number of integrations in DIME relevant to the advanced manufacturing domain have already been addressed.

Seen from an **Application domain** point of view, for example, the following have already been integrated:

- A IoT through (some parts of) EdgeX [19,20]
- Robotics through the UR command language [32]
- Persistency layer through various data storage alternatives, from CSV files, to relational (PostgreSQL) and no-SQL (MongoDB) databases (own work)
- Cloud services [10]
- Data analytics with R libraries (own work)

and own work is ongoing on

Table 1. SIBs information for REST services integration.

SIB name	Input(s)	Output(s)	Explanation
Rest_read_str_str	Url Input_var Input_val Output_var	Output_val (single var)	This SIB accepts inputs required to initiate the communication with an external REST service and receives a single variable as result
Rest_read_str_list	Url Input_var Input_val Output_var	Output_val (array/list)	This SIB accepts inputs required to initiate the communication with an external REST service, receives as result an array or a list and feeds it to the subsequent SIB for iterative processing of the elements

- some forms of AI and Machine Learning (classifiers, Grammatical Evolution [15], and more)
- Robotics through ROS, additional to [12,21,32]
- Distributed Ledger Technologies through blockchain
- Visualization tools with, e.g., Quickchart

Seen from a **Technology portfolio** point of view,

- REST services [10]
- R, seen as a programming language (own work)

are already supported, and the next months will see own work on

- Matlab and Julia, as programming languages/tools for simulations
- MQTT and other native IoT protocols, as in some cases it is impractical to have to use EdgeX.

In the following, we will provide some details on a few selected examples of these integrations.

4.1 REST Services

A case study [10] details a generic extension mechanism, where two LCDE platforms based on formal models were extended following the analogy of microservices. This extended the capabilities of DIME by integrating cloud and web services thorough REST. RESTful APIs are a standardized way how applications can communicate, firstly described by Roy in his PhD Thesis [13], have become one of the most used APIs schemas. DIME uses REST to share information between the front and the back end. While the commands are encoded via the widely supported HTTP standard, data can be exchanged in many formats. The most common data format is the Java Script Object Notation (JSON), but also Extended Markdown Language (XML) and others can be used.

In this context, this new DIME DSL allows to act as client for those APIs, i.e., to send request to external applications and to decode JSON responses into the data domain of DIME. Table 1 shows a list of sample SIBs with relevant IOs and explanation.

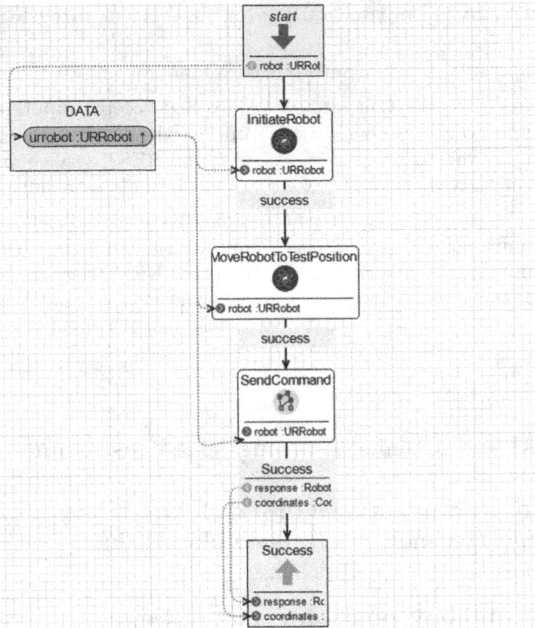

Fig. 3. DIME Process for the UR robot position control

4.2 Robotics with the UR Language

UR3 is a well-known lightweight collaborative robotic arm designed to work on assembly lines and production environments in the smart manufacturing context. The robotic arm is not only easy to install but has a simple command language to program all the tasks required, with a tethered tablet. The paper [32] showed how to build a remote controller through a DIME Web application that manages the remote communication with UR cobots and the commands through a UR-Family native DSL. Figure 3 shows the hierarchical process model in DIME for the outer working of the controller: the robot is initialized (started and ready to respond), it is sent to an initial position to test the correct functioning of the command channel, then the program with the real task is uploaded (this is itself a DIME a process) and the communication is then closed upon execution completion. Table 2 shows a list of sample SIBs with relevant IOs and explanation.

4.3 Data Management via Files and External Databases

DIME supports basic files handling operations, sufficient for text and Comma Separated Value (CSV) files. However, handling large datasets requires coordination with dedicated structured or non-structured databases. Recent work integrates MongoDB Atlas and Elephant SQL, two fully managed NOSQL cloud databases, and the PostgreSQL database service. The integrations use the MDD approach to provide functionalities to import and export data from/to these

Table 2. SIBs information for robotic arm integration.

SIB name	Input(s)	Output(s)	Explanation
InitiateRobot	No input	result (boolean)	The SIB does not need any input. It reads the robotic configurations from a pre-defined location, initiates a connection with the robotic arm and returns a boolean status code according to the execution outcome
MoveRobotToTestPosition	No input	result (boolean)	The SIB reads predefined coordinates from the application code, sends them to the robotic arm over a network connection. After the mechanical movement, it returns the according boolean status code
MoveCoordinatesRobot	x y z ax ay az	result (boolean)	The SIB accepts a set of coordinates (3D position, 3 angles) as input, sends them to the robotic arm requesting it to move to this position, then returns a boolean status code
StopRobot	No input	result (boolean)	The SIB sends to the robotic arm the stop command, with instructions to shut down and stop the communication, and returns a boolean status code

storage alternatives - an essential capability for the data interoperability and data migration in the Digital Thread platform. Table 3 shows a list of sample SIBs from the MongoDB integration with the relevant IOs and explanations.

4.4 Analytics with R

DIME is built upon J2EE and supports all its functionalities and capabilities. However, specialized languages and platforms like MATLAB for simulations and R for data analytics are optimized for those tasks and need to be supported in a proper Digital Thread platform. We recently extended DIME with the R environment by encapsulation through a Native DSL shown in Table 4. Figure 4 shows the runtime architecture: the application and the R environment are deployed in two different docker containers. The Rserve library is the entry point of the R environment, it handles all the external communication using TCP/IP. DIME uses this mechanism to provide the R data analytics capabilities.

The impact of having a platform mindset is that the functionality needs to be implemented only once and is reusable across multiple domains by very different domain experts, as illustrated in Fig. 5 and Fig. 6. The same plot_R_histogram SIB is used in fact in Fig. 5 (left) with a manufacturing domain dataset to draw

Table 3. SIBs information for external databases (MongoDB) integration

SIB name	Input(s)	Output(s)	Explanation
ConnectMongoDB	ConnectionString	result (boolean)	The SIB accepts as input a ConnectionString containing the address and credentials of the server. The boolean result tells whether or not the connection is successful
ReadfromDB	projectName databaseName attributeID	result	The SIB accepts the relevant project, database and attribute names and returns the result of the query as a single or multiple tuples

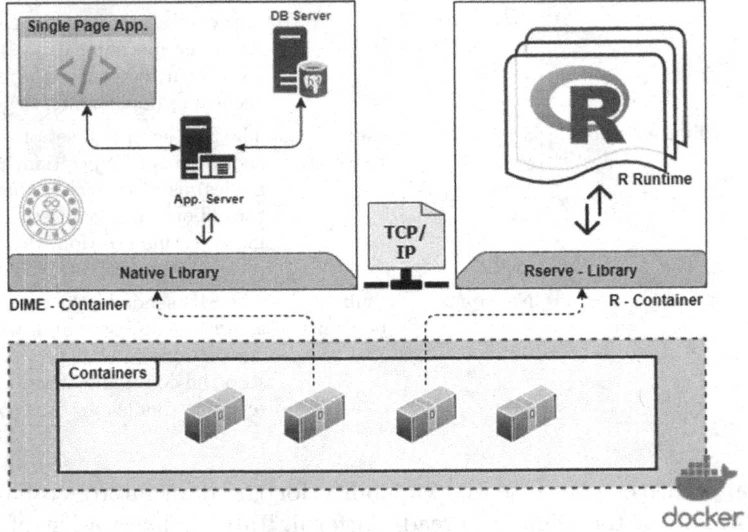

Fig. 4. Runtime infrastructure of DIME and R - environment

the histogram of manufacturing fitting failures per installation year (left), and in Fig. 6 on the Irish census data of 1901: in this history/humanities domain the same SIB is used to visualize the breakdown of the 1901 population by age.

5 Programming: What's Next?

Considering the questions posed to the authors in this Special Track, we answer them briefly from the point of view of the technologies described in this paper, considering also our experience in projects and education.

1. *What are the trends in classical programming language development?, both wrt. applications programming and systems/embedded programming?*
   While the state of the art in these domains is still dominated by traditional,

Table 4. SIBs information for the R – Environment integration.

SIB name	Input(s)	Output(s)	Explanation
execute_R_instructios	instruction	result	The SIB accepts a single R – language instruction as input and returns the execution result (if there is any) from the R – environment
execute_R_file	file_name	result	The SIB accepts a filename as input, executes the batch of R instructions contained in that file in the R environment and returns the execution result
plot_R_histogram	file_name col_name title x_label y_label color	image	The SIB accepts the dataset, parameters and formatting details as input, generates a histogram in the R environment and returns the resulting image
plot_R_wordcloud	file_name col_nam min_frequency max_words	image	The SIB accepts the dataset, parameters and specification details as input, generates a word cloud in the R environment and returns the resulting image

hand-coded software, the low-code development wave is reaching industry adoption and a certain degree of maturity. So far it is more prominent in the general application programming and not yet in the CPS/embedded systems domain, but that is in our opinion a matter of diffusing across communities. We are surely working to reach the embedded systems, CPS and Industry 4.0 industrial adopters for our methods.

2. *What are the trends in more experimental programming language development, where focus is on research rather than adoption? This includes topics such as e.g. program verification, meta-programming and program synthesis.* In this context, we see the evolution of meta-programming from the classic and traditional UML-driven community and mentality, that we see still prevail in recent surveys [46], towards the more radical approach promoted by Steffen et al. via Language Driven Engineering [54] and purpose driven collaboration using purpose specific languages (PSLs) [64]. This is a powerful, yet still niche, area of research and adoption. In this line of thought, also [6] advocates intent-based approaches and platforms as a way of channelling complexity by focusing on what matters. As adopters of the LDE and DSLs paradigms through the use of the Cinco-products DIME and Pyro/Pyrus [62,63], we see the advantages and the power of these new paradigms and tools. The need to understand the platforms, the various levels of "meta" and their interplay, which needs to be respected and embraced, require more understanding of the interna of these paradigms, their implementations, and also the limitations imposed by

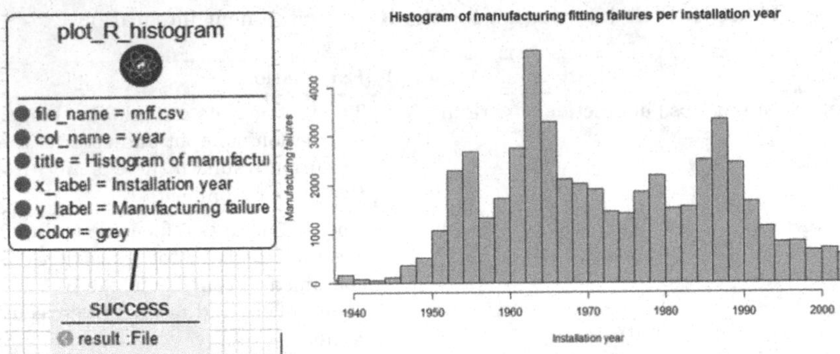

Fig. 5. Histogram plotting in R: SIB instance in the Manufacturing domain (manufacturing fitting failures per year)

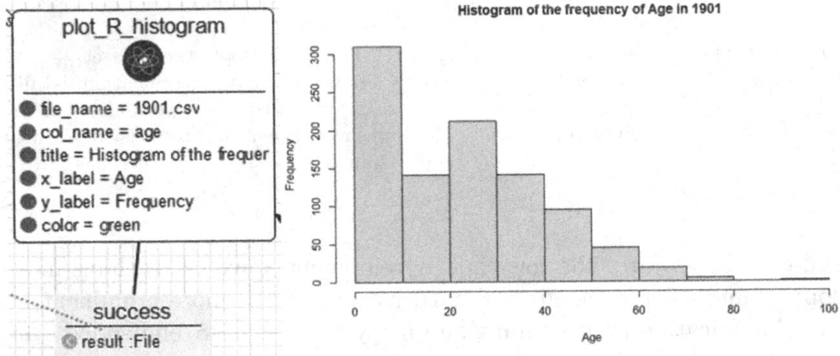

Fig. 6. Histogram plotting in R: SIB instance in the humanities domain (1901 census population breakdown by age)

the languages and platforms they at the end based upon (like Eclipse, E-core, and more). This is also underlined by Lethbridge [26], who provides also recommendations for the next generation of Low-code platforms. Core advantages of model-driven and low-code taken together are in the rapidity of evolution, and the precision of the generated artefacts. Taking out the human factor from a number of steps in the software implementation process may eliminate some genial solutions, but it also eliminates a wealth of errors, misunderstandings, and subjective local decisions that may be incoherent with other local decisions elsewhere. This enforced "uniformity by generation" has the advantage of enforcing a standard across the generated code base, and a generation standard is less unpredictable and easier to maintain and evolve.

In terms of program synthesis, we have a long experience in synthesis of workflows [33], of mashups and web services [29,31], of applications in robotics and bioinformatics [22,30] and of benchmark programs with well defined semantic profiles [55]. The potential for application to low-code and in particular no-code development environments that support a formal methods-underpinned semantics is certainly enticing. The fact is, so far the popular platforms of that kind do not have a formal semantics, and in this sense the Cinco-DIME-Pyro family of platforms is indeed quite unique.

3. *What role will domain-specific languages play and what is the right balance between textual and graphical languages?*
Concerning DSLs, we are keen adopters of them both at the language design level (as in DIME) and at the application domain level, with the External native DSLs. In our experience, they are useful to address the knowledge, the terminology and the concerns of both programmers and non-programmer stakeholders in a collaborative application development team. They are a key element of the bridge building [28] so necessary to get the right things right. Currently, most domain specific languages are at the coding level and do not leverage a model driven approach at the platform level. On the DSL side, the internal DSLs built in Scala of [16] address specific aspects in the design of embedded systems. They are an attractive step towards the preparation of abstractions that can connect well with the modelling level. The construction of meta-models behind these DSLs is challenging, since they must capture all the domain knowledge, i.e. provide both semantic and syntactic rules. For example, Ktrain [27] is a popular coding level DSL: a python wrapper that encapsulates Tensor Flow functionalities and facilitates developers to augment machine learning tasks with fewer lines of python code.
We see the graphical presentation of, specifically, coordination languages as an advantage for those tasks that privilege evidence and intuition. In this sense, "seeing" a workflow and a dataflow in a native representation as in DIME and Pyrus exposes some errors in a more self-evident way than if this representation had to be first derived from the linear syntax of customary code. Extracting again the Control Flow Graph and the Dataflow Graph, e.g., is common practice to then analyze dependencies or do the meanwhile well established program analysis and verification. We see an advantage to use them as the explicit, mathematically correct, representation facing the designers rather than to extract them from the traditional program code where they are only implicitly present.

4. *What is the connection between modeling and programming?*
In the light of the above, the connection is tight between, e.g., the program models used in DIME and the code they represent. We are here concentrating on the software that enables the operation, in particular the interoperation and control, of applications and systems, and therefore we do not delve into the kind of cyberphysical systems modelling that concerns the physics, mechanics, and general simulation models.
In terms of our own experience, being able to cover a variety of models in a single IME is a great advantage. The METAFrame [56] and jABC platforms [57] supported only process models, and even in DyWA [43] the integration between data model and process models happened through import/export

across two tools. In comparison, the current integration of language DSLs in DIME provides a level of comfort, ease of development and built-in checks that makes DIME a success in our teaching of agile development to undergraduates and postgraduates.

5. *Will system development continue to be dominated by programming or will there be radical changes in certain application areas/generally? E.g. driven by breakthroughs in AI and machine learning techniques and applications.* Next to the traditional hand-coded programming and the full AI/ML based approach, we see a significant and growing role for the XMDD style of modelling [36,37], that we see as an intermediate paradigm, more controllable, analyzable and explainable than those based on AI/ML. In our opinion it covers the sweet spot between these two schools of thought and practice. Several other approaches seem to inhabit this middle too: CaaSSET [40] is a Context-as-a-Service based framework to ease the development of context services. The transformation into executable services is semi-automatic. Agent-based modelling paradigm [53] is another popular approach to increase the development productivity in simulation environments.
In terms of AI support, for example, Xatkit [11], still in early stages of development, increases the reusability of chat bots by evolving NLP/NLU engine for text analytics. At the language level they support several versions of bots, but the generation of chatbots from existing data sources at the framework level is in future plans.
In terms of trends that have an influence on the programming and modelling philosophy, service orientation and more recently microservices play a significant role. This architectural style that tries to focus on building single-function modules with well-defined interfaces and operations can be seen in part as an evolution of web services [7], in a trend towards the production of fine-grained systems [44] that seems to conceptually align with the growing attention to limiting scope in order to tame complexity. There are graphical approaches [48], but mostly they use standard programming languages. Dedicated programming languages like Jolie [4] offer native abstractions for the creation and composition of services, but add to the layers of infrastructure needed to develop and then execute microservices. Here, we see our abstraction as one level higher, so that we integrate microservices as simply just one additional flavour of decentralized execution [10], building on previous experience with Webservices and WSDL.

6. *Is teaching classical programming as third discipline sensible/required?* We would advocate that an XMDD approach based on DSLs as we have presented is easier to understand, largely (programming) language and application domain independent. In our approach, the largest part of these technical, infrastructural and knowledge layers are dealt with by IT and programming professionals who integrate the domains and this way encapsulate them. What users do see, in terms of Native DSLs and the coordination layer, has a domain specific meaning but a language and domain independent general syntax and

semantics. Accordingly, we would consider it a better choice of abstraction level to bring to the masses of professionals as third discipline than the traditional programming in one paradigm/language, which is necessarily a very specialized choice.
There are also other frameworks in the making: for example, Aurera [58] is a low-code platform for automating business processes in manufacturing. It is standalone desktop system that addresses the challenges of frequent changes to IT solutions. It is however still in early stages of development and does not support communication with external systems.

7. *Can we imagine something like programming for everybody?*
Yes, we can! And the XMDD paradigm for Low-code and no-code application development is in our experience a strong candidate toward that aim.

6 Conclusion and Outlook

We addressed the principles, the architecture and the individual aspects of growing Digital Thread platform we are building, which conforms to the best practices of coordination languages. Through the adoption of the Low-Code Development Environment DIME it supports a level of reuse, refactoring and analysis at the coordination layer that goes beyond what is achieved today with the current practice of glue code. We illustrated the current status, and described various extension through generic REST services, to robotics through the UR family of robots, to the integration of various external databases (for data integration) and to the provision of data analytics capabilities in R.

We are currently working in various collaborative contexts to enrich the set of supported DSLs, as shown in Fig. 2. The choice of what to address next depends on the needs arising in various contexts, and it is limited by the time and staff available. The snowball effect of the impact has however already kicked in: in more than one case, a new application, sometimes in a completely different domain and collaboration, has already been able to avail of existing native DSLs, or even processes, developed in a totally different context.

Over time, we expect reuse to be increasingly the case, reducing the new integration and new development effort to a progressively smaller portion of the models and code needed for at least the most standard applications. We also expect this kind of paradigm to attract the attention of those sectors and industries that require a tighter cooperation between stakeholders with different expertise and knowledge, where there is a lack of skilled developers, and where the need for a faster turn around time can make code generation attractive as a form of automation.

Acknowledgement. This work was supported by the Science Foundation Ireland grants 16/RC/3918 (Confirm, the Smart Manufacturing Research Centre) and 13/RC/2094_2 (Lero, the Science Foundation Ireland Research Centre for Software).

References

1. Edgex foundry: The edgex foundry platform. https://www.edgexfoundry.org/. Accessed July 2021
2. Fi-ware: The open-source platform for our smart digital future. https://www.fiware.org/. Accessed July 2021
3. Gaia-x: A federated data infrastructure for Europe. https://www.data-infrastructure.eu/. Accessed July 2021
4. Jolie: The service-oriented programming language. https://www.jolie-lang.org/index.html. Accessed Sept 2021
5. Allian, A.P., Schnicke, F., Antonino, P.O., Rombach, D., Nakagawa, E.Y.: Architecture drivers for trustworthy interoperability in industry 4.0. IEEE Syst. J. (2021)
6. Balasubramanian, D., Coglio, A., Dubey, A., Karsai, G.: Towards model-based intent-driven adaptive software. In: Proceedings of ISoLA 2021. LNCS, vol. 13036 (2021)
7. Baresi, L., Garriga, M.: Microservices: the evolution and extinction of web services? Microservices, pp. 3–28 (2020)
8. Boßelmann, S., et al.: DIME: a programming-less modeling environment for web applications. In: Margaria, T., Steffen, B. (eds.) ISoLA 2016. LNCS, vol. 9953, pp. 809–832. Springer, Cham (2016). https://doi.org/10.1007/978-3-319-47169-3_60
9. Burns, T., Cosgrove, J., Doyle, F.: A review of interoperability standards for industry 4.0. Procedia Manuf. **38**, 646–653 (2019)
10. Chaudhary, H.A.A., Margaria, T.: Integration of micro-services as components in modeling environments for low code development. In: Proceedings of the Institute for System Programming of the RAS, vol. 33, no. 4 (2021, September (in print))
11. Daniel, G., Cabot, J., Deruelle, L., Derras, M.: Xatkit: a multimodal low-code chatbot development framework. IEEE Access **8**, 15332–15346 (2020). https://doi.org/10.1109/ACCESS.2020.2966919
12. Farulla, G.A., Indaco, M., Legay, A., Margaria, T.: Model driven design of secure properties for vision-based applications: a case study. In: Proceedings of the International Conference on Security and Management (SAM), p. 159. The Steering Committee of The World Congress in Computer Science, Computer (2016)
13. Fielding, R.T.: Architectural Styles and the Design of Network-Based Software Architectures. University of California, Irvine (2000)
14. Geraci, A.: IEEE Standard Computer Dictionary: Compilation of IEEE Standard Computer Glossaries. IEEE Press (1991)
15. Guevara, I., Margaria, T.: Mazegen: an evolutionary generator for bootstrapping robotic navigation scenarios. In: 37th International Manufacturing Conference, Irish Manufacturing Council, September 2021, Athlone, Ireland (2021)
16. Havelund, K., Bocchino, R.: Integrated modeling and development of component-based embedded software in scala. In: Proceedings ISoLA 2021. LNCS, vol. 13036 (2021)
17. Jepsen, S.C., Mørk, T.I., Hviid, J., Worm, T.: A pilot study of industry 4.0 asset interoperability challenges in an industry 4.0 laboratory. In: 2020 IEEE International Conference on Industrial Engineering and Engineering Management (IEEM), pp. 571–575. IEEE (2020)
18. Jirkovský, V., Obitko, M., Mařík, V.: Understanding data heterogeneity in the context of cyber-physical systems integration. IEEE Trans. Ind. Inform. **13**(2), 660–667 (2016)

19. John, J., Ghosal, A., Margaria, T., Pesch, D.: Dsls and middleware platforms in a model driven development approach for secure predictive maintenance systems in smart factories. In: Proceedings ISoLA 2021. LNCS, vol. 13036. Springer (2021)
20. John, J., Ghosal, A., Margaria, T., Pesch, D.: Dsls for model driven development of secure interoperable automation systems. In: Proceedings Forum for Specification and Design Languages (FDL). IEEE Press (September 2021 (in print))
21. Jorges, S., Kubczak, C., Pageau, F., Margaria, T.: Model driven design of reliable robot control programs using the jABC. In: Proceedings EASe 2007, vol. 07, pp. 137–148 (2007). https://doi.org/10.1109/EASE.2007.17
22. Jörges, S., Kubczak, C., Pageau, F., Margaria, T.: Model driven design of reliable robot control programs using the jABC. In: Proceedings of 4th IEEE International Workshop on Engineering of Autonomic and Autonomous Systems (EASe 2007), pp. 137–148 (2007)
23. Kovatsch, M., Hassan, Y.N., Mayer, S.: Practical semantics for the internet of things: physical states, device mashups, and open questions. In: 2015 5th International Conference on the Internet of Things (IOT), pp. 54–61. IEEE (2015)
24. Lee, H., Ryu, K., Cho, Y.: A framework of a smart injection molding system based on real-time data. Procedia Manuf. **11**, 1004–1011 (2017)
25. Lelli, F.: Interoperability of the time of industry 4.0 and the internet of things. Fut. Internet **11**(2), 36 (2019)
26. Lethbridge, T.C.: Low-code is often high-code, so we must design low-code platforms to enable proper software engineering. In: Proceedings ISoLA 2021. LNCS, vol. 13036 (2021)
27. Maiya, A.S.: ktrain: a low-code library for augmented machine learning. arXiv preprint arXiv:2004.10703 (2020)
28. Margaria, T., Steffen, B.: Service engineering: linking business and IT. Computer **39**(10), 45–55 (2006)
29. Margaria, T., Bakera, M., Kubczak, C., Naujokat, S., Steffen, B.: Automatic generation of the SWS-challenge mediator with jABC/ABC. In: Petrie, C., Margaria, T., Zaremba, M., Lausen, H. (eds.) Semantic Web Services Challenge. Results from the First Year, pp. 119–138. Springer Verlag (2008). https://doi.org/10.1007/978-0-387-72496-6
30. Margaria, T., Kubczak, C., Njoku, M., Steffen, B.: Model-based design of distributed collaborative bioinformatics processes in the jABC. In: Proceedings of the 11th IEEE International Conference on Engineering of Complex Computer Systems (ICECCS 2006), Los Alamitos, CA, USA, pp. 169–176. IEEE Computer Society, August 2006
31. Margaria, T., Meyer, D., Kubczak, C., Isberner, M., Steffen, B.: Synthesizing semantic web service compositions with jMosel and Golog. In: Bernstein, A., et al. (eds.) ISWC 2009. LNCS, vol. 5823, pp. 392–407. Springer, Heidelberg (2009). https://doi.org/10.1007/978-3-642-04930-9_25
32. Margaria, T., Schieweck, A.: The digital thread in Industry 4.0. In: Ahrendt, W., Tapia Tarifa, S.L. (eds.) IFM 2019. LNCS, vol. 11918, pp. 3–24. Springer, Cham (2019). https://doi.org/10.1007/978-3-030-34968-4_1
33. Margaria, T., Steffen, B.: Backtracking-free design planning by automatic synthesis in metaframe. In: Astesiano, E. (ed.) FASE 1998. LNCS, vol. 1382, pp. 188–204. Springer, Heidelberg (1998). https://doi.org/10.1007/BFb0053591
34. Margaria, T., Steffen, B.: Business process modeling in the jABC: the one-thing approach. In: Handbook of Research on Business Process Modeling, pp. 1–26. IGI Global (2009)

35. Margaria, T., Steffen, B.: Simplicity as a driver for agile innovation. Computer **43**(6), 90–92 (2010)
36. Margaria, T., Steffen, B.: Service-orientation: conquering complexity with XMDD. In: Hinchey, M., Coyle, L. (eds.) Conquering Complexity, pp. 217–236. Springer, London (2012). https://doi.org/10.1007/978-1-4471-2297-5_10
37. Margaria, T., Steffen, B.: extreme model-driven development (XMDD) technologies as a hands-on approach to software development without coding. In: Encyclopedia of Education and Information Technologies, pp. 732–750 (2020)
38. Mellor, S.J., Clark, T., Futagami, T.: Model-driven development: guest editors' introduction. IEEE Softw. 20(5), 14–18 (2003). ISSN 0740–7459
39. Merten, M., Steffen, B.: Simplicity driven application development. J. Integr. Des. Process Sci. **17**(3), 9–23 (2013)
40. Moradi, H., Zamani, B., Zamanifar, K.: CaaSSET: a framework for model-driven development of context as a service. Future Gener. Comput. Syst. **105**, 61–95 (2020)
41. Napoleone, A., Macchi, M., Pozzetti, A.: A review on the characteristics of cyber-physical systems for the future smart factories. J. Manuf. Syst. **54**, 305–335 (2020)
42. Naujokat, S., Lybecait, M., Kopetzki, D., Steffen, B.: CINCO: a simplicity-driven approach to full generation of domain-specific graphical modeling tools. Int. J. Softw. Tools Technol. Transf. **20**, 1–28 (2018). https://doi.org/10.1007/s10009-017-0453-6
43. Neubauer, J., Frohme, M., Steffen, B., Margaria, T.: Prototype-driven development of web applications with DyWA. In: Margaria, T., Steffen, B. (eds.) ISoLA 2014. LNCS, vol. 8802, pp. 56–72. Springer, Heidelberg (2014). https://doi.org/10.1007/978-3-662-45234-9_5
44. Newman, S.: Building Microservices: Designing Fine-Grained Systems. O'Reilly Media, Inc. (2015)
45. Nilsson, J., Sandin, F.: Semantic interoperability in Industry 4.0: survey of recent developments and outlook. In: 2018 IEEE 16th International Conference on Industrial Informatics (INDIN), pp. 127–132. IEEE (2018)
46. Ordoñez, K., Hilera, J., Cueva, S.: Model-driven development of accessible software: a systematic literature review. In: Universal Access in the Information Society, pp. 1–30 (2020)
47. Pang, T.Y., Pelaez Restrepo, J.D., Cheng, C.T., Yasin, A., Lim, H., Miletic, M.: Developing a digital twin and digital thread framework for an 'Industry 4.0' shipyard. Appl. Sci. **11**(3), 1097 (2021)
48. Rademacher, F., Sorgalla, J., Wizenty, P., Sachweh, S., Zündorf, A.: Graphical and textual model-driven microservice development. In: Microservices, pp. 147–179. Springer, Cham (2020). https://doi.org/10.1007/978-3-030-31646-4_7
49. da Rocha, H., Espirito-Santo, A., Abrishambaf, R.: Semantic interoperability in the Industry 4.0 using the IEEE 1451 standard. In: IECON 2020 The 46th Annual Conference of the IEEE Industrial Electronics Society, pp. 5243–5248. IEEE (2020)
50. Rumpe, B.: Modeling with UML. Springer, Cham (2016). https://doi.org/10.1007/978-3-319-33933-7
51. Sanchez, M., Exposito, E., Aguilar, J.: Industry 4.0: survey from a system integration perspective. Int. J. Comput. Integr. Manuf. **33**(10–11), 1017–1041 (2020)
52. Sanchis, R., García-Perales, Ó., Fraile, F., Poler, R.: Low-code as enabler of digital transformation in manufacturing industry. Appl. Sci. **10**(1), 12 (2020)
53. Santos, F., Nunes, I., Bazzan, A.L.: Quantitatively assessing the benefits of model-driven development in agent-based modeling and simulation. Simul. Model. Pract. Theory **104**, 102126 (2020)

54. Steffen, B., Gossen, F., Naujokat, S., Margaria, T.: Language-driven engineering: from general-purpose to purpose-specific languages. In: Steffen, B., Woeginger, G. (eds.) Computing and Software Science. LNCS, vol. 10000, pp. 311–344. Springer, Cham (2019). https://doi.org/10.1007/978-3-319-91908-9_17
55. Steffen, B., Howar, F., Isberner, M., Naujokat, S., Margaria, T.: Tailored generation of concurrent benchmarks. Softw. Tools Technol. Transf. **16**(5), 543–558 (2014). https://doi.org/10.1007/s10009-014-0339-9
56. Steffen, B., Margaria, T.: METAFrame in practice: design of intelligent network services. In: Olderog, E.-R., Steffen, B. (eds.) Correct System Design. LNCS, vol. 1710, pp. 390–415. Springer, Heidelberg (1999). https://doi.org/10.1007/3-540-48092-7_17
57. Steffen, B., Margaria, T., Nagel, R., Jörges, S., Kubczak, C.: Model-driven development with the jABC. In: Bin, E., Ziv, A., Ur, S. (eds.) HVC 2006. LNCS, vol. 4383, pp. 92–108. Springer, Heidelberg (2007). https://doi.org/10.1007/978-3-540-70889-6_7
58. Waszkowski, R.: Low-code platform for automating business processes in manufacturing. IFAC-PapersOnLine **52**(10), 376–381 (2019)
59. Windmüller, S., Neubauer, J., Steffen, B., Howar, F., Bauer, O.: Active continuous quality control. In: Proceedings of the 16th International ACM Sigsoft Symposium on Component-Based Software Engineering, pp. 111–120 (2013)
60. Xu, L.D.: The contribution of systems science to Industry 4.0. Syst. Res. Behav. Sci. **37**(4), 618–631 (2020)
61. You, Z., Feng, L.: Integration of Industry 4.0 related technologies in construction industry: a framework of cyber-physical system. IEEE Access **8**, 122908–122922 (2020)
62. Zweihoff, P., Naujokat, S., Steffen, B.: Pyro: generating domain-specific collaborative online modeling environments. In: Hähnle, R., van der Aalst, W. (eds.) FASE 2019. LNCS, vol. 11424, pp. 101–115. Springer, Cham (2019). https://doi.org/10.1007/978-3-030-16722-6_6
63. Zweihoff, P., Steffen, B.: Pyrus: an online modeling environment for no-code data-analytics service composition. In: Proceedings ISoLA 2021. LNCS, vol. 13036 (2021)
64. Zweihoff, P., Tegeler, T., Schürmann, J., Bainczyk, A., Steffen, B.: Aligned, purpose-driven cooperation: The future way of system development. In: Proceedings ISoLA 2021. LNCS, vol. 13036 (2021)

Programming vs. That Thing Subject Matter Experts Do

Markus Voelter(✉)

independent/itemis AG, Oetztaler Strasse 38, 70327 Stuttgart, Germany
voelter@acm.org

Abstract. Allowing subject matter experts to directly contribute their domain knowledge and expertise to software through DSLs and automation is a promising way to increase overall software development efficiency and the quality of the product. However, there are doubts of whether this will force subject matter experts to become programmers. In this paper I answer this question with "no". But at the same time, subject matter experts have to learn how to communicate clearly and unambiguously to a computer, and this requires *some* aspects of what is traditionally called programming. The main part of this paper discusses what these aspects are and why learning these does not make people programmers.

Keywords: Domain specific language · End-user programming · Language engineering

1 The Role of Subject Matter Experts

Subject matter experts, or SMEs, own the knowledge and expertise that is the backbone of software and the foundation of digitalization. But too often this rich expertise is not captured in a structured way and gets lost when translating it for software engineers (SEs) when they implement it. With the rate of change increasing, time-to-market shortening and product variability blooming, this indirect approach of putting knowledge into software is increasingly untenable: it causes delays, quality problems and frustration for everyone involved. A better approach is to *empower* subject matter experts to capture, understand, and reason about data, structures, rules, behaviors and other forms of knowledge and expertise in a precise and unambiguous form by providing them with *tailored software languages* (DSLs) and tools that allow them to directly edit, validate, simulate and test that knowledge. The models created this way are then executed either by interpretation or automatic transformed into program code. The software engineers focus their activities on building these languages, tools and transformations, plus robust execution platforms for the generated code. Figure 1 shows the overall process.

T. Margaria and B. Steffen (Eds.): ISoLA 2021, LNCS 13036, pp. 414–425, 2021.
https://doi.org/10.1007/978-3-030-89159-6_26

2 Can SMEs Use DSLs?

This paper is not about justifying the approach from a technical or economical perspective. I refer the reader to the Subject Matter First manifesto[1] Instead I want to focus on whether the SMEs are *able* to change from their typically imprecise, non-formal approach of specifying requirements using Word, Excel, User Stories or IBM Doors to this DSL-based approach.

Based on my experience over the years [10] my answer to this question is a clear yes, at least for the majority of subject matter experts I have worked with. But a key question is: to what extent do the subject matter experts who use DSLs have to become programmers? Do they have the *skills* to be programmers (hint: most do not), and do they *want* to become programmers (hint: most do not). But we still expect them to use "languages" and IDE-like tools. So:

Which parts of programming do they have to learn? How is SME'ing different from programming, and where does it overlap?

I answer this question in Sect. 5. To set the stage we briefly discuss the domains in which the approach works (Sect. 3) and how languages and applications are typically architected in such scenarios (Sect. 4). We conclude the paper with a wrap up in Sect. 7.

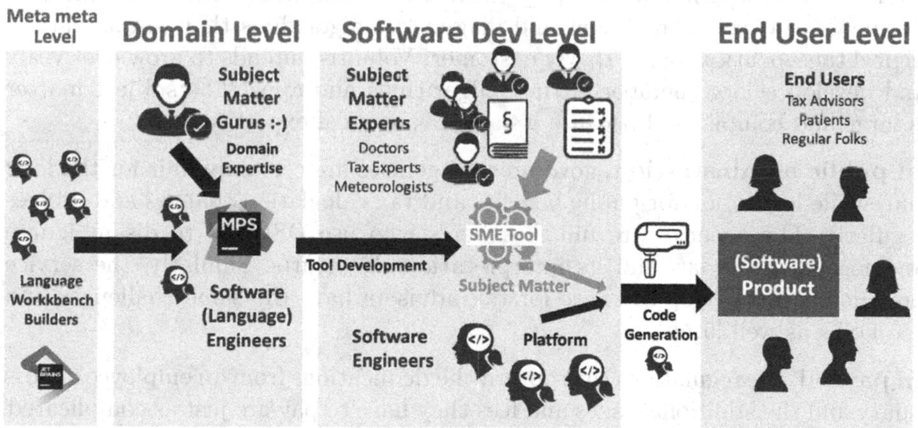

Fig. 1. The process from the SME's brain into software, based on tools and platforms developed by software engineers.

[1] http://subjectmatterfirst.org.

3 (Where) Does This Work?

Building the necessary language and IDE tooling and downstream automation requires investment, and this investment must pay off for the approach to make economical sense. Which is why this approach only works in domains that have the following characteristics. First, the subject matter has to have a minimum **size** and **complicatedness**. A consequence of this is often that there are people in the company who consider themselves **experts** in that subject matter. It is they who everybody asks about details in the domain. The second criterion is that this subject matter as a whole will remain **relevant over time** and that the business intends to continue developing software in that domain for a reasonably long time. Finally, even though the subject matter as a whole r relevant for a long time, a degree of **evolution** or **variety** within the domain is usually needed for the approach to make sense. I have seen this approach used in the following domains, among others:

In insurances, DSLs are used by insurance product definition staff to develop a variety of continuously evolving insurance products [4,7]. With increased differentiation and tailoring of products, these become more and more complicated while at the same time increasing in variety and number. The company itself is in the insurance business for the long run.

In healthcare, DSLs are used by medical doctors and other healthcare professionals to develop treatment and diagnostics algorithms that run as part of digital therapeutics apps [11]. My customer, Voluntis, intends to grow over years and develop a large number of these algorithms and apps. The subject matter is large and complicated because it captures medical expertise.

In public adminstration, government agencies are certainly in it for the long run, while legislation for public benefits and tax calculation changes and evolves regularly. The agencies are full of experts who use DSLs [1] to disambiguate and formalize the law and its interpretations by courts. Similarly, the service providers who develop software for tax advisors have the same challenges and use DSLs as well [5,6].

In payroll, the regulations that govern the deducations from an employee's gross salary and the additional taxes and fees they have to pay are just as complicated, long-lasting and ever changing as tax law (and of course directly related). Service provides who develop payroll software therefore also employ whole departments full of experts and benefit from the use of DSLs [12].

For an overview over this approach and a couple of easily readable case studies, see my InfoQ article [10].

4 Typical DSL Architecture

Many of the DSL I have built follow the general approach that is outlined in Fig. 2. The models created by the SMEs end up as the core of the system, usually

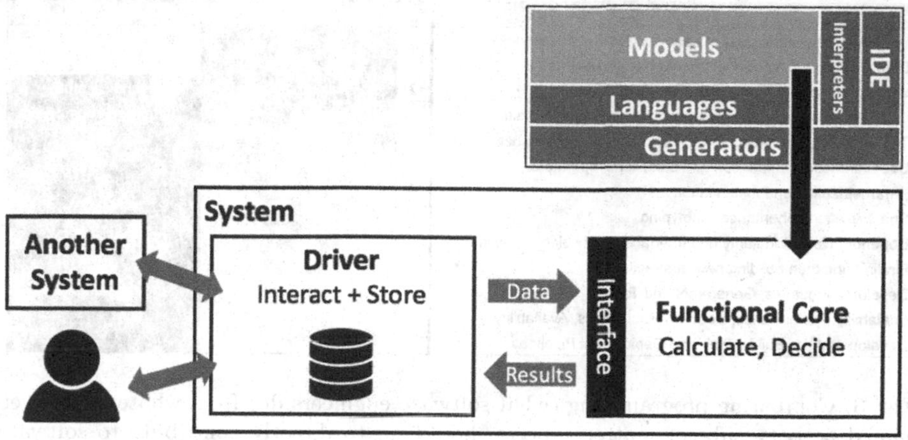

Fig. 2. Typical high-level systems architecture, where the models expressed with DSLs are transformed into code that forms the core of a larger application.

expressed with functional semantics, either via generation or via interpretation. That core implements a (manually defined) API that is used by a driver component to invoke the DSL-derived code. The driver interacts with users and other systems – potentially via additional architectural building blocks – and is often also responsible for managing and persisting state. Indeed, many of our DSLs are "funclarative" [8], where small, simple calculations are expressed with a functional-style language (so users do not have to care about effects at this level), and when things get more complicated, the DSL provides declarative first-class concepts to express those concisely without lots of low-level functional code.

In order to avoid reinventing the wheel with regards to the core functional expressions, the DSLs often embed (and then extend) a reusable language KernelF. I usually start by building a few of the domain-specific abstractions "around" KernelF. Then I iterate, building more abstractions, constraining away parts from KernelF that are not needed or replacing parts of KernelF with simpler abstractions. More details on KernelF and its use for DSLs can be found in [13].

If the DSL cannot be scoped to handling only the functional parts and thus has to manage state, I usually rely on variations of state machines. Generally it is a good idea to rely on established programming paradigms and DSL-ify them instead of trying to invent new fundamental paradigms.

5 Difference Between Programming and SME'ing

In this section we look at the work share between SMEs and SEs. We focus on what the SMEs do, because this paper is about the degree to which their activities resemble programming. We discuss the responsibilities of SEs mostly to contrast their work to that of the SMEs.

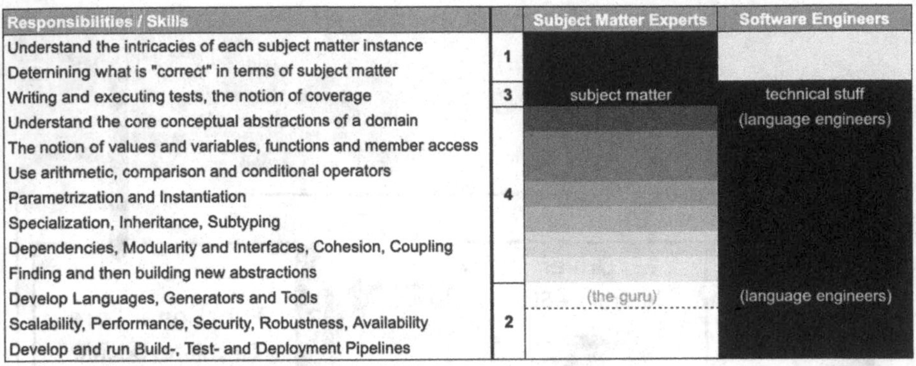

Responsibilities / Skills		Subject Matter Experts	Software Engineers
Understand the intricacies of each subject matter instance	1		
Determining what is "correct" in terms of subject matter			
Writing and executing tests, the notion of coverage	3	subject matter	technical stuff
Understand the core conceptual abstractions of a domain	4		(language engineers)
The notion of values and variables, functions and member access			
Use arithmetic, comparison and conditional operators			
Parametrization and Instantiation			
Specialization, Inheritance, Subtyping			
Dependencies, Modularity and Interfaces, Cohesion, Coupling			
Finding and then building new abstractions			
Develop Languages, Generators and Tools	2	(the guru)	(language engineers)
Scalability, Performance, Security, Robustness, Availability			
Develop and run Build-, Test- and Deployment Pipelines			

Fig. 3. Comparing programming (what software engineers do) from whatever not-yet-named activity subject matter experts should do to directly contribute to software. Darker shade means "is more relevant".

5.1 Skills and Responsibilities

Figure 3 shows the differences in responsibilities of SEs and SMEs. The darker the shade, the more responsibility the respective community has for that concern. We start our discussion with the two black and white cases, those where there is no overlap.

Region 1, SME only. Region 1 is completely the responsibility of SMEs. They have to understand every particular example, case, situation, and exception of the subject matter they want the software system to handle. This is their natural responsibility, this is why they exist. SEs on the other hand should not have to care at all. Achieving this separation – and then optimizing the tasks of both communities – is the reason for using DSLs and tools in the first place. Related to this, the SMEs are also in charge of determining what consistutes correct behavior in the subject matter, they write the tests. SMEs take full responsibility for what goes into test cases as well as for their completeness.

Region 2, SE only. Let us move on to region 2, which is completely the responsibility of SEs. Setting up and operating automated CI pipelines that build and package the software and run tests is nothing the SME should be concerned with, except for being notified if tests fail (after they have run correctly in their local environment, otherwise they should never reach the CI server).

The same is true for taking care of performance, scalability, safety, security, robustness and availability, all the operational (aka non-functional) concerns of the final software system. Keeping the subject matter segregated from these technical aspects of software is a key benefit of the approach, and it is clear that this should be handled in platforms, frameworks and code generators – all fully the domain of SEs.

Finally, the development of the DSLs and tools that will then be used by the SMEs for capturing, analysing and experimenting with subject matter is the responsibility of SEs. It might not be the domain of *all* of the software engineers, but maybe only of a certain specialization called language engineers who specialize in developing languages, IDEs, interpreters and generators. Also, a few of the most experienced subject matter experts – I sometimes refer to them as gurus – have to help survey, understand, analyse and abstract the domain so that the language engineers can build the languages. But the regular SME, the dozens or hundreds that many of our customers employ, are not involved with this task.

Note that in order to be able to build the languages, the SEs have to understand the domain at the meta level. Together with the gurus, they have to understand how to describe the structures, rules, behaviors and other forms of knowledge in the domain. But they do not have to know all the instances which are subsequently expressed by the SMEs using the DSL. This distinction is crucial and is often perceived as a contradiction with the goal of the approach of separating the work of the SMEs and SEs.

Region 3, Testing. Let us now look at region 3, one that apparently has full shared responsibility. However, in this case the illustration is a bit misleading. Indeed, both communities have to understand the purpose of testing, what a test case is, and appreciate the notion of coverage, i.e., understanding when they have enough tests to be (reasonably) sure that there are no more (reasonably few) bugs in the logic. But of course the SMEs care about this *only* for the subject matter expressed with the DSL, whereas the SEs care about it *only* in the platform, frameworks, language implementation and generators. So they both have to understand testing, but there are no artifacts for which they have shared responsibility.

Region 4, shared skills. This is the most interesting part: all the items in this region are native to programming and software engineering. So SEs care. But they are also relevant, to different degrees, to SMEs when they use DSLs. Let us explore them in detail.

Of course the SMEs have to understand the conceptual abstractions of the domain, because otherwise they cannot use the language. Understanding abstractions is not easy in general, but because in a DSL these abstractions are closely aligned with the subject matter, the SMEs – in my experience – are able to understand them. Maybe not every little detail (which is why the box is dark grey and not black) but sufficiently well to use the language. The SEs have to understand these abstractions as well, especially the language engieneers. Those who build the execution platform can usually deal with a black-box view of the generated code.

A note: the fact that there is shared understanding about the core abstractions of the subject matter in the domain for which the SMEs and the SEs co-create software is a major reason why DSLs are so useful here. The language definition, and its conceptual cousins, the core abstractions, are an unambiguous and clearly-scoped foundation for productive collaboration between the two communities. So when I write "xyz is the responsibility of SME/SE", it does not mean that there is not a *joint overall responsibility* of both communities together to deliver useful (in terms of subject matter) and robust (in terms of operational concerns) software.

Back to region 4. No real-world subject-matter focused DSL I have ever seen can make do without understanding the notion of values, and some notion of functions (entities that produce new values from inputs). It does not matter whether we are talking specifically about (textual) functions, (Excel-style) decision tables or (graphical) dataflow diagrams. The good thing is that essentially everybody has come across these at school or at university, even though using functions to assemble larger functionality from pieces and the explicit use of types is new to many. In practice, teaching the use of functions, at least in limited complexity situations, is feasible.

Similarly, the understanding of dot expressions to mean `the member X of entity Y` or `do Z with entity Y` is very hard to avoid, because working with parts of things or performing activities on things is ubiquitous. For many SMEs, this is harder to get used to. We've experimented with literally writing <member> of <object> instead of <object>.<member> but this results in less useful IDE support: with the latter syntax, one can easily scope the code completion menu to members of `object` because users write the object first. In contrast, with the former syntax, the code completion for the member has to show *all* members of *all* objects in the system because the context `object` is not yet specified.

In essentially every domain SMEs have to express decisions and calculations. So another set of constructs that is hard to avoid is arithmetic, logical and comparison operators (together with types like `number`), as well as notion of a conditional, such as `if ...then` or `switch{case, case, case}` and the associated `Boolean` type – independent of their concrete syntax (text, symbolic or graphical). Once again, most SMEs have come across these operators at school or university, so using them is not a big challenge.

The reason why these two lines are grey for SMEs and not totally black is because the complexity of the expressions built with these language concepts should (and usually can) be kept lower for SMEs. For example, for complicated decisions, we can support graphical decision tables of various forms which are much easier to grasp than nested `if` statements or the some form of `switch`-like statements.

Several of the DSLs I have built require an understanding of parametrization. For example, in function-like constructs, the values passed into the function are mapped (by position or by name) to parameters in the function signature that are then used in the body of the function. Most SMEs have no problems with this – again, school experience – but some do. Often parametrization is the threshold where the need for education and training starts (beyond building the shared understanding about the core concepts of a domain). A related concept is instantiation, where, usually, each instance has separate values for its state and can evolve independently. This is not taught in school, and it is not taught outside of computer science at university, so training is needed. On the other hand, many DSLs can do without instantiation which is why this box is a lighter shade of gray.

Thinking and mindset	Subject Matter Experts	Software Engineers
Notation	Tables, Diagrams, Symbols, Text	Text
Degrees of freedom, creativity	Picking options, selecting alternatives	Creatively constructing
Guidance (Scaffolding, Forms)	Appreciated	Only limited need/acceptance
Tool Support	Process/Use-Case oriented	Free modification of code / models
Thinking about problem	As a set of examples	Strive for complete algorithm
Validation	Try Out, Play, Simulate, Record	Try out, write tests, run automatically
Separating program from data	Challenging	Perfectly ok

Fig. 4. SMEs make different trade-offs than software engineers regarding the languages and tools they want to work with.

We are getting to more advanced concepts that are increasingly harder to grasp for many SMEs, but they are also not necessary in all DSLs (though unavoidable in some). The notion of specialization or subtyping is key here. While everybody understands subtyping intuitively ("an eagle *isa* bird *isa* animal *isa* living thing *isa* object"), many SMEs struggle with the consequences. Especially the mental assembly of everything that is in a subtype by (mentally) going through all its supertypes is hard: "we are not seeing the big picture" is what I often hear. Practice helps, but so can tools that optionally show all the inherited members inline in the subtype's definition.

For complex subject matter – tax calculation comes to mind – the models created with the DSLs become large, and complexity often rises along with size. Notions like delineating module boundaries, explicitly defined interfaces, reduction of unnecessary dependencies, and more generally, cohesion, coupling and reuse become an issue. Most SMEs struggle here. But on the other hand, 95% of the work of an SME can proceed without caring about these big picture concerns, except during initial design or downstream review phases, where SE or guru involvement can help to sort things out. Considering it is only 5% of the total work, such involvement is usually feasible.

The final ingredient in region 4 is discovering and then defining new abstractions. This is often not the strong suit of SMEs. Those that are good at it are usually the gurus who help with language definition, or they have been assimilated wholly by the software development team. But luckily it is quite rare that SMEs are required to define new abstractions, because those that are relevant in the domain should be available first-class in the DSL – or retrofitted for the next version once the need becomes obvious.

5.2 Different Emphasis

In my experience, (most) SMEs prioritize the features of languages and IDEs different from (most) developers. In this section we'll look at some of the more prominenet differences, Fig. 4 summarizes them.

Notation. Developers prefer textual notations, both for their conciseness, but also for reasons of homogeneity with regards to storing, editing, diffing and merging code. SMEs, in contrast, tend to emphasize readability and fit of the notation with established representations in the domain (e.g., tables in the tax law documents) over these efficiency concerns. Therefore, if you can build DSLs that are more diverse in notation – and not just colored text with curly braces and indentation – SME buy-in is usually easier to obtain.

Selecting vs. Creating. Developers love the creative freedom of coming up with an algorithm and crafting their own suitable abstractions from small, flexible building blocks. SMEs – because of their often limited experience with building their own abstractions – prefer picking from options and selecting alternatives. In my experience SMEs usually accept that they have to read a bit more documentation that (hopefully!) explains what the different options or alternatives mean. Consequently DSLs often contain many first-class concepts for the various needs of the domain, even if this requires the users to first understand what each of them means. The approach is usually also benefitial for domain-related semantic analysis (more first class concepts makes it easier to analyze programs) and it is easier to have a nice notation (because you can associate specific notations with these first-class concepts). In contrast, programming languages emphasize orthogonality and composability of their (fewer) first-class concepts.

Guidance. A related topic is guidance. Developers are happy with opening an empty editor and starting to write code. Code completion guides them a little bit. SMEs prefer more guidance, almost to the point where skeleton programs are pre-created after selection from a menu. DSLs that feel like a mix between a form-based application and program code seem to be particularly appreciated by many SMEs.

Tool Support. Taking this further, SEs prefer a toolbox approach, where the tool offers lots and lots of actions and it is the developer's job to use each action at the right time, in the right way. SMEs are more use-case oriented. They want tool support for their typical workflows and process steps, and specific tool support for each. To give an extreme example: I have built DSLs that included wizard-like functionality in the IDE, where using the wizard required more input gestures than just code-completion supported typing. Still the wizard was preferred by the SMEs.

Thinking about problems. It is almost a defining feature of SEs that they think about a problem (and its solution) as a complete algorithm that can cover all possible execution paths. Sure, tests then validate specific scenarios, but developers *think* in algorithms. SMEs often think in terms of examples first, and sometimes exclusively. For example, it is easier for them to deal with a (hopefully complete) set of sequence diagrams rather than with a state machine that captures the superset of the sequence diagrams. In terms of DSL design this means that more emphasis on case distinction in which distinct scenarios are specified separately (even if this incurs a degree of code duplication) is often a good idea.

Validation. Most developers are good at writing tests, writing them against APIs for a relatively small-size unit, and then running these tests automatically continuously. SMEs often think of validation more in terms of "playing with the system". They prefer "simulation GUIs" over writing repeatable tests as (a different kind of) program. So build those simulators first, and then allow the simulator to record "play sessions" and persist them as generated test cases for later automatic reexecution.

Recipe vs. Execution. A program is a recipe which, when combined with input data, behaves in a particular way. The specific behavior depends on the input data. So whenever SEs write code, they continuously imagine (and sometimes try out or trace with the debugger) how the program behaves for (all possible combinations of) input data. Many SMEs are not very good at doing this. One reason why Excel is so popular is because it does not make this distinction between the program and its execution: the program always runs (or, alternatively, a spreadsheet never runs, it just "is"). So anything from the universe of live programming is helpful for DSLs.

Despite these differences, there are lots of commonalities as well. Both communities want good tools (read: IDE support), relevant analyses with understandable and precise error messages, refactorings and other ways to make non-local changes to potentially large programs, low turnaround time plus various ways of illustrating, tracing and debugging the execution of programs. However, while software engineers are often willing to compromise on these features if the expressivity of the language is convincing, SMEs usually will not.

6 Where and How Can SMEs Learn

So where and how can SMEs learn the skills from the SME column of Fig. 3?

In school and at university. In my opinion, *everybody* should learn these basics in school and at university. While programming in the strict sense should be limited to computer science or software engineering curricula, this "SME'ing" should be mandatory for everybody, just like reading, writing or math. Of course such courses should not just teach Java or Python. They should emphasize the specific skills of "thinking like a programmer" with a range of dedicated and diverse languages and tools.

Programming Basics Course. A few years ago, based on the need to educate and trains a group of SMEs, I created a course called Programming Basics [9] that teaches these concepts relevant to SMEs step by step. It starts with simple values as cells of spreadsheets and then covers expressions, testing, types, functions, structured values, collections, decisions and calculations as well as instantiation. The course uses different varieties and notations for many of these concepts in order to try and emphasize the concepts. The course is built on the Jetbrains MPS language workbench[2] and KernelF, and allows extension and customization on language level towards particular DSLs. We are working on a way to get this into the browser for easier access.

[2] http://jetbrains.com/mps.

Hedy Language. Felienne Hermans has built Hedy [3], a gradual programming language. The goal is to teach "normal people" the basics of programming with a language that grows in capability step by step, with the need for each next capability motivated by user-understandable limitation in the previous step. Ultimately, when Hedy is fully developed, it is similar to Python. Hedy is free and works in the browser.

Computational Thinking. In the 2000s, a community of software engineers came up with the term computational thinking [2] as the "mental skills and practices for designing computations that get computers to do jobs for people, and explaining and interpreting the world as a complex of information processes." So the idea is similar to what I am advocating, although the relationship to DSLs and subject matter is missing. Computational thinking has been critizised as being just another name for computer science; but my discussions in this paper should make clear that there's a big difference between computer science and that thing SMEs should do.

7 Wrap Up

It is almost not worth saying because it is so obvious: almost all domains, disciplines, professions and sciences are becoming increasingly computational. And market forces require companies – especially those in the traditional industrial countries – to become more efficient. I am confident that providing "CAD programs for knowledge workers", i.e., DSL, tools and automation, is an important building block for future economic success.

With the comparison of programming and "that thing SMEs should do" in this paper I hope to make clear that everybody *does not* have to become a programmer. But: everybody has to be empowered to communicate the subject matter of their domain precisely to a computer (using DSLs or other suitable tools). And therefore, everybody has to learn to think like a programmer at least a little bit, enough to be able to understand and work with the things in the SME column of Fig. 3. And we software engineers have to adopt this subject-matter centric mindset and develop languages and tools that are built in line with the SME preferences in Fig. 4.

Acknowledgements. Thanks to Yulia Komarov and Federico Tomassetti for providing feedback on an earlier version of this paper, as well as the anonymous reviewers of the ISOLA 2021 conference.

References

1. Dutch Tax and Customs Administration. Challenges of the Dutch tax and customs administration (video) (2018). https://www.youtube.com/watch?v=_-XMjfz3RcU
2. Denning, P.J., Tedre, M.: Computational Thinking. MIT Press, Cambridge (2019)
3. Hermans, F.: Hedy, a gradual programming language (2020). https://hedy-beta.herokuapp.com/

4. itemis AG. The business DSL: Zurich insurance (2019). https://blogs.itemis.com/en/the-business-dsl-zurich-insurance
5. Markus Voelter, Y.K.: Streamlining der Steuersoftware-Entwicklung bei DATEV mittels Domänenspezifischer Sprachen (slides). In: OOP Conference 2021 (2021). http://voelter.de/data/presentations/oop2021-steuerDSLStreamlining.pdf
6. Markus Voelter, Y.K.: Streamlining der Steuersoftware-Entwicklung bei DATEV mittels Domänenspezifischer Sprachen (Video). In: OOP Conference 2021 (2021). https://youtu.be/q56wzLQkEho
7. Stotz, N., Birken, K.: Migrating insurance calculation rule descriptions from word to MPS. In: Bucchiarone, A., Cicchetti, A., Ciccozzi, F., Pierantonio, A. (eds.) Domain-Specific Languages in Practice, pp. 165–194. Springer, Cham (2021). https://doi.org/10.1007/978-3-030-73758-0_6
8. Voelter, M.: Fusing modeling and programming into language-oriented programming. In: Margaria, T., Steffen, B. (eds.) ISoLA 2018. LNCS, vol. 11244, pp. 309–339. Springer, Cham (2018). https://doi.org/10.1007/978-3-030-03418-4_19
9. Voelter, M.: Programming basics: how to think like a programmer (2018). https://markusvoelter.github.io/ProgrammingBasics/
10. Voelter, M.: Why DSLS? A collection of anecdotes (2020). https://www.infoq.com/articles/why-dsl-collection-anecdotes
11. Voelter, M., et al.: Using language workbenches and domain-specific languages for safety-critical software development. Softw. Syst. Model. **18**(4), 2507–2530 (2019)
12. Voelter, M., Koščejev, S., Riedel, M., Deitsch, A., Hinkelmann, A.: A domain-specific language for payroll calculations: an experience report from DATEV. In: Bucchiarone, A., Cicchetti, A., Ciccozzi, F., Pierantonio, A. (eds.) Domain-Specific Languages in Practice, pp. 93–130. Springer, Cham (2021). https://doi.org/10.1007/978-3-030-73758-0_4
13. Voelter, M.: The design, evolution, and use of KernelF. In: Rensink, A., Sánchez Cuadrado, J. (eds.) ICMT 2018. LNCS, vol. 10888, pp. 3–55. Springer, Cham (2018). https://doi.org/10.1007/978-3-319-93317-7_1

Aligned, Purpose-Driven Cooperation: The Future Way of System Development

Philip Zweihoff(✉), Tim Tegeler(✉), Jonas Schürmann, Alexander Bainczyk, and Bernhard Steffen

Chair for Programming Systems, TU Dortmund University, Dortmund, Germany
{philip.zweihoff,tim.tegeler,jonas.schuermann,alexander.bainczyk, steffen}@cs.tu-dortmund.de

Abstract. Collaborative system development requires a three-dimensional alignment: in *space*, in *time*, and in *mindset*: Traditionally, different developers typically have their own, local development environments, each of which may change over time due to updates and other version changes. The third dimension concerns so-called semantic gaps, which we proposed to address via Language-Driven Engineering using Purpose-Specific Language. In this paper we argue that web-based, collaborative development environments that support Language-Driven Engineering are capable of solving the three-dimensional alignment problem. Our illustration via a corresponding prototypical solution aims at illustrating that this vision has the power to radically improve the effectiveness of collaborative development and that it is realistic even in near future.

Keywords: Cloud IDE · Cloud Development · Programming · Domain-Specific Languages · Language-Driven Engineering

1 Introduction

The world of software development has changed dramatically in the last decades (Fig. 1). Today, e.g., the top five web frameworks, React.js, jQuery, Express, Angular, and Vue.js [57], have in average almost 800 contributors to their open-source repositories who develop their software on individual infrastructure, sometimes even using different Runtime Environments (REs). The required technological alignment concerning e.g., the used frameworks and their versions, lies in the hands of the individual developers. They have to make sure that their contributions fit some global, often rarely specified and frequently changing criteria, a complex and time-consuming task. Approaches like MIDAS aim at supporting users with this task by providing toolchains and dedicated specification languages that capture corresponding requirement changes and system evolutions [4]. An alternative approach is followed by general-purpose Cloud IDEs like Gitpod and Eclipse Che [15,21] which globally provide managed development environments in order to allow users to fully concentrate on their development tasks.

Another trend is to reduce the semantic gap between stakeholders of different expertise by directly involving them in the development process using

T. Margaria and B. Steffen (Eds.): ISoLA 2021, LNCS 13036, pp. 426–449, 2021.
https://doi.org/10.1007/978-3-030-89159-6_27

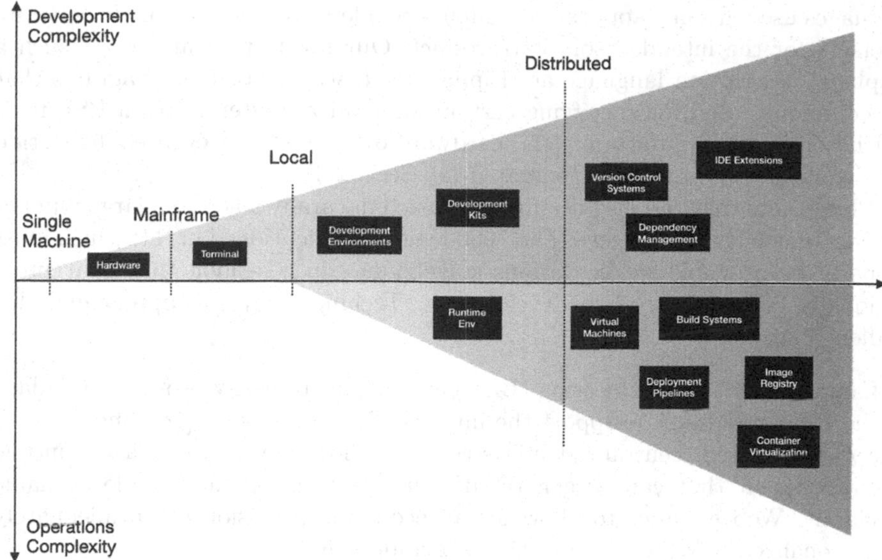

Fig. 1. The expanding universe of software system development.

domain/purpose-specific languages [29,58], without forcing them to become programmers [64] and as required in [60], to finally democratise software development. What is missing is a comprehensive development environment that aligns the IT infrastructure in *space* and *time*, and that provides different languages to adequately support the expertise of the different stakeholders.

In this paper, we sketch an IDE for collaborative system development (not only of web applications![1]) that support a three-dimensional alignment: in *space*, in *time*, and in *mindset* (cf. Sect. 2). Key is to provide the entire required infrastructure in the cloud, and to support even non-technical stakeholders via dedicated, Purpose-Specific Language (PSLs). We distinguish between PSLs and the commonly established notion of Domain-Specific Language (DSLs) which characterizes a certain class of languages as being domain-specific. In contrast, essentially every language has a purpose (why should it otherwise exist), making all languages a PSLs for some purpose, e.g., Java and C are PSLs for general purpose programming, class diagrams for data modeling, SQL for database interaction, BNFs for syntax definition.

The intent behind the introduction of the notion of PSLs is to advocate a purpose-first approach: Starting with a certain purpose we want to select/design dedicated PSLs for that very purpose, i.e., maximum language support allowing in particular non-technical stakeholders to specify their intended solutions in their established mindset (cf. Sect. 2.3). Technically, such PSLs typically arise as the result of enhancing (typically graphical) description and documentation

[1] Only the IDEs are in the Web/cloud, the class of to be developed software systems is not constraint.

languages used in some application domains to a level that allows one to generate artefacts for the intended solution/product. Our favourite example for such a graphical description language are Piping and Instrumentations Diagrams that are commonly used for specifying certain mechanical systems into a PSL from which corresponding data models, hardware diagrams, and even configuration code could be automatically generated (cf. Sect. 2.3).

Please note that the purpose-first approach naturally leads to a large number of PSLs, much larger than even the 7000 languages mentioned in [11] which must properly be provided to the various stakeholders in a fashion that guarantees a globally consistent system development. Technical key to approaching this challenge are (cf. Sect. 4):

- Language-Driven Engineering (LDE) as a means to easily provide and adapt the PSLs required to support the involved domain experts [58], and
- a cluster based, centralized infrastructure whose development and runtime environment that can be generated from specifications and made available via the Web in order to allow for an economic provision of an adequately personalized infrastructure to all stakeholders and

We will illustrate this approach to collaborative, purpose-driven software development along our prototypical implementation on the basis of CINCO, our language workbench for graphical modeling CINCO.

In the following three sections we describe the essential dimensions of collaborative system development that require an overarching alignment: *space* (Sect. 2.1), *time* (Sect. 2.2) and *mindset* (Sect. 2.3). Then we will describe the currently present Cloud IDE architecture and functionality in Sect. 3 based on the established open-source Tools Gitpod [21] and Eclipse Che [53]. Based on this, we will describe our vision of a cloud-based language workbench in Sect. 4. In Sect. 4 we describe our vision to extend the concept of a Cloud IDE to meet the given challenges. We will then discuss in Sect. 5 which steps are necessary to realize the CINCO language workbenches in the cloud to finally reach a realization of LDE. Finally, the results of the individual discussions are summarized in Sect. 6.

2 Challenges

As indicated by Fig. 1, the universe of software development is expanding: the systems themselves, their range of application, and the required/addressed infrastructure grow to an extent that they can hardly be controlled without computer assistance. Even in software development methodologies, which aim at increasing the productivity of developers (e.g. Model Based Software Engineering (MBSE)), the complexity of mastering change grows to an extent that computer support is needed [4]. Experts are able to survive in this highly complex landscape, but it remains very demanding to stay in synchrony with the evolving infrastructural requirements of a larger (open source) project. What is missing is a dedicated 'cross-dimensional' approach to achieve an overarching alignment. In this section, we will sketch the three dimensions we aim to align with our cloud-based, in our eyes trendsetting approach to purpose-driven cooperation.

2.1 Space

In Physics, *space* can be defined as *"the unlimited three-dimensional expanse in which all material objects are located"*[2]. In our context *space* includes everything that is necessary to develop a software project at a certain point in time (cf. Sect. 2.2). This includes the increasing language diversity (e.g. General-Purpose Languages and Domain-Specific Languages), the recent progression from software to system development (i.e. DevOps), and the growing need for tools and assistance (e.g. build-management, documentation).

In the early days, programs were typically written in a single General-Purpose Language (GPL) by a single person, using the same machine for development and execution. Since then, the way how software is developed has changed dramatically. Software is rarely developed in a single language anymore. In order to efficiently create more versatile applications, DSLs for individual components of a system were created (e.g. SQL). Every DSL is tailored to the respective task. It seems common to use multi languages in open-source projects nowadays [43]. Especially distributed systems, like full-stack web applications [63], are polyglot projects that combine a variety of GPLs and DSLs (e.g. JavaScript, Python, HTML), each of which requiring its own Software Development Kits (SDKs) and REs. The popularity of microservice architecture contributes to this trend, where every microservice can have its own different stack of technologies. In order to use multiple programming languages frameworks and runtime environments efficiently, modular Integrated Development Environments (IDEs) like Eclipse [26] were created in 2001. Through the integration of IDE extensions, different tools for development can be combined, but each developer has to manage his local setup still manually and independently.

The language diversity is not the only dimension that increases the complexity. Licensing models like Software as a Service, expand the scope of software projects from development to operating. Software is not just delivered as installable packages anymore, but provided as a service to the end user. This shifts more responsibility of managing the RE and infrastructure from the end user to the software developers and system administrators. The advent of DevOps [3,13] in the last decade is a response to the ongoing progression from software to system development. The focus shifts towards Infrastructure as Code (IaC) [28] and container virtualization [50] to ease the provisions of REs.

In order to face the challenge of this horizontal and vertically expansion, software projects rely more often on jigs and tools. Dependency and build systems such as Maven [30] were created in 2002 which allowed developers to easily integrate and reuse libraries located in a central repository, instead of managing dependencies manually. Building on that, complex Continuous Integration/Deployment (CI/CD) [54] workflows are maintained to completely automate remote

[2] https://www.collinsdictionary.com/dictionary/english/space.

test execution and deployment into production. Even in smaller software projects, CI/CD starts to become a standard, but writing correct configurations remains a tedious and error-prone task [61,62].

While the mono repository approach encourages to version all those artifacts in a singe repository (cf. Sect. 2.2), the fundamental problem with the distributed and at the same time heterogeneous development of software remains: The lack of alignment between the three dimension of *space*.

2.2 Time

According to the Merriam-Webster dictionary, *time* is *"a nonspatial continuum that is measured in terms of events which succeed one another from past through present to future"*[3]. This describes an important dimension for software development processes that generally extend over long periods of time, accumulating a huge amount of changes. New features are implemented, existing features are modified or removed, and the implementation code can be refactored or migrated to different languages and frameworks. As long as only one developer works on the project at one location, this is not much of a problem. But as discussed before, this is not the reality anymore. Projects are developed by teams with many developers in a distributed fashion, producing concurrent streams of changes to the development artifact. Managing and integrating these changes over time is a major challenge for development teams.

Distributed Version Control Systems (DVCSs) like Git [10] have become a very popular tool to manage the source code in a distributed development process. They embrace the distributed nature of the development process by explicitly supporting branches, on which different development efforts can be carried out concurrently. This also makes it possible for developers to work offline and later merge their changes with others. But while these systems are therefore very powerful and flexible, they fail to provide the alignment one would expect of them. Everyone who worked on a big project using a DVCS knows that the merging of concurrent development efforts is far from easy. To the contrary, systems like Git are known for the cryptic and complicated merge conflicts they produce in big merges, making them very hard to use and hindering collaboration. The growing size (i.e. *space*) of repositories amplifies this problem (cf. Sect. 2.1). And while realtime collaboration is the norm for many end-user applications, decentralized version control systems do not provide this facility, although remote pair programming could greatly strengthen the alignment of concurrent development efforts.

But implementation source code is not the only thing that changes with time. Nowadays, it is commonplace that software projects depend on a large number of open source libraries [20]. New dependencies can be added at any time, and existing dependencies have to be updated regularly to close security vulnerabilities and receive the latest bug fixes and improvements. And when a library is updated, the transitive dependencies brought in by that library might

[3] https://www.merriam-webster.com/dictionary/time.

change as well. The challenge lies in providing every developer with the same set of library versions that matches the source code implementation. Many programming languages bring their own package manager that writes (i.e. locks) all exact library versions into a lockfile[4] that is committed with the source code. This works reasonably well, but these package managers can only provide dependencies written in the same programming language, making them unsuitable to track system libraries or dependencies in polyglot projects. More powerful package managers like Nix [14] are able to build the complete system environment of a project regardless of programming languages used in a reproducible way. But they are complicated to set up and often hard to integrate into existing build processes, in part because every programming language brings their own, non-standardized package management philosophy. Moreover, they generally depend on certain operating systems and thus are not platform-independent.

Finally, the context of a software development project also includes IDEs, SDKs, and REs. These tools are used to develop, build and execute the software, and just like the source code and the library dependencies, they are ever-changing over time. Because these tools are so essential in the development process, local development environments commonly break whenever the requirements for these tools change, forcing each team member to fix their own development setup. This is also the time when the only answer you get from your teammates will be "works on my machine".

Finding configuration mismatches that cause development environments to break is a cumbersome and thankless task. As discussed in Sect. 2.1, IaC approaches can help remedy this problem, but they usually neither capture the complete context, nor are they platform-independent. The recently more widely adopted architectural pattern of microservices exacerbates these problems. The whole system consists of many loosely coupled services with each service potentially written in a different programming language that has certain requirements regarding development, build and deployment tools. The fact that individual services are often migrated from one programming language to another amplifies the amount of changes that have to be managed.

But not only does using Cloud IDEs provide remedy in terms of configuration issues, but it also counteracts the possible lack of available hardware resources of development machines. By shifting development environments, and thereby also resource intense tasks such as compile, build and test processes to the cloud, problems caused by a lack of resources should belong to the past. As a result of this, we expect to see an increase in a developer's productivity.

2.3 Mindset

The Cambridge Dictionary defines *mindset* as *"a person's way of thinking and their opinions"*[5]. In our case this comprises, in particular, thought patterns and best practices that have been established in the various application fields over

[4] Please note that lockfiles are not to be confused with log files.

[5] https://dictionary.cambridge.org/dictionary/english/mindset.

the years and that are reflected in the corresponding domain languages. The importance of mindset becomes apparent in interdisciplinary work where it is the main cause of so-called semantic gaps and false agreement: We often observed quite radical discrepancies between different stakeholders in the interpretation of one and the same diagram which often was even inconsistent in itself. E.g., in a larger industrial project we observed that class diagrams where 'naturally' interpreted as a kind of flow chart by the engineers which lateron cause major inconsistency between developed artefacts. But not only nodes and edges leave room for interpretation, also words like 'prototype' have quite a different meaning in, e.g., business and engineering: While business focusses on organizational aspects and therefore considers organization sketches as prototpyes, engineers are use to build concrete artefacts and therefore consider prototpyes to be tangible artefacts.

While developers are still the overwhelming majority of contributor roles, the diversity of contributors (i.e. manager, engineering, education) joining open-source projects is increasing over the last five years [20]. In order to address the growing problem of semantic gap low-code environments have been proposed that aim at enabling non-programmers to directly contribute to software/system development [7,44]. These environments ease the adoption of a typically very simple developer mindset, but they do not support the original mindset of the involved stakeholders. In contrast, the goal of Language-Driven Engineering (LDE) [58] is to enhance the languages used in the various domains typically for description and documentation purposes only to a level that allows one to generate significants parts of the intended concrete artefact. E.g., we turned Piping and Instrumentations Diagrams that are commonly used for specifying certain mechanical systems into a PSL from which corresponding data models and hardware diagrams could be automatically generated [68,69].

Language-Driven Engineering (LDE) supports this approach by easing the provision of new, Purpose-Specific Language in a services-oriented fashion at three levels:

- **IDE enhancement** via languages for modeling functionality that is then provided by the tools via plug-ins. Such plug-ins provide quality assurance in terms of model checking and testing, various code generators, and platform-specific CI/CD pipelines.
- **IDE support**, so that stakeholders can model in a PSL the user-level functionality, that is then included in a service-oriented fashion. Examples of such PSLs are dedicated (graphical) query languages, but also languages stemming from graphical languages traditionally used in application domains, like network layouts, workflow graphs, or piping and instrumentation diagrams.
- **Tailored interaction facilities** for specific users, like simple configuration languages (cf. CI/CD pipelines, canvases for business modeling, and spreadsheets or dataflow graphs for data analytics).

In practice, the following distinction between shallow and deep language integration is important:

- **Shallow language integration** provides separate special purpose IDEs that produce artifacts for the component library of the development IDE. In this case, the artifacts generated/produced with the special purpose IDE are integrated as a service into the development PSL. Typical examples of such artifacts are complex queries, decision procedures, or special visualization and routing algorithms.
- In **deep language integration** special purpose IDEs are integrated as a service into the global development IDE. The data, process and GUI PSL integration into DIME [5], our major development IDE for Web applications, are typical examples of deep integration.

Whereas shallow integration is meant to (easily) provide the users of a development IDE with additional external services,[6] deep integration increase the conceptual complexity of the development IDE.

Independently of the form of integration, the goal of the PSLs is to support the various stakeholders in a mindset aware/supporting fashion. We call IDEs that are tailored to special purposes and mindsets as mindset-supporting Integrated Development Environments (mIDEs) [58].

As shallow integration is conceptually rather straightforward, we will technologically concentrate on deep language integration in the rest of the paper, and on the provisioning of collaborative mIDEs in the cloud.

3 State of the Art

A promising approach to address at least the challenges of *space* and *time* is the use of so-called Cloud IDEs [19,70]. As recent examples show, Cloud IDEs are establishing themselves as a way to centrally manage complex development setups and make them generally accessible: Gitpod, a container-based development platform with over 400,000 users [21], raised 13 million Euro in 2021 [16]. GitHub, the market leader in source code hosting, made their own Cloud IDE called Codespaces publicly available as a limited beta in 2020 [49] and announced in 2021 that its very own engineering team has moved to Codespaces [67].

In contrast to traditional local development, Cloud IDEs offer an online project workspace accessible via the browser that is always up to date and ready for use. This completely decouples the development and execution of software from the developer's system by eliminating dependency on local infrastructure, performance, or resources [2].

The use of Cloud IDEs, which began in 2016 with Eclipse Che [15], now opens up the possibility of centralized management and provision of the development setup. This means that developers are no longer dependent on their own systems or local resources and can always work with the latest setup without having to migrate manually.

[6] Please note that (in fact manually) extending the service library for a generic, process-oriented basic language can be considered the main contribution of leading low code environments like Mendix and Bubble [7,44].

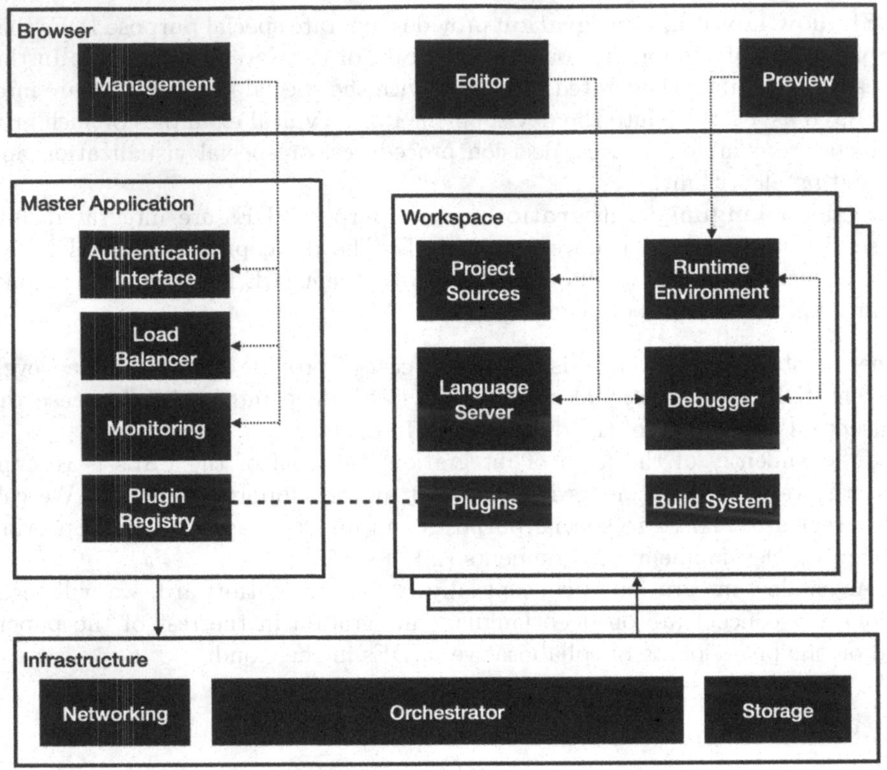

Fig. 2. Cloud IDE system architecture.

In this section, the concept of Cloud IDEs is analyzed and differentiated from classic local development. We describe the system architecture of a Cloud IDE (see Fig. 2) and give an overview of the individual components used to emulate the features of a desktop IDE. First, we explain the central cluster-based infrastructure that provides and scales an IDE as a distributed system in Sect. 3.1. Since a Cloud IDE can be used by a large number of users, a so-called Master Application (see Sect. 3.2) is used to manage and control the infrastructure. In contrast to local development, all tools, dependencies and source code of a project within a workspace (see Sect. 3.3) are aligned and delivered by the Cloud IDE.

3.1 Infrastructure

The infrastructure of a Cloud IDE orchestrates all workspaces and the master application in separate virtual containers build from predefined images. Gitpod currently provides six different example workspace images [21] which can be instantiated by a user to start a project. Each container has its own isolated resources and serves the required features of involved SDKs and REs in forms of so called plugins. The orchestrator manages all containers by dynamically allocating available resources for new workspaces for a user to work on a project.

In order to be able to edit the source code and other project resources, the corresponding files must be available within the infrastructure. Cloud IDEs use a central storage for this purpose, which is subdivided on the basis of the existing workspaces, so that each user can only access his files in isolation.

A workspace is represented by a container running on the infrastructure which can be accessed via corresponding URL. A network controller is used for traffic routing and scaling, by forwarding user requests to workspace containers.

3.2 Master Application

The master application controls the cluster behind a Cloud IDE. Since the entire load of development and execution lies on the infrastructure, the available resources must be continuously monitored. For this purpose, monitoring components [1] are used to observe the currently used workspaces including editors and REs. Based on the monitoring, the load balancer [52] can ensure that resources are allocated as needed and unused resources are released. In this way, the Cloud IDE infrastructure offers efficient use of the available computing capacity.

Besides the cluster, all user workspaces are managed by the master application, too. The user access and authentication mechanism provides SSO capabilities for established project management tools such as Github [12] and Gitlab [25].

3.3 Workspace

The workspace of a Cloud IDE symbolizes a combination of the source code of a project and a developer setup which are served by a user-specific container. To align all developers of a project, the development setup provides a composition of existing IDE components, which refer to specific SDKs, editors and REs. Thanks to this specification all dependencies and IDE plugins necessary for the development of the source can be loaded automatically to reduce the initial preparation time and eliminate manual setup. These steps can also be automated, reducing the initial preparation time of a workspace.

Listing 1.1 shows an example workspace specification for the Gitpod Cloud IDE used to develop the pet clinic project[7]. Lines 9 to 14 include several Java extensions and the Spring Boot extension, needed to develop a web application. The lines 1 to 3 specify how to load the dependencies for the project to prepare the runtime environment of the project. Lines 5 to 7 define an exposed port of the target application to be served and accessed inside the Cloud IDE.

4 Aligned, Purpose-Driven Cooperation

The challenges described in Sect. 2 not only concern the classical software development with GPLs but also the Model Driven Software Development (MDSD) [65]

[7] https://github.com/gitpod-io/spring-petclinic.

```
tasks:
- init: ./mvnw package -DskipTests
  command: java -jar target/*.jar
ports:
- port: 8080
  onOpen: open-preview
vscode:
  extensions:
    - redhat.java
    - vscjava.vscode-java-debug
    - vscjava.vscode-java-test
    - pivotal.vscode-spring-boot
```

Listing 1.1. Gitpod workspace specification file for the pet clinic example Spring Boot application.

and Extreme Model Driven Design (XMDD) [40]. Contrary to the classical development the concept of XMDD is based on the employment of as specific as possible and thus many DSL [18], which are embedded in likewise specialized environment. Accordingly, it is even more important for the domain-specific tool that the distributed use is supported by a cross-system alignment.

At this point it is obvious that the increasing setup complexity, faster cooperation and mindset support in system development requires new approaches for IDEs. Although the existing Cloud IDEs already made a step in the right direction by aligning the developer setup, neither the possibility to collaborate in real-time nor to use PSL exists. Current Cloud IDEs provide classical software development scenarios on the two levels of development and execution which is insufficient as described by Boßelmann et al. [6].

Our vision is based on the idea to extend the concept and architecture of Cloud IDEs for model-driven software development, extreme-model-driven design and ultimately LDE. As described in [58], the successful use of XMDD requires that new and refined PSLs are continuously created and made available. To achieve this goal, a Cloud IDE must be able to dynamically create new environments via bootstrapping [48] to directly deliver developed PSLs. This step opens new doors by making existing domain-specific tools like CINCO [47], Pyro [71] and DIME [5] easier to use than ever before. At the same time, a variety of new opportunities arise, such as the realization of LDE [58] in the cloud by the use of the one-thing-approach (OTA) [38]. Due to the fact that every PSL available in the Cloud IDE is at the same time a web-based service, LDE can be realized uniformly and comprehensively through service-oriented composition and integration [41]. As a result, mindset-supporting integrated development environments (mIDEs) [58] for intuitive and cooperative system development can be realized on the same central tool. The realization of a Cloud mIDE will accordingly bring the following advantages regarding LDE:

- **Modularization:** Each developed or refined PSL exists as an independent module which can be integrated within the Cloud mIDE as a service. A PSL module combines not only the respective language including editor, generator and execution environment but also a setup description (like Listing 1.1) which extends the plugin concept of Cloud IDEs. This way, a complete PSL with all dependencies can be integrated in an encapsulated manner. Due to the uniform structure of all created PSLs, users can independently use new specific combinations of PSLs in their workspace.

- **Publication:** In contrast to Cloud IDEs, the number of available languages is not limited but highly dynamic in LDE. Each PSL created within the Cloud mIDE is a service by construction and is available to all users of the environment immediately after creation. Thus, the distribution of new PSL modules is possible without any additional steps within the environment.
- **Maintenance:** Every change or refinement of a PSL takes place within the Cloud mIDE at a central location. Since each PSL is integrated as a service, it is accordingly not necessary for each user to make adjustments independently.

In the remainder of this section we illustrate the key design decisions of our Cloud mIDE beginning with the PSL Module that encapsulates the language editor, setup, and features of a PSL as a whole in Sect. 4.1. Subsequently, Sect. 4.2 shows the reflexive reuse and continuous refinement of a PSL inside the environment. Finally, it is described how different users can use specialized workspaces as a combination of selected PSLs in Sect. 4.3.

4.1 PSL Module

The PSL module (see Fig. 3) describes a self-contained component for using a PSL within the Cloud mIDE. Each language within a Cloud IDE requires an associated Language Server and an Editor Extension. Regarding different programming languages, language servers [8] are used to enrich the editor with language specific features such as keyword coloring, validation, content assist and reference jumping. Thanks to the Language Server Protocol (LSP) [22], the various language servers can be controlled by the editor via a uniform protocol. This loose coupling between language-specific support makes it possible to dynamically integrate new languages.

The Editor Extension is needed to associate an editor to a specific file type. As soon as a file of the corresponding type is opened, the language server is addressed via the standardized LSP. A language server provides all language specific features like syntax highlighting, syntax validation, auto-comprehension and jump to definition. For this purpose, the language server accesses the file currently opened by the user via the Storage API.

Unlike General-Purpose Languages, PSLs are complemented by generators and transformers that allow translation to other PSLs or executable code [66]. The PSL module thus extends the LSP so that users can trigger the generation or transformation via corresponding web services. The code generated during the generation process can be stored within the workspace via the corresponding storage API.

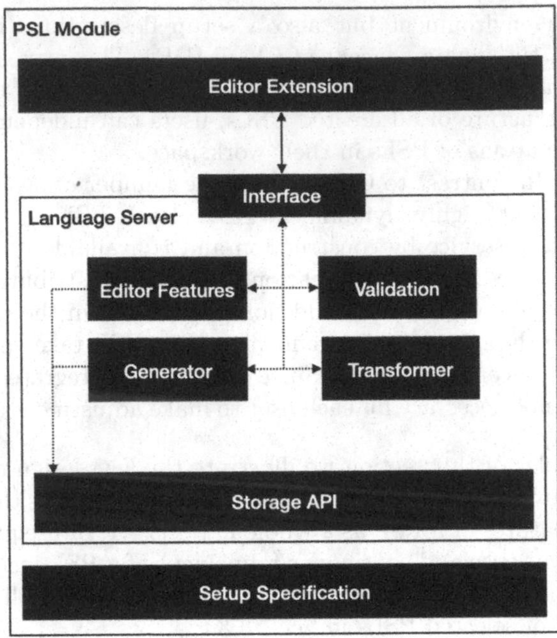

Fig. 3. PSL Module Concept to realize the PSL as a service.

In addition to the language server, a PSL module also contains the Setup Specification, which composes all dependent SDKs and REs for serving the PSL module. This way, a PSL module can be prepared by the environment automatically behind the scenes to be used by the users immediately. The combination of the unified language servers with the respective specification allows the environment to spawn instances of the PSL modules as needed.

4.2 Bootstrapping

A central component of the MDSD, XMDD and LDE approaches is the possibility to develop new PSL. In the context of the Cloud mIDE, this means the development and subsequent publishing of new PSL modules directly in the environment. For easy and intuitive development of PSLs, established language workbenches such as Xtext [17] and MPS [9] also use language definition PSLs. These PSLs can be used, for example, to describe the concrete and abstract syntax of a language and then automatically generate the necessary components such as parser and linker.

In order for the Cloud IDE to also offer the possibility of developing PSLs with PSLs, a reflexive structure must be provided. Figure 4 shows the concept for a workspace within the Cloud mIDE. Each workspace is served by a corresponding runtime, which provides the necessary features and in particular the language

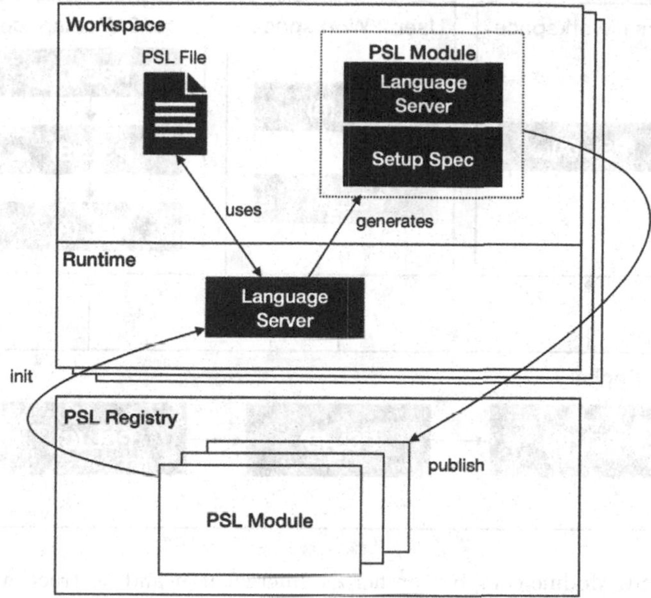

Fig. 4. Cloud mIDE bootstrapping concept, utilizing a PSL to create PSLs.

servers of the used PSL modules. In this way, a language server generates a new PSL module based on a language definition inside the workspace.

Afterwards, the generated PSL module can be included in the PSL registry and build by the corresponding setup specification. The newly added PSL as well as all previous ones can be reused accordingly in another workspace. The resulting reflexive structure allows to continuously develop, refine and use PSLs [51,58] inside the environment by all users.

4.3 Composition

According to the LDE approach [58], a PSL should always support a user on the appropriate level of abstraction. As a result, PSLs are often structured hierarchically by vertical refinement. In local development, however, this approach requires a user to manually prepare all transitively dependent PSLs. The Cloud mIDE can circumvent this problem by describing all required PSL modules inside the setup specification. Thanks to the uniform structure of all PSL modules, the corresponding workspace including all dependent PSLs can be provided automatically according to the mindset of a user.

Figure 5 shows an example for three different users, each with their own workspaces and level of abstraction. The underlying PSL Registry comprises three PSL modules which depend on each other by refining A by B and B by C. Depending on which level of abstraction a user chooses, the appropriate PSL module and all dependent ones can be instantiated inside a user's workspace.

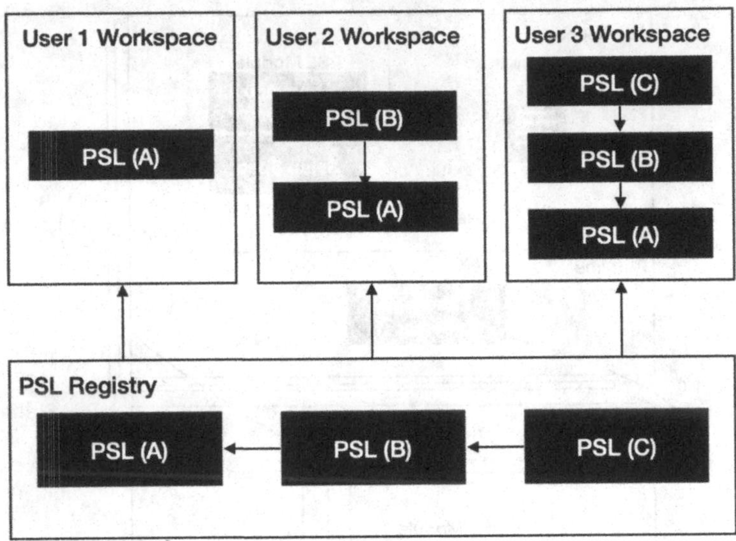

Fig. 5. PSL Module composition across different user and abstraction levels.

In this way all features of a selected PSL C can be used even if it depends on more abstract functionalities of PSL B and PSL A. Transformation sequences [24] can also be realized through this structure, by using the result of a PSL transformation as the input of a more abstract one.

5 Sketch: Aligned Cinco Environment

The Cinco Meta Tooling Suite [47] is an Eclipse Modeling Framework (EMF) based language workbench [59] for the specification and subsequent generation of graphical graph-based PSLs (gPSLs). In contrast to tools such as WebGME [42] and MetaEdit+ [56], Cinco focuses on ease of use by applying domain-specific concepts at the meta level. For this reason, Cinco is based on three core concepts: domain-specificity, full-code generation and service-orientation (DFS) [46].

This means that Cinco can generate a complete, directly executable mIDE based on three specialized specification languages. The specification takes place for the abstract and concrete syntax separately with the help of the Meta Graph Language (MGL) and the Meta Style Language (MSL). For the composition of several languages to a so-called Cinco Product the Cinco Product Definition (CPD) is offered. The corresponding generation process aggregates all information from the individual specification formats and creates a new environment. The integration of additional features or whole PSLs takes place service-oriented so that the users of Cinco can concentrate on the design of the PSL.

In this section, we describe the currently ongoing realization of the Aligned Cinco Environment (ACE) evolving the concepts of Cinco to a Cloud mIDE.

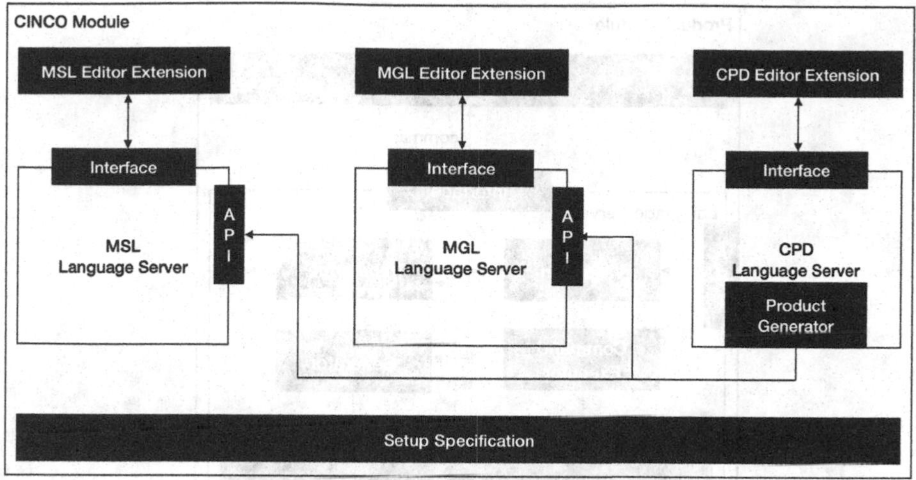

Fig. 6. The CINCO Module which composes the specifications languages for the MGL, MSL and CPD of CINCO.

The aim of the ACE is the creation and delivery of gPSLs in a web-based distributed environment. For this purpose, first a specific PSL module is designed which includes the specification languages and the product generator of CINCO. Afterwards, the approaches of the already existing Pyro [71] project are included which has already created several CINCO products for the web [23,35]. Based on Pyro, a corresponding gPSL module is designed which supports the use of gPSLs of CINCO in a real-time collaboration environment. Finally, it is shown how the service-oriented integration of gPSLs can be used in the context of the ACE to continuously refine gPSLs.

5.1 CINCO Module

The realization of the ACE is intended to map the features and concepts of the CINCO Meta Tooling Suite [47] by allowing gPSLs to be developed in a simple manner. For this purpose, CINCO provides three related PSLs describing the abstract and concrete syntax of graphical languages and the composition to a product. Based on the PSL module illustrated in Sect. 4.1, the CINCO Module can be created as a coherent composition of three PSLs. Figure 6 shows the schematic structure of the CINCO Module, which includes the MGL, MSL, and CPD specification languages. Similar to the PSL modules, each specification language has its own editor extension and a corresponding language server that provides the corresponding features. However, the languages can be used consistently in parallel thanks to the service-oriented API integration. In contrast to a direct file access, the API of a language server benefits from existing parsers and linkers so that a call can be described on the given metamodel instead of raw text. This connection enables for example cross-validation, reference jumping

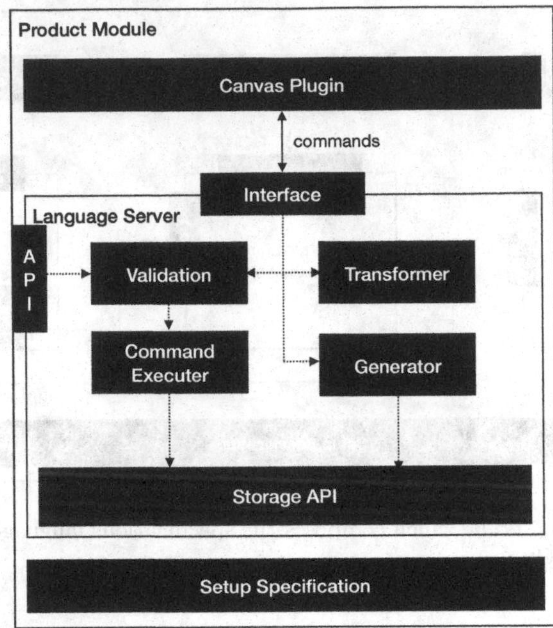

Fig. 7. The generated Product Module to use graphical graph-based PSLs in the ACE.

and generation [34] by establishing communication channels between the language servers. The generation process utilizes the APIs of all language servers, collects the entire gPSL specification and creates the Product Module.

5.2 Product Module

The product is generated by Pyro including the previously specified gPSL. Figure 7 visualizes the corresponding product module for the ACE. In contrast to textual PSLs, graphical languages require a canvas for modeling nodes and edges. To avoid the unnecessary and repetitive transfer of shapes, colors and styling, the canvas is generated as a specific editor plugin. Even though the editor must be adapted for each gPSL in this way, this can be done centrally within the ACE.

Another difference to textual languages is the communication between the editor and the server. Textual language server transfer text fragments as described in the LSP, which are used for a merge process. This technique is based on the same mechanisms as VCS and thus hinders fast collaboration in real-time between multiple users.

Graphical languages on the other hand offer the advantage that each element and action can be uniquely identified. For this reason, the language server generated by Pyro utilizes conflict-free replicated data types (CRDTs) [55] in form

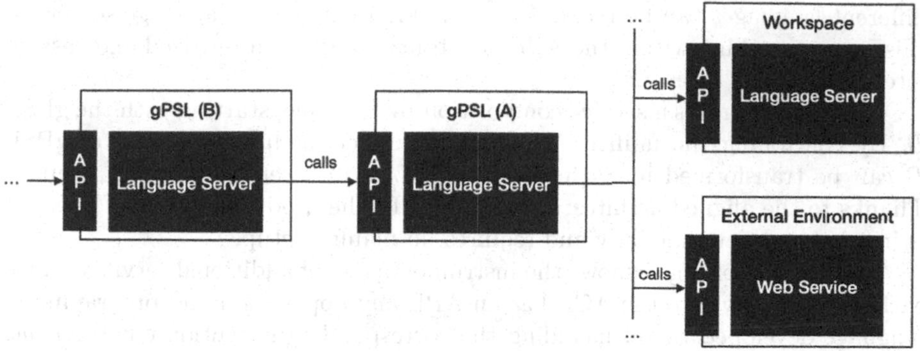

Fig. 8. Example for the service-oriented composition of ACE modules and external services.

of commands which can be used to unambiguously transmit a user's interactions with the canvas. This approach allows users to work in parallel on the same graphical model without interruptions and the need for merge operations.

Each command received is first validated within the server to ensure that it does not violate the previously specified syntax and any additional validators that may be present. According to the principles of CINCO [47], gPSLs should support the user as much as possible, which includes priority validation. Each valid command is then applied, distributed to all other users and finally persisted to a file via storage API.

Similar to the PSL modules described in Sect. 4.1, generators and transformers can be included that can be called via the editor. The generator has additionally still another connection to the Storage API to persist the generated files.

5.3 Service-Orientation

A key concept of the CINCO Meta Tooling Suite and LDE is the service-oriented integration of functionalities to reduce the complexity of a tool. This concept corresponds to the established micro-services, which provide functionalities via the web. In the area of scientific workflows, tools such as ETI [36], Bio-jETI [32] and Taverna [27] have already shown that the composition and instrumentation of reusable services facilitates the creation of complex applications as described by Lamprecht [31]. The achieved interoperability of service-oriented, model-driven environments can be used to align heterogeneous systems for e.g. internet-of-things (IoT) scenarios as described in [37].

In the context of the ACE, the set of reusable services can now be significantly increased by making each module a service by design. For this reason, each Language Server of a product module provides a unified API to grant other language servers and web services a convenient access to a model and corresponding editor functionalities. As a result, model transformations [34] between different languages can be realized by a simple request to a language server. In this way, everything within the ACE is automatically a fully-fledged and easy to integrate service.

Figure 8 illustrates a service composition by example, starting with the gPSL *B*. By controlling the unified API of the product modules, a model of gPSL *B* can be transformed into a model of gPSL *A* in a service-oriented manner. Thanks to the aligned architecture of the ACE, the product module of gPSL *A* is instantiated automatically and requires no manual setup.

The left side of Fig. 8 shows the instrumentation of additional services. Since each workspace within the ACE has an API, any application and programming language developed there, including the corresponding execution environment, can be reused. Besides the internal service connection, external environments and classical web services can also be used in a similar fashion.

As shown in Fig. 8, the service landscape can be extended and scaled both horizontally and vertically. Accordingly, each PSL inside the ACE can reuse and refine previously created PSLs, taking the service-oriented approach to the next level.

6 Conclusion and Perspectives

In this paper, we have sketched ACE, an IDE for collaborative system development that supports a three-dimensional alignment: in *space*, in *time*, and in *mindset*. Key is to provide the entire required infrastructure in the cloud, and to involve even non-technical stakeholders via dedicated PSLs. We address typical issues of low-code platforms, like the lacking support of good software engineering practices [33], by considering bootstrapping, simplicity and maintainability top-level priorities: Realised by our modularization strategy, even larger projects can be handled without perishing in an enormous amount of complex code. The complete development and runtime environment can be generated from self-documenting specifications [47]. Technically our approach uses centralized infrastructure, based on cluster technology and container virtualization, to support scalability and the rapid replacement of deprecated components, and LDE as a means to easily provide and adapt the PSLs required to support the involved domain experts [58].

ACE overcomes the problem that each developer of a cooperative project typically has to maintain her own, local development environment which changes over time due to updates and other version changes. Moreover, the easy integration of new Purpose-Specific Languages is an ideal means to reduce semantic gaps: Stakeholders with different expertise can contribute in the language supporting their mindset. This has a positive impact on the overall user experience, a quality that it is especially recommended for low-code platforms [33].

While our vision supports the separation of concerns very well for hierarchically organized PSLs, bidirectional dependencies between different models are not foreseen. Rather, cyclic dependencies have to be broken by introducing competence hierarchies following the one-thing-approach (OTA) [38]. In our experience, this structural restriction pays of due to its gained simplicity [39,45]. In contrast, the transformational approach presented in [60] aims at explicitly dealing with bidirectional dependencies which introduces conceptual challenges that do not fit our simplicity-oriented design style.

Basis for the ease of language definition and integration are PSL modules which provide languages as services with the help of a language server. PSL modules can be made available via a central repository forming a reflexive structure supporting languages that extend languages. Overall this results in Cloud mIDEs which are tailored to special purposes and mindsets of different stakeholders.

Our initial experience with ACE indicates a simplicity and uniformity which allows advanced users to even develop and refine Purpose-Specific Languages and then generate their own Cloud mIDEs independently. We are therefore convinced that our approach to an aligned, purpose-driven cooperation has the potential to open software system development to a much wider audience.

References

1. Aceto, G., Botta, A., De Donato, W., Pescapè, A.: Cloud monitoring: a survey. Comput. Netw. **57**(9), 2093–2115 (2013)
2. Aho, T., et al.: Designing IDE as a service. Commun. Cloud Softw. **1**(1), 1–10 (2011)
3. Allspaw, J., Hammond, P.: 10+ deploys per day: dev and ops cooperation at Flickr. In: Velocity: Web Performance and Operations Conference, June 2009. https://www.youtube.com/watch?v=LdOe18KhtT4
4. Balasubramanian, D., Coglio, A., Dubey, A., Karsai, G.: Towards model-based intent-driven adaptive software. In: Margaria, T., Steffen, B. (eds.) Proceedings of the 10th International Symposium on Leveraging Applications of Formal Method, Verification and Validation, ISoLA 2021. LNCS, vol. 13036, pp. 378–392. Springer, Cham (2021)
5. Boßelmann, S., et al.: DIME: a programming-less modeling environment for web applications. In: Margaria, T., Steffen, B. (eds.) ISoLA 2016. LNCS, vol. 9953, pp. 809–832. Springer, Cham (2016). https://doi.org/10.1007/978-3-319-47169-3_60
6. Boßelmann, S., Naujokat, S., Steffen, B.: On the difficulty of drawing the line. In: Margaria, T., Steffen, B. (eds.) ISoLA 2018. LNCS, vol. 11244, pp. 340–356. Springer, Cham (2018). https://doi.org/10.1007/978-3-030-03418-4_20
7. Bubble Group Inc: Bubble (2021). https://bubble.io/. Accessed 18 Aug 2021
8. Bünder, H.: Decoupling language and editor-the impact of the language server protocol on textual domain-specific languages. In: MODELSWARD, pp. 129–140 (2019)
9. Campagne, F.: The MPS Language Workbench, vol. 1. Fabien Campagne (2014)
10. Chacon, S., Straub, B.: Pro Git. The Expert's Voice. Apress (2014)
11. Chatley, R., Donaldson, A., Mycroft, A.: The next 7000 programming languages. In: Steffen, B., Woeginger, G. (eds.) Computing and Software Science. LNCS, vol. 10000, pp. 250–282. Springer, Cham (2019). https://doi.org/10.1007/978-3-319-91908-9_15

12. Dabbish, L., Stuart, C., Tsay, J., Herbsleb, J.: Social coding in GitHub: transparency and collaboration in an open software repository. In: Proceedings of the ACM 2012 Conference on Computer Supported Cooperative Work, pp. 1277–1286 (2012)
13. Debois, P., et al.: DevOps: a software revolution in the making. J. Inf. Technol. Manag. **24**(8), 3–39 (2011)
14. Dolstra, E.: The purely functional software deployment model. Ph.D. thesis (2006)
15. Eclipse: Eclipse Che. https://www.eclipse.org/che/. Accessed 10 May 2021
16. Efftinge, S., Landgraf, J.: Next Chapter for Gitpod. https://www.gitpod.io/blog/next-chapter-for-gitpod/. Accessed 10 May 2021
17. Eysholdt, M., Behrens, H.: Xtext: implement your language faster than the quick and dirty way. In: Proceedings of the ACM International Conference Companion on Object Oriented Programming Systems Languages and Applications Companion, pp. 307–309 (2010)
18. Fowler, M.: Domain-Specific Languages. Pearson Education (2010)
19. Gadhikar, L.M., Mohan, L., Chaudhari, M., Sawant, P., Bhusara, Y.: Browser based IDE to code in the cloud. In: Patnaik, S., Tripathy, P., Naik, S. (eds.) New Paradigms in Internet Computing, pp. 59–69. Springer, Cham (2013). https://doi.org/10.1007/978-3-642-35461-8_6
20. GitHub Inc: The 2020 State of the Octoverse (2020). https://octoverse.github.com. Accessed 5 Aug 2021
21. Gitpod: Gitpod. https://www.gitpod.io/. Accessed 10 May 2021
22. Gitpod: Lamguage Server Protocol. https://microsoft.github.io/language-server-protocol/. Accessed 10 May 2021
23. Gossen, F., Murtovi, A., Zweihoff, P., Steffen, B.: ADD-Lib: Decision Diagrams in Practice. arXiv preprint arXiv:1912.11308 (2019)
24. Hemel, Z., Kats, L.C.L., Visser, E.: Code generation by model transformation. In: Vallecillo, A., Gray, J., Pierantonio, A. (eds.) ICMT 2008. LNCS, vol. 5063, pp. 183–198. Springer, Heidelberg (2008). https://doi.org/10.1007/978-3-540-69927-9_13
25. Hethey, J.M.: GitLab Repository Management. Packt Publishing Ltd. (2013)
26. Holzner, S.: Eclipse. O'Reilly Media, Inc. (2004)
27. Hull, D., et al.: Taverna: a tool for building and running workflows of services. Nucleic Acids Res. **34**(Suppl. 2), W729–W732 (2006)
28. Hüttermann, M.: Infrastructure as code. In: Hüttermann, M. (ed.) DevOps for Developers, pp. 135–156. Springer, Heidelberg (2012). https://doi.org/10.1007/978-1-4302-4570-4_9
29. Kelly, S., Tolvanen, J.P.: Domain-Specific Modeling: Enabling Full Code Generation. Wiley-IEEE Computer Society Press, Hoboken (2008)
30. Lalou, J.: Apache Maven Dependency Management. Packt Publishing Ltd. (2013)
31. Lamprecht, A.-L.: User-Level Workflow Design. LNCS, vol. 8311. Springer, Heidelberg (2013). https://doi.org/10.1007/978-3-642-45389-2
32. Lamprecht, A.L., Margaria, T., Steffen, B.: Bio-jETI: a framework for semantics-based service composition. BMC Bioinform. **10**(10), 1–19 (2009)
33. Lethbridge, T.C.: Low-code is often high-code, so we must design low-code platforms to enable proper software engineering. In: Margaria, T., Steffen, B. (eds.) ISoLA 2021. LNCS, vol. 13036, pp. 202–212. Springer, Cham (2021)
34. Lybecait, M.: Meta-Model Based Generation of Domain-Specific Modeling Tools (2019)

35. Lybecait, M., Kopetzki, D., Zweihoff, P., Fuhge, A., Naujokat, S., Steffen, B.: A tutorial introduction to graphical modeling and metamodeling with CINCO. In: Margaria, T., Steffen, B. (eds.) ISoLA 2018. LNCS, vol. 11244, pp. 519–538. Springer, Cham (2018). https://doi.org/10.1007/978-3-030-03418-4_31
36. Margaria, T.: Web services-based tool-integration in the ETI platform. Softw. Syst. Model. **4**(2), 141–156 (2005)
37. Margaria, T., Chaudhary, H.A.A., Guevara, I., Ryan, S., Schieweck, A.: The interoperability challenge: building a model driven digital thread platform for CPS. In: Margaria, T., Steffen, B. (eds.) Proceedings of the the 37th International Manufacturing Conference, ISoLA 2021. LNCS, vol. 13036, pp. 393–413. Springer, Cham (2021)
38. Margaria, T., Steffen, B.: Business process modeling in the jABC: the one-thing approach. In: Handbook of Research on Business Process Modeling, pp. 1–26. IGI Global (2009)
39. Margaria, T., Steffen, B.: Simplicity as a driver for agile innovation. Computer **43**(6), 90–92 (2010)
40. Margaria, T., Steffen, B.: eXtreme Model-Driven Development (XMDD) technologies as a hands-on approach to software development without coding. In: Tatnall, A. (ed.) Encyclopedia of Education and Information Technologies, pp. 732–750. Springer, Cham (2020). https://doi.org/10.1007/978-3-319-60013-0_208-1
41. Margaria, T., Steffen, B., Reitenspieß, M.: Service-oriented design: the roots. In: Benatallah, B., Casati, F., Traverso, P. (eds.) ICSOC 2005. LNCS, vol. 3826, pp. 450–464. Springer, Heidelberg (2005). https://doi.org/10.1007/11596141_34
42. Maróti, M., et al.: Next generation (meta) modeling: web-and cloud-based collaborative tool infrastructure. In: MPM@ MoDELS, vol. 1237, pp. 41–60 (2014)
43. Mayer, P., Bauer, A.: An empirical analysis of the utilization of multiple programming languages in open source projects. In: Proceedings of the 19th International Conference on Evaluation and Assessment in Software Engineering, EASE 2015. Association for Computing Machinery, New York (2015). https://doi.org/10.1145/2745802.2745805
44. Mendix Technology BV 2021: Mendix (2021). https://www.mendix.com/. Accessed 18 Aug 2021
45. Merten, M., Steffen, B.: Simplicity driven application development. J. Integr. Des. Process Sci. (SDPS) **16** (2013)
46. Naujokat, S.: Heavy meta: model-driven domain-specific generation of generative domain-specific modeling tools. Ph.D. thesis (2017)
47. Naujokat, S., Lybecait, M., Kopetzki, D., Steffen, B.: CINCO: a simplicity-driven approach to full generation of domain-specific graphical modeling tools. Softw. Tools Technol. Transfer **20**(3), 327–354 (2017)
48. Naujokat, S., Neubauer, J., Margaria, T., Steffen, B.: Meta-level reuse for mastering domain specialization. In: Margaria, T., Steffen, B. (eds.) ISoLA 2016. LNCS, vol. 9953, pp. 218–237. Springer, Cham (2016). https://doi.org/10.1007/978-3-319-47169-3_16
49. Niyogi, S.: New from satellite 2020: Github discussions, codespaces, securing code in private repositories, and more (2020). https://github.blog/2020-05-06-new-from-satellite-2020-github-codespaces-github-discussions-securing-code-in-private-repositories-and-more/#codespaces. Accessed 18 Aug 2021
50. Pahl, C.: Containerization and the PaaS cloud. IEEE Cloud Comput. **2**(3), 24–31 (2015)

51. Prinz, A., Mezei, G.: The art of bootstrapping. In: Hammoudi, S., Pires, L.F., Selić, B. (eds.) MODELSWARD 2019. CCIS, vol. 1161, pp. 182–200. Springer, Cham (2020). https://doi.org/10.1007/978-3-030-37873-8_8
52. Rahman, M., Iqbal, S., Gao, J.: Load balancer as a service in cloud computing. In: 2014 IEEE 8th International Symposium on Service Oriented System Engineering, pp. 204–211. IEEE (2014)
53. Saini, R., Bali, S., Mussbacher, G.: Towards web collaborative modelling for the user requirements notation using eclipse che and theia IDE. In: 2019 IEEE/ACM 11th International Workshop on Modelling in Software Engineering (MiSE), pp. 15–18. IEEE (2019)
54. Shahin, M., Babar, M.A., Zhu, L.: Continuous integration, delivery and deployment: a systematic review on approaches, tools, challenges and practices. IEEE Access **5**, 3909–3943 (2017)
55. Shapiro, M., Preguiça, N., Baquero, C., Zawirski, M.: Conflict-free replicated data types. In: Défago, X., Petit, F., Villain, V. (eds.) SSS 2011. LNCS, vol. 6976, pp. 386–400. Springer, Heidelberg (2011). https://doi.org/10.1007/978-3-642-24550-3_29
56. Smolander, K., Lyytinen, K., Tahvanainen, V.-P., Marttiin, P.: MetaEdit—a flexible graphical environment for methodology modelling. In: Andersen, R., Bubenko, J.A., Sølvberg, A. (eds.) CAiSE 1991. LNCS, vol. 498, pp. 168–193. Springer, Heidelberg (1991). https://doi.org/10.1007/3-540-54059-8_85
57. Stack Exchange Inc: Stack Overflow Annual Developer Survey (2021). https://insights.stackoverflow.com/survey/2021. Accessed 5 Aug 2021
58. Steffen, B., Gossen, F., Naujokat, S., Margaria, T.: Language-driven engineering: from general-purpose to purpose-specific languages. In: Steffen, B., Woeginger, G. (eds.) Computing and Software Science. LNCS, vol. 10000, pp. 311–344. Springer, Cham (2019). https://doi.org/10.1007/978-3-319-91908-9_17
59. Steinberg, D., Budinsky, F., Merks, E., Paternostro, M.: EMF: Eclipse Modeling Framework. Pearson Education (2008)
60. Stevens, P.: The future of programming and modelling: a vision. In: Margaria, T., Steffen, B. (eds.) 9th International Symposium On Leveraging Applications of Formal Methods, Verification and Validation, ISoLA 2021. LNCS, vol. 13036, pp. 357–377. Springer, Cham (2021). https://www.research.ed.ac.uk/en/publications/the-future-of-programming-and-modelling-a-vision
61. Tegeler, T., Gossen, F., Steffen, B.: A model-driven approach to continuous practices for modern cloud-based web applications. In: 2019 9th International Conference on Cloud Computing, Data Science Engineering (Confluence), pp. 1–6 (2019)
62. Teumert, S.: Visual Authoring of CI/CD Pipeline Configurations. Bachelor's thesis, TU Dortmund University, April 2021. https://archive.org/details/visual-authoring-of-cicd-pipeline-configurations
63. Vainikka, J.: Full-stack web development using Django REST framework and React (2018)
64. Voelter, M.: Programming vs. that thing subject matter experts do. In: Margaria, T., Steffen, B. (eds.) Proceedings of the 10th International Symposium on Leveraging Applications of Formal Method, Verification and Validation. LNCS, vol. 13036, pp. 414–425. Springer, Cham (2021)
65. Völter, M., Stahl, T., Bettin, J., Haase, A., Helsen, S.: Model-Driven Software Development: Technology, Engineering, Management. Wiley, Hoboken (2013)

66. Völter, M., Visser, E.: Language extension and composition with language workbenches. In: Proceedings of the ACM International Conference Companion on Object Oriented Programming Systems Languages and Applications Companion, OOPSLA 2010, pp. 301–304. Association for Computing Machinery, New York (2010). https://doi.org/10.1145/1869542.1869623
67. Wilkerson, C.: Github's engineering team has moved to codespaces (2020). https://github.blog/2021-08-11-githubs-engineering-team-moved-codespaces/. Accessed 18 Aug 2021
68. Wortmann, N.: Modellbasierte Modellierung von industriellen Zentrifugen mit Codegenerierung für Steuerungssysteme. Bachelor thesis, Münster University of Applied Sciences (2015)
69. Wortmann, N., Michel, M., Naujokat, S.: A fully model-based approach to software development for industrial centrifuges. In: Margaria, T., Steffen, B. (eds.) ISoLA 2016, Part II. LNCS, vol. 9953, pp. 774–783. Springer, Cham (2016). https://doi.org/10.1007/978-3-319-47169-3_58
70. Wu, L., Liang, G., Kui, S., Wang, Q.: CEclipse: an online IDE for programing in the cloud. In: 2011 IEEE World Congress on Services, pp. 45–52. IEEE (2011)
71. Zweihoff, P., Naujokat, S., Steffen, B.: Pyro: generating domain-specific collaborative online modeling environments. In: Hähnle, R., van der Aalst, W. (eds.) FASE 2019. LNCS, vol. 11424, pp. 101–115. Springer, Cham (2019). https://doi.org/10.1007/978-3-030-16722-6_6

Software Verification Tools

sVerify: Verifying Smart Contracts Through Lazy Annotation and Learning

Bo Gao[1(✉)], Ling Shi[2], Jiaying Li[2], Jialiang Chang[3], Jun Sun[2], and Zijiang Yang[3]

[1] Singapore University of Technology and Design, Singapore, Singapore
[2] Singapore Management University, Singapore, Singapore
[3] Western Michigan University, Kalamazoo, USA

Abstract. Smart contracts have recently attracted much attention from industry as they aim to assure anonymous distributed secure transactions. It also becomes clear that they are not immune to code vulnerabilities. As smart contracts cannot be patched once deployed, it is crucial to verify their correctness before deployment. Existing approaches mainly focus on testing and bounded verification which do not guarantee the correctness of smart contracts. In this work, we develop a formal verifier called *sVerify* for Solidity smart contracts based on a combination of lazy annotation and automatic loop invariant learning techniques. The latter is essential as explicit or implicit loops (due to fallback function calls) are common in smart contracts. Patterns and features which are specific to smart contracts are used to facilitate invariant learning. *sVerify* has been evaluated with 4670 Solidity smart contracts, and the evaluation result shows that *sVerify* is effective and reasonably efficient for verifying smart contracts.

Keywords: Verification · Smart contracts · Loop invariant learning

1 Introduction

Blockchain is a fast-growing research area in recent years. It is first conceptualized in Bitcoin blockchain [23] by Satoshi Nakamoto based on multiple techniques like cryptographic chain of blocks by Stuart Haber and W. Scott Stornetta [12], distributed systems by Lamport [16], etc. The emergence of Bitcoin makes financial transactions among strangers possible without the help of a third-party authority. Later on, Buterin stepped forward to develop the platform Ethereum [29], which allows self-enforcing programs, called smart contracts, to run by themselves. Smart contracts have since attracted much attention in many domains, such as financial institutes and supply chains.

A smart contract is a computerized transaction protocol that executes the terms of a contract to satisfy user requirements, such as voting and trading. It can be regarded as a computer program, which is typically written in a Turing-complete language called Solidity in Ethereum. The immutability of blockchain makes smart contracts unpatchable once they are deployed on the blockchain. Furthermore, the Javascript-like syntax of Solidity and its many unique language features (e.g., storage variables and fallback functions) often confuse users, even if they are experienced with traditional programming languages. As a result, there are many attacks due to code vulnerabilities that caused huge economic losses. For instance, the DAO attack [1] resulted in a loss roughly

T. Margaria and B. Steffen (Eds.): ISoLA 2021, LNCS 13036, pp. 453–469, 2021.
https://doi.org/10.1007/978-3-030-89159-6_28

equivalent to 60 million USD at the time. The attacker found a loophole in the *splitDAO* function so that he could repeatedly withdraw Ether through an implicit loop in the *fallback* function in a single transaction.

To react on the increasing amount of attacks on smart contracts, multiple approaches and tools have been developed to analyze the correctness in recent years. For instance, Luu *et al.* [20] developed a symbolic engine for Solidity smart contracts called Oyente, which systematically analyzes individual functions in a smart contract to identify vulnerabilities. Nikolic *et al.* [24] developed a symbolic analyzer called MAIAN, which performs inter-procedural symbolic analysis to check suicidal, prodigal, and greedy contracts based on the bytecode of Ethereum smart contracts. These works, however, focus on testing smart contracts rather than verifying them. For instance, these symbolic execution engines set a bound on the loop iterations or the number of function calls and aim to cover those bounded program paths with generated test cases. There are also several attempts on verifying smart contracts, such as Securify [27], Zeus [15], *solc-verify* [13] and VerX [25]. The first three approaches translate Solidity programs into existing intermediate languages (i.e., Datalog, LLVM and Boogie) and reuse existing verification facilities. Such approaches are based on abstract interpretation, which is known to have problems like fixed abstract domains and false alarms due to coarse over-approximation. In particular, Securify does not support numerical properties like overflow; Zeus suffers from high numbers of false alarms and *solc-verify* lacks full coverage. VerX applies delayed predicate abstraction (which is based upon symbolic execution and abstraction) to verify real-world smart contracts. However, VerX only supports external-callback-free contracts [25] and a bound on the loop iteration within a function is required.

In this work, we develop a formal verification engine called *sVerify* which is designed for Solidity programs. *sVerify* is built upon lazy annotation [21] and state-of-the-art loop invariant generation techniques [17,31]. Given a smart contract with assertions, *sVerify* automatically constructs a labeled control-flow graph (CFG) of each function. Each node in the CFG is annotated lazily with an invariant (which is initially *true*) in a property-guided (i.e. assertion-guided) way. The invariants are monotonically strengthened through sound inference rules. More importantly, invariants associated with nodes contained in explicit or implicit loops are learned automatically with a combination of concrete testing, machine learning and symbolic execution techniques, based on features specific to smart contracts. The invariants are strengthened until the assertions are verified or falsified.

sVerify has been applied to verify against the common code vulnerabilities including overflow and re-entrancy which are two important types of vulnerabilities, on two sets of 835 and 3897 smart contracts respectively. It successfully verifies or falsifies 804 contracts on the first test set in the comparison experiment with Zeus. The result shows that *sVerify* suffers fewer false alarms than Zeus. In the second test subject set, 3859 contracts are successfully evaluated by *sVerify* against *solc-verify* and VeriSol. The manual examined results on 68 contracts with more than 100 transactions regarding to overflow show that *sVerify* gets fewer false alarms than *solc-verify* and more finished contracts than VeriSol. To further evaluate *sVerify* on verifying complex smart contracts against contract-specific assertions, we systematically apply *sVerify* to 7 different kinds

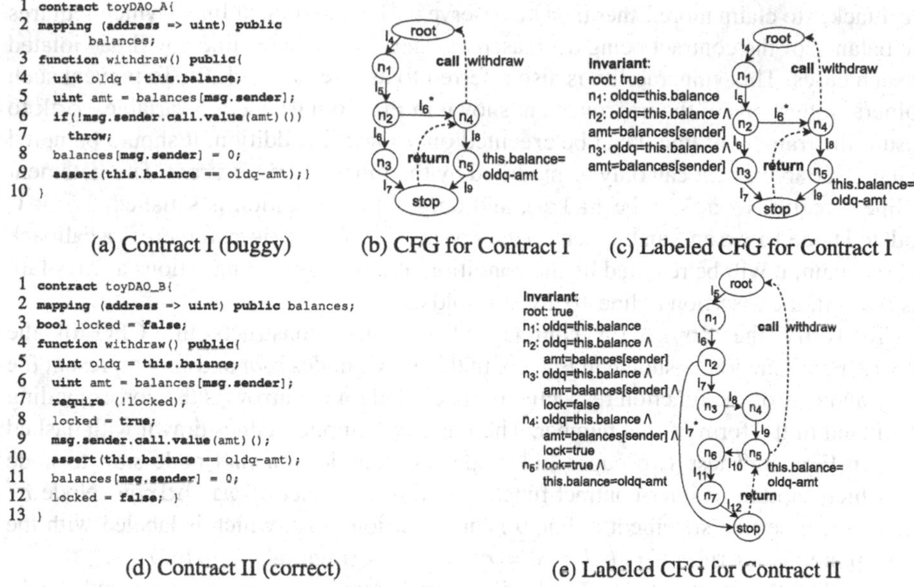

1 contract toyDAO_A{
2 mapping (address => uint) public balances;
3 function withdraw() public{
4 uint oldq = this.balance;
5 uint amt = balances[msg.sender];
6 if(!msg.sender.call.value(amt)())
7 throw;
8 balances[msg.sender] = 0;
9 assert(this.balance == oldq-amt);}}
10 }
root
call withdraw
return
this.balance=
oldq-amt
stop
Invariant:
root: true
n1: oldq=this.balance
n2: oldq=this.balance ∧
amt=balances[sender]
n3: oldq=this.balance ∧
amt=balances[sender]
1 contract toyDAO_B{
2 mapping (address => uint) public balances;
3 bool locked = false;
4 function withdraw() public{
5 uint oldq = this.balance;
6 uint amt = balances[msg.sender];
7 require (!locked);
8 locked = true;
9 msg.sender.call.value(amt)();
10 assert(this.balance == oldq-amt);
11 balances[msg.sender] = 0;
12 locked = false; }
13 }
Invariant:
root: true
n1: oldq=this.balance
n2: oldq=this.balance ∧
amt=balances[sender]
n3: oldq=this.balance ∧
amt=balances[sender] ∧
lock=false
n4: oldq=this.balance ∧
amt=balances[sender] ∧
lock=true
n6: lock=true ∧
this.balance=oldq-amt

(a) Contract I (buggy) (b) CFG for Contract I (c) Labeled CFG for Contract I

(d) Contract II (correct) (e) Labeled CFG for Contract II

Fig. 1. Example Contracts and corresponding labeled CFGs. (Color figure online)

of contracts that have the most balances with manually specified assertions. Three contracts have been verified successfully, and the falsified assertions reveal 2 vulnerabilities in these contracts.

To summarize, this paper makes the following contributions:

- We propose a method to verify the correctness of smart contracts through lazy annotation and invariant learning.
- We develop an end-to-end verification engine *sVerify* for Solidity contracts.
- We evaluate the effectiveness of *sVerify* with real-world smart contracts against overflow and re-entrancy vulnerabilities, and find *sVerify* can verify these contracts with fewer false alarms.

2 Overview Through Motivating Examples

In this section, we give an overview on how *sVerify* works by two example contracts (one is buggy and the other is correct, as shown in Fig. 1).

Figure 1a is a simplified version of the DAO contract. The function `withdraw` allows the investor `msg.sender` to claim back his investment and sets the investor's balance to 0. However, the `msg.sender` here is a contract account, which may be controlled by an attacker. The fallback function in this malicious contract is crafted to call back the `withdraw` function again. Note that the fallback function is invoked automatically when some Ether is transferred into the contract (triggered by line 6) according to the mechanism of Ethereum Virtual Machine (EVM). This action allows the attacker to claim more Ether than he deserves. The assertion at line 9 which requires the balance of the contract being decreased by `amt` exactly after line 8 will be violated in such cases. This vulnerability is also referred to as re-entrancy [20]. To prevent such vulnerabilities, one of the improvement shown in Fig. 1d introduces a variable `lock` to ensure the transfer at line 9 can be executed only once. In addition, it should be noted that the variable `lock` can only be modified by the function `withdraw`. The statement at line 7 requires `lock` to be `false`, and only if this condition is satisfied, `lock` is updated to be `true` and `amt` is sent to the investor `msg.sender`. If there is a callback action again, it will be reverted by the condition at line 7, such transactions always fail. As a result, the assertion at line 10 always holds.

To verify the `toyDAO_A` contract, *sVerify* first constructs the CFG of the `withdraw` function as shown in Fig. 1b. In this CFG, nodes *root* and *stop* represent the entry and exit of the function respectively. The label on the arrow is the corresponding command in the form of line number. There are two implicit edges drawn with dashed lines in Fig. 1b. These two edges link node n_4 to node *root* and node *stop* to node n_4, which capture an inter-contract function call to the function `withdraw`. Node n_5 before the assertion statement at line 9 is an assertion node, which is labeled with the corresponding assertion $this.balance = oldq - amt$ (highlighted in red).

Based on the constructed CFG, *sVerify* infers the invariant for each node and checks whether the invariant at node n_5 implies the assertion afterwards. Figure 1c shows the invariants of node n_1–n_3 with *root* node being true. Taking node n_2 as an example, its invariant is strengthened based on the invariant associated with node n_1 and statement at l_5. That is, the new invariant is the conjunction of the original invariant (which is $true$) at n_2 and $oldq = this.balance \wedge amt = balances[msg.sender]$ (which is the constraint that must be satisfied at n_2 since n_2 can only be reached from n_1). To infer the invariant at node n_4 which is the head node of the loop starting with an implicit edge labeled with **call** $withdraw$ and ended with an edge labeled with **return**, *sVerify* invokes the *loop invariant generator* to learn an invariant. It first generates random valuations of all relevant variables (including `amt`, `oldq`, and `this.balance`), then categorizes the valuations. After that it calls the learner to generate a candidate invariant which is validated by the validator thereafter. If the candidate invariant is not valid, a counterexample in the form of variable valuations is generated and used to learn a new candidate invariant. In this example, during the invariant learning process, an error sample (`amt=1, oldq=257, this.balance=256`) is generated. With this sample, the `msg.sender` will receive 1 wei (the smallest denomination of Ether) at line 6, and possibly will call back to this function again to get another 1 wei. While the second call satisfies the assertion at line 9 (`amt=1, oldq=256, balance=255`), the first call which completes subsequently violates the assertion (`amt=1, oldq=257, balance=255`). Thus, the verification terminates and the contract is falsified.

For the fixed contract `toyDAO_B` in Fig. 1d, the corresponding labeled CFG is shown in Fig. 1e where node n_5 is the head node of the loop. Similarly, *sVerify* infers the invariant for each node and invokes the *loop invariant generator* to generate the invariant for node n_5. The *loop invariant generator* generates a valid candidate invariant $locked = true \wedge this.balance = oldq - amt$ at node n_5 after a few iterations.

Afterwards, the contract is verified since the invariant at n_5 implies the assertion $this.balance = oldq - amt$ at that node successfully.

3 Our Approach

In this section, we present our approach step-by-step in detail.

3.1 Formalization of Smart Contracts

Unlike traditional programs in which the $main()$ function is the single entry, smart contracts can be accessed from any public function once they are deployed. Thus, it is important that each function is verified separately. Without loss of generality, we define the following commands which capture a core set of sequences of EVM instructions. Readers can refer to Ethereum yellow paper [29] and KSolidity [19] etc. for further details.

Definition 1 (Command). *A command in smart contracts is defined as follows.*

$$\begin{array}{lll} Com & ::= & sstore(p, v) \mid sload(p) \mid x := expr \mid \textbf{if } b \mid \textbf{assert } b \mid \textbf{call } f \mid \textbf{return} \\ expr & ::= & x \mid v \mid op(expr, expr) \\ op & ::= & add \mid mul \mid sub \mid div \mid mod \\ b & ::= & true \mid false \mid iszero(expr) \mid cmp(expr, expr) \mid not\ b \mid b\ and\ b \mid b\ or\ b \\ cmp & ::= & lt \mid gt \mid eq \end{array}$$

$sstore(p, v)$ writes a position p with value v (i.e., a 256-bit bitvector) to storage, while $sload(p)$ reads a value of p from storage. $x := expr$ assigns the valuation of expression $expr$ to variable x. The expression $expr$ can be a variable, a value, or an arithmetic operation on two expressions such as addition add, multiplication mul, and so on. Branching command **if** b evaluates a boolean expression b which can be boolean constants $true$ or $false$. The expression also includes comparison operators like $iszero$ and cmp (lt, gt, eq) together with boolean operators (not, and, or). Assertion **assert** b asserts the boolean expression b shall be true. Commands **call** f and **return** represent a call to function f and a return to the caller respectively.

Definition 2 (Function). *A smart contract function F is a tuple $(N, root, E, \mathcal{I}, \mathcal{A})$, where N is a set of nodes (representing control locations); $root \in N$ is the entry node; $E \subseteq N \times Com \times N$ is a set of edges labeled with a command defined in Definition 1; $\mathcal{I} : N -> Pred$ is a function that labels each node N with an invariant predicate; and $\mathcal{A} : N -> Pred$ is a function which labels each node N with an assertion predicate.*

The above defines a function of a smart contract to be a labeled control-flow graph (CFG) to simplify the discussion. In practice, given a function of a smart contract C, we first compile the source code into EVM bytecode [29] and subsequently disassemble the bytecode into EVM instructions. The CFG is then constructed through simulating the stack with the instructions, i.e., to figure out the targets of all `jump` instructions. To capture control flow due to the inter-contract function calls, two implicit edges are generated by linking the call node to the root node and linking the stop node to the call

$$\text{Sstore}\ \frac{n \xrightarrow{\mathbf{sstore}(p,v)}_e n', V' = V[storage[p] \mapsto v]}{(n, \Gamma, V) \xrightarrow{\mathbf{sstore}(p,v)}_s (n', \Gamma, V')} \quad \text{Assign}\ \frac{n \xrightarrow{x:=expr}_e n', V' = V[x \mapsto eval(expr, V)]}{(n, \Gamma, V) \xrightarrow{x:=expr}_s (n', \Gamma, V')}$$

$$\text{If-T}\ \frac{n \xrightarrow{\mathbf{if}\ b}_e n'}{(n, \Gamma, V) \xrightarrow{\mathbf{if}\ b}_s (n', \Gamma, V)} \quad \text{If-F}\ \frac{n \xrightarrow{\mathbf{if}\ !b}_e n''}{(n, \Gamma, V) \xrightarrow{\mathbf{if}\ !b}_s (n'', \Gamma, V)}$$

$$\text{Call}\ \frac{n \xrightarrow{\mathbf{call}\ f}_e n', V' = extract(V)}{(n, \Gamma, V) \xrightarrow{\mathbf{call}\ f}_s (n', \Gamma ^\frown \langle (f, V_\Gamma) \rangle, V')} \quad \text{Return}\ \frac{n \xrightarrow{\mathbf{return}}_e n', V' = V \oplus V_\Gamma}{(n, \Gamma ^\frown \langle (f, V_\Gamma) \rangle, V) \xrightarrow{\mathbf{return}}_s (n', \Gamma, V')}$$

Fig. 2. Execution rules, where $(n \xrightarrow{c}_e n') \in E$

node. Through these, a complete CFG is constructed. Readers are referred to [3,6] for further details.

Initially, the invariant function $\mathcal{I}$ is defined such that $\mathcal{I}(n) = true$ for every $n \in N$. Furthermore, the assertion function $\mathcal{A}$ is defined such that $\mathcal{A}(n) = b$ if n is a program location with a command **assert** b; otherwise $\mathcal{A}(n) = true$. For instance, as shown in the CFG of function *withdraw* in Fig. 1e, the invariant $\mathcal{I}(n_5)$ of node n_5 is $true$, and the assertion $\mathcal{A}(n_5)$ is $this.balance = oldq - amt$.

Definition 3 (Symbolic Semantics). *Let* $(N, root, E, \mathcal{I}, \mathcal{A})$ *be a function of a smart contract, its (symbolic) semantics is defined as a labeled transition system* $(S, init, \rightarrow_s, \mathcal{I}, \mathcal{A})$*, where* S *is a set of symbolic states, and each state* s *is a triple* (n, Γ, V) *where* $n \in N$*,* Γ *is a call stack,*[1] *and* V *is a symbolic valuation function which maps program variables to expressions of symbolic variables,* $init \in S$ *is the initial state,* $\rightarrow_s \subseteq S \times Com \times S$ *is the transition relation of the semantics while* E *is the transition relation at the code level.* $\rightarrow_s$ *conforms to the semantic rules defined in Fig. 2.*[2]

In Fig. 2, rule $Sstore$ captures how the value of the position in storage is updated. After the execution of the command, n is moved to the next node n' and position p in storage V' is updated by the value of v. Rule $Assign$ updates the value of variable x in V' based on the evaluation of expression $expr$ in the valuation V (denoted by function $eval$). The rules of *If-T* and *If-F* capture the branch situation, n is moved to either node n' or n'' after executing this command. Rule $Call$ captures the execution of any possible inter-contract function call. After the execution, n is moved to the root node of the called function n', function f and the valuation of the local variables V_Γ are added to the function call stack $\Gamma ^\frown \langle (f, V_\Gamma) \rangle$, and valuation V' is to extract the valuation of global variables in V that are only modified in current function by $extract$. Rule $Return$ pops the top element of the stack and moves to the node of the caller with the updated valuation which restores the local variable valuation at the calling node. Symbol $\oplus$ overrides the variable valuation in V with those in V_Γ.

---

[1] We omit the details on the content of the stack for brevity.

[2] Due to the page limit, only a core set of rules are presented here.

A path p of a function in a smart contract is a sequence of alternating nodes/commands in the form of $\langle n_0, c_0, n_1, c_1, \ldots, c_n, n_{n+1}\rangle$, where $n_0 = root$ and $n_i \xrightarrow{c_i}_e n_{i+1}$ for all $0 \leq i \leq n$. A (symbolic) trace is a path in the symbolic semantics, and each trace corresponds to a path in the contract by definition. Thus, a trace tr is a sequence of alternating states/commands in the form of $tr = \langle s_0, c_0, s_1, c_1, \ldots, c_n, s_{n+1}\rangle$, where $s_0 = init$ and $s_i \xrightarrow{c_i}_s s_{i+1}$ for all $0 \leq i \leq n$. We write $last(tr)$ to denote the last state of the trace s_{n+1}. The set of symbolic traces of a function F, written as $Trace(F)$, is the set of traces of its symbolic semantics, where each trace is a sequence whose head is the initial state and the alternating state/command conforms to the transition relation.

Definition 4 (Node Invariant). *Given a smart contract function* $F = (N, root, E, \mathcal{I}, \mathcal{A})$*, a predicate* ϕ *is an invariant at node* n *(denoted as* $\mathcal{I}(n) = \phi$*) if and only if* $last(tr) \models \phi$ *for all* $tr \in Trace(F)$ *s.t.* $\pi(last(tr)) = n$.

where $s \models \phi$ means ϕ is satisfied by the variable valuation s. Intuitively, the above definition states ϕ is an invariant at node n if and only if ϕ is satisfied by all traces leading to node n, i.e., when the trace reaches n, its variable valuation satisfies ϕ. Function $last$ returns the last element of the trace, and function π returns the node of the tuple.

Definition 5 (Contract Correctness). *Given a contract* C *with each function* $F_i = (N_i, root_i, E_i, \mathcal{I}_i, \mathcal{A}_i)$*,* F_i *is correct if* $\forall n_j \in N_i,\ \mathcal{I}_i(n_j) \Rightarrow \mathcal{A}_i(n_j)$*. Contract* C *is correct if all the functions* F_i *in* C *are correct.*

Based on the constructed CFG and its semantics, the verification of a smart contract can be achieved by checking whether the invariant of any node can imply the associated assertion. If yes, the program is verified to be correct. *sVerify* infers the node invariants with the method of strongest postcondition. Before presenting how the inference works, we first define how the strongest postcondition is computed.

Definition 6 (Strongest Postcondition). *Given a command* $c \in Com$ *and a precondition* ϕ*, the strongest postcondition* $sp(c, \phi)$ *is defined as:*

$$sp(sstore(p, v), \phi) = \exists y,\ \phi[y/storage[p]] \wedge storage[p] = v$$
$$sp(x := expr, \phi) = \exists y,\ x = expr[y/x] \ \wedge\ \phi[y/x]$$
$$sp(c, \phi) = \phi \wedge b \qquad \text{if } c = \textbf{if } b \text{ or } \textbf{assert } b$$
$$sp(c, \phi) = \phi \qquad \text{if } c = sload(x)$$
$$sp(\textbf{call } f, \phi) = \forall x \in LV,\ \forall y \in GV',\ \phi \ominus \phi(x) \ominus \phi(y)$$

In the above definition, the fresh variable y represents the previous values of $storage[p]$ and x in the strongest postconditions for command $sstore$ and assignment. For the branching and assertion commands, the strongest postcondition is the conjunction of ϕ and b. As command $sload$ only reads the storage, its strongest postcondition keeps the same. We remark that the strongest postcondition for command **call** f is ϕ except that all constraints related to local variables LV and global variables GV' are eliminated. Symbol $\ominus$ represents variable elimination of all variables in ϕ. GV' is global variables

Algorithm 1: Node Invariant Inference Algorithm $inferI(F, n)$

1 $\Psi \leftarrow false$;
2 **for** $(m_i, c_i, n) \in E$ **do**
3 $\quad \Psi \leftarrow \Psi \vee sp(c_i, \mathcal{I}(m_i))$;
4 **end**
5 **if** $\Psi \neq false$ **then** $\mathcal{I}(n) \leftarrow \mathcal{I}(n) \wedge \Psi$;

which can be modified by other functions besides the current function. This rule can be potentially improved with a contract-level invariant inference method. In *sVerify*, we conduct basic static analysis which allows us to identify the global variables that are modified by each function in the contract. With that information, we strengthen the above rule as follows: all constraints on global variables except those which are only modified by the current function, are eliminated. This is sound as all callback actions to the current function are captured in the CFG.

Algorithm 1 shows details on updating the invariant of a node n based on the strongest postcondition. Let Ψ be a predicate which is initially $false$. We compute $sp(c_i, \mathcal{I}(m_i))$ for each transition (m_i, c_i, n) to node n by command c_i. Their disjunction is a constraint which must be satisfied by the invariant at node n. Intuitively, this is because n can only be reached via one of its parents. Lastly, at line 5, we set the invariant at node n to be the conjunction of $\mathcal{I}(n)$ and Ψ so that it is monotonically strengthened over time. The condition at line 5 ensures that a node without a parent like the root node is not updated.

Proposition 1. *The invariant inferred by Algorithm 1 is indeed an invariant.* □

3.2 Loop Invariant Generation

While Algorithm 1 can be applied to infer invariants systematically, it may not be effective for loops. That is, given a loop of the form $\langle n_0, c_0, n_1, c_1, n_2 \ldots, n_k, c_k, n_0 \rangle$, the invariant of node n_0 is recursively inferred based on itself and thus may never terminate. Therefore, we distinguish head nodes of certain loops (i.e., a node representing the start of a loop statement or an external function call, it can be identified from the CFG) and apply a different approach to infer invariants for such nodes. The overall idea is an iterative "guess and check" approach for synthesizing loop invariants. This iterative approach consists of three phases, *data labeling*, *learning* (or guessing), and *validation*. The details are shown in Algorithm 2 where F is the CFG of the function and n is the head node of a loop.

In Algorithm 2, *Var* is the set of loop-related variables. The valuation set of variables in *Var* at node n (denoted as DS) is initiated by random sampling at line 1 and the size of the initial DS is decided empirically, e.g., 20. Note that an effective sampling method would allow us to learn the invariant efficiently, as shown in [17]. On the other hand, since the learned invariant is always validated by the validator, the learning is guaranteed to converge if there exists an invariant of the supported form. In general, a reasonably large set of random samples is often helpful in learning candidate invariants.

Algorithm 2: *genLI(F, n)*

```
1  DS = init(Var); DS' ← ∅; LDS ← ∅;
2  for ds ∈ DS do
3  |  DS' ← DS' ∪ concExLP(ds, n);
4  end
5  LDS ← label(DS', F, N) ;
6  while not timeout do
7  |  (flag, ds) ← checkErr(LDS);
8  |  if !flag then
9  |  |  return ("falsified", ds);
10 |  end
11 |  φ ← learnINV(LDS);
12 |  CE ← validate(φ, F, n);
13 |  if CE = ∅ then
14 |  |  return ("succeed", φ);
15 |  else
16 |  |  for ds ∈ CE do
17 |  |  |  DS' ← DS' ∪
   |  |  |    concExLP(ds, n);
18 |  |  end
19 |  |  LDS ← label(DS', F, N) ;
20 |  end
21 end
22 (CE, φ') ← heurAndVal(φ, F, n);
23 if CE = ∅ then return ("succeed", φ') ;
24 else return ("timeout", null) ;
```

Algorithm 3: Overall Algorithm

```
{F1, F2, ..., Fm} ← CFG_build(C);
for F ∈ {F1, F2, ..., Fm} do
|  I' ← ∅; I ← {true | n ∈ N};
|  while I' ≠ I do
|  |  I' ← I;
|  |  for n ∈ N do
|  |  |  if n is loop head then
|  |  |  |  (msg, v) ← genLI(F, n);
|  |  |  |  if msg = "succeed" then
|  |  |  |  |  I(n) ← v;
|  |  |  |  else if msg = "falsified" then
|  |  |  |  |  return ("falsified", v);
|  |  |  |  else
|  |  |  |  |  return ("timeout", null);
|  |  |  else
|  |  |  |  I(n) ← inferI(F, n) ;
|  |  |  end
|  |  end
|  end
|  for n ∈ N do
|  |  if I(n) ⇏ A(n) then
|  |  |  return ("falsified", ce)
|  |  end
|  end
end
return "verified" ;
```

LDS is labeled DS', which is updated at line 5 by *label* function. The data samples are collected through lines 2–4 by concretely executing the loop part with the valuations from DS. During the execution, node n may be visited iteratively and all the variable valuations upon reaching n are added to DS' as well. Labeling for valuations in DS' is based on three categories, i.e., '+' for positive, '−' for negative, and 'e' for error. A valuation s which starts from an initial valuation s_0 and becomes s after zero or more iterations is labeled based on whether s_0 satisfies $\mathcal{I}(n)$ and whether eventually an assertion is violated. Specifically,

- '+': if s_0 satisfies $\mathcal{I}(n)$, and no assertion is violated during the execution.
- '−': if s_0 violates $\mathcal{I}(n)$ and an assertion is violated during the execution.
- 'e': if s_0 satisfies $\mathcal{I}(n)$, and an assertion is violated during the execution.

Intuitively, the valuations labeled with '+' must satisfy the (unknown) loop invariant; the one labeled with '−' must not satisfy the loop invariant; and a valuation labeled with 'e' is a concrete counterexample which falsifies the assertion. Take the contract in Fig. 1d as an example, assume 2 valuations $(2, 0, 20, 18)$, $(5, 1, 30, 25)$ for variables (`amt`, `lock`, `oldq` and `this.balance`) are randomly sampled at line 1. After executing function *concExLP* with these valuations at line 3, 1 more valuation is added to DS': $(2, 0, 20, 16)$, which violates the assertion. Afterwards, valuation $\{(5, 1, 30, 25)\}$ is labeled with '+'; and $\{(2, 0, 20, 18), (2, 0, 20, 16)\}$ are labeled with '−'.

After labeling the initial dataset, we try to strengthen a valid invariant from lines 6–21. Lines 7–10 check whether there is any 'e' valuation and return "falsified" together with the valuation as a counterexample. 'e' valuation is a concrete valuation in LDS which violates any assertions. A candidate invariant is expected from function *learnINV* at line 11. The primary idea is to guess a candidate invariant in the form of a classifier which separates the valuations labeled with '+' from those labeled with '−'. Specifically, we adopt the LINEARARBITRARY algorithm proposed in [31], which is built upon SVM and decision tree classification, to infer candidate invariants in the form of arbitrary combination of conjunction or disjunction of linear inequalities. Line 12 invokes the function *validate* to check whether the candidate invariant ϕ is indeed an invariant (i.e., it is inductive through every path in the loop). That is, we tentatively label the node n with the candidate and apply Algorithm 1 to propagate it through nodes starting from n and ending with a parent of n. The invariant is inductive if and only if, for all m such that $(m, c, n) \in E$, $sp(\mathcal{I}(m), c) \Rightarrow \phi$, which means ϕ is a valid invariant and returned at line 14. Otherwise, a counterexample in the form of variable valuation is generated and added to CE, which is further subsumed into LDS for the next round invariant generation.

We remark that the loop invariants learned through this way are property-guided. Although the learning algorithm adopted from [31] is guaranteed to terminate given a finite set LDS, the overall learning process may timeout due to too many guess-and-check iterations. We adopt a simple heuristics of conjuncting the assertion with the current candidate as a candidate invariant for validation at line 22. This is justified intuitively as the learned invariant should be strong enough to imply the assertion. For example, in contract `toyDAO_B` shown in Fig. 1d, a candidate invariant $lock = true$ is generated by Algorithm 2. However, timeout occurs when *sVerify* validates it. Applying the heuristics, the candidate invariant is strengthened to be $lock = true \wedge this.balance = oldq - amt$, which is subsequently validated. Otherwise, timeout is returned at line 24.

3.3 Overall Verification Algorithm

With the above discussion, we are ready to present the overall algorithm which is shown in Algorithm 3. Given a smart contract C with m functions, we first construct the CFG for each function at line 1. For each node n in each function F, we initiate the node's invariant with $true$ and update them at lines 4–19. If node n is a loop head node, Algorithm 2 is invoked and an invariant is returned when it is "succeed" at line 10. Otherwise, the algorithm will return "falsified" or "timeout" at lines 12 and 14. Whenever the invariants stabilize (i.e., reaches a fixed point), we check whether, for each node, its invariant implies its assertion at lines 20–24. If the implication fails at any node, the counterexample (*ce*) from the SMT solver that violates the node assertion is returned to the user. If all assertions are implied by their corresponding invariants, the contract is successfully verified.

Theorem 1. *The contract is safe if Algorithm 3 returns "verified".*

Proof. The claim follows the fact that all inferred invariants are indeed invariants. There are two ways of inferring invariants, either by Algorithm 1 or 2. In the former case, the inferred invariant is indeed an invariant according to Proposition 1. In the latter case, the correctness of the inferred invariant generated by *genLI* is ensured by function *validate* in Algorithm 2 which checks whether the learned invariant is inductive. Given that all inferred invariants are sound, Algorithm 3 is sound as it returns "verified" when all assertions are implied by the invariants (by Definition 5). □

In practice, Algorithm 3 is made always terminating with a timeout on the $genLI$ method. The complexity of the algorithm is hard to analyze due to the many components. We thus evaluate it empirically in the next section.

4 Implementation and Evaluations

We have implemented our approach in *sVerify* with C++. Given a Solidity smart contract, *sVerify* first compiles it into EVM bytecode and subsequently disassembles the bytecode into instructions for constructing the CFG. Then, LIBSVM [5] and C5.0 [26] are adopted for invariant learning, and Z3 SMT solver is used for invariant validation. We conduct two sets of experiments to evaluate *sVerify* on real-world smart contracts. In particular, we attempt to address the following two questions.

1. How effective is *sVerify* in verifying common code vulnerabilities?
2. How effective is *sVerify* in verifying contract-specific assertions?

All experiments are conducted on a machine with an Intel Core i7-7700HQ CPU with 8 cores clocked at 2.8 GHz, and 23.4 GB of RAM, running the system of 64-bit Ubuntu 18.04LTS. The dependancies of *sVerify* include Z3 (version 4.8.0) and the boost library (version 1.68.0). As of now, it is developed for Solidity before version 0.5.19 and Ethereum Virtual Machine (EVM) before version 1.8.21.

4.1 Verification Against Common Code Vulnerabilities

In this set of experiments, we evaluate the performance of *sVerify* on verifying against common code vulnerabilities including overflow and re-entrancy. These two kinds of vulnerabilities are particularly interesting and relevant.

First, most of the vulnerabilities (90.2% (476/528)) reported in the CVE list [9] between 2018 and 2020 are overflow problems. The DAO attack [1], one of the most famous attacks which caused huge monetary loss, has evidenced the importance of re-entrancy. Furthermore, re-entrancy is a vulnerability which is associated with implicit loops due to fallback function calls and thus would put our loop invariant generation approach under test. Assertions for capturing overflow vulnerabilities are systematically generated and assertions for capturing re-entrancy vulnerabilities are manually specified regarding the balance after each call transaction like the example in Sect. 2.

For baseline comparison, we focus on three state-of-the-art verification tools Zeus, *solc-verify* and VeriSol. Zeus [15] is a framework for automatic verification of smart contracts based on abstract interpretation techniques. *solc-verify* [13] and VeriSol [28] are tools that allow specification and modular verification of Solidity contracts which are built upon the Boogie verifier.

Setup. To compare with Zeus, we adopt the test subjects reportedly analyzed by Zeus in [15] and systematically run *sVerify* on them. We did not compare with the other two tools because (1) solc-verify lacks the support of complex data types and memory models before version 0.5.0 and thus fails to verify most of the test subjects; (2) VeriSol

Table 1. Comparison results between Zeus and *sVerify*

	Zeus					*sVerify*				
Category	Safe	Unsafe	Unk.	FP	FN	Safe	Unsafe	Unk.	FP	FN
Overflow	234	592	9	33	5	255	549	31	4	0
Re-entrancy	803	28	4	2	20	754	50	31	0	0

```
function split() payable public {
   uint fee = msg.value / 100; ...
   etcDestination.call.value(msg.value - fee)(); }
function process(bytes32 _destination) payable returns (bool) {
  if (msg.value < 100) throw;
  var tax = msg.value * taxPerc / 100; ... }
function testNumberRequest(address randomreality, ...) payable {...
   uint256 cost = randomrealityapi.getPrice(200000);
   bytes32 id = randomrealityapi.requestNumber.value(cost)(...);  ... }
function transferFrom() returns (bool success) {
   ... if(now < startTime + 1 years) ... }
function multisend(..., address[] dests, uint256[] values){ ...
   while (i < dests.length) {
      assert( i < values.length);
      ERC20(_tokenAddr).transfer(dests[i], values[i]);
      i+=1; ... }
```

Fig. 3. Functions incorrectly analyzed by tools

requires manual-specified assertions for specific properties and thus we leave the comparison to the second experiment. Note that the code of Zeus is not open source and thus it is not possible to apply it to other smart contracts. Among 1524 contracts reportedly analyzed by Zeus, 898 of them are still available online. As nested loops are yet to be supported mainly due to the required engineering effort as well as lack of motivation - there are relatively small amount of nested loop contracts on the blockchain. Thus, the remaining 835 contracts are taken as the test subjects.

We further evaluate *sVerify* on 3897 contracts against open-source tools, *solc-verify* with version of v0.4.25-boogie to include the support of arithmetic mod-overflow and VeriSol[3] of 0.1.5-alpha. Note that only 68 contracts that have more than 100 transactions are demonstrated in the paper, which are also the same subjects discussed by *solc-verify* [13]. The option of flag "arithmetic" for *solc-verify* is "mod-overflow". Similar flag with the option of "useModularArithmetic" is also set for VeriSol. Timeout for verifying each contract is 3600 s for all tools. Furthermore, a 10 s timeout is set for each z3 solver request.

Results. The experiment results on Zeus's 835 test subjects are summarized in Table 1.[4] Each result is either "Safe" or "Unsafe" (i.e., there is a potential issue). "Unk." means unknown, due to either exception or timeout. "FP" and "FN" stand for false positives and false negatives. A false positive occurs when tools return "Unsafe" but the contract

[3] Necessary assertions regarding overflow and reentrancy are inserted manually.
[4] Details and benchmarks can be found at https://doi.org/10.5281/zenodo.5168441.

Table 2. Comparison results on Overflow with *solc-verify* and VeriSol.

	solc-verify					VeriSol					*sVerify*				
Category	Safe	Unsafe	Unk.	FP	FN	Safe	Unsafe	Unk.	FP	FN	Safe	Unsafe	Unk.	FP	FN
Overflow	34	34	0	30	0	18	12	38	1	0	41	25	2	9	0

is actually "Safe" after we manually examined the alarmed code, while a false negative occurs when tools return "Safe" but the contract is actually "Unsafe".

We have multiple observations based on the results. First, compared with Zeus, *sVerify*'s verification results are more reliable since there are fewer false positives and false negative. In particular, for overflow, Zeus generates 33 false positives and 5 false negatives, whereas *sVerify* has 4 false positives and 0 false negative; for re-entrancy, *sVerify* has 0 false positive and 0 false negative.

Since Zeus is not open source, there is no way to know why some contracts are not correctly analyzed. We show some examples in Fig. 3 in the following which may offer clues. Zeus generates a false alarm of overflow for function `split` in Fig. 3 which sends tokens to two accounts. We speculate the false alarm is due to line 3, since examining this line alone would suggest that overflow is possible due to the arithmetic operation. In comparison, *sVerify* keeps track of relationship between `fee` and `msg.value` due to line 2 and correctly concludes there is no overflow. Zeus misses the overflow in function `process` where the statement `msg.value*taxPerc/100` may exceed the maximum value at line 6. For re-entrancy, one example Zeus misses is the one in function `testNumberRequest` where attackers may input some address to exploit the re-entrancy vulnerability at line 9. The reason of four false positives by *sVerify* is because *sVerify* verifies each function in isolation. Namely, symbolic values are assigned to global variables so that they may have arbitrary values. In reality, these variables may be constrained in certain ways. For instance, `startTime` in function `transferFrom` is only set in constructor and the overflow at line 11 is impossible. Finally, we notice that *sVerify* missed reporting one re-entrancy vulnerability as *sVerify* terminates the analysis once an issue is identified, e.g., an overflow issue is identified before a re-entrancy issue is encountered.

Table 2 demonstrates the results of 68 contracts by three tools. It can be observed that *solc-verify* has more false positives compared to VeriSol and *sVerify*. There are multiple reasons why false alarms are generated by *solc-verify*. For instance, missing range assumptions for array lengths causes false alarms for loop counters [13], which contributes the most false alarms. On the contrary, *sVerify* identifies more true vulnerabilities. One example is the function `multisend` shown in Fig. 3. *solc-verify* reports `i+=1` might overflow, which is regarded as a false alarm (FP). However, *sVerify* reports the index of variable `values` at line 15 might cause overflow if `i` is larger than the length of array `values`, which is a true issue that is missed by *solc-verify*. VeriSol can also find such problems if only an assertion shown at line 14 is inserted. Only 30 contracts are successfully analyzed by VeriSol. 9 false alarms are generated by *sVerify*. Besides the missing constraints on time like the case in func-

Table 3. Real-world Contracts Analysis.

Contract	#loc	#pubfns	#lpfns	*sVerify*	*solc-verify*
MultisigWallet	304	14	7	Unsafe	Unk.
Imt	65	4	1	Safe	FP
WithdrawDAO	15	2	0	FP	FP
LifCrowdsale	800	37	1	Safe	Unk.
WETH	50	6	0	FP	FP
KyberReserve	298	19	2	Safe	Unk.
TokenStore	240	20	3	Unsafe	Unk.

tion `transferFrom`, other run-time variables also matter like the amount of Ether in `amt=msg.value*2000`, which is safe as the total Ether is limited.

Efficiency sVerify successfully analyzed 804 (out of 835) contracts and 3859 (out of 3897) contracts for two sets of benchmarks, and each contract takes an average of 38.5 s and 14.8 s respectively. On the contrary, Zeus finishes 97% of the contracts within 60s, there is no further detailed data provided. *solc-verify* finishes all the contracts with an average time of 1.24 s and VeriSol finishes 30 (out of 68) contracts with 2.28 s. Longer time is needed to learn invariants for loops in the verification process, which is an essential step to acquire an accurate result, but also leads to more timeouts.

4.2 Verifying Contract-Specific Assertions

While verification against common vulnerabilities is important, it is far from sufficient for the functional correctness. In this section, we identify several high-profile smart contracts, manually specify assertions relevant to their functional correctness and apply *sVerify* to verifying those assertions. The assertions are mainly targeted at functions with loops as those are non-trivial to verify. Since most of the loops operate on arrays, we define several patterns specific to them, e.g., `assert(ret==ARRAY_MAX)` to check whether the returned value `ret` by the program is the maximum. The test subjects consist of 7 representative contracts from accounts ranking top 1000 in terms of balance, including the wallet contracts which receive and transfer Ether for users, like *multiSig*, *Imt* and *WithdrawDAO*, the token contracts which work for token issuance and crowdsale, like *LifCrowdsale* and *WETH*, the decentralized exchange contracts which work for crypto asset transaction, like *KyberReserve* and *TokenStore*. Many contracts are built upon these contracts. Table 3 shows the results of *sVerify* and *solc-verify*, where columns $\#loc$, $\#pubfns$, and $\#lpfns$ stand for lines of code, number of public functions, and number of loop functions. The results by VeriSol are ignored because of version problem.

sVerify successfully analyzes all the contracts whereas *solc-verify* finishes three. Two out of four alarms reported by *sVerify* are real vulnerabilities. In function `getTxIds` shown in Fig. 4, the statement at line 2 overflows if the assigned value

```
1 function getTxIds(uint from, uint to, ...) public returns(uint[] _txIds){ ...
2     _txIds = new uint[](to - from); ... }
3 function withdraw(uint _amount){
4     ... tokens[0][msg.sender] = safeSub(tokens[0][msg.sender], amount);
5     uint oldq = this.balance;
6     if (!msg.sender.call.value(amount)()) ...
7     assert(this.balance == oldq - amount); }
```

Fig. 4. Alarmed functions by *sVerify*

of variable `to` is smaller than `from` (which may spawn new arrays and cost up all the gas). The other one is in function `withdraw`, the assertion statement at line 7 is violated if the fallback function in `msg.sender` calls back to function `withdraw` again. Although this, in practical runtime, the smart contract decreases the token amount of the `msg.sender` at line 4, which ensures the `msg.sender` cannot claim more Ether than he deserves. The other two false alarms are due to limitations on analyzing functions in isolation, as explained for the constraints of time and Ether balance in Sect. 4.1. Two false alarms are all eliminated after inserting `require` statements for restricting the arithmetic overflow. In comparison, *solc-verify* reports 3 alarms which are all false alarms. This test shows that *sVerify* can be helpful to verify some contract-specific assertions.

5 Related Work

In the last five years, several approaches have been proposed to test or verify smart contracts through various techniques. For instance, the fuzzing tools reported in [2,14,30] try to selectively generate test inputs with both static and dynamic techniques to find critical vulnerabilities. Inevitably, they are prone to false negatives which are of great concern for verification of smart contracts. Other works adopt symbolic techniques to analyze smart contracts [8,20,22,24]. To avoid the path explosion problem, these approaches usually bound the search space by, for instance, setting a limit on the number of blocks or function calls.

Unlike these approaches, Securify [27] is based on abstract interpretation and dependency graph to produce vulnerability patterns through inference rule-based generation and analyze the correctness accordingly. However, Securify does not support numerical properties like overflow. VerX [25] introduces delayed predicate abstraction approach based upon symbolic execution to verify smart contracts during transaction execution. However, VerX only supports external-call-free contracts whose behavior is equivalent to the behavior of the contracts without callbacks. Some other approaches like the work in [4] and Zeus [15] translated smart contracts into intermediate representations like F* programs and LLVM bitcode respectively, then leverage existing tools for F* and Seahorn to reason about contract correctness. *solc-verify* [13] and verisol [28] translate smart contracts into the Boogie intermediate language, and leverages the verification toolchain for Boogie programs for analysis. The translation is on the source code level, which allows the users to write annotations directly in the contract. However, since Boogie was not designed for smart contracts, some features are not supported for the translation.

In this work, we propose a verification approach based on lazy annotation and automatic loop invariant generation. A number of loop invariant generation approaches have been proposed, including those based on abstraction interpretation [11], counterexample-guided abstraction refinement [7] or interpolation [18], logical inference [10] and learning [17,31]. The former three depend on constraint solving and thus suffer from scalability. We adopt the learning-based invariant generation approach in this work.

6 Conclusion

We leverage the techniques of lazy annotation and state-of-the-art loop invariant generation method to implement the formal verifier *sVerify*. With the help of invariant inference, *sVerify* can be helpful to verify or falsify smart contracts. We evaluated *sVerify* on 4670 real-world smart contracts and the results show that *sVerify* is effective and reasonably efficient. We will extend our work to contract-level verification in the future.

References

1. Dao (2016). https://www.coindesk.com/understanding-dao-hack-journalists
2. Akca, S., Rajan, A., Peng, C.: SolAnalyser: a framework for analysing and testing smart contracts, pp. 482–489 (2019). https://doi.org/10.1109/APSEC48747.2019.00071
3. Albert, E., Correas, J., Gordillo, P., Román-Díez, G., Rubio, A.: Analyzing smart contracts: from EVM to a sound control-flow graph. arXiv preprint arXiv:2004.14437 (2020)
4. Bhargavan, K., Delignat-Lavaud, A., Fournet, C., Gollamudi, A., Gonthier, G., Kobeissi, N.: Formal verification of smart contracts: short paper. In: PLAS, pp. 91–96. ACM (2016)
5. Chang, C.C., Lin, C.J.: LIBSVM: a library for support vector machines. ACM TIST **2**, 27:1–27:27 (2011). http://www.csie.ntu.edu.tw/~cjlin/libsvm
6. Chang, J., Gao, B., Xiao, H., Sun, J., Cai, Y., Yang, Z.: sCompile: critical path identification and analysis for smart contracts. In: Ait-Ameur, Y., Qin, S. (eds.) ICFEM 2019. LNCS, vol. 11852, pp. 286–304. Springer, Cham (2019). https://doi.org/10.1007/978-3-030-32409-4_18
7. Clarke, E., Grumberg, O., Jha, S., Lu, Y., Veith, H.: Counterexample-guided abstraction refinement for symbolic model checking. J. ACM **50**(5), 752–794 (2003)
8. ConsenSys: Mythril: Security analysis of ethereum smart contracts (2018). https://github.com/ConsenSys/mythril. Accessed 30 May 2019. online
9. CVE: CVE list. https://cve.mitre.org/data/downloads/index.html. Accessed 4 June 2021
10. Dillig, I., Dillig, T., Li, B., McMillan, K.: Inductive invariant generation via abductive inference. In: OOPSLA, pp. 443–456 (2013)
11. Flanagan, C., Qadeer, S.: Predicate abstraction for software verification. In: POPL, pp. 191–202. ACM (2002)
12. Haber, S., Stornetta, W.S.: How to time-stamp a digital document. In: Menezes, A.J., Vanstone, S.A. (eds.) CRYPTO 1990. LNCS, vol. 537, pp. 437–455. Springer, Heidelberg (1991). https://doi.org/10.1007/3-540-38424-3_32
13. Hajdu, Á., Jovanović, D.: SOLC-VERIFY: a modular verifier for solidity smart contracts. In: Chakraborty, S., Navas, J.A. (eds.) VSTTE 2019. LNCS, vol. 12031, pp. 161–179. Springer, Cham (2020). https://doi.org/10.1007/978-3-030-41600-3_11
14. Jiang, B., Liu, Y., Chan, W.: ContractFuzzer: fuzzing smart contracts for vulnerability detection, pp. 259–269 (2018). https://doi.org/10.1145/3238147.3238177

15. Kalra, S., Goel, S., Dhawan, M., Sharma, S.: ZEUS: analyzing safety of smart contracts. In: NDSS. The Internet Society (2018)
16. Lamport, L.: Time, clocks, and the ordering of events in a distributed system. Commun. ACM **21**(7), 558–565 (1978)
17. Li, J., Sun, J., Li, L., Le, Q.L., Lin, S.: Automatic loop-invariant generation and refinement through selective sampling. In: ASE, pp. 782–792 (2017)
18. Lin, S., Sun, J., Nguyen, T.K., Liu, Y., Dong, J.S.: Interpolation guided compositional verification (t). In: ASE, pp. 65–74 (2015)
19. Lin, S.: K-framework Solidity (2018). https://github.com/kframework/solidity-semantics
20. Luu, L., Chu, D.H., Olickel, H., Saxena, P.: Making smart contracts smarter. In: CCS, pp. 254–269. ACM (2016)
21. McMillan, K.L.: Lazy annotation for program testing and verification. In: Touili, T., Cook, B., Jackson, P. (eds.) CAV 2010. LNCS, vol. 6174, pp. 104–118. Springer, Heidelberg (2010). https://doi.org/10.1007/978-3-642-14295-6_10
22. Mossberg, M., Manzano, F., Hennenfent, E., Groce, A.: Manticore: a user-friendly symbolic execution framework for binaries and smart contracts. In: ASE, pp. 1186–1189. IEEE (2019)
23. Nakamoto, S.: Bitcoin: a peer-to-peer electronic cash system. Technical report, Manubot (2019)
24. Nikolic, I., Kolluri, A., Sergey, I., Saxena, P., Hobor, A.: Finding the greedy, prodigal, and suicidal contracts at scale. In: ACSAC, pp. 653–663. ACM (2018)
25. Permenev, A., Dimitrov, D., Tsankov, P., Drachsler-Cohen, D., Vechev, M.: VerX: safety verification of smart contract. In: IEEE Symposium on Security and Privacy (2020)
26. Quinlan, J.: C5.0: an informal tutorial (2017). http://www.rulequest.com/see5-unix.html
27. Tsankov, P., Dan, A., Drachsler-Cohen, D., Gervais, A., Buenzli, F., Vechev, M.: Securify: practical security analysis of smart contracts. In: CCS, pp. 67–82. ACM (2018)
28. Wang, Y., et al.: Formal verification of workflow policies for smart contracts in azure blockchain. In: Chakraborty, S., Navas, J.A. (eds.) VSTTE 2019. LNCS, vol. 12031, pp. 87–106. Springer, Cham (2020). https://doi.org/10.1007/978-3-030-41600-3_7
29. Wood, G.: Ethereum: a secure decentralised generalised transaction ledger. Ethereum Project Yellow Paper **151**, 1–32 (2014)
30. Wüstholz, V., Christakis, M.: Harvey: a greybox fuzzer for smart contracts. In: ESEC/FSE, pp. 1398–1409 (2020)
31. Zhu, H., Magill, S., Jagannathan, S.: A data-driven CHC solver. In: PLDI, pp. 707–721. ACM (2018)

Rigorous Engineering of Collective Adaptive Systems

Verifying Temporal Properties of Stigmergic Collective Systems Using CADP

Luca Di Stefano(✉) and Frédéric Lang

Univ. Grenoble Alpes, Inria, CNRS, Grenoble INP (Institute of Engineering Univ. Grenoble Alpes), LIG, 38000 Grenoble, France
luca.di-stefano@inria.fr
http://convecs.inria.fr

Abstract. We introduce an automated workflow to verify a variety of temporal properties on systems of agents that interact through virtual stigmergies. By mechanically reducing the property and the system under verification to an MCL query and a sequential LNT program (both MCL and LNT being languages available in the CADP formal verification toolbox), we may reuse efficient model-checking procedures that can give us a verdict on whether the property is satisfied by the system. Among other things, this procedure allows us to verify that a system satisfies a given predicate infinitely often during its execution, which is an improvement over previous verification approaches. We demonstrate the capabilities of this workflow by verifying a selection of example systems. Additionally, we present preliminary results showing that this workflow may also generate parallel LNT programs and exploit compositional verification techniques, which is likely to improve the analysis performance.

Keywords: Collective adaptive systems · Virtual stigmergy · Temporal logics · Model checking

1 Introduction

Collective adaptive systems (CAS) are composed of several *agents*, with limited capabilities and knowledge, that interact together to reach a common goal [41]. When studying the evolution of these systems, one can often witness global phenomena that arise from the seemingly chaotic interaction of agents, such as the emergence of a coherent pattern of movement in a flock of birds or the spread of a popular opinion on a social network. While collective systems have traditionally been analyzed by looking at their aggregate features (for instance, by using general equilibrium theory to describe an economy), there is a growing interest in understanding what kind of local behaviour and which communication mechanisms may give rise to such global effects. These *individual-based* approaches are increasingly being used in hard and soft sciences alike, with applications ranging from economics [32], to epidemiology [27], to social sciences [18]. Additionally, replicating those mechanisms in man-made systems is likely to make them more adaptive, autonomous, and robust with respect to individual failures [3,34].

T. Margaria and B. Steffen (Eds.): ISoLA 2021, LNCS 13036, pp. 473–489, 2021.
https://doi.org/10.1007/978-3-030-89159-6_29

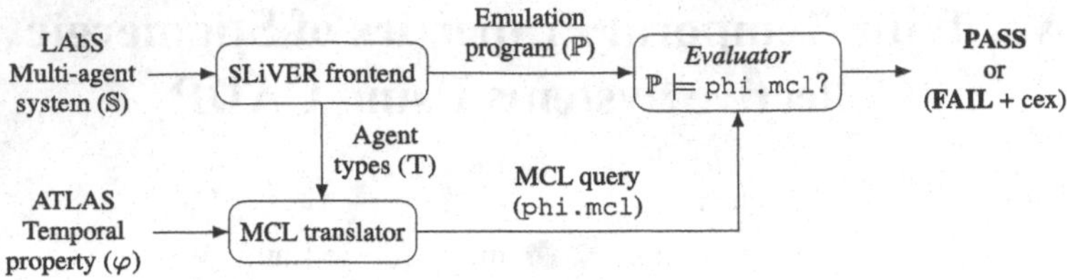

Fig. 1. Our verification workflow.

Stigmergies are one example of such a mechanism. A stigmergy is a mode of communication where agents interact by means of traces in a shared environment. Stigmergic systems feature agents that can coordinate and reach common goals just by leaving and interpreting these traces, even though no direct communication ever happens between them. While stigmergies were originally introduced to model the construction of termite nests [19], they have found widespread adoption as a conceptual tool to describe several collective systems, from colonies of foraging ants [33] to the Wikipedia collaborative encyclopedia [5]. Thus, they may be useful to scholars across many different disciplines which aim at understanding self-organization and spontaneous coordination [22]. However, the asynchronous nature of stigmergic interaction, coupled with the potentially nondeterministic behaviour and interleaving of agents, results in systems with a large state space. Thus, automated procedures are needed to formally guarantee the correctness of such systems.

In this paper, we introduce ATLAS (A Temporal Logic for Agents with State), a small formalism to express a variety of temporal properties about stateful agents. Then, we put forward an automated workflow to verify properties expressed in this formalism against stigmergic systems specified in the LAbS language [6]. This language allows to describe systems where the stigmergic medium is a distributed data structure [35], and where interaction among agents may be constrained by predicates on their exposed features. Our workflow reduces the system's specification to what we call an *emulation program* in the LNT process language [16], and translates the desired property into a query in the MCL property language [31]. Both LNT and MCL are languages available in the CADP formal verification toolbox[1] [15]. Our workflow can then use CADP tools to model-check the query against the program to obtain a verdict about whether the original specification satisfies the given property (Fig. 1). This workflow brings several improvements over previous LAbS verification approaches [11]. For instance, the present work introduces the capability of verifying that a system satisfies a given property infinitely often during its evolution. We demonstrate the effectiveness of this approach by verifying a selection of illustrative stigmergic systems.

As an additional contribution, we describe an alternative approach based on the generation of *parallel* LNT programs, i.e., where components of the system are implemented as separate processes. We then provide preliminary experimental results,[2]

[1] http://cadp.inria.fr.

[2] Artifacts related to the experiments presented in this work are available as a repository (https://gitlab.inria.fr/ldistefa/labs2lnt-artifacts).

showing that these programs can be efficiently verified by means of compositional techniques [28].

This paper is structured as follows. Section 2 introduces the necessary background information. Section 3 describes recent improvements to our emulation programs, as well as the ATLAS property language and its reduction to MCL queries. In Sect. 4, we demonstrate our approach by performing verification tasks on a collection of illustrative systems. Section 5 discusses how this workflow can be naturally extended to take advantages of compositional verification techniques, and presents some preliminary experimental results in that direction. Lastly, Sect. 6 discusses related work and Sect. 7 contains our conclusions, together with directions for future work.

2 Background

2.1 The CADP Toolbox

CADP [15] is a software toolbox for the analysis of asynchronous concurrent systems, described in languages whose semantics is expressed in terms of an LTS (labelled transition system). It contains a wide range of tools for simulation, test generation, verification (model checking and equivalence checking), performance evaluation, etc.

LNT is one of the input languages available in CADP to formally describe asynchronous concurrent systems [16]. A system is modeled as a process, generally composed of several, possibly concurrent processes, which may perform communication actions on gates and exchange information by multiway (value-passing) rendezvous, in the style of the Theoretical CSP [23] and LOTOS [24] process algebras. The syntax of LNT is inspired from both imperative languages (assignments, sequential composition, loops) and functional languages (pattern matching, recursion), with many static checks, such as binding, typing, and dataflow analysis ensuring the proper definition of variables and function results. A compiler for LNT generates the LTS corresponding to a main process, either as an explicit enumeration of its states and transitions (BCG graph) or in the form of an API (initial state and successor function) for on-the-fly verification.

MCL [31] is an action-based temporal logic based on the alternation-free fragment of the modal μ-calculus [26], extended with regular action formulas and value-passing constructs. It subsumes both branching-time and linear-time formalisms (e.g., CTL [4] and LTL [36]), allowing to express a quite wide range of temporal properties. The MCL language is built upon action formulas α, path formulas β, and state formulas φ. Basically, an action formula is a pattern that is intended to match some of the system's actions. So doing, MCL allows data-values present in the matched system's actions to be captured and stored in data variables, in order to be used in subsequent action or state formulas. For instance, if the system has an action of the form "*G* !1 !2", then it is matched by the action formula "*G* ?*x* : *int* !2" and the value of x takes the value 1. A path formula is basically a regular expression built on action formulas, which enables arbitrarily long sequences of actions to be specified. State formulas are built from: Boolean operators; predicates on data variables; the possibility modality $\langle\beta\rangle\varphi$ denoting the states with an outgoing path matching β and leading to a state satisfying φ; the necessity modality $[\beta]\varphi$ denoting the states all outgoing paths of which satisfying β lead to states satisfying φ; and two parameterized fixed point operators: the minimal fixed point operator

$\mu X(x_1 : T_1 = e_1, \ldots, x_n : T_n = e_n).\varphi$ (to specify finite sequences recursively), and the maximal parameterized fixed point operator $\nu X(x_1 : T_1 = e_1, \ldots, x_n : T_n = e_n).\varphi$ (to specify infinite sequences), where X is called a propositional variable and φ usually contains occurrences of X with actual values for the parameters $x_1, \ldots, x_n$ of types $T_1, \ldots, T_n$; the expressions $e_1, \ldots, e_n$ denote the parameter's initial values. MCL also allows action and state formulas to be embedded in parameterized macro definitions, to enable code reuse. Many additional high-level constructs inspired from programming languages (such as loops and conditionals) also exist, mostly introduced as syntactic sugar. A complete description can be found online in the MCL manual page.[3] The *Evaluator* model checker available in CADP can be used to evaluate temporal properties expressed in MCL, either on a BCG graph or on-the-fly through the API representing an LTS. A complete description of *Evaluator*'s features can be found in its online manual page.[4]

2.2 LAbS and SLiVER

In our experimental evaluation, we will consider emulation programs generated from LAbS specifications. The LAbS language [6] allows to describe systems of agents that communicate indirectly via *virtual stigmergies*. A virtual stigmergy [35] is a distributed key-value store that allows an agent to asynchronously diffuse its own (local) knowledge to neighboring agents. An agent can manipulate a stigmergy simply by assigning values to specific local variables (which we call *stigmergic variables*). Whenever this happens, the agent also computes a *timestamp* to record the moment when the assignment took place. Then, the agent asynchronously advertises the new value by sending messages to its neighbors containing the name of the variable, the new value, and the computed timestamp. Receivers will accept *newer* values for a variable (i.e., those with a higher timestamp than their local value) and advertise them as well, while they will reject *older* ones and react by advertising their own, newer, value. Agents will also send similar messages whenever they access the values of these variables (e.g., during evaluation of an expression). While the concept of *neighborhood* is commonly associated with spatial closeness, LAbS allows the user to define it in terms of *predicates* over the exposed features of agents. Furthermore, the user may equip different stigmergic variables with different definitions of neighborhood.

To illustrate LAbS, let us discuss a simplified version of the *Boids* algorithm for flocking agents [39]. An excerpt of the LAbS specification is shown in Listing 1. In this model, N "birds" are scattered on a 2D grid of size G. Every bird has a *position* $(x, y) \in [0, G-1] \times [0, G-1]$ and a *direction* of movement (dx, dy), for which we assume four possible values, i.e., those in the set $\{\pm 1\} \times \{\pm 1\}$. Lastly, the *behaviour* of each bird simply makes it move by repeatedly updating its position according to its direction: specifically, its new position is the sum (modulo G) of its current position and direction. The modulo operation, informally, means that the grid wraps around: for instance, an agent in position $(0, 0)$ can reach $(G-1, G-1)$ in a single step. It is worth noticing that the behaviour does not feature any communication constructs.

[3] http://cadp.inria.fr/man/mcl.html.

[4] http://cadp.inria.fr/man/evaluator.html.

Listing 1. A simple model of flocking behaviour in LAbS.

```
stigmergy Dir {
  link=√((x1−x2)² + (y1−y2)²) ≤ δ
  dx, dy: {-1, 1}, {-1, 1}
}

agent Bird {
  interface= x:[0..G], y:[0..G]
  stigmergies= Dir
  Behaviour=
    x, y←(x+dx) mod G, (y+dy) mod G;
    Behaviour
}
```

Rather, we declare (dx, dy) as stigmergic variables, so that agents will advertise their direction every time they use it to update their position. We use a check on the Euclidean distance as the link predicate: two agents a_1 (the sender) and a_2 (the potential receiver) may only exchange a message if their distance is not greater than a given value δ. Intuitively, given a big enough δ and enough time, all birds should eventually have the same values for dx, dy, and thus they should move in the same direction.

The features described above lead to compact specifications of systems which may nonetheless display very large state spaces. Thus, formal verification becomes essential to prove that the specified systems do behave correctly and do not reach unwanted states. A possible way to verify a LAbS system $\mathbb{S}$ is by crafting and analyzing a sequential emulation program [10], i.e., a program $\mathbb{P}$ that can reproduce all possible executions of $\mathbb{S}$, without introducing spurious executions. $\mathbb{P}$ is *sequential* in the sense that the concurrent execution of the agents in $\mathbb{S}$ is reproduced by means of a nondeterministic, but non-concurrent scheduler, similarly to the way sequentialization is used to verify a piece of concurrent software by reducing it to an equivalent sequential program [37]. The SLiVER tool[5] aims at verifying LAbS systems by generating emulation programs in several languages, including LNT [11]. In fact, we will rely on a slightly modified version of SLiVER as part of our workflow.

3 Model Checking Sequential LNT Emulation Programs

As stated earlier, the automated workflow of Fig. 1 translates a LAbS system and an ATLAS property into an LNT program and an MCL query, respectively. Then, it uses CADP's Evaluator to determine whether the program satisfies the query. This gives us a verdict on whether the system satisfies the property. In this section, we describe our workflow in more detail: we first outline several improvements in the generation of LNT programs (Sect. 3.1), and then introduce ATLAS (Sect. 3.2) and describe how we can encode ATLAS properties into MCL queries (Sect. 3.3).

3.1 Improving LNT Emulation Programs for LAbS

The SLiVER tool already demonstrated the feasibility of building and analyzing LNT emulation programs for LAbS specifications, by means of a provably correct structural

[5] https://github.com/labs-lang/sliver.

encoding procedure [10]. In a previous version of SLiVER [11], the emulation program contained a *monitor* that encoded the property under verification; then, one simply used *Evaluator* to check the behaviour of the monitor and obtain a verdict on the satisfaction of the property. The emulation program also contained "diagnostic" transitions that were used to extract a counterexample in case of a property violation. However, these transitions did not follow a rigorous scheme: for instance, transitions resulting from assignments were different from those caused by stigmergic messages. In contrast, the current LNT code generator does not introduce a monitor, and its diagnostic transitions have been systematically revised to allow for MCL-based property verification (see Sect. 3.3). Namely, we let the emulation program signal every change of state (i.e., any change to one of the program's variables) by means of a visible transition, labelled as `assign !<id> !<varName> !<value>`, where `<id>` is the agent's unique identifier, `<varName>` the name of the changed variable, and `<value>` its new value. MCL queries are generally more efficient than the previous approach, and allow to verify multiple properties on the same program. Furthermore, this change allows us to progressively increase the fragment of supported properties without altering the LAbS-to-LNT code generator.

Additionally, we introduce a more efficient encoding of virtual stigmergies, resulting in emulation programs with a smaller state space that are thus easier to verify. While the original encoding explicitly modelled timestamps as natural numbers, we observed that the semantics of stigmergic interaction only ever needs to *compare* the timestamps of two agents. Thus, the new encoding just records these comparisons by associating to each stigmergic variable `var` a matrix $M_{\texttt{var}}$ of symbolic values `GREATER`, `SAME`, `LESS`. The intuition is that $M_{\texttt{var}}(i, j)$ is `GREATER` (resp. `LESS`) iff the value of `var` stored by the i-th agent is newer (resp. older) than that of the j-th agent, and it is `SAME` iff the two values have the same timestamp. To enforce this rule, we must maintain the matrix in two ways. First, whenever agent i assigns a new value to `var`, we set $M_{\texttt{var}}(i, j)$ to `GREATER` for all agents $j \neq i$. Respectively, we set $M_{\texttt{var}}(j, i)$ to `LESS`. Furthermore, whenever an agent j successfully receives a value for `var` from another agent i, we update both $M_{\texttt{var}}(i, j)$ and $M_{\texttt{var}}(j, i)$ to `SAME`.

3.2 A Basic Property Language for Systems of Stateful Agents

We are interested in verifying temporal properties on an emulation program that represents a system of stateful agents. Naturally, we could encode any such property by manually writing an MCL query. However, doing so requires a good knowledge of both MCL and the structure of our emulation programs, and thus would be unsuitable for most users without a strong background in model checking. Furthermore, since agents are stateful, users may want to express *state-based* properties about them. Even though action- and state-based logics are essentially interchangeable [9], these users may feel at odds with the action-based MCL. What we propose, instead, is that the user should define properties in a higher-level language that trades off some of the expressiveness of MCL in exchange for more compact and intuitive properties, and encode such properties into MCL by means of a mechanizable procedure. We call this language ATLAS (A Temporal Logic for Agents with State).

$$
\begin{aligned}
e &::= \kappa \mid x.var \mid e \circ e \mid |e| && \text{(value expression)} \\
p &::= e \bowtie e \mid x = x \mid \neg p \mid p \wedge p && \text{(predicate)} \\
\psi &::= p \mid \exists x \in \mathrm{T} \bullet \psi \mid \forall x \in \mathrm{T} \bullet \psi && \text{(quantified predicate)} \\
\phi &::= \mathsf{always}\,\psi \mid \mathsf{fairly}\,\psi \mid \mathsf{fairly}_\infty\,\psi && \text{(temporal property)}
\end{aligned}
$$

Fig. 2. Syntax of ATLAS, a temporal property language for collective adaptive systems.

The syntax of ATLAS is presented in Fig. 2, where $\circ$ is a generic binary arithmetic operator ($+$, $-$, ...), $\bowtie$ is a generic comparison ($=$, $>$, ...), and $|e|$ is the absolute value of e. Furthermore, we assume that the agents in the system are partitioned into user-defined *types*, ranged over by T. A *value expression* is an arithmetic expression that may contain constants (κ) or refer to of agents' local variables: given a quantified *agent variable* x, $x.var$ evaluates to the value that x currently gives to its local variable var. A *predicate* can either compare two expressions ($e \bowtie e$), or check whether two agent variables refer to the same agent ($x = x$). Predicates can be negated, or can contain a conjunction of other predicates ($\neg p$, $p \wedge p$). Other compound predicates ($x \neq x$, $p \vee p, \ldots$) can be derived from these ones in the usual way. A *quantified predicate* is a predicate preceded by zero or more universal or existential (typed) quantifiers. We will only consider *sentences*, i.e., predicates where all agent variables are in the scope of some quantifier. Every sentence has a definite truth value in every state of a system: that is, a state either satisfies a sentence or not. Finally, a *temporal property* specifies *when* a quantified predicate should hold during the execution of a system. Property $\mathsf{always}\,\psi$ states that ψ should be satisfied in every state of the system: $\mathsf{fairly}\,\psi$ says that every *fair* execution of the system should contain at least one state satisfying ψ; lastly, $\mathsf{fairly}_\infty\,\psi$ says that every fair execution should satisfy ψ infinitely many times. The precise definition of a fair execution will be given below.

Informal semantics of quantified predicates. We think of a *state* of a given system as a function $\sigma : A \to V \cup \{id, type\} \to \mathbb{Z}$ that maps every agent $a \in A$ to a valuation function that, in turn, maps each local variable $var \in V$ to its current value, which we assume to be an integer. This valuation function also defines two special variables, id and $type$. The value of id is unique to each agent, while the value of $type$ will be the same for agents of the same type. Both values are constant across all states of the system.

To check whether a state σ satisfies a quantified predicate, we repeatedly apply quantifier elimination until we obtain a propositional predicate. Thus, $\forall x \in \mathrm{T} \bullet p$ reduces to $\bigwedge_{a \in A} a \in \mathrm{T} \Rightarrow p[a/x]$ and $\exists x \in \mathrm{T} \bullet p$ reduces to $\bigvee_{a \in A} a \in \mathrm{T} \wedge p[a/x]$, where predicate $a \in \mathrm{T}$ holds iff the type of agent a is T (and can be implemented as a check on $\sigma(a)(type)$), and $p[a/x]$ is the predicate p where all occurrences of agent variable x are replaced by the actual agent a. Then, we replace all expressions of $a.var$, and all predicates of the form $a = b$ (where a and b are agents), by $\sigma(a)(var)$ and $\sigma(a)(id) = \sigma(b)(id)$. The truth value of the resulting Boolean formula tells whether the original predicate holds in σ.

Informal semantics of temporal properties. We can give an informal explanation of our temporal modalities by means of CTL operators [4]. A predicate always ψ holds iff all reachable states in the system satisfy ψ. Thus, it corresponds to the CTL property $\mathsf{AG}\psi$. The fairly modality represents a form of *fair reachability* [38]. An execution is *unfair* if it ends in an infinite cycle, such that there is at least one state along the cycle from which one could break out of the loop by performing some transition. The fairness assumption here is that such a transition is enabled infinitely often, and thus it should be fired at least once during the evolution of the system. Therefore, fairly ψ holds if every path such that ψ does not hold leads to a state from which we may reach a state that satisfies ψ. We can slightly abuse CTL's notation and express such a property as $\mathsf{AG}_{\neg\psi}\mathsf{EF}\psi$, where $\mathsf{AG}_{\neg\psi}$ represents those paths on which ψ is never satisfied. Lastly, fairly_∞ ψ holds if every fair execution of the system contains infinitely many states where ψ holds, and may be represented in CTL as $\mathsf{AGEF}\psi$. This modality was not supported by previous verification workflows for LAbS specifications.

3.3 Encoding State-Based Properties as MCL Queries

We now focus on the problem of mechanically translating a temporal property espressed in the (state-based) ATLAS formalism into the (action-based) MCL language. Regardless of the temporal modality used in the formula, we will always have to reduce ψ to a propositional predicate and encode the result as a *parameterized macro*. For instance, consider the quantified predicate $\forall x \in \mathrm{T} \bullet x.var > 0$, and assume that our system of interest contains 3 agents of type T (which we will denote by $a_{1,2,3}$). Then, we can reduce such predicate to the conjunction $a_1.var > 0 \wedge a_2.var > 0 \wedge a_3.var > 0$, which we encode as the following macro:

```
macro Predicate(a1_var, a2_var, a3_var) =
  (a1_var > 0) and (a2_var > 0) and (a3_var > 0)
end_macro
```

To mechanically perform this translation we only need ψ and some information about agent types featured in ψ, which can be provided by SLiVER. In general, a formula may have to consider n agents and m variables, resulting in a macro with nm parameters. For simplicity, from now on we assume that the identifiers of these n agents are $1, 2, \ldots, n$, and that the variables relevant to ψ are named $\mathtt{v}_1, \ldots, \mathtt{v}_m$. We will denote by x_{ij} the value that the i-th agent gives to variable $\mathtt{v}_j$, and we will write $x_{11}, \ldots, x_{nm}$ to range over all nm such values.

*Encoding **always**.* An MCL query that encodes always ψ should evaluate ψ (actually, the `Predicate` macro encoding it) on every reachable state of the emulation program, and report a property violation iff it finds a state where this evaluation yields *false*. To do so, it should first capture the initial values for all mn variables that are relevant to ψ, and then use a *parameterized fixed point* formula to check that ψ is indeed an invariant of the system, while capturing those assignments that may affect its satisfaction by means of parameters. The structure of such a query is shown on Listing 2. Informally, the initial "box" operator captures the initial values of $\mathtt{v}_1, \ldots, \mathtt{v}_m$ for all agents, while

Listing 2. Checking invariance of `Predicate` in MCL.

```
[{assign !1 !"v1" ?x̄11:Int} . ... . {assign !n !"vm" ?x̄nm:Int}]
nu Inv (x11:Int=x̄11, ..., xnm:Int=x̄nm) . (
  Predicate(x11,...,xnm) and
  [not {assign ...} or {assign to other variables}] Inv(x11,...,xnm) and
  [{assign !1 !"v1" ?v:Int}] Inv(v,x12,...,xnm) and ... and
  [{assign !n !"vm" ?v:Int}] Inv(x11,x12,...,v) )
```

Listing 3. An MCL macro to check that a state satisfying `Predicate` is fairly reachable from the current state.

```
macro Reach (v11,...,vnm) =
  mu R (x11:Int=v11, ..., xnm:Int=vnm) . (
  Predicate(x11,...,xnm) or
  <not {assign ...} or {assign to other variables}>R(x11,...,xnm) or
  <{assign !1 !"v1" ?v:Int}>R(v,...,xnm) or ... or
  <{assign !n !"vm" ?v:Int}>R(x11,...,v) )
end_macro
```

also specifying that the subsequent formula should hold for all paths. Then, we pass these values to a parameterized maximal fixed point formula `Inv`, which is satisfied in a given state iff the current parameters satisfy ψ, and additionally:

1. Every assignment that does not affect ψ leads to a state that satisfies `Inv` (without changing its parameters);
2. If an assignment changes the value of the ij-th relevant variable, the resulting state still satisfies `Inv` (after using the new value as its ij-th parameter).

Encoding **fairly**$_\infty$ *and* **fairly**. To encode "infinitely-often" properties (**fairly**$_\infty$ ψ) in MCL, we similarly start by encoding ψ as a macro `Predicate`. Then, we need to write another macro `Reach` that says "A state satisfying `Predicate` is reachable from this state", by means of a *minimal* fixed point formula (Listing 3). Lastly, we check that `Reach` is an invariant of the system by using the same query shown in Listing 2, but with `Reach` instead of `Predicate`.

Checking fair reachability of ψ (**fairly** ψ) is just a variation on the "infinitely-often" case. Informally, we want to stop exploring an execution of our system as soon as we find a state where ψ holds. To do so, we check `Predicate` within the body of the `Inv` formula, so that its satisfaction is sufficient to satisfy the whole formula.

4 Verification of Sequential Emulation Programs

In this section, we evaluate our suggested verification workflow (Fig. 1) by performing a selection of verification tasks on a selection of LAbS specifications. For each specification, we generated a corresponding LNT emulation program and verified one or more temporal properties against it.

Description of the benchmark and properties. Here, we briefly describe our systems of interest and the temporal property (or properties) that we have verified on them.

`formation` describes a system of line-forming agents. $N = 3$ robots are randomly placed on a segment of length $L = 10$. They can asynchronously inform other agents about their position, but their communication range is limited to $\delta = 2$. Property `safety` asks that the position of all robots is always in the interval $[0, L-1]$. (`safety` $\triangleq$ **always** $\forall x \in \text{Robot} \bullet x.pos \geq 0 \land x.pos < L$). Property `distance` states that, eventually, the distance between any two robots should not be smaller than δ. (`distance` $\triangleq$ $\textsf{fairly}_\infty$ $\forall x \in \text{Robot} \bullet \forall y \in \text{Robot} \bullet x \neq y \implies |a.pos - b.pos| \geq \delta$).

`flock` is the simple flocking model described in Sect. 2.2. In our experiments we used $N = 3$ birds, a 5×5 arena, and a communication radius $\delta = 5$.

Property `consensus` states that the system reaches a state where every bird moves in the same direction infinitely often. (`consensus` $\triangleq$ $\textsf{fairly}_\infty$ $\forall x \in \text{Bird} \bullet \forall y \in \text{Bird} \bullet x.dir = y.dir$).

`leader` is a bully algorithm for leader election [17]. N agents must elect one of them as their leader, or coordinator. Each agent starts by advertising itself as the leader, by sending asynchronous messages containing its own identifier id. However, an agent will stop doing so if they receive a message with an id lower than their own. Property `consensus0` states that all agents eventually agree to choose the one with identifier 0 as their leader. (`consensus0` $\triangleq$ $\textsf{fairly}_\infty$ $\forall x \in \text{Agent} \bullet x.leader = 0$).

`twophase` is a two-phase commit system [20]. A coordinator asks N workers if they agree to commit a transaction or not. If all of them agree, the coordinator commits the transaction; otherwise, it performs a rollback operation. We represent those operations by equipping the coordinator with two local variables `commit`, `rollback`, initially set to 0, and later assigning a value of 1 to either of them. After either operation has been performed, the coordinator resets both variables to 0 and the system starts over. In our specification, workers always agree to perform the commit: thus, we expect the system to perform infinitely many commits. This expectation is encoded by the `infcommits` property (`infcommits` $\triangleq$ $\textsf{fairly}_\infty$ $\exists x \in \text{Coordinator} \bullet x.commit = 1$).

Experimental setup and results. Each verification task consists of two steps. First, we generate an LTS in BCG format from the given program. Then, we check that this LTS satisfies the requested property. This procedure is generally faster than asking *Evaluator* to model-check the LNT program on the fly, and also allows us to quantify the complexity of a program by looking at the size of its LTS. All the experiments were performed with CADP version 2021-e on the Grid'5000 testbed,[6] specifically on the *Dahu* cluster in Grenoble. Each node in this cluster is equipped with two Intel Xeon Gold 6130 CPUs. We set a timeout of 3 h and a memory limit of 16 GiB for all experiments.

---

[6] https://www.grid5000.fr.

Table 1. Experimental results for sequential emulation programs.

System	States	Transitions	Property	Time (s)	Memory (kiB)
`formation-rr`	8786313	160984587	`safety`	1931	1723492
			`distance`	2147	2062872
`flock-rr`	58032296	121581762	`consensus`	3772	14122756
`flock`	60121704	223508430	`consensus`	4375	14108608
`leader5`	41752	1630955	`consensus0`	11	43456
`leader6`	421964	27873756	`consensus0`	240	224392
`leader7`	4438576	497568001	`consensus0`	3963	3240356
`twophase2`	19246	1124680	`infcommits`	17	54584
`twophase3`	291329	22689137	`infcommits`	849	145904

Table 1 shows the results of our experimental evaluation. Columns from left to right contain, respectively, the name of the system under verification; the number of states and transitions of its corresponding LTS; the name of the property we are checking; and the resources (time and memory) that were used to check the property. Specifically, the *Time* column reports the total amount of time spent on generating and model-checking the LTS, while the *Memory* column reports the maximum amount of memory that was used during the whole task. In the first column, an `-rr` suffix denotes that we have assumed round-robin scheduling of agents, i.e., we only verified those executions where agents performed their action in circular order. In systems without the suffix, we have instead assumed free interleaving of agents. We have verified increasingly larger versions of `leader` and `twophase`. For `leader` systems, the numerical suffix denotes the number of agents; For `twophase` systems, it denotes the number of workers.

Every task resulted in a positive verdict. For `formation` and `flock`, this is consistent with previous verification results [10]. For `leader` and `twophase`, the positive verdict is consistent with the existing literature on the two algorithms [17,20].

In the `leader` and `twophase` systems, we can observe that adding one agent makes the LTS grow by roughly one order of magnitude. This is likely the effect of two factors, namely the free interleaving of agents and the asynchronous nature of stigmergic messages. We can similarly appreciate the effect of using free interleaving instead of round-robin scheduling by comparing the `flock` and `flock-rr` experiments. The number of *states* is not particularly affected, but the *transitions* nearly double: respectively, they increase by roughly 3.6% and 83.8%. Informally, free interleaving mainly allows for alternative ways of moving between one state and the next. This has an obvious impact on the overall verification time, which increases by roughly 15%.

5 Compositional Verification of Parallel Emulation Programs

Compositional verification is a family of *divide and conquer* approaches, which exploit the parallel structure of a concurrent model to palliate state space explosion. In this work, we consider compositional (property-dependent) state space reduction (available in CADP [14,28]) which, given a property of interest, identifies both a maximal set

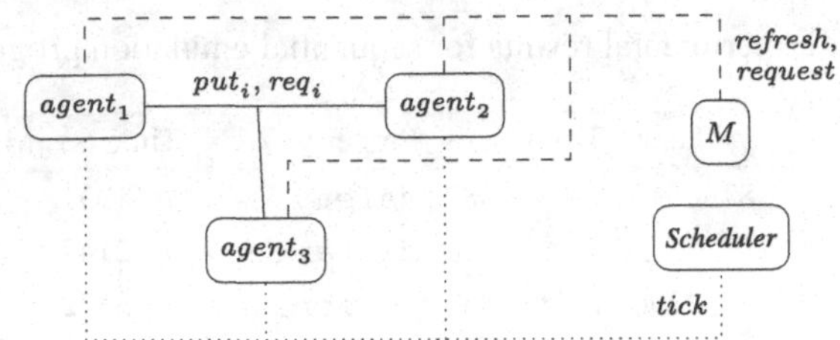

Fig. 3. Structure of a 3-agent parallel emulation program.

of actions that can be hidden and a reduction with respect to an equivalence relation, in a way that guarantees to preserve the truth-value of the property. In general, the equivalence relation is based on bisimulations (strong, divbranching,[7] or sharp bisimulation [28]), which are congruences with respect to parallel composition. It is hence possible to apply action hiding and bisimulation reduction incrementally, first to individual agents and then to intermediate compositions. Choosing an appropriate composition order is a key of success of the approach.

To exploit the potential of compositional verification in our context, we consider in this section the feasibility of creating *parallel* emulation programs from LAbS specifications, and verify them compositionally. Figure 3 shows a simplified network diagram of a 3-agent parallel emulation program. Each agent is implemented as its own process $agent_i$, which can send stigmergic messages to the others via gates put_i and req_i. This means that a system with n agents would require $2n$ gates. Information about *timestamps* is stored in a separate process, which essentially maintains the $M_{\mathtt{var}}$ matrices introduced in Sect. 4. Each agent can signal that they have updated a stigmergic variable by means of a *refresh* gate, or can ask how their timestamp for a value compares to that of another agent via a *request* gate. Lastly, a *scheduler* process ensures that agents perform their actions either in round-robin or nondeterministic fashion, without producing interleavings that are forbidden by the semantics of LAbS. Notice that a program with such an architecture can be mechanically generated from a LAbS specification by simply altering the "program template" used by the SLiVER code generator.

A potential issue that arises when using a compositional approach is that, when a process P can receive values of type T over a gate `G` (expressed in LNT as `G(?x)`, with `x` a variable of type T), the associated LTS as generated by CADP will have to consider *every* possible value of type T. If P is part of a larger system, it may be the case that only a small subset of those values are ever sent to P by other processes, and an LTS that only considered such subset would be sufficient.

To generate such an LTS from our emulation program, we had to constrain the values accepted over the communication gates depicted in Fig. 3, by decorating LNT reception statements with `where` clauses. Thus, a statement `G(?x)` becomes `G(?x) where f(x)` (with `f(x)` a predicate over `x`). In this preliminary experiment we added such `where` clauses manually, but this step may be mechanized, for instance, by computing the clauses via an interval analysis.

[7] We use divbranching as shorthand for divergence-preserving branching.

Table 2. Compositional verification of `flock-rr`.

Process	States	Transitions	Time (s)	Memory (kiB)
M	13	234	3	34360
Scheduler	6	12	2	34212
$Agent_1$	25637	1989572	537	3102904
$Agent_2$	25637	1989572	537	3102908
$Agent_3$	25637	1989572	538	3100408
Main	28800	74906	73	70828
Main $\models$ `consensus`	–	–	2	43428
Total time, max memory			1692	3102908

5.1 Experimental Evaluation

As a preliminary evaluation of this approach, we considered the `flock-rr` system from Sect. 4, and reduced it to a parallel emulation program whose architecture matches that of Fig. 3. Then, we asked CADP to generate the individual LTSs of each process, reduce them with respect to divbranching bisimulation, and finally compose them. We used the same experimental setup described in Sect. 4. Finally, we asked to evaluate the `consensus` property on the resulting LTS.

Details about this experiment are shown in Table 2. For each row except the last two, the first three columns contain the name of a process in the emulation program and the size of its corresponding LTS (in terms of its states and transitions). Then, the *Time* column contains the total time spent by CADP to generate and reduce the LTS with respect to divbranching bisimulation. The *Memory* column, instead, contains the maximum amount of memory required by these two operations. Notice that *Main* is the process encoding the whole system. The last rows, instead, show the resources used by CADP to evaluate whether the LTS of `Main` satisfies `consensus`, and an overall account of the resources (total time and maximum amount of physical memory used) needed for the whole experiment. CADP provided a positive verdict after 1692 s (roughly half an hour), by spending roughly 3 GiB of memory. Most of the time was spent in the generation and reduction of the LTSs for the three agents. These numbers appear to improve over the sequential approach, which by comparison requires 3772 s and around 14 GiB of memory (Table 1).

6 Related Work

Several other works investigate the use of on-the-fly model checking to verify multi-agent systems [2,30]. Recently, formal verification of *open* systems (where countably many agents may join or leave during its evolution) has been addressed in [25], which also uses properties that are quantified over the agents. So far, SLiVER does not support open systems, and the problem appears to be decidable only for a specific class of systems. It would be interesting to investigate whether LAbS systems belong to such a class.

Verifying higher-level languages by means of mechanized translations to process algebras or similar kinds of formal models has been explored by several other works, allowing to verify diverse classes of systems, including web choreographies [13], agents with attribute-based communication [8], information systems with trace-dependent attributes [40], or component-based ensembles [21]. Compositional verification has also been shown to be effective in dealing with component-based [1] and asynchronous concurrent systems [14]. An alternative approach relies on encodings into some general-purpose programming language, such as C: the resulting emulation programs can then be verified by any off-the-shelf analysis tool supporting said language [7]. SLiVER's modular architecture allows to support both approaches, exemplified respectively by LNT and C, and to add new modules implementing additional translations [10].

Our encoding of temporal properties bears some resemblance to the *specification pattern system* of [12]. Similarly to us, the authors of these patterns contend that higher-level logical formalisms are needed to facilitate the adoption of formal verification. While their approach focuses on capturing temporal relationships between states or actions (which are left unspecified), we focused on specifying state properties by means of quantified predicate and then implemented some of these patterns on top of a data-aware, action-based logic. Extending our approach to other patterns may be a worthwhile effort.

7 Conclusions

We have introduced an automated workflow for the verification of a variety of temporal properties on stigmergic systems, which are encoded as sequential emulation programs in the LNT language. This workflow reuses an expressive property language and state-of-the-art procedures for on-the-fly model checking. We have demonstrated our approach by carrying out a selection of verification tasks. Then, we have presented some preliminary results about the feasibility of using parallel emulation programs, combined with compositional verification techniques. This direction of research appears to be promising for large systems and should be investigated as part of our future work. Another possible approach would consist in generating the LTS of a sequential emulation program in a distributed fashion, using other tools provided by CADP.[8]

We should stress that our proposed property language and verification workflow can be applied to other types of concurrent systems, as long as they can be reduced to emulation programs. This aspect should also be analysed in further depth, by finding other formalisms and case studies. Lastly, our property language could be improved in multiple ways, e.g., by supporting predicates about shared memory; introducing the capability to count [29] the agents that satisfy some predicate; or extending the range of temporal properties supported by our procedure.

Acknowledgments. The authors wish to thank Radu Mateescu for his precious insights into MCL. Experiments presented in this paper were carried out using the Grid'5000 testbed, supported by a scientific interest group hosted by Inria and including CNRS, RENATER and several Universities as well as other organizations.

[8] E.g., the *Distributor* tool: see https://cadp.inria.fr/man/distributor.html.

References

1. Bensalem, S., Bozga, M., Sifakis, J., Nguyen, T.-H.: Compositional verification for component-based systems and application. In: Cha, S.S., Choi, J.-Y., Kim, M., Lee, I., Viswanathan, M. (eds.) ATVA 2008. LNCS, vol. 5311, pp. 64–79. Springer, Heidelberg (2008). https://doi.org/10.1007/978-3-540-88387-6_7
2. Bordini, R.H., Fisher, M., Visser, W., Wooldridge, M.: Verifying multi-agent programs by model checking. Auton. Agents Multi-Agent Syst. **12**(2), 239–256 (2006). https://doi.org/10.1007/s10458-006-5955-7
3. Brooks, R.A., Flynn, A.M.: Fast, cheap and out of control: a robot invasion of the solar system. J. Br. Interplanet. Soc. **42**, 478–485 (1989)
4. Clarke, E.M., Emerson, E.A.: Design and synthesis of synchronization skeletons using branching time temporal logic. In: Kozen, D. (ed.) Logic of Programs 1981. LNCS, vol. 131, pp. 52–71. Springer, Heidelberg (1982). https://doi.org/10.1007/BFb0025774
5. Crowston, K., Rezgui, A.: Effects of stigmergic and explicit coordination on Wikipedia article quality. In: HICSS. ScholarSpace (2020)
6. De Nicola, R., Di Stefano, L., Inverso, O.: Multi-agent systems with virtual stigmergy. Sci. Comput. Program. **187**, 102345 (2020). https://doi.org/10.1016/j.scico.2019.102345
7. De Nicola, R., Duong, T., Inverso, O.: Verifying AbC specifications via emulation. In: Margaria, T., Steffen, B. (eds.) ISoLA 2020. LNCS, vol. 12477, pp. 261–279. Springer, Cham (2020). https://doi.org/10.1007/978-3-030-61470-6_16
8. De Nicola, R., Duong, T., Inverso, O., Mazzanti, F.: A systematic approach to programming and verifying attribute-based communication systems. In: ter Beek, M.H., Fantechi, A., Semini, L. (eds.) From Software Engineering to Formal Methods and Tools, and Back. LNCS, vol. 11865, pp. 377–396. Springer, Cham (2019). https://doi.org/10.1007/978-3-030-30985-5_22
9. De Nicola, R., Vaandrager, F.: Action versus state based logics for transition systems. In: Guessarian, I. (ed.) LITP 1990. LNCS, vol. 469, pp. 407–419. Springer, Heidelberg (1990). https://doi.org/10.1007/3-540-53479-2_17
10. Di Stefano, L.: Modelling and verification of multi-agent systems via sequential emulation. Ph.D. thesis, Gran Sasso Science Institute (2020)
11. Di Stefano, L., Lang, F., Serwe, W.: Combining SLiVER with CADP to analyze multi-agent systems. In: Bliudze, S., Bocchi, L. (eds.) COORDINATION 2020. LNCS, vol. 12134, pp. 370–385. Springer, Cham (2020). https://doi.org/10.1007/978-3-030-50029-0_23
12. Dwyer, M.B., Avrunin, G.S., Corbett, J.C.: Patterns in property specifications for finite-state verification. In: ICSE. ACM (1999). https://doi.org/10.1145/302405.302672
13. Foster, H., Uchitel, S., Magee, J., Kramer, J.: WS-engineer: a model-based approach to engineering web service compositions and choreography. In: Baresi, L., Nitto, E.D. (eds.) Test and Analysis of Web Services. Springer, Heidelberg (2007). https://doi.org/10.1007/978-3-540-72912-9_4
14. Garavel, H., Lang, F., Mateescu, R.: Compositional verification of asynchronous concurrent systems using CADP. Acta Informatica **52**(4), 337–392 (2015)
15. Garavel, H., Lang, F., Mateescu, R., Serwe, W.: CADP 2011: a toolbox for the construction and analysis of distributed processes. Softw. Tools Technol. Transf. **15**(2), 89–107 (2013). https://doi.org/10.1007/s10009-012-0244-z
16. Garavel, H., Lang, F., Serwe, W.: From LOTOS to LNT. In: Katoen, J.-P., Langerak, R., Rensink, A. (eds.) ModelEd, TestEd, TrustEd. LNCS, vol. 10500, pp. 3–26. Springer, Cham (2017). https://doi.org/10.1007/978-3-319-68270-9_1
17. Garcia-Molina, H.: Elections in a distributed computing system. IEEE Trans. Comput. **31**(1), 48–59 (1982). https://doi.org/10.1109/TC.1982.1675885

18. Geller, A., Moss, S.: Growing qawm: an evidence-driven declarative model of Afghan power structures. Adv. Complex Syst. **11**(2), 321–335 (2008). https://doi.org/10.1142/S0219525908001659
19. Grassé, P.P.: La reconstruction du nid et les coordinations interindividuelles chez Bellicositermes natalensis et Cubitermes sp. la théorie de la stigmergie: Essai d'interprétation du comportement des termites constructeurs. Insectes Sociaux **6**(1) (1959). https://doi.org/10.1007/BF02223791
20. Gray, J.N.: Notes on data base operating systems. In: Bayer, R., Graham, R.M., Seegmüller, G. (eds.) Operating Systems. LNCS, vol. 60, pp. 393–481. Springer, Heidelberg (1978). https://doi.org/10.1007/3-540-08755-9_9
21. Hennicker, R., Klarl, A., Wirsing, M.: Model-checking HELENA ensembles with spin. In: Martí-Oliet, N., Ölveczky, P.C., Talcott, C. (eds.) Logic, Rewriting, and Concurrency. LNCS, vol. 9200, pp. 331–360. Springer, Cham (2015). https://doi.org/10.1007/978-3-319-23165-5_16
22. Heylighen, F.: Stigmergy as a universal coordination mechanism I: definition and components. Cogn. Syst. Res. **38**, 4–13 (2016). https://doi.org/10.1016/j.cogsys.2015.12.002
23. Hoare, C.A.R.: Communicating Sequential Processes. Prentice-Hall, Hoboken (1985)
24. ISO/IEC: Information processing systems - Open systems interconnection - LOTOS - A formal description technique based on the temporal ordering of observational behaviour. International Standard 8807, ISO (1989)
25. Kouvaros, P., Lomuscio, A., Pirovano, E., Punchihewa, H.: Formal verification of open multi-agent systems. In: AAMAS. IFAAMAS (2019)
26. Kozen, D.: Results on the propositional mu-calculus. Theor. Comput. Sci. **27** (1983)
27. Kuylen, E., Liesenborgs, J., Broeckhove, J., Hens, N.: Using individual-based models to look beyond the horizon: the changing effects of household-based clustering of susceptibility to measles in the next 20 years. In: Krzhizhanovskaya, V.V., Závodszky, G., Lees, M.H., Dongarra, J.J., Sloot, P.M.A., Brissos, S., Teixeira, J. (eds.) ICCS 2020. LNCS, vol. 12137, pp. 385–398. Springer, Cham (2020). https://doi.org/10.1007/978-3-030-50371-0_28
28. Lang, F., Mateescu, R., Mazzanti, F.: Sharp congruences adequate with temporal logics combining weak and strong modalities. In: TACAS 2020. LNCS, vol. 12079, pp. 57–76. Springer, Cham (2020). https://doi.org/10.1007/978-3-030-45237-7_4
29. Libkin, L.: Logics with counting and local properties. ACM Trans. Comput. Logic **1**(1), 33–59 (2000). https://doi.org/10.1145/343369.343376
30. Lomuscio, A., Qu, H., Raimondi, F.: MCMAS: an open-source model checker for the verification of multi-agent systems. Int. J. Softw. Tools Technol. Transfer **19**(1), 9–30 (2015). https://doi.org/10.1007/s10009-015-0378-x
31. Mateescu, R., Thivolle, D.: A model checking language for concurrent value-passing systems. In: Cuellar, J., Maibaum, T., Sere, K. (eds.) FM 2008. LNCS, vol. 5014, pp. 148–164. Springer, Heidelberg (2008). https://doi.org/10.1007/978-3-540-68237-0_12
32. Olner, D., Evans, A.J., Heppenstall, A.J.: An agent model of urban economics: digging into emergence. Comput. Environ. Urban Syst. **54**, 414–427 (2015). https://doi.org/10.1016/j.compenvurbsys.2014.12.003
33. Panait, L.A., Luke, S.: Ant foraging revisited. In: ALIFE. MIT Press (2004). https://doi.org/10.7551/mitpress/1429.003.0096
34. Parunak, H.V.D.: "Go to the ant": engineering principles from natural multi-agent systems. Ann. Oper. Res. **75**, 69–101 (1997). https://doi.org/10.1023/A:1018980001403
35. Pinciroli, C., Beltrame, G.: Buzz: an extensible programming language for heterogeneous swarm robotics. In: IROS. IEEE (2016). https://doi.org/10.1109/IROS.2016.7759558
36. Pnueli, A.: The temporal logic of programs. In: FOCS. IEEE (1977). https://doi.org/10.1109/SFCS.1977.32

37. Qadeer, S., Wu, D.: KISS: Keep it simple and sequential. In: PLDI. ACM (2004). https://doi.org/10.1145/996841.996845
38. Queille, J.P., Sifakis, J.: Fairness and related properties in transition systems - a temporal logic to deal with fairness. Acta Informatica **19**, 195–220 (1983). https://doi.org/10.1007/BF00265555
39. Reynolds, C.W.: Flocks, herds and schools: a distributed behavioral model. In: SIGGRAPH. ACM (1987). https://doi.org/10.1145/37402.37406
40. Vekris, D., Lang, F., Dima, C., Mateescu, R.: Verification of EB^3 specifications using CADP. Formal Aspects Comput. **28**(1), 145–178 (2016). https://doi.org/10.1007/s00165-016-0362-6
41. Wirsing, M., Banâtre, J.P., Hölzl, M., Rauschmayer, A. (eds.): Software-Intensive Systems and New Computing Paradigms - Challenges and Visions. LNCS, vol. 5380. Springer, Heidelberg (2008). https://doi.org/10.1007/978-3-540-89437-7

Formal Methods for DIStributed COmputing in Future RAILway Systems

RAILS: Roadmaps for AI integration in the raiL Sector

Francesco Flammini[1] and Valeria Vittorini[2]

[1] Linnaeus University and Mälardalen University, Västerås, Sweden
francesco.flammini@lnu.se
[2] CINI and University of Naples "Federico II", Naples, Italy
valeria.vittorini@unina.it

Abstract. Artificial Intelligence (AI) is dominating the prominent emerging technologies, especially the ones used in autonomous vehicles. Among those emerging technologies, Machine Learning, Digital Twins, Internet of Things and Self-Healing are expected to reach their plateau of productivity in less than 10 years.

The Shift2Rail RAILS project[1] has its roots in the new wave of research and applications that goes under the name of Industry 4.0. This term refers to the application of machine learning and cognitive computing to leverage an effective data exchange and processing in manufacturing technologies, services and transportation [1], laying the foundation of what is commonly known as the fourth industrial revolution. Several industries are impacted and, although until now the ones that have benefitted the most are logistics [2] and manufacturing [3], transport systems rep-resent one of the fields in which machine learning and other techniques is expected to have a very important impact in the near future.

RAILS takes up the challenge in the rail sector supporting the definition of new research directions: the ultimate goal of RAILS is to investigate the potential of AI in the rail sector in continuity with ongoing research in railways, in particular within the Shift2Rail innovation pro-gram, and to contribute to the definition of roadmaps for future research in next generation signalling systems, operational intelligence, smart-maintenance and network management.

To reach its goal RAILS aims at: a) ***determining the gaps*** between AI potential, possible future scenarios and applications with the status-quo in the rail sector, in order ***to recognize the required innovation shifts***, b) ***developing*** methodological and experimental proof-of-concepts through ***feasibility studies*** for the adoption of AI and related techniques in safety and rail automation, predictive maintenance and defect detection, traffic planning and management, c) ***de-signing transition pathways*** toward the rail system scenario: identification of the new research directions to improve reliability, maintainability, safety, and performance through the adoption of AI.

In pursuing these objectives, RAILS wants to take a critical approach to the opportunities offered by AI in the rail sector, addressing the need for explainable, reliable and trustworthy AI technologies, to support the development of the new "Railway 4.0".

[1] https://rails-project.eu/.

T. Margaria and B. Steffen (Eds.): ISoLA 2021, LNCS 13036, pp. 493–494, 2021.
https://doi.org/10.1007/978-3-030-89159-6

Hence, the main ambition of RAILS is to understand and identify which approaches within the broad area of AI can have a meaningful impact on railway systems, with possible migration and technology transfer from other transport sectors and other relevant industries, like avionics, robotics and automotive, where the application of AI has proven to be feasible and advantageous. Some preliminary results described in [4] show that the integration of AI solutions and techniques to railways is still in its infancy despite of the work done in maintenance and traffic planning and management, as well as in investigating safety and security issues but also reveal that there is a great potential for principles driving research and real world applications in other sectors to be transferable to railways.

With respect to safety related aspects, emerging threats (e.g. the so-called adversarial attacks) and certification issues could be addressed when adopting AI in autonomous and cooperative driving (e.g. *virtual coupling*), based on the concepts of explainable AI (XAI) and trustworthy AI.

With respect to cyber-physical threat detection, innovative approaches could be developed based on AI models like Artificial Neural Networks (ANN) and Bayesian Networks together with multi-sensor data fusion and artificial vision. Resilience and optimization techniques based on genetic algorithms and self-healing could be addressed to face failures and service disruptions, as well as to increase efficiency and line capacity. Transport management problems, such as timetabling and real-time traffic rescheduling, are notoriously difficult, and commonly referred as to NP-hard problems. Recently, machine learning has been applied to solve NP-hard scheduling problems, giving a promising direction as an alternative to heuristics.

Acknowledgements and Disclaimer. RAILS has received funding from the European Union's Horizon 2020 research and innovation programme under grant agreement No. 881782. The information and views set out in this document are those of the author(s) and do not necessarily reflect the official opinion of Shift2Rail Joint Undertaking. The JU does not guarantee the accuracy of the data included in this article. Neither the JU nor any person acting on the JU's behalf may be held responsible for the use which may be made of the information contained therein.

References

1. Rojko, A.: Industry 4.0 concept: background and overview. Int. J. Interact. Mob. Technol. (IJIM) **11**(5), 77–90 (2017)
2. Barreto, L., Amaral, A., Pereira, T.: Industry 4.0 implications in logistics: an overview. Procedia Manuf. **13**, 1245–1252 (2017)
3. Stock, T., Günther S.: Opportunities of sustainable manufacturing in industry 4.0. Procedia Cirp **40**, 536–541 (2016)
4. RAILS Deliverable 1.1.: Definition of a reference taxonomy of AI in railways, August 2020. https://rails-project.eu/

A Journey Through Software Model Checking of Interlocking Programs

Simon Chadwick[1], Phillip James[2], Faron Moller[2], Markus Roggenbach[2(✉)], and Thomas Werner[1]

[1] Siemens Mobility, Chippenham, UK
{simon.chadwick,tom.werner}@siemens.com
[2] Swansea University, Sketty, UK
{p.d.james,f.g.moller,m.roggenbach}@swansea.ac.uk

In this paper, we report and reflect upon successful technology transfer from Swansea University to Siemens Mobility over the years 2007–2021. This transfer concerns formal software verification technology for programming interlocking computers from Technology Readiness Level TRL 1–7.

Interlockings are safety-critical systems which form an essential part of rail control systems. They are often realised as *programmable logic controllers* programmed in the language *ladder logic*. In the context of rail signalling systems, they provide a safety layer between a (human or automatic) controller and the physical track which guarantees safety rules such as: *before a signal can show proceed, all train detection devices in the route indicate the line is clear.* Rail authorities such as the UK Rail Safety and Standards Board as well as rail companies such as Siemens Mobility have defined such safety rules (we work with about 300 rules) that shall guarantee safe rail operation. This poses the question of how one can verify that a given program written in ladder logic fulfils a safety property.

Theoretical Foundations (TRL 1&2). Software model checking verification of interlockings is well established within the railway domain. Already 25 years ago, Groote et al. [3] used it to verify the interlocking of Hoorn Kersenbooger station. In this approach, ladder logic programs are represented in temporal propositional logic. Generic safety properties are formulated in temporal first order logic; for concrete track layouts these generic properties can equivalently be expressed in the same temporal propositional logic as used for representing the programs. This allows interlocking verification to be formulate as software model checking for temporal propositional logic [2, 5].

Academic Experiments (TRL 3&4). Software model checking for ladder logic programs requires the automation of two steps. First, one needs to transform a program into a logical formula Ψ via the Tseitin transformation. Then, one needs to instantiate a generic safety property with track plan information and derive a formula ϕ in temporal propositional logic. One can then verify that ϕ is a consequence of Ψ using a standard SAT solver.

Our experiences [4, 6], using a mix of programming languages (Haskell, Java, Prolog) and experimenting with two ladder logic programs and c. 5 safety properties, suggest the following: the verification concept works and scales up to

T. Margaria and B. Steffen (Eds.): ISoLA 2021, LNCS 13036, pp. 495–497, 2021.
https://doi.org/10.1007/978-3-030-89159-6

real world programs; applying program slicing is worthwhile in order to reduce verification times; rather than looking purely for *hold/does not hold* decisions, bounded model checking is useful for debugging; visualisation of counter examples turns out to be a challenge; and verification via k-induction fails.

Technology Transfer (TRL 5–7). Further development required deeper collaboration between academic and industrial partners, in order to interpret verification failures and to expand the number of examples treated concerning the encoding of safety properties [1, 7]. The software architecture needed revision to cater for tool interoperability, usability and error treatment. The resulting tool is able to find mistakes in ladder logic programs that cannot be found with traditional testing methods. Also, it has a turn-around time in the order of hours, as compared to turn-around times in the order of a week for testing.

Reflections. A number of themes permeate the described technology transfer, including faithful modelling, scalability, accessibility, and interoperability. Depending on the TRL, these themes recurred with a different focus. For instance, when considering the theoretical foundations, faithful modelling concerned the definitions of the logic and the transformations. When it came to the academic experiments, it meant correctness of slicing, and true representation of selected properties and track layouts. Finally, in technology transfer, we had to reflect how "complete" the set of safety properties was.

Future Development (Towards TRL 8&9). Until now, we have only analysed artefacts from completed projects. However, we have concrete plans for a trial under real software production conditions. For this, we need to revisit the theoretical foundations. For example, rather than a one-step next operator, the logic needs to provide k-step next operators (for $k > 1$), to cater for *fleeting outputs* of ladder logic programs: outputs which are "unstable" for a limited number of cycles. This will allow to "relativise" safety properties up to fleeting. Also, experiments with model checking algorithms are needed to mitigate the effect of *false positives*: the reporting of an error where there is none.

References

1. Chadwick, S.: Formal verification, 2020. Invited Talk at BCTCS (2020). https://cs.swansea.ac.uk/bctcs2020/Slides/Chadwick.pdf
2. Gruner, S., Kumar, A., Maibaum, T., Roggenbach, M.: Conclusions and prospects for future work. In: On the Construction of Engineering Handbooks. SCS, pp. 77–78. Springer, Cham (2020). https://doi.org/10.1007/978-3-030-44648-2_6
3. Groote, J.K.J., van Vlijmen, S.: The safety-guaranteeing system at station Hoorn-Kersenboogerd. In: COMPASS 1995. IEEE (1995)
4. James, P.: SAT-based model checking and its applications to train control software. Swansea University, Master of Research (2010)
5. James, P., et al.: Verification of solid state interlocking programs. In: Counsell, S., Núñez, M. (eds.) SEFM 2013. LNCS, vol. 8368, pp. 253–268. Springer, Cham (2014). https://doi.org/10.1007/978-3-319-05032-4_19

6. Kanso, K.: Formal verification of ladder logic. Swansea University, Master of Research (2010)
7. Werner, T.: Safety verification of ladder logic programs for railway interlockings. Swansea University, Master of Research (2017)

Supporting the Development of Hybrid ERTMS/ETCS Level 3 with Formal Modelling, Analysis and Simulation

Maarten Bartholomeus[1], Rick Erkens[2], Bas Luttik[2(✉)], and Tim Willemse[2]

[1] ProRail, Utrecht, The Netherlands
[2] Eindhoven University of Technology, Eindhoven, The Netherlands
s.p.luttik@tue.nl

Abstract. Hybrid ERTMS/ETCS Level 3 is a recent proposal for a train control system specification that serves to increase the capacity of the railway network by allowing multiple trains with an integrity monitoring system and a GSM-R connection to the trackside on a single section. The development of the principles of ETCS Hybrid Level 3 has been supported with formal modelling, analysis and simulation, using the mCRL2 toolset.

Keywords: ERTMS/ETCS · Hybrid level 3 · Formal analysis · Simulation · mCRL2

The main innovation of ERTMS/ETCS Level 3 is that it implements full radio-based train separation. It introduces the notion of virtual block, which facilitates partitioning tracks into sections without the need for installing expensive train detection hardware. Since these sections can be arbitrarily small, a capacity increase of the network is realised. The original proposal of Level 3 does away entirely with train detection hardware, but this has several drawbacks. For instance, all trains need to be equipped with a train integrity monitoring system. Also, it is hard to recover from a failing radio connection between train and trackside. To mitigate these drawbacks, the EEIG ERTMS Users Group is developing a hybrid version of Level 3 (HL3), which allows partitioning sections protected by train detection hardware into smaller virtual blocks.

The HL3 principles describe how a trackside system should determine the occupancy statuses of the virtual blocks on the basis of position reports from trains and the train detection system. Besides the statuses FREE and OCCUPIED, according to the HL3 principles a virtual block may assume two more statuses UNKNOWN and AMBIGUOUS, through which the trackside manages potential hazardous situations. Various waiting and propogation timers are defined that should prevent that situations are qualified as hazardous too quickly.

The research was partly sponsored by ProRail. The vision put forward in this extended abstract reflects the personal views of the authors and is not part of the strategy of ProRail.

T. Margaria and B. Steffen (Eds.): ISoLA 2021, LNCS 13036, pp. 498–499, 2021.
https://doi.org/10.1007/978-3-030-89159-6

There has been quite some attention from the formal methods research community for the HL3 principles, since version 1A of the principles [4] served as a case study promoted by the ABZ conference (see [3] and references therein). We also contributed to these efforts [1], presenting a formal analysis of version 1A of the principles in the mCRL2 toolset [2]. We developed an mCRL2 model that specifies a trackside system responsible for computing the statuses of the virtual blocks. Furthermore, we specified the behaviour of trains and a train detection system to the extent that it was relevant for the status computations of the trackside system. Our formal verification focussed on whether the trackside system prevents collisions of trains, and also considered to what extent the computation of the statuses of the virtual blocks was terminating and deterministic. Our analyses, then, resulted in suggestions for improvement of the principles that were taken into account in subsequent versions.

Recently, we have updated our mCRL2 model to reflect version 1D of the principles [5]. In the update, we addressed the role of the various timers, which were left out from detailed consideration in the earlier analysis. This brought to light some further issues with the formulation of the principles. Our analyses revealed new potentially dangerous scenarios involving the behaviour of timers and led to further improvements of the formulation of the principles. We have included a sophisticated train model, allowing trains to split multiple times.

ProRail is going to use the mCRL2 model for the simulation of scenarios using the simulator of mCRL2 and is currently building a graphical tool that visualises simulations. To support that activity, we have added a mechanism to our model that facilitates a straightforward configuration with a track layout and train specification.

References

1. Bartholomeus, M., Luttik, B., Willemse, T.: Modelling and analysing ERTMS hybrid level 3 with the mCRL2 toolset. In: Howar, F., Barnat, J. (eds.) FMICS 2018. LNCS, vol. 11119, pp. 98–114. Springer, Cham (2018). https://doi.org/10.1007/978-3-030-00244-2_7
2. Bunte, O., et al.: The mCRL2 toolset for analysing concurrent systems. In: Vojnar, T., Zhang, L. (eds.) TACAS 2019, Part II. LNCS, vol. 11428, pp. 21–39. Springer, Cham (2019). https://doi.org/10.1007/978-3-030-17465-1_2
3. Butler, M.J., Hoang, T.S., Raschke, A., Reichl, K.: Introduction to special section on the ABZ 2018 case study: hybrid ERTMS/ETCS level 3. Int. J. Softw. Tools Technol. Transf. **22**(3), 249–255 (2020). https://doi.org/10.1007/s10009-020-00562-3
4. EEIG ERTMS Users Group: Hybrid ERTMS/ETCS Level 3, ref: 16E045, Version: 1A. Accessed 14 July 2017
5. EEIG ERTMS Users Group: Hybrid ERTMS/ETCS Level 3. Ref: 16E042, Version: 1D. https://ertms.be/workgroups/level3. Accessed 15 Oct 2020

Formal Methods in Railway Signalling Infrastructure Standardisation Processes

Mark Bouwman[1], Bas Luttik[1](✉), Arend Rensink[2], Mariëlle Stoelinga[2,3], and Djurre van der Wal[2]

[1] Eindhoven University of Technology, Eindhoven, The Netherlands
{m.s.bouwman,s.p.luttik}@tue.nl
[2] University of Twente, Enschede, The Netherlands
{arend.rensink,m.i.a.stoelinga,d.vanderwal-1}@utwente.nl
[3] Radboud University Nijmegen, Nijmegen, The Netherlands

Abstract. The EULYNX initiative of the European railway infrastructure managers aims to standardise the interfaces between the interlocking and field elements. To support these standardisation efforts, the goal of the *FormaSig* project, an initiative of the Dutch and German railway infrastructure managers and two Dutch universities, is to deliver a formal framework in which the EULYNX interface standard can be formally analysed and conformance to the standard of an interface implementation can be efficiently established.

Keywords: Railway interface standardisation · Formal analysis · Model-based testing · mCRL2 · SysML.

European infrastructure managers have joined forces in the EULYNX[1] organisation with the aim to arrive at standardised interfaces between interlockings and trackside equipment (signals, points, level crossings). Standardisation efforts will significantly reduce the cost of ownership of signalling systems. Indeed, if the interfaces and architecture of a signalling system are standardised, then different components can be procured from different suppliers, thereby enabling competition and preventing vendor lock-in situations. Furthermore, approval processes can be harmonised and simplified, and will thus become more efficient.

To be effective, the quality of the standard is crucial. Not only should it be clear and unambiguous, but, to stay in control of procurement, railway infrastructure managers should also be able to verify efficiently and effectively whether a delivered product conforms to the standard. In 2019, infrastructure managers DB Netz AG and ProRail together with Eindhoven University of Technology and the University of Twente started the four-year research project *Formal Methods in Railway Signalling Infrastructure Standardisation Processes (FormaSig)*

The FormaSig project is fully funded by DB Netz AG and ProRail. The vision put forward in this extended abstract reflects the personal views of the authors and is not part of the strategy of DB Netz AG or ProRail.

[1] https://www.eulynx.eu.

T. Margaria and B. Steffen (Eds.): ISoLA 2021, LNCS 13036, pp. 500–501, 2021.
https://doi.org/10.1007/978-3-030-89159-6

to investigate how the use of formal models can support the EULYNX standardisation process as well as the approval processes for delivered components.

The EULYNX standard specifies the interfaces through semi-formal SysML[2] models. The approach of FormaSig is to derive, from these SysML models, a formal model in the process specification language mCRL2 [4]. The mCRL2 toolset[3] [3] then offers model-checking facilities to formally analyse the correctness of the interface model with respect to high-level requirements formulated in an extension of the modal μ-calculus. Moreover, since the semantics of an mCRL2 model is a labelled transition system, it also facilitates automated testing of compliance of implementations to the standard in accordance with formal testing theory [5].

In a first case study, presented in [2], we have manually derived an mCRL2 model from the SysML models specifying the EULYNX Point interface. A formal analysis of the model using the mCRL2 toolset revealed a deadlock caused by event buffers overflowing. We also performed some preliminary model-based testing experiments using JTorX to automatically generate tests from the mCRL2 model, running those tests on a simulator of the EULYNX interface. The case study showed the feasibility of our approach.

We are currently working on improving the framework, and, in particular, on automating the translation of EULYNX SysML models to mCRL2. As a stepping stone towards an automated translation, we have now defined an executable formal semantics of EULYNX SysML directly in mCRL2 [1]. From there, it is fairly straightforward to automatically generate mCRL2 models from EULYNX SysML models.

References

1. Bouwman, M., Luttik, B., van der Wal, D.: A formalisation of SysML state machines in mCRL2. In: Peters, K., Willemse, T.A.C. (eds.) FORTE 2021. LNCS, vol. 12719, pp. 42–59. Springer, Cham (2021). https://doi.org/10.1007/978-3-030-78089-0_3
2. e point: Formal analysis and test generation for a railway standard. In: Baraldi, P., di Maio, F., Zio, E. (eds.) Proceedings of ESREL 2020 and PSAM 15. Research Publishing, Singapore (2020). https://www.rpsonline.com.sg/proceedings/esrel2020/html/4410.xml
3. Vojnar, T., Zhang, L. (eds.): TACAS 2019, Part II. LNCS, vol. 11428. Springer, Cham (2019). https://doi.org/10.1007/978-3-030-17465-1
4. Groote, J.F., Mousavi, M.R.: Modeling and Analysis of Communicating Systems. MIT Press (2014). https://mitpress.mit.edu/books/modeling-and-analysis-communicating-systems
5. Tretmans, J.: Model based testing with labelled transition systems. In: Hierons, R.M., Bowen, J.P., Harman, M. (eds.) Formal Methods and Testing. LNCS, vol. 4949, pp. 1–38. Springer, Heidelberg (2008). https://doi.org/10.1007/978-3-540-78917-8_1

[2] https://www.omg.org/spec/SysML/.
[3] https://www.mcrl2.org.

Author Index

Printed in the United States
by Baker & Taylor Publisher Services